SUPER LCCS™

Gale's
Library of Congress
Classification Schedules

Combined
with Additions
and Changes
through 2002

ISSN 1088-1921

Class E-F

History: America

SUPER LCCS™

Gale's
Library of Congress
Classification Schedules

Combined
with Additions
and Changes
through 2002

Compiled from sources enumerated on verso

GALE®

THOMSON
GALE™

Detroit • New York • San Diego • San Francisco • Cleveland • New Haven, Conn • Waterville, Maine • London • Munich

THOMSON

GALE

SUPERLCCS

Gale's Library of Congress Classification Schedules Combined with Additions and Changes Through 2002

Classification: Classes E-F, History: America, Washington, 2000, issued by Library of Congress, Cataloging Policy and Support Office, Library Services, and combined with revisions published in *L.C. Classification—Additions and Changes,* List 281 (Jan.-Mar., 2001) through List 284 (Oct. Dec., 2001) and *Library of Congress Classification Weekly Lists, 2002.*

Project Editor
Kathleen Droste

Editorial
Michael Reade

Technical Support Services
Mira Bossowska

Manufacturing
Keith Helmling

Product Design
Cynthia Baldwin

LIBRARY OF CONGRESS CATALOG CARD NUMBER 2001027702

ISBN 0-7876-6128-7 (This cumulation)
ISBN 0-7876-6082-5 (Complete Set)
ISBN 0-7876-6090-6 (Microfiche cumulation)
ISBN 0-7876-6106-6 (Microfiche complete set)

Printed in the United States of America
10 9 8 7 6 5 4 3 2 1

CONTENTS

PREFACE

This publication integrates each of the latest editions of the Library of Congress classification schedules with all pertinent changes found in the Library's quarterly publication *LC Classification—Additions and Changes*. The material included in each volume covers the period from the publication date of each schedule through December, 2001 (List 284) and *Library of Congress Classification Weekly Lists, 2002*. This series of cumulations has been prepared by a staff of professional librarians at Gale Group.

A Valuable Tool

The use of this publication eases the painstaking task of classification immeasurably. No longer is it necessary to determine where and how the additions and changes relate to the schedule. All classification information from the lists through 2002 has been interfiled into one sequence.

Validation Procedures

The full text of each schedule and its index have been meticulously combined with the changes from the quarterly *LC Classification—Additions and Changes* and *Library of Congress Classification Weekly Lists*. Although there is no official connection between Gale and the Library of Congress (LC) in the preparation of this publication, LC generously provided the editors with information when questions of form or problems of interpretation arose during the integration process.

Frequency of publication

Completely updated volumes of *Library of Congress Classification Schedules Combined with Additions and Changes and Weekly Lists* are published annually.

A Standardized Gale Style

In 1994 a new Gale classification database was constructed that allowed for a more efficient, accurate, and flexible interaction with the data. Data elements were normalized and the varying styles of the printed schedules were standardized into one Gale style. Much of this style originated with the announced Library of Congress changes in which footnotes would be eliminated; "Divide like" notes would be replaced with developments; "General works" captions would be reinstated; and many internal tables changed into external tables.

A Noteworthy Gale Feature

In the schedules Gale is adding editorial notes in textual situations where such notes would be beneficial to users. These notes direct the user to another location or define, clarify, or elaborate abbreviated or ambiguous instruction or description. These notes are easily identified by the label "GALE NOTE."

For example, many times in the Library of Congress text, the word "modified" appears after a table reference when subtopics are listed below such a caption that contains a table reference. In these cases, the cataloger would adjust the table by integrating the subtopics into the table development. Whenever a table modification is implied or when the word "modified" appears following a table reference in the Library of Congress text, the following GALE NOTE will appear:

> GALE NOTE To develop this number range, integrate the subtopics
> into the table structure.

Some Gale notes reiterate Library of Congress instruction in places lacking such direction. For example, the Library of Congress occasionally adds the definition of ".x" in cutter number tables. Gale will add this following definition to all tables that contain this symbolic cutter number:

> GALE NOTE ".x" represents the cutter number for ...

Each year Gale will systematically add new notes to make *SUPERLCCS* easier to use and to make its content more accessible to its users.

The GALE NOTE is just one of the many suggestions adopted from recommendations made by an Advisory Board.

Notes Relating to Specific Volumes

The Library of Congress recently released a new edition of *Class H: Social Sciences.* Gale is publishing the data from this new edition and adding the subsequent updating lists. The Library of Congress is planning a new schedule: *Subclasses KB-KBZ: Religious Legal Systems.* If this appears during Gale's publication cycle of January-July, the editors will make every effort to incorporate this new data.

In 1999 Library of Congress issued a new schedule, *K Tables, Form Division Tables for Law.* Since some of the law schedules already include tables at the end of the text, Gale, as a convenience to its customers, will include these new K Tables at the end of those schedules to which they apply. Tables of subdivisions referred to in the text of the Class P schedules are found in a separate schedule, *Language and Literature Tables,* reissued by the Library of Congress in 1998.

Suggestions Are Welcome

The editors welcome your comments and suggestions for enhancing or improving this work. Please write to: The Editors, SUPERLCCS, Gale Group, 27500 Drake Rd., Farmington Hills, MI 48331-4253. Phone no.: 1-800-877-4253; Fax no. 248-699-8062. E-mail address: SUPERLCCS@gale.com.

SYNOPSIS

OUTLINE

F	1-975	United States local history
	1-15	New England
	16-30	Maine
	31-45	New Hampshire
	46-60	Vermont
	61-75	Massachusetts
	76-90	Rhode Island
	91-105	Connecticut
	106	Atlantic coast. Middle Atlantic States
	116-130	New York
	131-145	New Jersey
	146-160	Pennsylvania
	161-175	Delaware
	176-190	Maryland
	191-205	District of Columbia. Washington
	206-220	The South. South Atlantic States
	221-235	Virginia
	236-250	West Virginia
	251-265	North Carolina
	266-280	South Carolina
	281-295	Georgia
	296-301	Gulf States. West Florida
	306-320	Florida
	321-335	Alabama
	336-350	Mississippi
	350.5-355	Mississippi River and Valley. Middle West
	366-380	Louisiana
	381-395	Texas
	396	Old Southwest. Lower Mississippi Valley
	406-420	Arkansas
	431-445	Tennessee
	446-460	Kentucky
	461-475	Missouri
	476-485	Old Northwest. Northwest Territory
	486-500	Ohio
	516-520	Ohio River and Valley
	521-535	Indiana
	536-550	Illinois
	550.5-553.2	The Lake region. Great Lakes
	561-575	Michigan
	576-590	Wisconsin
	590.3-596.3	The West. Trans-Mississippi Region. Great Plains
	597	The Northwest
	598	Missouri River and Valley
	601-615	Minnesota
	616-630	Iowa
	631-645	North Dakota
	646-660	South Dakota
	661-675	Nebraska
	676-690	Kansas
	691-705	Oklahoma
	721-722	Rocky Mountains. Yellowstone National Park
	726-740	Montana
	741-755	Idaho
	756-770	Wyoming
	771-785	Colorado
	786-790	New Southwest. Colorado River, Canyon, and Valley
	791-805	New Mexico
	806-820	Arizona
	821-835	Utah
	836-850	Nevada

F		United States local history - Continued
	850.5-851.5	Pacific States
	851.7	Cascade Range
	852-854	Pacific Northwest. Columbia River and Valley. Northwest boundary since 1846
	856-870	California
	871-885	Oregon
	886-900	Washington
	901-951	Alaska
	951	Bering Sea and Aleutian Islands
	965	The territories of the United States (General)
	970	Insular possessions of the United States (General)
	975	Central American, West Indian, and other countries protected by and having close political affiliations with the United States (General)
F	1001-1140	British America
	1001-1140	Canada
	1001-1035	General
	1035.8	Maritime provinces. Atlantic coast of Canada
	1036-1040	Nova Scotia. Acadia
	1041-1045	New Brunswick
	1046-1049.7	Prince Edward Island
	1050	St. Lawrence Gulf, River, and Valley (General)
	1051-1055	Quebec
	1056-1059.7	Ontario
	1060-1060.97	Canadian Northwest. Northwest Territories
	1061-1065	Manitoba
	1067	Assiniboia
	1070-1074.7	Saskatchewan
	1075-1080	Alberta
	1086-1089.7	British Columbia
	1090	Rocky Mountains of Canada
	1090.5	Arctic regions
	1091-1095.5	Yukon
	1096-1100.5	Mackenzie
	1101-1105.7	Franklin
	1106-1110.5	Keewatin
	1121-1139	Newfoundland
	1135-1139	Labrador
	1140	The Labrador Peninsula
		Other than Canada
		Bahamas, *see* F1650+
		Bermudas, *see* F1630+
		British East and West Florida, 1763-1783, *see* F301, F314
		British Guiana, *see* F2361+
		British Honduras (Belize), *see* F1441+
		British West Indies, *see* F2131+
		Falkland Islands, *see* F3031+
		Thirteen North American Colonies before 1776, *see* E186+
F		Dutch America
		Colony in Brazil, 1625-1661, *see* F2532
		Dutch Guiana, *see* F2401+
		Dutch West Indies, *see* F2141
		New Netherlands to 1664, *see* F122.1
		New Sweden (Dutch possession, 1655-1664), *see* F167
F	1170	French America
	1170	Saint Pierre and Miquelon
		Other French America
		Colony in Brazil, 1555-1567, *see* F2529
		Colony in Florida, 1562-1565, *see* F314

F		French America
		Other French America - Continued
		French Guiana, *see* F2441+
		French West Indies, *see* F2151
		Louisiana, 1698-1803, *see* F372
		New France and Acadia, 1600-1763, *see* F1030, F1038
F	1201-3799	Latin America. Spanish America
	1201-1392	Mexico
	1218.5-1221	Antiquities. Indians
	1401-1419	Latin America (General)
	1421-1440	Central America
	1435-1435.3	Mayas
	1441-1457	Belize
	1461-1477	Guatemala
	1481-1497	Salvador (El Salvador)
	1501-1517	Honduras
	1521-1537	Nicaragua
	1541-1557	Costa Rica
	1561-1577	Panama
	1569.C2	Canal Zone. Panama Canal
	1601-1629	West Indies
	1630-1640	Bermudas
	1650-1660	Bahamas
	1741-1991	Greater Antilles
	1751-1854.9	Cuba
	1788-1788.22	Communist regime
	1861-1896	Jamaica
	1900-1941	Haiti (Island). Hispaniola
	1912-1930	Haiti (Republic)
	1931-1941	Dominican Republic
	1951-1983	Puerto Rico
	1991	Navassa
	2001-2151	Lesser Antilles
		Groups of islands, by geographical distribution
	2006	Leeward Islands
	2011	Windward Islands
	2016	Islands along Venezuela coast
	2033-2129	Individual islands
		Groups of islands, by political allegiance
	2131-2133	British West Indies
	2136	Virgin Islands of the United States
	2141	Netherlands West Indies. Dutch West Indies
	2151	French West Indies
	2155-2191	Caribbean area. Caribbean Sea
	2201-3799	South America
	2201-2239	General
	2251-2299	Colombia
	2301-2349	Venezuela
	2351	Guiana
	2361-2391	Guyana. British Guiana
	2401-2431	Surinam
	2441-2471	French Guiana
	2501-2659	Brazil
	2661-2699	Paraguay
	2701-2799	Uruguay
	2801-3021	Argentina
	3031-3031.5	Falkland Islands
	3051-3285	Chile
	3301-3359	Bolivia
	3401-3619	Peru
	3701-3799	Ecuador

General

E11-E29 are reserved for works which are actually comprehensive in scope. A book on travel would only occasionally be classified here; the numbers for the United States, Spanish America, etc., would usually accomodate all works, the choice being determined by the main country or region covered

11	**Periodicals. Societies. Collections (serial)**
	For international American Conferences, see F1404+
	Collections (Nonserial). Collected works
12	Several authors
13	Individual authors
14	**Dictionaries. Gazetteers. Geographic names**
	General works, *see* E18
	History
16	Historiography
16.5	Study and teaching
	Biography
17	Collective
	Individual, *see* country, period, etc.
18	General works
	Including comprehensive works on America
18.5	Chronology, chronological tables, etc.
18.7	Juvenile works
18.75	General special
	By period
	Pre-Columbian period, *see* E51+, E103+
18.82	1492-1810
	Cf. E101+, Discovery and exploration of America
	Cf. E141+, Earliest accounts of America to 1810
18.83	1810-1900
18.85	1901-
19	**Pamphlets, addresses, essays, etc.**
	Including radio programs, pageants, etc.
20	**Social life and customs. Civilization. Intellectual life**
21	**Historic monuments (General)**
21.5	**Antiquities (Non-Indian)**
21.7	**Historical geography**
	Description and travel. Views
	Cf. F851, Pacific Coast
	Cf. G419+, Travels around the world and in several parts of the world including America and other countries
	Cf. G575+, Polar discoveries
	Earliest to 1606, *see* E141+
	1607-1810, *see* E143
27	1811-1950
27.2	1951-1980
27.5	1981-
	Elements in the population
29.A1	General works
29.A2-.Z	Individual elements, A-Z
29.B35	Basques
	Blacks, *see* E29.N3
29.B75	British
29.C35	Canary Islanders
29.C37	Catalans
29.C5	Chinese
29.C73	Creoles
29.C75	Croats
29.C94	Czechs
29.D25	Danube Swabians
29.E37	East Indians

	General
	Elements in the population — Continued
29.E87	Europeans
29.F8	French
29.G26	Galicians (Spain)
29.G3	Germans
29.H9	Huguenots
29.I74	Irish
29.I8	Italians
29.J3	Japanese
29.J5	Jews
29.N3	Negroes. Blacks
29.O6	Orientals
	Cf. E29.C5, Chinese
29.P6	Poles
29.R83	Russian Germans
29.R84	Russians
29.S65	Spaniards
29.S83	Swedes

North America

The numbers "E31-46" like "E11-29" are to be assigned to works actually comprehensive in scope; for example, a book dealing principally with British America with a few pages at the end on the United States would be classed in F1001-1035, regardless of title. Most works having United States in the title relate so largely to this country that they are classed in E151-839

31	**Periodicals. Societies. Collections**
35	**Dictionaries. Gazetteers. Geographic names**
	Biography
36	Collective
	Individual, *see* country, period, etc.
38	**General works**
38.5	**Juvenile works**
39	**Pamphlets, addresses, essays, etc.**
39.5	**Pictorial works**
40	**Social life and customs. Civilization. Intellectual life**
40.5	**Geography**
41	**Description and travel**
43	**Antiquities (non-Indian)**
43.5	**National and state parks and reservations (Collective descriptive works)**
	History
	Cf. E101+, Discovery and exploration of America
	Cf. F1411+, History of Latin America
45	General works
46	General special
46.5	Military history
	Elements in the population
49	General works
49.2.A-.2.Z	Individual elements, A-Z
	For a list of racial, ethnic, and religious elements (with cutter numbers), see E184.A+

South America, *see* F2201+

Pre-Columbian America. The Indians

For language, see Subclass PM

51	**Periodicals. Societies. Collections (Serial)**
	Including anthropological records, Archaeological Institute of America
	For American Antiquarian Society, see E172
51.5	**Congresses**
	Collections (nonserial). Collected works
53	Several authors
54	Individual authors
54.5	**Dictionaries. Directories. Guides to tribes**

Pre-Columbian America. The Indians — Continued
Study and teaching. Research

55.5	General works
55.6	Audiovisual aids
55.6.Z9A-.Z9Z	Catalogs of materials
56	**Museums. Exhibitions**
	Including collections of antiquities
	Subarrange by author
57	**Theory. Methods of investigation**
	Including biography (Arranged by biographee), e.g. William Jones
58	**General works**
58.4	**Juvenile works**
59.A-.Z	**Topics, A-Z**
59.A32	Aesthetics
59.A35	Agriculture
59.A5	Anthropometry
	Antiquities, *see* E61
59.A67	Architecture
59.A68	Arms and armor. Weapons
59.A7	Art
59.A73	Arts
59.A8	Astronomy
59.B3	Baskets
59.B43	Beadwork
	Boats, *see* E59.C2
59.C18	Cannibalism
59.C2	Canoes. Boats
59.C22	Captivities
59.C25	Cartography
59.C46	Children
59.C5	Chronology
59.C55	City planning
59.C59	Commerce
59.C6	Costume. Adornment
59.C73	Craniology
59.C9	Cremation
	Culture, *see* E58
59.D35	Dance
59.D45	Dentistry
59.D58	Diseases
59.D66	Dolls
59.D69	Domestic animals
59.D9	Dwellings
59.E3	Economic conditions
	Including employment
59.E4	Education
59.E75	Ethnic identity
59.F53	First contact with Europeans
59.F6	Folklore. Legends
59.F63	Food
59.G3	Games. Recreation. Sports
59.G55	Goldwork
	Government, Tribal, *see* E59.T75
	Government and politics, *see* E59.P73
59.G6	Government relations
59.H54	Hindu influences
59.I4	Implements
59.I5	Industries
59.I53	Influence on other civilizations
59.L3	Land tenure

Pre-Columbian America. The Indians

59.A-.Z	**Topics, A-Z — Continued**
59.L4	Leatherwork. Tanning
	Legends, *see* E59.F6
	Literature, *see* PM151+
59.M3	Masks
59.M33	Material culture
59.M34	Mathematics
59.M4	Medicine
59.M47	Metalwork
59.M65	Missions
59.M66	Mixed descent
59.M7	Money
59.M8	Mortuary customs
59.N5	Narcotics
59.N8	Numeration
59.P42	Petroglyphs. Rock painting
59.P45	Philosophy
	Picture writing, *see* E59.W9
	Popular attitudes toward Indians, *see* E59.P89
59.P73	Politics and government
59.P75	Population
59.P8	Pottery
59.P87	Psychology
59.P89	Public opinion. Popular attitudes toward Indians
59.P92	Public welfare
	Recreation, *see* E59.G3
59.R38	Religion. Mythology
59.R56	Rites and ceremonies
59.R6	Roads. Trails
	Rock paintings, *see* E59.P42
59.S35	Science
59.S37	Sculpture
59.S45	Sexual behavior
59.S54	Shell engraving
59.S64	Social conditions
59.S65	Social life and customs
	Sports, *see* E59.G3
59.S7	Statistics
59.T35	Textile fabrics
59.T6	Tobacco pipes
	Trails, *see* E59.R6
59.T73	Transpacific influences
59.T75	Tribal government
59.W3	Warfare
	Weapons, *see* E59.A68
59.W8	Women
59.W9	Writing. Picture writing
61	**Archaeology of the Americans. Origin of the Indians in general**
65	**Latin America (General)**
	For Spanish treatment of the Indians, see F1411
	For special, class in local history, usually under the country; in certain cases with state or province; e.g., F1219, Mexico; F1529.M9, Mosquito Reservation
	North America (north of Mexico)
71	General works
	For works on Indians only, see E77+
	Mound builders. Mounds
	Class here general works only
	For mounds in a particular state, province, or region, see E78.A+
(74.A-.Z)	By state, province, or region, A-Z

	Indians of North America
75	**Periodicals. Societies. Collections**
76	**Congresses**
76.2	**Dictionaries. Directories. Guides to tribes**
	Biographies of Indianists
76.4	Collective
76.45.A-.45.Z	Individual, A-Z
	Subarrange by Table E1 at the end of the text
76.6	**Study and teaching**
76.7	Research
76.8	**Historiography**
76.85	**Museums. Exhibitions**
	General works
77	Comprehensive works
77.2	Addresses, essays, lectures
77.4	Juvenile works
77.5	Pictorial works
77.6	Minor works
	Archaeology
77.8	Periodicals. Societies. Collections. Congresses
77.9	General treatises
77.92	Juvenile works
77.94	Minor works
78.A-.Z	**By state, province, or region ,A-Z**
	Including Indian antiquities
	Class all mounds and archaeological sites within a county or toher division of a state, with the state, subarranging by author, e.g., mounds in Franklin County, Ohio, are classed in E78.O3
	Class Indian reservations here under state unless held by a single tribe, when they are classes in E99
	For Canada (General), see E78.C2
	For works limited to specific tribes, see E99.A+
78.A28	Alabama
78.A3	Alaska
78.A34	Alberta
78.A66	Appalachian Region
	Including Blue Ridge Mountains
78.A7	Arizona
78.A8	Arkansas
78.A88	Atlantic States
	Blue Ridge Mountains, *see E78.A66*
78.B9	British Columbia
78.C15	California
78.C2	Canada (General)
	Including the Canadian Northwest
	Cf. E92, Government relations
	Cf. E78.B9, British Columbia; E78.N9, Nova Scotia; etc.
78.C45	Chattahoochee River Valley
78.C5	Churchill River Watershed (Sask. and Man.)
78.C6	Colorado
78.C617	Colorado Plateau
78.C62	Colorado River Valley
78.C63	Columbia Plateau
78.C64	Columbia River Valley
78.C7	Connecticut
78.D2	Dakota Territory
	For North Dakota, see E78.N75
	For South Dakota, see E78.S63
78.D3	Delaware
78.D5	Delaware Valley
78.D54	Delmarva Peninsula

	Indians of North America
78.A-.Z	**By state, province, or region ,A-Z — Continued**
78.D6	District of Columbia
78.E2	Eastern North America. Woodlands
78.F6	Florida
78.F73	Franklin (District)
78.G3	Georgia
78.G67	Great Basin
78.G7	Great Lakes
78.G73	Great Plains
78.H83	Hudson Valley
78.I18	Idaho
78.I3	Illinois
78.I5	Indian Territory
	Including the five civilized tribes before 1907
	For the five civilized tribes after 1907, see E78.O45
78.I53	Indiana
78.I6	Iowa
78.K15	Kankakee Valley
78.K16	Kansas
78.K25	Keewatin (District)
78.K3	Kentucky
78.L3	Labrador
78.L58	Little Colorado River Valley (New Mexico and Arizona)
78.L8	Louisiana
78.M16	Mackenzie
78.M2	Maine
78.M25	Manitoba
78.M28	Maritime Provinces
78.M3	Maryland
78.M4	Massachusetts
78.M6	Michigan
78.M65	Middle Atlantic States
78.M67	Middle West
78.M7	Minnesota
78.M73	Mississippi
78.M75	Mississippi Valley
78.M8	Missouri
78.M82	Missouri Valley
78.M9	Montana
78.N3	Nebraska
78.N4	Nevada
78.N46	New Brunswick
78.N5	New England
78.N54	New Hampshire
78.N6	New Jersey
78.N65	New Mexico
78.N7	New York
78.N72	Newfoundland
78.N74	North Carolina
78.N75	North Dakota
	Northeastern States, *see* E78.E2
78.N76	Northwest (Old)
78.N77	Northwest (Pacific)
78.N78	Northwest coast of North America
78.N79	Northwest Territories
78.N8	Northwestern States
78.N9	Nova Scotia. Acadia
78.O3	Ohio
78.O4	Ohio Valley

Indians of North America

                        Indians of North America
                           Indian wars
83   Individual wars — Continued
83.71   Tuscarora War, 1711-1713
83.713   Yamassee War, 1715-1716
83.72   Eastern Indian Wars (New England), 1722-1726
                                        Including Pigwacket Fight, 1725; Sebastien Rasles (Rale, Rasle); etc.
83.73   Natchez Massacre, 1729
83.739   Chickasaw War, 1739-1740
                                    King George's War, 1744-1748, *see* E198
                                    French and Indian War, 1755-1763, *see* E199
83.759   Cherokee War, 1759-1761
83.7595   Wyoming Massacre, 1763
83.76   Pontiac's Conspiracy, 1763-1765
                                        Biography: Henry Bouquet, etc.
83.77   Dunmore's War, 1774. Battle of Point Pleasant
83.775   Indian Wars, 1775-1783
                                        Campaigns of the Revolution, see E230+
                                        Wyoming Massacre, 1778, see E241.W9
                                        Cherry Valley Massacre, 1778, see E241.C5
                                        Sullivan's Campaign, 1779, see E235
                                        Crawford's Campaign, 1782, see E238
83.79   Northwestern Indian Wars (Ohio Valley), 1790-1795
                                        Including Harmar's Expedition, 1790; Scott's Expedition, May 1791; Wilkinson's
                                            Expedition, August 1791; St. Clair's Campaign, November 1791
83.794   Wayne's Campaign, 1793-1795
83.81   Battle of Tippecanoe, 1811
83.812   Indian Wars, 1812-1815
                                    Campaigns of the War of 1812, *see* E355.2
83.813   First Creek War, 1813-1814
                                            Including Jackson's execution of the Tennessee militiamen
83.817   First Seminole War, 1817-1818
                                        Including the execution of Ambrister and Arbuthnot
83.818   Arikara War, 1823
83.83   Black Hawk War, 1832
                                        Biography: Black Hawk, the Sauk chief, etc.
83.835   Second Seminole War, 1835-1842
83.836   Second Creek War, 1836
                                        Thomas Sidney Jesup, etc.
83.837   Comanche War, 1840
83.838   Temecula Massacre, 1847
83.84   Pacific Northwest Indian wars, 1847-1865
                                        Including Cayuse War, 1847-1850; Rogue River War, 1850; Yakima War, 1855-1858;
                                            Spokane Expedition, 1858
83.854   Dakota Indian or Sioux War, 1855-1856
                                        Including Harney's Expedition
83.855   Third Seminole War, 1855-1858
83.8565   Battle of Maricopa Wells, 1857
                                    Mountain Meadow Massacre, 1857, *see* F826
83.857   Spirit Lake Massacre, 1857
83.8575   Battle of Solomon's Fork, 1857
83.8577   Battle of Crooked Creek, 1859
83.858   Mill Creek War, 1857-1865
83.859   Navaho (Navajo) War, 1858-1868
83.86   Dakota Indian or Sioux War, 1862-1865
                                        Including uprising in Minnesota (Battles of Birch Coulee, Fort Ridgely, New Ulm, Wood
                                            Lake), 1862; Battle of Whitestone Hill, 1863; Battle of Killdeer Mountain, July 1864;
                                            Platt Bridge Fight, July 1865; Powder River Campaign, July-October 1865

	Indians of North America
	Indian wars
83	Individual wars — Continued
83.863	Indian wars, 1862-1865
	Including Shoshoni War, 1863-1865; Cheyenne War, 1864; Sand Creek Massacre, 1864;
	Battle of Adobe Walls, 1864
	Cf. E83.858, Mill Creek War
	Cf. E83.859, Navaho War
	Cf. E83.86, Sioux War
83.866	Indian wars, 1866-1898
	Including Fort Phil Kearney Massacre, 1866; Warren Wagon Train Massacre, 1871; Red
	Cloud War, 1866-1867
	Biography: George Crook, Nelson Appleton Miles, etc.
83.867	Black Hawk War (Utah), 1865-1872
83.8675	Battle of Camp Cady, 1866
83.868	Battle of Beecher Island, 1868
83.869	Washita Campaign, 1868-1869
83.8695	Battle of Summit Springs, 1869
83.8697	Battle of Belly River, 1870
83.87	Modoc War, 1872-1873
83.875	Red River War, 1874-1875
	Including Cheyenne Outbreak
83.876	Dakota Indian or Sioux War, 1876
	Including Battle of the Little Big Horn
83.8765	Battle of the Butte, 1877
83.877	Nez Percé War, 1877
	Including Battle of the Big Hole
83.879	Ute War, 1879
	Riel Rebellion, *see* F1060.9
83.88	Apache War, 1882-1886
83.89	Dakota Indian or Sioux War, 1890-1891. Messiah War
	Including Death of Chief Sitting Bull; Wounded Knee Massacre, 1890
83.895	Chippewa War, 1898
	Captivities
	Including adventures and experiences of those taken captive by the Indians
85	General works. Collected narratives
87.A-.Z	Individual captivities, A-Z
	Prefer classification in E83 or E99 if captivity relates to a particular war or tribe
88	**Individual memoirs of early explorers, traders, trappers, etc., giving accounts of their experiences**
	among the Indians
	For memoirs relating to a specific tribe, see E99.A+
	Biography
89	Collective
	Including portraits
90.A-.Z	Individual, A-Z
	Class individuals identified with specific tribes in E99 unless better known in connection with
	specific wars in which case class with the war in E83.63-.895
	Subarrange by Table E1 at the end of the text
	GALE NOTE *The cutter number(s) listed below have been given only as examples by the*
	Library of Congress
	Black Hawk, Sauk chief, *see* E83.83
	Pocahontas, *see* E99.P85
	Sitting Bull, Dakota chief, *see* E99.D1
90.T2	Tegakouita, Catharine
	Government relations
	Including government agencies dealing with Indians, Indian rights associations, biography,
	treatment of Indians, reservations (General), and government services for Indians (General)
	For works limited to specific regions or states, see E78.A+
	For works limited to specific tribes, see E99.A+
91	General works

	Indians of North America
	Government relations — Continued
92	Canada
	Cf. E78.C2, Indians in Canada
93	United States
(94)	Law, *see* Class K
(95)	Treaties, *see* Class K
	Social life and customs, *see E98.S7*
	Education
	For works limited to specific tribes, see E99.A+
96	General works
	Canada
96.2	General works
	Indian schools
96.5	General works
96.6.A-.6.Z	Individual schools. By name, A-Z
	GALE NOTE *The cutter number(s) listed below have been given only as examples by the Library of Congress*
96.6.S17	St. Pauls's Indian Residential School, Cardston, Alta.
96.65.A-.65.Z	By region or province, A-Z
	United States
97	General works
97.3	Finance
	Indian schools
97.5	General works
97.55	Tribal colleges. Indian community colleges
97.6.A-.6.Z	Individual schools. By name, A-Z
	GALE NOTE *The cutter number(s) listed below have been given only as examples by the Library of Congress*
97.6.B87	Bureau of Indian Affairs School, Bethel, Alaska
97.6.C35	Cherokee National Female Seminary, Tahlequah, Okla.
97.6.F66	Fort Shaw Indian School (Great Falls, Mont.)
97.6.H3	Hampton Institute, Hampton, Va.
	Cf. LC2851.H27+, African-American education at Hampton Institute
97.6.J69	Johnson's Indian School, White Sulphur, Ky.
97.6.M5	Moor's Indian Charity School, Lebanon, Conn.
	Cf. LD1420+, Dartmouth College, Hanover, N.H.
97.6.R35	Rapid City Indian School
97.6.S2	Santee Normal Training School, Santee, Nebr.
97.6.T4	Thomas Indian School, Iroquois, N.Y.
97.6.U54	University of California. Tecumseh Center
97.65.A-.65.Z	By region or state, A-Z
97.8	**Indian libraries. Library service to Indians**
97.9	**Indian archives**
98.A-.Z	**Other topics, A-Z**
	For works limited to specific geographic areas, if specific tribes are not indicated, see E78.A+
	For works limited to specific tribes, see E99.A+
98.A15	Adoption
98.A2	Aesthetics
	Afro-American relations, *see E98.R28*
98.A27	Aged
98.A3	Agriculture
	Alcohol use, *see E98.L7*
98.A55	Anthropometry
	Antiquities, *see E77.8+, E78.A+*
	Appropriations, *see E91+*
98.A63	Architecture
98.A65	Arms and armor. Weapons

Indians of North America

98.A-.Z	**Other topics, A-Z — Continued**
98.A7	Art
	For modern art by Indian artists, see Class N
98.A73	Arts
98.A84	Asian influences
98.A88	Astronomy
98.B3	Baskets
98.B46	Beadwork
98.B54	Biology. Ethnobiology
98.B6	Boats. Canoes
98.B7	Botany (Economic). Ethnobotany
98.B8	Buffalo
	Burial customs, *see* E98.M8
98.B87	Business enterprises
98.C14	Calendar
	Captivities, *see* E85+
98.C17	Cartography
	Including works about maps of Indian lands
98.C3	Census
98.C47	Charitable contributions. Philanthropy
98.C5	Children
	Citizenship, *see* E91+
98.C55	Chronology
	Claims
98.C6	By Indians
98.C62	Against Indians
98.C7	Commerce
98.C73	Communication
98.C76	Copperwork
98.C79	Cosmology
98.C8	Costume. Adornment
	Crafts, *see* E98.I5
98.C85	Craniology
98.C87	Crime. Police
	Including Indian reservation police
	Criminal justice system, *see* Class K
98.C89	Cultural assimilation
	Cf. E91+, Government relations and treatment of Indians
	Culture, *see* E77
98.D2	Dance
98.D6	Diseases
98.D65	Dolls
98.D67	Domestic animals
98.D8	Drama
98.D9	Dwellings. Furniture
98.E2	Economic conditions
	Education, *see* E97+
98.E5	Embroidery
98.E6	Employment
98.E83	Ethics
98.E85	Ethnic identity
	Ethnobiology, *see* E98.B54
	Ethnobotany, *see* E98.B7
98.F3	Financial affairs
	Including trust estates, revolving credit fund, relief
	Cf. E98.P3, Pensions
98.F38	Fire use
98.F39	First contact with Europeans
98.F4	Fishing

	Indians of North America
98.A-.Z	**Other topics, A-Z — Continued**
98.F58	Folk literature
	For legends and tales, see E98.F6
98.F6	Folklore. Legends
	For individual tribes, see E99.A+
98.F7	Food
98.F73	Footwear
98.G18	Gambling
	Including gambling on Indian reservations
98.G2	Games. Recreation. Sports
98.G44	Genealogy
	Government relations, *see E91+*
	Handicraft, *see E98.I5*
98.H35	Handicapped
	History, *see E77+*
	Homosexuality, *see E98.S48*
98.H55	Horses
	Hospitals, *see RA981.A35*
98.H58	Housing
98.H77	Humor
98.H8	Hunting
98.I4	Implements. Utensils
98.I5	Industries
	Including handicraft, mining, etc.
	For basketry, see E98.B3
	For silversmithing, see E98.S55
	For textile industry, see E98.T35
98.I54	Interviews
98.I75	Irrigation
98.J48	Jewelry
98.K48	Kinship
98.K54	Knives
98.L3	Land tenure
	Land transfers, *see E91+*
	Language, *see PM1+*
98.L4	Leatherwork. Tanning
	Legends, *see E98.F6*
98.L7	Liquor use. Alcohol use
98.M2	Magic
98.M27	Marriage customs and rites
98.M3	Masks
	Mass media, *see P94.5.I53*
98.M34	Material culture
98.M35	Medals
98.M4	Medicine. Medicine men
	Cf. E98.D6, Diseases
	Mental health, *see RC451.5.I5*
98.M45	Metalwork
98.M5	Military capacity and organization. Indians as soldiers
98.M6	Missions (General)
	Including biography of missionaries
	Prefer tribe or local
	For Jesuit missions in New France, see F1030.7+
98.M63	Mixed descent
98.M7	Money. Wampum
98.M8	Mortuary customs
	Music (Music scores), *see M1669, ML3557*
98.N2	Names
98.N5	Narcotics. Drugs

	Indians of North America
98.A-.Z	**Other topics, A-Z — Continued**
	Newspapers, *see* PN4883
	Origin, *see* E61
98.O7	Oratory. Speeches, addresses, etc.
	Ornaments, *see* E98.C8
98.O76	Orphanages
98.P23	Painting
98.P3	Pensions
98.P34	Petroglyphs. Rock paintings
	Philanthropy, *see* E98.C47
98.P5	Philosophy
98.P53	Physical anthropology
	Including physical characteristics, beauty, etc.
	Cf. E98.A55, Anthropometry
(98.P74)	Poetry
	For poetry in Indian languages, see PM151+
	For poetry by Indians in non-Indian languages, see Subclasses PR, PS, etc.
	Police, *see* E98.C87
	Politics and government, *see* E98.T77
98.P76	Population
	Portraits (Collected), *see* E89+
98.P8	Pottery
98.P86	Powwows
98.P9	Property
	Including appraisal, removal of restrictions, timber contracts, wills, etc.
98.P95	Psychology
	Cf. BF432.I5, Intelligence of Indians
98.P99	Public opinion about Indians. Popular attitudes toward Indians
	Recreation, *see* E98.G2
98.R28	Relations with Afro-Americans
98.R3	Religion. Mythology
	Including creation, future life, katcinas, occultism, revivalism, rites and ceremonies, shamanism, etc.
98.R4	Removal
	Reservations, *see* E78.A+, E91+, E99.A+
98.R5	Riding gear
98.R53	Rites and ceremonies
	Rock paintings, *see* E98.P34
98.S26	Salt
98.S3	Sandpaintings
	Scalping, *see* E98.W2
98.S43	Science
98.S46	Services for
98.S48	Sexual behavior
	Including homosexuality
98.S5	Sign language
98.S55	Silversmithing
98.S6	Slavery
	Smoking, *see* E98.T6
98.S67	Social conditions
98.S7	Social life and customs
98.S75	Societies
	Speeches, addresses, etc., *see* E98.O7
	Sports, *see* E98.G2
	Suffrage, *see* E91+
98.S9	Suicide
98.S94	Sweatbaths
98.T2	Tattooing
98.T24	Taxation

	Indians of North America
98.A-.Z	**Other topics, A-Z — Continued**
98.T35	Textile fabrics. Weaving
	Including blankets, rugs, etc.
98.T6	Tobacco pipes. Smoking
98.T65	Totems
	Including totem poles
98.T7	Trails
98.T73	Transatlantic influences
98.T75	Trapping
	Treaties, *see* Class K
98.T77	Tribal government. Politics and government
98.U72	Urban residence
	Utensils, *see* E98.I4
98.W2	Warfare. Scalping
	Wars, *see* E81+
	Weapons, *see* E98.A65
	Weaving, *see* E98.T35
98.W49	Wife abuse
	Wills, *see* E98.P9
98.W8	Women
98.W86	Writing
98.Y68	Youth
	Tribes and cultures, A-Z
	Including those Mexican tribes which are also found in the United States
	For biographies, assign second cutter for biographees
99.A12	Abitibi
99.A13	Abnaki. Abenaki
99.A15	Achomawi
99.A16	Acoma
99.A18	Adena culture
99.A28	Ahtena
99.A34	Aleuts
99.A349	Algonkin
99.A35	Algonquian
99.A4	Alibamu
99.A45	Alsea
	Anasazi culture, *see* E99.P9
99.A6	Apache
99.A62	Apalachee
99.A63	Apalachicola
99.A7	Arapaho
99.A8	Arikara
99.A82	Arosaguntacook
99.A83	Assateague
99.A84	Assiniboin
99.A86	Athapascan
99.A87	Atsina
99.A875	Atsugewi
99.A88	Attacapa
99.B33	Bannock
99.B37	Basket-Maker
99.B376	Bearlake
(99.B38)	Bellabella, *see* E99.H45
99.B39	Bellacoola
99.B4	Beothuk
99.B5	Biloxi
99.B6	Bocootawwonauke
99.B7	Brotherton
99.B8	Brulé

Indians of North America
Tribes and cultures, A-Z —   Continued

99.C12	Caddo
99.C13	Caddoan
99.C15	Cahokia
99.C155	Cahuilla
99.C18	Calusa
99.C19	Campo
99.C2	Capote
	Carrier, *see* E99.T17
99.C23	Casas Grandes culture
99.C24	Catawba
99.C26	Cathlamet
(99.C27)	Caughnawaga, *see* E99.M8
99.C3	Cayuga
99.C32	Cayuse
99.C4	Chakchiuma
99.C48	Chasta
99.C483	Chastacosta
99.C49	Chehalis
99.C4925	Chelan
99.C493	Chemehuevi
99.C495	Cheraw
99.C5	Cherokee
99.C526	Chetco
99.C53	Cheyenne
99.C55	Chickasaw
	Chilcotin, *see* E99.T78
99.C552	Chilkat
99.C5523	Chilliwack
99.C553	Chilula
99.C56	Chimariko
99.C565	Chimmesyan
99.C57	Chinook
99.C58	Chinookan
99.C59	Chipewyan
99.C6	Chippewa
99.C68	Chiricahua
99.C7	Chitimacha
99.C8	Choctaw
99.C815	Chumash. Chumashan
99.C82	Clallam
99.C83	Clayoquot
99.C832	Clovis culture
99.C834	Coahuiltecan
99.C835	Cochimi
99.C84	Cochiti
99.C842	Cocopa
99.C844	Colville
99.C85	Comanche
99.C86	Comox
99.C87	Conestoga
99.C873	Conoy
	Including Piscataway
99.C874	Coos
99.C87414	Coosa
99.C8742	Coquille
99.C8743	Coree
(99.C8744)	Costanoan, *see* E99.O32
99.C875	Cowichan

Indians of North America
Tribes and cultures, A-Z — Continued

99.C877	Cowlitz
99.C88	Cree
99.C9	Creek
99.C91	Croatan. Lumbee
99.C92	Crow
99.C94	Cupeño
99.D1	Dakota. Sioux
	Including Chief Sitting Bull
	For death of Chief Sitting Bull, see E83.89
99.D2	Delaware
	Dena'ina, *see* E99.T185
99.D25	Dene Thá
99.D4	Dhegiha
99.D5	Diegueño
99.D8	Dudley
99.D9	Duwamish
99.E42	Entiat
99.E5	Erie
99.E7	Eskimos
	Including Inuit
99.E8	Esopus
99.E85	Esselen
99.E9	Eyak
	Five civilized tribes, *see* E78.I5, E99.C5, E99.C55, E99.C8, E99.C9, E99.S28
99.F65	Folsom culture
99.F67	Fort Ancient culture
99.F7	Fox
99.G15	Gabrieleño
	Gitksan, *see* E99.K55
99.G67	Gosiute
99.G82	Guale
99.H15	Hackensack
99.H2	Haida
99.H23	Haisla
99.H26	Han
99.H28	Hasinai
99.H3	Havasupai
99.H45	Heiltsuk
99.H6	Hidatsa
99.H65	Hitchiti
99.H68	Hohokam culture
99.H69	Hopewell culture
99.H7	Hopi
99.H72	Houma
99.H75	Hualapai
99.H795	Hunkpapa
99.H8	Hupa
99.H9	Huron
	Including Wyandot Indians
99.I2	Illinois
99.I5	Ingalik
	Inuit, *see* E99.E7
99.I6	Iowa
99.I69	Iroquoian
99.I7	Iroquois
99.I8	Isleta
99.J4	Jemez
99.J5	Jicarilla

Indians of North America
Tribes and cultures, A-Z — Continued

99.J8	Juaneño
99.J9	Jumano
99.K15	Kainah
99.K16	Kalapuyan
99.K17	Kalispel
99.K18	Kamia
99.K2	Kansa
99.K23	Karankawa
99.K25	Karok
99.K258	Kashaya
99.K26	Kaska
99.K264	Kaskaskia
99.K267	Kato
99.K269	Kawaiisu
99.K28	Kawchottine
99.K3	Keeche
99.K39	Keresan
99.K396	Kichai
99.K4	Kickapoo
99.K5	Kiowa
99.K52	Kiowa Apache
99.K55	Kitksan. Gitksan
99.K59	Kiyuksa
99.K7	Klamath
99.K76	Klikitat
99.K77	Koasati
99.K79	Koyukon
99.K82	Kuitsh
99.K83	Kusso
99.K84	Kutchin
99.K85	Kutenai
99.K9	Kwakiutl
99.L2	Laguna
	Lakes, *see* E99.S546
99.L25	Lamar culture
99.L3	Lassik
99.L35	Lekwungen. Songhees
99.L4	Lillooet
99.L5	Lipan
99.L9	Luiseño
	Lumbee, *see* E99.C91
99.L95	Lummi
99.L98	Lutuamian
99.M115	Madehsi
99.M12	Mahican
99.M18	Maidu
99.M19	Makah
99.M195	Malecite
99.M198	Manahoac
99.M2	Mandan
99.M22	Manhattan
99.M23	Manso
99.M25	Maricopa
99.M27	Martis culture
99.M3	Mascouten
99.M4	Mashpee
99.M42	Massachuset
99.M424	Massawomeck

Indians of North America
Tribes and cultures, A-Z — Continued

99.M43	Mattole
99.M433	Mayas
	Cf. F1435+, Central America
	Cf. F1445+, British Honduras
	Cf. F1465+, Guatemala
99.M435	Mdewakanton
99.M44	Menominee
99.M45	Mescalero
99.M46	Methow
99.M47	Métis
99.M48	Miami
99.M6	Micmac
99.M615	Mikasuki
99.M62	Mikinakwadshiwininiwak
99.M625	Mill Creek
99.M63	Mimbreño
99.M64	Mingo
99.M642	Miniconjou
99.M65	Minisink
99.M68	Missisauga
99.M6815	Mississippian culture
99.M682	Missouri
99.M683	Mistassin
99.M69	Miwok
99.M693	Mixed descent
	For Métis, see E99.M47
99.M697	Moache
99.M698	Mobile
99.M7	Modoc
99.M75	Mogollon Apache
99.M76	Mogollon culture
	Including Mimbres culture
99.M77	Mohave
99.M8	Mohawk
99.M83	Mohegan
99.M84	Molala
99.M85	Monacan
99.M86	Mono
99.M87	Montagnais
99.M88	Montauk
99.M89	Moquelumnan
99.M9	Moravian
99.M917	Muckleshoot
99.M92	Multnomah
99.M93	Munsee
99.M95	Muskhogean
99.N125	Nahane
99.N14	Nanticoke
99.N16	Narranganset
99.N18	Naskapi
99.N19	Natchesan
99.N2	Natchez
99.N22	Natsitkutchin
99.N23	Naugatuck
99.N25	Nauset
99.N3	Navajo
99.N45	Nehalem
99.N46	Nespelim

Indians of North America
Tribes and cultures, A-Z — Continued

99.48	Neutral Nation
99.N5	NezPercé
99.N6	Niantic
99.N65	Nipissing
99.N7	Nipmuc
99.N73	Nisenan
99.N734	Niska
99.N74	Nisqually
99.N815	Nomlaki
99.N84	Nooksack
99.N85	Nootka
99.N9	Norridgewock
99.N93	Nottoway
99.N96	Ntlakyapamuk
99.N97	Numic
99.O22	Occaneechi
99.O3	Oglala
99.O32	Ohlone
	Ojibwa, *see* E99.C6
(99.O33)	Oka, *see* E99.M8
99.O35	Okinagan
99.O4	Omaha
99.O45	Oneida
99.O5	Oneota (Great Plains)
99.O58	Onondaga
99.O63	Oohenonpa
99.O68	Oowekeeno
99.O8	Osage
99.O87	Oto
99.O9	Ottawa
99.P2	Paiute
99.P215	Palaihnihan
99.P22	Paloos
99.P225	Pamlico
99.P23	Pamunkey
99.P24	Panamint
99.P244	Panhandle culture
99.P25	Papago. Tohono O'Odham
99.P26	Pascagoula
99.P27	Passamaquoddy
99.P29	Patwin
99.P292	Paugusset
99.P3	Pawnee
99.P32	Payaya
99.P34	Pecos
99.P35	Pee Dee
99.P4	Pennacook
99.P5	Penobscot
99.P515	Peoria
99.P52	Pequawket
99.P53	Pequot
99.P57	Piankashaw
99.P575	Picuris
99.P58	Piegan
99.P6	Pima
99.P62	Piman
99.P63	Piro Pueblo
	Piscataway, *see* E99.C873

Indians of North America

Tribes and cultures, A-Z — Continued

Plains Indians, *see* E78.G73

99.P64	Pocasset
99.P65	Pomo
99.P7	Ponca
99.P8	Potawatomi
99.P83	Potomac
99.P84	Poverty Point culture
99.P85	Powhatan
	Including Pocahontas
99.P9	Pueblo
	Including Anasazi culture and cliff dwellings
99.P98	Puyallup
99.Q2	Quapaw
99.Q5	Quileute
99.Q6	Quinaielt
99.Q7	Quinnipiac
99.R18	Rappahannock
99.S14	Saclan
(99.S15)	Saint Regis, *see* E99.M8
99.S16	Sakonnet
	Salado culture, *see* E99.S547
99.S17	Salinan
99.S2	Salish
99.S21	Salishan
	Including Coast Salish and Puget Sound Salish
99.S2115	Samish
99.S212	San Felipe
99.S213	San Ildefonso
99.S214	Sandia
99.S215	Sanpoil
99.S217	Sans Arc
99.S22	Santee
99.S223	Santo Domingo
99.S225	Saone
99.S226	Saponi
99.S227	Sarsi
99.S23	Sauk
99.S25	Scaticook (Connecticut)
99.S252	Scaticook (New York)
99.S258	Sechelt
99.S26	Sekani
99.S28	Seminole
99.S3	Seneca
99.S31	Serrano
99.S32	Sewee
99.S325	Shahaptian
99.S33	Shasta
99.S332	Shastan
99.S35	Shawnee
99.S38	Shinnecock
99.S39	Shoshonean
99.S4	Shoshoni
99.S45	Shuswap
99.S5	Sia
99.S53	Sihasapa
99.S54	Siksika
99.S544	Siletz
99.S546	Sin Aikst. Lakes Indians

Indians of North America
Tribes and cultures, A-Z — Continued

99.S547	Sinagua culture
	Including Salado culture
99.S55	Sinkiuse-Columbia
99.S56	Sinkyone
99.S6	Siouan
	Sioux, *see* E99.D1
99.S62	Sisseton
99.S622	Siuslaw
99.S623	Siwanoy
99.S627	Skagit
99.S63	Skitswish
99.S64	Skokomish
99.S65	Slave
99.S66	Snoqualmie
99.S665	Sokoki
	Songhees, *see* E99.L35
99.S68	Spokan
99.S7	Squawmish
99.S72	Stalo
99.S75	Stillaquamish
99.S8	Stockbridge
99.S85	Suquamish
99.S95	Susquehanna
99.T114	Tabeguache
99.T115	Taensa
99.T12	Tahltan
99.T15	Takelma
99.T17	Takulli
99.T18	Tamaroa
99.T185	Tanai. Dena'ina
99.T187	Tanana
99.T2	Taos
99.T315	Tawakoni
99.T32	Tenino
99.T325	Tequesta
99.T33	Têtes de Boule
99.T34	Teton
99.T35	Tewa
99.T4	Thlingchadinne
99.T52	Tigua. Tiwa
99.T53	Tillamook
99.T54	Timiskaming
99.T55	Timucua
99.T56	Tinne
99.T57	Tionontati
	Tiwa, *see* E99.T52
99.T58	Tlakluit
99.T6	Tlingit
	Tohono O'Odham, *see* E99.P25
99.T7	Tolowa
99.T73	Tonikan
99.T75	Tonkawa
99.T77	Tsattine
99.T772	Tsetsaut
99.T78	Tsilkotin
99.T8	Tsimshian
99.T83	Tubatulabal
99.T845	Tukkuthkutchin

Indians of North America

Tribes and cultures, A-Z — Continued

99.T85	Tukuarika
99.T87	Tulalip
99.T875	Tunica
99.T88	Tunxis
99.T9	Tuscarora
99.T92	Tutchone
99.T96	Tutelo
99.T97	Tututni
99.T98	Twana
99.T986	Tzotzil

Cf. F1221.T9, Mexico

99.U35	Uinta
99.U4	Umatilla
99.U45	Umpqua
99.U8	Ute
99.U85	Uto-Aztecan
99.V8	Vuntakutchin
99.W114	Waccamaw
99.W12	Wachuset
99.W125	Waco
99.W13	Wahpekute
99.W135	Wahpeton
99.W15	Wailaki
99.W16	Wakashan
99.W18	Walla Walla
99.W185	Walpapi
99.W19	Wamesit
99.W2	Wampanoag
99.W3	Wanapum
99.W34	Wappinger
99.W35	Wappo
99.W36	Warm Spring Apache
99.W37	Wasco
99.W38	Washo
99.W4	Wawenock
99.W45	Wea
99.W48	Weeden Island culture
99.W5	Welsh

Including the tradition and theories about this mythic tribe

99.W53	Wenatchi
99.W54	Wenrohronon
99.W56	Wet'suwet'en
99.W6	Wichita
99.W63	Wiechquaeskeck
99.W65	Wiminuche
99.W7	Winnebago
99.W78	Wintu
99.W79	Wintun
99.W8	Wiyat
99.W84	Woodland culture
99.W9	Wyam
99.Y18	Yahuskin
99.Y2	Yakama. Yakima
99.Y212	Yakonan
99.Y22	Yamassee
99.Y225	Yampa
99.Y23	Yana
99.Y25	Yankton

	Indians of North America
	Tribes and cultures, A-Z — Continued
99.Y26	Yanktonai
	Yaqui, *see* F1221.Y3
99.Y5	Yavapai
99.Y7	Yokayo
99.Y75	Yokuts
99.Y77	Yoncalla
99.Y9	Yuchi
99.Y92	Yukian
99.Y94	Yuma
99.Y95	Yuman
99.Y97	Yurok
99.Z9	Zuñi
	Discovery of America and early explorations
	Including early to about 1607
101	**General works**
	Pre-Columbian period
103	General works
	Special
105	Norse. Vinland
	Including biography of Liev Eiriksson, Kensington rune stone
	For Greenland, see G725+
109.A-.Z	Other, A-Z
109.A35	African
109.B3	Basque
109.C37	Catalan
109.C44	Celtic
109.C5	Chinese
109.D2	Danish
109.D9	Dutch
109.E2	East Indian
109.E3	Egyptian
109.G7	Greek
109.I57	Indonesian
109.I6	Irish
109.I8	Italian
	Including voyages of the brothers Niccolò and Antonio Zeno
109.M34	Malian
109.P5	Phoenician
109.P8	Portuguese
109.S7	Spanish
109.T74	Trojan
109.W4	Welsh
	For the tradition of the Welsh Indians, see E99.W5
	Background factors of the discovery, and resulting conditions
	Including the influence of Paolo del Pozzo Toscanelli, Martin Behaim
	Columbus (Cristoforo Colombo)
111	General works
	Including biography
112	Special
	Including autographs, birthplace, canonization, celebrations, coat of arms, education, friends, iconography, landfall, language, marriage, monuments, name. relics, ships, tomb
	For bibliography of Columbus, see Z8187
113	Family
	Including the Colombo, Colón, Moniz, and Perestrello families
	Writings of Columbus
114	Collected works
	Including collected letters and collectiond of documents concerning him
	Arranged alphabetically by editor

Discovery of America and early explorations
Columbus (Cristoforo Colombo)
Writings of Columbus — Continued
Individual works
First letter (Santangel)

115   Spanish text. By date
                Including facsimiles and reprints without translation

115.2   Translations. By language, A-Z, and date of imprint
                With or without facsimiles or reprints of Spanish text

115.3   Pharaphrases and works about the letter. By author
Second letter (Sánchez)

116   Spanish text. By date
                Including facsimiles and reprints without translation
Translations

116.1   Latin. By date
                Including the earliest translation as well as others made from it; facsimiles and texts

116.2   Other. By initial letter of language and date
                With or without facsimiles or reprints of Spanish text

116.3   Pharaphrases and works about the letter. By author
117   Other writings
                For his journal, see E118

118   Voyages. Journal of Columbus
119   Coluimbus celebrations, 1892-1893
            Arranged alphabetically by place
            Cf. T400+, National and international exhibitions

119.2   Columbus quincentennial, 1192-1993
120   Pamphlets, addresses, essays, etc.
            Including poetry, drama, Columbus Day celebrations and programs
            Cf. Subclasses PN-PZ, Literature

Post-Columbian period. El Dorado
            Including successors of Columbus to about 1607

121   General works
            Cf. G199.2+, History of geographical discoveries, explorations, and travels
            Cf. G575+, Polar discoveries
            Cf. G640+, Search for the Northwest Passage
Spanish and Portuguese

123   General works
            Including Line of Demarcation drawn by Pope Alexander VI in 1493 and modified by Treaty of Tordesillas, 1494
            Cf. E141+, Descriptive accounts of America before 1607
            Cf. F314, Spanish settlement in Florida before 1821
            Cf. F1230, Spanish settlement in Mexico before 1810
            Cf. F1411, History of Spanish America before 1600
            Cf. F3442, Spanish settlement in Peru before 1820
            Cf. G278+, History of geographical discoveries by the Spanish and the Portuguese
Individual explorers, A-Z
           GALE NOTE *The cutter number(s) listed below have been given only as examples by the Library of Congress*

125.A3   Aguilar, Jerónimo de
            Subarrange by Table E1 at the end of the text

125.A35   Aguirre, Lope de
            Subarrange by Table E1 at the end of the text

125.B2   Balboa, Vasco Núñez de
            Subarrange by Table E1 at the end of the text

125.B7   Boyl, Bernardo
            Subarrange by Table E1 at the end of the text

125.C11   Cabral, Pedro Alvares
            Subarrange by Table E1 at the end of the text

                Discovery of America and early explorations
                 Post-Columbian period. El Dorado
                   Spanish and Portuguese
                   Individual explorers, A-Z — Continued

125.C12	Cabrillo, Juan Rodríquez
	Subarrange by Table E1 at the end of the text
125.C2	Caminha, Pedro Vaz de
	Subarrange by Table E1 at the end of the text
125.C4	Casas, Bartolomé de las
	Subarrange by Table E1 at the end of the text
	For the tracts of Las Casas, see F1411
125.C8	Cosa, Juan de la
	Subarrange by Table E1 at the end of the text
125.F3	Federmann, Nikolaus
	Subarrange by Table E1 at the end of the text
125.F35	Fernández, Juan
	Subarrange by Table E1 at the end of the text
125.F9	Fuca, Juan de
	Subarrange by Table E1 at the end of the text
125.G2	García, Diego de Moguer
	Subarrange by Table E1 at the end of the text
125.G6	Gómez, Esteban
	Subarrange by Table E1 at the end of the text
125.G8	Grijalva, Juan de
	Subarrange by Table E1 at the end of the text
125.M3	Marco da Nizza, Father
	Subarrange by Table E1 at the end of the text
125.N3	Narváez, Pánfilo de
	Subarrange by Table E1 at the end of the text
125.N9	Núñez Cabeza de Vaca, Alvar
	Subarrange by Table E1 at the end of the text
125.O58	Ordás, Diego de
	Subarrange by Table E1 at the end of the text
125.O6	Orellano, Francisco de
	Subarrange by Table E1 at the end of the text
125.P2	Pancaldo, León
	Subarrange by Table E1 at the end of the text
125.P5	Pinzón, Martín Alonso
	Subarrange by Table E1 at the end of the text
125.P52	Pinzón, Vincente Yáñez
	Subarrange by Table E1 at the end of the text
125.P7	Ponce de León, Juan
	Subarrange by Table E1 at the end of the text
125.S23	Sarmiento de Gamboa, Pedro
	Subarrange by Table E1 at the end of the text
125.S3	Schmidel, Ulrich
	Subarrange by Table E1 at the end of the text
125.S7	Soto, Hernando de
	Subarrange by Table E1 at the end of the text
125.U8	Ursúa, Pedro de
	Subarrange by Table E1 at the end of the text
125.V3	Vásquez de Coronado, Francisco
	Subarrange by Table E1 at the end of the text
125.V5	Vespucci, Amerigo
	Subarrange by Table E1 at the end of the text
125.V6	The name "America"
	English
127	General works

                          Discovery of America and early explorations
                          Post-Columbian period. El Dorado
                              English — Continued
129.A-.Z   Individual explorers, A-Z
129.C1   Cabot, John an d Sebastian
                                          Subarrange by Table E1 at the end of the text
129.D7   Drake, Sir Francis
                                          Subarrange by Table E1 at the end of the text
                                          Cf. G420.D7, Voyage of circumnavigation
129.G4   Gilbert, Sir Humphrey
                                          Subarrange by Table E1 at the end of the text
129.H4   Hawkins, Sir Richard
                                          Subarrange by Table E1 at the end of the text
129.H8   Hudson, Henry
                                          Subarrange by Table E1 at the end of the text
                                          Cf. F127.H8, Hudson: Fulton celebration, 1909
129.R2   Raleigh, Sir Walter
                                          Subarrange by Table E1 at the end of the text
                                          Cf. DA86.22.R2, Biography
                                          Cf. F229, Raleigh's Roanoke colonies, 1584-1590
                              French
                                          Cf. F314, French colony in Florida
                                          Cf. 1030, New France
131   General works
133.A-.Z   Individual explorers, A-Z
133.C3   Cartier, Jacques
                                          Subarrange by Table E1 at the end of the text
133.P3   Paulmier de Gonneville, Binot
                                          Subarrange by Table E1 at the end of the text
133.T47   Thevet, André
                                          Subarrange by Table E1 at the end of the text
133.V5   Verrazzano, Giovanni da
                                          Subarrange by Table E1 at the end of the text
135.A-.Z   Other, A-Z
                                  GALE NOTE *The cutter number(s) listed below have been given only as examples by the*
                                      Library of Congress
135.D9   Dutch
135.G3   German. Welsers
135.I8   Italian
                          Allusions
                              Including works on subjetcs other than America, containing illusions to the discovery and to the
                              New World
                              For the books being classified with the subjects of which they treat or the literature to which they
                                  belong, e.g., the polyglot Psalter edited by Agostino Giustiniani, see BS1419, and the
                                  Sentencias catholocias del divi, poeta Dant, compiled by Jaume Ferrer de Blanes,
                                  seePS3937.F4
                          Descriptive accounts of America. Earliest to 1810
141   **Earliest to 1606**
                                  cluding 16th century travels
                                  Cf. E101+, Discoveries
                                  Cf. F1411, History of Latin America to 1600
143   **1607-1810. Latin America**
                                  For English colonies, see E162
                                  For Latin America since 1810, see F1409
                                  For New France, 1603-1763, see F1030
                                  For other local, see corresponding country and period divisions in Class F

	General
151	**Periodicals. Societies. Collections**
	Including general societies for the preservation of places of historic or other national interest, e.g.
	American Scenic and Historic Preservation Society
	For geographic societies, see G3
	For historical periodicals and societies, see E171-172 , E186 , etc.
	For patriotic societies, see E172.7, E181, E182, E186, E202, etc.
154	**Gazetteers**
	Directories
154.5	General
154.7	Social directories. Social registers
(154.9)	Business and trade directories, *see* HF5035-5068
	Recreational directories, *see* E158
155	**Geographic names**
	Cf. E98.N2, Indian names
	Cf. G104+, Geographic names and terms (General)
156	**General works**
	Electronic information resource catalogs, *see* E175.88
158	**Guidebooks. Handbooks**
	Including directories of summer and winter resorts, excursions, etc.
159	**Historic monuments (General)**
	Including mansions, mission buildings, public buildings
	For individual mansions, mission buildings, public buildings, etc., see local divisions
	For roads, see HE356.A+
	For historical and descriptive works on regions traversed by a road, see Class F
	For general questions of the location and removal of the national capital, see F195
	Cf. E179.5, Boundaries
	Cf. G109, Distances
	Cf. GB494+, Altitudes
159.5	**Antiquities (Non-Indian)**
160	**National and state parks and reservations (Collective descriptive works)**
	Including national forests as parks
	Cf. SD426+, Forest reserves
	For works on individual parks, including theory, management and description, see the subject or local division, e.g. E475.81, Chickamauga and Chattanooga National Military Park; F868.Y6, Yosemite National Park
	For works on theory, management and history, etc., of U.S. parks and public reservations in general, see SB482.A1+
161	**Social life and customs (General)**
	Including antiquities, museums, etc., illustrative of American life, e.g. Henry Ford Museum and Greenfield Village, Dearborn, Mich.
	Cf. E169.1+, Civilization, Intellectual life
	By period, *see* E162+
161.3	**Geography**
	Description and travel
	For travel before era of settlement, see E141+
	For regions, see Class F, Local history, e.g. F106, Atlantic coast; F206-220, Southern States; F351-354, Mississippi Valley; F476-485, Old Northwest; F591-595, The West
161.5	History of travels. Travel anthologies
	By period
	Including works on civilization, social life
	Class general works of travel through the country in 1785 in E164, not in F106, Atlantic States
162	1607-1764
	Including general descriptive works on the British colonies in America including Thanksgiving Day and customs
	Cf. F7, Thanksgiving Day in New England
	Cf. GT4975, Festivals
163	1765-1783
164	1784-1811

General

Description and travel

By period — Continued

165	1812-1844
166	1845-1860
167	1861-1865
	For travels in the Confederate States, see F214
168	1866-1913
169	1914-1944
169.02	1945-1980
169.04	1981-

Civilization. Intellectual life

Including national characteristics, ideals, Americanization

Cf. E161, Social life and customs (General)

Cf. JK1758, Manuals for foreign-born citizens

169.1	General works
	By period
	Early to 1865, *see* E162+
	1866-1945, *see* E169.1
169.12	1945-
	Biography (Americanization literature), *see* E184+

History

171	**Periodicals. Yearbooks**
172	**Societies**
	Including historical departments of other organizations, e.g. Museums, libraries
	Cf. E175.4, Historiography
	Geographic societies, *see* G3
	Patriotic hereditary societies
172.7	General works
	Individual societies, *see* E181-182, E186, E202, etc.
	Political and patriotic societies primarily interested in social objectives, *see* HS2321+
172.9	**Congresses, seminars, etc.**
173	**Sources and documents. Collections. Collected works**
	Including exhibitions of source materials
174	**Dictionaries and encyclopedias**
174.5	**Chronology. Chronological tables, etc.**
	Historiography
	For general works on state and local historiography, see E180.5
175	General works. History
175.1	Pamphlets, etc.
175.4	Institutions
	Including programs, reports, methods of organization and work
	Including the work of government commissions, historical societies, etc.
175.4.C3	Carnegie Institution of Washington. Division of Historical Research
	Biography of historians
	Including general criticism of their works
	Class criticism of a particular work with the work
175.45	Collective
175.5.A-.5.Z	Individual, A-Z
	Subarrange by Table E1 at the end of the text
	GALE NOTE *The cutter number(s) listed below have been given only as examples by the Library of Congress*
175.5.B38	Beard, Charles Austin
175.7	Methodology
	Including theory, comparison and criticism, etc. Research
	Study and teaching
	Class here study and teaching in colleges, universities, and secondary schools
175.8	General works
175.85	Criticism of textbooks (General)
	Cf. E468.5, Criticism of textbooks on the Civil War

	History — Continued
175.87	**Film catalogs**
175.88	**Electronic information resource catalogs**
175.9	**Philosophy of American history**
	Biography (Collective)
176	General
	For general United States biography not limited to political life, see CT210+
	For biography of individual periods, see the period, e.g. E302.5, 1775-1829
	Presidents
	For the biography of each president, see his administration, e.g. E312, Washington; E322, Jefferson
	Presidential inaugurations are classed in local history, e.g. F128.44, New York City, for Washington's first inauguration in 1789; but F158.44, Philadelphia, for his second in 1793; F197-200, Washington, D.C., for the inaugurations of Jefferson and succeeding presidents
	For the White House, see F204.W5
176.1	General works
176.2	Wives of Presidents
176.25	Fathers of Presidents
176.3	Mothers of Presidents
176.4	Relations with women
176.45	Children and grandchildren of Presidents
176.47	Staff
176.472.A-.472.Z	Relations with specific ethnic groups, A-Z
176.472.A34	African Americans
176.472.J47	Jews
176.48	Pets
176.49	Vice-Presidents
176.5	Portraits
	Class here works emphasizing historical aspects
	For works emphasizing the artistic aspects or the artist, see N7593+
176.6	Hall of Fame, New York University
176.8	Juvenile works
	Biography (Individual), *see* under periods in national or state history, e.g. E195, United States, 1689-1775; E207, Revolution; F122, New York State before 1775; and under topics, e.g E181-182, Military and naval leaders; E185.97, Afro-Americans
	For the life of a representative in Congress and governor of a state, see state history unless his national career has been decidedly more prominent
	General works
178	Comprehensive works
178.1	Textbooks
178.2	Outlines, syllabi, etc.
	For chronology, see E174.5
178.25	Examinations, questions, etc.
178.3	Juvenile works
	Including collections of stories from American history for children
	Cf. PE1127.H5+, English readers on United States history
178.4	Comic and satirical works
	Including humor of American history
178.5	Pictorial works
178.6	Addresses, essays, lectures, etc.
178.9	Poetical works. Rhyming histories
	For general collections of American historical poems, see PS595.H5
	Collections or single poems on a particular event are classed with the subject, e.g. E233, Ballads and poems relating to the Burgoyne campaign
179	General special
	Including topics such as disasters, floods, pageants, vigilance committees, etc. in general not otherwise provided for
	For local, see Class F

History — Continued

179.5   **Historical geography**

Including Boundaries (General), the frontier, history of territorial expansion, public domain, regionalism, etc.

For boundaries (Special), see F912.B7, Alaska; F550.5+, F597, North; E398, F27.B7, F42.B7, F57.B7, F127.B7, Northeast; F854, F880, Northwest; F317.B7, Southeast before 1819; F392.B7, F786, Southwest

For anthropogeography, see GF503+

Cf. E713, Expansion controversy, imperialism, etc.

Cf. JK2551+, Territorial government and administration

History of states and counties, collectively

Class counties limited to one state with that state

180   General works

180.5   State and local historiography

General special

181   Military history

Including battles of more than two wars

For battles of more than two wars in the twentieth century, see E745

Including military societies, veterans' organizations, etc., covering more than one war: Medal of Honor Legion of the United States, Military Order of Foreign Wars of the United States, Military Order of the Purple Heart, Society of American Wars of the United States, Veterans of Foreign Wars of the United States, etc.

For Grand Army of the Republic (Civil War), see E462.1

Including military biography not limited to one war: William Selby Harney, John Joseph Pershing, Hugh Lenox Scott, Leonard Wood, etc.

Cf. U52-53, Biography (Military science)

For military history of the twentieth century, see E745

For military history of individual wars, see the war, e.g. E230-239, Revolution; E470-478, Civil War

182   Naval history (United States Navy and Marine Corps)

Including naval battles of more than two wars

Including naval societies, veterans' organizations, etc., covering more than one war: Naval Order of the United States, United States Navy Veteran Association, etc.

For National Association of Naval Veterans (Civil War), see E462.5

Naval biography not limited to one war: Smedley Darlington Butler; Stephen Decatur, 1752-1808; Robley Dunglison Evans; Ernest Joseph King; Edward Yorke Macauley; Alfred Thayer Mahan; Richard Worsam Meade; Hiram Paulding; Matthew Calbraith Perry; John Woodward Philip; George Henry Preble; Francis Asbury Roe; Stephen Clegg Rowan; Benjamin Franklin Sands; Charles Steedman; Thomas Truxtun; etc.

Cf. V62+, Biography (Naval science)

For naval history of the twentieth century, see E746

For naval history of individual wars, see the war, e.g. E271, Revolution; E591-600, Civil War

Political history

Political history of a period or administration is classed with the period or administration, e.g. E188, Colonial history; E801, Hoover's administration

183   General works

183.3   Political collectibles. Political Americana

Diplomatic history. Foreign and general relations

General works on the diplomatic history of a period or administration are classed with the period or administration, e.g. E313, Washington's administration; E661.7, Period since Civil War; E744, Twentieth century

All the works on relations with a specific country are classed in E183.8, regardless of administration or period

Cf. JZ1482, Monroe Doctrine

183.7   General works

(183.75)   Relations with special groups of countries

For Africa, see DT38

For Barbary States (1801-1809), see E335

	History
	General special
	Diplomatic history. Foreign and general relations
(183.75)	Relations with special groups of countries — Continued
	For Central American, West Indian, and other countries protected by and having close political affiliations with the United States, see F975
	For Europe (1945-), see D1065.U5
	For The Far East (Far Eastern question), see DS518.8
	For Latin America, see F1418
	For International American Conference, see F1405
	For Near East, see DS63.2.U5
	For Oceania, see DU30
	For West Indies, see F1622
183.8.A-.8.Z	Relations with individual countries, A-Z
183.9	Other (not A-Z)
	Elements in the population
184.A-.Z	**Elements, A-Z**
	The cutter numbers are intended to be used as a guide for the best distribution of numbers and not to be used as a fixed standard or to affect numbers already assigned
	Including racial and ethnic groups and religious bodies which have significance in the history of the United States
	Elements in individual regions, states, cities, etc., are classed with the region, state, city, etc., e.g. F128.9.G3, Germans in New York (City)
	For voyages of discovery by various nationalities, see E101+; G220+
184.A1	General works
	Including foreign elements (General), minorities, race conflicts, and problems, etc.
184.A2	Acadians. Cajuns
184.A23	Afghans
184.A24	Africans
	For works on Afro-Americans in the United States in general or in individual regions or states, see E185.5+ *or* E441+
	For works on Afro-Americans in individual counties, cities, or towns, see Class F. If the pertinent number in Class F provides for an A-Z arrangement for elements in the population, assign ".N4"
184.A26	Afrikaners
184.A3	Albanians
184.A4	Alsatians
	Amish, *see* E184.M45
184.A65	Arabs
184.A7	Armenians
	Asians, *see* E184.O6
184.A8	Assyrians
184.A9	Austrians
184.A95	Azoreans
184.B13	Bangladeshis
184.B15	Basques
184.B2	Belgians
184.B26	Bengalis
184.B67	Bohemians. Czechs
184.B674	Bolivians
184.B676	Brass Ankles
184.B68	Brazilians
184.B7	British
	Including the English
	For other nationalities, see the nationality, e.g. E184.S3, Scotch
184.B8	Bulgarians
	Byelorussians, *see* E184.W6
	Cajuns, *see* E184.A2
	Cambodians, *see* E184.K45
184.C2	Canadians

	Elements in the population
184.A-.Z	**Elements, A-Z — Continued**
184.C22	Canary Islanders
184.C24	Cape Verdeans
184.C27	Caribbeans
184.C29	Catalans
184.C3	Catholics
	Cf. E184.C36, Chaldean Catholics
184.C34	Central Americans
184.C36	Chaldean Catholics
184.C4	Chileans
184.C5	Chinese
184.C58	Colombians
184.C6	Cornish
184.C8	Covenanters
184.C87	Creoles
184.C9	Cretans
184.C93	Croats. Croatians
184.C97	Cubans
	Czechs, *see* E184.B67
	Danes, *see* E184.S19
184.D6	Dominicans (Dominican Republic)
184.D78	Druzes
184.D9	Dutch
184.E17	East Europeans
184.E2	East Indians
	Cf. E184.G84, Gujaratis
	Cf. E184.K35, Kanarese
	Cf. E184.M37, Marathas
	Cf. E184.P28, Pakistanis
	Cf. E184.P36, Panjabis
184.E28	Ecuadorians
184.E38	Egyptians
(184.E5)	English, *see* E184.B7
184.E7	Estonians
184.E74	Ethiopians
184.E95	Europeans
	Cf. E184.E17, East Europeans
184.F4	Filipinos
184.F5	Finns
184.F57	Flemings
184.F8	French
	Cf. E184.A2, Acadians
	Cf. E184.F85, French Canadians
	Cf. E184.H9, Huguenots
184.F85	French Canadians
	Cf. E184.A2, Acadians
184.F89	Friends. Society of Friends. Quakers
184.F894	Frisians
184.G24	Gambians
184.G27	Georgians (Transcaucasians)
184.G3	Germans
	Cf. E184.M7, Moravians
	Cf. E184.R85, Russian Germans
	Cf. E184.S78, Swabians
	For Palatines, see E184.P3
184.G44	Ghanaians
184.G7	Greeks
184.G75	Grenadians
184.G82	Guatemalans

	Elements in the population
184.A-.Z	**Elements, A-Z — Continued**
184.G84	Gujaratis
184.G86	Guyanese
184.H27	Haitians
184.H3	Hawaiians
	Hispanic Americans, *see* E184.S75
184.H55	Hmong (Asian people)
184.H9	Huguenots
184.H95	Hungarians
184.H97	Hutterite Brethren
184.I3	Icelanders
	Indians, *see* E75+
184.I43	Indochinese
184.I45	Indonesians
184.I5	Iranians
184.I55	Iraquis
184.I6	Irish
	Cf. E184.S4, Scotch-Irish
184.I7	Israelis
	Cf. E184.J5, Jews
184.I8	Italians
	Jackson Whites, *see* E184.R3
184.J27	Jamaicans
184.J3	Japanese
	For Japanese-American war relocation centers, see D769.8.A6
(184.J5)	Jews, *see* E184.3+
	This number is not valid for works about Jews in the United States as a whole. The Cutter number .J5 may be used under those numbers in United States local history that are subarranged by this list of Cutter numbers, e.g. F73.9.J5, Jews in Massachusetts
	Jugoslavs, *see* E184.Y7
184.K3	Kalmyks
184.K35	Kanarese
184.K45	Khmers. Cambodians
184.K6	Koreans
184.L27	Laos
184.L34	Lebanese
184.L4	Letts. Latvians
184.L53	Liberians
184.L55	Liechtensteiners
184.L7	Lithuanians
184.L88	Luxemburgers
184.M3	Macedonians
184.M34	Maltese
184.M37	Marathas
184.M44	Melungeons
184.M45	Mennonites. Amish
184.M47	Mestizos
184.M5	Mexicans
184.M53	Minorcans
184.M7	Moravians
184.M8	Mormons
184.M83	Mountain people
	Cf. F210, Southern States
184.M88	Muslims
(184.N4)	Negroes, *see* E184.5+, E441+, or Class F
	Assign the cutter .N4 only for numbers in Class F that provide for an A-Z arrangement for elements in the population
184.N53	Nicaraguans
184.N55	Nigerians

	Elements in the population
184.A-.Z	**Elements, A-Z — Continued**
	Norwegians, *see* E184.S2
184.O6	Orientals. Asians
	Cf. E184.C5, Chinese
	Cf. E184.F4, Filipinos
	Cf. E184.J3, Japanese
184.P25	Pacific Islanders
184.P28	Pakistanis
184.P3	Palatines
184.P33	Palestinians
184.P35	Panamanians
184.P36	Panjabis
	Persians, *see* E184.I5
184.P47	Peruvians
184.P7	Poles
184.P8	Portuguese
184.P85	Puerto Ricans
184.R3	Ramapo Mountain people
184.R8	Romanians
184.R85	Russian Germans
184.R9	Russians
	Ruthenians, *see* E184.U5
184.R93	Rwandans
184.S15	Salvadorans
184.S16	Sami Americans
184.S17	Samoans
	Scandinavians
184.S18	General
184.S19	Danes
184.S2	Norwegians
184.S23	Swedes
184.S3	Scotch. Scots
184.S4	Scotch-Irish
184.S5	Serbs
184.S53	Shakers
184.S55	Sikhs
184.S6	Slavs
	Cf. E184.B67, Bohemians. Czechs
	Cf. E184.B8, Bulgarians
	Cf. E184.C93, Croats
	Cf. E184.P7, Poles
	Cf. E184.R9, Russians
	Cf. E184.S5, Serbs
	Cf. E184.S64, Slovaks
	Cf. E184.S65, Slovenes
	Cf. E184.U5, Ukrainians
	Cf. E184.Y7, Yugoslavs
184.S64	Slovaks
184.S65	Slovenes
184.S67	Somalis
184.S68	Sorbs
184.S69	South Asians
184.S7	Spaniards
184.S75	Spanish Americans
	Cf. E184.C34, Central Americans
	Cf. E184.M5, Mexicans
184.S77	Sudanese
184.S78	Swabians
	Swedes, *see* E184.S23

	Elements in the population
184.A-.Z	**Elements, A-Z — Continued**
184.S9	Swiss
184.S98	Syrians
184.T35	Taiwanese
184.T4	Thais
184.T53	Tibetans
184.T88	Turks
184.U5	Ukrainians
	Including Ruthenians
184.V53	Vietnamese
184.W35	Walloons
184.W4	Welsh
184.W5	Wesorts
184.W54	West Indians
184.W6	White Russians
184.Y36	Yao (Southeast Asian people)
184.Y44	Yemenites
184.Y66	Yoruba
184.Y7	Yugoslavs
184.2	**Americans in foreign countries**
	Americans in a particular country are classified with that country
	Jews
	Including Italian Jews, Russian Jews, etc.
184.3	Periodicals
184.312	Congresses
184.32	Collections. Sources
184.33	Historiography
184.34	Study and teaching
184.35	History (General). General works
	For history of Judaism in the United States, including synagogues and congregations, see BM203+
	By period
184.3512	Colonial period to 1776
184.352	1776-1880
184.353	1880-1925
184.354	1925-1945
184.355	1945-
184.36.A-.36.Z	Special topics, A-Z
184.36.A34	Afro-American-Jewish relations
	Antisemitism, *see* DS146.U6
184.36.E25	Economic conditions
	For special aspects of economic conditions, see Class H
184.36.E84	Ethnic identity
	For relations between American Jews and Israel, see DS132
184.36.E86	Ethnic relations
184.36.P64	Politics and government
184.36.S65	Social conditions. Social life and customs
	Including family, youth, children, etc.
	For special aspects of social conditions, including specific activities, services, etc., see Class H
	For religious life, see BM723+
184.36.W64	Women
	Including collective biography
	By region, state, etc., *see* Class F
	Biography and memoirs
184.37.A1-.37.A19	Collective
184.37.A2-.37.Z	Individual, A-Z
	For collective biography of women, see E184.36.W64

Elements in the population — Continued
Afro-Americans
                    Including works on free Afro-Americans in the United States before 1863
                    Periodicals, societies, etc., *see* E185.5

184.5	Congresses
184.6	Collections. Sources
184.65	Historiography
184.7	Study and teaching. Afro-American studies
184.7.Z9	Catalogs of audiovisual materials
185	General works. History (General)

           Cf. E440.92+, Slavery in the United States
           Cf. E448, Colonization
           Cf. E453, Emancipation
           Cf. GN645, Black race (Anthropology)
           Cf. HT973.2+, Slave trade (General)
           Cf. HV3181+, Protection, assistance, and relief for Afro-Americans
           Cf. JX4447, Slave trade (International law)
           Cf. LC2701+, Education of Afro-Americans

History (By period)

185.18	To 1863

        Including free Afro-Americans
        For free Afro-Americans in an individual state, see E185.93.A+

185.2	1863-1877

        Including from emancipation to the end of the reconstruction period, the Afro- American as a ward of the nation, ex-slaves, slave pensions, Freedmen's Bureau (Bureau of Refugees, Freedmen, and Abandoned Lands)
        For Reconstruction in the United States, 1865-1877, see E668
        For Reconstruction in individual southern states, see the state, e.g. F231, Virginia; F259, North Carolina
        For Freedmen, by state, see E185.93.A+

1877-1964. Reconstruction to Civil Rights Act of 1964

185.5	Periodicals. Societies. Collections

        Including periodicals and societies before emancipation, and post 1964
          Cf. HS2259+, Fraternal and social societies

Museums. Exhibitions, etc.

185.53.A1	General works
185.53.A3-.53.Z	By city and museum, A-Z
185.6	General works
185.61	Race relations

        Including attitudes, discriminations, loyalties, prejudices; civil rights; interracial cooperation, movements, and practices; segregation
          Cf. BP221+, Black Muslims
          Cf. JK1923+, Afro-American suffrage
          Cf. LC212.5+, Racial segregation in schools
          For relations with indians, see E98.R28
          For relations with Jewish Americans, see E184.36.A34

185.615	1964-

        For periodicals, societies, etc., see E185.5

Special topics

185.62	Intermarriage of races. Miscegnation. Mulattoes
185.625	Psychosocial factors. Race identity
185.63	Afro-Americans in the Armed Forces

           Cf. D639.N4, Afro-Americans in World War I, 1914-1918
           Cf. D810.N4, Afro-Americans in World War II, 1939-1945
           Cf. E269.N3, Afro-Americans in the Revolution, 1775-1783
           Cf. E540.N3, Afro-Americans in the Civil War, 1861-1865 (Union Army)
           Cf. E585.A35, Afro-Americans in the Civil War, 1861-1865 (Confederate Army)
           Cf. E725.5.N3, Afro-Americans in the Spanish-American War, 1898
        Crime. Delinquency, *see* HV6197.A+

	Elements in the population
	Afro-Americans
	Special topics — Continued
(185.7)	Religion. Afro-American churches
	For Black Muslims, see BP221+
	For Afro-American churches (General), Afro-American clergy, etc., see BR563.N4
	For Afro-American religions not limited to Christianity, see BL1+
185.8	Economic conditions
	For special aspects of economic conditions, see Class H
	The professions, *see* the individual profession
185.86	Social conditions. Social life and customs
	Including family, women, youth, children, etc.
	Health. Physical condition, *see* Class R
185.89.A-.89.Z	Other topics, A-Z
185.89.E8	Ethnobotany
	Housing, *see* HD7293.A1+
	Iconography, *see* Class N
185.89.N3	Names
	Relations with Jewish Americans, *see* E184.36.A34
	Relations with Indians, *see* E98.R28
185.89.R45	Reparations
	Transportation, *see* HE1+
	By region, state, etc.
185.9	Afro-Americans in the North
185.912	Afro-Americans in the Appalachian Region
185.915	Afro-Americans in the Middle West and Old Northwest
185.917	Afro-Americans in New England
185.92	Afro-Americans in the South
	For pre-1964 material, see E185 *or* E185.6
185.925	Afro-Americans in the West
185.93.A-.93.W	By state, A-W
	For Afro-Americans in an individual county, city, or town, see Class F, *e.g.* F128.9.N3,
	Afro-Americans in New York
	For slavery in an individual state, see E445.A+
185.93.A3	Alabama
185.93.A4	Alaska
185.93.A7	Arizona
185.93.A8	Arkansas
185.93.C2	California
185.93.C6	Colorado
185.93.C7	Connecticut
185.93.D4	Delaware
185.93.D6	District of Columbia
185.93.F5	Florida
185.93.G4	Georgia
185.93.H3	Hawaii
185.93.I15	Idaho
185.93.I2	Illinois
185.93.I4	Indiana
185.93.I64	Iowa
185.93.K16	Kansas
185.93.K3	Kentucky
185.93.L6	Louisiana
185.93.M15	Maine
185.93.M2	Maryland
185.93.M3	Massachusetts
185.93.M5	Michigan
185.93.M55	Minnesota
185.93.M6	Mississippi
185.93.M7	Missouri

	Elements in the population
	Afro-Americans
	By region, state, etc.
185.93.A-.93.W	By state, A-W — Continued
185.93.M8	Montana
185.93.N5	Nebraska
185.93.N52	Nevada
185.93.N53	New Hampshire
185.93.N54	New Jersey
185.93.N55	New Mexico
185.93.N56	New York
185.93.N6	North Carolina
185.93.N7	North Dakota
185.93.O2	Ohio
185.93.O4	Oklahoma
185.93.O7	Oregon
185.93.P41	Pennsylvania
185.93.R4	Rhode Island
185.93.S7	South Carolina
	Including the Sea Islands
185.93.S8	South Dakota
185.93.T3	Tennessee
185.93.T4	Texas
185.93.U8	Utah
185.93.V4	Vermont
185.93.V8	Virginia
185.93.W3	Washington
185.93.W5	West Virginia
185.93.W58	Wisconsin
185.93.W9	Wyoming
185.94	Afro-Americans living in foreign countries (Collectively)
	For Afro-Americans in a particular country, see the country
	Biography. Genealogy
185.96	Collective
	Including biographical dictionaries and directories
	Class here general collected biography, including collected biography of Afro- Americans in public life covering several or all periods of United States history
	For biography of Afro-Americans in public life covering a single period of United States history, see the period
	For Afro-Americans associated with a special field, see the field
	For Afro-Americans of special regions or states, see E185.9+
	For Afro-Americans of an individual county, city, or town, see Class F
185.97.A-.97.Z	Individual, A-Z
	For biography of slaves, see E444, E449+
	For Afro-Americans associated with a special field (including politics), see the field or period of activity
	For Afro-Americans of special regions or states, see E185.9+
	For Afro-Americans in an individual county, city, or town, see Class F, e.g. F128.9.N3, New York (City)
	GALE NOTE *The cutter number(s) listed below have been given only as examples by the Library of Congress*
	Carver, George Washington, *see* S417.A+
185.97.R63	Robeson, Paul
	Subarrange by Table E1 at the end of the text
	For Robeson as a singer, see ML420.R73
185.97.T8	Truth, Sojourner
	Subarrange by Table E1 at the end of the text
185.97.W4	Washington, Booker Taliaferro
	Subarrange by Table E1 at the end of the text
185.97.Z9	Anonymous

                Elements in the population
                  Afro-Americans
                     Biography. Genealogy — Continued

185.98	Biography of persons other than Afro-Americans identified primarily with Afro-Americans
185.98.A1	Collective
185.98.A3-.98.Z	Individual, A-Z
	Subarrange by Table E1 at the end of the text

                Colonial history, 1607-1775
                  Including earliest permanent English settlements on the Atlantic Coast to the American Revolution
                  Including the thirteen colonies

186	**Periodicals. Societies**
	e.g. The Prince Society and its publications
186.3-.99	**Patriotic societies**

                  Under each (unless otherwise indicated):
                     Official publications

.A1-.A4	Serial publications
.A5-.A69	Monographs
.A7	Nonofficial publications
.A8-.W	State branches. By state, A-W

                     Under each:
                        Official publications

A1-A4	Serial publications
A5-A7	Monographs
A8-Z	Nonofficial publications

186.3	Society of Colonial Wars
	Subarrange by table below E186.3-.99
186.4	National Society of the Colonial Dames of America
	Subarrange by table below E186.3-.99
186.5	Colonial Dames of America
	Subarrange by table below E186.3-.99
186.6	Order of the Founders and Patriots of America
	Subarrange by table below E186.3-.99
186.7	Colonial Daughters of the Seventeenth Century
	Subarrange by table below E186.3-.99
186.8	Daughters of Founders and Patriots of America
	Subarrange by table below E186.3-.99
186.99.A-.99.Z	Other, A-Z

                  Under each:
                    GALE NOTE *".x" represents the cutter number for the patriotic society*
                     Official publications

.xA1-.xA4	Serial publications
.xA5-.xA7	Monographs
.xA8-.xZ	Nonofficial publications

186.99.C55	Colonial Dames of the XVII Century
	Subarrange by table below E186.99.A-.99.Z
186.99.D3	Daughters of the American Colonists
	Subarrange by table below E186.99.A-.99.Z
186.99.H55	Hereditary Order of Descendants of Colonial Governors
	Subarrange by table below E186.99.A-.99.Z
186.99.N33	National Society of the Colonial Daughters of America
	Subarrange by table below E186.99.A-.99.Z
186.99.O6	Order of Colonial Lords of Manors in America
	Subarrange by table below E186.99.A-.99.Z
	Order of Washington, *see* E202.7
186.99.P6	The Pilgrims
	Subarrange by table below E186.99.A-.99.Z
186.99.S5	Sons and Daughters of the Pilgrims
	Subarrange by table below E186.99.A-.99.Z

	Colonial history, 1607-1775 — **Continued**
187	**Collections. Collected works**
	Including monographs, essays, documents, sources, etc.
187.A5	American colonial tracts monthly
187.A53	American political tracts
187.C72	Colonial pamphlets
187.F69	Force, Peter. Tracts and other papers
187.H42	Hazard, Ebenezer. Historical collections
187.O7	Original narratives of early American history
187.2	**Historiography**
	Biography
187.5	Collective. Genealogy
	Including comprehensive lists of English immigrants
	For lists of immigrants of non-English nationalities, see E184.A+
	For biography of later colonial period, beginning with French and Indian War, see E302.5; *genealogy of New England in F3; etc.*
	Individual, *see* E191-199, E302.6, and individual wars
188	**General works**
	Cf. E82-83, Indian wars
	Cf. E101+, Discovery and exploration of America to 1607
	Cf. E141+, General accounts of America to 1810
	Cf. E162, Travel and description
	Cf. F7, New England to 1775
	Cf. F229, Raleigh's Roanoke colonies, 1584-1590
	Cf. F314, French Huguenot colonies
	Cf. F1030, British North America
	Cf. F2131, British West Indies
	Cf. F2361+, British Guiana
	Cf. JV1000+, Administration of British colonies
188.5	**Addresses, essays, lectures, sermons, etc.**
189	**Minor works**
	Including pamphlets, pageants, etc., and otherwise unprovided-for topics
	For discussions on European origin of American institutions, see Class D, *unless largely American history*
	By period
191	1607-1689
	Cf. E83.63, Pequot War, 1636-1638
	Cf. E83.663, War with Esopus Indians, 1658-1664
	Cf. E83.67, King Philip's War, 1675-1676
	Cf. F7, Council for New England, 1620; Plymouth Company, 1606; United Colonies of New England, 1643-1684; etc.
	Cf. F7.5, Governor Andros and his government, 1688
	Cf. F22, Popham Colony, Maine
	Cf. F229, Virginia Company of London
	1689-1775
	Including attempts at union; Albany Congress of 1754; last years of colonial government, 1763- 1775; etc.
	Including biography: Sir William Johnson, William Shirley, etc.
	Cf. E83.71, Tuscarora War, 1711-1713
	Cf. E83.72, Wars with the eastern Indians (New England), 1722-1726
	Cf. E83.739, Wars with the Chickasaw Indians, 1739-1740
	Cf. E83.76, Pontiac's Conspiracy, 1763-1765
	Cf. E210+, Political history, disputes with Great Britain
	Cf. E215.2, Stamp Act Congress, 1765
	Cf. F517, Ohio Company
	Cf. F1032, Quebec Act, 1774
	Cf. F2272.5, Cartagena Expedition, 1741
195	General works

	Colonial history, 1607-1775
	By period
	1689-1775 — Continued
196	King William's War, 1689-1697
	Including the destruction of Schenectady, 1690; capture of Port Royal (Nova Scotia), 1690; Quebec Expedition, 1690; Massacre at Haverhill, 1697; etc.
197	Queen Anne's War, 1702-1713
	Including Massacres at Deerfield (1704), Haverhill (1708), etc.; Church's expedition to the eastward; capture of Port Royal (Nova Scotia), 1710; Walker's expedition to Quebec, 1711; etc.
	Cf. D281+, War of Spanish Succession, 1710-1714
	Cf. E83.71, Tuscarora War, 1711-1713
198	King George's War, 1744-1748
	Including the siege and capture of Louisburg (Cape Breton Island), 1745
	Including biography: Sir William Pepperell, etc.
	Cf. D291+, War of the Austrian Succession, 1740-1748
	Cf. F1036+, Nova Scotia, Acadia, Cape Breton Island
199	French and Indian War, 1755-1763
	Including Washington at Fort Necessity, 1754; Braddock's defeat, 1755; Battle of Lake George, 1755; siege of Fort William Henry, 1757; expeditions against Ticonderoga and Crown Point, 1755-1759; second siege and capture of Louisburg, 1758; capture of Fort Frontenac, 1758; Niagara and Quebec campaigns, 1759
	Including biography: John Bradstreet; François Gaston, duc de Lévis; Louis Joseph de Montcalm-Gozon, marquis de Saint-Veran; Robert Rogers; etc.
	Cf. E83.759, Cherokee War, 1759-1761
	Cf. E195+, Albany Congress, 1754
	Cf. F1038, Winslow's expedition for expulsion of the Acadians, 1755
	Cf. F1781, Siege of Havana, 1762-1763
	Elements in the population, *see* E184.A+
	The Revolution, 1775-1783
201	**Periodicals. Societies (Research)**
202	**Societies (Patriotic and hereditary)**
	Including reports, registers, etc.
	For collections of documents, memoirs, etc., see E203, e.g. E203.S49, Publications of the Seventy-Six Society
202.1	Society of the Cincinnati
	Subarrange by table below E186.3-.99
202.2	Daughters of the Cincinnati
	Subarrange by table below E186.3-.99
202.3	Sons of the American Revolution
	Subarrange by table below E186.3-.99
202.4	Sons of the Revolution
	Subarrange by table below E186.3-.99
	Including proposals for the union of Sons of the Revolution and Sons of the American Revolution
202.5	Daughters of the American Revolution
	Subarrange by table below E186.3-.99
202.6	Daughters of the Revolution
	Subarrange by table below E186.3-.99
202.7	Order of Washington
	Subarrange by table below E186.3-.99
202.8	Washington Society of Maryland
	Subarrange by table below E186.3-.99
202.9	Children of the American Revolution
	Subarrange by table below E186.3-.99
202.99.A-.99.Z	Other, A-Z
	Subarrange by table below E186.99.A-.99.Z
	GALE NOTE *The cutter number(s) listed below have been given only as examples by the Library of Congress*

The Revolution, 1775-1783

202	**Societies (Patriotic and hereditary)**
202.99.A-.99.Z	Other, A-Z — Continued
202.99.M64	Military Order of Pulaski
	Subarrange by table below E186.99.A-.99.Z
202.99.O63	Order of LaFayette
	Subarrange by table below E186.99.A-.99.Z
202.99.O65	Order of the Descendants of the Signers of the Secret Pact or Prior Declaration of Independence
	Subarrange by table below E186.99.A-.99.Z
	Museums, exhibitions, *see* E289
203	**Collections. Collected works**
	Including documents, essays, letters, journals, memoirs, etc.
	For collections of anecdotes, see E296
204	**Congresses, seminars, etc.**
	Biography
	Including portraits
206	Collective
	Especially military and naval leaders
	For signers of the Declaration of Independence, see E221
	For statesmen of the Revolutionary period, see E302.5
207.A-.Z	Individual, A-Z
	Including lives of military and naval commanders and staff officers
	For regimental officers and privates, see regimental histories in E263.A+, or personal narratives in E275.A2+
	For Scouts and spies, see E279+
	Cf. E302.6.A+, Lives of individual statesmen
	GALE NOTE *The cutter number(s) listed below have been given only as examples by the Library of Congress*
207.A3	Alexander, William
	Subarrange by Table E1 at the end of the text
	Called Lord Stirling
207.A4	Allen, Ethan
	Subarrange by Table E1 at the end of the text
207.B2	Barry, John
	Subarrange by Table E1 at the end of the text
207.B48	Biddle, Nicholas
	Subarrange by Table E1 at the end of the text
207.B5	Biddle, Owen
	Subarrange by Table E1 at the end of the text
207.B58	Bigelow, Timothy
	Subarrange by Table E1 at the end of the text
207.B8	Brown, John, 1744-1780
	Subarrange by Table E1 at the end of the text
207.C5	Clark, George Rogers
	Subarrange by Table E1 at the end of the text
207.C62	Clinton, James
	Subarrange by Table E1 at the end of the text
207.D3	Davidson, William Lee
	Subarrange by Table E1 at the end of the text
207.D9	Duportail, Louis Lebègue de Presle
	Subarrange by Table E1 at the end of the text
207.E3	Elbert, Samuel
	Subarrange by Table E1 at the end of the text
207.G2	Gadsden, Christopher
	Subarrange by Table E1 at the end of the text
207.G3	Gates, Horatio
	Subarrange by Table E1 at the end of the text
207.G56	Glover, John
	Subarrange by Table E1 at the end of the text

The Revolution, 1775-1783
Biography

207.A-.Z	Individual, A-Z — Continued
207.G9	Greene, Nathanael
	Subarrange by Table E1 at the end of the text
207.H7	Hopkins, Ezek
	Subarrange by Table E1 at the end of the text
207.H85	Howe, Robert
	Subarrange by Table E1 at the end of the text
207.J7	Jones, John Paul
	Subarrange by Table E1 at the end of the text
207.K14	Kalb, Jean, baron de
	Subarrange by Table E1 at the end of the text
207.K74	Knox, Henry
	Subarrange by Table E1 at the end of the text
207.K8	Kósciusko, Tadeusz Andrzej
	Subarrange by Table E1 at the end of the text
	Cf. DK4348.K67, Polish patriot
207.L2	Lafayette, Marquis de
	Subarrange by Table E1 at the end of the text
	Including Lafayette in America
	Cf. DC146.L2, Lafayette in France
207.L22	Lamb, John
	Subarrange by Table E1 at the end of the text
207.L47	Lee, Charles
	Subarrange by Table E1 at the end of the text
207.L5	Lee, Henry
	Subarrange by Table E1 at the end of the text
207.M3	Marion, Francis
	Subarrange by Table E1 at the end of the text
207.M5	Mercer, Hugh
	Subarrange by Table E1 at the end of the text
207.M6	Mifflin, Thomas
	Subarrange by Table E1 at the end of the text
207.M7	Montgomery, Richard
	Subarrange by Table E1 at the end of the text
207.M8	Morgan, Daniel
	Subarrange by Table E1 at the end of the text
207.M85	Moultrie, William
	Subarrange by Table E1 at the end of the text
207.M9	Moylan, Stephen
	Subarrange by Table E1 at the end of the text
207.M95	Muhlenberg, John Peter Gabriel
	Subarrange by Table E1 at the end of the text
207.N2	Nash, Francis
	Subarrange by Table E1 at the end of the text
207.O13	O'Brien, Jeremiah
	Subarrange by Table E1 at the end of the text
207.P2	Parsons, Samuel Holden
	Subarrange by Table E1 at the end of the text
207.P3	Paterson, John
	Subarrange by Table E1 at the end of the text
207.P63	Pickens, Andrew
	Subarrange by Table E1 at the end of the text
207.P68	Pitcairn, John
	Subarrange by Table E1 at the end of the text
207.P7	Pomeroy, Seth
	Subarrange by Table E1 at the end of the text
207.P75	Prescott, William
	Subarrange by Table E1 at the end of the text

	The Revolution, 1775-1783
	Biography
207.A-.Z	Individual, A-Z — Continued
207.P8	Pułaski, Kazimierz
	Subarrange by Table E1 at the end of the text
	Cf. DK4348.P8, Polish patriot
207.P9	Putnam, Israel
	Subarrange by Table E1 at the end of the text
207.R32	Reed, James
	Subarrange by Table E1 at the end of the text
207.S3	Schuyler, Philip John
	Subarrange by Table E1 at the end of the text
207.S79	Stark, John
	Subarrange by Table E1 at the end of the text
207.S8	Steuben, Friedrich Wilhelm, Baron von
	Subarrange by Table E1 at the end of the text
207.S9	Sullivan, John
	Subarrange by Table E1 at the end of the text
207.S95	Sumter, Thomas
	Subarrange by Table E1 at the end of the text
207.T13	Talbot, Silas
	Subarrange by Table E1 at the end of the text
207.T45	Thomas, John
	Subarrange by Table E1 at the end of the text
207.T57	Tilghman, Tench
	Subarrange by Table E1 at the end of the text
207.T8	Tucker, Samuel
	Subarrange by Table E1 at the end of the text
207.W2	Ward, Artemas
	Subarrange by Table E1 at the end of the text
207.W26	Ward, Samuel
	Subarrange by Table E1 at the end of the text
207.W27	Warner, Seth
	Subarrange by Table E1 at the end of the text
207.W35	Wayne, Anthony
	Subarrange by Table E1 at the end of the text
207.W63	Wickes, Lambert
	Subarrange by Table E1 at the end of the text
207.W65	Willett, Marinus
	Subarrange by Table E1 at the end of the text
207.W7	Williams, Otho Holland
	Subarrange by Table E1 at the end of the text
207.W78	Wood, James
	Subarrange by Table E1 at the end of the text
207.W8	Woodhull, Nathaniel
	Subarrange by Table E1 at the end of the text
207.W9	Wooster, David
	Subarrange by Table E1 at the end of the text
208	**General works. History (General)**
	For travel, manners, and customs of the period, see E163
209	**General special**
	Including pamphlets, pictorial works, chronological tables, etc., and otherwise unprovided-for
	topics, such as historiography, the Revolution as a social movement, religious aspects, legends
	Political history
	Including the causes and origins of the Revolution and the controversies which preceded it, 1763-
	1775; the influence of the American clergy, legal aspects, trade, western lands, etc.
	For controversies in individual colonies before 1763, see E263.A+, e.g. E263.M4, Massachusetts
210	General works (Other than contemporary)

The Revolution, 1775-1783

Political history — Continued

211	Contemporary works
	For sermons and addresses of a general character, see E297
	Special questions and events
215	General works
215.1	Commercial restrictions (General). Enforcement of trade and navigation laws. Writs of assistance
215.2	Stamp Act, 1765. Stamp Act Congress, New York, 1765
215.3	Townshend Acts, 1767. Nonimportation agreements of 1768-1769
	Including Townshend Acts repealed in April 1770, except for a tax on tea
215.4	Mutiny Act, 1765. Boston Massacre, March 5, 1770
	Including the quartering of troops in Boston
215.5	Taxation and representation
215.6	Gaspee affair, June 1772
215.7	Resistance to the tea tax. Boston Tea Party, December 1773
215.8	Boston Port Bill, 1774
215.9	Mecklenburg Resolves, 1775
	Including the so-called Mecklenburg Declaration of Independence
215.95	The "Olive branch" petition to George III, 1775
216	Other special topics (not A-Z)
	Including Committees of correspondence and safety; efforts to enlist aid of other British possessions, as Canada and Ireland; Paul Revere's ride; Sons of Liberty; the Duché letters; etc.
	For Loyalists in the colonies, see E277+
	For The parsons' cause, Va., see F229
	For War of the Regulators, N.C., see F257
221	**Declaration of Independence**
	Including collective biography of the signers
	Military operations
	Cf. E271+, Naval history
230	General works
	Including campaigns and battles (General) and lists of battles
	For individual battles, see E241.A+
	Class orderly books with campaigns in E231-239 or in E255-268 with the military organization to which they belong
	For Indian wars, 1775-1783, see E83.775
230.5.A-.5.Z	By region, A-Z
	Class regions within a state under the name of the state
	GALE NOTE *The cutter number(s) listed below have been given only as examples by the Library of Congress*
230.5.M6	Middle States
230.5.N4	New York (State). Hudson Valley
230.5.O3	Ohio Valley
230.5.V3	Vermont. Mount Independence
	Campaigns. By year
231	1775
	Including Beginnings, Canadian invasion, siege of Boston (1775-1776), Patriots' Day (April 19), etc.
232	1776
	Including British occupation of New York, Washington's retreat up the Hudson and through New Jersey, etc.
233	1777
	Including Burgoyne's invasion, St. Leger's invasion, Howe's occupation of Philadelphia, Jane McCrea, etc.
	For Saratoga Campaign, see E241.S2
234	1778
	Including Clark's Expedition, Butler's Indian Campaign, Valley Forge, etc.
235	1779
	Including Penobscot Expedition, Sullivan's Indian Campaign, etc.

	The Revolution, 1775-1783
	Military operations
	Campaigns. By year — Continued
236	1780

Including Benedict Arnold's treason, campaigns in the South, etc.
Cf. E278.A7, Arnold as a loyalist

237	1781

Including Campaigns in the Carolinas and Virginia, Clark's Expedition against Detroit, etc.
For Mutiny of the Pennsylvania line, see E255

238	1782

Including Crawford's Indian Campaign, etc.

239	1783

Including British evacuation of New York, Evacuation Day, etc.
For Newburgh addresses, see E255

241.A-.Z	Individual battles, A-Z

Including attacks, capture and burning of cities, massacres, sieges, etc.
Class battles, sieges, etc., in E231+, if preferred

241.B33	Bedford, N.Y. (Westchester Co.), 1779
241.B4	Bennington, Vt., 1777
241.B65	Blue Licks, Ky., 1782
	Boston siege, 1775-1776, *see* E231
241.B76	Bound Brook, N.J., 1777
241.B8	Brandywine, Pa., 1777
	Brooklyn, N.Y., 1776, *see* E241.L8
241.B87	Bull's Ferry, N.J., 1780
241.B9	Bunker Hill, Mass., 1775
241.C17	Camden, S.C., 1780
241.C2	Carleton's Raid, 1778
241.C4	Charleston, S.C., 1780
241.C48	Chelsea, Mass., 1775
241.C5	Cherry Valley, N.Y., 1778
241.C52	Chestnut Hill, Pa., 1777
241.C56	Clapps Mill, N.C., 1781
241.C7	Concord, Mass., 1775
241.C73	Cooch's Bridge, Del., 1777
241.C8	Cowan's Ford, Tenn., 1781
241.C9	Cowpens, S.C., 1781
241.C94	Crooked Billet, Pa., 1778
241.C96	Cumberland, Fort, N.B., 1776
241.D2	Danbury, Conn., 1777
241.E39	Elizabeth, N.J., 1780
241.E4	Elizabethtown, N.C., 1781
241.F16	Fairfield, Conn., 1779
	Falmouth, Me., *see* E241.P8
241.F55	Flamborough Head, England, 1779
241.F74	Freeland, Fort, Warrior Run, Pa., 1779
241.G3	Germantown, Pa., 1777
241.G6	Great Bridge, Va., 1775
241.G8	Groton Heights, Conn., 1781
241.G9	Guilford Court House, N.C., 1781
241.H2	Harlem Heights, N.Y., 1776
241.H8	Hubbardton, Vt., 1777
241.K48	Kettle Creek, Ga., 1779
241.K5	King's Mountain, S.C., 1780
241.K6	Kingston, N.Y., 1777
241.L6	Lexington, Mass., 1775
241.L65	Lindley's Mill, N.C., 1781
241.L7	Little Egg Harbor, N.J., 1778
241.L8	Long Island, N.Y., 1776

The Revolution, 1775-1783

Military operations

241.A-.Z	Individual battles, A-Z — Continued
241.M5	Mercer, Fort, N.J., 1777
241.M6	Minisink, N.Y., 1779
241.M7	Monmouth, N.J., 1778
241.M8	Moore's Creek Bridge, N.C., 1776
241.M9	Moultrie, Fort, S.C., 1776
241.N5	New Haven, Conn., 1779
241.N56	Newtown, N.Y., 1779
241.O6	Oriskany, N.Y., 1777
241.P2	Paoli, Pa., 1777
241.P24	Paulus Hook, N.J., 1779
241.P3	Pell's Point, N.Y., 1776
241.P55	Piqua, Ohio, 1780
241.P8	Portland, Me., 1775
241.P9	Princeton, N.J., 1777
241.Q3	Quebec (City), 1775-1776
241.R3	Red Bank, N.J., 1777
241.R4	Rhode Island, 1778
241.R53	Ridgefield, Conn., 1777
241.S2	Saratoga, N.Y., 1777
241.S26	Savannah, Ga., 1779
241.S53	Short Hills, N.J., 1777
241.S6	Springfield, N.J., 1780
241.S7	Stanwix, Fort, N.Y., 1777
241.S8	Stony Point, N.Y., 1779
241.T5	Ticonderoga, N.Y., 1775
241.T7	Trenton, N.J., 1776
241.V14	Valcour Island, Lake Champlain, 1776
241.W3	Washington, Fort, N.Y., 1776
241.W5	White Plains, N.Y., 1776
241.W9	Wyoming, Pa., 1778
241.Y6	Yorktown, Va., 1781

249	**Diplomatic history. Treaty of Paris, 1783**
	Including alliances, claims of foreigners against the United States, diplomatic relations with individual countries, missions to foreign powers, propaganda, Treaty of 1778
	Cf. E265, French participation in the war, French auxiliaries
	Cf. E313+, Final withdrawal of British troops from western posts
249.3	**Foreign public opinion**
	Armies. Troops
251	General works
	The American Army
255	General works
	Including bounties; the Conway Cabal; Mutiny of the Pennsylvania Line, 1781; Newburgh addresses; pensioners; registers and lists not confined to single states; war claims; etc.
	For orderly books, see E231+
	Cf. E281, Lists of prisoners
	Cf. UB373+, Military pensions (General)
	Continental army
259	General works
260	Military organizations raised by Congress directly
	Including Commander in Chief's Guard, Lee's Legion, etc.
263.A-.W	By state, A-W
	Including the British American colonies; each state's part in the war and previous controversy
	Including collections; histories (General, and regimental); rolls and orderly books; registers; addresses honoring patriots; diaries, journals, letters, and memoirs of officers, etc.; state continental line; state troops and militia, including minutemen

          The Revolution, 1775-1783
            Armies. Troops
              The American Army

263.A-.W	By state, A-W — Continued
	For histories of counties and towns in the war, see local history, e.g. F74.W9, Worcester, Mass.
	Cf. E230+, Military operations in a state
	Cf. E277+, American loyalists in individual states
263.C2	Canada (Province of Quebec)
	Including biography: Antoine Paulint, etc.
	Cf. E216, Efforts to enlaid of Canada
	Cf. E263.N9, Nova Scotia and dependencies
	Cf. E269.C27, Canadians in the American army
263.C5	Connecticut
	Including biography: Jonathan Trumbull, etc.
263.D3	Delaware. Delmarva Peninsula
	Including biography: Thomas Rodney, etc.
263.F6	Florida (East and West)
263.G3	Georgia
	Including biography: Lyman Hall, etc.
263.I5	Indiana
263.K4	Kentucky
263.L68	Louisiana
	Maine, *see* E263.M4
263.M3	Maryland
	Including biography: John Gunby, John Eager Howard, etc.
	Cf. E263.D3, Delmarva Peninsula
263.M4	Massachusetts (and Maine)
	Including biography: Joseph Hawley, Josiah Quincy (1744-1775), Joseph Warren, etc.
263.N4	New Hampshire
	Including biography: Joseph Cilley, etc.
263.N5	New Jersey
	Including biography: Moore Furman, Margaret (Hill) Morris, etc.
263.N6	New York
	Including biography: Simon Boerum, Henry Ludington, etc.
263.N8	North Carolina (and Tennessee)
	Including biography: Joseph Graham, etc.
	For Tennessee alone, see E263.T4
	Cf. E215.9, Mecklenburg Resolutions, 1775
	Cf. F257, War of the Regulators, 1766-1771
263.N84	Old Northwest
263.N9	Nova Scotia (and dependencies)
	Cf. E263.C2, Canada (Province of Quebec)
263.O3	Ohio
263.P4	Pennsylvania and Delaware Valley (General)
	Including biography: John Bayard, John Rosbrugh, etc.
	Quebec, *see* E263.C2
263.R4	Rhode Island
	Including biography: Israel Angell, etc.
	Cf. E215.6, Gaspee Affair, June 1772
263.S7	South Carolina
	Including biography: John Drayton, Eliza (Yonge) Wilkinson, etc.
263.T4	Tennessee
	For Tennessee with North Carolina, see E263.N8
263.T45	Texas
263.V5	Vermont
263.V8	Virginia
	Including biography: Theodorick Bland, John Champe, Filippo Mazzei, Leven Powell, etc.
	Cf. E83.77, Dunmore's War, 1774

	The Revolution, 1775-1783
	Armies. Troops
	The American Army
263.A-.W	By state, A-W
263.V8	Virginia — Continued
	Cf. E263.D3, Delmarva Peninsula
263.W5	West Indies. Bermudas
265	Auxiliaries
	Including French participation; histories; lists; personal letters, journals, and narratives of soldiers and sailors; etc.
	Including biography: Comte de Rochambeau, etc.
	For Marquis de Lafayette, see E207.L2
	The British Army
	Including histories; lists; personal diaries; journals, letters, and narratives; etc.
	For Tory regiments, see E277.6.A+
267	General works
268	German mercenaries. Hessians
	For Germans in the American Army, see E269.G3
269.A-.Z	**Participation by race, ethnic group, religious group, etc., A-Z**
	Afro-Americans, *see* E269.N3
269.B2	Baptists
269.C27	Canadians
269.C3	Catholics
269.C5	Church of England (Anglicans)
269.D88	Dutch
269.F67	Foreigners (General)
	French auxiliaries, *see* E265
269.F8	Friends. Quakers
	German mercenaries, *see* E268
269.G3	Germans
269.H3	Haitians
269.I5	Indians
269.I6	Irish
269.J5	Jews
	Loyalists, *see* E277+
269.M6	Moravians
269.N3	Negroes. Afro-Americans
269.P6	Poles
269.P9	Presbyterians
269.S36	Scots-Irish
269.S63	Spaniards
269.S8	Swedes
269.W4	Welsh
	Colleges and their participation
270.A1	General works
270.A2-.Z	Individual colleges, A-Z
	GALE NOTE *The cutter number(s) listed below have been given only as examples by the Library of Congress*
270.P9	Princeton University
270.Y2	Yale University
	Naval history. Naval operations
	Including British and French fleets in the West Indies; narratives of sailors, privateers, etc.
	For the lives of naval leaders, see E206+
	For naval operations forming part of military movements, see E231+
271	General works
273.A-.Z	Individual ships, A-Z
273.P75	Providence
	Personal narratives and other accounts (General)
	Including diaries, journals, letters, memoirs, reminiscences, etc.

           The Revolution, 1775-1783
              Personal narratives and other accounts (General) — Continued
                 For narratives relating to special campaigns, battles, or regiments, see E231+ or E263.A+
                 For narratives of British soldiers, see E267+
                 For narratives of French auxiliaries, see E265
                 For narratives of German mercenaries, see E268
                 For narratives of loyalists, see E278.A+
                 For narratives of prisoners, see E281
                 For narratives of naval service, see E271
                 Cf. E203, Collections of source material
                 Cf. E296, Anecdotes

275.A2	Collections
275.A3-.Z	Individual narratives
276	**Women and the war**
	Loyalists. Traitors

                 Including biography and narratives of loyalists; loyalists in exile (General) and in England;
                    treatment of Tories, e.g. sequestration, confiscation, and sale of estates; etc.
                 For Loyalists in individual provinces of Canada, see F1036+, F1041+, F1056+

277	General works
277.6.A-.6.Z	Loyalist regiments, etc.

                    GALE NOTE *The cutter number(s) listed below have been given only as examples by the*
                      Library of Congress

277.6.B9	Butler's Rangers
277.6.D3	De Lancey's Brigade (Loyalist)
277.6.M2	Maryland Loyalists Regiment
277.6.N5	New Jersey Volunteers
277.6.Q6	Queen's Rangers
278.A-.Z	Individual loyalists, A-Z

                    GALE NOTE *The cutter number(s) listed below have been given only as examples by the*
                      Library of Congress

278.A3	Alexander, Robert
	Subarrange by Table E1 at the end of the text
278.A4	Allen, Jolley
	Subarrange by Table E1 at the end of the text
278.A7	Arnold, Benedict
	Subarrange by Table E1 at the end of the text
	Cf. E236, Arnold's treason
278.A72	Arnold, Margaret (Shippen)
	Subarrange by Table E1 at the end of the text
278.B9	Butler, Walter
	Subarrange by Table E1 at the end of the text
278.C4	Chandler, John
	Subarrange by Table E1 at the end of the text
278.C5	Christie, James
	Subarrange by Table E1 at the end of the text
278.C7	Connolly, John
	Subarrange by Table E1 at the end of the text
278.C8	Cornell, Samuel
	Subarrange by Table E1 at the end of the text
278.C9	Curwen, Samuel
	Subarrange by Table E1 at the end of the text
278.D94	Dulany, Daniel
	Subarrange by Table E1 at the end of the text
278.F2	Fanning, David
	Subarrange by Table E1 at the end of the text
278.G14	Galloway, Joseph
	Subarrange by Table E1 at the end of the text
278.G4	Gilbert, Thomas
	Subarrange by Table E1 at the end of the text

The Revolution, 1775-1783
Loyalists. Traitors

278.A-.Z	Individual loyalists, A-Z — Continued
278.L5	Leonard, Daniel
	Subarrange by Table E1 at the end of the text
278.M13	McAlpine, John
	Subarrange by Table E1 at the end of the text
278.M8	Moody, James
	Subarrange by Table E1 at the end of the text
278.M98	Murray, James
	Subarrange by Table E1 at the end of the text
278.S6	Smyth, John Ferdinand Dalziel
	Subarrange by Table E1 at the end of the text
278.T9	Tuttle, Stephen
	Subarrange by Table E1 at the end of the text
278.V27	Van Schaack, Henry Cruger
	Subarrange by Table E1 at the end of the text
278.V54	Vernon, Thomas
	Subarrange by Table E1 at the end of the text
278.W6	Wilkins, Isaac
	Subarrange by Table E1 at the end of the text

Secret service. Spies

279	General works
280.A-.Z	Individual spies, A-Z
	GALE NOTE *The cutter number(s) listed below have been given only as examples by the Library of Congress*
280.A5	André, John
	Subarrange by Table E1 at the end of the text
	Including his captors: John Paulding, Isaac Van Wart, David Williams
280.C95	Crosby, Enoch
	Subarrange by Table E1 at the end of the text
280.H2	Hale, Nathan
	Subarrange by Table E1 at the end of the text
280.H8	Howe, John
	Subarrange by Table E1 at the end of the text
280.T7	Townsend, Robert
	Subarrange by Table E1 at the end of the text
281	**Prisoners and prisons**
	Including exchanges, prison life, prison ships, prisoners' narratives, etc.
283	**Medical and hospital services. Hospitals, etc.**
	Including biography: Jonathan Potts, etc.
	Celebrations. Anniversaries
	For special celebrations in the form of expositions, see T400+
	For monuments and memorials, see by place in Class F
285	General works
	Special centennials
	1876
	For works limited to the 1876 exposition, see T825
285.2	General works
285.25.A-.25.W	By state, A-W
	Under each:
	GALE NOTE *".x" represents the cutter number for the state*
	.x General works
	.x2A-.x2Z By city, A-Z
	1926 exposition, *see* T826.3
	1976
285.3	General works
285.4.A-.4.W	By state, A-W
	Subarrange by table below E285.25.A-.25.W

	The Revolution, 1775-1783
	Celebrations. Anniversaries — Continued
	Special days
	Evacuation Day, November 25, *see* E239
	Fourth of July
	Class here general works on the observance of the day, including specific celebrations and addresses
	For works of distinct local interest, see Class F
286.A1-.A19	General works
286.A2-.Z	Individual celebrations and addresses. By place and date
	GALE NOTE *The cutter number(s) listed below have been given only as examples by the Library of Congress*
286.B74 1774	Boston, 1774
286.B74 1933	Boston, 1933
	Patriots' Day, April 19, *see* E231
289	**Museums. Exhibitions**
	Including bells, flags, relics, trophies, etc.
	Cf. NK806, Collectibles
(295)	**Poetry, ballads, songs. Drama, pageants,** *see* Class P
296	**Anecdotes**
	Cf. E203, Collections of source material
	Cf. E275.A2+, Personal narratives
297	**Sermons. Prayers**
	For sermons on a specific subject, see the subject
298	**Comic and satirical histories. Humor, caricatures, etc.**
	Revolution to the Civil War, 1775/1783-1861
	For history of the Revolutionary War, see E201+
	For history of the Civil War, see E461+
300	**Historiography**
301	**General works**
	Including works covering the preliminaries of the Revolution to the close of the Civil War, 1765-1865
	For political history of slavery, see E338-459
	Cf. E183.7+, Diplomatic history, 1783-1865
	Cf. E398, Northeast boundary question
	Cf. E440.92+, Slavery and the antislavery movement
	Cf. F550.5+; F597, Northern boundary
	Cf. F854; F880, Northwest boundary
302.A-.Z	**Collected works of American statesmen (Revolutionary group), A-Z**
	For works of statesmen of the early nineteenth century, see E337.8.A+
	For works of statesmen of the middle nineteenth century, see E415.6.A+
	GALE NOTE *The cutter number(s) listed below have been given only as examples by the Library of Congress*
302.A26	Adams, John
	Subarrange by Table E3 at the end of the text
302.F8	Franklin, Benjamin
	Subarrange by Table E3 at the end of the text
	For his literary works and biography, see PS745+
302.J44	Jefferson, Thomas
	Subarrange by Table E3 at the end of the text
302.M19	Madison, James
	Subarrange by Table E3 at the end of the text
	Washington, George, *see* E312.7
302.1	**Political history**
	Including the supremacy of the fathers of the republic
	Cf. E210+, Political history of the Revolution
	Cf. E357+, Political history of the War of 1812
	Cf. E407, Political history of the War with Mexico
	Biography (Late eighteenth century)
	For Revolutionary leaders, especially military commanders, see E206+

Revolution to the Civil War, 1775/1783-1861
Biography (Late eighteenth century) — Continued

302.5	Collective
	For signers of the Declaration of Independence, collectively, see E221
302.6.A-.6.Z	Individual, A-Z
	GALE NOTE *The cutter number(s) listed below have been given only as examples by the Library of Congress*
302.6.A2	Adams, Samuel
	Subarrange by Table E2A at the end of the text
302.6.A5	Ames, Fisher
	Subarrange by Table E2A at the end of the text
302.6.A7	Armstrong, John
	Subarrange by Table E2A at the end of the text
302.6.B14	Bache, Benjamin Franklin
	Subarrange by Table E2A at the end of the text
302.6.B17	Baldwin, Abraham
	Subarrange by Table E2A at the end of the text
302.6.B19	Baldwin, Simeon
	Subarrange by Table E2A at the end of the text
302.6.B2	Bartlett, Josiah
	Subarrange by Table E2A at the end of the text
302.6.B3	Bayard, James Asheton
	Subarrange by Table E2A at the end of the text
302.6.B6	Blount, William
	Subarrange by Table E2A at the end of the text
302.6.B7	Boudinot, Elias
	Subarrange by Table E2A at the end of the text
302.6.B8	Bradley, Stephen Row
	Subarrange by Table E2A at the end of the text
302.6.B84	Breckinridge, John
	Subarrange by Table E2A at the end of the text
302.6.B9	Burr, Aaron
	Subarrange by Table E2A at the end of the text
	For Burr's conspiracy, see E334
302.6.B91	Jumel, Eliza (Bowen)
	Subarrange by Table E2A at the end of the text
302.6.B93	Burr, Esther (Edwards)
	Subarrange by Table E2A at the end of the text
302.6.C11	Cabot, George
	Subarrange by Table E2A at the end of the text
302.6.C2	Campbell, George Washington
	Subarrange by Table E2A at the end of the text
302.6.C3	Carroll, Charles (Charles Carroll of Carrollton)
	Subarrange by Table E2A at the end of the text
302.6.C33	Carroll, Daniel
	Subarrange by Table E2A at the end of the text
302.6.C4	Chase, Samuel
	Subarrange by Table E2A at the end of the text
302.6.C55	Clark, Abraham
	Subarrange by Table E2A at the end of the text
302.6.C6	Clinton, George
	Subarrange by Table E2A at the end of the text
302.6.C7	Cooper, Thomas
	Subarrange by Table E2A at the end of the text
302.6.D14	Dallas, Alexander James
	Subarrange by Table E2A at the end of the text
302.6.D16	Dana, Francis
	Subarrange by Table E2A at the end of the text
302.6.D2	Davie, William Richardson
	Subarrange by Table E2A at the end of the text

Revolution to the Civil War, 1775/1783-1861
Biography (Late eighteenth century)

302.6.A-.6.Z	Individual, A-Z — Continued
302.6.D25	Deane, Silas
	Subarrange by Table E2A at the end of the text
302.6.D3	Dearborn, Henry
	Subarrange by Table E2A at the end of the text
302.6.D45	Dexter, Samuel
	Subarrange by Table E2A at the end of the text
302.6.D5	Dickinson, John
	Subarrange by Table E2A at the end of the text
302.6.D8	Duane, James
	Subarrange by Table E2A at the end of the text
302.6.D82	Duane, William
	Subarrange by Table E2A at the end of the text
302.6.E15	Eaton, William
	Subarrange by Table E2A at the end of the text
302.6.E3	Ellery, William
	Subarrange by Table E2A at the end of the text
302.6.E4	Ellsworth, Oliver
	Subarrange by Table E2A at the end of the text
302.6.F24	Farragut, George
	Subarrange by Table E2A at the end of the text
302.6.F56	FitzSimons, Thomas
	Subarrange by Table E2A at the end of the text
302.6.F6	Fowler, John
	Subarrange by Table E2A at the end of the text
302.6.F7-.6.F8	Franklin, Benjamin
	For his collected works, see E302.F8
	Autobiography
302.6.F7A2	English. By date
302.6.F7A3-.6.F7Z3	Translations. By language and date
302.6.F7Z4-.6.F7Z99	Commentaries
302.6.F75	Letters
302.6.F75A1-.6.F75A6	Collections. By title
302.6.F75A7	Single letters. By date
302.6.F8	Biography
302.6.G16	Gallatin, Albert
	Subarrange by Table E2A at the end of the text
302.6.G37	Gerry, Elbridge
	Subarrange by Table E2A at the end of the text
302.6.G47	Giles, William Branch
	Subarrange by Table E2A at the end of the text
302.6.G66	Gorham, Nathaniel
	Subarrange by Table E2A at the end of the text
302.6.G95	Gwinnett, Button
	Subarrange by Table E2A at the end of the text
302.6.H2	Hamilton, Alexander
	Subarrange by Table E2A at the end of the text
	For his collected works, see E302.H2
302.6.H22	Hamilton, Elizabeth (Schuyler)
	Subarrange by Table E2A at the end of the text
	Hancock, John
302.6.H23	General works
	Subarrange by Table E2A at the end of the text
302.6.H24	Hancock, Dorothy (Quincy)
	Subarrange by Table E2A at the end of the text
302.6.H27	Hanson, John
	Subarrange by Table E2A at the end of the text

Revolution to the Civil War, 1775/1783-1861
Biography (Late eighteenth century)

302.6.A-.6.Z	Individual, A-Z — Continued
302.6.H29	Harper, Robert Goodloe
	Subarrange by Table E2A at the end of the text
302.6.H4	Henry, John
	Subarrange by Table E2A at the end of the text
302.6.H5	Henry, Patrick
	Subarrange by Table E2A at the end of the text
302.6.H6	Hillegas, Michael
	Subarrange by Table E2A at the end of the text
302.6.H63	Hillhouse, James
	Subarrange by Table E2A at the end of the text
302.6.H65	Hindman, William
	Subarrange by Table E2A at the end of the text
302.6.H7	Hooper, William
	Subarrange by Table E2A at the end of the text
302.6.H78	Hopkins, Stephen
	Subarrange by Table E2A at the end of the text
302.6.H8	Hosmer, Titus
	Subarrange by Table E2A at the end of the text
302.6.H89	Humphreys, David
	Subarrange by Table E2A at the end of the text
302.6.H9	Huntington, Benjamin
	Subarrange by Table E2A at the end of the text
302.6.H93	Husbands, Herman
	Subarrange by Table E2A at the end of the text
302.6.I6	Ingersoll, Jared
	Subarrange by Table E2A at the end of the text
302.6.I7	Iredell, James
	Subarrange by Table E2A at the end of the text
302.6.J4	Jay, John
	Subarrange by Table E2A at the end of the text
	For Jay's Treaty, see E314
302.6.J65	Johnson, Thomas
	Subarrange by Table E2A at the end of the text
302.6.J7	Johnson, William Samuel
	Subarrange by Table E2A at the end of the text
302.6.K3	Kavanagh, Edward
	Subarrange by Table E2A at the end of the text
302.6.K5	King, Rufus
	Subarrange by Table E2A at the end of the text
302.6.L26	Langdon, John
	Subarrange by Table E2A at the end of the text
302.6.L3	Laurens, Henry
	Subarrange by Table E2A at the end of the text
302.6.L4	Lee, Richard Henry
	Subarrange by Table E2A at the end of the text
302.6.L6	Lewis, Francis
	Subarrange by Table E2A at the end of the text
302.6.L66	Livermore, Edward St. Loe
	Subarrange by Table E2A at the end of the text
302.6.L67	Livingston, Anne Home (Shippen)
	Subarrange by Table E2A at the end of the text
	Livingston, Edward
302.6.L68	General works
	Subarrange by Table E2A at the end of the text
302.6.L684	Livingston, Louise (Davezac) Moreau
	Subarrange by Table E2A at the end of the text

Revolution to the Civil War, 1775/1783-1861
Biography (Late eighteenth century)

302.6.A-.6.Z	Individual, A-Z — Continued
302.6.L7	Livingston, Philip
	Subarrange by Table E2A at the end of the text
302.6.L72	Livingston, Robert R.
	Subarrange by Table E2A at the end of the text
302.6.L75	Livingston, William
	Subarrange by Table E2A at the end of the text
302.6.L8	Logan, George
	Subarrange by Table E2A at the end of the text
302.6.L9	Lyon, Matthew
	Subarrange by Table E2A at the end of the text
302.6.M12	McHenry, James
	Subarrange by Table E2A at the end of the text
302.6.M13	McKean, Thomas
	Subarrange by Table E2A at the end of the text
302.6.M14	Maclay, William
	Subarrange by Table E2A at the end of the text
302.6.M17	Macon, Nathaniel
	Subarrange by Table E2A at the end of the text
302.6.M35	Marshall, Humphrey
	Subarrange by Table E2A at the end of the text
302.6.M4	Marshall, John
	Subarrange by Table E2A at the end of the text
	Including John Marshall Day
302.6.M432	Mason, Armistead Thomson
	Subarrange by Table E2A at the end of the text
302.6.M45	Mason, George
	Subarrange by Table E2A at the end of the text
302.6.M7	Morris, Gouverneur
	Subarrange by Table E2A at the end of the text
	Morris, Robert
302.6.M8	General works
	Subarrange by Table E2A at the end of the text
302.6.M81	Morris, Mary (White)
	Subarrange by Table E2A at the end of the text
302.6.M88	Mulligan, Hercules
	Subarrange by Table E2A at the end of the text
302.6.O8	Otis, James
	Subarrange by Table E2A at the end of the text
302.6.P14	Paine, Robert Treat
	Subarrange by Table E2A at the end of the text
	Paine, Thomas, *see* JC178.V2
302.6.P3	Paterson, William
	Subarrange by Table E2A at the end of the text
302.6.P5	Pickering, Timothy
	Subarrange by Table E2A at the end of the text
302.6.P54	Pinckney, Charles
	Subarrange by Table E2A at the end of the text
302.6.P55	Pinckney, Charles Cotesworth
	Subarrange by Table E2A at the end of the text
32.6.P57	Pinckney, Thomas
	Subarrange by Table E2A at the end of the text
302.6.P6	Pinkney, William
	Subarrange by Table E2A at the end of the text
302.6.P73	Plumer, William
	Subarrange by Table E2A at the end of the text
302.6.P84	Pollock, Oliver
	Subarrange by Table E2A at the end of the text

Revolution to the Civil War, 1775/1783-1861
Biography (Late eighteenth century)

302.6.A-.6.Z	Individual, A-Z — Continued
302.6.P86	Pope, John
	Subarrange by Table E2A at the end of the text
302.6.P93	Preston, Francis
	Subarrange by Table E2A at the end of the text
302.6.Q7	Quincy, Josiah, 1772-1864
	Subarrange by Table E2A at the end of the text
302.6.R18	Randolph, Edmund
	Subarrange by Table E2A at the end of the text
302.6.R2	Randolph, John
	Subarrange by Table E2A at the end of the text
302.6.R27	Read, George
	Subarrange by Table E2A at the end of the text
302.6.R3	Reed, Joseph
	Subarrange by Table E2A at the end of the text
302.6.R6	Rodney, Caesar
	Subarrange by Table E2A at the end of the text
302.6.R61	Rodney, Caesar Augustus
	Subarrange by Table E2A at the end of the text
302.6.R77	Ross, Betsy (Griscom)
	Subarrange by Table E2A at the end of the text
302.6.R79	Ross, George, 1730-1779
	Subarrange by Table E2A at the end of the text
302.6.R8	Ross, James
	Subarrange by Table E2A at the end of the text
302.6.R85	Rush, Benjamin
	Subarrange by Table E2A at the end of the text
302.6.R89	Rutledge, John, 1739-1800
	Subarrange by Table E2A at the end of the text
302.6.R9	Rutledge, John, 1766-1819
	Subarrange by Table E2A at the end of the text
302.6.S13	Sailly, Peter
	Subarrange by Table E2A at the end of the text
302.6.S17	Salomon, Haym
	Subarrange by Table E2A at the end of the text
302.6.S3	Sawyer, Lemuel
	Subarrange by Table E2A at the end of the text
302.6.S45	Sevier, John
	Subarrange by Table E2A at the end of the text
302.6.S5	Sherman, Roger
	Subarrange by Table E2A at the end of the text
302.6.S57	Smith, Jeremiah
	Subarrange by Table E2A at the end of the text
302.6.S59	Smith, William Stephens
	Subarrange by Table E2A at the end of the text
302.6.S7	Spaight, Richard Dobbs
	Subarrange by Table E2A at the end of the text
302.6.S85	Stockton, Richard
	Subarrange by Table E2A at the end of the text
302.6.S98	Symmes, John Cleves
	Subarrange by Table E2A at the end of the text
302.6.T18	Tait, Charles
	Subarrange by Table E2A at the end of the text
302.6.T2	Tallmadge, Benjamin
	Subarrange by Table E2A at the end of the text
302.6.T23	Taylor, John
	Subarrange by Table E2A at the end of the text

Revolution to the Civil War, 1775/1783-1861
Biography (Late eighteenth century)

302.6.A-.6.Z	Individual, A-Z — Continued
302.6.T4	Thomas, Ebenezer Smith
	Subarrange by Table E2A at the end of the text
302.6.T48	Thomson, Charles
	Subarrange by Table E2A at the end of the text
302.6.T8	Tompkins, Daniel D.
	Subarrange by Table E2A at the end of the text
302.6.T93	Tyler, Mary Hunt (Palmer)
	Subarrange by Table E2A at the end of the text
302.6.V33	Varnum, James Mitchell
	Subarrange by Table E2A at the end of the text
302.6.V4	Varnum, Joseph Bradley
	Subarrange by Table E2A at the end of the text
302.6.W15	Washington, Bushrod
	Subarrange by Table E2A at the end of the text
302.6.W2	Webster, Pelatiah
	Subarrange by Table E2A at the end of the text
302.6.W4	Weems, Mason Locke
	Subarrange by Table E2A at the end of the text
302.6.W5	Whipple, William
	Subarrange by Table E2A at the end of the text
302.6.W55	Williams, William
	Subarrange by Table E2A at the end of the text
302.6.W6	Williamson, Hugh
	Subarrange by Table E2A at the end of the text
302.6.W62	Willing, Thomas
	Subarrange by Table E2A at the end of the text
302.6.W64	Wilson, James
	Subarrange by Table E2A at the end of the text
302.6.W67	Wingate, Paine
	Subarrange by Table E2A at the end of the text
302.6.W68	Wisner, Henry
	Subarrange by Table E2A at the end of the text
302.6.W7	Witherspoon, John
	Subarrange by Table E2A at the end of the text
302.6.W85	Wolcott, Oliver
	Subarrange by Table E2A at the end of the text
	By period
	1775-1789. The Confederation, 1783-1789
303	General works
	Including Continental Congress, 1774-1788. Articles of Confederation. The Constitution.
	Foreign relations, 1783-1789
	For Constitutional history, see JK111+
	For Revolution, see E201+
	For Shay's Rebellion, see F69
303.2	Bicentennial celebrations for the Constitution
309	Territorial questions
	Including cession of western land claims to the general government by Connecticut,
	Massachusetts, New York, North Carolina, and Virginia, 1781-1786. Northwest
	Ordinance, 1787
	For Georgia land cessions of 1802, see F290
	For South Carolina cession of 1787, see F292.B7
	1789-1809. Constitutional period
310	General works
310.7	Diplomatic history. Foreign and general relations
	For diplomatic history of special periods, see E313-314,E323,E333-336,E357, etc.
	Washington's administrations, 1789-1797
	For wars with the northwestern Indians, 1790-1795, see E83.79
	Cf. HG2525+, United States banks (First and second)

Revolution to the Civil War, 1775/1783-1861
    By period
        1789-1809. Constitutional period
            Washington's administrations, 1789-1797 — Continued

311	General works
	Biography of George Washington, 1732-1799
	For bibliography, see Z8950
312	General works. Washington as president
312.1	Societies
312.15	Reminiscences of contemporaries, anecdotes, calendars, etc.
312.17	Special
	Including personality, character, religion, etc.; relations with special classes or individuals; etc.
312.19	Ancestry. Family. Servants
	Including biography, e.g. Martha Washington
	For genealogy of the Washingtons and genealogical tables, see CS71.A+
312.195	Sulgrave Manor
	Including the home of the Washington family in England
	Including publications of Sulgrave Institution
	By period
312.2	Early life to 1775
312.23	Expeditions to the Ohio, 1753-1754. Participation in French and Indian War
	For general accounts of Braddock's campaign, see E199
	Military career as commander-in-chief, 1775-1783
312.25	General works
	Cf. E201+ , The American Revolution
312.27	Itineraries, etc.
	Class individual headquarters with locality in Class F
312.29	Period after the Revolution, 1783-1799
	For period of the Presidency, 1789-1797, see E311+
312.3	Death. Funeral. Memorial services
	Including memorial publications
	For funeral addresses and sermons, see E312.62+
	For tomb, see E312.5
	Iconography
312.4	General works
312.43	Portraits, etc.
	For medals, see CJ5801+
	Monuments, statues, etc.
312.45	General works
	Local monuments, statues, etc., see Class F, e.g. F203.4.W3 , Washington monument in Washington, D.C.
312.5	Homes and haunts
	Including birthplace, Wakefield, Va.; Mount Vernon; Washington estate; Washington's tomb and relics
312.6	Anniversaries. Celebrations. Memorials (since 1800 only)
	Including Washington's birthday, centennial celebrations, etc.
	For funeral and memorial services, 1799-1800, see E312.3
	Addresses, essays, lectures. Sermons
312.62	Collections
312.63	Individual
(312.65)	Poetry. Drama. Fiction, *see* Subclasses P-PZ
312.66	Juvenile works
	Music, *see* Class M
312.67	Other works
	Including questions and answers on his life
	Writings of Washington
312.7	Collected works. By date
312.72	Partial collections. Selected works. By date

Revolution to the Civil War, 1775/1783-1861
    By period
        1789-1809. Constitutional period
           Washington's administrations, 1789-1797
              Writings of Washington — Continued
                Letters
                  Collections

312.74	General. By date
312.75.A-.75.Z	By subject, A-Z
	GALE NOTE *The cutter number(s) listed below have been given only as examples by the Library of Congress*
312.75.A2-.75.A3	Agriculture
312.75.M4-.75.M5	Freemasons
312.75.R3-.75.R4	Religion
	Revolution, *see* E203
312.75.S6-.75.S7	Society of the Cincinnati
312.76	Individual letters. By date
312.77	Spurious letters. Editions. By date
312.78	Rules of civility. By date
312.79	Selections. Extracts
	Including maxims, prayers, sayings, etc.
312.8	Diaries. Journals. By date
	For selected Revolutionary orders, see E230
312.81	Accounts. Editions. By date
	Addresses and messages
312.83	Addresses to officers of the army, March 15, 1783
312.85	Circular letter, June 18, 1783
	Another edition has title "Last official address ... to the legislatures of the United States"
	Addressed to the governors of the several states
	Editions arranged by place of publication
312.87	Farewell address to the army, November 2, 1783
312.9	Speeches and messages as President. By date
312.95	Farewell address, 1796. By date
	Subarrange by place of publication
312.952	History and criticism
312.99	Will. Editions, by date
	Diplomatic history. Foreign relations
	Including Neutrality proclamation of 1793; withdrawal of British garrisons from western posts; embargo of 1794; Treaty with Spain, 1795; etc.
	Including activities of foreign ministers Adet, Genet, and Casa Yrujo
313	General works
314	Jay's Treaty
	Signed November 1794, ratified August 1795
	For British right of search, see E357.2
315	Whisky insurrection of Pennsylvania, 1794
320	Presidential campaign of 1796
	John Adams' administration, 1797-1801
	For Washington, D.C., selected as capital, see F195
321	General works
	Biography of John Adams, 1735-1826
	For his collected works, see E302.A26
	For his speeches and messages as President, see J82.A2+
322	General works
	Subarrange by Table E2 at the end of the text
322.1	Adams family (not genealogy)
323	Troubles with France, 1796-1800
	Including "XYZ" letters, naval conflicts, etc.
	For French spoilation claims before 1800, see JX238.F72+
326	Fries Rebellion, 1798-1799

Revolution to the Civil War, 1775/1783-1861
    By period
        1789-1809. Constitutional period
          John Adams' administration, 1797-1801 — Continued
            Alien and sedition laws, 1798

327	General works
328	Kentucky and Virginia Resolutions
330	Presidential campaign of 1800

          Jefferson's administrations, 1801-1809
            For the Chesapeake affair, see E357.2
            For impressment of American seamen, see E357.2
            For Lewis and Clark Expedition, 1804-1806, see F592.3+

331	General works

          Biography of Thomas Jefferson, 1743-1826
            For bibliography, see Z8452

332	General works. Jefferson as president and statesman

            For autobiography, see E332.9.A8

332.15	Reminiscences of contemporaries. Anecdotes
332.2	Special

            Including Jefferson's personality, character, religion, catholicity, etc.; his attitude toward civil and religious liberty, state rights, freedom of the press, etc.; his knowledge of government, language, science, the fine and useful arts, etc.
            Including Jefferson as scholar, humanist, author, architect, musician, educator, social reformer, farmer, inventor, etc.
            For Jefferson as president and statesman, see E332
            For Jefferson as legislator, see E332.3+
            For Jefferson as diplomat, see E332.45
            For Jefferson as traveler, see E332.745
            For Jefferson as philosopher, see B885
            Including Jefferson's relations with special classes, e.g. Jews; Slaves; Relations with contemporaries, e.g. Alexander Hamilton; James Madison

332.25	Ancestry. Family. Family life

            Including biography, e.g. Martha (Jefferson) Randolph, his daughter
          By period

332.27	Early life

            Including frontier life in western Virginia; education; admission to the bar, 1764; professional career, 1767-1774; marriage
          Public life

332.3	General works
332.4	State politics

            Including service in Virginia House of Burgesses, 1770; Virginia legislature, 1776-1778; governor, 1779-1781

332.45	International diplomacy

            Including Jefferson as treaty negotiator with European powers, 1784; Minister to France, 1785-1789

332.5	National politics

            Including Jefferson as delegate to the Continental Congress, 1775-1776, 1781, 1783-1784; Secretary of State, 1790-1793; Vice-president, 1796-1800
            Cf. E221, Declaration of Independence
            Cf. E320, Presidential campaign of 1796
            Cf. E330, Presidential campaign of 1800
            Cf. E337, Presidential campaigns of 1808
            Cf. HG521, History of United States money, 1783-1860
            Cf. JK2311+, Democratic (Democratic-Republican) Party
            For Presidency, 1801-1809, see E331+

332.6	Later life

            Including his financial difficulties; sale of library to Congress, 1815; death and burial; funeral and memorial services, 1826-1827; Memorial publications
            For the founding of the University of Virginia, 1819, see LD5660+
            For funeral addresses and sermons, see E332.76+

Revolution to the Civil War, 1775/1783-1861
By period

	1789-1809. Constitutional period
	Jefferson's administrations, 1801-1809
	Biography of Thomas Jefferson, 1743-1826
	By period
332.6	Later life — Continued
	For his tomb, see E332.74
	Iconography
332.7	General works
332.72	Portraits, etc.
	Cf. Subclass NE, Engraved portraits
	For medals, see CJ5801+
332.73	Monuments, statues, etc.
	Including foreign monuments and statues, e.g. the Jefferson statue at Angers, France
	For local monuments and statues, see Class F, e.g. the Thomas Jefferson Memorial in Washington, F203.4.J4
332.74	Homes and haunts
	Including his birthplace, Shadwell, Va.; Monticello with tomb and relics; Graff House, Philadelphia; Hőel de Langear, Paris; etc.
332.745	Journeys
	Including those in America and Europe
332.75	Anniversaries. Celebrations. Memorials
	Including memorials since 1827; Jefferson's birthday; centennial celebrations, etc.
	For funeral and memorial services, 1826-1827, see E332.6
	Addresses, essays, lectures. Sermons
332.76	Collections
332.77	Individual
(332.78)	Poetry. Drama. Fiction, *see* Subclasses P-PZ
	Music, *see* Class M
332.79	Juvenile works
332.795	Other works
	Including the Thomas Jefferson quiz book
332.799	Uncataloged pamphlets, clippings, etc.
	Writings of Jefferson
	For speeches and messages as President, see J82.A3+
(332.8)	Collected works, *see* E302.J44
(332.82)	Selected works, *see* E302.J44
	Correspondence
332.84	Calendar of correspondence
332.85	Collections of letters (General). By date
332.86	Selected letters (General). By date
	Special
332.87	Letters. By subject, A-Z
	In general, prefer classification in Classes A-Z, e.g. PA70.U6, Letters concerning philology and the classics
332.88.A-.88.Z	Letters. By correspondent, A-Z
	GALE NOTE *The cutter number(s) listed below have been given only as examples by the Library of Congress*
332.88.D8	Dupont de Nemours, Pierre Samuel
332.88.J4	Jefferson, Randolph
332.9.A-.9.Z	Individual works, A-Z
	In general, prefer classification by subject in Classes A-Z
	GALE NOTE *The cutter number(s) listed below have been given only as examples by the Library of Congress*
332.9.A8	Autobiography (1743-1790)
332.9.C6	Commonplace books. Literary Bible
	Declaration of Independence, *see* E221

Revolution to the Civil War, 1775/1783-1861

By period

1789-1809. Constitutional period

Jefferson's administrations, 1801-1809

Writings of Jefferson

332.9.A-.9.Z	Individual works, A-Z — Continued
	Jefferson Bible, *see* BS2549.J3+
	Literary Bible, *see* E332.9.C6
	Notes on the state of Virginia, *see* F230
	Summary view of the rights of British America, *see* E211
(332.95)	Addresses, essays, lectures, *see* E302.J44
(332.98)	Doubtful or spurious works, *see* classification by subject
(332.99)	Criticism and evaluation of Jefferson's writings, *see* E332.2
333	Purchase of Louisiana, 1803
	Including Treaty of Paris, 1803; diplomatic and political aspects; etc.
	For the region purchased, see F351+, F366+
333.7	Presidential campaign of 1804
334	Burr's conspiracy, 1805-1807. Wilkinson's participation
	For Burr, Aaron (Biography), see E302.6.B9
	For Mississippi Valley, see F353
	For Wilkinson, James (Biography), see E353.1.W6
335	War with Tripoli, 1801-1805
	Called also Tripolitan War or Tripoline War
	Including general relations with Barbary States; Treaty of Peace and Amity; the capture and destruction of the frigate Philadelphia; etc.
	Including biography: James Barron, Richard Valentine Morris, Mordecai Manuel Noah, Edward Preble, Richard Somers, etc.
	For war with Algeria, see E365
	Neutral trade and its restriction, 1800-1810
	Including French spoliations after 1800
	For controversies with England, see E357+
	For orders in Council, see HF3505.9
336	General works
336.5	Embargo, December 1807-March 1809
	For Embargo acts: Text, and effects on commerce, see HF3027.1
337	Presidential campaign of 1808
337.5	Nineteenth century (General)
	Early nineteenth century, 1801/1809-1845
	Including Slavery controversy in politics, general works on "manifest destiny," territorial expansion, etc.
	For Antimasonic controversy, 1827-1845, see HS525-527
	Cf. E440.92, Moral and economic aspects of slavery in the United States
337.8.A-.8.Z	Collected works of American statesmen, A-Z
	For works of statesmen of the middle nineteenth century, see E415.6.A+
	GALE NOTE *The cutter number(s) listed below have been given only as examples by the Library of Congress*
337.8.A2	Adams, John Quincy
337.8.C13	Calhoun, John Caldwell
337.8.C55	Clay, Henry
337.8.E9	Everett, Edward
337.8.J3	Jackson, Andrew
337.8.W24	Webster, Daniel
338	General works
	Biography
	For the middle nineteenth century, see E415.8+
339	Collective
340.A-.Z	Individual, A-Z
	GALE NOTE *The cutter number(s) listed below have been given only as examples by the Library of Congress*

Revolution to the Civil War, 1775/1783-1861
    By period
        Early nineteenth century, 1801/1809-1845
           Biography

340.A-.Z	Individual, A-Z — Continued
340.A4	Allen, Charles
	Subarrange by Table E2A at the end of the text
340.B2	Bancroft, George
	Subarrange by Table E2A at the end of the text
340.B4	Benton, Thomas Hart
	Subarrange by Table E2A at the end of the text
340.B57	Binney, Horace, 1780-1875
	Subarrange by Table E2A at the end of the text
340.B6	Birney, James Gillespie
	Subarrange by Table E2A at the end of the text
340.B67	Branch, John
	Subarrange by Table E2A at the end of the text
340.B8	Brockenbrough, William Henry
	Subarrange by Table E2A at the end of the text
340.B88	Brown, James
	Subarrange by Table E2A at the end of the text
340.B9	Burges, Tristam
	Subarrange by Table E2A at the end of the text
340.B98	Butler, Benjamin Franklin, 1795-1858
	Subarrange by Table E2A at the end of the text
340.C15	Calhoun, John Caldwell
	Subarrange by Table E2A at the end of the text
340.C3	Cass, Lewis
	Subarrange by Table E2A at the end of the text
340.C4	Choate, Rufus
	Subarrange by Table E2A at the end of the text
340.C5	Cilley, Jonathan
	Subarrange by Table E2A at the end of the text
	Including the Graves-Cilley duel
340.C6	Clay, Henry
	Subarrange by Table E2A at the end of the text
340.C62	Clayton, Augustin Smith
	Subarrange by Table E2A at the end of the text
340.C65	Clinton, De Witt
	Subarrange by Table E2A at the end of the text
340.C7	Cook, Daniel Pope
	Subarrange by Table E2A at the end of the text
340.C76	Corwin, Thomas
	Subarrange by Table E2A at the end of the text
340.C89	Crawford, William Harris
	Subarrange by Table E2A at the end of the text
340.C9	Crittenden, John Jordan
	Subarrange by Table E2A at the end of the text
340.D14	Dallas, George Mifflin
	Subarrange by Table E2A at the end of the text
340.D4	DeForest, David Curtis
	Subarrange by Table E2A at the end of the text
340.D7	Dodge, Henry
	Subarrange by Table E2A at the end of the text
340.E8	Everett, Edward
	Subarrange by Table E2A at the end of the text
340.E9	Ewing, Thomas
	Subarrange by Table E2A at the end of the text
340.F16	Fairfield, John
	Subarrange by Table E2A at the end of the text

Revolution to the Civil War, 1775/1783-1861

    By period

        Early nineteenth century, 1801/1809-1845

            Biography

340.A-.Z	Individual, A-Z — Continued
340.F86	Frelinghuysen, Theodore
	Subarrange by Table E2A at the end of the text
340.G2	Gaston, William
	Subarrange by Table E2A at the end of the text
340.G48	Gilpin, Henry Dilworth
	Subarrange by Table E2A at the end of the text
340.G8	Grundy, Felix
	Subarrange by Table E2A at the end of the text
340.H2	Hammond, Charles
	Subarrange by Table E2A at the end of the text
340.H26	Hardin, Benjamin
	Subarrange by Table E2A at the end of the text
340.H4	Hayne, Robert Young
	Subarrange by Table E2A at the end of the text
340.H9	Huntington, Jabez Williams
	Subarrange by Table E2A at the end of the text
340.I5	Ingersoll, Charles Jared
	Subarrange by Table E2A at the end of the text
340.I53	Ingersoll, Joseph Reed
	Subarrange by Table E2A at the end of the text
340.J3	Jarvis, Leonard
	Subarrange by Table E2A at the end of the text
340.J69	Johnson, Richard Mentor
	Subarrange by Table E2A at the end of the text
340.K2	Kaufman, David Spangler
	Subarrange by Table E2A at the end of the text
340.K33	Kendall, Amos
	Subarrange by Table E2A at the end of the text
340.K54	King, William Rufus
	Subarrange by Table E2A at the end of the text
340.L4	Lawrence, Abbott
	Subarrange by Table E2A at the end of the text
340.L5	Legaré, Hugh Swinton
	Subarrange by Table E2A at the end of the text
340.L7	Linn, Lewis Fields
	Subarrange by Table E2A at the end of the text
340.M17	McDuffie, George
	Subarrange by Table E2A at the end of the text
340.M2	McLean, John
	Subarrange by Table E2A at the end of the text
340.M3	Mangum, Willie Person
	Subarrange by Table E2A at the end of the text
340.M34	Mason, Jeremiah
	Subarrange by Table E2A at the end of the text
340.M4	Menefee, Richard Hickman
	Subarrange by Table E2A at the end of the text
340.M5	Mercer, Charles Fenton
	Subarrange by Table E2A at the end of the text
340.M7	Monroe, James, 1799-1870
	Subarrange by Table E2A at the end of the text
340.M8	Morris, Thomas
	Subarrange by Table E2A at the end of the text
340.M83	Morrow, Jeremiah
	Subarrange by Table E2A at the end of the text

Revolution to the Civil War, 1775/1783-1861
By period
Early nineteenth century, 1801/1809-1845
Biography

340.A-.Z	Individual, A-Z — Continued
340.O8	Otis, Harrison Gray
	Subarrange by Table E2A at the end of the text
340.P3	Pearce, James Alfred
	Subarrange by Table E2A at the end of the text
340.P54	Phelps, Samuel Shethar
	Subarrange by Table E2A at the end of the text
340.P75	Poindexter, George
	Subarrange by Table E2A at the end of the text
340.P77	Poinsett, Joel Roberts
	Subarrange by Table E2A at the end of the text
340.P88	Prentiss, Samuel
	Subarrange by Table E2A at the end of the text
340.P9	Prentiss, Seargent Smith
	Subarrange by Table E2A at the end of the text
	Including the Prentiss-Tucker duel
340.R6	Ritchie, Thomas
	Subarrange by Table E2A at the end of the text
340.R7	Robertson, George
	Subarrange by Table E2A at the end of the text
340.R88	Royall, Anne (Newport)
	Subarrange by Table E2A at the end of the text
340.R9	Rush, Richard
	Subarrange by Table E2A at the end of the text
340.S18	Saltonstall, Leverett
	Subarrange by Table E2A at the end of the text
340.S75	Stevenson, Andrew
	Subarrange by Table E2A at the end of the text
	Story, Joseph, *see* KF8745.A+
	Taney, Roger Brooke, *see* KF8745.A+
340.T47	Thompson, Richard Wigginton
	Subarrange by Table E2A at the end of the text
340.V7	Vinton, Samuel Finley
	Subarrange by Table E2A at the end of the text
340.W3	Wayne, James Moore
	Subarrange by Table E2A at the end of the text
340.W4	Webster, Daniel
	Subarrange by Table E2A at the end of the text
340.W53	White, Hugh Lawson
	Subarrange by Table E2A at the end of the text
340.W65	Wilmot, David
	Subarrange by Table E2A at the end of the text
340.W73	Winthrop, Robert Charles
	Subarrange by Table E2A at the end of the text
340.W79	Wirt, William
	Subarrange by Table E2A at the end of the text
340.W8	Woodbury, Levi
	Subarrange by Table E2A at the end of the text
340.W95	Wright, Silas
	Subarrange by Table E2A at the end of the text

Jefferson's administrations, 1801-1809, *see* E331+
Madison's administrations, 1809-1817
For war with Algeria, 1815, see E365
For Presidential campaign of 1816, see E370
Cf. E83.81, Battle of Tippecanoe, 1811
Cf. E83.813, First Creek War, 1813-1814

Revolution to the Civil War, 1775/1783-1861

By period

Early nineteenth century, 1801/1809-1845

Madison's administrations, 1809-1817 — Continued

	Cf. E357+, Troubles with England since 1797
	Cf. F314, Seizure of West Florida west of the Perdido
341	General works
	Biography of James Madison, 1751-1836
	For his collected works, see E302.M19
	For his speeches and messages as President, see J82.A4+
342	General
	Subarrange by Table E2 at the end of the text
342.1	Madison's family (not genealogy)
	Including biography, e.g. Dorothy (Payne) Todd Madison (Dolly Madison)
349	Presidential campaign of 1812
	War of 1812
	Periodicals. Societies. Collections
351	General works
	Societies of veterans
351.2	National Convention of the Soldiers of the War of 1812
351.23	Pennsylvania Association of the Defenders of the Country in the War of 1812
351.27	New England Association of Soldiers of the War of 1812
351.28	New York State Convention of the Soldiers of the War of 1812
351.3-353.6	Patriotic societies of descendants
	Under each:
	.A1-.A49 Official publications
	.A5A-.A5Z History of the society
	.A6-.Z By state
351.3	Society of the War of 1812
	Subarrange by table below E351.3-353.6
351.32	Society of the Second War with Great Britain in the State of New York
	Subarrange by table below E351.3-353.6
351.5	Military Society of the War of 1812
	Subarrange by table below E351.3-353.6
351.6	National Society of United States Daughters of 1812
	Subarrange by table below E351.3-353.6
	Biography
353	Collective
	Including chiefly military and naval leaders
	For statesmen and politicians, see E302.5+, E339+
353.1.A-.1.Z	Individual, A-Z
	GALE NOTE *The cutter number(s) listed below have been given only as examples by the Library of Congress*
353.1.A19	Adair, John
	Subarrange by Table E1 at the end of the text
353.1.B2	Bainbridge, William
	Subarrange by Table E1 at the end of the text
353.1.B26	Barney, Joshua
	Subarrange by Table E1 at the end of the text
353.1.B5	Biddle, James
	Subarrange by Table E1 at the end of the text
353.1.B8	Brock, Sir Isaac
	Subarrange by Table E1 at the end of the text
353.1.B9	Brown, Jacob
	Subarrange by Table E1 at the end of the text
353.1.C75	Covington, Leonard
	Subarrange by Table E1 at the end of the text
353.1.C8	Croghan, George
	Subarrange by Table E1 at the end of the text

Revolution to the Civil War, 1775/1783-1861

By period

Early nineteenth century, 1801/1809-1845

Madison's administrations, 1809-1817

War of 1812

Biography

353.1.A-.1.Z	Individual, A-Z — Continued
353.1.D29	Decatur, Stephen, 1779-1820
	Subarrange by Table E1 at the end of the text
353.1.E4	Elliot, Jesse Duncan
	Subarrange by Table E1 at the end of the text
353.1.G14	Gaines, Edmund Pendleton
	Subarrange by Table E1 at the end of the text
353.1.H2	Hampton, Wade, 1754-1835
	Subarrange by Table E1 at the end of the text
353.1.H8	Hull, Isaac
	Subarrange by Table E1 at the end of the text
353.1.H9	Hull, William
	Subarrange by Table E1 at the end of the text
353.1.J7	Jones, Jacob
	Subarrange by Table E1 at the end of the text
353.1.L4	Lawrence, James
	Subarrange by Table E1 at the end of the text
353.1.M15	McArthur, Duncan
	Subarrange by Table E1 at the end of the text
353.1.M2	Macdonough, Thomas
	Subarrange by Table E1 at the end of the text
353.1.M3	Macomb, Alexander
	Subarrange by Table E1 at the end of the text
353.1.M8	Morris, Charles
	Subarrange by Table E1 at the end of the text
353.1.P4	Perry, Oliver Hazard
	Subarrange by Table E1 at the end of the text
353.1.P7	Porter, David
	Subarrange by Table E1 at the end of the text
353.1.R5	Ripley, Eleazer Wheelock
	Subarrange by Table E1 at the end of the text
353.1.R7	Rodgers, John
	Subarrange by Table E1 at the end of the text
353.1.S8	Stewart, Charles
	Subarrange by Table E1 at the end of the text
353.1.W6	Wilkinson, James
	Subarrange by Table E1 at the end of the text
354	General works
	Cf. E165, Manners and customs, and general travel, 1812-1845
	Military operations, 1812-1815
	Cf. E83.812, Indian wars, 1812-1815
355	General works
	Including campaigns and battles (General) and lists of battles
	For individual battles, see E356.A+
355.1.A-.1.Z	By region, A-Z
	Including campaigns of the northwestern army, the war in the north, in the south, etc., in general
E355.1.N5	Campaigns upon the Niagara frontier
	Campaigns. By year
355.2	1812
	Including campaigns in the north and northwest covering Detroit, Lake Champlain, Niagara, etc.

Revolution to the Civil War, 1775/1783-1861
   By period
      Early nineteenth century, 1801/1809-1845
         Madison's administrations, 1809-1817
            War of 1812
               Military operations, 1812-1815
                  Campaigns. By year — Continued

355.4	1813
	Including campaigns in the east, north, and northwest covering Chesapeake Bay, Lake Champlain, Lake Erie, Lake Ontario, St Lawrence River, etc.
	Cf. E83.813, First Creek War, 1813-1814
355.6	1814-1815
	Including campaigns in the east, north, and south covering Chesapeake Bay, Lake Champlain, New Orleans, Niagara, etc.
	For the capture and burning of Washington, see E356.W3
356.A-.Z	Individual battles, A-Z
	Including attacks; capture and burning of cities; sieges
	Battles, sieges, etc., may be classed in E355.2+
356.B2	Baltimore, 1814
	Including the battle of North Point and the bombardment of Fort McHenry
	Class here also the Fort McHenry National Monument and Historic Shrine
356.B3	Beaver Dams, Ont., 1813
356.B5	Bladensburg, Md., 1814
356.B6	Boquet River, N.Y., 1814
	Bridgewater, Ont., *see* E356.L9
356.B8	Brownstown, Mich., 1812
356.C2	Campbell's Island, 1814
	In Mississippi River east of Moline, Ill.
356.C3	Caulk's Field, Md., 1814
	Champlain, Lake, *see* E356.P7
356.C4	Chateauguay, N.Y., 1813
356.C53	Chicago, 1812
356.C55	Chippewa, Ont., 1814
356.C74	Cook's Mills, Ont., 1814
356.C8	Craney Island, Va., 1813
	Dearborn, Fort, *see* E356.C53
356.D4	Detroit, 1812
356.D8	Dudley's defeat
356.E5	Erie, Fort, Ont., 1814
356.E6	Erie, Lake, 1813
	Including Perry Memorial, Put-in-Bay, Ohio
	Frenchtown, Mich., *see* E356.R2
356.G4	George, Fort, Ont., 1812
356.H3	Harrison, Fort, Ind., 1812
356.L9	Lundy's Lane, Ont., 1814
356.M15	Mackinac, Mich., 1812
	On Mackinac Island, Lake Huron
356.M19	Malcolm's Mills, Ont., 1814
	McHenry, Fort, *see* E356.B2
356.M5	Meigs, Fort, Ohio, 1813
356.N5	New Orleans, 1815
	Including Chalmette National Historical Park
	Niagara, Ont., *see* E356.L9
	North Point, *see* E356.B2
356.P6	Pigeon Roost, Ind., 1812
356.P7	Plattsburg, N.Y., 1814
356.Q3	Queenston (Queenston Heights), Ont., 1812
356.R2	Raisin River, Mich., 1813
356.S34	Sackets Harbor, N.Y., 1813
356.S7	Stephenson, Fort, Ohio, 1813

Revolution to the Civil War, 1775/1783-1861

By period

Early nineteenth century, 1801/1809-1845

Madison's administrations, 1809-1817

War of 1812

Military operations, 1812-1815

356.A-.Z	Individual battles, A-Z — Continued
356.S8	Stonington, Conn., 1814
356.T3	Thames, Ont., 1813
356.T68	Toronto, 1813
356.W3	Washington, D.C., 1814
	York, Ont., *see* E356.T68
	Political history
	Including controversy with England, 1797-1812
	Cf. E314, Jay's Treaty
	Cf. E336+, Neutral trade and its restrictions, 1800-1810
	Cf. E336.5, Embargo, December 1807-March 1809
357	General works
	Right of search and impressment
357.2	General works
357.3	The Chesapeake-Leopard Affair, 1807
	Opposition to the war by the New England Federalists
357.6	General works
357.7	Hartford Convention, 1814
357.9	Effects of the war
358	Diplomatic history. Foreign relations
	Treaty of Ghent, 1814; Treatment of Alien enemies; Fisheries; Boundaries; etc.
	Armies. Troops
359	General works
	The American Army
359.2	Regulars
359.24	Infantry
359.25	Cavalry
359.26	Artillery
359.3	Militia
359.4	Pensioners. Bounties. Claims
359.5.A-.5.W	The states and their participation, A-W
359.5.C7	Connecticut
359.5.F6	Florida
359.5.G4	Georgia
359.5.I53	Indiana
359.5.K5	Kentucky
359.5.L8	Louisiana
359.5.M2	Maryland
359.5.M3	Massachusetts
359.5.N3	New Hampshire
359.5.N4	New Jersey
359.5.N6	New York
359.5.N7	North Carolina
359.5.O2	Ohio
359.5.P3	Pennsylvania
359.5.T47	Texas
359.5.V3	Vermont
359.5.V8	Virginia
	The British Army
359.8	General works
359.85	Canadian participation
359.9.A-.9.Z	Participation by race, ethnic group, etc., A-Z
359.9.A35	Afro-Americans
359.9.J5	Jews

Revolution to the Civil War, 1775/1783-1861
By period
Early nineteenth century, 1801/1809-1845
Madison's administrations, 1809-1817
War of 1812
Armies. Troops
Participation by race, ethnic group, etc., A-Z — Continued

359.9.A-.9.Z

Negroes, *see* E359.9.A35

360 Naval history

Including naval battles on the ocean; naval blockades; narratives of sailors,
privateers; etc.
For biography of naval leaders, see E353+
For Chesapeake-Leopard Affair, see E357.3
For naval battles in connection with military operations, see E355+
Secret service. Spies

360.5 General works
360.6.A-.6.Z Individual spies, A-Z
360.6.H5 Henry, John (British)
Subarrange by Table E1 at the end of the text
361.A-.Z Personal narratives, A-Z
For prisoners' narratives, see E362
For sailors' narratives, see E360
362 Prisoners and prisons
Including lists of prisoners, prison life, prisoners' narratives, etc., as well as accounts
of the Dartmoor Massacre, 1815 (Dartmoor Military Prison, England)
362.5 Medical and hospital services. Hospitals
363 Celebrations. Anniversaries. Museums
Including exhibitions
Illustrative material
(364) Poetry, ballads, songs. Drama, pageants, *see* Class P
364.3 Anecdotes
Cf. E360, Personal narratives of sailors and soldiers
Cf. E361.A+, Personal narratives of sailors and soldiers
Cf. Subclasses PN-PT, Literature
364.5 Addresses, essays, lectures. Sermons. Prayers
364.9 Other (not A-Z)
365 War with Algeria, 1815
Cf. E335, Relations with the Barbary States in general
370 Presidential campaign of 1816
Monroe's administrations, 1817-1825
For the First Seminole War, 1817-1818, see E83.817
371 General works
372 Biography of James Monroe, 1758-1831
Subarrange by Table E2 at the end of the text
For his collected works, see E302.M72+
For his speeches and messages as President, see J82.A5+
373 Missouri Compromise, 1820
Cf. E433, Repeal of the Missouri Compromise, 1854
Cf. E446, Early American slavery and political agitation growing out of it
Cf. F466, Missouri history
374 Diplomatic history. Foreign relations
For the execution of Arbuthnot and Ambrister, 1818, see E83.817
For Monroe doctrine, see JZ1482
For the Spanish Treaty of 1819 and cession of Florida, see F314
375 Presidential campaign of 1824
Including charge of a corrupt bargain between Adams and Clay
John Quincy Adams' administration, 1825-1829
For Northeastern boundary dispute, see E398
For Panama Congress, 1826, see F1404
For Tariff of 1828, see HF1754

Revolution to the Civil War, 1775/1783-1861
  By period
    Early nineteenth century, 1801/1809-1845 — Continued
    W.H. Harrison's administration, March 4-April 4, 1841

391	General works
392	Biography of William H. Harrison, 1773-1841

  Subarrange by Table E2 at the end of the text
  For his collected works, see E337.8.A+
  For his speeches and messages as President, see J82.B1+
    Tyler's administration, April 4, 1841-1845
      For his attempt to reestablish Bank of the United States, see HG2525+
      For Dorr's Rebellion, 1842, see F83.4
      For question of the annexation of Texas, see F390
      For tariff, see HF1754

396	General works

  Including explosion of the frigate "Princeton," 1844

397	Biography of John Tyler, 1790-1862

  Subarrange by Table E2 at the end of the text
  For his collected works, see E337.8.A+
  For his speeches and messages as President, see J82.B2+

398	Northeastern boundary dispute, 1783-1845

  Including the Aroostook War, 1839; Webster-Ashburton Treaty (known also as Treaty of Washington, Ashburton Treaty), 1842
  After 1845 reports on boundary disputes are classed with locality, e.g. F27.B7, Maine; F42.B7, New Hampshire; F127.B7, New York

400	Presidential campaign of 1844

    Mexican War, 1846-1848

401	Periodicals. Collections (Serial)

      Societies

401.1	Aztec Club of 1847
401.2	Guadalupe Club of 1848, Washington, D.C
401.3	National Association of Veterans of the Mexican War
401.34	Michigan Association of Veterans of the War with Mexico
401.36	Ohio State Association of Mexican War Veterans
401.7	Dames of 1846

      Biography
        Includes chiefly military and naval leaders
        For statesmen and politicians, see E339+ and E415.8+

403	Collective
403.1.A-.1.Z	Individual, A-Z

        GALE NOTE *The cutter number(s) listed below have been given only as examples by the Library of Congress*

403.1.B9	Butler, William Orlando

  Subarrange by Table E1 at the end of the text

403.1.C7	Connor, David

  Subarrange by Table E1 at the end of the text
  Cf. E410, Naval history

403.1.D6	Doniphan, Alexander William

  Subarrange by Table E1 at the end of the text

403.1.H2	Hamer, Thomas Lyon

  Subarrange by Table E1 at the end of the text

403.1.H87	Hungerford, Daniel Elihu

  Subarrange by Table E1 at the end of the text

403.1.K2	Kearny, Stephen Watts

  Subarrange by Table E1 at the end of the text

403.1.P6	Pillow, Gideon Johnson

  Subarrange by Table E1 at the end of the text
  For Pillow's court-martial, see E405.6

403.1.Q8	Quitman, John Anthony

  Subarrange by Table E1 at the end of the text

Revolution to the Civil War, 1775/1783-1861

By period

Mexican War, 1846-1848

Biography

403.1.A-.1.Z	Individual, A-Z — Continued
403.1.R2	Ransom, Truman Bishop
	Subarrange by Table E1 at the end of the text
403.1.S4	Scott, Winfield
	Subarrange by Table E1 at the end of the text
403.1.S5	Shields, James
	Subarrange by Table E1 at the end of the text
403.1.S6	Sloat, John Drake
	Subarrange by Table E1 at the end of the text
403.1.S8	Stockton, Robert Field
	Subarrange by Table E1 at the end of the text
403.1.W8	Wool, John Ellis
	Subarrange by Table E1 at the end of the text
	Cf. E405.4, Wool's campaign in Mexico
	Cf. E601+, Civil War reminiscences
403.1.W9	Worth, William Jenkins
	Subarrange by Table E1 at the end of the text
404	General works
	Military operations
	Cf. E410, Naval history
	For individual battles, see E406.A+
405	General works
	Campaigns
	For general works, see E405
405.1	Taylor's campaign, 1846-1847
	Including campaign along the Rio Grande and in northern Mexico
405.2	Campaigns in and the occupation of New Mexico and California
	Including expeditions made by Doniphan, Kearny, Stockton, etc.
405.4	Chihuahua Campaign, 1846-1848
	Including Wool's march from San Antonio to Saltillo
405.6	Scott's Campaign, 1847
	From Veracruz to Mexico City
406.A-.Z	Individual battles, etc., A-Z
406.A48	Alvarado, Veracruz, Mexico, 1846
406.B9	Buena Vista, Mexico, 1847
406.C4	Cerro Gordo, Mexico, 1847
406.C47	Chapultepec, Mexico, 1847
406.C5	Churubusco, Mexico, 1847
406.C6	Contreras, Mexico, 1847
406.M3	Matamoros, Mexico, 1846
406.M6	Mexico City, 1847
406.M65	Molino del Rey, Mexico, 1847
406.M7	Monterrey, Mexico, 1846
406.P3	Palo Alto, Mexico, 1846
406.R4	Resaca de la Palma, Mexico, 1846
406.S2	San Pasqual, Calif., 1846
406.S25	Santa Clara, Calif., 1847
406.V4	Veracruz, Mexico, 1847
407	Political history
	Including causes of the war
	Cf. F390, Revolt and annexation of Texas
408	Diplomatic history. Treaty of Guadalupe Hidalgo, 1848
	Including the Mexican cessions of 1848
	Cf. F786, Mexican boundary after 1848, and the Gadsden Purchase, 1853
	Armies. Troops
409	General works

Revolution to the Civil War, 1775/1783-1861
  By period
    Mexican War, 1846-1848
      Armies. Troops — Continued
        The American Army

409.2	Regulars
409.4	Pensioners. Bounties. Claims
	For United States military pensions (General), see UB373+
409.5.A-.5.W	The states and their participation, A-W
409.5.C6	Connecticut
409.5.D6	District of Columbia
409.5.I4	Illinois
409.5.I7	Indiana
409.5.I72	Iowa
409.5.K4	Kentucky
409.5.M2	Maryland
409.5.M56	Mississippi
409.5.N6	New York
409.5.O3	Ohio
409.5.P3	Pennsylvania
409.5.S7	South Carolina
409.5.T4	Tennessee
409.5.T45	Texas
409.7	Registers, lists of the dead and wounded, etc.
409.8	The Mexican Army
410	Naval history
	Including narratives of sailors
	For biography of naval leaders, see E403+
	For operations in connection with military campaigns, see E405+
411	Personal narratives
	For prisoners' narratives, see E412
	For sailors' narratives, see E410
412	Prisoners and prisons
	Including lists of prisoners, prison life, prisoners' narratives, etc.
412.5	Medical and hospital services. Hospitals
413	Celebrations. Anniversaries
	Cf. E401.1+, Societies of veterans
	War poetry, drama, etc., *see* Class P
415	Addresses, essays, lectures. Sermons
415.2.A-.2.Z	Special topics, A-Z
415.2.A78	Art and the war
415.2.D48	Desertions
415.2.P82	Public opinion
415.2.S43	Secret service

    Middle nineteenth century, 1845/1848-1861

415.6.A-.6.Z	Collected works of American statesmen, A-Z
	For works of statesmen of the early nineteenth century, see E337.8.A+
	GALE NOTE *The cutter number(s) listed below have been given only as examples by the Library of Congress*
415.6.D16	Dana, Richard Henry
	Subarrange by Table E3 at the end of the text
415.6.J65	Johnson, Andrew
	Subarrange by Table E3 at the end of the text
415.6.J94	Julian, George Washington
	Subarrange by Table E3 at the end of the text
	Lincoln, Abraham, *see* E457.91+
415.6.P55	Phillips, Wendell
	Subarrange by Table E3 at the end of the text
415.6.S51	Seward, William Henry
	Subarrange by Table E3 at the end of the text

Revolution to the Civil War, 1775/1783-1861
By period
Middle nineteenth century, 1845/1848-1861

415.6.A-.6.Z	Collected works of American statesmen, A-Z — Continued
415.6.S93	Sumner, Charles
	Subarrange by Table E3 at the end of the text
415.6.T57	Tilden, Samuel Jones
	Subarrange by Table E3 at the end of the text
415.7	General works
	From the outbreak of the Mexican War through the period of reconstruction after the Civil War, 1845-1877
	Including political aspects of the slavery question, extension of slavery to the territories, squatter sovereignty, etc.
	For wars with the Pacific coast Indians, 1847-1865, see E83.84
	Cf. F1783, Cuban question, 1810-1899
	Cf. JK2341, American Party (Know-Nothing Party)
	Biography
	For military leaders of the Civil War, see E467+
	For military leaders of the Mexican War, see E403+
415.8	Collective
415.9.A-.9.Z	Individual, A-Z
	GALE NOTE *The cutter number(s) listed below have been given only as examples by the Library of Congress*
415.9.B4	Bell, John
	Subarrange by Table E2A at the end of the text
415.9.B45	Belmont, August
	Subarrange by Table E2A at the end of the text
415.9.B6	Black, Jeremiah Sullivan
	Subarrange by Table E2A at the end of the text
415.9.B79	Breckinridge, John Cabell
	Subarrange by Table E2A at the end of the text
415.9.B84	Broderick, David Colbreth
	Subarrange by Table E2A at the end of the text
415.9.B88	Browning, Orville Hickman
	Subarrange by Table E2A at the end of the text
415.9.B9	Brownlow, William Gannaway
	Subarrange by Table E2A at the end of the text
415.9.C18	Cameron, Simon
	Subarrange by Table E2A at the end of the text
415.9.C19	Campbell, John Archibald
	Subarrange by Table E2A at the end of the text
415.9.C4	Chase, Salmon Portland
	Subarrange by Table E2A at the end of the text
415.9.C55	Clay, Cassius Marcellus
	Subarrange by Table E2A at the end of the text
415.9.C6	Clayton, John Middleton
	Subarrange by Table E2A at the end of the text
415.9.C63	Clingman, Thomas Lanier
	Subarrange by Table E2A at the end of the text
415.9.C68	Colfax, Schuyler
	Subarrange by Table E2A at the end of the text
415.9.C96	Curtis, Benjamin Robbins
	Subarrange by Table E2A at the end of the text
415.9.C98	Cushing, Caleb
	Subarrange by Table E2A at the end of the text
415.9.D15	Dana, Richard Henry
	Subarrange by Table E2A at the end of the text
	For his collected works, see E415.6.D16
415.9.D26	Davis, Henry Winter
	Subarrange by Table E2A at the end of the text

Revolution to the Civil War, 1775/1783-1861
By period
Middle nineteenth century, 1845/1848-1861
Biography
Individual, A-Z

415.9.A-.9.Z	Individual, A-Z
415.9.D26	Davis, Henry Winter — Continued
	For his collected works, see E415.6.A+
415.9.D27	Dayton, William Lewis
	Subarrange by Table E2A at the end of the text
415.9.D48	Dickinson, Anna Elizabeth
	Subarrange by Table E2A at the end of the text
415.9.D5	Dickinson, Daniel Stevens
	Subarrange by Table E2A at the end of the text
415.9.D6	Dix, John Adams
	Subarrange by Table E2A at the end of the text
415.9.D73	Douglas, Stephen Arnold
	Subarrange by Table E2A at the end of the text
	For Lincoln-Douglas debates, see E457.4
415.9.D9	Dunn, William McKee
	Subarrange by Table E2A at the end of the text
415.9.F4	Fessenden, William Pitt
	Subarrange by Table E2A at the end of the text
415.9.F5	Field, David Dudley
	Subarrange by Table E2A at the end of the text
415.9.F55	Field, Maunsell Bradhurst
	Subarrange by Table E2A at the end of the text
415.9.F64	Floyd, John Buchanan
	Subarrange by Table E2A at the end of the text
415.9.F7	Foote, Henry Stuart
	Subarrange by Table E2A at the end of the text
415.9.F8	Frémont, John Charles
	Subarrange by Table E2A at the end of the text
415.9.G4	Giddings, Joshua Reed
	Subarrange by Table E2A at the end of the text
415.9.G7	Graham, William Alexander
	Subarrange by Table E2A at the end of the text
415.9.G8	Greeley, Horace
	Subarrange by Table E2A at the end of the text
	For the presidential campaign of 1872, see E675
415.9.G85	Grimes, James Wilson
	Subarrange by Table E2A at the end of the text
415.9.G86	Grinnell, Josiah Bushnell
	Subarrange by Table E2A at the end of the text
415.9.G89	Grow, Galusha Aaron
	Subarrange by Table E2A at the end of the text
415.9.H15	Hale, John Parker
	Subarrange by Table E2A at the end of the text
415.9.H2	Hamlin, Hannibal
	Subarrange by Table E2A at the end of the text
415.9.H28	Harris, Benjamin Gwinn
	Subarrange by Table E2A at the end of the text
	For the Harris court-martial, 1865, see E458.8
415.9.H35	Haskin, John Bussing
	Subarrange by Table E2A at the end of the text
415.9.H6	Hicks, Thomas Holliday
	Subarrange by Table E2A at the end of the text
415.9.H65	Hilliard, Henry Washington
	Subarrange by Table E2A at the end of the text
415.9.H9	Hunter, Robert Mercer Taliaferro
	Subarrange by Table E2A at the end of the text

Revolution to the Civil War, 1775/1783-1861
By period
Middle nineteenth century, 1845/1848-1861
Biography

415.9.A-.9.Z	Individual, A-Z — Continued
415.9.J5	Jenckes, Thomas Allen
	Subarrange by Table E2A at the end of the text
415.9.J6	Jones, George Wallace
	Subarrange by Table E2A at the end of the text
415.9.J7	Jones, J. Glancy
	Subarrange by Table E2A at the end of the text
415.9.J95	Julian, George Washington
	Subarrange by Table E2A at the end of the text
	For his collected works, see E415.6.J94
415.9.K35	Kennedy, John Pendleton
	Subarrange by Table E2A at the end of the text
415.9.K52	King, Horatio
	Subarrange by Table E2A at the end of the text
415.9.K7	Körner, Gustav Philipp
	Subarrange by Table E2A at the end of the text
415.9.L2	Lane, Joseph
	Subarrange by Table E2A at the end of the text
415.9.L38	Lawrence, Amos Adams
	Subarrange by Table E2A at the end of the text
415.9.L4	Lawrence, William Beach
	Subarrange by Table E2A at the end of the text
415.9.L7	Lieber, Francis
	Subarrange by Table E2A at the end of the text
415.9.L89	Lovejoy, Owen
	Subarrange by Table E2A at the end of the text
415.9.M16	Maclay, William Brown
	Subarrange by Table E2A at the end of the text
415.9.M18	Marcy, William Learned
	Subarrange by Table E2A at the end of the text
415.9.M19	Mason, Charles
	Subarrange by Table E2A at the end of the text
415.9.M2	Mason, James Murray
	Subarrange by Table E2A at the end of the text
415.9.M3	Maury, Dabney Herndon
	Subarrange by Table E2A at the end of the text
415.9.M4	Memminger, Christopher Gustavus
	Subarrange by Table E2A at the end of the text
415.9.M5	Meredith, William Morris
	Subarrange by Table E2A at the end of the text
415.9.P4	Pendleton, George Hunt
	Subarrange by Table E2A at the end of the text
415.9.P78	Pomeroy, Samuel Clarke
	Subarrange by Table E2A at the end of the text
415.9.R75	Rollins, Edward Henry
	Subarrange by Table E2A at the end of the text
415.9.R76	Rollins, James Sidney
	Subarrange by Table E2A at the end of the text
415.9.S4	Seward, William Henry
	Subarrange by Table E2A at the end of the text
	For his collected works, see E415.6.S51
415.9.S5	Seymour, Horatio
	Subarrange by Table E2A at the end of the text
415.9.S53	Sickles, Daniel Edgar
	Subarrange by Table E2A at the end of the text

Revolution to the Civil War, 1775/1783-1861
By period
Middle nineteenth century, 1845/1848-1861
Biography

415.9.A-.9.Z	Individual, A-Z — Continued
415.9.S58	Slidell, John
	Subarrange by Table E2A at the end of the text
415.9.S64	Smith, Gerrit
	Subarrange by Table E2A at the end of the text
415.9.S72	Soulé, Pierre
	Subarrange by Table E2A at the end of the text
415.9.S74	Speed, James
	Subarrange by Table E2A at the end of the text
415.9.S84	Stevens, Thaddeus
	Subarrange by Table E2A at the end of the text
415.9.S88	Stuart, Alexander Hugh Holmes
	Subarrange by Table E2A at the end of the text
415.9.S9	Sumner, Charles
	Subarrange by Table E2A at the end of the text
	For his collected works, see E415.6.S93
	For works on Brooks' assault, see E434.8
415.9.T12	Taft, Alphonso
	Subarrange by Table E2A at the end of the text
415.9.T45	Thompson, Jacob
	Subarrange by Table E2A at the end of the text
415.9.T5	Tilden, Samuel Jones
	Subarrange by Table E2A at the end of the text
	For his collected works, see E415.6.T57
415.9.T6	Toombs, Robert Augustus
	Subarrange by Table E2A at the end of the text
415.9.T86	Trumbull, Lyman
	Subarrange by Table E2A at the end of the text
415.9.T88	Tuck, Amos
	Subarrange by Table E2A at the end of the text
415.9.T93	Tyler, Robert
	Subarrange by Table E2A at the end of the text
415.9.V2	Vallandigham, Clement Laird
	Subarrange by Table E2A at the end of the text
415.9.W16	Wade, Benjamin Franklin
	Subarrange by Table E2A at the end of the text
415.9.W2	Walker, Robert James
	Subarrange by Table E2A at the end of the text
415.9.W39	Weed, Thurlow
	Subarrange by Table E2A at the end of the text
415.9.W6	Wilson, Henry
	Subarrange by Table E2A at the end of the text
415.9.W8	Wise, Henry Alexander
	Subarrange by Table E2A at the end of the text
415.9.Y2	Yancey, William Lowndes
	Subarrange by Table E2A at the end of the text
415.9.Y9	Yulee, David Levy
	Subarrange by Table E2A at the end of the text
	Polk's administration, 1845-1849
	Including government of the newly acquired Spanish possessions in the Southwest; slavery in the territories; slavery question in politics; Wilmot Proviso, 1846; etc.
	For annexation of Texas, 1845, see F390
	For Oregon question and Northwestern boundary to 1846, see F880
416	General works
	Biography of James K. Polk, 1795-1849
	For his collected works, see E415.6.A+

Revolution to the Civil War, 1775/1783-1861
By period
Middle nineteenth century, 1845/1848-1861
Polk's administration, 1845-1849
Biography of James K. Polk, 1795-1849 — Continued
For his speeches and messages as President, see J82.B3+

417	General works
	Subarrange by Table E2 at the end of the text
417.1	Polk, Sarah (Childress)
420	Presidential campaign of 1848

Taylor's administration, 1849-July 9, 1850
For admission of California, see F864
For organization of New Mexico and Utah territories, see F801, F826
For payment to Texas for claim on part of New Mexico, see F801

421	General works
422	Biography of Zachary Taylor, 1784-1850
	Subarrange by Table E2 at the end of the text
	For his collected works, see E415.6.A+
	For his speeches and messages as President, see J82.B4+
	For his campaign, 1846-1847, see E405.1
423	Slavery question, 1849-1853
	Including Clay's Omnibus Bill (Compromise of 1850); Southern Convention, Nashville, 1850
	For fugitive slaves and the new law of 1850, see E450

Fillmore's administration, July 9, 1850-1853

426	General works
427	Biography of Millard Fillmore, 1800-1874
	Subarrange by Table E2 at the end of the text
	For his collected works, see E415.6.A+
	For his speeches and messages as President, see J82.B5+
429	Diplomatic history, 1849-1853. Foreign relations
	Including intervention; political refugees from abroad; etc.
	For Clayton-Bulwer Treaty, 1850, see F1438
	For Cuban question, see F1783
430	Presidential campaign of 1852

Pierce's administration, 1853-1857
For American Party (Know-Nothing Party), see JK2341
For bombardment of Greytown, Nicaragua, 1854, see F1536.S2
For the Cuban question, see F1783
For the Filibuster War in Nicaragua, 1855-1857, see F1526
For the Gadsden purchase, 1853, see F786
For the Third Seminole War, 1855-1858, see E83.855
For the Wars with Pacific coast Indians, see E83.84

431	General works
	Including diplomatic history; the Ostend Manifesto, October 1854
	Biography of Franklin Pierce, 1804-1869
	For his collected works, see E415.6.A+
	For his speeches and messages as President, see J82.B6+
432	General
	Subarrange by Table E2 at the end of the text
432.2	Pierce family (not genealogy)
	Including biography of individual members
433	Slavery question, 1853-1857
	Including repeal of the Missouri Compromise, 1854; Kansas-Nebraska Bill, May 1854
	For Kansas troubles, see F685
	For moral and economic aspects of the slavery question, see E449+
	For squatter sovereignty, see E415.7
434.5	Election of speaker of the House
434.8	Brooks' assault on Senator Sumner, 1856
435	Presidential campaign of 1856

Revolution to the Civil War, 1775/1783-1861
    By period
        Middle nineteenth century, 1845/1848-1861 — Continued
            Buchanan's administration, 1857-1861
                For Cuban question, see F1783
                For Mill Creek War, 1857-1865, see E83.858
                For Mormon Rebellion, 1857-1859, see F826
                For Paraguay Expedition, see F2686
                For Spirit Lake Massacre, 1857, see E83.857
                For Walker's Filibuster wars, 1855-1860, see F1526

436	General works
	Biography of James Buchanan, 1791-1868
	For his collected works, see E337.8.A+
	For his speeches and messages as President, see J82.B7+
437	General works
	Subarrange by Table E2 at the end of the text
437.1	Buchanan family (not genealogy)
	Including biography, e.g. Harriet Lane, 1830-1903
438	Slavery question, 1857-1861
	Including attempt to revive slave trade, 1858, Lincoln's Cooper Institute address
	For Dred Scott decision, 1857, see E450
	For Harpers Ferry raid, 1859, see E451
	For Kansas and the Lecompton Constitution, see F685
	For Lincoln-Douglas debates, 1858, see E457.4
	For squatter sovereignty, see E415.7
440	Presidential campaign of 1860
440.5	State of the country, November 1860- March 4, 1861
	Including attempts at compromise (Crittenden Compromise, December 18, 1860;
	Crittenden Resolution, July 22, 1861; etc.); Peace Conference at Washington (Border
	Slave State Convention), 1861; secession of certain states
	Cf. E458.1, Political history, March 4-December 31, 1861
	Cf. E471.1, Opening events of Civil War

Slavery in the United States. Antislavery movements
    Including general works on slavery in the South
    Cf. HT851+, Slavery and the slave trade (General)
    For various political aspects of the slavery question of the Revolution to the Civil War period, see
       E301+, including especially E373, E407, E415.7, E416, E423, E433, E438, E440.5
    For general works on Afro-Americans, including the period since the Civil War, see E185
    Periodicals, *see E446, E449*

441	General works
	Including history of slavery in general
	For history by period, see E446+
442	The internal slave trade. Slave markets and auctions
443	Slave life
	Including duties of slaves and masters, overseers
444	Biography. Personal narratives of slaves
	For biography of fugitive slaves, see E450
	Cf. E449, Life and writings of Frederick Douglass
445.A-.W	By state, A-W
	Including history of antislavery movements
	For slavery in an individual county, see under the state
	Cf. E185.93.A+, Afro-Americans in individual states
445.A3	Alabama
445.C7	Connecticut
445.D3	Delaware
445.D6	District of Columbia
445.F6	Florida
445.G3	Georgia
445.I2	Illinois
445.I3	Indiana

Revolution to the Civil War, 1775/1783-1861
Slavery in the United States. Antislavery movements

445.A-.W	By state, A-W — Continued	
445.K16	Kansas	
		Cf. F685, Struggle between pro-slavery and antislavery parties
445.K5	Kentucky	
445.L8	Louisiana	
445.M3	Maryland	
445.M4	Massachusetts	
445.M6	Mississippi	
445.M67	Missouri	
445.N2	Nebraska	
445.N5	New England	
445.N54	New Jersey	
445.N55	New Mexico	
445.N56	New York	
		Cf. F128.4, Negro plot in New York City, 1741
445.N8	North Carolina	
445.P3	Pennsylvania	
445.R4	Rhode Island	
445.S7	South Carolina	
		Cf. F273, Trouble with Massachusetts over its Afro-American citizens in South Carolina
		Cf. F279.C4, Charleston Insurrection (Denmark Vesey's Rebellion), 1822
445.T3	Tennessee	
445.T47	Texas	
445.V8	Virginia	
		Cf. F232.S7, Southampton Insurrection (Nat Turner's Rebellion), 1831
		Cf. F234.R5, Richmond Insurrection (Gabriel's Insurrection), 1800
445.W8	Wisconsin	
	History of slavery to 1830	
		Including controversial literature
446	General works	
		Including attempts to revive slave trade, early anti-slavery movements, etc.
		Cf. E309, Northwest Ordinance of 1787
		Cf. E373, Missouri Compromise, 1820
447	Slave insurrections (General)	
		Including mutiny on slave ships, e.g Amistad (Schooner); Creole (Brig)
		For individual insurrections, see local history, e.g. F279.C4, Charleston Insurrection (Denmark Vesey's Rebellion), 1822; F128.4, New York Negro plot, 1741; F234.R5, Richmond Insurrection (Gabriel's Insurrection), 1800; F232.S7, Southampton Insurrection (Nat Turner's Rebellion), 1831
448	Colonization	
		Including the American Colonization Society and affiliated organizations: their origin, plans, history, etc.; also modern colonization societies
		Cf. DT621+, Liberia
	History of slavery, 1830-1863. Period of abolition agitation	
		Including controversial literature
		Cf. E337.8+, Political aspects of slavery question
		Cf. E416+, Wilmot Proviso, 1846
		Cf. E423, Compromise of 1850
		Cf. E434.8, Brooks' assault on Senator Sumner, 1856
		Cf. F273, Dispute between Massachusetts and South Carolina over Afro-American citizens of Massachusetts, 1845
		Cf. F549.A4, Alton Riot, 1837
		Cf. F685, Struggle between proslavery and antislavery parties in Kansas
449	General works	
		Including biography: Frederick Douglass, William Lloyd Garrison, William Jay, Lucretia (Coffin) Mott, Wendell Phillips

Revolution to the Civil War, 1775/1783-1861

Slavery in the United States. Antislavery movements

History of slavery, 1830-1863. Period of abolition agitation — Continued

450   Fugitive slaves

Including biographies and narratives of fugitive slaves, e.g. John Anderson, Eliza Harris, James Williams; fugitive slave law; personal liberty laws; slaves in free states; underground railroad; biographies and narratives of protectors of slaves, e.g. Levi Coffin, Jonathan Walker, Laura S. Haviland

Including such events and cases as the Garrison mob, Boston, 1835; case of the slave child, Med Slater, 1836; Isaac Brown case, 1847; Dred Scott case, 1848-1857; South Bend slave case, 1849; Randolph epistles, 1850; Christiana Riot, 1851, and trial of Castner Hanway and others for assault on Edward Gorsuch; Sherman M. Booth case, 1854; Anthony Burns case in Boston, 1854; Addison White rescue, 1857; Oberlin-Wellington rescue, 1858; Jonathan Lemmon slave case, 1860

Cf. KF4545.S5, Fugitive slave act

For court records of individual trials, see KF223+

451   John Brown's Raid at Harpers Ferry, W. Va., 1859

Including the capture, trial, execution, and biography of John Brown

Cf. F685, John Brown in Kansas

453   Slaves and the slavery question in the Civil War

Including "Contrabands"; slavery in the Confederate States of America; emancipation of the slaves in general; Emancipation Proclamation (Manifesto by Abraham Lincoln on September 22, 1862, that on January 1, 1863, he would declare free all slaves held in parts of the United States not in the possession of the Union armies)

For local material, see E445.A+ or E185.93.A+

Cf. E185.2, Freedmen, Freedmen's Bureau (Bureau of Refugees, Freedmen, and Abandoned Lands), etc.

Cf. E185.93.S7, Port Royal Mission, S.C.

Cf. E540.N3, Afro-American soldiers in the Union Army

Cf. E585.A35, Afro-American soldiers in the Confederate Army

Cf. JK169, Thirteenth, fourteenth, and fifteenth amendments to the Constitution

Civil War period, 1861-1865

Lincoln's administrations, 1861-April 15, 1865

For election and events preceding inauguration, see E440+

For presidential campaign of 1864, see E458.4

For wars with Dakota Indians, 1862-1863, see E83.86

For other Indian wars, 1862-1863, see E83.863

456   General works

Biography of Abraham Lincoln, 1809-1865

For his collected works, see E457.91+

For his speeches and messages as President, see E457.94

457   General works. Lincoln as president and statesman

Subarrange by Table E2 at the end of the text

Including campaign biographies of 1860, 1864

Cf. E456,E458+, Political history of the country, 1861-1865

457.1   Societies

457.15   Anecdotes relating to Lincoln

Including personal reminiscences of contemporaries, but not formal biographies

457.2   Special

Including Lincoln's personality (Character, kindness, loyalty, etc.), religion, education, books and reading, etc. Attitude toward slavery, temperance and prohibition, etc.

Including Lincoln as lawyer, freemason, writer, speaker, etc.

For Lincoln as president and statesman, see E457

Including Lincoln's relations with special classes, e.g. Jews, private soldiers, etc.

457.25   Family life

Including biography, e.g. Mary (Todd) Lincoln; Thomas (Tad) Lincoln

By period

Early life to 1861

For campaign biographies, see E457

Cf. F532.S6, Lincoln Boyhood National Memorial

Civil War period, 1861-1865
Lincoln's administrations, 1861-April 15, 1865
Biography of Abraham Lincoln, 1809-1865
By period
Early life to 1861 — Continued
Cf. F549.S7, Lincoln's home in Springfield, Ill

457.3	General works
457.32	To 1830

Including lineage, family, and parents (Thomas Lincoln, Nancy (Hanks) Lincoln, Sarah (Bush) Johnston Lincoln), etc.
Including birthplace (Hodgenville, Ky.), boyhood and youth in Kentucky and Indiana
Cf. F532.S6, Nancy Hanks Lincoln Memorial

457.35	1830-1846

Including first years in Illinois; Black Hawk War, 1832; Illinois legislature, professional career; etc.
Including Ann Rutledge, marriage, etc.
Cf. E457.25, Family life

457.4	1846-1861

Including national politics; congressional service; Lincoln-Douglas debates, 1858; journey to Washington; etc.
Cf. E415.7, E449, The slavery question
Cf. E440, Presidential campaign of 1860
Cf. E440.5, State of the country, November 1860-March 1861

1861-1865
Cf. E458.4, Presidential campaign of 1864
Cf. E461+, The Civil War
Cf. E475.35, Gettysburg address

457.5	Assassination

Including the conspirators (Booth, Surratt, etc.)
For the trials of Booth, Surratt, etc., see KF223+

457.52	Death

Including funeral journey to Springfield, burial, memorial services throughout the country and abroad, guard of honor, tomb, etc.
Cf. E457.8, Funeral sermons

457.6	Monuments. Statues. Portraits

Including life and death masks, etc.; monuments, statues, etc. located in foreign countries
For local monuments, statues, etc., in the United States, see Class F, e.g. in Washington, D.C., F203.4.L72, Lincoln statue (Lincoln Park); F203.4.L73, Lincoln Memorial
Cf. E457.32, Birthplace, Hodgenville, Kentucky
Cf. E457.52, Lincoln Tomb, Springfield, Ill.
For medals, see CJ5801+

457.63	Caricatures and cartoons

Including satirical and comic works

457.64	Homes and haunts of Lincoln (General)

For early years, see E457.32 or E457.35
For Springfield home, see F549.S7

457.65	Museums. Exhibitions. Lincoln relics

Including Lincoln Museum (Ford Theatre), Washington, D.C.; Oldroyd collection of Lincoln relics
For medals, see CJ5801+

457.7	Anniversaries. Celebrations. Memorials since 1865

Including centennials, Lincoln Day
For funeral and memorial services, see E457.52

457.8	Addresses, essays, lectures. Sermons (Funeral, etc.)

Class here addresses which have been delivered since the assassination
For addresses delivered before April 1865, see E440, E457, or E458.1-.5
Cf. E457.15, Personal reminiscences
Cf. E457.52, Funeral services

	Civil War period, 1861-1865
	Lincoln's administrations, 1861-April 15, 1865
	Biography of Abraham Lincoln, 1809-1865 — Continued
(457.9)	Poetry. Drama. Fiction, *see* Class P
	Music, *see* Class M
457.905	Juvenile works
457.909	Lincolniana
	Including miscellaneous printed matter, minor pamphlets
	Reserved for material not separately cataloged
	Writings of Lincoln
	Classification by subject is preferred
457.91	Collected works. By date
457.92	Partial collections. Selected works. Selections. By date
	Including collections of speeches (Three or more)
457.94	State papers, messages, inaugural addresses. By date
457.95	Addresses, essays, lectures. By date
	For collections of speeches, see E457.92
	For Lincoln-Douglas debates, 1858, see E457.4
	Letters
457.96	Individual. By date
457.962	Collections. By date
457.98	Minor works
	Including history of the Fisher murder mystery; a facsimile of an indenture drawn up,
	October 25, 1841, by Lincoln and signed by his father
457.99	Stories, anecdotes, poems, axioms, brief extracts, etc., attributed to Lincoln
	Arrange alphabetically by editor or title
	Political history (Contemporary works)
	Including questions at issue between North and South, the internal policies of the United States,
	etc.
	For treaties published after the close of the war, see E459
	For sermons and addresses, see E649+
	For foreign public opinion, see E469.8
458	General works
	Including collections and works covering more than a single year
458.1	March 4-December 31, 1861
	Cf. E440.5, State of the nation, November 1860-March 4, 1861
458.2	1862
458.3	1863
	Cf. E453, Emancipation of the slaves
458.4	1864
	Including presidential campaign of 1864; campaign literature; etc.
458.5	January-May 1865
458.7	Union men in the South. Refugees
458.8	Confederate sympathizers in the North. "Copperheads," "Butternuts," etc.
	Including conspiracies, e.g. Northwestern Conspiracy, 1864; disloyal organizations: Knights
	of the Golden Circle, Order of American Knights or Sons of Liberty, Order of the Lone Star,
	etc.; suspension of the writ of habeas corpus; prisoners of state; Harris court-martial, 1865;
	etc.
	Cf. E615+, Union prisons
	Cf. JK343, Military rule, martial law, etc., within states or districts during the Civil War
459	Political history (Non-contemporary works)
	Including publications since May 1865
	For treatises only
	For addresses, sermons, etc., see E649+
	For contemporary publications, see E458+
	The Civil War, 1861-1865
461	**Periodicals**
	For Confederate periodicals, see E482

	The Civil War, 1861-1865 — Continued		
	Societies of veterans, etc.		

       For Confederate societies, see E483

       For regimental associations of veterans, see regiment in E492

462   General works

462.Z7   Minor publications not separately cataloged

        Individual societies, etc.

         Under each (unless otherwise indicated):

          Official publications

          .A1-.A4   Serial publications

          .A5-.A69   Monographs

          .A7A-.A7Z   Nonofficial publications

          .A8-.W   State branches. By state, A-W

            Under each:

              Official publications

            A1-A4   Serial publications

            A5-A7   Monographs

            A8-Z   Nonofficial publications

462.1   Grand Army of the Republic

         Subarrange by table above E462.1

462.15   Women's Relief Corps

         Subarrange by table above E462.1

462.17   Ladies of the Grand Army of the Republic

         Subarrange by table above E462.1

462.18   Legion of Loyal Women, Washington, D.C.

         Subarrange by table above E462.1

462.2   Military Order of the Loyal Legion of the United States

         Subarrange by table above E462.1

462.25   Dames of the Loyal Legion

         Subarrange by table above E462.1

462.3   Military Order of the Medal of Honor

         Subarrange by table above E462.1

462.4   Union Veteran Legion of the United States

         Subarrange by table above E462.1

462.5   National Association of Naval Veterans

         Subarrange by table above E462.1

462.6   Veteran Brotherhood of the State of Kansas

         Subarrange by table above E462.1

462.7   Union League of America

         Subarrange by table above E462.1

462.84   Union clubs

         Subarrange by table above E462.1

         For local Union clubs, see HS2721+

462.9   Sons of Union Veterans of the Civil War

         Subarrange by table above E462.1

462.92   Soldiers' and Sailors' National Union League of Washington, D.C.

         Subarrange by table above E462.1

462.93   Washington, D.C. Old Guard

         Subarrange by table above E462.1

462.94   Order of American Freemen

         Subarrange by table above E462.1

462.96   Union White Boys in Blue

         Subarrange by table above E462.1

462.97   Philadelphia. War Veterans' Club

         Subarrange by table above E462.1

462.98   National Soldiers Historical Association

         Subarrange by table above E462.1

462.99.A.99.Z   Other societies, etc., A-Z

         GALE NOTE *The cutter number(s) listed below have been given only as examples by the Library of Congress*

	The Civil War, 1861-1865
	Societies of veterans, etc.
	Individual societies, etc.
462.99.A.99.Z	Other societies, etc., A-Z — Continued
462.99.D2	Daughters of Union Veterans of the Civil War
	Subarrange by table below E186.99.A-.99.Z
	First Defenders, *see* E493.9
	National Association of Civil War Army Nurses, *see* E621
462.99.N27	National Veteran Club of the United States
	Subarrange by table below E186.99.A-.99.Z
462.99.O65	Order of Stars and Stripes
	Subarrange by table below E186.99.A-.99.Z
462.99.S6	Society for Correct Civil War Information
	Subarrange by table below E186.99.A-.99.Z
462.99.S62	Society of the Army and Navy of the Gulf
	Subarrange by table below E186.99.A-.99.Z
462.99.U53	Union Society of the Civil War
	Subarrange by table below E186.99.A-.99.Z
462.99.U57	Union Soldiers' Alliance, Washington, D.C.
	Subarrange by table below E186.99.A-.99.Z
462.99.U63	Union Veterans' Union
	Subarrange by table below E186.99.A-.99.Z
	United States Veteran Signal Corps Association, *see* E608
463	Patriotic societies during the war
	Including Loyal League of Union Citizens, Loyal National League of the State of New York,
	Loyal Publication Society, etc.
	For Loyal Union League clubs, see HS2721+
464	Collections. Collected works
	Including papers read before Loyal Legion, Grand Army of the Republic
	Cf. E458+, Collections of political pamphlets
	Cf. E484, Confederate collections
	Cf. E655, Anecdotes of the Civil War
	Biography
467	Collective (Union and Confederate)
	For nurses, see E621+
	For prisoners of war, see E611+
	For rolls of college men in the war, see E541.A+ and E586.A+
467.1.A-.1.Z	Individual, A-Z
	Including chiefly lives of commanders and other officers
	Cf. E415.9.A+, Biography of political leaders except a few like Davis, Stanton, and Benjamin
	whose careers culminated in the war
	Cf. E495+, E545+, Regimental officers and privates
	Cf. E601+, Personal narratives of war service
	GALE NOTE *The cutter number(s) listed below have been given only as examples by the*
	Library of Congress
467.1.A2	Adams, Charles Francis, 1807-1886
	Subarrange by Table E1 at the end of the text
467.1.A3	Alexander, Andrew Jonathan
	Subarrange by Table E1 at the end of the text
467.1.A4	Allen, Henry Watkins
	Subarrange by Table E1 at the end of the text
467.1.A54	Anderson, Richard Heron
	Subarrange by Table E1 at the end of the text
467.1.A78	Arrowsmith, George
	Subarrange by Table E1 at the end of the text
467.1.A8	Ashby, Turner
	Subarrange by Table E1 at the end of the text
467.1.B14	Bailey, Theodorus
	Subarrange by Table E1 at the end of the text

The Civil War, 1861-1865
Biography

467.1.A-.1.Z	Individual, A-Z — Continued
467.1.B16	Baker, Edward Dickenson
	Subarrange by Table E1 at the end of the text
467.1.B23	Banks, Nathaniel Prentice
	Subarrange by Table E1 at the end of the text
467.1.B25	Barlow, Francis Channing
	Subarrange by Table E1 at the end of the text
467.1.B26	Barnes, James
	Subarrange by Table E1 at the end of the text
467.1.B29	Bartlett, William Francis
	Subarrange by Table E1 at the end of the text
467.1.B3	Bayard, George Dashiell
	Subarrange by Table E1 at the end of the text
467.1.B38	Beauregard, Pierre Gustave
	Subarrange by Table E1 at the end of the text
467.1.B39	Beaver, James Addams
	Subarrange by Table E1 at the end of the text
467.1.B397	Benedict, Lewis
	Subarrange by Table E1 at the end of the text
467.1.B4	Benjamin, Judah Philip
	Subarrange by Table E1 at the end of the text
467.1.B5	Berry, Hiram Gregory
	Subarrange by Table E1 at the end of the text
467.1.B6	Birney, David Bell
	Subarrange by Table E1 at the end of the text
467.1.B7	Boomer, George Boardman
	Subarrange by Table E1 at the end of the text
467.1.B73	Bowen, John Steven
	Subarrange by Table E1 at the end of the text
467.1.B75	Bragg, Braxton
	Subarrange by Table E1 at the end of the text
467.1.B77	Brown, Joseph Newton
	Subarrange by Table E1 at the end of the text
467.1.B8	Burnside, Ambrose Everett
	Subarrange by Table E1 at the end of the text
467.1.B87	Butler, Benjamin Franklin (1818-1893)
	Subarrange by Table E1 at the end of the text
467.1.B9	Butterfield, Daniel
	Subarrange by Table E1 at the end of the text
467.1.C52	Chetlain, Augustus Louis
	Subarrange by Table E1 at the end of the text
467.1.C97	Curtis, Samuel Ryan
	Subarrange by Table E1 at the end of the text
467.1.C98	Cushing, William Barker
	Subarrange by Table E1 at the end of the text
467.1.C99	Custer, George Armstrong
	Subarrange by Table E1 at the end of the text
467.1.D13	Dahlgren, John Adolphus
	Subarrange by Table E1 at the end of the text
467.1.D24	Davis, Charles Henry
	Subarrange by Table E1 at the end of the text
467.1.D26	Davis, Jefferson
	Subarrange by Table E1 at the end of the text
467.1.D27	Davis, Varina (Howell). "Mrs. Jefferson Davis"
	Subarrange by Table E1 at the end of the text
467.1.D28	Davis, Varina Anne Jefferson
	Subarrange by Table E1 at the end of the text

The Civil War, 1861-1865
Biography

467.1.A-.1.Z	Individual, A-Z — Continued
467.1.D6	Dodge, Grenville Mellen
	Subarrange by Table E1 at the end of the text
467.1.D9	Du Pont, Samuel Francis
	Subarrange by Table E1 at the end of the text
467.1.E13	Early, Jubal Anderson
	Subarrange by Table E1 at the end of the text
467.1.E4	Elliott, Stephen
	Subarrange by Table E1 at the end of the text
467.1.E47	Ellsworth, Ephraim Elmer
	Subarrange by Table E1 at the end of the text
467.1.E86	Ewell, Richard Stoddert
	Subarrange by Table E1 at the end of the text
467.1.E9	Ewing, Charles
	Subarrange by Table E1 at the end of the text
467.1.F23	Farragut, David Glasgow
	Subarrange by Table E1 at the end of the text
467.1.F64	Flusser, Charles Williamson
	Subarrange by Table E1 at the end of the text
467.1.F68	Foote, Andrew Hull
	Subarrange by Table E1 at the end of the text
467.1.F72	Forrest, Nathan Bedford
	Subarrange by Table E1 at the end of the text
467.1.F83	Franklin, William Buel
	Subarrange by Table E1 at the end of the text
467.1.F87	French, Samuel Gibbs
	Subarrange by Table E1 at the end of the text
467.1.F9	Fritchie, Barbara (Hauer)
	Subarrange by Table E1 at the end of the text
467.1.G29	Geary, John White
	Subarrange by Table E1 at the end of the text
467.1.G6	Gooding, Oliver Paul
	Subarrange by Table E1 at the end of the text
467.1.G66	Gordon, John Brown
	Subarrange by Table E1 at the end of the text
467.1.G68	Gorgas, Josiah
	Subarrange by Table E1 at the end of the text
467.1.G79	Greene, George Sears
	Subarrange by Table E1 at the end of the text
467.1.G88	Grout, William Wallace
	Subarrange by Table E1 at the end of the text
467.1.H18	Halleck, Henry Wager
	Subarrange by Table E1 at the end of the text
467.1.H19	Hampton, Wade, 1818-1902
	Subarrange by Table E1 at the end of the text
467.1.H2	Hancock, Winfield Scott
	Subarrange by Table E1 at the end of the text
467.1.H4	Hartranft, John Frederick
	Subarrange by Table E1 at the end of the text
467.1.H44	Hatton, Robert
	Subarrange by Table E1 at the end of the text
467.1.H58	Hood, John Bell
	Subarrange by Table E1 at the end of the text
467.1.H6	Hooker, Joseph
	Subarrange by Table E1 at the end of the text
467.1.H7	Hovey, Alvin Peterson
	Subarrange by Table E1 at the end of the text

The Civil War, 1861-1865
Biography

467.1.A-.1.Z	Individual, A-Z — Continued
467.1.H8	Howard, Oliver Otis
	Subarrange by Table E1 at the end of the text
467.1.H885	Humphreys, Andrew
	Subarrange by Table E1 at the end of the text
467.1.H89	Hunt, Henry Jackson
	Subarrange by Table E1 at the end of the text
467.1.H9	Hunter, David
	Subarrange by Table E1 at the end of the text
467.1.J15	Jackson, Thomas Jonathan
	Subarrange by Table E1 at the end of the text
467.1.J73	Johnston, Albert Sidney
	Subarrange by Table E1 at the end of the text
467.1.J74	Johnston, Joseph Eggleston
	Subarrange by Table E1 at the end of the text
467.1.K24	Kearny, Philip
	Subarrange by Table E1 at the end of the text
467.1.L4	Lee, Robert Edward
	Subarrange by Table E1 at the end of the text
467.1.L5	Logan, Thomas Muldrup
	Subarrange by Table E1 at the end of the text
467.1.L55	Longstreet, James
	Subarrange by Table E1 at the end of the text
467.1.L6	Lowell, Charles Russell
	Subarrange by Table E1 at the end of the text
467.1.L9	Lyon, Nathaniel
	Subarrange by Table E1 at the end of the text
467.1.M2	McClellan, George Brinton
	Subarrange by Table E1 at the end of the text
	Cf. E458.4, Presidential campaign of 1864
467.1.M24	McCulloch, Ben
	Subarrange by Table E1 at the end of the text
467.1.M35	Maffitt, John Newland
	Subarrange by Table E1 at the end of the text
467.1.M38	Meade, George Gordon
	Subarrange by Table E1 at the end of the text
467.1.M4	Meagher, Thomas Francis
	Subarrange by Table E1 at the end of the text
467.1.M6	Mitchel, Ormsby Macknight
	Subarrange by Table E1 at the end of the text
467.1.M86	Morgan, John Hunt
	Subarrange by Table E1 at the end of the text
467.1.M87	Mosby, John Singleton
	Subarrange by Table E1 at the end of the text
467.1.O7	Ord, Edward Otho Cresap
	Subarrange by Table E1 at the end of the text
467.1.P26	Parsons, Lewis Baldwin
	Subarrange by Table E1 at the end of the text
467.1.P365	Pemberton, John Clifford
	Subarrange by Table E1 at the end of the text
467.1.P37	Pendleton, William Nelson
	Subarrange by Table E1 at the end of the text
467.1.P4	Perkins, George Hamilton
	Subarrange by Table E1 at the end of the text
467.1.P51	Pettigrew, James Johnston
	Subarrange by Table E1 at the end of the text
467.1.P57	Pickett, George Edward
	Subarrange by Table E1 at the end of the text

The Civil War, 1861-1865
Biography

467.1.A-.1.Z	Individual, A-Z — Continued
467.1.P7	Polk, Leonidas
	Subarrange by Table E1 at the end of the text
467.1.P78	Porter, David Dixon
	Subarrange by Table E1 at the end of the text
467.1.P8	Porter, Fitz-John
	Subarrange by Table E1 at the end of the text
	For conduct at 2d battle of Bull Run and court-martial, see E473.772
467.1.P82	Porter, Horace
	Subarrange by Table E1 at the end of the text
467.1.R2	Ramseur, Stephen Dodson
	Subarrange by Table E1 at the end of the text
467.1.R25	Rawlins, John Aaron
	Subarrange by Table E1 at the end of the text
467.1.R4	Reynolds, John Fulton
	Subarrange by Table E1 at the end of the text
467.1.R7	Rosecrans, William Starke
	Subarrange by Table E1 at the end of the text
467.1.S32	Schenck, Robert Cumming
	Subarrange by Table E1 at the end of the text
467.1.S35	Schofield, John McAllister
	Subarrange by Table E1 at the end of the text
467.1.S4	Sedgwick, John
	Subarrange by Table E1 at the end of the text
467.1.S47	Semmes, Raphael
	Subarrange by Table E1 at the end of the text
467.1.S54	Sheridan, Philip Henry
	Subarrange by Table E1 at the end of the text
467.1.S55	Sherman, William Tecumseh
	Subarrange by Table E1 at the end of the text
467.1.S552	Sherman, Ellen (Ewing)
	Subarrange by Table E1 at the end of the text
467.1.S58	Sigel, Franz
	Subarrange by Table E1 at the end of the text
467.1.S63	Slocum, Henry Warner
	Subarrange by Table E1 at the end of the text
467.1.S75	Smith, William Farrar
	Subarrange by Table E1 at the end of the text
467.1.S8	Stanton, Edwin McMasters
	Subarrange by Table E1 at the end of the text
467.1.S84	Steedman, James Barrett
	Subarrange by Table E1 at the end of the text
467.1.S85	Stephens, Alexander Hamilton
	Subarrange by Table E1 at the end of the text
467.1.S87	Stone, Charles Pomeroy
	Subarrange by Table E1 at the end of the text
467.1.S9	Stuart, James Ewell Brown
	Subarrange by Table E1 at the end of the text
467.1.T4	Thomas, George Henry
	Subarrange by Table E1 at the end of the text
467.1.T8	Tucker, John Randolph
	Subarrange by Table E1 at the end of the text
467.1.T9	Tyler, Daniel
	Subarrange by Table E1 at the end of the text
467.1.T98	Tyndale, Hector
	Subarrange by Table E1 at the end of the text
467.1.W13	Wadsworth, James Samuel
	Subarrange by Table E1 at the end of the text

The Civil War, 1861-1865
Biography

467.1.A-.1.Z   Individual, A-Z — Continued
467.1.W2   Wallace, Lewis
                                 Subarrange by Table E1 at the end of the text
                                 Cf. PS3130+, Wallace as an author, his works, and criticism of those works
467.1.W3   Wallace, William Henry Lamme
                                 Subarrange by Table E1 at the end of the text
467.1.W4   Warren, Gouverneur Kemble
                                 Subarrange by Table E1 at the end of the text
                                 Cf. E477.675, Warren court-martial
467.1.W46   Welles, Gideon
                                 Subarrange by Table E1 at the end of the text
467.1.W5   Wheeler, Joseph
                                 Subarrange by Table E1 at the end of the text
467.1.W61   Whiting, William Henry Chase
                                 Subarrange by Table E1 at the end of the text
467.1.W69   Wilder, John Thomas
                                 Subarrange by Table E1 at the end of the text
467.1.W72   Williams, Alpheus Starkey
                                 Subarrange by Table E1 at the end of the text
467.1.W74   Wilson, James Harrison
                                 Subarrange by Table E1 at the end of the text
467.1.W77   Winslow, John Ancrum
                                 Subarrange by Table E1 at the end of the text
467.1.W81   Wistar, Isaac Jones
                                 Subarrange by Table E1 at the end of the text
467.1.W94   Wright, Marcus Joseph
                                 Subarrange by Table E1 at the end of the text

Comprehensive works. General histories
                                 Cf. E167, Description and travel, 1861-1865
                                 Cf. E458+, Causes, aims, etc., of the war
                                 Cf. E470+, Military operations
                                 Cf. E482+, F214, The Confederate States of America
468   General works
468.3   Chronology
                                 Cf. E470.1, Chronological lists of battles
468.5   Historiography
                                 Including criticism of histories and textbooks, accuracy and bias of writers, etc.
                                 Cf. E175.85, Criticisms of textbooks, (General)
468.7   Pictorial works
                                 Including works important solely or chiefly for the illustrations
468.8   Soldiers' almanacs
468.9   General special
                                 Including otherwise unprovided for topics such as propaganda, name of the war, influence, etc.
                                 Cf. E488.5, Confederate propaganda in foreign countries

Diplomatic history
                                 Including Trent Affair, 1861; Gilmore and Jacquess' conference with Jefferson Davis, 1864;
                                 Hampton Roads Conference, 1865; construction of Confederate war vessels in England; etc.
                                 Cf. E440.5, Washington Peace Conference, 1860
                                 Cf. E470.95, Confederates in Canada, and St. Albans Raid
                                 Cf. E488, Confederate diplomatic history
                                 Cf. E596+, Confederate navy
                                 Cf. F1233, French intervention in Mexico
                                 Cf. JX238.A4+, Alabama claims
469   General works
469.8   Foreign public opinion
                                 Cf. E458+, Contemporary addresses on the war

The Civil War, 1861-1865 — Continued
Military operations

470   General works
         Including campaigns and battles (General); military histories of the war; narratives of
           commanders; etc.
         For works restricted to a special region, campaign, or battle, see E470+
         For lists of battles, see E470.1
         Cf. E468+, General history of the war
         Cf. E601+, Personal narratives of minor officers and privates

470.1   Battles (Alphabetical or chronological lists)
         For individual battles, see E471+
         By region
           Including military operations of individual armies
           Eastern border states
             Including Virginia, Maryland, District of Columbia, and Pennsylvania, Army of the James,
               Army of the Potomac, Army of Virginia, Army of Northern Virginia (C.S.A.)
             Personal narratives of service in the Army of the Potomac, if not classed under campaign or
               regiment, should be classed in E601 rather than E470.2

470.2   General works
470.3   Shenandoah Valley
           Western border states
             Including Ohio Valley and central Mississippi Valley (West Virginia, Kentucky, Tennessee,
               Ohio, Indiana, Illinois, Missouri, Arkansas), Army of West Virginia

470.4   General works
470.45   Border warfare. Guerrillas
470.5   Cumberland and Tennessee Valleys. Chattanooga region
             Including armies of the Cumberland and the Tennessee, Army of Tennessee (C.S.A.)

470.6   Lower South
             Including North Carolina, South Carolina, Georgia, and region west
             For Sherman's march, see E476.69

470.65   South Atlantic coast line
             Including Siege of Charleston, 1863-1865; supplies for Savannah
             Cf. E475.6+, Engagements in Charleston Harbor, 1863
             Cf. E476.4+, Engagements in Charleston Harbor, 1864
             For Naval operations and blockade running, see E591+

470.7   Gulf States
             Including Florida, Alabama, Mississippi, Louisiana, Texas
             For Society of the Army and Navy of the Gulf, see E462.99.S62
             For naval operations and blockade running, see E591+

470.8   Mississippi Valley
470.9   Trans-Mississippi region
             Including Texas, Indian Territory, Kansas, New Mexico, Missouri, Arkansas, etc., Army of
               the Pacific

470.95   Northern frontier of the United States
             Including Confederates in Canada; St. Albans (Vt.) Raid, 1864
           By campaign and battle
             Cf. E467.1.A+, Biography of leaders
             Cf. E468+, Comprehensive histories of the war
             Cf. E470, General military histories, and memoirs of commanders
             Cf. E470.2+, Military operations by region, and history of armies
             Cf. E493.1, History of corps and divisions
             Cf. E493.5, History of brigades
             Cf. E495+, E551+, History of regiments
             Cf. E547, History of corps, divisions, amd brigades
             A history of a regiment in a particular campaign or battle is classed in E471-478, rather than
               E495-582
             The literature of the national military parks at Chickamauga and Chattanooga, Gettysburg,
               Vicksburg, etc., and descriptive works dealing with the battlefield are classed with the battle
             For local guidebooks, see Class F, e.g. F444.C4, Chattanooga

The Civil War, 1861-1865
  Military operations
    By campaign and battle — Continued
      For naval operations in connection with military movements, see E471-478 rather than E591
      Opening events

471	General works
471.1	South Carolina, December 20, 1860- April 14, 1861
	Including Charleston Harbor (Fort Sumter)
	Other southern states
	Cf. E440.5, E458.1, E551+, General political history
471.5	General works
471.51	Georgia, January 3-26, 1861
471.52	Alabama and Mississippi, January 4-20, 1861
471.53	Florida, January 6-August 31, 1861
	Including Fort Jefferson, Dry Tortugas
471.54	North Carolina, January 9-May 20, 1861
471.55	Louisiana, January 10-February 19, 1861
471.56	Texas and New Mexico, February 1-June 11, 1861
471.57	Arkansas, Indian Territory, and Missouri, February 7-May 9, 1861
	Maryland, Pennsylvania, Virginia, and West Virginia, April 16-July 31, 1861
472.1	General works
472.13	Conflict between United States troops and mob in Baltimore, April 19
472.14	Engagement at Big Bethel, June 10
472.16	Operations in Shenandoah Valley, July 2-25
472.17	Campaign in West Virginia, July 6-17
	Including Battle of Rich Mountain, July 11
	Bull Run Campaign, July 16-22
	Including First battle of Bull Run (Manassas), July 21
472.18	General works
472.182	Manassas Battlefield Confederate Park
472.183	Manassas National Battlefield Park
	Missouri, Arkansas, Kansas and Indian Territory, May 10-November 19, 1861
472.2	General works
472.23	Battle of Wilson's Creek, August 10
472.25	Siege of Lexington, Mo., September 13-20
472.28	Engagement at Belmont, Mo., and demonstration from Paducah upon Columbus, Ky., November 7
	Texas, New Mexico, and Arizona, June 11-February 1, 1862
472.3	General works
472.32	Skirmish at Mesilla, evacuation of Fort Fillmore, and surrender of Union forces at San Augustine, July 25-27
472.4	Kentucky and Tennessee, July 1-November 19, 1861
472.5	North Carolina and southeastern Virginia, August 1, 1861-January 11, 1862
	Maryland, northern Virginia, and West Virginia, August 1, 1861-March 17, 1862
472.6	General works
472.63	Operations on the Potomac near Leesburg, Va.
	Including engagement at Ball's Bluff and action near Edward's Ferry, October 21-24
	Coasts of South Carolina, Georgia, and middle and east Florida, August 21, 1861-April 11, 1862
	Including Port Royal Expedition, November, 1861
472.7	General works
472.79	Bombardment and capture of Fort Pulaski, Ga., April 10-11
	West Florida, southern Alabama, southern Mississippi, and Louisiana, September 1, 1861-May 12, 1862
472.8	General works
472.88	Bombardment and capture of Forts Jackson and Saint Philip and occupation of New Orleans, by Union forces, April 18-May 1
	Cf. E510, General Butler's government of Louisiana
	Kentucky, Tennessee, north Alabama, and southwest Virginia, November 19, 1861- March 4, 1862
	Including Anna E. Carroll's claim
472.9	General works
472.96	Capture of Fort Henry, Tenn., February 6

The Civil War, 1861-1865
   Military operations
      By campaign and battle
         Kentucky, Tennessee, north Alabama, and southwest Virginia, November 19, 1861- March 4, 1862 — Continued

472.97	Siege and capture of Fort Donelson, Tenn., February 12-16
	Missouri, Arkansas, Kansas, and Indian Territory, November 19, 1861-April 10, 1862
473.1	General works
473.15	Operations at New Madrid, Mo., and Island No. 10, and descent upon Union City, Tenn., February 28-April 8
473.17	Battle of Pea Ridge, March 6-8
473.2	Southeastern Virginia, January 11-March 17, 1862
	Including naval engagement in Hampton Roads, Merrimac and Monitor
	North Carolina, January 11-August 20, 1862
	Including Burnside's Expedition, capture of Elizabeth City, N.C., September 10
473.3	General works
473.31	Battle of Roanoke Island, February 8
473.34	Battle of New Bern, March 14
	Texas, New Mexico, and Arizona, February 1- September 20, 1862
	Including Battle of Nueces River, August 10
473.4	General works
473.46	Expedition from southern California through Arizona to northwestern Texas and New Mexico, April 13-September 20
	Including California column
	Kentucky, Tennessee, northern Mississippi, northern Alabama, and southwest Virginia, March 4-June 10, 1862
473.5	General works
473.52	Cumberland Gap campaign, March 28-June 18
473.54	Battle of Shiloh, April 6-7
	Including Shiloh National Military Park
473.55	Raid on Confederate line of communication between Chattanooga, Tenn., and Marietta, Ga., April 7-12
	Including Andrews' railroad raid
473.56	Advance upon and siege of Corinth, Miss., and pursuit of the Confederate forces, April 29-June 10
473.59	Attack on Chattanooga, Tenn., June 7-8
	Peninsular campaign, Va., March 17-September 2, 1862
473.6	General works
473.61	Siege of Yorktown, April 5-May 4
473.63	Battle of Williamsburg, May 5
473.64	Occupation of Norfolk and Portsmouth, May 10
473.65	Battle of Fair Oaks, May 31-June 1
473.66	Stuart's raid, June 13-15
473.68	Seven days' battles, June 25-July 1
	Including Battles of Mechanicsville (Beaver Dam Creek), June 26; Gaines' Mill, June 27; Savage Station, June 29; Glendale (Frayser's Farm), June 30; Malvern Hill, July 1
	Northern Virginia, West Virginia, and Maryland, March 17-September 2, 1862
	Including General Pope's Virginia campaign
473.7	General works
473.72	Battle of Kernstown, Va., March 23
473.74	Operations in the Shenandoah Valley, May 15-June 17
473.76	Battle of Cedar Mountain, August 9
	Campaign in northern Virginia, August 16-September 2
	Including Battles of Groveton, August 28-29; Bull Run (Second battle), August 30; Chantilly, September 1
473.77	General works
473.772	Fitz-John Porter case
473.8	Missouri, Arkansas, Kansas, Indian Territory, and the Department of the Northwest, April 10-November 20, 1862
	Cf. E83.86, Sioux Indian War, 1862-1865

The Civil War, 1861-1865
Military operations
By campaign and battle — Continued
Coasts of South Carolina, Georgia, and middle and east Florida, April 12, 1862-June 11, 1863
473.9   General works
473.92   Engagement at Secessionville (James Island), S.C., June 16, 1862
473.96   Engagement in Charleston Harbor, April 7, 1863
West Florida, southern Alabama, southern Mississippi, and Louisiana, May 12, 1862- May 14, 1863. Texas, New Mexico, and Arizona, September 20, 1862-May 14, 1863
    Including Battle of Galveston, January 1, 1863
    For Grierson's raid, April 17-May 2, 1863, see E475.23
474.1   General works
474.11   Operations against Vicksburg, Miss., and Baton Rouge, La., May 18-August 6, 1862
    Including The Essex (U.S. ironclad) and Arkansas (Confederate ironclad)
474.17   Operations against and about Port Hudson, La., March 7-27, 1863
474.18   Operations in west Louisiana, April 9-May 14, 1863
Kentucky, middle and east Tennessee, north Alabama, and southwest Virginia, June 10-October 31, 1862
474.3   General works
474.32   Morgan's first Kentucky raid, July 4-28
474.34   Action at and surrender of Murfreesboro, Tenn., July 13
474.37   Battle of Richmond, Ky., August 30
474.38   Evacuation of Cumberland Gap, Tenn., September 17-October 3
474.39   Battle of Perryville, Ky., October 8
West Tennessee and northern Mississippi, June 10, 1862-January 20, 1863
474.4   General works
474.42   Engagement at Iuka, Miss., September 19
474.44   Battle of Corinth, Miss., and pursuit of the Confederate forces, October 3-12
474.46   Forrest's expedition into west Tennessee, December 15-January 2
474.47   Operations against Vicksburg, December 20-January 3
474.48   Expedition against Arkansas Post or Fort Hindman, Ark., and operations in that vicinity, January 4-17
North Carolina and southeastern Virginia, August 20, 1862-June 3, 1863
474.5   General works
474.52   Expedition from New Bern, to Goldsboro, N.C., December 11-20, 1862
474.55   Siege of Washington, N.C. and pursuit of the Confederate forces, March 30-April 20, 1863
Northern Virginia, West Virginia, Maryland, and Pennsylvania, September 3-November 14, 1862
474.6   General works
The Maryland campaign, September 3-20
    Including siege of Harper's Ferry, September 14-15
474.61   General works
474.65   Battle of Antietam, September 17
    Including Antietam National Cemetery
474.67   Stuart's expedition into Maryland and Pennsylvania, October 9-12
Kentucky, middle and east Tennessee, north Alabama, and southwest Virginia, November 1, 1862-January 20, 1863
474.7   General works
474.75   Morgan's second Kentucky raid, December 22-January 2
474.77   The Stone's River or Murfreesboro, Tenn. campaign, December 26-January 5
    Including Stones River National Military Park
Northern Virginia, West Virginia, Maryland, and Pennsylvania, November 15, 1862-January 25, 1863
474.8   General works
474.85   Battle of Fredericksburg, Va., December 11-15
    Including Fredericksburg and Spotsylvania County National Military Park
Missouri, Arkansas, Kansas, Indian Territory, and the Department of the Northwest, November 20, 1862-December 31, 1863
    Including Battles of Helena, Ark., July 4; and Baxter Springs, Kans., October 6
    Cf. E83.86, Sioux Indian War, 1862-1865
474.9   General works

The Civil War, 1861-1865

  Military operations

    By campaign and battle

      Missouri, Arkansas, Kansas, Indian Territory, and the Department of the Northwest, November 20, 1862-December 31, 1863 — Continued

474.92	Battle of Prairie Grove, Ark., December 7, 1862
474.94	Battle of Fayetteville, Ark., April 18, 1863
474.96	Advance of Union forces upon Little Rock, Ark., August 1-September 14, 1863
474.97	Quantrill's raid into Kansas and pursuit by Union forces, August 20-28
	Including the Lawrence massacre and burning, August 21
474.98	Shelby's raid in Arkansas and Missouri, September 22-October 26

      Kentucky, middle and east Tennessee, north Alabama, and southwest Virginia, January 21-August 10, 1863

        Including Streight's raid toward Rome, Ga., April-May 1863

475.1	General works
475.16	The middle Tennessee or Tullahoma campaign, June 23-July 7
475.18	Morgan's raid in Kentucky, Indiana, and Ohio, July 2-26

      Mississippi and West Tennessee

        Including operations in Arkansas and Louisiana connected with the siege of Vicksburg, January 20-August 10, 1863

475.2	General works
475.22	Yazoo Pass expedition, February 24-April 8
475.23	Grierson's raid from La Grange, Tenn., to Baton Rouge, La., April 17-May 2
475.24	Battle of Port Gibson, Miss., May 1
475.26	Battle of Champion's Hill, May 16
475.27	Siege of Vicksburg, Miss., May 19-July 4
	Including Vicksburg National Military Park
475.29	The Jackson, Miss., campaign, July 5-25

      Northern Virginia, West Virginia, Maryland, and Pennsylvania, January 26-June 3, 1863

        Including Battle of Kelly's Ford, March 17

475.3	General works
475.35	The Chancellorsville campaign, April 27- May 6
475.38	The Stoneman raid, April 29-May 7

      West Florida, southern Alabama, southern Mississippi, Louisiana, Texas, and New Mexico, May 14-December 31, 1863

        Including engagements at Milliken's Bend, June 7, and Sabine Pass, September 8

        For siege of Vicksburg, see E475.27

475.4	General works
475.42	Siege of Port Hudson, La., May 22-July 8

      475.5   North Carolina, Virginia, West Virginia, Maryland, Pennsylvania, and Department of the East, June 3-August 3, 1863

        Including Battle of Middleburg, Va., June 17-18

        Cf. F128.44, Draft riots in New York City, June 13-16

      The Gettysburg campaign, June 3-August 1

        Including Battle of Hanover, Pa., June 30

475.51	General works
475.53	Battle of Gettysburg
475.55	Gettysburg National Cemetery
	Including dedication, national monument, and Lincoln's Gettysburg address
475.56	Gettysburg National Military Park
	Including state, regimental, and other monuments
	For acccounts of the battle, see E475.53
475.57	Fiftieth anniversary celebration, 1913
475.58	Seventy-fifth anniversary celebration, 1938
475.582	One-hundredth anniversary celebration, 1963

      Coasts of South Carolina and Georgia. Middle and east Florida, June 12- December 31, 1863

475.6	General works
475.62	Charleston Harbor, April-December, 1863
475.63	Operations on Morris Island, S.C., July 10-September 7
	Including attack and fall of Battery Wagner

The Civil War, 1861-1865
Military operations
By campaign and battle
Coasts of South Carolina and Georgia. Middle and east Florida, June 12- December 31, 1863 —
Continued

475.65	Bombardment of Fort Sumter, August 17- December 31
475.68	Engagement in Charleston Harbor, September 7-8
	North Carolina, Virginia, West Virginia, Maryland, and Pennsylvania, August 4-December 31, 1863
475.7	General works
475.75	The Bristoe, Va., campaign, October 9-22
475.76	Expeditions from Beverly and Charleston against Lewisburg, W. Va., November 1-7
	Including Battle of Droop Mountain, W. Va., November 6
475.78	Mine Run, Va., campaign, November 26- December 2
	Kentucky, southwest Virginia, Tennessee, Mississippi, north Alabama, and north Georgia, August 11-October 19, 1863
475.8	General works
475.81	Chickamauga, Ga., campaign, August 16- September 22
	Including Chickamauga and Chattanooga National Park
475.85	East Tennessee campaign, August 16-October 19
475.87	Wheeler and Roddey's raid, September 30- October 17
475.88	Chalmer's raid in west Tennessee and northern Mississippi, October 4-17
	Kentucky, southwest Virginia, Tennessee, Mississippi, north Alabama, and north Georgia, October 20-December 31, 1863
475.9	General works
475.92	Reopening of the Tennessee River, October 26-29
	Including skirmish at Brown's Ferry and engagement at Wauhatchie, Tenn., October 29
475.94	Knoxville, Tenn., campaign, November 4- December 23
	Including Attack upon Fort Sanders, November 29
475.97	Chattanooga-Ringgold campaign, November 23-27
	Including Battles of Lookout Mountain and Missionary Ridge
	Kentucky, southwest Virginia, Tennessee, Mississippi, Alabama, and north Georgia, January 1- April 30, 1864
476.1	General works
476.14	The Meridian, Miss., expedition, February 3-March 6
	Including cooperating expeditions from Memphis and up the Yazoo River
476.17	Forrest's expedition into west Tennessee and Kentucky, March 16-April 14
	Including Massacre at Fort Pillow, April 12
	North Carolina, Virginia, West Virginia, Maryland, and Pennsylvania, January 1-April 30, 1864
476.2	General works
476.23	Expedition against New Bern, N.C., January 28-February 10
476.27	Kilpatrick's expedition against Richmond, February 28-March 4
	Including Dahlgren's raid
	Louisiana and the trans-Mississippi states and territories, January 1-June 30, 1864
476.3	General works
476.33	Red River, La., campaign, March 10-May 22
	Including Battle of Pleasant Hill, La., April 9
476.35	Camden, Ark., expedition, March 23-May 3
	Including Battle of Fitzhugh's Woods, April 1
	South Carolina, Florida, and coast of Georgia, January 1-November 13, 1864
476.4	General works
476.41	Operations in Charleston Harbor and vicinity, January 1-November 13
476.43	Florida expedition, February 5-22
	Including Battle of Olustee, February 20
	Southeastern Virginia and North Carolina, May 1-June 12, 1864
476.5	General works
476.52	Campaign from the Rapidan to the James, May 4-June 12
	Including Battle of the Wilderness, May 5-7; Spottsylvania, May 8-21; Cold Harbor, June 3
476.57	Operations on the south side of the James, May 4-June 2
	Including Bermuda Hundred, Va., May 16-30

The Civil War, 1861-1865
  Military operations
    By campaign and battle
      Southeastern Virginia and North Carolina, May 1-June 12, 1864 — Continued
476.59 | Engagement at Petersburg, Va., June 9
      Northern Virginia, West Virginia, Maryland, and Pennsylvania, May 1-August 3, 1864
476.6 | General works
476.62 | Expedition against the Virginia and Tennessee Railroad, May 2-19
476.64 | Engagement at New Market, Va., May 15
476.65 | Lynchburg campaign, May 26-June 29
476.66 | Operations in the Shenandoah Valley, Maryland, and Pennsylvania, June 23-August 3
        Including Maryland campaign: Battle of Monocacy River, July 9; attack on Fort Stevens, Washington, D.C., July 11-12
        For burning of Chambersburg, Pa., July 30, see F159.C4
476.69 | Sherman's march, May 1864-April 1865
        Cf. E476.7, Atlanta, Ga., campaign, May 1-September 8, 1864
        Cf. E476.87, Operations in north Georgia and north Alabama, September 29-November 13, 1864
        Cf. E477.41, Savannah campaign, November 15-December 21
        Cf. E477.7, North Carolina (from February 1), South Carolina, southern Georgia, and east Florida, January 1-June 30, 1865
476.7 | Atlanta, Ga., campaign, May 1-September 8, 1864
        Including Battles of New Hope Church, May 24-28; Kennesaw Mountain, June 27; Peachtree Creek, July 20; Jonesboro (Jonesborough), August 31-September 1; capture of Atlanta, September 1
        Including Kennesaw Mountain National Battlefield Park
      Kentucky, southwest Virginia, Tennessee, Mississippi, Alabama, and north Georgia, May 1-November 13, 1864
        For Atlanta campaign, see E476.7
476.8 | General works
476.82 | Morgan's raid into Kentucky, May 31-June 20
476.83 | Expedition from Memphis, Tenn., into Mississippi, June 1-13
476.84 | Expedition from La Grange, Tenn., to Tupelo, Miss., July 5-21
476.85 | Operations in Mobile Bay, August 2-23
476.87 | Operations in north Georgia and north Alabama, September 29-November 13
        Including Battle of Allatoona, October 5
      Southeastern Virginia and North Carolina, June 13-July 31, 1864
476.9 | General works
      Richmond campaign, June 13-July 31
476.91 | General works
476.93 | Siege of Petersburg. Battle of Petersburg Crater
        Including Petersburg National Military Park
      Louisiana and the trans-Mississippi states and territories, July 1-December 31, 1864
        Cf. E83.863, Indian campaigns in Dakota
477.1 | General works
477.16 | Price's Missouri expedition, August 29- December 2
        Including Battles of Pilot Knob, September 27; Westport, October 21-23; Big Blue, October 22
      Southeastern Virginia and North Carolina, August 1-December 31, 1864
477.2 | General works
477.21 | Richmond campaign, August 1-December 31
        Including Weldon Railroad; battle and capture of Fort Harrison, September 29-30
477.28 | Expedition to and operations against Fort Fisher, N.C., December 7-27
      Northern Virginia, West Virginia, Maryland, and Pennsylvania, August 4-December 31, 1864
477.3 | General works
477.33 | Shenandoah Valley campaign, August 7- November 28
        Including Battles of Winchester, September 19; Fisher's Hill, September 22; Cedar Creek, October 19
      South Carolina, Georgia, and Florida, November 14-December 31, 1864
477.4 | General works

The Civil War, 1861-1865
Military operations
By campaign and battle
South Carolina, Georgia, and Florida, November 14-December 31, 1864 — Continued

477.41	Savannah campaign, November 15-December 21
477.44	Engagement at Honey Hill, S.C., November 30
	Kentucky, southwest Virginia, Tennessee, Mississippi, Alabama, and north Georgia, November 14, 1864-January 23, 1865
477.5	General works
477.52	Campaign in north Alabama and middle Tennessee, November 14, 1864-January 23, 1865
	Including Battles of Spring Hill, Tenn., November 29; Franklin, Tenn., November 30; Nashville, December 15-16
	Northern and southeastern Virginia, North Carolina (January 1-31), West Virginia, Maryland, and Pennsylvania, January 1-June 30, 1865
477.6	General works
477.61	Richmond campaign, January 1-April 3
	Including attack on Fort Stedman, March 25; evacuation of Petersburg, April 2
477.63	Expedition to and capture of Fort Fisher, N.C., January 3-17
477.65	Expedition from Winchester to the front of Petersburg, February 27-March 28
	Appomattox campaign, March 29-April 9
	Including Battles of Gravelly Run, Dinwiddie Courthouse, Five Forks
477.67	General works
477.675	Warren court-martial
	North Carolina (from February 1), South Carolina, southern Georgia, and east Florida, January 1-June 30, 1865
	Including Campaign of the Carolinas
477.7	General works
477.75	Capture and burning of Columbia, S.C., February 17-18
477.8	Louisiana and the trans-Mississippi states and territories, January 1-June 30, 1865
	Cf. E83.863, Indian campaigns
	Kentucky, southwestern Virginia, Tennessee, northern and central Georgia, Mississippi, Alabama, and west Florida, January 1-June 30, 1865
	Including Stoneman's raid, March 24-April 15; Gillem's raid, April 15-25
477.9	General works
477.94	Mobile campaign, March 17-May 4
477.96	Wilson's raid from Chickasaw to Selma, Ala., and Macon, Ga., March 22-April 24
	Including Capture of Columbus, Ga., April 16
477.98	Pursuit and capture of Jefferson Davis, May 1-10
478.1	Pacific coast, January 1, 1861-June 30, 1865
	For expedition from southern California through Arizona to northwestern Texas and New Mexico, April 13-September 20, 1862, see E473.46
	Cf. E83.86, Indian campaigns
	Cf. E83.863, Indian wars

Finance. Commerce. Confiscations, etc.
Including abandoned and confiscable property, blockade, government contracts, purchase of products from insurgents, war claims
Cf. HF3027.6, History of United States commerce during Civil War
Cf. HJ251+, Public finance of Civil War
Cf. HJ2371+, Revenue and taxation during Civil War
Cf. JK347, Military rule, martial law, etc., during Civil War

480	General works
480.5	Confederate States of America

Confederate States of America

482	Periodicals
483	Societies
483.1	United Confederate Veterans
483.2	Confederate Veteran Association of Kentucky
483.25	Society of the Army and Navy of the Confederate States, Maryland
483.28	Grand Camp Confederate Veterans, Department of Virginia

	The Civil War, 1861-1865
	Confederate States of America
483	Societies — Continued
483.4	Sons of Confederate Veterans
	Formerly United Sons of Confederate Veterans
483.5	United Daughters of the Confederacy
483.55	Children of the Confederacy
483.7	Southern Historical Society
483.72	Confederate Southern Memorial Association
483.75	Confederate Memorial Literary Society
483.99.A-.99.Z	Other societies, A-Z
483.99.C78	Confederate Veterans' Association of Fulton County, Georgia
484	Collections. Collected works
	Biography (Collective and individual), *see* E467+
	Description and travel, social conditions, etc., *see* F214
487	History (General). Political history
	Including administration of Jefferson Davis and memoirs and reminiscences of civil officials
	and noncombatants
	Cf. E458+, Political history and causes of the war
	Cf. E468, General histories of the war
	Cf. E470+, Military operations
	Cf. JK9663+, C.S.A. documents
488	Diplomatic history
	Cf. E469+, Diplomatic history of the United States
	Cf. E596+, Foreign-built Confederate cruisers
	Military history, *see* E470.2+, E545+
	Naval history, *see* E591+
	Economic history, *see* HC105.65
	Addresses, sermons, etc., *see* E650
	Commemorations, Memorial Day, *see* E645
	Battle Abbey, Richmond, *see* F234.R5
	Flags, *see* E646
	Hospitals, *see* E625
	Military prisons, *see* E611
488.5	Propaganda in foreign countries
	Secret Service, Signal Corps., *see* E608
	Union men in the South, *see* E458.7
489	Other (not A-Z)
	Armies. Troops
	The Union Army
491	General works
	Including administration, organization, volunteering, conscription, Southern federals,
	statistics, numbers and losses, Civil War medals of honor, transportation, supplies, etc.
	Arms of the service
492	General works
	United States regular troops
	For general histories of regular army organizations, see UA24+
492.3	General works
492.4	Infantry
	Subarrange by number or name of regiment, A-Z. By author, A-Z
492.5	Cavalry
	Subarrange by number or name of regiment, A-Z. By author, A-Z
492.6	Artillery
	Subarrange by number or name of regiment, A-Z. By author, A-Z
492.7	Other (not A-Z)
	Including Balloon Service, Corps of Engineers, Sharpshooters, etc.
	For Secret Service, Signal Corps, see E608
	Afro-American regiments
	For general subject of Afro-Americans in the war, see E540.N3
	For various state regiments of Afro-Americans, see E495+

The Civil War, 1861-1865
Armies. Troops
The Union Army
Arms of the service
Afro-American regiments — Continued

492.9	General works
492.94	Infantry
	Subarrange by number or name of regiment, A-Z. By author, A-Z
492.95	Cavalry
	Subarrange by number or name of regiment, A-Z. By author, A-Z
493.1	Corps. Divisions
	Including associations, societies, unions, etc., of individual corps
	Subarrange by number or name of corps, A-Z. By author, A-Z
493.5	Brigades
	Subarrange by number or name of brigade, A-Z. By author, A-Z
	Including associations, reunions, etc., of individual brigades
	For a brigade consisting entirely of troops from a single state whether infantry or cavalry, see E495-537, subdivision .4 under state number, e.g. E507.4.C9, Crocker's Iowa Brigade
493.9	First defenders or Minute Men of 1861
	Including works on the troops who responded to President Lincoln's first call of April 15, 1861
494	Registers, lists of the dead and wounded, etc.
	Including lists of soldiers and officers from more than one state and veterans residing in particular states
	For veterans residing in a county or town, see local biography in Class F
	For lists of prisoners, see E611
495-537	By state
	Including state political history, 1861-1865; quotas in war; war governors
	For a comprehensive history of a state militia regiment, see UA50+
	For military operations in a state, see E470.2+
	For relief associations, see E629
	Alabama
	For campaigns and battles, see E471+
	For Civil War, campaigns and battles, see E470.6, E470.7
	For Confederate history, see E471.52, E551.1+
495	General works
495.1	Official publications on the raising, equipment, and service of the troops in the war
495.2	Adjutant Generals' reports for 1861-1865
495.3	Lists of soldiers. Lists of the state's dead
	For the seceded states, this subdivision is used for Union troops
495.4	Histories of the states' troops
	Including collected biographies or lists of officers, general associations of survivors, the draft, state brigades, state memorials and monuments, the state's battle flags, lists of citizens serving in organizations of other states
	For the seceded states, this subdivision is used for Union troops
	Military organizations
	For the seceded states, this subdivision is used for Union troops
495.5	Infantry
	For the seceded states, this subdivision is used for Union troops
	Subarrange by number or name of regiment, A-Z. By author, A-Z, e.g. E527.5.L6, Logan Guards
495.6	Cavalry
	For the seceded states, this subdivision is used for Union troops
	Subarrange by number or name of regiment, A-Z. By author, A-Z
495.7	Artillery, Heavy
	For the seceded states, this subdivision is used for Union troops
	Subarrange by number or name of regiment, A-Z. By author, A-Z
495.8	Artillery, Light
	For the seceded states, this subdivision is used for Union troops

The Civil War, 1861-1865
Armies. Troops
The Union Army
495-537   By state
Alabama
Military organizations
495.8   Artillery, Light — Continued
Subarrange by number or name of regiment, A-Z. By author, A-Z
495.9   Other (not A-Z)
For the seceded states, this subdivision is used for Union troops
History of a town or county's participation in the Civil War, and local lists of soldiers, are classed in local history (F1-900). If, however, the town was the seat of military operations, as Chambersburg, Pa., the literature is found in E471-478, or where several sieges or battles are covered, in E470.2-.9 (e.g., a history of all military operations around Richmond)
495.95   Arizona
Not to be further subdivided
Arkansas
For Confederate history, see E471.57, E553.1+
For campaigns and battles, see E470.4+, E470.8-.9, E471+
496   General works
496.1   Official publications on the raising, equipment, and service of the troops in the war
496.2   Adjutant Generals' reports for 1861-1865
496.3   Lists of soldiers. Lists of the state's dead
For the seceded states, this subdivision is used for Union troops
496.4   Histories of the states' troops
Including collected biographies or lists of officers, general associations of survivors, the draft, state brigades, state memorials and monuments, the state's battle flags, lists of citizens serving in organizations of other states
For the seceded states, this subdivision is used for Union troops
Military organizations
For the seceded states, this subdivision is used for Union troops
496.5   Infantry
For the seceded states, this subdivision is used for Union troops
Subarrange by number or name of regiment, A-Z. By author, A-Z, e.g. E527.5.L6, Logan Guards
496.6   Cavalry
For the seceded states, this subdivision is used for Union troops
Subarrange by number or name of regiment, A-Z. By author, A-Z
496.7   Artillery, Heavy
For the seceded states, this subdivision is used for Union troops
Subarrange by number or name of regiment, A-Z. By author, A-Z
496.8   Artillery, Light
For the seceded states, this subdivision is used for Union troops
Subarrange by number or name of regiment, A-Z. By author, A-Z
496.9   Other (not A-Z)
For the seceded states, this subdivision is used for Union troops
History of a town or county's participation in the Civil War, and local lists of soldiers, are classed in local history (F1-900). If, however, the town was the seat of military operations, as Chambersburg, Pa., the literature is found in E471-478, or where several sieges or battles are covered, in E470.2-.9 (e.g., a history of all military operations around Richmond)
California
Cf. E473.46, The California column, 1862
497   General works
497.1   Official publications on the raising, equipment, and service of the troops in the war
497.2   Adjutant Generals' reports for 1861-1865
497.3   Lists of soldiers. Lists of the state's dead
For the seceded states, this subdivision is used for Union troops

The Civil War, 1861-1865

Armies. Troops

The Union Army

495-537   By state

             California — Continued

497.4   Histories of the states' troops

Including collected biographies or lists of officers, general associations of survivors, the draft, state brigades, state memorials and monuments, the state's battle flags, lists of citizens serving in organizations of other states

For the seceded states, this subdivision is used for Union troops

              Military organizations

For the seceded states, this subdivision is used for Union troops

497.5   Infantry

For the seceded states, this subdivision is used for Union troops

Subarrange by number or name of regiment, A-Z. By author, A-Z, e.g. E527.5.L6, Logan Guards

497.6   Cavalry

For the seceded states, this subdivision is used for Union troops

Subarrange by number or name of regiment, A-Z. By author, A-Z

497.7   Artillery, Heavy

For the seceded states, this subdivision is used for Union troops

Subarrange by number or name of regiment, A-Z. By author, A-Z

497.8   Artillery, Light

For the seceded states, this subdivision is used for Union troops

Subarrange by number or name of regiment, A-Z. By author, A-Z

497.9   Other (not A-Z)

For the seceded states, this subdivision is used for Union troops

History of a town or county's participation in the Civil War, and local lists of soldiers, are classed in local history (F1-900). If, however, the town was the seat of military operations, as Chambersburg, Pa., the literature is found in E471-478, or where several sieges or battles are covered, in E470.2-.9 (e.g., a history of all military operations around Richmond)

             Colorado

498   General works

498.1   Official publications on the raising, equipment, and service of the troops in the war

498.2   Adjutant Generals' reports for 1861-1865

498.3   Lists of soldiers. Lists of the state's dead

For the seceded states, this subdivision is used for Union troops

498.4   Histories of the states' troops

Including collected biographies or lists of officers, general associations of survivors, the draft, state brigades, state memorials and monuments, the state's battle flags, lists of citizens serving in organizations of other states

For the seceded states, this subdivision is used for Union troops

              Military organizations

For the seceded states, this subdivision is used for Union troops

498.5   Infantry

For the seceded states, this subdivision is used for Union troops

Subarrange by number or name of regiment, A-Z. By author, A-Z, e.g. E527.5.L6, Logan Guards

498.6   Cavalry

For the seceded states, this subdivision is used for Union troops

Subarrange by number or name of regiment, A-Z. By author, A-Z

498.7   Artillery, Heavy

For the seceded states, this subdivision is used for Union troops

Subarrange by number or name of regiment, A-Z. By author, A-Z

498.8   Artillery, Light

For the seceded states, this subdivision is used for Union troops

Subarrange by number or name of regiment, A-Z. By author, A-Z

498.9   Other (not A-Z)

For the seceded states, this subdivision is used for Union troops

The Civil War, 1861-1865
Armies. Troops
The Union Army
	By state
495-537	

Colorado
Military organizations
498.9 Other (not A-Z) — Continued

History of a town or county's participation in the Civil War, and local lists of soldiers, are classed in local history (F1-900). If, however, the town was the seat of military operations, as Chambersburg, Pa., the literature is found in E471-478, or where several sieges or battles are covered, in E470.2-.9 (e.g., a history of all military operations around Richmond)

Connecticut
Including biography: William Alfred Buckingham, etc.

499	General works
499.1	Official publications on the raising, equipment, and service of the troops in the war
499.2	Adjutant Generals' reports for 1861-1865
499.3	Lists of soldiers. Lists of the state's dead

For the seceded states, this subdivision is used for Union troops

499.4	Histories of the states' troops

Including collected biographies or lists of officers, general associations of survivors, the draft, state brigades, state memorials and monuments, the state's battle flags, lists of citizens serving in organizations of other states
For the seceded states, this subdivision is used for Union troops

Military organizations
For the seceded states, this subdivision is used for Union troops

499.5	Infantry

For the seceded states, this subdivision is used for Union troops
Subarrange by number or name of regiment, A-Z. By author, A-Z, e.g. E527.5.L6, Logan Guards

499.6	Cavalry

For the seceded states, this subdivision is used for Union troops
Subarrange by number or name of regiment, A-Z. By author, A-Z

499.7	Artillery, Heavy

For the seceded states, this subdivision is used for Union troops
Subarrange by number or name of regiment, A-Z. By author, A-Z

499.8	Artillery, Light

For the seceded states, this subdivision is used for Union troops
Subarrange by number or name of regiment, A-Z. By author, A-Z

499.9	Other (not A-Z)

For the seceded states, this subdivision is used for Union troops
History of a town or county's participation in the Civil War, and local lists of soldiers, are classed in local history (F1-900). If, however, the town was the seat of military operations, as Chambersburg, Pa., the literature is found in E471-478, or where several sieges or battles are covered, in E470.2-.9 (e.g., a history of all military operations around Richmond)

Dakota Territory, *see* E530.1+
Delaware

500	General works
500.1	Official publications on the raising, equipment, and service of the troops in the war
500.2	Adjutant Generals' reports for 1861-1865
500.3	Lists of soldiers. Lists of the state's dead

For the seceded states, this subdivision is used for Union troops

500.4	Histories of the states' troops

Including collected biographies or lists of officers, general associations of survivors, the draft, state brigades, state memorials and monuments, the state's battle flags, lists of citizens serving in organizations of other states
For the seceded states, this subdivision is used for Union troops

Military organizations
For the seceded states, this subdivision is used for Union troops

The Civil War, 1861-1865
Armies. Troops
The Union Army
495-537   By state
Delaware
Military organizations — Continued
500.5   Infantry

For the seceded states, this subdivision is used for Union troops

Subarrange by number or name of regiment, A-Z. By author, A-Z, e.g. E527.5.L6, Logan Guards

500.6   Cavalry

For the seceded states, this subdivision is used for Union troops

Subarrange by number or name of regiment, A-Z. By author, A-Z

500.7   Artillery, Heavy

For the seceded states, this subdivision is used for Union troops

Subarrange by number or name of regiment, A-Z. By author, A-Z

500.8   Artillery, Light

For the seceded states, this subdivision is used for Union troops

Subarrange by number or name of regiment, A-Z. By author, A-Z

500.9   Other (not A-Z)

For the seceded states, this subdivision is used for Union troops

History of a town or county's participation in the Civil War, and local lists of soldiers, are classed in local history (F1-900). If, however, the town was the seat of military operations, as Chambersburg, Pa., the literature is found in E471-478, or where several sieges or battles are covered, in E470.2-.9 (e.g., a history of all military operations around Richmond)

District of Columbia

For campaigns and battles, see E470.2+, E471+

501   General works
501.1   Official publications on the raising, equipment, and service of the troops in the war
501.2   Adjutant Generals' reports for 1861-1865
501.3   Lists of soldiers. Lists of the state's dead

For the seceded states, this subdivision is used for Union troops

501.4   Histories of the states' troops

Including collected biographies or lists of officers, general associations of survivors, the draft, state brigades, state memorials and monuments, the state's battle flags, lists of citizens serving in organizations of other states

For the seceded states, this subdivision is used for Union troops

Military organizations

For the seceded states, this subdivision is used for Union troops

501.5   Infantry

For the seceded states, this subdivision is used for Union troops

Subarrange by number or name of regiment, A-Z. By author, A-Z, e.g. E527.5.L6, Logan Guards

501.6   Cavalry

For the seceded states, this subdivision is used for Union troops

Subarrange by number or name of regiment, A-Z. By author, A-Z

501.7   Artillery, Heavy

For the seceded states, this subdivision is used for Union troops

Subarrange by number or name of regiment, A-Z. By author, A-Z

501.8   Artillery, Light

For the seceded states, this subdivision is used for Union troops

Subarrange by number or name of regiment, A-Z. By author, A-Z

501.9   Other (not A-Z)

For the seceded states, this subdivision is used for Union troops

History of a town or county's participation in the Civil War, and local lists of soldiers, are classed in local history (F1-900). If, however, the town was the seat of military operations, as Chambersburg, Pa., the literature is found in E471-478, or where several sieges or battles are covered, in E470.2-.9 (e.g., a history of all military operations around Richmond)

The Civil War, 1861-1865
Armies. Troops
The Union Army

495-537   By state — Continued

Florida

For Confederate history, see E471.53, E558.1+

For campaigns and battles, see E470.6-.7, E471+

502   General works

502.1   Official publications on the raising, equipment, and service of the troops in the war

502.2   Adjutant Generals' reports for 1861-1865

502.3   Lists of soldiers. Lists of the state's dead

For the seceded states, this subdivision is used for Union troops

502.4   Histories of the states' troops

Including collected biographies or lists of officers, general associations of survivors, the draft, state brigades, state memorials and monuments, the state's battle flags, lists of citizens serving in organizations of other states

For the seceded states, this subdivision is used for Union troops

Military organizations

For the seceded states, this subdivision is used for Union troops

502.5   Infantry

For the seceded states, this subdivision is used for Union troops

Subarrange by number or name of regiment, A-Z. By author, A-Z, e.g. E527.5.L6, Logan Guards

502.6   Cavalry

For the seceded states, this subdivision is used for Union troops

Subarrange by number or name of regiment, A-Z. By author, A-Z

502.7   Artillery, Heavy

For the seceded states, this subdivision is used for Union troops

Subarrange by number or name of regiment, A-Z. By author, A-Z

502.8   Artillery, Light

For the seceded states, this subdivision is used for Union troops

Subarrange by number or name of regiment, A-Z. By author, A-Z

502.9   Other (not A-Z)

For the seceded states, this subdivision is used for Union troops

History of a town or county's participation in the Civil War, and local lists of soldiers, are classed in local history (F1-900). If, however, the town was the seat of military operations, as Chambersburg, Pa., the literature is found in E471-478, or where several sieges or battles are covered, in E470.2-.9 (e.g., a history of all military operations around Richmond)

Georgia

For Confederate history, see E471.51, E559.1+

For campaigns and battles, see E470.6, E471+

503   General works

503.1   Official publications on the raising, equipment, and service of the troops in the war

503.2   Adjutant Generals' reports for 1861-1865

503.3   Lists of soldiers. Lists of the state's dead

For the seceded states, this subdivision is used for Union troops

503.4   Histories of the states' troops

Including collected biographies or lists of officers, general associations of survivors, the draft, state brigades, state memorials and monuments, the state's battle flags, lists of citizens serving in organizations of other states

For the seceded states, this subdivision is used for Union troops

Military organizations

For the seceded states, this subdivision is used for Union troops

503.5   Infantry

For the seceded states, this subdivision is used for Union troops

Subarrange by number or name of regiment, A-Z. By author, A-Z, e.g. E527.5.L6, Logan Guards

503.6   Cavalry

For the seceded states, this subdivision is used for Union troops

The Civil War, 1861-1865
Armies. Troops
The Union Army

495-537	By state
	Georgia
	Military organizations
503.6	Cavalry — Continued
	Subarrange by number or name of regiment, A-Z. By author, A-Z
503.7	Artillery, Heavy
	For the seceded states, this subdivision is used for Union troops
	Subarrange by number or name of regiment, A-Z. By author, A-Z
503.8	Artillery, Light
	For the seceded states, this subdivision is used for Union troops
	Subarrange by number or name of regiment, A-Z. By author, A-Z
503.9	Other (not A-Z)
	For the seceded states, this subdivision is used for Union troops
	History of a town or county's participation in the Civil War, and local lists of soldiers, are classed in local history (F1-900). If, however, the town was the seat of military operations, as Chambersburg, Pa., the literature is found in E471-478, or where several sieges or battles are covered, in E470.2-.9 (e.g., a history of all military operations around Richmond)
	Illinois
	For campaigns and battles, see E470.4+, E471+
505	General works
505.1	Official publications on the raising, equipment, and service of the troops in the war
505.2	Adjutant Generals' reports for 1861-1865
505.3	Lists of soldiers. Lists of the state's dead
	For the seceded states, this subdivision is used for Union troops
505.4	Histories of the states' troops
	Including collected biographies or lists of officers, general associations of survivors, the draft, state brigades, state memorials and monuments, the state's battle flags, lists of citizens serving in organizations of other states
	For the seceded states, this subdivision is used for Union troops
	Military organizations
	For the seceded states, this subdivision is used for Union troops
505.5	Infantry
	For the seceded states, this subdivision is used for Union troops
	Subarrange by number or name of regiment, A-Z. By author, A-Z, e.g. E527.5.L6, Logan Guards
505.6	Cavalry
	For the seceded states, this subdivision is used for Union troops
	Subarrange by number or name of regiment, A-Z. By author, A-Z
505.7	Artillery, Heavy
	For the seceded states, this subdivision is used for Union troops
	Subarrange by number or name of regiment, A-Z. By author, A-Z
505.8	Artillery, Light
	For the seceded states, this subdivision is used for Union troops
	Subarrange by number or name of regiment, A-Z. By author, A-Z
505.9	Other (not A-Z)
	For the seceded states, this subdivision is used for Union troops
	History of a town or county's participation in the Civil War, and local lists of soldiers, are classed in local history (F1-900). If, however, the town was the seat of military operations, as Chambersburg, Pa., the literature is found in E471-478, or where several sieges or battles are covered, in E470.2-.9 (e.g., a history of all military operations around Richmond)
505.95	Indian Territory
	Not to be further subdivided
	For Confederate history, see E471.57, E561
	For campaigns and battles, see E470.9, E471+
	For preliminaries of the war, see E471.57

The Civil War, 1861-1865
Armies. Troops
The Union Army
By state
Indian Territory — Continued

495-537

505.95

For Indian tribes, see E99.A+

Indiana
Including biography: Oliver Perry Morton, etc.
For campaigns and battles, see E470.4+, E471+

506   General works
506.1   Official publications on the raising, equipment, and service of the troops in the war
506.2   Adjutant Generals' reports for 1861-1865
506.3   Lists of soldiers. Lists of the state's dead
                 For the seceded states, this subdivision is used for Union troops
506.4   Histories of the states' troops
                 Including collected biographies or lists of officers, general associations of survivors,
                     the draft, state brigades, state memorials and monuments, the state's battle flags,
                     lists of citizens serving in organizations of other states
                 For the seceded states, this subdivision is used for Union troops
             Military organizations
                 For the seceded states, this subdivision is used for Union troops
506.5   Infantry
                     For the seceded states, this subdivision is used for Union troops
                     Subarrange by number or name of regiment, A-Z. By author, A-Z, e.g. E527.5.L6,
                         Logan Guards
506.6   Cavalry
                     For the seceded states, this subdivision is used for Union troops
                     Subarrange by number or name of regiment, A-Z. By author, A-Z
506.7   Artillery, Heavy
                     For the seceded states, this subdivision is used for Union troops
                     Subarrange by number or name of regiment, A-Z. By author, A-Z
506.8   Artillery, Light
                     For the seceded states, this subdivision is used for Union troops
                     Subarrange by number or name of regiment, A-Z. By author, A-Z
506.9   Other (not A-Z)
                     For the seceded states, this subdivision is used for Union troops
                     History of a town or county's participation in the Civil War, and local lists of
                         soldiers, are classed in local history (F1-900). If, however, the town was the seat
                         of military operations, as Chambersburg, Pa., the literature is found in E471-
                         478, or where several sieges or battles are covered, in E470.2-.9 (e.g., a history
                         of all military operations around Richmond)

             Iowa
                 Including biography: Samuel Jordan Kirkwood
507   General works
507.1   Official publications on the raising, equipment, and service of the troops in the war
507.2   Adjutant Generals' reports for 1861-1865
507.3   Lists of soldiers. Lists of the state's dead
                 For the seceded states, this subdivision is used for Union troops
507.4   Histories of the states' troops
                 Including collected biographies or lists of officers, general associations of survivors,
                     the draft, state brigades, state memorials and monuments, the state's battle flags,
                     lists of citizens serving in organizations of other states
                 For the seceded states, this subdivision is used for Union troops
             Military organizations
                 For the seceded states, this subdivision is used for Union troops
507.5   Infantry
                     For the seceded states, this subdivision is used for Union troops
                     Subarrange by number or name of regiment, A-Z. By author, A-Z, e.g. E527.5.L6,
                         Logan Guards

The Civil War, 1861-1865
Armies. Troops
The Union Army

495-537   By state
Iowa
Military organizations — Continued

507.6   Cavalry
For the seceded states, this subdivision is used for Union troops
Subarrange by number or name of regiment, A-Z. By author, A-Z

507.7   Artillery, Heavy
For the seceded states, this subdivision is used for Union troops
Subarrange by number or name of regiment, A-Z. By author, A-Z

507.8   Artillery, Light
For the seceded states, this subdivision is used for Union troops
Subarrange by number or name of regiment, A-Z. By author, A-Z

507.9   Other (not A-Z)
For the seceded states, this subdivision is used for Union troops
History of a town or county's participation in the Civil War, and local lists of
soldiers, are classed in local history (F1-900). If, however, the town was the seat
of military operations, as Chambersburg, Pa., the literature is found in E471-
478, or where several sieges or battles are covered, in E470.2-.9 (e.g., a history
of all military operations around Richmond)

Kansas
For campaigns and battles, see E470.9, E471+

508   General works
508.1   Official publications on the raising, equipment, and service of the troops in the war
508.2   Adjutant Generals' reports for 1861-1865
508.3   Lists of soldiers. Lists of the state's dead
For the seceded states, this subdivision is used for Union troops

508.4   Histories of the states' troops
Including collected biographies or lists of officers, general associations of survivors,
the draft, state brigades, state memorials and monuments, the state's battle flags,
lists of citizens serving in organizations of other states
For the seceded states, this subdivision is used for Union troops

Military organizations
For the seceded states, this subdivision is used for Union troops

508.5   Infantry
For the seceded states, this subdivision is used for Union troops
Subarrange by number or name of regiment, A-Z. By author, A-Z, e.g. E527.5.L6,
Logan Guards

508.6   Cavalry
For the seceded states, this subdivision is used for Union troops
Subarrange by number or name of regiment, A-Z. By author, A-Z

508.7   Artillery, Heavy
For the seceded states, this subdivision is used for Union troops
Subarrange by number or name of regiment, A-Z. By author, A-Z

508.8   Artillery, Light
For the seceded states, this subdivision is used for Union troops
Subarrange by number or name of regiment, A-Z. By author, A-Z

508.9   Other (not A-Z)
For the seceded states, this subdivision is used for Union troops
History of a town or county's participation in the Civil War, and local lists of
soldiers, are classed in local history (F1-900). If, however, the town was the seat
of military operations, as Chambersburg, Pa., the literature is found in E471-
478, or where several sieges or battles are covered, in E470.2-.9 (e.g., a history
of all military operations around Richmond)

Kentucky
For Confederate history, see E564.1+
For campaigns and battles, see E470.4+, E470.5, E470.8, E471+

509   General works

The Civil War, 1861-1865
Armies. Troops
The Union Army
By state
Kentucky — Continued

495-537

509.1   Official publications on the raising, equipment, and service of the troops in the war
509.2   Adjutant Generals' reports for 1861-1865
509.3   Lists of soldiers. Lists of the state's dead
For the seceded states, this subdivision is used for Union troops
509.4   Histories of the states' troops
Including collected biographies or lists of officers, general associations of survivors, the draft, state brigades, state memorials and monuments, the state's battle flags, lists of citizens serving in organizations of other states
For the seceded states, this subdivision is used for Union troops
Military organizations
For the seceded states, this subdivision is used for Union troops
509.5   Infantry
For the seceded states, this subdivision is used for Union troops
Subarrange by number or name of regiment, A-Z. By author, A-Z, e.g. E527.5.L6, Logan Guards
509.6   Cavalry
For the seceded states, this subdivision is used for Union troops
Subarrange by number or name of regiment, A-Z. By author, A-Z
509.7   Artillery, Heavy
For the seceded states, this subdivision is used for Union troops
Subarrange by number or name of regiment, A-Z. By author, A-Z
509.8   Artillery, Light
For the seceded states, this subdivision is used for Union troops
Subarrange by number or name of regiment, A-Z. By author, A-Z
509.9   Other (not A-Z)
For the seceded states, this subdivision is used for Union troops
History of a town or county's participation in the Civil War, and local lists of soldiers, are classed in local history (F1-900). If, however, the town was the seat of military operations, as Chambersburg, Pa., the literature is found in E471-478, or where several sieges or battles are covered, in E470.2-.9 (e.g., a history of all military operations around Richmond)
Louisiana
Including the administration of the Department of the Gulf by General Benjamin Franklin Butler in 1862
For Confederate history, see E471.55, E565.1+
For campaigns and battles, see E470.7, E471+
510   General works
510.1   Official publications on the raising, equipment, and service of the troops in the war
510.2   Adjutant Generals' reports for 1861-1865
510.3   Lists of soldiers. Lists of the state's dead
For the seceded states, this subdivision is used for Union troops
510.4   Histories of the states' troops
Including collected biographies or lists of officers, general associations of survivors, the draft, state brigades, state memorials and monuments, the state's battle flags, lists of citizens serving in organizations of other states
For the seceded states, this subdivision is used for Union troops
Military organizations
For the seceded states, this subdivision is used for Union troops
510.5   Infantry
For the seceded states, this subdivision is used for Union troops
Subarrange by number or name of regiment, A-Z. By author, A-Z, e.g. E527.5.L6, Logan Guards
510.6   Cavalry
For the seceded states, this subdivision is used for Union troops
Subarrange by number or name of regiment, A-Z. By author, A-Z

The Civil War, 1861-1865

Armies. Troops

The Union Army

495-537	By state
	Louisiana
	Military organizations — Continued
510.7	Artillery, Heavy
	For the seceded states, this subdivision is used for Union troops
	Subarrange by number or name of regiment, A-Z. By author, A-Z
510.8	Artillery, Light
	For the seceded states, this subdivision is used for Union troops
	Subarrange by number or name of regiment, A-Z. By author, A-Z
510.9	Other (not A-Z)
	For the seceded states, this subdivision is used for Union troops
	History of a town or county's participation in the Civil War, and local lists of soldiers, are classed in local history (F1-900). If, however, the town was the seat of military operations, as Chambersburg, Pa., the literature is found in E471-478, or where several sieges or battles are covered, in E470.2-.9 (e.g., a history of all military operations around Richmond)
	Maine
	Including biography: Abner Coburn, Israel Washburn, etc.
511	General works
511.1	Official publications on the raising, equipment, and service of the troops in the war
511.2	Adjutant Generals' reports for 1861-1865
511.3	Lists of soldiers. Lists of the state's dead
	For the seceded states, this subdivision is used for Union troops
511.4	Histories of the states' troops
	Including collected biographies or lists of officers, general associations of survivors, the draft, state brigades, state memorials and monuments, the state's battle flags, lists of citizens serving in organizations of other states
	For the seceded states, this subdivision is used for Union troops
	Military organizations
	For the seceded states, this subdivision is used for Union troops
511.5	Infantry
	For the seceded states, this subdivision is used for Union troops
	Subarrange by number or name of regiment, A-Z. By author, A-Z, e.g. E527.5.L6, Logan Guards
511.6	Cavalry
	For the seceded states, this subdivision is used for Union troops
	Subarrange by number or name of regiment, A-Z. By author, A-Z
511.7	Artillery, Heavy
	For the seceded states, this subdivision is used for Union troops
	Subarrange by number or name of regiment, A-Z. By author, A-Z
511.8	Artillery, Light
	For the seceded states, this subdivision is used for Union troops
	Subarrange by number or name of regiment, A-Z. By author, A-Z
511.9	Other (not A-Z)
	For the seceded states, this subdivision is used for Union troops
	History of a town or county's participation in the Civil War, and local lists of soldiers, are classed in local history (F1-900). If, however, the town was the seat of military operations, as Chambersburg, Pa., the literature is found in E471-478, or where several sieges or battles are covered, in E470.2-.9 (e.g., a history of all military operations around Richmond)
	Maryland
	For Confederate history, see E566.1+
	For campaigns and battles, see E470.2+, E471+
	For prisoners of state, see E458.8
512	General works
512.1	Official publications on the raising, equipment, and service of the troops in the war
512.2	Adjutant Generals' reports for 1861-1865

The Civil War, 1861-1865
Armies. Troops
The Union Army

495-537	By state
	Maryland — Continued
512.3	Lists of soldiers. Lists of the state's dead

For the seceded states, this subdivision is used for Union troops

512.4   Histories of the states' troops

Including collected biographies or lists of officers, general associations of survivors, the draft, state brigades, state memorials and monuments, the state's battle flags, lists of citizens serving in organizations of other states

For the seceded states, this subdivision is used for Union troops

Military organizations

For the seceded states, this subdivision is used for Union troops

512.5   Infantry

For the seceded states, this subdivision is used for Union troops

Subarrange by number or name of regiment, A-Z. By author, A-Z, e.g. E527.5.L6, Logan Guards

512.6   Cavalry

For the seceded states, this subdivision is used for Union troops

Subarrange by number or name of regiment, A-Z. By author, A-Z

512.7   Artillery, Heavy

For the seceded states, this subdivision is used for Union troops

Subarrange by number or name of regiment, A-Z. By author, A-Z

512.8   Artillery, Light

For the seceded states, this subdivision is used for Union troops

Subarrange by number or name of regiment, A-Z. By author, A-Z

512.9   Other (not A-Z)

For the seceded states, this subdivision is used for Union troops

History of a town or county's participation in the Civil War, and local lists of soldiers, are classed in local history (F1-900). If, however, the town was the seat of military operations, as Chambersburg, Pa., the literature is found in E471-478, or where several sieges or battles are covered, in E470.2-.9 (e.g., a history of all military operations around Richmond)

Massachusetts

Including biography: John Albion Andrew

513	General works
513.1	Official publications on the raising, equipment, and service of the troops in the war
513.2	Adjutant Generals' reports for 1861-1865
513.3	Lists of soldiers. Lists of the state's dead

For the seceded states, this subdivision is used for Union troops

513.4   Histories of the states' troops

Including collected biographies or lists of officers, general associations of survivors, the draft, state brigades, state memorials and monuments, the state's battle flags, lists of citizens serving in organizations of other states

For the seceded states, this subdivision is used for Union troops

Military organizations

For the seceded states, this subdivision is used for Union troops

513.5   Infantry

For the seceded states, this subdivision is used for Union troops

Subarrange by number or name of regiment, A-Z. By author, A-Z, e.g. E527.5.L6, Logan Guards

513.6   Cavalry

For the seceded states, this subdivision is used for Union troops

Subarrange by number or name of regiment, A-Z. By author, A-Z

513.7   Artillery, Heavy

For the seceded states, this subdivision is used for Union troops

Subarrange by number or name of regiment, A-Z. By author, A-Z

513.8   Artillery, Light

For the seceded states, this subdivision is used for Union troops

The Civil War, 1861-1865
Armies. Troops
The Union Army

495-537	By state
	Massachusetts
	Military organizations
513.8	Artillery, Light — Continued

Subarrange by number or name of regiment, A-Z. By author, A-Z

513.9	Other (not A-Z)

For the seceded states, this subdivision is used for Union troops

History of a town or county's participation in the Civil War, and local lists of soldiers, are classed in local history (F1-900). If, however, the town was the seat of military operations, as Chambersburg, Pa., the literature is found in E471-478, or where several sieges or battles are covered, in E470.2-.9 (e.g., a history of all military operations around Richmond)

	Michigan
514	General works
514.1	Official publications on the raising, equipment, and service of the troops in the war
514.2	Adjutant Generals' reports for 1861-1865
514.3	Lists of soldiers. Lists of the state's dead

For the seceded states, this subdivision is used for Union troops

514.4	Histories of the states' troops

Including collected biographies or lists of officers, general associations of survivors, the draft, state brigades, state memorials and monuments, the state's battle flags, lists of citizens serving in organizations of other states

For the seceded states, this subdivision is used for Union troops

Military organizations

For the seceded states, this subdivision is used for Union troops

514.5	Infantry

For the seceded states, this subdivision is used for Union troops

Subarrange by number or name of regiment, A-Z. By author, A-Z, e.g. E527.5.L6, Logan Guards

514.6	Cavalry

For the seceded states, this subdivision is used for Union troops

Subarrange by number or name of regiment, A-Z. By author, A-Z

514.7	Artillery, Heavy

For the seceded states, this subdivision is used for Union troops

Subarrange by number or name of regiment, A-Z. By author, A-Z

514.8	Artillery, Light

For the seceded states, this subdivision is used for Union troops

Subarrange by number or name of regiment, A-Z. By author, A-Z

514.9	Other (not A-Z)

For the seceded states, this subdivision is used for Union troops

History of a town or county's participation in the Civil War, and local lists of soldiers, are classed in local history (F1-900). If, however, the town was the seat of military operations, as Chambersburg, Pa., the literature is found in E471-478, or where several sieges or battles are covered, in E470.2-.9 (e.g., a history of all military operations around Richmond)

	Minnesota

For Indian wars, see E83.86, E83.863

515	General works
515.1	Official publications on the raising, equipment, and service of the troops in the war
515.2	Adjutant Generals' reports for 1861-1865
515.3	Lists of soldiers. Lists of the state's dead

For the seceded states, this subdivision is used for Union troops

515.4	Histories of the states' troops

Including collected biographies or lists of officers, general associations of survivors, the draft, state brigades, state memorials and monuments, the state's battle flags, lists of citizens serving in organizations of other states

For the seceded states, this subdivision is used for Union troops

The Civil War, 1861-1865
  Armies. Troops
    The Union Army
495-537   By state
                  Minnesota — Continued
                    Military organizations
                        For the seceded states, this subdivision is used for Union troops
515.5   Infantry
                            For the seceded states, this subdivision is used for Union troops
                            Subarrange by number or name of regiment, A-Z. By author, A-Z, e.g. E527.5.L6,
                                Logan Guards
515.6   Cavalry
                            For the seceded states, this subdivision is used for Union troops
                            Subarrange by number or name of regiment, A-Z. By author, A-Z
515.7   Artillery, Heavy
                            For the seceded states, this subdivision is used for Union troops
                            Subarrange by number or name of regiment, A-Z. By author, A-Z
515.8   Artillery, Light
                            For the seceded states, this subdivision is used for Union troops
                            Subarrange by number or name of regiment, A-Z. By author, A-Z
515.9   Other (not A-Z)
                            For the seceded states, this subdivision is used for Union troops
                            History of a town or county's participation in the Civil War, and local lists of
                                soldiers, are classed in local history (F1-900). If, however, the town was the seat
                                of military operations, as Chambersburg, Pa., the literature is found in E471-
                                478, or where several sieges or battles are covered, in E470.2-.9 (e.g., a history
                                of all military operations around Richmond)
                  Mississippi
                      For Confederate history, see E471.52, E568.1+
                      For campaigns and battles, see E470.6-.7, E471+
516   General works
516.1   Official publications on the raising, equipment, and service of the troops in the war
516.2   Adjutant Generals' reports for 1861-1865
516.3   Lists of soldiers. Lists of the state's dead
                        For the seceded states, this subdivision is used for Union troops
516.4   Histories of the states' troops
                        Including collected biographies or lists of officers, general associations of survivors,
                            the draft, state brigades, state memorials and monuments, the state's battle flags,
                            lists of citizens serving in organizations of other states
                        For the seceded states, this subdivision is used for Union troops
                    Military organizations
                        For the seceded states, this subdivision is used for Union troops
516.5   Infantry
                            For the seceded states, this subdivision is used for Union troops
                            Subarrange by number or name of regiment, A-Z. By author, A-Z, e.g. E527.5.L6,
                                Logan Guards
516.6   Cavalry
                            For the seceded states, this subdivision is used for Union troops
                            Subarrange by number or name of regiment, A-Z. By author, A-Z
516.7   Artillery, Heavy
                            For the seceded states, this subdivision is used for Union troops
                            Subarrange by number or name of regiment, A-Z. By author, A-Z
516.8   Artillery, Light
                            For the seceded states, this subdivision is used for Union troops
                            Subarrange by number or name of regiment, A-Z. By author, A-Z
516.9   Other (not A-Z)
                            For the seceded states, this subdivision is used for Union troops

The Civil War, 1861-1865
Armies. Troops
The Union Army

495-537   By state

Mississippi

Military organizations

516.9   Other (not A-Z) — Continued

*History of a town or county's participation in the Civil War, and local lists of
soldiers, are classed in local history (F1-900). If, however, the town was the seat
of military operations, as Chambersburg, Pa., the literature is found in E471-
478, or where several sieges or battles are covered, in E470.2-.9 (e.g., a history
of all military operations around Richmond)*

Missouri

For Confederate history, see E471.57, E569.1+
For campaigns and battles, see E470.4+, E470.9, E471+

517   General works
517.1   Official publications on the raising, equipment, and service of the troops in the war
517.2   Adjutant Generals' reports for 1861-1865
517.3   Lists of soldiers. Lists of the state's dead
For the seceded states, this subdivision is used for Union troops
517.4   Histories of the states' troops
*Including collected biographies or lists of officers, general associations of survivors,
the draft, state brigades, state memorials and monuments, the state's battle flags,
lists of citizens serving in organizations of other states*
For the seceded states, this subdivision is used for Union troops

Military organizations
For the seceded states, this subdivision is used for Union troops

517.5   Infantry
For the seceded states, this subdivision is used for Union troops
*Subarrange by number or name of regiment, A-Z. By author, A-Z, e.g. E527.5.L6,
Logan Guards*
517.6   Cavalry
For the seceded states, this subdivision is used for Union troops
Subarrange by number or name of regiment, A-Z. By author, A-Z
517.7   Artillery, Heavy
For the seceded states, this subdivision is used for Union troops
Subarrange by number or name of regiment, A-Z. By author, A-Z
517.8   Artillery, Light
For the seceded states, this subdivision is used for Union troops
Subarrange by number or name of regiment, A-Z. By author, A-Z
517.9   Other (not A-Z)
For the seceded states, this subdivision is used for Union troops
*History of a town or county's participation in the Civil War, and local lists of
soldiers, are classed in local history (F1-900). If, however, the town was the seat
of military operations, as Chambersburg, Pa., the literature is found in E471-
478, or where several sieges or battles are covered, in E470.2-.9 (e.g., a history
of all military operations around Richmond)*

Nebraska

518   General works
518.1   Official publications on the raising, equipment, and service of the troops in the war
518.2   Adjutant Generals' reports for 1861-1865
518.3   Lists of soldiers. Lists of the state's dead
For the seceded states, this subdivision is used for Union troops
518.4   Histories of the states' troops
*Including collected biographies or lists of officers, general associations of survivors,
the draft, state brigades, state memorials and monuments, the state's battle flags,
lists of citizens serving in organizations of other states*
For the seceded states, this subdivision is used for Union troops

Military organizations
For the seceded states, this subdivision is used for Union troops

The Civil War, 1861-1865
Armies. Troops
The Union Army

	By state
495-537	Nebraska

Military organizations — Continued

518.5   Infantry
For the seceded states, this subdivision is used for Union troops
Subarrange by number or name of regiment, A-Z. By author, A-Z, e.g. E527.5.L6,
Logan Guards

518.6   Cavalry
For the seceded states, this subdivision is used for Union troops
Subarrange by number or name of regiment, A-Z. By author, A-Z

518.7   Artillery, Heavy
For the seceded states, this subdivision is used for Union troops
Subarrange by number or name of regiment, A-Z. By author, A-Z

518.8   Artillery, Light
For the seceded states, this subdivision is used for Union troops
Subarrange by number or name of regiment, A-Z. By author, A-Z

518.9   Other (not A-Z)
For the seceded states, this subdivision is used for Union troops
History of a town or county's participation in the Civil War, and local lists of
soldiers, are classed in local history (F1-900). If, however, the town was the seat
of military operations, as Chambersburg, Pa., the literature is found in E471-
478, or where several sieges or battles are covered, in E470.2-.9 (e.g., a history
of all military operations around Richmond)

Nevada

519   General works
519.1   Official publications on the raising, equipment, and service of the troops in the war
519.2   Adjutant Generals' reports for 1861-1865
519.3   Lists of soldiers. Lists of the state's dead
For the seceded states, this subdivision is used for Union troops

519.4   Histories of the states' troops
Including collected biographies or lists of officers, general associations of survivors,
the draft, state brigades, state memorials and monuments, the state's battle flags,
lists of citizens serving in organizations of other states
For the seceded states, this subdivision is used for Union troops

Military organizations
For the seceded states, this subdivision is used for Union troops

519.5   Infantry
For the seceded states, this subdivision is used for Union troops
Subarrange by number or name of regiment, A-Z. By author, A-Z, e.g. E527.5.L6,
Logan Guards

519.6   Cavalry
For the seceded states, this subdivision is used for Union troops
Subarrange by number or name of regiment, A-Z. By author, A-Z

519.7   Artillery, Heavy
For the seceded states, this subdivision is used for Union troops
Subarrange by number or name of regiment, A-Z. By author, A-Z

519.8   Artillery, Light
For the seceded states, this subdivision is used for Union troops
Subarrange by number or name of regiment, A-Z. By author, A-Z

519.9   Other (not A-Z)
For the seceded states, this subdivision is used for Union troops
History of a town or county's participation in the Civil War, and local lists of
soldiers, are classed in local history (F1-900). If, however, the town was the seat
of military operations, as Chambersburg, Pa., the literature is found in E471-
478, or where several sieges or battles are covered, in E470.2-.9 (e.g., a history
of all military operations around Richmond)

	The Civil War, 1861-1865
	Armies. Troops
	The Union Army
495-537	By state — Continued
	New Hampshire
520	General works
520.1	Official publications on the raising, equipment, and service of the troops in the war
520.2	Adjutant Generals' reports for 1861-1865
520.3	Lists of soldiers. Lists of the state's dead

For the seceded states, this subdivision is used for Union troops

| 520.4 | Histories of the states' troops |

Including collected biographies or lists of officers, general associations of survivors, the draft, state brigades, state memorials and monuments, the state's battle flags, lists of citizens serving in organizations of other states

For the seceded states, this subdivision is used for Union troops

Military organizations

For the seceded states, this subdivision is used for Union troops

| 520.5 | Infantry |

For the seceded states, this subdivision is used for Union troops

Subarrange by number or name of regiment, A-Z. By author, A-Z, e.g. E527.5.L6, Logan Guards

| 520.6 | Cavalry |

For the seceded states, this subdivision is used for Union troops

Subarrange by number or name of regiment, A-Z. By author, A-Z

| 520.7 | Artillery, Heavy |

For the seceded states, this subdivision is used for Union troops

Subarrange by number or name of regiment, A-Z. By author, A-Z

| 520.8 | Artillery, Light |

For the seceded states, this subdivision is used for Union troops

Subarrange by number or name of regiment, A-Z. By author, A-Z

| 520.9 | Other (not A-Z) |

For the seceded states, this subdivision is used for Union troops

History of a town or county's participation in the Civil War, and local lists of soldiers, are classed in local history (F1-900). If, however, the town was the seat of military operations, as Chambersburg, Pa., the literature is found in E471-478, or where several sieges or battles are covered, in E470.2-.9 (e.g., a history of all military operations around Richmond)

New Jersey

Including biography: Joel Parker, etc.

521	General works
521.1	Official publications on the raising, equipment, and service of the troops in the war
521.2	Adjutant Generals' reports for 1861-1865
521.3	Lists of soldiers. Lists of the state's dead

For the seceded states, this subdivision is used for Union troops

| 521.4 | Histories of the states' troops |

Including collected biographies or lists of officers, general associations of survivors, the draft, state brigades, state memorials and monuments, the state's battle flags, lists of citizens serving in organizations of other states

For the seceded states, this subdivision is used for Union troops

Military organizations

For the seceded states, this subdivision is used for Union troops

| 521.5 | Infantry |

For the seceded states, this subdivision is used for Union troops

Subarrange by number or name of regiment, A-Z. By author, A-Z, e.g. E527.5.L6, Logan Guards

| 521.6 | Cavalry |

For the seceded states, this subdivision is used for Union troops

Subarrange by number or name of regiment, A-Z. By author, A-Z

| 521.7 | Artillery, Heavy |

For the seceded states, this subdivision is used for Union troops

	The Civil War, 1861-1865
	Armies. Troops
	The Union Army
495-537	By state
	New Jersey
	Military organizations
521.7	Artillery, Heavy — Continued
	Subarrange by number or name of regiment, A-Z. By author, A-Z
521.8	Artillery, Light
	For the seceded states, this subdivision is used for Union troops
	Subarrange by number or name of regiment, A-Z. By author, A-Z
521.9	Other (not A-Z)
	For the seceded states, this subdivision is used for Union troops
	History of a town or county's participation in the Civil War, and local lists of soldiers, are classed in local history (F1-900). If, however, the town was the seat of military operations, as Chambersburg, Pa., the literature is found in E471-478, or where several sieges or battles are covered, in E470.2-.9 (e.g., a history of all military operations around Richmond)
	New Mexico
	For Confederate history, see E471.56, E571.1+
	For campaigns and battles, see E470.9, E471+
522	General works
522.1	Official publications on the raising, equipment, and service of the troops in the war
522.2	Adjutant Generals' reports for 1861-1865
522.3	Lists of soldiers. Lists of the state's dead
	For the seceded states, this subdivision is used for Union troops
522.4	Histories of the states' troops
	Including collected biographies or lists of officers, general associations of survivors, the draft, state brigades, state memorials and monuments, the state's battle flags, lists of citizens serving in organizations of other states
	For the seceded states, this subdivision is used for Union troops
	Military organizations
	For the seceded states, this subdivision is used for Union troops
522.5	Infantry
	For the seceded states, this subdivision is used for Union troops
	Subarrange by number or name of regiment, A-Z. By author, A-Z, e.g. E527.5.L6, Logan Guards
522.6	Cavalry
	For the seceded states, this subdivision is used for Union troops
	Subarrange by number or name of regiment, A-Z. By author, A-Z
522.7	Artillery, Heavy
	For the seceded states, this subdivision is used for Union troops
	Subarrange by number or name of regiment, A-Z. By author, A-Z
522.8	Artillery, Light
	For the seceded states, this subdivision is used for Union troops
	Subarrange by number or name of regiment, A-Z. By author, A-Z
522.9	Other (not A-Z)
	For the seceded states, this subdivision is used for Union troops
	History of a town or county's participation in the Civil War, and local lists of soldiers, are classed in local history (F1-900). If, however, the town was the seat of military operations, as Chambersburg, Pa., the literature is found in E471-478, or where several sieges or battles are covered, in E470.2-.9 (e.g., a history of all military operations around Richmond)
	New York
	Cf. F128.44, Draft riots, New York City
523	General works
523.1	Official publications on the raising, equipment, and service of the troops in the war
523.2	Adjutant Generals' reports for 1861-1865
523.3	Lists of soldiers. Lists of the state's dead
	For the seceded states, this subdivision is used for Union troops

The Civil War, 1861-1865
Armies. Troops
The Union Army

495-537	By state
	New York — Continued
523.4	Histories of the states' troops

Including collected biographies or lists of officers, general associations of survivors, the draft, state brigades, state memorials and monuments, the state's battle flags, lists of citizens serving in organizations of other states
For the seceded states, this subdivision is used for Union troops

Military organizations
For the seceded states, this subdivision is used for Union troops

523.5	Infantry

For the seceded states, this subdivision is used for Union troops
Subarrange by number or name of regiment, A-Z. By author, A-Z, e.g. E527.5.L6, Logan Guards

523.6	Cavalry

For the seceded states, this subdivision is used for Union troops
Subarrange by number or name of regiment, A-Z. By author, A-Z

523.7	Artillery, Heavy

For the seceded states, this subdivision is used for Union troops
Subarrange by number or name of regiment, A-Z. By author, A-Z

523.8	Artillery, Light

For the seceded states, this subdivision is used for Union troops
Subarrange by number or name of regiment, A-Z. By author, A-Z

523.9	Other (not A-Z)

For the seceded states, this subdivision is used for Union troops
History of a town or county's participation in the Civil War, and local lists of soldiers, are classed in local history (F1-900). If, however, the town was the seat of military operations, as Chambersburg, Pa., the literature is found in E471-478, or where several sieges or battles are covered, in E470.2-.9 (e.g., a history of all military operations around Richmond)

North Carolina
For Confederate history, see E471.54, E573.1+
For campaigns and battles, see E470.6, E471+

524	General works
524.1	Official publications on the raising, equipment, and service of the troops in the war
524.2	Adjutant Generals' reports for 1861-1865
524.3	Lists of soldiers. Lists of the state's dead

For the seceded states, this subdivision is used for Union troops

524.4	Histories of the states' troops

Including collected biographies or lists of officers, general associations of survivors, the draft, state brigades, state memorials and monuments, the state's battle flags, lists of citizens serving in organizations of other states
For the seceded states, this subdivision is used for Union troops

Military organizations
For the seceded states, this subdivision is used for Union troops

524.5	Infantry

For the seceded states, this subdivision is used for Union troops
Subarrange by number or name of regiment, A-Z. By author, A-Z, e.g. E527.5.L6, Logan Guards

524.6	Cavalry

For the seceded states, this subdivision is used for Union troops
Subarrange by number or name of regiment, A-Z. By author, A-Z

524.7	Artillery, Heavy

For the seceded states, this subdivision is used for Union troops
Subarrange by number or name of regiment, A-Z. By author, A-Z

524.8	Artillery, Light

For the seceded states, this subdivision is used for Union troops
Subarrange by number or name of regiment, A-Z. By author, A-Z

	The Civil War, 1861-1865
	Armies. Troops
	The Union Army
495-537	By state
	North Carolina
	Military organizations — Continued
524.9	Other (not A-Z)

For the seceded states, this subdivision is used for Union troops

History of a town or county's participation in the Civil War, and local lists of soldiers, are classed in local history (F1-900). If, however, the town was the seat of military operations, as Chambersburg, Pa., the literature is found in E471-478, or where several sieges or battles are covered, in E470.2-.9 (e.g., a history of all military operations around Richmond)

North Dakota, *see* E530.1+

Ohio

For campaigns and battles, see E470.4+, E471+

525	General works
525.1	Official publications on the raising, equipment, and service of the troops in the war
525.2	Adjutant Generals' reports for 1861-1865
525.3	Lists of soldiers. Lists of the state's dead

For the seceded states, this subdivision is used for Union troops

525.4	Histories of the states' troops

Including collected biographies or lists of officers, general associations of survivors, the draft, state brigades, state memorials and monuments, the state's battle flags, lists of citizens serving in organizations of other states

For the seceded states, this subdivision is used for Union troops

Military organizations

For the seceded states, this subdivision is used for Union troops

525.5	Infantry

For the seceded states, this subdivision is used for Union troops

Subarrange by number or name of regiment, A-Z. By author, A-Z, e.g. E527.5.L6, Logan Guards

525.6	Cavalry

For the seceded states, this subdivision is used for Union troops

Subarrange by number or name of regiment, A-Z. By author, A-Z

525.7	Artillery, Heavy

For the seceded states, this subdivision is used for Union troops

Subarrange by number or name of regiment, A-Z. By author, A-Z

525.8	Artillery, Light

For the seceded states, this subdivision is used for Union troops

Subarrange by number or name of regiment, A-Z. By author, A-Z

525.9	Other (not A-Z)

For the seceded states, this subdivision is used for Union troops

History of a town or county's participation in the Civil War, and local lists of soldiers, are classed in local history (F1-900). If, however, the town was the seat of military operations, as Chambersburg, Pa., the literature is found in E471-478, or where several sieges or battles are covered, in E470.2-.9 (e.g., a history of all military operations around Richmond)

Oklahoma, *see* E505.95

Oregon

526	General works
526.1	Official publications on the raising, equipment, and service of the troops in the war
526.2	Adjutant Generals' reports for 1861-1865
526.3	Lists of soldiers. Lists of the state's dead

For the seceded states, this subdivision is used for Union troops

526.4	Histories of the states' troops

Including collected biographies or lists of officers, general associations of survivors, the draft, state brigades, state memorials and monuments, the state's battle flags, lists of citizens serving in organizations of other states

For the seceded states, this subdivision is used for Union troops

The Civil War, 1861-1865
    Armies. Troops
       The Union Army

495-537   By state
           Oregon — Continued
             Military organizations
               For the seceded states, this subdivision is used for Union troops

526.5   Infantry
                 For the seceded states, this subdivision is used for Union troops
                 Subarrange by number or name of regiment, A-Z. By author, A-Z, e.g. E527.5.L6,
                   Logan Guards

526.6   Cavalry
                 For the seceded states, this subdivision is used for Union troops
                 Subarrange by number or name of regiment, A-Z. By author, A-Z

526.7   Artillery, Heavy
                 For the seceded states, this subdivision is used for Union troops
                 Subarrange by number or name of regiment, A-Z. By author, A-Z

526.8   Artillery, Light
                 For the seceded states, this subdivision is used for Union troops
                 Subarrange by number or name of regiment, A-Z. By author, A-Z

526.9   Other (not A-Z)
                 For the seceded states, this subdivision is used for Union troops
                 History of a town or county's participation in the Civil War, and local lists of
                   soldiers, are classed in local history (F1-900). If, however, the town was the seat
                   of military operations, as Chambersburg, Pa., the literature is found in E471-
                   478, or where several sieges or battles are covered, in E470.2-.9 (e.g., a history
                   of all military operations around Richmond)

           Pennsylvania
            For campaigns and battles, see E470.2+, E471+

527   General works
527.1   Official publications on the raising, equipment, and service of the troops in the war
527.2   Adjutant Generals' reports for 1861-1865
527.3   Lists of soldiers. Lists of the state's dead
            For the seceded states, this subdivision is used for Union troops
527.4   Histories of the states' troops
            Including collected biographies or lists of officers, general associations of survivors,
              the draft, state brigades, state memorials and monuments, the state's battle flags,
              lists of citizens serving in organizations of other states
            For the seceded states, this subdivision is used for Union troops
            Military organizations
            For the seceded states, this subdivision is used for Union troops

527.5   Infantry
                 For the seceded states, this subdivision is used for Union troops
                 Subarrange by number or name of regiment, A-Z. By author, A-Z, e.g. E527.5.L6,
                   Logan Guards

527.6   Cavalry
                 For the seceded states, this subdivision is used for Union troops
                 Subarrange by number or name of regiment, A-Z. By author, A-Z

527.7   Artillery, Heavy
                 For the seceded states, this subdivision is used for Union troops
                 Subarrange by number or name of regiment, A-Z. By author, A-Z

527.8   Artillery, Light
                 For the seceded states, this subdivision is used for Union troops
                 Subarrange by number or name of regiment, A-Z. By author, A-Z

527.9   Other (not A-Z)
                 For the seceded states, this subdivision is used for Union troops

The Civil War, 1861-1865
    Armies. Troops
       The Union Army

495-537	By state
	Pennsylvania
	Military organizations
527.9	Other (not A-Z) — Continued
	History of a town or county's participation in the Civil War, and local lists of soldiers, are classed in local history (F1-900). If, however, the town was the seat of military operations, as Chambersburg, Pa., the literature is found in E471-478, or where several sieges or battles are covered, in E470.2-.9 (e.g., a history of all military operations around Richmond)
	Rhode Island
528	General works
528.1	Official publications on the raising, equipment, and service of the troops in the war
528.2	Adjutant Generals' reports for 1861-1865
528.3	Lists of soldiers. Lists of the state's dead
	For the seceded states, this subdivision is used for Union troops
528.4	Histories of the states' troops
	Including collected biographies or lists of officers, general associations of survivors, the draft, state brigades, state memorials and monuments, the state's battle flags, lists of citizens serving in organizations of other states
	For the seceded states, this subdivision is used for Union troops
	Military organizations
	For the seceded states, this subdivision is used for Union troops
528.5	Infantry
	For the seceded states, this subdivision is used for Union troops
	Subarrange by number or name of regiment, A-Z. By author, A-Z, e.g. E527.5.L6, Logan Guards
528.6	Cavalry
	For the seceded states, this subdivision is used for Union troops
	Subarrange by number or name of regiment, A-Z. By author, A-Z
528.7	Artillery, Heavy
	For the seceded states, this subdivision is used for Union troops
	Subarrange by number or name of regiment, A-Z. By author, A-Z
528.8	Artillery, Light
	For the seceded states, this subdivision is used for Union troops
	Subarrange by number or name of regiment, A-Z. By author, A-Z
528.9	Other (not A-Z)
	For the seceded states, this subdivision is used for Union troops
	History of a town or county's participation in the Civil War, and local lists of soldiers, are classed in local history (F1-900). If, however, the town was the seat of military operations, as Chambersburg, Pa., the literature is found in E471-478, or where several sieges or battles are covered, in E470.2-.9 (e.g., a history of all military operations around Richmond)
	South Carolina
	For Confederate history, see E471.1, E577.1+
	For campaigns and battles, see E470.6, E471+
	Cf. E185.93.S7, Afro-Americans in the Sea Island District
529	General works
529.1	Official publications on the raising, equipment, and service of the troops in the war
529.2	Adjutant Generals' reports for 1861-1865
529.3	Lists of soldiers. Lists of the state's dead
	For the seceded states, this subdivision is used for Union troops
529.4	Histories of the states' troops
	Including collected biographies or lists of officers, general associations of survivors, the draft, state brigades, state memorials and monuments, the state's battle flags, lists of citizens serving in organizations of other states
	For the seceded states, this subdivision is used for Union troops

The Civil War, 1861-1865
Armies. Troops
The Union Army
By state
South Carolina — Continued
Military organizations
For the seceded states, this subdivision is used for Union troops
529.5 Infantry
For the seceded states, this subdivision is used for Union troops
Subarrange by number or name of regiment, A-Z. By author, A-Z, e.g. E527.5.L6, Logan Guards
529.6 Cavalry
For the seceded states, this subdivision is used for Union troops
Subarrange by number or name of regiment, A-Z. By author, A-Z
529.7 Artillery, Heavy
For the seceded states, this subdivision is used for Union troops
Subarrange by number or name of regiment, A-Z. By author, A-Z
529.8 Artillery, Light
For the seceded states, this subdivision is used for Union troops
Subarrange by number or name of regiment, A-Z. By author, A-Z
529.9 Other (not A-Z)
For the seceded states, this subdivision is used for Union troops
History of a town or county's participation in the Civil War, and local lists of soldiers, are classed in local history (F1-900). If, however, the town was the seat of military operations, as Chambersburg, Pa., the literature is found in E471-478, or where several sieges or battles are covered, in E470.2-.9 (e.g., a history of all military operations around Richmond)
South Dakota. Dakota Territory
For Indian wars, see E83.86, E83.863
530 General works
530.1 Official publications on the raising, equipment, and service of the troops in the war
530.2 Adjutant Generals' reports for 1861-1865
530.3 Lists of soldiers. Lists of the state's dead
For the seceded states, this subdivision is used for Union troops
530.4 Histories of the states' troops
Including collected biographies or lists of officers, general associations of survivors, the draft, state brigades, state memorials and monuments, the state's battle flags, lists of citizens serving in organizations of other states
For the seceded states, this subdivision is used for Union troops
Military organizations
For the seceded states, this subdivision is used for Union troops
530.5 Infantry
For the seceded states, this subdivision is used for Union troops
Subarrange by number or name of regiment, A-Z. By author, A-Z, e.g. E527.5.L6, Logan Guards
530.6 Cavalry
For the seceded states, this subdivision is used for Union troops
Subarrange by number or name of regiment, A-Z. By author, A-Z
530.7 Artillery, Heavy
For the seceded states, this subdivision is used for Union troops
Subarrange by number or name of regiment, A-Z. By author, A-Z
530.8 Artillery, Light
For the seceded states, this subdivision is used for Union troops
Subarrange by number or name of regiment, A-Z. By author, A-Z
530.9 Other (not A-Z)
For the seceded states, this subdivision is used for Union troops

The Civil War, 1861-1865
Armies. Troops
The Union Army
495-537   By state
South Dakota. Dakota Territory
Military organizations
530.9   Other (not A-Z) — Continued
History of a town or county's participation in the Civil War, and local lists of
soldiers, are classed in local history (F1-900). If, however, the town was the seat
of military operations, as Chambersburg, Pa., the literature is found in E471-
478, or where several sieges or battles are covered, in E470.2-.9 (e.g., a history
of all military operations around Richmond)
Tennessee
For Confederate history, see E579.1+
For campaigns and battles, see E470.4+, E471+
531   General works
531.1   Official publications on the raising, equipment, and service of the troops in the war
531.2   Adjutant Generals' reports for 1861-1865
531.3   Lists of soldiers. Lists of the state's dead
For the seceded states, this subdivision is used for Union troops
531.4   Histories of the states' troops
Including collected biographies or lists of officers, general associations of survivors,
the draft, state brigades, state memorials and monuments, the state's battle flags,
lists of citizens serving in organizations of other states
For the seceded states, this subdivision is used for Union troops
Military organizations
For the seceded states, this subdivision is used for Union troops
531.5   Infantry
For the seceded states, this subdivision is used for Union troops
Subarrange by number or name of regiment, A-Z. By author, A-Z, e.g. E527.5.L6,
Logan Guards
531.6   Cavalry
For the seceded states, this subdivision is used for Union troops
Subarrange by number or name of regiment, A-Z. By author, A-Z
531.7   Artillery, Heavy
For the seceded states, this subdivision is used for Union troops
Subarrange by number or name of regiment, A-Z. By author, A-Z
531.8   Artillery, Light
For the seceded states, this subdivision is used for Union troops
Subarrange by number or name of regiment, A-Z. By author, A-Z
531.9   Other (not A-Z)
For the seceded states, this subdivision is used for Union troops
History of a town or county's participation in the Civil War, and local lists of
soldiers, are classed in local history (F1-900). If, however, the town was the seat
of military operations, as Chambersburg, Pa., the literature is found in E471-
478, or where several sieges or battles are covered, in E470.2-.9 (e.g., a history
of all military operations around Richmond)
Texas
For Confederate history, see E471.56, E580.1+
For campaigns and battles, see E470.7, E470.9, E471+
532   General works
532.1   Official publications on the raising, equipment, and service of the troops in the war
532.2   Adjutant Generals' reports for 1861-1865
532.3   Lists of soldiers. Lists of the state's dead
For the seceded states, this subdivision is used for Union troops
532.4   Histories of the states' troops
Including collected biographies or lists of officers, general associations of survivors,
the draft, state brigades, state memorials and monuments, the state's battle flags,
lists of citizens serving in organizations of other states
For the seceded states, this subdivision is used for Union troops

The Civil War, 1861-1865

Armies. Troops

The Union Army

495-537	By state
	Texas — Continued
	Military organizations
	For the seceded states, this subdivision is used for Union troops
532.5	Infantry
	For the seceded states, this subdivision is used for Union troops
	Subarrange by number or name of regiment, A-Z. By author, A-Z, e.g. E527.5.L6, Logan Guards
532.6	Cavalry
	For the seceded states, this subdivision is used for Union troops
	Subarrange by number or name of regiment, A-Z. By author, A-Z
532.7	Artillery, Heavy
	For the seceded states, this subdivision is used for Union troops
	Subarrange by number or name of regiment, A-Z. By author, A-Z
532.8	Artillery, Light
	For the seceded states, this subdivision is used for Union troops
	Subarrange by number or name of regiment, A-Z. By author, A-Z
532.9	Other (not A-Z)
	For the seceded states, this subdivision is used for Union troops
	History of a town or county's participation in the Civil War, and local lists of soldiers, are classed in local history (F1-900). If, however, the town was the seat of military operations, as Chambersburg, Pa., the literature is found in E471-478, or where several sieges or battles are covered, in E470.2-.9 (e.g., a history of all military operations around Richmond)
532.95	Utah
	Not to be further subdivided
	Vermont
	Cf. E470.95, St. Albans Raid, 1864
533	General works
533.1	Official publications on the raising, equipment, and service of the troops in the war
533.2	Adjutant Generals' reports for 1861-1865
533.3	Lists of soldiers. Lists of the state's dead
	For the seceded states, this subdivision is used for Union troops
533.4	Histories of the states' troops
	Including collected biographies or lists of officers, general associations of survivors, the draft, state brigades, state memorials and monuments, the state's battle flags, lists of citizens serving in organizations of other states
	For the seceded states, this subdivision is used for Union troops
	Military organizations
	For the seceded states, this subdivision is used for Union troops
533.5	Infantry
	For the seceded states, this subdivision is used for Union troops
	Subarrange by number or name of regiment, A-Z. By author, A-Z, e.g. E527.5.L6, Logan Guards
533.6	Cavalry
	For the seceded states, this subdivision is used for Union troops
	Subarrange by number or name of regiment, A-Z. By author, A-Z
533.7	Artillery, Heavy
	For the seceded states, this subdivision is used for Union troops
	Subarrange by number or name of regiment, A-Z. By author, A-Z
533.8	Artillery, Light
	For the seceded states, this subdivision is used for Union troops
	Subarrange by number or name of regiment, A-Z. By author, A-Z
533.9	Other (not A-Z)
	For the seceded states, this subdivision is used for Union troops

The Civil War, 1861-1865
Armies. Troops
The Union Army

	By state
495-537	By state

                   Vermont

                       Military organizations

533.9   Other (not A-Z) — Continued

History of a town or county's participation in the Civil War, and local lists of soldiers, are classed in local history (F1-900). If, however, the town was the seat of military operations, as Chambersburg, Pa., the literature is found in E471-478, or where several sieges or battles are covered, in E470.2-.9 (e.g., a history of all military operations around Richmond)

                   Virginia

Including biography of Governor Francis Harrison Pierpont
For Confederate history, see E581.1+
For campaigns and battles, see E470.2+, E471+

534   General works

534.1   Official publications on the raising, equipment, and service of the troops in the war

534.2   Adjutant Generals' reports for 1861-1865

534.3   Lists of soldiers. Lists of the state's dead

For the seceded states, this subdivision is used for Union troops

534.4   Histories of the states' troops

Including collected biographies or lists of officers, general associations of survivors, the draft, state brigades, state memorials and monuments, the state's battle flags, lists of citizens serving in organizations of other states
For the seceded states, this subdivision is used for Union troops

                     Military organizations

For the seceded states, this subdivision is used for Union troops

534.5   Infantry

For the seceded states, this subdivision is used for Union troops
Subarrange by number or name of regiment, A-Z. By author, A-Z, e.g. E527.5.L6, Logan Guards

534.6   Cavalry

For the seceded states, this subdivision is used for Union troops
Subarrange by number or name of regiment, A-Z. By author, A-Z

534.7   Artillery, Heavy

For the seceded states, this subdivision is used for Union troops
Subarrange by number or name of regiment, A-Z. By author, A-Z

534.8   Artillery, Light

For the seceded states, this subdivision is used for Union troops
Subarrange by number or name of regiment, A-Z. By author, A-Z

534.9   Other (not A-Z)

For the seceded states, this subdivision is used for Union troops
History of a town or county's participation in the Civil War, and local lists of soldiers, are classed in local history (F1-900). If, however, the town was the seat of military operations, as Chambersburg, Pa., the literature is found in E471-478, or where several sieges or battles are covered, in E470.2-.9 (e.g., a history of all military operations around Richmond)

                   Washington (State)

535   General works

535.1   Official publications on the raising, equipment, and service of the troops in the war

535.2   Adjutant Generals' reports for 1861-1865

535.3   Lists of soldiers. Lists of the state's dead

For the seceded states, this subdivision is used for Union troops

535.4   Histories of the states' troops

Including collected biographies or lists of officers, general associations of survivors, the draft, state brigades, state memorials and monuments, the state's battle flags, lists of citizens serving in organizations of other states
For the seceded states, this subdivision is used for Union troops

	The Civil War, 1861-1865
	Armies. Troops
	The Union Army
495-537	By state
	Washington (State) — Continued
	Military organizations
	For the seceded states, this subdivision is used for Union troops
535.5	Infantry
	For the seceded states, this subdivision is used for Union troops
	Subarrange by number or name of regiment, A-Z, and by author, A-Z
535.6	Cavalry
	For the seceded states, this subdivision is used for Union troops
	Subarrange by number or name of regiment, A-Z. By author, A-Z
535.7	Artillery, Heavy
	For the seceded states, this subdivision is used for Union troops
	Subarrange by number or name of regiment, A-Z. By author, A-Z
535.8	Artillery, Light
	For the seceded states, this subdivision is used for Union troops
	Subarrange by number or name of regiment, A-Z. By author, A-Z
535.9	Other (not A-Z)
	For the seceded states, this subdivision is used for Union troops
	History of a town or county's participation in the Civil War, and local lists of soldiers, are classed in local history (F1-900). If, however, the town was the seat of military operations, as Chambersburg, Pa., the literature is found in E471-478, or where several sieges or battles are covered, in E470.2-.9 (e.g., a history of all military operations around Richmond)
	West Virginia
	For Confederate history, see E582.1+
	For campaigns and battles, see E470.4+, E471+
536	General works
536.1	Official publications on the raising, equipment, and service of the troops in the war
536.2	Adjutant Generals' reports for 1861-1865
536.3	Lists of soldiers. Lists of the state's dead
	For the seceded states, this subdivision is used for Union troops
536.4	Histories of the states' troops
	Including collected biographies or lists of officers, general associations of survivors, the draft, state brigades, state memorials and monuments, the state's battle flags, lists of citizens serving in organizations of other states
	For the seceded states, this subdivision is used for Union troops
	Military organizations
	For the seceded states, this subdivision is used for Union troops
536.5	Infantry
	For the seceded states, this subdivision is used for Union troops
	Subarrange by number or name of regiment, A-Z. By author, A-Z, e.g. E527.5.L6, Logan Guards
536.6	Cavalry
	For the seceded states, this subdivision is used for Union troops
	Subarrange by number or name of regiment, A-Z. By author, A-Z
536.7	Artillery, Heavy
	For the seceded states, this subdivision is used for Union troops
	Subarrange by number or name of regiment, A-Z. By author, A-Z
536.8	Artillery, Light
	For the seceded states, this subdivision is used for Union troops
	Subarrange by number or name of regiment, A-Z. By author, A-Z
536.9	Other (not A-Z)
	For the seceded states, this subdivision is used for Union troops

The Civil War, 1861-1865
Armies. Troops
The Union Army

495-537	By state
	West Virginia
	Military organizations
536.9	Other (not A-Z) — Continued

History of a town or county's participation in the Civil War, and local lists of soldiers, are classed in local history (F1-900). If, however, the town was the seat of military operations, as Chambersburg, Pa., the literature is found in E471-478, or where several sieges or battles are covered, in E470.2-.9 (e.g., a history of all military operations around Richmond)

	Wisconsin
537	General works
537.1	Official publications on the raising, equipment, and service of the troops in the war
537.2	Adjutant Generals' reports for 1861-1865
537.3	Lists of soldiers. Lists of the state's dead

For the seceded states, this subdivision is used for Union troops

537.4	Histories of the states' troops

Including collected biographies or lists of officers, general associations of survivors, the draft, state brigades, state memorials and monuments, the state's battle flags, lists of citizens serving in organizations of other states
For the seceded states, this subdivision is used for Union troops

Military organizations
For the seceded states, this subdivision is used for Union troops

537.5	Infantry

For the seceded states, this subdivision is used for Union troops
Subarrange by number or name of regiment, A-Z, and by author, A-Z

537.6	Cavalry

For the seceded states, this subdivision is used for Union troops
Subarrange by number or name of regiment, A-Z. By author, A-Z

537.7	Artillery, Heavy

For the seceded states, this subdivision is used for Union troops
Subarrange by number or name of regiment, A-Z. By author, A-Z

537.8	Artillery, Light

For the seceded states, this subdivision is used for Union troops
Subarrange by number or name of regiment, A-Z. By author, A-Z

537.9	Other (not A-Z)

For the seceded states, this subdivision is used for Union troops
History of a town or county's participation in the Civil War, and local lists of soldiers, are classed in local history (F1-900). If, however, the town was the seat of military operations, as Chambersburg, Pa., the literature is found in E471-478, or where several sieges or battles are covered, in E470.2-.9 (e.g., a history of all military operations around Richmond)

540.A-.Z	Participation by race, ethnic group, religious group, etc., A-Z
	Afro-Americans, *see* E540.N3
540.B4	Belgians
540.C3	Catholics
540.C47	Children
540.C5	Christians. Clergy. Churches (General)
540.C94	Czechs
540.F6	Foreigners (General). Immigrants
	Cf. E540.G3, Germans
	Cf. E540.H6, Hungarians
	Cf. E540.I6, Irish
540.F8	Friends
540.G3	Germans
540.H6	Hungarians
	Immigrants, *see* E540.F6

The Civil War, 1861-1865
  Armies. Troops
   The Union Army

540.A-.Z	Participation by race, ethnic group, religious group, etc., A-Z — Continued
540.I3	Indians
	For Indian wars, 1861-1865, see E83.86, E83.863
540.I6	Irish
540.I8	Italians
540.J5	Jews
540.M5	Methodists
540.M54	Mexicans
540.N3	Negroes. Afro-Americans
	For United States Afro-American regiments, see E492.9
	For state Afro-American regiments, see E495+
	Cf. E453, Slavery as affected by the war
540.P64	Poles
540.P9	Presbyterians
540.S8	Swedes
541.A-.Z	Colleges, schools, etc., and their participation, A-Z
	Cf. E586.A+, Confederate colleges, schools, etc.
	GALE NOTE *The cutter number(s) listed below have been given only as examples by the Library of Congress*
541.A5	Amherst College
541.B7	Bowdoin College
541.B8	Brown University
541.D22	Dartmouth College
541.E13	East Maine Conference Seminary, Bucksport
541.H2	Harvard University
541.I6	Iowa. University
541.M3	Marietta College
541.N2	Nazareth Hall, Nazareth, Pa
541.N5	New York. City College
541.O2	Oberlin College
541.P4	Pennsylvania. University
541.P9	Princeton University
541.U5	Union University, Schenectady, N.Y
541.W7	Williams College
541.Y2	Yale University

   The Confederate States Army

545	General works
	Including administration, organization, volunteering, conscription, statistics, transportation, supplies
	For amnesty, see E668
	For flags, see E646
	For separate armies, see E470.2+

    Arms of service

546	General works
	For individual corps, divisions, etc., which are confined to a single state, see E551-582 with subdivision .4 under each
546.4	Infantry
546.5	Cavalry
546.6	Artillery
546.7	Other (not A-Z)
	For Secret Service, Signal Corps, see E608
547	Corps. Divisions. Brigades
	Including associations, etc.
	For corps, divisions, and brigades confined to one state, see E551-582 with subdivision .4 under each
	GALE NOTE *The cutter number(s) listed below have been given only as examples by the Library of Congress*

The Civil War, 1861-1865
Armies. Troops
The Confederate States Army
Arms of service

547	Corps. Divisions. Brigades — Continued
547.C6	Cleburne's Division
547.F6	Forrest's Cavalry Corps
547.H2	Hampton's Cavalry Division
547.M8	Morgan's Cavalry Division
547.P5	Pickett's Division
547.W5	Wheeler's Cavalry Corps
548	Registers, lists of the dead and wounded, etc.

In general, lists of soldiers and officers from more than one state and veterans residing in particular states are classed here

For veterans residing in a county or town, see local biography in Class F

For lists of prisoners, see E615+

By state

Including individual Confederate States and border states with troops in the Confederate States Army

Under the border states (Kentucky, Maryland, Missouri, and West Virginia, and territory of New Mexico), the subdivisions ".3-.9" are used for Confederate troops, all general and political history of the state being classed in E509, E512, E517, E522, and E536

For military operations in a state, see E470.2+

For southern relief agencies, see E634

Alabama

For preliminaries of the war, see E471.52

For Union history, see E495.1+

For campaigns and battles, see E470.6, E471+

551	General works
551.1	Official publications on the raising, equipment, and service of the troops in the war
551.2	Adjutant Generals' reports for 1861-1865
551.3	Lists of soldiers. Lists of the state's dead
551.4	Histories of the states' troops

Including collected biographies or lists of officers, general associations of survivors, the draft, state brigades, state memorials and monuments, the state's battle flags, lists of citizens serving in organizations of other states

Military organizations

A comprehensive history of a state militia regiment is classed in UA50-549 even if Civil War service is given

For regimental associations of veterans, see the regiment

551.5	Infantry

Subarrange by number or name of regiment, A-Z. By author, A-Z, e.g. E527.5.L6, Logan Guards

551.6	Cavalry

Subarrange by number or name of regiment, A-Z. By author, A-Z

551.7	Artillery, Heavy

Subarrange by number or name of regiment, A-Z. By author, A-Z

551.8	Artillery, Light

Subarrange by number or name of regiment, A-Z. By author, A-Z

551.9	Other (not A-Z)

Arizona

552	General works
552.1	Official publications on the raising, equipment, and service of the troops in the war
552.2	Adjutant Generals' reports for 1861-1865
552.3	Lists of soldiers. Lists of the state's dead
552.4	Histories of the states' troops

Including collected biographies or lists of officers, general associations of survivors, the draft, state brigades, state memorials and monuments, the state's battle flags, lists of citizens serving in organizations of other states

The Civil War, 1861-1865
Armies. Troops
The Confederate States Army
By state
Arizona — Continued
Military organizations
552.5   Infantry
Subarrange by number or name of regiment, A-Z. By author, A-Z, e.g. E527.5.L6, Logan Guards
552.6   Cavalry
Subarrange by number or name of regiment, A-Z. By author, A-Z
552.7   Artillery, Heavy
Subarrange by number or name of regiment, A-Z. By author, A-Z
552.8   Artillery, Light
Subarrange by number or name of regiment, A-Z. By author, A-Z
552.9   Other (not A-Z)
Arkansas
For preliminaries of the war, see E471.57
For Union history, see E496.1+
For campaigns and battles, see E470.4+, E471+
553   General works
553.1   Official publications on the raising, equipment, and service of the troops in the war
553.2   Adjutant Generals' reports for 1861-1865
553.3   Lists of soldiers. Lists of the state's dead
553.4   Histories of the states' troops
Including collected biographies or lists of officers, general associations of survivors, the draft, state brigades, state memorials and monuments, the state's battle flags, lists of citizens serving in organizations of other states
Military organizations
553.5   Infantry
Subarrange by number or name of regiment, A-Z. By author, A-Z, e.g. E527.5.L6, Logan Guards
553.6   Cavalry
Subarrange by number or name of regiment, A-Z. By author, A-Z
553.7   Artillery, Heavy
Subarrange by number or name of regiment, A-Z. By author, A-Z
553.8   Artillery, Light
Subarrange by number or name of regiment, A-Z. By author, A-Z
553.9   Other (not A-Z)
Florida
For preliminaries of the war, see E471.53
For Union history, see E502.1+
For campaigns and battles, see E471+
558   General works
558.1   Official publications on the raising, equipment, and service of the troops in the war
558.2   Adjutant Generals' reports for 1861-1865
558.3   Lists of soldiers. Lists of the state's dead
558.4   Histories of the states' troops
Including collected biographies or lists of officers, general associations of survivors, the draft, state brigades, state memorials and monuments, the state's battle flags, lists of citizens serving in organizations of other states
Military organizations
558.5   Infantry
Subarrange by number or name of regiment, A-Z. By author, A-Z, e.g. E527.5.L6, Logan Guards
558.6   Cavalry
Subarrange by number or name of regiment, A-Z. By author, A-Z
558.7   Artillery, Heavy
Subarrange by number or name of regiment, A-Z. By author, A-Z

The Civil War, 1861-1865
Armies. Troops
The Confederate States Army
By state
Florida
Military organizations — Continued

558.8	Artillery, Light
	Subarrange by number or name of regiment, A-Z. By author, A-Z
558.9	Other (not A-Z)

Georgia
For preliminaries of the war, see E471.51
For Union history, see E503.1+
For campaigns and battles, see E470.6, E471+

559	General works
559.1	Official publications on the raising, equipment, and service of the troops in the war
559.2	Adjutant Generals' reports for 1861-1865
559.3	Lists of soldiers. Lists of the state's dead
559.4	Histories of the states' troops

Including collected biographies or lists of officers, general associations of survivors, the draft, state brigades, state memorials and monuments, the state's battle flags, lists of citizens serving in organizations of other states

Military organizations

559.5	Infantry
	Subarrange by number or name of regiment, A-Z. By author, A-Z, e.g. E527.5.L6, Logan Guards
559.6	Cavalry
	Subarrange by number or name of regiment, A-Z. By author, A-Z
559.7	Artillery, Heavy
	Subarrange by number or name of regiment, A-Z. By author, A-Z
559.8	Artillery, Light
	Subarrange by number or name of regiment, A-Z. By author, A-Z
559.9	Other (not A-Z)
561	Indian Territory

Not to be further subdivided
For preliminaries of the war, see E471.57
For campaigns and battles, see E470.9, E471+
For individual Indian tribes, see E99.A+

Kentucky
For Union history, see E509.1+
For campaigns and battles, see E470.4-.5, E470.8, E471+

564	General works
564.1	Official publications on the raising, equipment, and service of the troops in the war
564.2	Adjutant Generals' reports for 1861-1865
564.3	Lists of soldiers. Lists of the state's dead
564.4	Histories of the states' troops

Including collected biographies or lists of officers, general associations of survivors, the draft, state brigades, state memorials and monuments, the state's battle flags, lists of citizens serving in organizations of other states
This subdivision is used for Confederate troops

Military organizations

564.5	Infantry
	This subdivision is used for Confederate troops
	Subarrange by number or name of regiment, A-Z. By author, A-Z, e.g. E527.5.L6, Logan Guards
564.6	Cavalry
	This subdivision is used for Confederate troops
	Subarrange by number or name of regiment, A-Z. By author, A-Z
564.7	Artillery, Heavy
	This subdivision is used for Confederate troops
	Subarrange by number or name of regiment, A-Z. By author, A-Z

The Civil War, 1861-1865
Armies. Troops
The Confederate States Army
By state
Kentucky
Military organizations — Continued
564.8   Artillery, Light
This subdivision is used for Confederate troops
Subarrange by number or name of regiment, A-Z. By author, A-Z
564.9   Other (not A-Z)
This subdivision is used for Confederate troops
Louisiana
For preliminaries of the war, see E471.55
For campaigns and battles, see E471+
565   General works
565.1   Official publications on the raising, equipment, and service of the troops in the war
565.2   Adjutant Generals' reports for 1861-1865
565.3   Lists of soldiers. Lists of the state's dead
565.4   Histories of the states' troops
Including collected biographies or lists of officers, general associations of survivors, the draft, state brigades, state memorials and monuments, the state's battle flags, lists of citizens serving in organizations of other states
Military organizations
565.5   Infantry
Subarrange by number or name of regiment, A-Z. By author, A-Z, e.g. E527.5.L6, Logan Guards
565.6   Cavalry
Subarrange by number or name of regiment, A-Z. By author, A-Z
565.7   Artillery, Heavy
Subarrange by number or name of regiment, A-Z. By author, A-Z
565.8   Artillery, Light
Subarrange by number or name of regiment, A-Z. By author, A-Z
565.9   Other (not A-Z)
Maryland
For Union history, see E512.1+
For campaigns and battles, see E470.2+, E471+
566   General works
566.1   Official publications on the raising, equipment, and service of the troops in the war
566.2   Adjutant Generals' reports for 1861-1865
566.3   Lists of soldiers. Lists of the state's dead
566.4   Histories of the states' troops
Including collected biographies or lists of officers, general associations of survivors, the draft, state brigades, state memorials and monuments, the state's battle flags, lists of citizens serving in organizations of other states
This subdivision is used for Confederate troops
Military organizations
566.5   Infantry
This subdivision is used for Confederate troops
Subarrange by number or name of regiment, A-Z. By author, A-Z, e.g. E527.5.L6, Logan Guards
566.6   Cavalry
This subdivision is used for Confederate troops
Subarrange by number or name of regiment, A-Z. By author, A-Z
566.7   Artillery, Heavy
This subdivision is used for Confederate troops
Subarrange by number or name of regiment, A-Z. By author, A-Z
566.8   Artillery, Light
This subdivision is used for Confederate troops
Subarrange by number or name of regiment, A-Z. By author, A-Z

The Civil War, 1861-1865
  Armies. Troops
    The Confederate States Army
      By state
        Maryland
          Military organizations — Continued

566.9	Other (not A-Z)
	This subdivision is used for Confederate troops

        Mississippi
          For preliminaries of the war, see E471.52
          For Union history, see E516.1+
          For campaigns and battles, see E470.6, E471+

568	General works
568.1	Official publications on the raising, equipment, and service of the troops in the war
568.2	Adjutant Generals' reports for 1861-1865
568.3	Lists of soldiers. Lists of the state's dead
568.4	Histories of the states' troops

            Including collected biographies or lists of officers, general associations of survivors, the draft, state brigades, state memorials and monuments, the state's battle flags, lists of citizens serving in organizations of other states
          Military organizations

568.5	Infantry
	Subarrange by number or name of regiment, A-Z. By author, A-Z, e.g. E527.5.L6, Logan Guards
568.6	Cavalry
	Subarrange by number or name of regiment, A-Z. By author, A-Z
568.7	Artillery, Heavy
	Subarrange by number or name of regiment, A-Z. By author, A-Z
568.8	Artillery, Light
	Subarrange by number or name of regiment, A-Z. By author, A-Z
568.9	Other (not A-Z)

        Missouri
          For preliminaries of the war, see E471.57
          For Union history, see E517.1+
          For campaigns and battles, see E470.4+, E471+

569	General works
569.1	Official publications on the raising, equipment, and service of the troops in the war
569.2	Adjutant Generals' reports for 1861-1865
569.3	Lists of soldiers. Lists of the state's dead
569.4	Histories of the states' troops

            Including collected biographies or lists of officers, general associations of survivors, the draft, state brigades, state memorials and monuments, the state's battle flags, lists of citizens serving in organizations of other states
            This subdivision is used for Confederate troops
          Military organizations

569.5	Infantry
	This subdivision is used for Confederate troops
	Subarrange by number or name of regiment, A-Z. By author, A-Z, e.g. E527.5.L6, Logan Guards
569.6	Cavalry
	This subdivision is used for Confederate troops
	Subarrange by number or name of regiment, A-Z. By author, A-Z
569.7	Artillery, Heavy
	This subdivision is used for Confederate troops
	Subarrange by number or name of regiment, A-Z. By author, A-Z
569.8	Artillery, Light
	This subdivision is used for Confederate troops
	Subarrange by number or name of regiment, A-Z. By author, A-Z
569.9	Other (not A-Z)
	This subdivision is used for Confederate troops

The Civil War, 1861-1865
 Armies. Troops
  The Confederate States Army
   By state — Continued
    New Mexico
     For preliminaries of the war, see E471.56
     For campaigns and battles, see E470.9, E471+

571	General works
571.1	Official publications on the raising, equipment, and service of the troops in the war
571.2	Adjutant Generals' reports for 1861-1865
571.3	Lists of soldiers. Lists of the state's dead
571.4	Histories of the states' troops

Including collected biographies or lists of officers, general associations of survivors, the draft, state brigades, state memorials and monuments, the state's battle flags, lists of citizens serving in organizations of other states

Military organizations

571.5	Infantry

Subarrange by number or name of regiment, A-Z. By author, A-Z, e.g. E527.5.L6, Logan Guards

571.6	Cavalry

Subarrange by number or name of regiment, A-Z. By author, A-Z

571.7	Artillery, Heavy

Subarrange by number or name of regiment, A-Z. By author, A-Z

571.8	Artillery, Light

Subarrange by number or name of regiment, A-Z. By author, A-Z

571.9	Other (not A-Z)

North Carolina
 For preliminaries of the war, see E471.54
 For Union history, see E524.1+
 For campaigns and battles, see E470.6, E471+

573	General works
573.1	Official publications on the raising, equipment, and service of the troops in the war
573.2	Adjutant Generals' reports for 1861-1865
573.3	Lists of soldiers. Lists of the state's dead
573.4	Histories of the states' troops

Including collected biographies or lists of officers, general associations of survivors, the draft, state brigades, state memorials and monuments, the state's battle flags, lists of citizens serving in organizations of other states

Military organizations

573.5	Infantry

Subarrange by number or name of regiment, A-Z. By author, A-Z, e.g. E527.5.L6, Logan Guards

573.6	Cavalry

Subarrange by number or name of regiment, A-Z. By author, A-Z

573.7	Artillery, Heavy

Subarrange by number or name of regiment, A-Z. By author, A-Z

573.8	Artillery, Light

Subarrange by number or name of regiment, A-Z. By author, A-Z

573.9	Other (not A-Z)

Oklahoma, *see* E561
South Carolina
 For preliminaries of the war, see E471.1
 For Union history, see E529.1+
 For campaigns and battles, see E470.6, E471+

577	General works
577.1	Official publications on the raising, equipment, and service of the troops in the war
577.2	Adjutant Generals' reports for 1861-1865
577.3	Lists of soldiers. Lists of the state's dead

The Civil War, 1861-1865
  Armies. Troops
    The Confederate States Army
      By state
        South Carolina — Continued

577.4	Histories of the states' troops
	Including collected biographies or lists of officers, general associations of survivors, the draft, state brigades, state memorials and monuments, the state's battle flags, lists of citizens serving in organizations of other states
	Military organizations
577.5	Infantry
	Subarrange by number or name of regiment, A-Z. By author, A-Z, e.g. E527.5.L6, Logan Guards
577.6	Cavalry
	Subarrange by number or name of regiment, A-Z. By author, A-Z
577.7	Artillery, Heavy
	Subarrange by number or name of regiment, A-Z. By author, A-Z
577.8	Artillery, Light
	Subarrange by number or name of regiment, A-Z. By author, A-Z
577.9	Other (not A-Z)
	Tennessee
	For campaigns and battles, see E470.4-.5, E471+
579	General works
579.1	Official publications on the raising, equipment, and service of the troops in the war
579.2	Adjutant Generals' reports for 1861-1865
579.3	Lists of soldiers. Lists of the state's dead
579.4	Histories of the states' troops
	Including collected biographies or lists of officers, general associations of survivors, the draft, state brigades, state memorials and monuments, the state's battle flags, lists of citizens serving in organizations of other states
	Military organizations
579.5	Infantry
	Subarrange by number or name of regiment, A-Z. By author, A-Z, e.g. E527.5.L6, Logan Guards
579.6	Cavalry
	Subarrange by number or name of regiment, A-Z. By author, A-Z
579.7	Artillery, Heavy
	Subarrange by number or name of regiment, A-Z. By author, A-Z
579.8	Artillery, Light
	Subarrange by number or name of regiment, A-Z. By author, A-Z
579.9	Other (not A-Z)
	Texas
	For preliminaries of the war, see E471.56
	For Union history, see E532.1+
	For campaigns and battles, see E470.9
580	General works
580.1	Official publications on the raising, equipment, and service of the troops in the war
580.2	Adjutant Generals' reports for 1861-1865
580.3	Lists of soldiers. Lists of the state's dead
580.4	Histories of the states' troops
	Including collected biographies or lists of officers, general associations of survivors, the draft, state brigades, state memorials and monuments, the state's battle flags, lists of citizens serving in organizations of other states
	Military organizations
580.5	Infantry
	Subarrange by number or name of regiment, A-Z. By author, A-Z, e.g. E527.5.L6, Logan Guards
580.6	Cavalry
	Subarrange by number or name of regiment, A-Z. By author, A-Z

           The Civil War, 1861-1865
             Armies. Troops
               The Confederate States Army
                 By state
                   Texas
                     Military organizations — Continued

580.7	Artillery, Heavy
	Subarrange by number or name of regiment, A-Z. By author, A-Z
580.8	Artillery, Light
	Subarrange by number or name of regiment, A-Z. By author, A-Z
580.9	Other (not A-Z)
	Virginia
	For Union history, see E534.1+
581	General works
581.1	Official publications on the raising, equipment, and service of the troops in the war
581.2	Adjutant Generals' reports for 1861-1865
581.3	Lists of soldiers. Lists of the state's dead
581.4	Histories of the states' troops
	Including collected biographies or lists of officers, general associations of survivors, the draft, state brigades, state memorials and monuments, the state's battle flags, lists of citizens serving in organizations of other states
	Military organizations
581.5	Infantry
	Subarrange by number or name of regiment, A-Z. By author, A-Z, e.g. E527.5.L6, Logan Guards
581.6	Cavalry
	Subarrange by number or name of regiment, A-Z. By author, A-Z
581.7	Artillery, Heavy
	Subarrange by number or name of regiment, A-Z. By author, A-Z
581.8	Artillery, Light
	Subarrange by number or name of regiment, A-Z. By author, A-Z
581.9	Other (not A-Z)
	West Virginia
	For Union history, see E536.1+
	For campaigns and battles, see E470.4+
582	General works
582.1	Official publications on the raising, equipment, and service of the troops in the war
582.2	Adjutant Generals' reports for 1861-1865
582.3	Lists of soldiers. Lists of the state's dead
582.4	Histories of the states' troops
	Including collected biographies or lists of officers, general associations of survivors, the draft, state brigades, state memorials and monuments, the state's battle flags, lists of citizens serving in organizations of other states
	This subdivision is used for Confederate troops
	Military organizations
582.5	Infantry
	This subdivision is used for Confederate troops
	Subarrange by number or name of regiment, A-Z. By author, A-Z, e.g. E527.5.L6, Logan Guards
582.6	Cavalry
	This subdivision is used for Confederate troops
	Subarrange by number or name of regiment, A-Z. By author, A-Z
582.7	Artillery, Heavy
	This subdivision is used for Confederate troops
	Subarrange by number or name of regiment, A-Z. By author, A-Z
582.8	Artillery, Light
	This subdivision is used for Confederate troops
	Subarrange by number or name of regiment, A-Z. By author, A-Z
582.9	Other (not A-Z)
	This subdivision is used for Confederate troops

	The Civil War, 1861-1865
	Armies. Troops
	The Confederate States Army — Continued
585.A-.Z	Participation by race, ethnic group, religious group, etc., A-Z
585.A35	Afro-Americans
585.C54	Children
585.I53	Indians
	Negroes, *see* E585.A35
586.A-.Z	Colleges, schools, etc., and their participation, A-Z
	GALE NOTE *The cutter number(s) listed below have been given only as examples by the Library of Congress*
586.N8	North Carolina. University
586.S5	Shreveport, La. Centenary College of Louisiana
586.S7	South Carolina. University
586.U5	U.S. Military Academy, West Point
586.V5	Virginia Military Institute, Lexington, Va.
586.V6	Virginia. Univerity
	Naval history
591	General works. The Union Navy
	Including naval operations, registers, naval reminiscences, individual fleets or squadrons
	Cf. E462.5, National Association of Naval Veterans
	Cf. E467+, Lives of naval commanders
	Cf. E470+, Naval operations in combination with military campaigns, e.g Monitor-Merrimac battle
	Cf. E480, Naval contracts
595.A-.Z	Individual ships, A-Z
	GALE NOTE *The cutter number(s) listed below have been given only as examples by the Library of Congress*
595.C5	Cherokee (Steamer)
595.C9	Cumberland (Frigate)
595.H2	Hartford (Sloop)
595.K2	Kearsarge (Corvette)
595.L5	Lehigh (Monitor)
595.M7	Monitor (Ironclad)
595.R6	Roanoke (Steamer)
	The Confederate States Navy
	Including registers, naval reminiscences, privateers and cruisers
	Cf. E469+, Construction of cruisers abroad
596	General works
599.A-.Z	Individual ships, A-Z
	GALE NOTE *The cutter number(s) listed below have been given only as examples by the Library of Congress*
599.A3	Alabama (Confederate cruiser)
599.A4	Albemarle (Ram)
599.A8	Atlanta (Ram)
599.F6	Florida (Privateer)
599.M5	Merrimac (Frigate)
599.S2	Savannah (Privateer)
599.S5	Shenandoah (Cruiser)
599.S8	Sumter (Cruiser)
600	Blockade and blockade running
	Personal narratives and other accounts
	The narratives of general or staff officers are usually classed in E470, unless relating to special armies or campaigns, in which case they are classed in E470.2-.9 or E471-478
	For biography of commanding officers, see E467+
	The narratives of regimental officers and privates are usually classed in E495-537 or E551-552 if they contain rolls or are otherwise valuable for regimental histories. If they are of value for military history of special campaigns, they are classed in E471+
	The narratives of noncombatants are usually classed in E470-478, if relating to military operations; otherwise in E456, E468, E491, E545; F214; or under state in E495-582

The Civil War, 1861-1865
　　　Personal narratives and other accounts — Continued
　　　　　Cf. E464, E484, Collections of narratives
　　　　　Cf. E591+, Sailors' narratives
　　　　　Cf. E611+, Prisoners' narratives
　　　　　Cf. E628, Women's narratives
　　　　　Cf. E621+, Nurses' narratives
　　　　　Cf. E655, Collections of anecdotes

601	Union narratives
	Including journals, diaries, letters, etc.
	Cf. E458.7, Refugees from the South
605	Confederate narratives
	Cf. E487, Memoirs and reminiscences of Confederate civil officials and noncombatants
	Cf. F214, The South (Travel and description during the Civil War)
607	**Army life. The private soldier**
608	**Secret Service. Signal Corps**
	Including United States Veteran Signal Corps Association, telegraph service, United States Military Telegraph Corps, spies, scouts, etc. (North and South)
	Cf. E473.55, Andrews' Railroad Raid, 1862
609	**Press. Censorship**
	Prisoners and prisons
	Including prison life
	Confederate prisons
611	General works
	Including general lists of prisoners, exchanges
612.A-.Z	Individual prisons. By name of prison or city, A-Z
	GALE NOTE *The cutter number(s) listed below have been given only as examples by the Library of Congress*
612.A5	Andersonville, Ga. Military Prison
612.B3	Belle Isle Prison, Richmond
612.C2	Cahaba, Ala. Military Prison
612.D2	Danville, Va. Military Prison
612.L6	Libby Prison, Richmond
612.L7	Liggon's Tobacco Warehouse Prison, Richmond
612.M1	Macon, Ga. Military Prison
612.M2	Madison, Ga. Military Prison
612.R6	Richmond prisons (Collective)
612.S15	Salisbury, N.C. Military Prison
612.T9	Tyler, Tex. Camp Ford
	Union prisons
	Cf. E458.8, Treason and traitors in the North, prisoners of state, and suspension of habeas corpus
	Cf. JK343+, Military rule, martial law, etc., within states during a civil war
615	General works
616.A-.Z	Individual prisons. By name of prison or city, A-Z
	GALE NOTE *The cutter number(s) listed below have been given only as examples by the Library of Congress*
616.A4	Alton, Ill. Military Prison
616.C4	Camp Chase, Columbus, Ohio
616.D3	Fort Delaware, Del.
616.D4	Camp Dennison, Ohio
616.D7	Camp Douglas, Chicago, Ill.
616.E4	Elmira, N.Y. Military Prison
616.J7	Johnson's Island, Lake Erie
616.L2	Fort Lafayette, N.Y.
616.L8	Point Lookout, Md.
616.M8	Camp Morton, Ind.
616.O4	Old Capitol Prison, Washington, D.C.
616.R6	Rock Island, Ill. Military Prison
	Washington, D.C. Old Capitol, *see* E616.O4

The Civil War, 1861-1865 — Continued
Medical and hospital services. Sanitary services
Including ambulance service; hospitals; mortality and health statistics; nurses, physicians, surgeons; transportation of the wounded

621 General, and the North
Including National Association of Army Nurses of the Civil War
Including biography: Mary Ann Bickerdyke, John Hill Brinton

625 The South
Including biography

628 **Women's work**
Relief. Charities

629 General, and the North
Including southern relief agencies and associations
United States Sanitary Commission
631.A1-.A7 Official publications
631.A8-.Z4 Branch societies. By name
Including publications of and about these societies
631.Z5 General works
Western Sanitary Commission
631.5.A1-.5.A7 Official publications
631.5.A8-.5.Z General works
631.7.A-.7.Z Local sanitary commissions. By state, city, etc., A-Z
631.7.A1 General works
632 Sanitary fairs
634 The South
Including southern relief agencies

635 **Religion in the armed forces (North and South)**
Including religious life of the personnel; work of chaplains, church denominations, United States Christian Commission, Young Men's Christian Association, etc.
Including religious and other tracts
Celebrations. Memorials. Monuments
Cf. E495+, Civil War history of the states
For national cemeteries located on battlefields, see E471-478. Those located elsewhere are classed in local history, e.g. F234.A7, Arlington, Va.
For registers of the dead (General), see E494, E548
For registers of deceased prisoners of war, see E611+
For reunion of veterans of a single state or group of states, see E494, E548

641 General, and the North
642 Memorial Day services and addresses
645 The South. Confederate Memorial Day
Including services and addresses
646 War museums. Exhibitions. Flags. Trophies
Cf. E495+, subdivision ".4", Battle flags of individual states
646.5 **Antiquities**
Illustrative material
647 Cartoons
Addresses, essays, lectures. Sermons, prayers
649 The North
Including those delivered since the war
For those delivered during the war, see E458+
For Lincoln memorial address, see E457.8
For Memorial Day addresses, see E642
650 The South
Including southern addresses and sermons made during the war and after
For Confederate Memorial Day addresses, see E645
655 Anecdotes. Collections of short narratives
Cf. E464, General collections
Cf. E484, Confederate collections
For literature, see Subclasses PN-PT
656 Motion pictures about the war

	Late nineteenth century, 1865-1900
660.A-.Z	**Collected works of American statesmen, A-Z**
	Including works of statesmen of the twentieth century to 1921
	GALE NOTE *The cutter number(s) listed below have been given only as examples by the Library of Congress*
660.B6	Blaine, James Gillespie
	Subarrange by Table E3 at the end of the text
660.B87	Bryan, William Jennings
	Subarrange by Table E3 at the end of the text
660.D3	Depew, Chauncey Mitchell
	Subarrange by Table E3 at the end of the text
660.G2	Garfield, James Abram
	Subarrange by Table E3 at the end of the text
660.G756	Grant, Ulysses Simpson
	Subarrange by Table E3 at the end of the text
660.H29	Harrison, Benjamin
	Subarrange by Table E3 at the end of the text
660.L75	Lodge, Henry Cabot
	Subarrange by Table E3 at the end of the text
660.M14	McKinley, William
	Subarrange by Table E3 at the end of the text
660.R7	Roosevelt, Theodore
	Subarrange by Table E3 at the end of the text
660.S3	Schurz, Carl
	Subarrange by Table E3 at the end of the text
660.T11	Taft, William Howard
	Subarrange by Table E3 at the end of the text
660.W71	Wilson, Woodrow
	Subarrange by Table E3 at the end of the text
661	**General works**
	Cf. E83.866, Indian wars, 1866-1898
	Cf. E185, Afro-Americans, the race question
	Cf. E668, Reconstruction, 1865-1877
	Cf. E741, Twentieth century
661.7	**Diplomatic history. Foreign and general relations**
	For relations with individual countries, see E183.8.A+
	For relations with Latin America, see F1418
	Biography
	Including biography of statesmen of the early twentieth century
663	Collective
664.A-.Z	Individual, A-Z
	GALE NOTE *The cutter number(s) listed below have been given only as examples by the Library of Congress*
664.A19	Adams, Charles Francis, 1835-1915
	Subarrange by Table E2A at the end of the text
664.A55	Angell, James Burrill
	Subarrange by Table E2A at the end of the text
664.A6	Anthony, Henry Bowen
	Subarrange by Table E2A at the end of the text
664.B123	Bacon, Robert
	Subarrange by Table E2A at the end of the text
664.B2	Bailey, Joseph Weldon
	Subarrange by Table E2A at the end of the text
664.B3	Bayard, Thomas Francis
	Subarrange by Table E2A at the end of the text
664.B5	Belmont, Perry
	Subarrange by Table E2A at the end of the text
664.B55	Bigelow, John
	Subarrange by Table E2A at the end of the text

Late nineteenth century, 1865-1900
Biography

664.A-.Z	Individual, A-Z — Continued
664.B6	Blaine, James Gillespie
	Subarrange by Table E2A at the end of the text
	For his collected works, see E660.B6
664.B62	Blaine, Harriet Bailey
	Subarrange by Table E2A at the end of the text
	"Mrs. J.G. Blaine"
664.B64	Bland, Richard Parks
	Subarrange by Table E2A at the end of the text
664.B69	Bonaparte, Charles Joseph
	Subarrange by Table E2A at the end of the text
664.B819	Brandeis, Louis Dembitz
	Subarrange by Table E2A at the end of the text
664.B87	Bryan, William Jennings
	Subarrange by Table E2A at the end of the text
	For his collected works, see E660.B87
664.C22	Cannon, Joseph Gurney
	Subarrange by Table E2A at the end of the text
664.C29	Carpenter, Matthew Hale
	Subarrange by Table E2A at the end of the text
664.C4	Chandler, Zachariah
	Subarrange by Table E2A at the end of the text
664.C45	Choate, Joseph Hodges
	Subarrange by Table E2A at the end of the text
664.C49	Clark, Champ
	Subarrange by Table E2A at the end of the text
664.C543	Cockran, William Bourke
	Subarrange by Table E2A at the end of the text
664.C75	Conkling, Roscoe
	Subarrange by Table E2A at the end of the text
664.C78	Cox, Jacob Dolson
	Subarrange by Table E2A at the end of the text
664.C8	Cox, Samuel Sullivan
	Subarrange by Table E2A at the end of the text
664.D28	Davis, Jeff
	Subarrange by Table E2A at the end of the text
664.D4	Depew, Chauncey Mitchell
	Subarrange by Table E2A at the end of the text
	For his collected works, see E660.D3
664.D58	Dingley, Nelson, Jr.
	Subarrange by Table E2A at the end of the text
664.E88	Evarts, William Maxwell
	Subarrange by Table E2A at the end of the text
664.F46	Field, Stephen Johnson
	Subarrange by Table E2A at the end of the text
664.F52	Fish, Hamilton
	Subarrange by Table E2A at the end of the text
664.F53	Fisk, Clinton Bowen
	Subarrange by Table E2A at the end of the text
664.F69	Foraker, Joseph Benson
	Subarrange by Table E2A at the end of the text
664.G2	Gardner, Augustus Peabody
	Subarrange by Table E2A at the end of the text
664.G34	George, James Zachariah
	Subarrange by Table E2A at the end of the text
664.G67	Gorman, Arthur Pue
	Subarrange by Table E2A at the end of the text

Late nineteenth century, 1865-1900
Biography

664.A-.Z	Individual, A-Z — Continued
664.G73	Grady, Henry Woodfin
	Subarrange by Table E2A at the end of the text
664.H24	Hanna, Marcus Alonzo
	Subarrange by Table E2A at the end of the text
664.H27	Harlan, James
	Subarrange by Table E2A at the end of the text
664.H31	Harris, Isham Green
	Subarrange by Table E2A at the end of the text
664.H41	Hay, John
	Subarrange by Table E2A at the end of the text
664.H49	Hendricks, Thomas Andrews
	Subarrange by Table E2A at the end of the text
664.H53	Hill, Benjamin Harvey
	Subarrange by Table E2A at the end of the text
664.H65	Hoar, George Frisbie
	Subarrange by Table E2A at the end of the text
664.H73	Hobart, Garret Augustus
	Subarrange by Table E2A at the end of the text
664.H86	Hughes, Charles Evans
	Subarrange by Table E2A at the end of the text
664.I4	Ingalls, John James
	Subarrange by Table E2A at the end of the text
664.K4	Kerr, Michael Crawford
	Subarrange by Table E2A at the end of the text
664.L16	LaFollette, Robert Marion
	Subarrange by Table E2A at the end of the text
664.L2	Lamar, Lucius Quintus Cincinnatus
	Subarrange by Table E2A at the end of the text
664.L7	Lodge, Henry Cabot
	Subarrange by Table E2A at the end of the text
	For his collected works, see E660.L75
664.L83	Logan, John Alexander
	Subarrange by Table E2A at the end of the text
664.M8	Morrill, Justin Smith
	Subarrange by Table E2A at the end of the text
664.M82	Morton, Julius Sterling
	Subarrange by Table E2A at the end of the text
664.M85	Morton, Levi Parsons
	Subarrange by Table E2A at the end of the text
664.N4	Nelson, Knute
	Subarrange by Table E2A at the end of the text
664.P15	Page, Walter Hines
	Subarrange by Table E2A at the end of the text
664.P2	Palmer, John McAuley
	Subarrange by Table E2A at the end of the text
664.P41	Penrose, Boies
	Subarrange by Table E2A at the end of the text
664.P53	Phelps, William Walter
	Subarrange by Table E2A at the end of the text
664.P62	Pinchot, Gifford
	Subarrange by Table E2A at the end of the text
664.P7	Platt, Orville Hitchcock
	Subarrange by Table E2A at the end of the text
664.P72	Platt, Thomas Collier
	Subarrange by Table E2A at the end of the text
664.P73	Plumb, Preston B.
	Subarrange by Table E2A at the end of the text

	Late nineteenth century, 1865-1900
	Biography
664.A-.Z	Individual, A-Z — Continued
664.Q2	Quay, Matthew Stanley
	Subarrange by Table E2A at the end of the text
664.R3	Reed, Thomas Brackett
	Subarrange by Table E2A at the end of the text
664.R35	Reid, Whitelaw
	Subarrange by Table E2A at the end of the text
664.R7	Root, Elihu
	Subarrange by Table E2A at the end of the text
664.R93	Rusk, Jeremiah McLain
	Subarrange by Table E2A at the end of the text
664.S39	Schurz, Carl
	Subarrange by Table E2A at the end of the text
	For his collected works, see E660.S3
664.S57	Sherman, John
	Subarrange by Table E2A at the end of the text
664.S68	Smoot, Reed
	Subarrange by Table E2A at the end of the text
664.S78	Stanford, Leland
	Subarrange by Table E2A at the end of the text
664.S896	Straus, Oscar Solomon
	Subarrange by Table E2A at the end of the text
664.T2	Teller, Henry Moore
	Subarrange by Table E2A at the end of the text
664.T57	Tillman, Benjamin Ryan
	Subarrange by Table E2A at the end of the text
664.V2	Vance, Zebulon Baird
	Subarrange by Table E2A at the end of the text
664.W24	Wanamaker, John
	Subarrange by Table E2A at the end of the text
664.W337	Watson, Thomas Edward
	Subarrange by Table E2A at the end of the text
664.W55	Wharton, Francis
	Subarrange by Table E2A at the end of the text
664.W675	Williams, John Sharp
	Subarrange by Table E2A at the end of the text
664.W76	Windom, William
	Subarrange by Table E2A at the end of the text
664.W8	Wolcott, Edward Oliver
	Subarrange by Table E2A at the end of the text
	Johnson's administration, April 15, 1865-1869
666	General works
	Including impeachment of the President
	Cf. E83.868, Beecher Island Fight
	Cf. F1032, Fenian invasion of Canada, 1866
	Cf. KF5076.J6, Impeachment (Legal aspects)
667	Biography of Andrew Johnson, 1808-1875
	Subarrange by Table E2 at the end of the text
	For his collected works, see E415.6.J65
	For his speeches and messages as President, see J82.B9+
668	Reconstruction, 1865-1877
	Including Amnesty; Ku-Klux Klan; relations of seceded states to the Union; removal of
	political disabilities
	Cf. E185.2, Afro-Americans during reconstruction
	Cf. F216, Travel in the South during reconstruction
	For reconstruction in individual states, see the state in Class F
669	Diplomatic history. Foreign relations
	Including proposed annexation of Danish West Indies, 1867-1869; purchase of Alaska, 1867

Late nineteenth century, 1865-1900

Johnson's administration, April 15, 1865-1869

669   Diplomatic history. Foreign relations — Continued

          Cf. F901+, Alaska, Klondike region, Bering Sea, and Aleutian Islands

          Cf. F1233, French in Mexico

670   Presidential campaign of 1868

Grant's administrations, 1869-1877

671   General works

          Including Grant and Sumner controversy; Liberal Republicans; etc.

          Cf. E83.87, Modoc War, 1872-1873

          Cf. E83.876, Dakota Indian War, Custer Massacre, 1876

          Cf. E668, Reconstruction

          Cf. HB3717, Panic of 1873

          Cf. HG527, Specie Resumption Act, January 1875

          Cf. HJ5021, Whisky Ring, 1875

          Cf. JK681+, Civil service reform

          Cf. T825, Centennial Exposition, Philadelphia, 1876

        Biography of Ulysses Simpson Grant, 1822-1885

          For his collected works, see E660.G756

          For his speeches and messages as President, see J82.C1+

672   General works

          Subarrange by Table E2 at the end of the text

672.1   Grant family (not genealogy)

          Including biography of individual members

673   Diplomatic history. Foreign relations

          Including proposed annexation of Santo Domingo, 1869-1871; sale of arms to France

          Cf. F854, Northwest San Juan border

          Cf. F1033, Fenian invasions of Canada, 1870-1871

          Cf. F1785, Cuban question; Virginius affair, October-December, 1873

          Cf. F1938.2+, Dominican Republic foreign relations

675   Presidential campaign of 1872

680   Presidential campaign of 1876

          Including Hayes-Tilden contest, Electoral Commission

Hayes' administration, 1877-1881

681   General works

          Cf. E83.877, Nez Percé War, 1877

          Cf. E83.879, Ute War, 1879

          Cf. HG527, Resumption of gold payments, 1879

         Biography of Rutherford Birchard Hayes, 1822-1893

          For his collected works, see E660.A+

          For his speeches and messages as President, see J82.C2+

682   General works

          Subarrange by Table E2 at the end of the text

682.1   Hayes family (not genealogy)

          Including biography of individual members

685   Presidential campaign of 1880

Garfield's administration, March 4-September 19, 1881

686   General works

          Including Blaine's foreign policy

          Cf. E691, Arthur's administration

          Cf. E701, Harrison's administration

         Biography of James Abram Garfield, 1831-1881

          For his collected works, see E660.A+

          For his speeches and messages as President, see J82.C3+

687   General works

          Subarrange by Table E2 at the end of the text

687.2   Garfield's family (not genealogy)

          Including biography of individual families

687.9   Assassination. Guiteau

154   **SUPERLCCS: GALE'S LIBRARY OF CONGRESS CLASSIFICATION SCHEDULES**

COMBINED WITH ADDITIONS AND CHANGES THROUGH 2002

Late nineteenth century, 1865-1900 — Continued

Arthur's administration, September 19, 1881-1885

691 General works
Cf. E83.88, Apache War, 1883-1886

692 Biography of Chester Alan Arthur, 1830-1886
Subarrange by Table E2 at the end of the text
For his collected works, see E660.A+
For his speeches and messages as President, see J82.C4+

695 Presidential campaign of 1884

Cleveland's first administration, 1885-1889

696 General works
For Cleveland's second administration, see E706+
Cf. E83.88, Apache War, 1883-1886

697 Biography of Grover Cleveland, 1837-1908
Subarrange by Table E2 at the end of the text
For his collected works, see E660.A+
For his speeches and messages as President, see J82.C5+

697.5 Cleveland family (not genealogy)
Including biography of individual members

700 Presidential campaign of 1888

Benjamin Harrison's administration, 1889-1893

701 General works
Cf. E83.89, Dakota Indian War, 1890-1891
Cf. F1405, International American Conference, 1889-1890
Cf. HF1755, McKinley Tariff Act, 1890
Cf. JX238.F8+, Bering Sea fur seal controversy

702 Biography of Benjamin Harrison, 1833-1901
Subarrange by Table E2 at the end of the text
For his collected works, see E660.H29
For his speeches and messages as President, see J82.C6+

705 Presidential campaign of 1892

Cleveland's second administration, 1893-1897

706 General works
For Cleveland's first administration, see E696+
Cf. DU627.19+, Hawaiian Revolution, 1893-1898
Cf. F2331.B7, Venezuela-British Guiana boundary controversy
Cf. HF1755, Wilson-Gorman Tariff Act, 1894
Cf. HG529+, Currency question, 1890-1900

710 Presidential campaign of 1896

McKinley's first administration, 1897-1901

711 General works
For McKinley's second administration, see E751+
Cf. DS771, Boxer Insurrection in China, 1900
Cf. E713, Territorial expansion
Cf. HF1756+, Dingley tariff
Biography of William McKinley, 1843-1901
For his collected works, see E660.M14
For his speeches and messages as President, see J82.C8+

711.6 General works
Subarrange by Table E2 at the end of the text

711.9 Assassination. Czolgosz

711.95 McKinley, Ida (Saxton)

713 Diplomatic history. Foreign relations
Including imperialism; territorial expansion, e. g. Hawaiian Islands; Philippine Islands
Cf. DS679+, Annexation of Philippine Islands, 1898
Cf. DU627.3+, Annexation of Hawaiian Islands, 1898
Cf. E179.5, Historical geography of United States
Cf. F970, Insular possessions of the United States as a whole
Cf. F1786, Question of Cuban annexation
Cf. F1975, Annexation of Puerto Rico, 1898

Late nineteenth century, 1865-1900

McKinley's first administration, 1897-1901 — Continued

War of 1898 (Spanish-American War)

714	Periodicals. Collections
714.3.A-.3.Z	Societies
	GALE NOTE *The cutter number(s) listed below have been given only as examples by the*
	Library of Congress
714.3.A12	Spanish War Veterans (1899-1904)
714.3.N2-.3.N8	Naval and Military Order of the Spanish-American War
714.3.S48-.3.S5	Service Men of the Spanish War (1899-1904)
714.3.S67-.3.S68	Society of the Army of Santiago de Cuba
714.3.U57-.3.U95	United Spanish War Veterans
	Biography
	For individual narratives, see E729
714.5	Collective
714.6.A-.6.Z	Individual, A-Z
	GALE NOTE *The cutter number(s) listed below have been given only as examples by the*
	Library of Congress
714.6.D51	Dewey, George
	Subarrange by Table E2A at the end of the text
714.6.D55	Dickinson, Walter Mason
	Subarrange by Table E2A at the end of the text
714.6.R8	Rowan, Andrew Summers
	Subarrange by Table E2A at the end of the text
714.6.S3	Schley, Winfield Scott
	Subarrange by Table E2A at the end of the text
	Cf. E727, Court-martial
715	Comprehensive works. General histories
	Military operations. Campaigns and battles
717	General works
717.1	Cuban Campaign
	Including Santiago Campaign; battles of El Caney, San Juan Hill, Santiago
	Cf. E727 , Naval battle off Santiago
	Cf. F1786 , Cuban Revolution, 1895-1898
717.3	Puerto Rican Campaign
717.7	Philippine Campaign. Battle of Manila Bay
	Cf. DS679+, Philippine Insurrection
	Battles, *see E717+*
	Political history
	Including question of intervention after destruction of the "Maine"; public opinion
721	General works
721.6	Destruction of the Maine (Battleship), February 15, 1898
723	Diplomatic history. Treaty of Paris, 1898
	For legal works, including texts of the treaty and related documents, see KZ1389+
	Armies. Troops
725	General works
	United States Army. Corps. Brigades
725.3	General works
725.4	Infantry
	Including regulars and volunteers
	Subarranged by regiment, e.g E725.4.9th for Ninth regiment (Volunteer)
725.45	Cavalry
	Including regulars and volunteers
	Subarranged by regiment, e.g E725.45.1st for First regiment (Volunteer), "The Rough
	Riders"
725.46	Artillery
725.47	Other (not A-Z)
	Including engineers, Signal Corps
725.5.A-.5.Z	Participation by race, ethnic group, etc., A-Z
	Afro-Americans, *see E725.5.N3*

Late nineteenth century, 1865-1900
McKinley's first administration, 1897-1901
War of 1898 (Spanish-American War)
Armies. Troops
United States Army. Corps. Brigades

725.5.A-.5.Z	Participation by race, ethnic group, etc., A-Z — Continued
725.5.C5	Churches
725.5.G3	Germans
725.5.J4	Jews
725.5.N3	Negroes. Afro-Americans
725.6.A-.6.Z	Colleges, schools, etc., and their participation, A-Z
	GALE NOTE *The cutter number(s) listed below have been given only as examples by*
	the Library of Congress
725.6.H3	Harvard University
725.6.P7	Princeton University
725.8	Registers, lists of the dead and wounded, etc.
725.9	Spanish Army
726.A-.W	By state, A-W. Regimental histories
726.A3	Alabama
726.C1	California
726.C7	Connecticut
726.F6	Florida
726.I2	Illinois
726.I3	Indiana
726.I4	Iowa
726.K2	Kansas
726.K37	Kentucky
726.L8	Louisiana
726.M4	Massachusetts
726.M6	Michigan
726.M7	Minnesota
726.M8	Missouri
726.N3	New Hampshire
726.N4	New Jersey
726.N5	New York
726.N8	North Carolina
726.O3	Ohio
726.P4	Pennsylvania
726.R4	Rhode Island
726.T4	Tennessee
726.V5	Vermont
726.W6	Wisconsin
	Naval history
727	General works. United States Navy
	Naval operations including battle of Santiago and destruction of Cervera's fleet but not
	battle of Manila Bay, which is classed in E717.7 ; court-martial of Schley; individual
	squadrons and ships
	Cf. E721.6 , Destruction of the Maine (Battleship)
727.8	Spanish Navy
729	Personal narratives and other accounts
	Including diaries, letters, reminiscences
	Cf. E727 , Sailors' narratives
	Cf. E730 , Prisoners' narratives
730	Prisoners and prisons
	Including prison life
731	Medical and hospital services. War relief work
	Including camps, Red Cross, sanitary services
733	Celebrations. Monuments
734	Museums. Exhibitions. Flags. Trophies
735	Addresses, essays, lectures

	Late nineteenth century, 1865-1900
	McKinley's first administration, 1897-1901 — Continued
738	Presidential campaign of 1900
	Twentieth century
740	**Periodicals. Societies. Collections (Serial)**
740.5	**Sources and documents**
740.7	**Dictionaries and encyclopedias**
741	**General works**
742	**Addresses, essays, lectures, etc. (Collected). By several authors or an individual author**
742.5.A-.5.Z	**Collected works of American statesmen, A-Z**

       For works of statesmen of the early 20th century to 1921, see E660.A+
       For works of statesmen prominent after 1960, see E838.5.A+

742.5.E37	Eisenhower, Dwight David

       Subarrange by Table E3 at the end of the text

742.5.H66	Hoover, Herbert Clark

       Subarrange by Table E3 at the end of the text

742.5.R6	Roosevelt, Franklin Delano

       Subarrange by Table E3 at the end of the text

742.5.T6	Truman, Harry S.

       Subarrange by Table E3 at the end of the text

	Political history
743	General works
743.5	Un-American activities

       Including propaganda, spies and espionage, subversive activities, fifth column
       For Soviet propaganda in the United States, see DK272.U6
       For Anti-Soviet propaganda in the United States, see DK272.7.U6

	Diplomatic history. Foreign and general relations

       For relations with individual countries, or groups of countries, see E183.8.A+; F1418

744	General works
744.5	Cultural relations (General)

       e.g. The work and publications of the U.S Department of State's Office of Information and
          Educational Exchange; the U.S. Information Agency; Voice of America
       For works treating only of American information libraries, see Z675.G7
       Cultural relations with individual countries or groups of countries are classed with foreign
          relations, e.g. E183.6; F1418; etc.

745	**Military history**

       For military societies established before 1951, see E181
       Including military biography of World Wars I-II and the Korean War, e.g. Claire Lee Chennault;
          Douglas MacArthur; George Catlett Marshall; George Smith Patton; Jonathan Mayhew
          Wainright, etc.
       For biographees whose careers extend into the Vietnamese Conflict, see E840.5.A+
       For military history of individual wars, see the war, e.g. D509-680, World War I, 1914-1918;
          D731-838, World War II, 1939-1945; DS918-921.7, Korean War, 1950-1953

746	**Naval history**

       Including naval battles of more than two wars
       Including naval biography, not limited to one war (Collective and individual): William Frederick
          Halsey
       For naval history of individual wars, see the war, e.g. DS920, Korean War

	Biography
747	Collective
748.A-.Z	Individual, A-Z

       GALE NOTE *The cutter number(s) listed below have been given only as examples by the*
          Library of Congress

748.B32	Baruch, Bernard Mannes

       Subarrange by Table E2A at the end of the text

748.B63	Bloom, Sol

       Subarrange by Table E2A at the end of the text

748.B7	Borah, William Edgar

       Subarrange by Table E2A at the end of the text

	Twentieth century
	Biography
748.A-.Z	Individual, A-Z — Continued
748.D22	Dawes, Charles Gates
	Subarrange by Table E2A at the end of the text
748.D48	Dewey, Thomas Edmund
	Subarrange by Table E2A at the end of the text
748.D868	Dulles, John Foster
	Subarrange by Table E2A at the end of the text
748.F24	Farley, James Aloysius
	Subarrange by Table E2A at the end of the text
748.G23	Garner, John Nance
	Subarrange by Table E2A at the end of the text
748.G53	Glass, Carter
	Subarrange by Table E2A at the end of the text
748.H93	Hull, Cordell
	Subarrange by Table E2A at the end of the text
748.I28	Ickes, Harold Le Claire
	Subarrange by Table E2A at the end of the text
748.L23	La Guardia, Fiorello Henry
	Subarrange by Table E2A at the end of the text
748.L7	Lilienthal, David Eli
	Subarrange by Table E2A at the end of the text
748.L86	Long, Huey Pierce
	Subarrange by Table E2A at the end of the text
748.L893	Lucas, Scott Wike
	Subarrange by Table E2A at the end of the text
748.M52	Mellon, Andrew William
	Subarrange by Table E2A at the end of the text
748.M75	Morrow, Dwight Whitney
	Subarrange by Table E2A at the end of the text
748.N65	Norris, George William
	Subarrange by Table E2A at the end of the text
748.S63	Smith, Alfred Emanuel
	Subarrange by Table E2A at the end of the text
748.S88	Stimson, Frederic Jesup
	Subarrange by Table E2A at the end of the text
748.T2	Taft, Robert Alphonso
	Subarrange by Table E2A at the end of the text
748.W225	Walker, Frank C.
	Subarrange by Table E2A at the end of the text
748.W23	Wallace, Henry Agard
	Subarrange by Table E2A at the end of the text
748.W7	Wilke, Wendell Lewis
	Subarrange by Table E2A at the end of the text
748.Y74	Young, Owen D.
	Subarrange by Table E2A at the end of the text
749	**Pamphlets, addresses, etc.**
	McKinley's second administration, March 4-September 14, 1901
	For McKinley's first administration, see E711+
	For presidential campaign of 1900, see E738
751	General works
	Biography and assassination of McKinley, *see* E711.6+
	Theodore Roosevelt's administrations, September 14, 1901-1909
756	General works
	Including negotiations for purchase of Danish West Indies, policy in Russo-Japanese War
	Cf. F912.B7 , Alaska boundary question, 1903
	Cf. F1566.5 , Panama foreign relations, 1903
	Cf. HD6250.A+ , Child labor legislation

	Twentieth century
	Theodore Roosevelt's administrations, September 14, 1901-1909 — Continued
	Biography of Theodore Roosevelt, 1858-1919
	For his collected works, see E660.R7
	For his speeches and messages as President, see J82.C9+
757	General works
	Subarrange by Table E2 at the end of the text
757.2	Roosevelt memorials
	Including reports
	Cf. F129.O98 , Sagamore Hill, Oyster Bay, N.Y.
	Cf. F203.4.T5 , Theodore Roosevelt Island, D.C.
757.3	Roosevelt family (not genealogy)
758	Presidential campaign of 1904
760	Presidential campaign of 1908
	Taft's administration, 1909-1913
761	General works
	Cf. HD2771+ , Regulation of corporations
	Cf. HF1732+ , Reciprocity with Canada
	Cf. HF1756+ , Payne-Aldrich tariff, 1909
	Biography of William Howard Taft, 1857-1930
	For his collected works, see E660.T11
	For his speeches and messages as President, see J82.D1+
762	General works
	Subarrange by Table E2 at the end of the text
762.1	Taft family (not genealogy)
	Including biography, e.g. Helen (Herron) Taft
765	Presidential campaign of 1912
	Wilson's administrations, 1913-1921
766	General works
	For period of World War I, see E780
	Cf. HG2559+ , Establishment of Federal Reserve System
	Cf. HV5089 , 18th amendment to Constitution, 1919 (Prohibition)
	Cf. JK1888-1896 , 19th amendment to Constitution, 1920 (Woman suffrage)
	Biography of Woodrow Wilson, 1856-1924
	For his collected works, see E660.W71
	For his speeches and messages as President, see J82.D2+
767	General works
	Subarrange by Table E2 at the end of the text
767.1	Special (not A-Z)
767.3	Wilson family (not genealogy)
	Including biography, e.g. Edith (Bolling) Galt Wilson
768	Diplomatic history. Foreign relations
	Including purchase of Danish West Indies (Virgin Islands)
	Cf. D570, Participation of the United States in World War I
	Cf. D619, Relation of United States to World War I prior to its entry
	For frontier troubles with Mexico, 1913, see F1234
	For Occupation of Veracruz, 1914, see F1234
	For Pershing Expedition, 1916, see F1234
769	Presidential campaign of 1916
772	Woodrow Wilson Foundation
780	Internal history during World War I
783	Presidential campaign of 1920
784	**1919-1933. Harding-Coolidge-Hoover era. "The twenties"**
	Harding's administration, 1921-August 2, 1923
785	General works
	Including history of Teapot Dome oil scandal
	Cf. HD242.5 , Oil leases
	Cf. HF1756+ , Fordney-McCumber Tariff Act, 1922
	Cf. JX235+ , Conference on the Limitation of Armament, Washington, 1921-1922; Four-Power Treaty Relating to Pacific Possessions

	Twentieth century
784	**1919-1933. Harding-Coolidge-Hoover era. "The twenties"**
	Harding's administration, 1921-August 2, 1923 — Continued
786	Biography of Warren Gamaliel Harding, 1865-1923
	Subarrange by Table E2 at the end of the text
	For his collected works, see E742.5.A+
	For his speeches and messages as President, see J82.D3+
786.2	Harding family (not genealogy)
	Including biography, e.g. Florence Kling Harding
	Coolidge's administrations, August 2, 1923-1929
791	General works
	Cf. D649.G3A+ , Dawes and Young plans
	Cf. JX1952, JX1987+, Kellogg-Briand Pact of 1928 (Pact of Paris renouncing war)
	Biography of Calvin Coolidge, 1872-1933
	For his collected works, see E742.5.A+
	For his speeches and messages as President, see J82.D4+
792	General works
	Subarrange by Table E2 at the end of the text
792.1	Coolidge family (not genealogy)
	Including biography, e.g. Calvin Coolidge, Jr.
795	Presidential campaign of 1924
796	Presidential campaign of 1928
796.Z9	Campaign literature not separately cataloged
796.Z93	Democratic
796.Z95	Republican
	Hoover's administration, 1929-1933
801	General works
	Cf. HB3717 , Stock market crash, 1929
	Cf. HF1756+ , Hawley-Smoot Tariff Act, 1930
	Cf. HG3729.A+, Reconstruction Finance Corporation (created 1932)
	Cf. JX1974+, London Naval Conference and Treaty, Three-Power Treaty (Limitation of naval armament)
	Biography of Herbert Clark Hoover, 1874-1964
	For his collected works, see E742.5.A+
	For his speeches and messages as President, see J82.D5+
802	General works
	Subarrange by Table E2 at the end of the text
802.1	Hoover family (not genealogy)
	Including biography, e.g. Lou (Henry) Hoover
805	Presidential campaign of 1932
	F.D. Roosevelt's administrations, 1933-April 12, 1945
806	General works
	Period of the "New Deal"
	Including works covering the Roosevelt and Truman administrations, 1933-1953
	Cf. D731+, World War II, 1939-1945
	Cf. DS686+, Commonwealth of the Philippines, 1935-1946
	Cf. HD7121+, Social security
	Cf. HF1732+, Reciprocal Trade Agreement Act, 1934, and trade agreements
	Cf. TK1421+, Tennessee Valley Authority (created 1932)
	Biography of Franklin Delano Roosevelt, 1882-1945
	Cf. F129.H99, Hyde Park
	For his collected works, see E742.5.R6
	For his speeches and messages as President, see J82.D6+
807	General works
	Subarrange by Table E2 at the end of the text
807.1	Roosevelt family (not genealogy)
	Including biography, e.g. Eleanor Roosevelt
807.3	Assassination attempt
	Including biography of Giuseppe Zangara
810	Presidential campaign of 1936

	Twentieth century
	F.D. Roosevelt's administrations, 1933-April 12, 1945 — Continued
811	Presidential campaign of 1940
812	Presidential campaign of 1944
	Truman's administrations, April 12, 1945-1953
813	General works
	Including Period of the "Fair Deal"
	Cf. D845, North Atlantic Treaty, 1949
	Cf. DS686.5, Republic of the Philippines, 1946-
	Cf. HC60, Point four program, Technical assistance program
	Cf. HC240, Marshall Plan (European Recovery Program), Foreign Assistance Act, 1948
	Cf. JX1976+, United Nations
	Cf. UA646.3+, North Atlantic Treaty Organization
	Cf. UB343, Selective Service Act, 1948
	Biography of Harry S. Truman, 1884-1972
	For his collected works, see E742.5.T6
	For his speeches and messages as President, see J82.D7+
814	General works
	Subarrange by Table E2 at the end of the text
814.1	Truman family (not genealogy)
	Including biography, e.g. Margaret (Truman) Daniels
815	Presidential campaign of 1948
816	Presidential campaign of 1952
	Eisenhower's administrations, 1953-1961
835	General works
	Cf. D839, Geneva Conference, 1955
	Cf. DS921.7, Korean armistice, 1953
	Cf. E743.5, Internal security, subversive activities, etc.
	Cf. HD242.5, Tidelands oil controversy
	Cf. HD9698+, Atoms for peace program
	Cf. LC212.5+, Segregation in schools
	Biography of Dwight David Eisenhower, 1890-1969
	For his collected works, see E742.5.E37
	For his speeches and messages as President, see J82.D8+
836	General works
	Subarrange by Table E2 at the end of the text
837	Eisenhower family (not genealogy)
	Including biography, e.g. Mamie (Doud) Eisenhower
837.5	Presidential campaign of 1956
837.7	Presidential campaign of 1960
	Later twentieth century, 1961-2000
838	**Periodicals. Societies**
	Collections
838.3	Sources and documents
838.5.A-.5.Z	Collected works of American statesmen, A-Z
838.5.K4	Kennedy, John Fitzgerald
	Subarrange by Table E3 at the end of the text
838.6	**Dictionaries and encyclopedias**
839	**General works**
839.3	**Minor works. Pamphlets**
839.4	**Addresses, essays, lectures, etc. (Collected). By several authors or an individual author**
	Political history
839.5	General works
839.8	Un-American activities
	Including propaganda, spies and espionage, subversive activities
	Diplomatic history. Foreign and general relations
	For relations with individual countries or groups of countries, see E183.8.A+
840	General works

Later twentieth century, 1961-2000

Diplomatic history. Foreign and general relations — Continued

840.2	Cultural relations (General)

e.g. The work and publications of the U.S. Department of State's Office of Information and Educational Exchange; the U.S. Information Agency; Voice of America; etc.

Cultural relations with individual countries or groups of countries are classed with foreign relations, e.g. E183.8; F1418; etc.

Military, naval, and air force history

840.4	General works
840.5.A-.5.Z	Biography, A-Z

Subarrange by Table E1 at the end of the text

Biography (General)

840.6	Collective
840.8.A-.8.Z	Individual, A-Z

GALE NOTE *The cutter number(s) listed below have been given only as examples by the Library of Congress*

840.8.K4	Kennedy, Robert F.

Subarrange by Table E2A at the end of the text

840.8.K58	Kissinger, Henry

Subarrange by Table E2A at the end of the text

Kennedy's administration, 1961-November 22, 1963

Including Cuban missile crisis

841	General works

Biography of John Fitzgerald Kennedy, 1917-1963

842.A-.Z8	General works. Kennedy as President and statesman

Subarrange by Table E2 at the end of the text

For his collected works, see E838.5.K4

For his speeches and messages issued as official documents, see KF70.A47+

For his speeches and messages as President, see J82.D9+

842.Z9	Juvenile works on all or portions of Kennedy's life
842.1	Special (not A-Z)
	By period
842.3	Naval career, 1941-1945
842.47	Visit to Ireland, 1963
842.5	Monuments, portraits, statues, etc.

Class here also monuments, etc. located in foreign countries

For medals, see CJ5801+

842.9	Assassination, funeral, memorial services, etc.
843	Kennedy family (not genealogy)

Including biography, e.g. Jacqueline (Bouvier) Kennedy

For Jacqueline (Kennedy) Onassis, see CT275.A+

Johnson's administrations, November 22, 1963-1969

846	General works

Biography of Lyndon Baines Johnson, 1908-1973

For his collected works, see E838.5.A+

For his speeches and messages as President, see J82.E1+

847	General works

Subarrange by Table E2 at the end of the text

847.2	Special (not A-Z)
848	Johnson family (not genealogy)

Including biography, e.g. Claudia Alta (Taylor) Johnson

850	Presidential campaign of 1964
851	Presidential campaign of 1968

Nixon's administrations, 1969-August 9, 1974

855	General works

Biography of Richard Milhous Nixon, 1913-1994

For his collected works, see E838.5.A+

For his speeches and messages as President, see J82.E2+

856	General works

Subarrange by Table E2 at the end of the text

Later twentieth century, 1961-2000

Nixon's administrations, 1969-August 9, 1974

Biography of Richard Milhous Nixon, 1913-1994 — Continued

857   Nixon family (not genealogy)
                  Including biography, e.g. Thelma (Ryan) Nixon
859   Presidential campaign of 1972
860   Watergate Affair, 1972-1974
861   Impeachment question. Resignation

Ford's administration, August 9, 1974-1977

865   General works
                  Biography of Gerald R. Ford, 1913-
                      For his collected works, see E838.5.A+
                      For his speeches and messages as President, see J82.E3+
866   General works
                      Subarrange by Table E2 at the end of the text
866.3   Assassination attempts
                      Including biography of Lynette Fromme
867   Ford family (not genealogy)
                      Including biography of individual members
868   Presidential campaign of 1976

Carter's administration, 1977-1981

872   General works
                  Biography of Jimmy Carter, 1924-
                      For his collected works, see E838.5.A+
                      For his speeches and messages as President, see J82.E4+
873   General works
                      Subarrange by Table E2 at the end of the text
873.2   Special (not A-Z)
874   Carter family (not genealogy)
                      Including biography of individual members
                  Iran Hostage Crisis, 1979-1981, *see E183.8.A+*
875   Presidential campaign of 1980

Reagan's administration, 1981-1989

876   General works
                  Biography of Ronald Reagan, 1911-
                      For his collected works, see E838.5.A+
                      For his speeches and messages as President, see J82.E5+
                      For his acting career, see PN2287.R25
877   General works
                      Subarrange by Table E2 at the end of the text
877.2   Special (not A-Z)
877.3   Assassination attempt
                      Including biography of John Hinckley
878   Reagan family (not genealogy)
                      Including biography of individual members
879   Presidential campaign of 1984
880   Presidential campaign of 1988

881   **Bush administration, 1989-1993**
                  Biography of George Bush, 1924-
                      For his collected works, see E838.5.A+
                      For his speeches as President, see J82.E6
882   General works
                      Subarrange by Table E2 at the end of the text
882.2   Special (not A-Z)
883   Bush family (not genealogy)
                      Including biography of individual members
884   Presidential campaign of 1992

Clinton's administrations, 1993-2001

885   General works

Later twentieth century, 1961-2000

Clinton's administrations, 1993-2001 —   Continued

Biography of Bill Clinton, 1946-

For his collected works, see E838.5.A+

For his speeches as President, see J82.E7

886   General works

Subarrange by Table E2 at the end of the text

886.2   Special (not A-Z)

887   Clinton family (not genealogy)

Including biography of individual members

888   Presidential campaign of 1996

889   Presidential campaign of 2000

Twenty-first century

895   **Diplomatic history. Foreign and general relations**

For relations with individual countries, see E183.8.A-.8.Z

For relations with Latin America, see F1418

George W. Bush's administration, 2001-

902   General works

Biography of G. W. Bush, 1946-

For his collected works, see E838.5

For speeches and messages as president, see J82.E8

903   General works

Subarrange by Table E2 at the end of the text

903.2   Special (not A-Z)

904   Bush family (not genealogy)

Including biography of individual members

901.1   biography

	New England
1	**Periodicals. Societies. Collections**
1.5	**Museums. Exhibitions, exhibits**
2	**Gazetteers. Dictionaries. Geographic names**
2.3	**Guidebooks**
3	**Biography (Collective). Genealogy (Collective)**
3.2	**Historiography**
	Historians, *see* E175.5.A+
3.5	**Study and teaching**
4	**General works. Histories**
4.3	**Juvenile works**
	Pamphlets, addresses, essays, etc.
4.5	General
4.6	Anecdotes, legends, pageants, etc.
5	**Historic monuments (General). Illustrative material**
6	**Antiquities (Non-Indian)**
	By period
7	Early to 1775

Including the Plymouth Company, 1606; Council for New England, 1620; United Colonies of New England, 1643-1684; Puritans; Pilgrims; Thanksgiving Day in New England
Including individual voyagers after 1607, e.g. Bartholomew Gosnold, John Smith, George Waymouth
Cf. BF1575+, Witchcraft in New England
Cf. E83.63, Pequot War, 1636-1638
Cf. E83.67, King Philip's War, 1675-1676
Cf. E83.72, War with eastern Indians, 1722-1726
Cf. E105, Norsemen, Vinland
Cf. E121+, Early voyages before 1607
Cf. E162, Thanksgiving Day in the United States
Cf. E196, King William's War, 1689-1697
Cf. E197, Queen Anne's War, 1702-1713
Cf. E198, King George's War, 1744-1748
Cf. E199, French and Indian War, 1755-1763
Cf. F22, Popham Colony
Cf. F67, Puritans in Massachusetts
Cf. F68, Pilgrims in New Plymouth Colony

| 7.5 | Dominion of New England, 1686-1689 |

Including consolidation of New England colonies and regions into one province; later (1688), enlarged by the addition of New York and New Jersey
Including relations with Governor Edmund Andros; Revolution of 1689

| 8 | 1775-1865 |

Cf. E357.6+, Opposition to War of 1812

| 9 | 1865-1950 |

Including New England hurricane, 1938
For effects of hurricane on an individual state or city, see the local classification number

| 10 | 1951- |
| 12.A-.Z | **Regions, A-Z** |

For Berkshire Hills, see F72.B5

| 12.A74 | Atlantic Coast |
| 12.C7 | Connecticut River and Valley |

Cf. F42.C65, New Hampshire
Cf. F57.C7, Vermont
Cf. F72.C7, Massachusetts
Cf. F102.C7, Connecticut

Isle of Shoals, *see* F42.I8
Merrimac River and Valley, *see* F42.M4, F72.M6
White Mountains, *see* F41

| | **Elements in the population** |
| 15.A1 | General works |

	New England
	Elements in the population — Continued
15.A2-.Z	Individual elements
	For list of racial, ethnic, and religious elements (with cutter numbers), see E184.A+
	Maine
16	**Periodicals. Societies. Collections**
16.5	**Museums. Exhibitions, exhibits**
17	**Gazetteers. Dictionaries. Geographic names**
17.3	**Guidebooks**
18	**Biography (Collective). Genealogy (Collective)**
18.2	**Historiography**
	Historians, *see E175.5.A+*
18.5	**Study and teaching**
19	**General works. Histories**
19.3	**Juvenile works**
	Pamphlets, addresses, essays, etc.
19.5	General
19.6	Anecdotes, legends, pageants, etc.
20	**Historic monuments (General). Illustrative material**
21	**Antiquities (Non-Indian)**
	By period
22	Early to 1620
	Including attempts at colonization: Pemaquid, Me.; Popham Colony
23	1620-1775
	Including Lygonia Colony (Plough Patent); Trelawney Plantation
	Including biography: Edward Godfrey
	Cf. E83.72, War with Eastern Indians, 1722-1726
	Cf. F27.K3, Kennebec Patent
	Cf. F27.M95, Muscongus or Waldo Patent
	Cf. F29.B9, Pejepscot Purchase
	Cf. F1036+, Acadia
	Cf. F1039.B7, Boundary between French and English possessions in Acadia
24	1775-1865
	Including separation from Massachusetts and admission as a state, March 15, 1820
	Including biography: William King
	Cf. E230+, Military operations and battles
	Cf. E263.M4, Maine in the Revolution (General)
	Cf. E398, International boundary troubles and the Aroostook War, 1839
	Cf. E511.1+, Civil War, 1861-1865 (General)
25	1865-1950
	Including biography: Harris Merrill Plaisted, etc.
	Cf. D570.85.M2+ , World War I, 1914-1918
	Cf. D769.85.M2+ , World War II, 1939-1945
	1951-
26	General works
	Biography
26.3	Collective
26.32.A-.32.Z	Individual, A-Z
	GALE NOTE *See note at the head of Table F5 at the end of the text for further instructions on how to subdivide this number*
27.A-.Z	**Regions, counties, etc., A-Z**
27.A15	Counties
27.A16	Regions
27.A17	Rivers
27.A18	Lakes
27.A19	Islands
	Acadia National Park, *see F27.M9*
27.A4	Allagash River and Valley
27.A5	Androscoggin Co.
	Including Lake Androscoggin, Snow Falls

	Maine
27.A-.Z	**Regions, counties, etc., A-Z — Continued**
27.A53	Androscoggin River and Valley
27.A7	Aroostook Co.
	Including Aroostook River and Valley (General, and Maine)
	Cf. F1044.A7 , New Brunswick
27.A75	Atlantic Coast
	Bartlett Island, *see F27.M9*
	Baxter State Park, *see F27.P5*
27.B49	Blue Hill Bay
	Bluff Island, *see F27.Y6*
27.B7	Boundaries
	Cf. E398, Northeastern boundary disputes, 1783-1845
	Cf. F42.B7, New Hampshire boundary
	Cf. F1039.B7, Ancient boundary of Acadia
27.C3	Casco Bay and islands (Collectively)
	For individual islands, see F27.C9
27.C9	Cumberland Co.
	Including Orr's Island, Peak Island, Sebago Lake
	For Saco Bay, see F27.Y6
	For Saco River and Valley, see F27.S15
27.D2	Dead River and Valley
	Dochet Island, *see F27.W3*
27.F8	Franklin Co.
	Friendship Long Island, *see F27.K7*
	Great Gott Island, *see F27.H3*
27.H3	Hancock Co.
	Including Great Gott Island, Little Cranberry Island, Little Gott Island, Long Island, Swans Island, Union River and Valley, Union River Bay
	For Mount Desert Island, see F27.M9
	Isles of Shoals, *see F42.I8*
	Islesboro Island, *see F27.W16*
	Kennebago Lake, *see F27.R2*
27.K2	Kennebec Co.
	Including Lake Cobbosseecontee
27.K3	Kennebec Patent. Plymouth Company (1749-1816)
27.K32	Kennebec River and Valley
27.K7	Knox Co.
	Including Friendship Long Island
	For Matinicus Island, see F27.M3
27.L7	Lincoln Co.
	For Monhegan Island, see F27.M7
	Little Cranberry Island, *see F27.H3*
	Little Gott Island, *see F27.H3*
	Long Island, *see F27.H3*
27.M18	Magalloway Island
27.M3	Matinicus Island
27.M7	Monhegan Island
27.M8	Moosehead Lake region
27.M9	Mount Desert Island
	Including Acadia National Park, Bartlett Island
	Cf. F1038, Jesuit station, 1609
	Moxie Pond, *see F27.S7*
27.M95	Muscongus or Waldo Patent
	Including greater part of Waldo and Knox and a portion of Lincoln counties
27.O9	Oxford Co.
	Including Oxford Hills, Parmachenee Lake
	Oxford Hills, *see F27.O9*
	Parmachenee Lake, *see F27.O9*

	Maine
27.A-.Z	**Regions, counties, etc., A-Z — Continued**
27.P3	Passamaquoddy Bay, Maine
	Cf. F1044.P3 , New Brunswick
	Pejepscot Patent (Brunswick), *see* F29.B9
27.P37	Penobscot Bay region
27.P38	Penobscot Co.
27.P4	Penobscot River and Valley
27.P48	Piscataqua River and Valley, Maine
	Cf. F42.P4 , General, and New Hampshire
27.P5	Piscataquis Co.
	Including Baxter State Park, Debsconeag Lake region, Mount Katahdin, Chesuncook Lake, Sebec Lake
	Pond Island, *see* F27.W3
27.R2	Rangeley Lakes. Kennebago Lake
	Roque Island, *see* F27.W3
	Saco Bay, *see* F27.Y6
27.S15	Saco River and Valley
27.S18	Sagadahoc Co.
	St. Croix (Dochet) Island, *see* F27.W3
27.S2	St. Croix River and Valley (General, and Maine)
	Cf. F1044.S17 , New Brunswick
27.S25	St. George (George's) River
27.S3	St. John River and Valley, Maine
	Cf. F1044.S2, General, and New Brunswick
	Sebec Lake, *see* F27.P5
	Sheepscot River and Valley, *see* F27.W16
	Snow Falls, *see* F27.A5
27.S7	Somerset Co.
	Including Moxie Pond
	Stratton Island, *see* F27.Y6
	Swans Island, *see* F27.H3
27.T48	Thompson Lake and Region
	Union River and Valley. Union River Bay, *see* F27.H3
27.W16	Waldo Co.
	Including Islesboro Island, Sheepscot River and Valley
	For Waldo Patent, see F27.M95
27.W3	Washington Co.
	Including Narraguagus Valley, Pond Island, St. Croix (Dochet) Island, Roque Island
27.Y6	York Co.
	Including Bluff Island, Boon Island, Saco Bay, Stratton Island
	For Saco River and Valley, see F27.S15
29.A-.Z	**Cities, towns, etc., A-Z**
	GALE NOTE *The cutter number(s) listed below have been given only as examples by the Library of Congress*
29.A9	Augusta
29.B2	Bangor
29.B3	Bar Harbor
29.B9	Brunswick
	Including Pejepscot Purchase. Pejepscot Company (Brunswick Proprietors)
29.K3	Kennebunk
29.P9	Portland
29.Y6	York
	Elements in the population
30.A1	General works
30.A2-.Z	Individual elements
	For list of racial, ethnic, and religious elements (with cutter numbers), see E184.A+
	New Hampshire
31	**Periodicals. Societies. Collections**
31.5	**Museums. Exhibitions, exhibits**

                 New Hampshire — Continued

32	**Gazetteers. Dictionaries. Geographic names**
32.3	**Guidebooks**
33	**Biography (Collective). Genealogy (Collective)**
33.2	**Historiography**
	Historians, *see* E175.5.A+
33.5	**Study and teaching**
34	**General works. Histories**
34.3	**Juvenile works**
	Pamphlets, addresses, essays, etc.
34.5	General
34.6	Anecdotes, legends, pageants, etc.
35	**Historic monuments (General). Illustrative material**
36	**Antiquities (Non-Indian)**
	By period
37	Early to 1775. Mason's Grant
	Including biography: John Mason
	Cf. E83.72 , Wars with eastern Indians, 1722-1726
	Cf. E199 , French and Indian War, 1755-1763
	Cf. F52 , New Hampshire Grants
38	1775-1865
	Including biography: William Henry Young Hackett, Isaac Hill, etc.
	Cf. E263.N4 , New Hampshire in the Revolution
	Cf. E359.5.N3 , War of 1812
	Cf. E520.1+ , Civil War, 1861-1865 (General)
39	1865-1950
	Including biography: Harry Bingham, Charles Doe
	Cf. D570.85.N25+ , World War I, 1914-1918
	Cf. D769.85.N25+ , World War II, 1939-1945
	Cf. E726.N3 , War of 1898 (Spanish-American War)
40	1951-
41	**White Mountains**
41.1	Periodicals. Societies. Collections
41.2	Gazetteers. Dictionaries. Geographic names
41.25	Guidebooks
41.3	General works
41.32	Pamphlets, addresses, essays, etc.
41.37	Historic monuments (General). Illustrative material
	By period
41.44	Early to 1865
41.5	1865-1950
41.52	1951-
41.6.A-.6.Z	Regions, places, etc., A-Z
	For political divisions, see F42-44
	GALE NOTE *The cutter number(s) listed below have been given only as examples by the Library of Congress*
41.6.F8	Franconia Notch
	Old Man of the Mountain, *see* F41.6.P9
41.6.P9	The Profile
41.6.W3	Mount Washington
42.A-.Z	**Regions, counties, etc., A-Z**
42.A15	Counties
42.A16	Mountains
42.A17	Rivers
42.A18	Lakes
42.A19	Islands
42.B4	Belknap Co.
42.B7	Boundaries
	For New York-New Hampshire dispute over New Hampshire Grants, see F52

	New Hampshire
42.A-.Z	**Regions, counties, etc., A-Z — Continued**
42.C3	Carroll Co.
	Including Mount Pequawkwet (Kearsarge), Ossipee Mountain Park
	For Mount Kearsarge, Merrimack Co., see F42.M5
42.C5	Cheshire Co.
	Including Mount Monadnock
42.C65	Connecticut River and Valley, N.H.
	Cf. F12.C7 , New England
42.C7	Coos Co.
	Including Indian Stream
42.G7	Grafton Co.
	Including Newfound (Pasquaney) Lake, Mount Moosilaukee
42.H6	Hillsboro (Hillsborough) Co.
	Including Uncanoonuc Mountains
42.I8	Isles of Shoals
	Kearsarge, Mount, Carroll Co., *see* F42.C3
	Kearsarge, Mount, Merrimack Co., *see* F42.M5
	Magalloway Valley, *see* F27.M18
42.M4	Merrimac River and Valley, N.H.
	Cf. F72.M6 , General, and Massachusetts
42.M5	Merrimack Co.
	Including Mount Kearsarge
	Odiorne Point Stat Park, *see* F42.R7
42.P4	Piscataqua River and Valley (General, and N.H.)
	Cf. F27.P48 , Maine
42.R7	Rockingham Co.
	Including Lake Massabesic, Odiorne Point State Park
	For Isles of Shoals, see F42.I8
42.S8	Strafford Co.
42.S87	Sullivan Co.
42.S9	Sunapee Lake
	Waterville Valley, *see* F44.W32
	Welch Island, *see* F42.W7
	White Mountains, *see* F41
42.W7	Lake Winnipesaukee
	Including Welch Island
44.A-.Z	**Cities, towns, etc., A-Z**
	GALE NOTE *The cutter number(s) listed below have been given only as examples by the Library of Congress*
44.C7	Concord
44.D7	Dover
44.M2	Manchester
44.N2	Nashua
44.P8	Portsmouth
44.W32	Waterville
	Including Waterville Valley
	Elements in the population
45.A1	General works
45.A2-.Z	Individual elements
	For a list of racial, ethnic, and religious elements (with cutter numbers), see E184.A+
	Vermont
46	**Periodicals. Societies. Collections**
46.5	**Museums. Exhibitions, exhibits**
47	**Gazetteers. Dictionaries. Geographic names**
47.3	**Guidebooks**
48	**Biography (Collective). Genealogy (Collective)**
48.2	**Historiography**
	Historians, *see* E175.5.A+
48.5	**Study and teaching**

	Vermont — Continued
49	**General works. Histories**
49.3	**Juvenile works**
	Pamphlets, addresses, essays, etc.
49.5	General
49.6	Anecdotes, legends, pageants, etc.
50	**Historic monuments (General). Illustrative material**
51	**Antiquities (Non-Indian)**
	By period
52	Early to 1791

> *Including New Hampshire Grants; Green Mountain boys*
> *Including biography: Ira Allen, Thomas Chittenden*
> *Cf. E263.V5 , Vermont in the Revolution (General)*
> *Cf. E230+ , Military operations and battles*
> *Cf. F37 , New Hampshire colonial history*
> *Cf. F122 , New York colonial history*
> *Cf. F127.A3 , Albany Co., N.Y.*
> *Cf. F127.W3 , Charlotte (now Washington) County, N.Y.*

| 53 | 1791-1865 |

> *Including admission as a state, March 4, 1791*
> *Including biography: Jacob Collamer, etc.*
> *Cf. E359.5.V3, War of 1812*
> *Cf. E355, Military operations*
> *Cf. E533.1+, Civil War, 1861-1865 (General)*
> *Cf. E470.95, St. Alban's Raid*

| 54 | 1865-1950 |

> *Cf. D570.85.V5+, World War I, 1914-1918*
> *Cf. D769.85.V5+, World War II, 1939-1945*
> *Cf. E726.V5, War of 1898 (Spanish-American War)*

	1951-
55	General works
	Biography
55.2	Collective
55.22.A-.22.Z	Individual, A-Z

> GALE NOTE *See note at the head of Table F5 at the end of the text for further instructions on how to subdivide this number*

57.A-.Z	**Regions, counties, etc., A-Z**
57.A15	Counties
57.A16	Mountains
57.A17	Rivers
57.A18	Lakes
57.A19	Islands
57.A2	Addison Co.

> *Including Lake Dunmore*

| 57.B4 | Bennington Co. |

> *Including Hoosic River and Valley, Vt.*
> *Cf. F72.B5, Massachusetts*
> *Cf. F127.H73, General, and New York*

| 57.B7 | Boundaries |

> *Cf. F42.B7, New Hampshire boundary*
> *Cf. F72.B7, Massachusetts boundary*
> *Cf. F127.B7, New York boundary*
> *For New Hampshire-New York dispute over land in the present state of Vermont, see F52*

| 57.C2 | Caledonia Co. |
| 57.C4 | Lake Champlain region, Vt. |

> *Cf. F57.G7 , Grand Isle Co.*
> *Cf. F127.C6 , General, and New York*

| 57.C5 | Chittenden Co. |
| 57.C7 | Connecticut River and Valley, Vt. |

> *Cf. F12.C7 , New England*

	Vermont
57.A-.Z	**Regions, counties, etc., A-Z — Continued**
57.E7	Essex Co.
57.F8	Franklin Co.
	For Missisquoi River and Valley, see F57.M7
57.G7	Grand Isle Co.
57.G8	Green Mountains
	Hoosic River and Valley, Vt., *see F57.B4*
57.L2	Lamoille Co.
57.L22	Lamoille River and Valley
57.M3	Mount Mansfield
57.M5	Lake Memphremagog region, Vt.
	Cf. F1054.M5 , Quebec
57.M7	Missisquoi River and Valley, Vt.
	Cf. F1054.B8 , General, and Quebec
57.O56	Ompompanoosuc Parish
	Cf. F59.N9 , Norwich
	Cf. F59.T4 , Thetford
57.O6	Orange Co.
57.O7	Orleans Co.
	Including Willoughby Lake
	For Missisquoi River and Valley, see F57.M7
57.R9	Rutland Co.
	Including Lake Bomoseen
57.W3	Washington Co.
	Willoughby Lake, *see F57.O7*
57.W6	Windham Co.
57.W7	Windsor Co.
57.W73	Winooski River
59.A-.Z	**Cities, towns, etc., A-Z**
	GALE NOTE *The cutter number(s) listed below have been given only as examples by the Library of Congress*
59.B4	Bennington
59.B8	Brattleboro
59.B9	Burlington
59.M7	Montpelier
59.N9	Norwich
	Ompompanoosuc Parish, *see F57.O56*
59.T4	Thetford
	Elements in the population
60.A1	General works
60.A2-.Z	Individual elements
	For a list of racial, ethnic, and religious elements (with cutter numbers), see E184.A+
	Massachusetts
61	**Periodicals. Societies. Collections**
61.5	**Museums. Exhibitions, exhibits**
62	**Gazetteers. Dictionaries. Geographic names**
62.3	**Guidebooks**
63	**Biography (Collective). Genealogy (Collective)**
63.2	**Historiography**
	Historians, *see E175.5.A+*
63.5	**Study and teaching**
64	**General works. Histories**
64.3	**Juvenile works**
	Pamphlets, addresses, essays, etc.
64.5	General
64.6	Anecdotes, legends, pageants, etc.
65	**Historic monuments (General). Illustrative material**
66	**Antiquities (Non-Indian)**

                         Massachusetts — Continued
                         By period
                             Early to 1775

67   General

             Including Dorchester Company; Massachusetts Bay Company; persecution of Quakers; Province of Massachusetts; Puritans; etc.

             Including biography: Roger Conant, Thomas Dudley, John Endecott, Daniel Gookin, Anne (Marbury) Hutchinson, Thomas Hutchinson, Cotton Mather, Increase Mather, Peter Oliver, Thomas Pownall, John Read, Timothy Ruggles, Samuel Sewall, John Winthrop (1588-1649), etc.

             Cf. BF1575, Witchcraft delusion

             Cf. E83.67, King Philip's War, 1675-1676

             Cf. E83.72, War with the eastern Indians, 1722-1726

             Cf. E196, King William's War, 1689-1697

             Cf. E197, Queen Anne's War, 1702-1713

             Cf. E198, King George's War, 1744-1748

             Cf. E199, French and Indian War, 1755-1763

             Cf. F7.5, Andros and his province of New England, 1688-1689

68   New Plymouth Colony

             Including pilgrims; annexation to Massachusetts, 1691 (forming the counties of Barnstable, Bristol, and Plymouth); etc.

             Including Pilgrim Society, Plymouth; Society of Mayflower Descendants; etc.

             For Old Colony Historical Society, Taunton, see F74.T2

             Including biography: Isaac Allerton, William Bradford, William Brewster, Miles Standish, etc.

69   1775-1865

             Including Shays' Rebellion, 1786-1787

             Including biography: James Bowdoin, Christopher Gore, David Henshaw, Samuel Howe, Amos Lawrence, Theophilus Parsons, Samuel Phillips, William Phillips, Paul Revere, Caleb Strong

             Cf. E263.M4 , Massachusetts and the Revolution

             Cf. E210+, Preliminaries (Revolution)

             Cf. E216, Paul Revere's ride

             Cf. E230+, Military operations and battles

             Cf. E309, F483, Cession of western lands

             Cf. E359.5.M3, War of 1812

             Cf. E513.1+, Civil War, 1861-1865 (General)

             Cf. F127.G2, F127.H7, F127.T6, Lands in western New York

             Cf. F273, Trouble with South Carolina over Afro-American citizens, 1845

70   1865-1950

             Including biography: James Michael Curley, Frederic Thomas Greenhalge, Samuel Hoar, Roger Wolcott, etc.

             Cf. D570.85.M4+, World War I, 1914-1918

             Cf. D769.85.M4+, World War II, 1939-1945

             Cf. E726.M4, War of 1898 (Spanish-American War)

                        1951-

71   General works

                        Biography

71.2   Collective

71.22.A-.22.Z   Individual, A-Z

                        GALE NOTE *See note at the head of Table F5 at the end of the text for further instructions on how to subdivide this number*

72.A-.Z   **Regions, counties, etc., A-Z**

72.A15   Counties

72.A16   Mountains

72.A17   Rivers

72.A18   Lakes

72.A19   Islands

                        Barnstable Co., *see* F72.C3

72.B5   Berkshire Co.

             Including Berkshire Hills, Greylock Mountain, Hoosic River and Valley, Mass., Mohawk Trail, Mount Everett

	Massachusetts
72.A-.Z	**Regions, counties, etc., A-Z**
72.B5	Berkshire Co. — Continued
	Cf. F57.B4, Vermont
	Cf. F127.H73, General, and New York, Hoosic River and Valley
	Cf. F127.M55, New York, Mohawk Trail
72.B57	Blackstone River and Valley
	Cf. F87.B55 , General, and Rhode Island
	Boon Lake, *see F72.M7*
	"Boston Ten Townships," N.Y., *see F127.T6*
72.B7	Boundaries
	Cf. F42.B7 , New Hampshire boundary
	Cf. F1039.B7 , Ancient boundary of Acadia
	For Massachusetts territorial claims to western New York, see F127.G2
72.B8	Bristol Co.
72.B9	Buzzards Bay region
72.C3	Cape Cod. Barnstable Co.
	Including Cape Cod Bay, Sparrow-hawk (Ship) wreck (1626)
	Chappaquiddick Island, *see F72.M5*
72.C46	Charles River
72.C7	Connecticut River and Valley, Mass.
	Cf. F12.C7, New England
	Dukes Co., *see F72.M5*
72.E5	Elizabeth Islands
	Including Cuttyhunk, Nashawena, Naushon, Nonamesset, Pasque, and Penikese Islands
72.E7	Essex Co.
	Including Cape Ann, Ipswich (Agawam) River, North Shore, Saugus River
72.F8	Franklin Co.
	Including Deerfield River, Pocumtuck Valley
72.H2	Hampden Co.
72.H3	Hampshire Co.
	Including Mill River, Mount Holyoke, Mount Tom
72.H7	Housatonic River and Valley, Mass.
	Cf. F102.H7 , General, and Connecticut
72.M5	Martha's Vineyard. Dukes Co.
	Including Chappaquiddick Island
	"Massachusetts Ten Townships," N.Y., *see F127.T6*
72.M6	Merrimac River and Valley (General, and Mass.)
	Cf. F42.M4, New Hampshire
72.M7	Middlesex Co.
	Including Lake Boon, Concord River, Middlesex Fells Reservation, Minute Man National Historical Park, Walden Pond
	Middlesex Fells Reservation, *see F72.M7*
72.M73	Millers River and Valley
	Minute Man National Historical Park, *see F72.M7*
72.N2	Nantucket Co.
	Including Nantucket, Muskeget, and Tuckernuck Islands
72.N6	No Mans Land (Island)
72.N8	Norfolk Co.
	Pioneer Valley, *see F72.C7*
72.P6	Plum Island
72.P7	Plymouth Co.
	Including North River, South Shore
72.S86	Sudbury River and Valley
72.S9	Suffolk Co.
	Cf. F73 , Boston
72.S94	Swift River Valley. Quabbin Reservoir. Ware River Valley
	Walden Pond, *see F72.M7*
72.W9	Worcester Co.
	Including Wachusett Mountain, Lake Quinsigamond

Massachusetts — Continued

73		**Boston**
73.1		Periodicals. Societies. Collections
73.15		Museums. Exhibitions, exhibits
		For Foreign Exhibition, 1883, see T460
73.18		Guidebooks
73.25		Biography (Collective). Genealogy (Collective)
		Including vital records, epitaphs
73.27		Historiography
73.29		Study and teaching
73.3		General works. Histories
73.33		Juvenile works
		Pamphlets, addresses, essays, etc.
73.35		General
73.36		Anecdotes, legends, pageants, etc.
73.37		Historic monuments (General). Illustrative material
73.39		Antiquities (Non-Indian)
		By period
73.4		Early to 1775
		Including the fires of 1711, 1737, 1760, etc.
		Including biography: William Blackstone, etc.
		Cf. E215, Events just prior to the Revolution
73.44		1775-1865
		Cf. E450, Fugitive slave riots
73.5		1865-1950
		Including fire of 1872
		1951-
73.52		General works
		Biography
73.53		Collective
73.54.A-.54.Z		Individual, A-Z
		GALE NOTE *See note at the head of Table F5 at the end of the text for further instructions on how to subdivide this number*
		Sections. Localities. Districts, etc.
73.6		General works
73.61		Cemeteries
		Including Copp's Hill Burial Ground, Granary Burial Ground, King's Chapel Burial Ground, Mount Hope Cemetery
73.62		Churches
73.625		Hotels, taverns, etc.
73.627		Places of amusement
73.63		Harbor
73.64		Monuments. Statues
		GALE NOTE *The cutter number(s) listed below have been given only as examples by the Library of Congress*
73.64.A1		General works
73.64.B4		Beacon Hill Monument
73.64.W4		Wendell Phillips Statue
73.65		Parks. Squares. Circles
		Including Boston Common, Franklin Park
73.67		Streets. Bridges. Railroads, etc.
		GALE NOTE *The cutter number(s) listed below have been given only as examples by the Library of Congress*
73.67.A1		General works
73.67.P3		Park Street
73.67.S7		State Street
73.67.T7		Tremont Street
73.67.W3		Washington Street
73.68.A-.68.Z		Suburbs. Sections of the city. Rivers
73.68.B4		Beacon Hill

	Massachusetts
73	**Boston**
	Sections. Localities. Districts, etc.
73.68.A-.68.Z	Suburbs. Sections of the city. Rivers — Continued
	Brighton, *see* F74.B73
73.68.C3	Castle Island
	Charlestown, *see* F74.C4
	Dorchester, *see* F74.D5
73.68.E2	East Boston
73.68.L43	Leather District
73.68.N65	North End
73.68.R2	Rainsford Island
73.68.R67	Roslindale
	Roxbury, *see* F74.R9
73.68.S7	South Boston
73.68.T5	Thompson Island
73.68.W47	West End
	West Roxbury, *see* F74.W59
73.69	Wards
	Buildings
73.7	Collective
73.8.A-.8.Z	Individual, A-Z
	GALE NOTE *The cutter number(s) listed below have been given only as examples by the Library of Congress*
73.8.C9	Crown Coffee House
73.8.F2	Faneuil Hall Market
73.8.O4	Old State House
73.8.P3	Parker House
73.8.S8	State House
	Elements in the population
73.9.A1	General works
73.9.A2-.9.Z	Individual elements
	For a list of racial, ethnic, and religious elements (with cutter numbers), see E184.A+
74.A-.Z	**Other cities, towns, etc., A-Z**
	GALE NOTE *The cutter number(s) listed below have been given only as examples by the Library of Congress*
74.B73	Brighton
74.C1	Cambridge
74.C4	Charlestown
74.C8	Concord
74.D5	Dorchester
74.G9	Groton
74.L98	Lynn
74.P8	Plymouth
74.P96	Provincetown
74.R9	Roxbury
74.S1	Salem
74.S8	Springfield
	Subarrange by Table F2 at the end of the text
74.T2	Taunton
	Including Old Colony Historical Society
74.W59	West Roxbury
74.W9	Worcester
	Elements in the population
75.A1	Collective
75.A2-.Z	Individual elements
	For a list of racial, ethnic, and religious elements (with cutter numbers), see E184.A+
	Rhode Island
76	**Periodicals. Societies. Collections**
76.5	**Museums. Exhibitions, exhibits**

	Rhode Island — Continued
77	**Gazetteers. Dictionaries. Geographic names**
77.3	**Guidebooks**
78	**Biography (Collective). Genealogy (Collective)**
78.2	**Historiography**
	Historians, *see* E175.5.A+
78.5	**Study and teaching**
79	**General works. Histories**
79.3	**Juvenile works**
	Pamphlets, addresses, essays, etc.
79.5	General
79.6	Anecdotes, legends, pageants, etc.
80	**Historic monuments (General). Illustrative material**
81	**Antiquities (Non-Indian)**
	By period
82	Early to 1775
	Including First Rhode Island Charter, 1663; the Narragansett country; union of plantations at Newport, Portsmouth, Providence, and Warwick, 1636-1643
	Including biography: John Clarke, Samuel Gorton, Roger Williams, etc.
	Cf. E83.67, King Philip's War, 1675-1676
	1775-1865
83	General
	Cf. E215.6, Gaspee affair
	Cf. E263.R4, Rhode Island in the Revolution (General)
	Cf. E230+, Military operations and battles
	Cf. E528.1+, Civil War, 1861-1865 (General)
83.4	Dorr Rebellion, 1842
	Including biography: Thomas Wilson Dorr, etc.
84	1865-1950
	Cf. D570.85.R4+, World War I, 1914-1918
	Cf. D769.85.R4+, World War II, 1939-1945
	Cf. E726.R4, War of 1898 (Spanish-American War)
85	1951-
87.A-.Z	**Regions, counties, etc., A-Z**
87.A15	Counties
87.A16	Mountains
87.A17	Rivers
87.A18	Lakes
87.A19	Islands
87.B55	Blackstone River and Valley (General, and Rhode Island)
	Cf. F72.B57 , Massachusetts
87.B6	Block Island (Manisees)
87.B7	Boundaries
	Cf. F72.B7, Massachusetts boundary
	Cf. F82, Massachusetts claims to Narragansett country
	Cf. F102.B7, Connecticut boundary
87.B86	Bristol Co.
87.K3	Kent Co.
87.N2	Narragansett Bay region
87.N5	Newport Co.
	For Block Island, see F87.B6
	For Rhode Island (Island), see F87.R4
87.P3	Pawtuxet River and Valley
87.P5	Pettaquamscutt Purchase
87.P9	Providence Co.
87.R4	Rhode Island (Island) (Aquidneck)
87.S25	Sakonnet River and Region
87.W3	Washington Co.

	Rhode Island — Continued
89.A-.Z	**Cities, towns, etc., A-Z**
	GALE NOTE *The cutter number(s) listed below have been given only as examples by the Library of Congress*
89.N5	Newport
89.P9	Providence
	Subarrange by Table F2 at the end of the text
	Elements in the population
90.A1	General works
90.A2-.Z	Individual elements
	For a list of racial, ethnic, and religious elements (with cutter numbers), see E184.A+
	Connecticut
91	**Periodicals. Societies. Collections**
91.5	**Museums. Exhibitions, exhibits**
92	**Gazetteers. Dictionaries. Geographic names**
92.3	**Guidebooks**
93	**Biography (Collective). Genealogy (Collective)**
93.2	**Historiography**
	Historians, *see* E175.5.A+
93.5	**Study and teaching**
94	**General works. Histories**
94.3	**Juvenile works**
	Pamphlets, addresses, essays, etc.
94.5	General
94.6	Anecdotes, legends, pageants, etc.
94.8	**Geography**
95	**Historic monuments (General). Illustrative material**
96	**Antiquities (Non-Indian)**
	By period
	Early to 1775
	Including early grants by the Council for New England; Dutch posts; etc.
	Including biography: John Winthrop, 1606-1676
	Cf. E83.63, Pequot War, 1636-1638
	Cf. E83.67, King Philip's War, 1675-1676
	Cf. E199, French and Indian War, 1755-1763
	Cf. F7.5, Government of Andros, 1688-1689
	Cf. F157.W9, Claims to Wyoming Valley, Susquehanna Company
97	General works
98	New Haven Colony
	Cf. F102.N5, New Haven County
	Cf. F104.N6, New Haven
99	1775-1865
	Cf. E263.C5, Connecticut in the Revolution (General)
	Cf. E230+, Military operations and battles in the Revolution
	Cf. E309, F483, F497.W5, Cession of western lands
	Cf. E357.7, Hartford Convention, 1814
	Cf. E359.5.C7, War of 1812
	Cf. E409.5.C6, War with Mexico, 1845-1848
	Cf. E499.1+, Civil War, 1861-1865 (General)
	Cf. F157.W9, Susquehanna claims
100	1865-1950
	Cf. D570.85.C8+, World War I, 1914-1918
	Cf. D769.85.C8+, World War II, 1939-1945
	Cf. E726.C7, War of 1898 (Spanish-American War)
101	1951-
102.A-.Z	**Regions, counties, etc., A-Z**
102.A15	Counties
102.A16	Mountains
102.A17	Rivers
102.A18	Lakes

	Connecticut
102.A-.Z	**Regions, counties, etc., A-Z — Continued**
102.A19	Islands
102.B7	Boundaries

> Cf. F72.B7, Massachusetts boundary
> Cf. F127.B7, New York boundary
> Cf. F157.W9, Pennsylvania-Connecticut boundary dispute ("Connecticut Gore," Susquehanna Company)

102.C2	Lake Candlewood
102.C7	Connecticut River and Valley, Conn.

> Cf. F12.C7, New England

102.F2	Fairfield Co.

> Including Norwalk Islands and Sheffield Island

	Firelands, see F497.W5
	Fishers Island, see F127.F5
102.H3	Hartford Co.
102.H7	Housatonic River and Valley (General, and Conn.)

> Cf. F72.H7, Massachusetts

102.L6	Litchfield Co.

> Including Highland Lake, Litchfield Hills
> For Berkshire Hills, see F72.B5

	Long Island, see F127.L8
102.M6	Middlesex Co.
102.N2	Naugatuck River and Valley
102.N5	New Haven Co.

> Including Leetes Island
> Cf. F98, New Haven Colony

102.N7	New London Co.
102.T4	The Thimbles
102.T6	Tolland Co.
	Western Reserve, see F497.W5
	Westmoreland (township, 1774; county, 1775), see F157.W9
102.W7	Windham Co.
104.A-.Z	**Cities, towns, etc., A-Z**

> GALE NOTE *The cutter number(s) listed below have been given only as examples by the Library of Congress*

104.H3	Hartford
104.L7	Litchfield
104.N6	New Haven

> Subarrange by Table F2 at the end of the text

104.N7	New London
104.N93	Norwich
104.S8	Stamford
	Elements in the population
105.A1	General works
105.A2-.Z	Individual elements

> For a list of racial, ethnic, and religious elements (with cutter numbers), see E184.A+

106	**Atlantic coast of North America. Middle Atlantic States**

> Including the eastern United States as a whole; Atlantic States (Maine to Florida); Middle States; Appalachian Mountains (General)
> Class here descriptive and historic works after 1825
> For earlier works, see E162-165 , E186-375
> Cf. F157.D4, Delaware River and Valley
> Cf. F157.S8, Susquehanna River and Valley
> Cf. F172.D3, Delaware Bay and region
> Cf. F187.C5, Chesapeake Bay and region
> Cf. F187.P8, Potomac River and Valley
> Cf. F217.A65, Appalachian Mountains, Southern
> Cf. F1035.8, Atlantic coast of Canada

	New York
116	**Periodicals. Societies. Collections**
	New York Historical Society
	Collections
116.N62	First and second series, 1811-1859
116.N63	John Watts de Peyster Publication Fund series
	Formerly Publication Fund series
116.N638	Quarterly bulletin, 1917-
116.N64	Proceedings, 1843-1849
116.N65	Annual report of the Executive Committee
116.N66	Charter, constitution, etc. Editions by date
116.N67	Lists of members. Editions by date
116.N68	Anniversary address. By date
116.N69	Inaugural address of President. By date
116.N7-.N76	Other official publications. By title
116.N77A-.N77Z	Publications about the society or its officers. By author or name of officer
116.5	**Museums. Exhibitions, exhibits**
117	**Gazetteers. Dictionaries. Geographic names**
117.3	**Guidebooks**
118	**Biography (Collective). Genealogy (Collective)**
118.2	**Historiography**
	Historians, *see* E175.5.A+
118.5	**Study and teaching**
119	**General works. Histories**
119.3	**Juvenile works**
	Pamphlets, addresses, essays, etc.
119.5	General
119.6	Anecdotes, legends, pageants, etc.
120	**Historic monuments (General). Illustrative material**
121	**Antiquities (Non-Indian)**
	By period
	Early to 1775
	Including English province, 1664-1774; Dutch reconquest, 1673-1674; Leisler's Rebellion, 1689; Agrarian conflicts, 1711-1715
	Including biography: Nicholas Bayard; William Burnet; Cadwallader Colden; Thomas Dongan, Earl of Limerick; Caleb Heathcote; Jacob Leisler; etc.
	Cf. E101+, Early voyages to America
	Cf. E196, King William's War, 1689-1697
	Cf. E199, French and Indian War, 1755-1763
	Cf. F7.5, Andros and his government, 1688-1689
	Cf. F52, New Hampshire Grants
	Cf. F1030, French explorations, invasions, and missionaries in western New York
	Cf. HD196.A+, Agrarian conflicts, 1711-1715
122	General works
122.1	New Netherlands. Dutch Colony, 1610-1664
	Including biography: Arent van Curler, Adriaen van der Donck, Jonas Michaelius, Peter Minuit, Peter Stuyvesant, etc.
	Cf. E83.655, Indian uprising of 1655
	Cf. E83.663, Esopus Indian War, 1663-1664
	Cf. F127.R32, Rensselaerswyck
	Cf. F167, Subjugation of the Swedes on the Delaware, 1655
123	1775-1865
	Including biography: John Watts DePeyster, James Kent, John Alsop King, Elias Warner Leavenworth, Henry Cruse Murphy, Daniel D. Tompkins, Stephen Van Rensselaer, etc.
	Cf. E263.N6, New York in the Revolution (General)
	Cf. E230+, Military operations and battles in the Revolution
	Cf. E359.5.N6, War of 1812 (General)
	Cf. E355+, Military operations and battles in the War of 1812
	Cf. E409.5.N6, War with Mexico, 1845-1848 (General)
	Cf. E523.1+, Civil War, 1861-1865 (General)

	New York
	By period
123	1775-1865 — Continued
	Cf. F1032, Burning of the "Caroline"; the McLeod case
	Cf. HD199, Antirent movement, 1835-1846
	Cf. HS525+, Antimasonic Controversy, 1827-1845
	Cf. TC625.E6, Erie Canal
124	1865-1950
	Including biography: John Alden Dix, Daniel Drew, Roswell Pettibone Flower, Herbert Henry Lehman, Patrick Henry McCarren, James Aloysius O'Gorman, John Boyd Thacher, etc.
	Cf. D570.85.N4+, World War I, 1914-1918
	Cf. D769.85.N4+, World War II, 1939-1945
	Cf. E726.N5, War of 1898 (Spanish-American War)
	1951-
125	General works
	Biography
125.2	Collective
125.3.A-.3.Z	Individual, A-Z
	GALE NOTE *See note at the head of Table F5 at the end of the text for further instructions on how to subdivide this number*
127.A-.Z	**Regions, counties, etc., A-Z**
127.A15	Counties
127.A16	Mountains
127.A17	Rivers
127.A18	Lakes
127.A19	Islands
127.A2	Adirondack Mountains
	Including Esther Mountain, Mount Marcy, etc.
127.A3	Albany Co.
	Including Helderberg Mountains
	Cf. F52 , New Hampshire
	Cf. F127.R32 , Rensselaerswyck
127.A4	Allegany Co.
127.A43	Allegany State Park
127.A45	Allegheny River and Valley, N.Y.
	Cf. F157.A5, General, and Pennsylvania
	Allens Creek and Valley, *see F127.M6*
	Altona Flat Rock, *see F127.C77*
	Au Sable River and Valley, *see F127.E8*
127.B4	Beaver Kill and Beaver Kill Valley
127.B48	Black River
	"Boston Ten Townships," *see F127.T6*
127.B7	Boundaries
	Cf. F72.B7, Massachusetts boundary
	Cf. F142.B7, New Jersey boundary
	For Massachusetts territorial claims to western New York, see F127.G2
	For New Hampshire-New York dispute over New Hampshire Grants, see F52
	Bronx Co., *see F128.68.B8*
127.B8	Broome Co.
	Cf. F127.G2, Genesee region
	Cf. F127.T6, "Massachusetts (or Boston) Ten Townships"
127.C28	Castleton Island State Park
127.C3	Catskill Mountains
	Including Kaaterskill Park, Rip Van Winkle Trail
127.C4	Cattaraugus Co.
127.C5	Cayuga Co.
127.C52	Cayuga Lake
127.C6	Lake Champlain region (General, and N.Y.)
	Including Champlain Valley; Lake Champlain Tercentenary, 1909
	Cf. F57.C4, Vermont

	New York
127.A-.Z	**Regions, counties, etc., A-Z**
127.C6	Lake Champlain region (General, and N.Y.) — Continued
	Cf. F57.G7, Grand Isle Co., Vt.
	Charlotte Co. (1772), see F127.W3
127.C7	Chautauqua Co.
	Including Chautauqua Creek and Valley, Lake Chautauqua, Portage Trail
127.C72	Chemung Co.
127.C73	Chemung River and Valley (General, and N.Y.)
	Cf. F157.C37 , Pennsylvania
127.C76	Chenango Co.
127.C765	Chenango River and Valley. Chenango Canal
	Clermont State Park, see F127.L73
127.C77	Clinton Co.
	Including Altona Flat Rock
127.C8	Columbia Co.
127.C83	Constitution Island
	Cornwall Co., see F23
127.C85	Cortland Co.
	Cumberland Co. (1768), see F52
127.D3	Delaware Co.
127.D4	Delaware River and Valley, N.Y.
	Cf. F142.D4, New Jersey
	Cf. F157.D4, General, and Pennsylvania
	Cf. F172.D4, Delaware
127.D8	Dutchess Co.
	Including Little (or Upper) Nine Partners Patent, etc.
127.E5	Erie Canal
127.E6	Erie Co.
127.E65	Lake Erie region, N.Y.
	Cf. F555, Lake Erie (General)
127.E8	Essex Co.
	Including Au Sable River and Valley, Au Sable Chasm, etc.
	Esther Mountain, see F127.A2
127.F4	Finger Lakes region
	Cf. F127.C52, Cayuga Lake, etc.
	Fire Island, see F127.S9
127.F5	Fishers Island
	Cf. F129.S74 , Southold
127.F8	Franklin Co.
	Including Mount Seward, Saranac Lakes
127.F88	Fulton Chain Lakes and Region
127.F9	Fulton Co.
	Gardiner's Island, see F129.E13
127.G15	Gateway National Recreation Area (General, and New York)
	Cf. F142.G37, New Jersey
127.G19	Genesee Co.
127.G2	Genesee region. Genesee River and Valley
	Including Phelps-Gorham Purchase (1788), etc.
	Cf. F127.H7, Holland Purchase
	Cf. F127.T6, "Massachusetts (or Boston) Ten Townships"
127.G3	Lake George
	Gloucester Co. (1770), see F52
	Grand Island, see F129.G68
127.G7	Greene Co.
	For Catskill Mountains, see F127.C3
	Grindstone Island, see F127.T5
127.H2	Hamilton Co.
	Including Blue Mountain Lake, Long Lake, Raquette Lake
	Hamptons, see F127.S9

	New York
127.A-.Z	**Regions, counties, etc., A-Z — Continued**
	Helderberg Mountains, *see* F127.A3
127.H5	Herkimer Co.
	Including West Canada Creek
	Hiawatha Island, *see* F127.S96
127.H7	Holland Purchase. Treaty of Big Tree, 1797
127.H73	Hoosic River and Valley (General, and N.Y.)
	Cf. F57.B4, Vermont
	Cf. F72.B5, Massachusetts
127.H8	Hudson River and Valley (General, and N.Y.)
	Including Highlands; Hudson-Fulton Celebration, 1909; Palisades
	Cf. F142.B4, New Jersey Palisades
	Cf. F142.H83, New Jersey
	Irondequoit Creek and Valley, *see* F127.M6
127.J4	Jefferson Co.
127.K4	Keuka Lake
127.K5	Kings Co.
	Cf. F129.B7 , Borough of Brooklyn
127.L6	Lewis Co.
127.L7	Livingston Co.
	Including Hemlock Lake
127.L73	Livingston Manor. Clermont State Park
127.L8	Long Island
	For Fishers Island, see F127.F5
	For Shelter Island, see F127.S54
	Cf. F127.K5, Kings Co.
	Cf. F127.N2, Nassau Co.
	Cf. F127.Q3, Queens Co.
	Cf. F127.S9, Suffolk Co.
127.M2	Madison Co.
	Manhasset Neck, *see* F127.N2
	Marcy, Mount, *see* F127.A2
	"Massachusetts (or Boston) Ten Townships," *see* F127.T6
127.M4	Military tract (set off from Tryon Co., 1782)
127.M5	Minisink region
	For Minisink Patent (1704), see F142.B7
127.M55	Mohawk River and Valley
	Including Mohawk Trail, N.Y.
	For Mohawk Trail, Mass., see F72.B5
127.M6	Monroe Co.
	Including Allens Creek and Valley, Irondequoit Creek and Valley
127.M7	Montgomery Co.
	Including Tryon Co. (1772-1784)
127.N2	Nassau Co.
	Including Manhasset Neck
	New Hampshire Grants, *see* F52
	New York Co., *see* F128+
127.N38	New York State Seaway Trail
127.N5	Niagara Co.
127.N6	Niagara River and region (General, and N.Y.)
	Including Niagara frontier, Niagara River and Valley, etc.
	Cf. F1059.N5, Niagara Peninsula, Ontario
127.N8	Niagara Falls
	Including State Reservation, Goat Island
	Cf. F1059.Q3 , Queen Victoria Niagara Falls Park, Ontario
127.O5	Oneida Co.
127.O52	Oneida Lake
127.O6	Onondaga Co.
	Including Onondaga Lake

127.A-.Z	**New York** **Regions, counties, etc., A-Z — Continued**
127.O7	Ontario Co. *Cf. F127.G2, Genesee region* *Cf. F127.H7, Holland Purchase*
127.O72	Lake Ontario region, N.Y. *Cf. F556, Lake Ontario (General)*
127.O8	Orange Co. *Including Newburgh Bay* *For Highlands, see F127.H8* *For Minisink region, see F127.M5* *For Wawayanda Patent (1703), see F142.B7*
127.O9	Orleans Co.
127.O91	Oswego Co.
127.O93	Otsego Co. Ozonia Lake, *see F127.S2* Palisades of the Hudson, *see F127.H8* Phelps-Gorham Purchase (1788), *see F127.G2*
127.P9	Putnam Co.
127.Q3	Queens Co. *Cf. F128.68.Q4, Borough of Queens* Raquette Lake, *see F127.H2*
127.R3	Rensselaer Co. *Including Taconic Mountains*
127.R32	Rensselaerswyck. The Van Rensselaer Manor *Cf. HD199, Antirent movement, 1835-1846* Richmond Co., *see F127.S7* Robins Island, *see F127.S9*
127.R6	Rockland Co.
127.S2	St. Lawrence Co. *Including Black Lake, Ozonia Lake*
127.S23	St. Lawrence River and Valley, N.Y. *Cf. F127.T5, Thousand Islands* *Cf. F1050, General, and Canada*
127.S235	Sampson State Park Saranac Lakes, *see F127.F8*
127.S26	Saratoga Co. *Including Mount McGregor, etc.*
127.S27	Schenectady Co.
127.S3	Schoharie Co. *Including Schoharie Creek and Valley, etc.*
127.S33	Schroon River and Valley
127.S34	Schuyler Co. *Including Watkins Glen* Seaway Trail, *see F127.N38*
127.S4	Seneca Co.
127.S43	Seneca Lake Shawangunk Mountains, *see F127.U4*
127.S54	Shelter Island
127.S7	Staten Island. Richmond Co. Borough of Richmond
127.S8	Steuben Co. *Including Canisteo River*
127.S9	Suffolk Co. *Including Fire Island, Fire Island State Park, Hamptons, Robins Island* *For Fishers Island, see F127.F5*
127.S91	Sullivan Co. *For Minisink region, see F127.M5*
127.S96	Susquehanna River and Valley, N.Y. *Including Hiawatha Island* *Cf. F157.S8, General, and Pennsylvania*

	New York
127.A-.Z	**Regions, counties, etc., A-Z**
127.S96	Susquehanna River and Valley, N.Y. — Continued
	Cf. F187.S8, Maryland
127.T5	Thousand Islands
	Including Carleton Island, Grenell Island, Grindstone Island
127.T6	Tioga Co. "Massachusetts (or Boston) Ten Townships"
	Cf. F127.G2, Genesee region
127.T7	Tompkins Co.
	Tryon Co. (1772-1784), *see* F127.M7
127.T83	Tug Hill region
127.U4	Ulster Co.
	Including Lake Minnewaska, Mohonk Lake, Mount Meenahga, Shawangunk Mountains
	For Catskill Mountains, see F127.C3
	For Minisink region, see F127.M5
127.U54	Unadilla River and Valley
127.W2	Warren Co.
	Including Luzerne Lake
	Cf. F127.G3 , Lake George
127.W3	Washington Co.
	Including Charlotte County (1772)
	Cf. F52, New Hampshire Grants
	Cf. F127.G3, Lake George
	Wawayanda Patent (1703), *see* F142.B7
127.W4	Wayne Co.
127.W5	Westchester Co.
	Including Fordham Manor, Philipsburg Manor, Van Cortlandt Manor
	Cf. F128.68.B8, Borough of the Bronx
127.W9	Wyoming Co.
127.Y3	Yates Co.
	New York (City). New York (County)
128.1	Periodicals. Societies. Collections
128.15	Museums. Exhibitions, exhibits
	For World's Fair, 1939-1940, see T785
128.18	Guidebooks
128.25	Biography (Collective). Genealogy (Collective)
128.27	Historiography
128.29	Study and teaching
128.3	General works. Histories
128.33	Juvenile works
	Pamphlets, addresses, essays, etc.
128.35	General
128.36	Anecdotes, legends, pageants, etc.
128.37	Historic monuments. Illustrative material
128.39	Antiquities (Non-Indian)
	By period
128.4	Early to 1775
	Including New Amsterdam; Negro plot, 1741
	Including biography: Annetje Jane Bogardus, etc.
	Cf. F122+, New York (State)
128.44	1775-1865
	Including fire, 1835; Draft riot, 1863
	Including biography: Michael Floy, Philip Hone, Fernando Wood, etc.
	Cf. E263.N6, New York in the Revolution
	Cf. E230+, Military operations and battles in the Revolution
128.47	1865-1900
	Including Riot, 1871; Blizzard, 1888
	Including biography: Richard Croker, Andrew Haswell Green, John Kelly, Abram Stevens Hewitt, William Marcy Tweed, etc.

	New York
	New York (City). New York (County)
	By period — Continued
128.5	1901-1950. Greater New York
	Including "General Slocum" disaster, 1904
	Including biography: Edward Joseph Flynn, William Jay Gaynor, Seth Low, James John Walker, etc.
	Cf. F127.Q3, Queens County
	Cf. F127.S7, Staten Island, Richmond County
	Cf. F129.B7, Brooklyn
	1951-1980
128.52	General works
	Biography
128.53	Collective
128.54.A-.54.Z	Individual, A-Z
	GALE NOTE *See note at the head of Table F5 at the end of the text for further instructions on how to subdivide this number*
	1981-
128.55	General works
	Biography
128.56	Collective
128.57.A-.57.Z	Individual, A-Z
	Sections. Localities. Districts, etc.
128.6	General works
128.61.A-.61.Z	Cemeteries
	GALE NOTE *The cutter number(s) listed below have been given only as examples by the Library of Congress*
128.61.A1	General works
128.61.W8	Woodlawn Cemetery
128.62	Churches
	For architecture, see Subclass NA
	For religious aspects, see Subclass BX
128.625	Hotels, taverns, etc.
128.627	Places of amusement
128.63	Harbor
128.64.A-.64.Z	Monuments. Statues
	GALE NOTE *The cutter number(s) listed below have been given only as examples by the Library of Congress*
128.64.A1	General works
128.64.G7	Grant Monument (Grant's Tomb)
128.64.L6	Statue of Liberty
128.65.A-.65.Z	Parks. Squares. Circles
	GALE NOTE *The cutter number(s) listed below have been given only as examples by the Library of Congress*
128.65.A1	General works
128.65.B3	Battery
128.65.B8	Bronx Parkway
128.65.C3	Central Park
128.65.C5	City Hall Park
128.65.R5	Riverside Park
128.65.Z6	Zoological Park
128.67.A-.67.Z	Streets. Bridges. Railroads, etc.
	GALE NOTE *The cutter number(s) listed below have been given only as examples by the Library of Congress*
128.67.A1	General works
128.67.B6	Bowery
128.67.B7	Broadway
128.67.F4	Fifth Avenue
128.67.F7	Forty-second Street
128.67.P3	Park Avenue

	New York
	New York (City). New York (County)
	Sections. Localities. Districts, etc.
128.67.A-.67.Z	Streets. Bridges. Railroads, etc. — Continued
128.67.R6	Riverside Drive
128.67.W2	Wall Street
128.68.A-.68.Z	Suburbs. Sections of the city. Rivers
	GALE NOTE *The cutter number(s) listed below have been given only as examples by the Library of Congress*
128.68.A1	General works
128.68.B6	Bloomingdale
128.68.B8	Bronx (Borough)
	Including Morrisania Manor, Pelham Manor, etc.
	Cf. F127.W5, Westchester Co.
	Brooklyn (Borough), *see* F129.B7
128.68.C47	Chinatown
128.68.C5	City Island
	Coney Island, *see* F129.C75
128.68.G7	Governor's Island
128.68.G8	Greenwich Village
128.68.H3	Harlem
128.68.H4	Harlem River
	Long Island City, *see* F129.L78
128.68.Q4	Queens (Borough)
	Cf. F127.Q3, Queens County
	Richmond (Borough), *see* F127.S7
	Rockaway Beach, *see* F129.R8
	Staten Island, *see* F127.S7
128.68.S9	Stuyvesant Village
128.68.W2	Washington Heights
128.69	Wards
	Buildings
128.7	General works. Collective
128.8.A-.8.Z	Individual, A-Z
	GALE NOTE *The cutter number(s) listed below have been given only as examples by the Library of Congress*
128.8.M8	Morris Mansion (Jumel Mansion)
128.8.P4	Pennsylvania Station
128.8.R7	Rockefeller Center
128.8.V2	Van Cortlandt Mansion
128.8.W82	Woolworth Building
	Elements in the population
128.9.A1	General works
128.9.A2-.9.Z	Individual elements
	For a list of racial, ethnic, and religious elements (with cutter numbers), see E184.A+
129.A-.Z	**Other cities, towns, etc., A-Z**
	GALE NOTE *The cutter number(s) listed below have been given only as examples by the Library of Congress*
129.A1	General works
129.A3	Albany
	Subarrange by Table F2 at the end of the text
129.B7	Brooklyn
	A borough of New York (City)
129.B8	Buffalo
	Subarrange by Table F2 at the end of the text
129.C75	Coney Island
129.E13	East Hampton
	Including Gardiner's Island, Gardiner Manor
129.G68	Grand Island
129.H99	Hyde Park

	New York
129.A-.Z	**Other cities, towns, etc., A-Z — Continued**
129.L78	Long Island City
129.O98	Oyster Bay
	Including Sagamore Hill
129.R7	Rochester
	Subarrange by Table F2 at the end of the text
129.R8	Rockaway Beach
129.S3	Saratoga Springs
129.S74	Southold
	Cf. F127.F5, Fishers Island
	Elements in the population
130.A1	General works
130.A2-.Z	Individual elements
	For a list of racial, ethnic, and religious elements (with cutter numbers), see E184.A+
	New Jersey
131	**Periodicals. Societies. Collections**
131.5	**Museums. Exhibitions, exhibits**
132	**Gazetteers. Dictionaries. Geographic names**
132.3	**Guidebooks**
133	**Biography (Collective). Genealogy (Collective)**
133.2	**Historiography**
	Historians, *see* E175.5.A+
133.5	**Study and teaching**
134	**General works. Histories**
134.3	**Juvenile works**
	Pamphlets, addresses, essays, etc.
134.5	General
134.6	Anecdotes, legends, pageants, etc.
135	**Historic monuments (General). Illustrative material**
136	**Antiquities (Non-Indian)**
	By period
137	Early to 1775
	Including Plowden's New Albion Grant; East and West Jersey, 1676-1702
	Including biography: Sir George Carteret, John Fenwick, William Franklin, etc.
	Cf. E198, King George's War, 1744-1748
	Cf. F142.S2, Fenwick's Colony
	Cf. F167, New Sweden
138	1775-1865
	Including biography: Richard Stockton Field, William Churchill Houston, Andrew Kirkpatrick, etc.
	Cf. E263.N5, New Jersey in the Revolution
	Cf. E230+, Military operations and battles in the Revolution
	Cf. E359.5.N4, War of 1812 (General)
	Cf. E521.1+, Civil War, 1861-1865 (General)
139	1865-1950
	Including biography: Harold Giles Hoffman, John Peter Jackson, Henry Cooper Pitney, etc.
	Cf. D570.85.N3+, World War I, 1914-1918
	Cf. D769.85.N3+, World War II, 1939-1945
	Cf. E726.N4, War of 1898 (Spanish-American War)
	1951-
140	General works
	Biography
140.2	Collective
140.22.A-.22.Z	Individual, A-Z
	GALE NOTE *See note at the head of Table F5 at the end of the text for further instructions on how to subdivide this number*
142.A-.Z	**Regions, counties, etc., A-Z**
142.A15	Counties
142.A16	Mountains

	New Jersey
142.A-.Z	**Regions, counties, etc., A-Z — Continued**
142.A17	Rivers
142.A18	Lakes
142.A19	Islands
142.A79	Atlantic Coast
142.A8	Atlantic Co.
	Barnegat Bay, *see* F142.O2
142.B4	Bergen Co.
	Including Hackensack River and Valley; New Jersey Palisades
	Cf. F127.H8, New York
142.B7	Boundaries
	Including Minisink and Wawayanda Patents
	Cf. F172.B7, Delaware boundary
142.B9	Burlington Co.
	Including Rancocas Valley
142.C16	Camden Co.
142.C2	Cape May Co.
142.C9	Cumberland Co.
	Deal Lake, *see* F142.M7
142.D3	Delaware Bay region, N.J.
	Cf. F172.D3 , General, and Delaware
142.D4	Delaware River and Valley, N.J.
	Cf. F127.D4, New York
	Cf. F157.D4, General, and Pennsylvania
	Cf. F172.D4, Delaware
	Delaware Water Gap, *see* F157.D5
142.E8	Essex Co.
	Including Nutley area
142.G37	Gateway National Recreation Area
	Cf. F127.G15, General, and New York
142.G5	Gloucester Co.
142.H35	Hackensack Meadowlands
142.H7	Lake Hopatcong
142.H8	Hudson Co.
142.H83	Hudson River and Valley, N.J.
	Cf. F127.H8, General, and New York
	Cf. F142.B4, New Jersey Palisades
142.H9	Hunterdon Co.
142.J4	Jersey Shore
142.L65	Long Beach Island
142.M5	Mercer Co.
142.M6	Middlesex Co.
142.M64	Millstone River and Valley
142.M7	Monmouth Co.
	Including Deal Lake, Monmouth Patent, Navesink River and Valley, Shark River
142.M8	Morris Co.
142.M85	Morristown National Historical Park
142.M9	Mullica River
	Navesink River and Valley, *see* F142.M7
	New Albion Grant, *see* F137
142.N48	New Jersey Coastal Heritage Trail
142.O2	Ocean Co.
	Including Barnegat Bay, Long Beach, Sedge Islands
	Palisades of New Jersey, *see* F142.B4
	Palisades of the Hudson (Interstate park), *see* F127.H8
142.P2	Passaic Co.
	Including Ringwood Manor
142.P3	Passaic River and Valley
142.P5	Pine Barrens. Pinelands National Reserve

	New Jersey
142.A-.Z	**Regions, counties, etc., A-Z — Continued**
	Pinelands National Reserve, *see* F142.P5
142.R16	Ramapo River and Valley, N.J.
142.R2	Raritan River and Valley
142.S2	Salem Co.
	Including John Fenwick's colony
	Sedge Islands, *see* F142.O2
142.S6	Somerset Co.
	Staten Island, *see* F127.S7
142.S9	Sussex Co.
	For Minisink Patent, see F142.B7
	For Minisink region, see F127.M5
142.U5	Union Co.
142.W2	Warren Co.
	For Delaware Water Gap, see F157.D5
142.W47	Wharton State Forest
144.A-.Z	**Cities, towns, etc., A-Z**
	GALE NOTE *The cutter number(s) listed below have been given only as examples by the Library of Congress*
144.A1	General works
144.A8	Atlantic City
144.C2	Camden
	East Orange, *see* F144.O6
144.E4	Elizabeth
144.J5	Jersey City
	Subarrange by Table F2 at the end of the text
144.N6	Newark
	Subarrange by Table F2 at the end of the text
144.O6	Orange (East, South, West)
144.P4	Paterson
	South Orange, *see* F144.O6
144.T7	Trenton
	Subarrange by Table F2 at the end of the text
	West Orange, *see* F144.O6
	Elements in the population
145.A1	General works
145.A2-.Z	Individual elements
	For a list of racial, ethnic, and religious elements (with cutter numbers), see E184.A+
	Pennsylvania
146	**Periodicals. Societies. Collections**
146.5	**Museums. Exhibitions, exhibits**
147	**Gazetteers. Dictionaries. Geographic names**
147.3	**Guidebooks**
148	**Biography (Collective). Genealogy (Collective)**
148.2	**Historiography**
	Historians, *see* E175.5.A+
148.5	**Study and teaching**
149	**General works. Histories**
149.3	**Juvenile works**
	Pamphlets, addresses, essays, etc.
149.5	General
149.6	Anecdotes, legends, pageants, etc.
149.8	**Geography**
150	**Historic monuments (General). Illustrative material**
151	**Antiquities (Non-Indian)**
	By period
	Early to 1775
152	General
	Including Grant to Penn, 1681; the Paxton boys

                           Pennsylvania
                             By period
                               Early to 1775

152	General — Continued

            Including biography: Andrew Hamilton, Sir William Keith, James Logan, Francis Daniel Pastorius, Richard Peters, Michael Schlatter, Conrad Weiser, etc.

            Cf. E83.76, Pontiac's Conspiracy, 1763-1765

            Cf. E198, King George's War, 1744-1748

            Cf. E199, French and Indian War, 1755-1763

            Cf. F157.W5, Virginia claims in southwestern Pennsylvania

            Cf. F157.W9, Connecticut claims in northeastern Pennsylvania

| 152.2 | The proprietors: William Penn and family |
| 153 | 1775-1865 |

            Including Harrisburg Convention, 1788; Buckshot War, 1838

            Including biography: Charles Biddle, Benjamin Chew, James Cooper, William John Duane, Thomas Earle, John Bannister Gibson, Joseph Hiester, Ellis Lewis, Joseph Ritner, William Rodman, George Washington Woodward, etc.

            Cf. E263.P4, Pennsylvania in the Revolution

            Cf. E230+, Military operations and battles in the Revolution

            Cf. E315, Whisky Rebellion, 1794

            Cf. E326, Fries' Rebellion, 1798-1799

            Cf. E359.5.P3, War of 1812

            Cf. E409.5.P3, War with Mexico, 1845-1848

            Cf. E527+, Civil War, 1861-1865 (General)

            Cf. E470.2, E471+, Campaigns and battles in the Civil War

            Cf. F157.W9, Connecticut settlers in Wyoming Valley, Susquehanna claim

| 154 | 1865-1950 |

            Including biography: John Wallace Crawford; John A. Lemon; Arthur George Olmsted; Samuel Whitaker Pennypacker; George Ross, 1841-1894; etc.

            Cf. D570.85.P4+, World War I, 1914-1918

            Cf. D769.85.P4+, World War II, 1939-1945

            Cf. E726.P4, War of 1898 (Spanish-American War)

            Cf. HV6452.A+, Molly Maguires

                             1951-

155	General works
	Biography
155.2	Collective
155.3.A-.3.Z	Individual, A-Z

            GALE NOTE *See note at the head of Table F5 at the end of the text for further instructions on how to subdivide this number*

157.A-.Z	**Regions, counties, etc., A-Z**
157.A15	Counties
157.A16	Mountains
157.A17	Rivers
157.A18	Lakes
157.A19	Islands
157.A2	Adams Co.

            For Conewago Creek and Valley, see F157.C75

| 157.A4 | Allegheny Co. |
| 157.A5 | Allegheny River and Valley (General, and Pa.) |

            Cf. F127.A45, New York

157.A7	Armstrong Co.
157.B16	Bald Eagle Mountain
157.B2	Beaver Co.

            Including Ohio River and Valley, Pa.

            Cf. F516+, General

157.B23	Beaver River and Valley
157.B25	Bedford Co.
157.B3	Berks Co.

            Including Oley Valley

	Pennsylvania
157.A-.Z	**Regions, counties, etc., A-Z — Continued**
157.B5	Blair Co.
157.B65	Blue Mountains
157.B7	Boundaries. Mason and Dixon's Line

	For Connecticut claims in northeastern Pennsylvania, see F157.W9
	For Virginia claim to land south and east of the Ohio River, see F157.W5
	Cf. F127.B7, New York boundary
	Cf. F497.B7, Ohio boundary

157.B76	Bradford Co.
157.B77	Brandywine Creek and Valley (General, and Pennsylvania)
	Cf. F172.B78, Delaware
157.B8	Bucks Co.
	For Perkiomen River and Valley, see F157.M7
	Buffalo Creek and Valley, *see F157.U5*
157.B87	Butler Co.
157.C16	Cambria Co.
157.C18	Cameron Co.
157.C2	Carbon Co.
157.C3	Centre Co.
	Including Penn's Cave, etc.
157.C37	Chemung River and Valley, Pa.
	Cf. F127.C73, General, and New York
157.C4	Chester Co.
157.C5	Clarion Co.
157.C52	Clarion River
157.C53	Clearfield Co.
157.C6	Clinton Co.
157.C67	Cocalico Creek and Valley
157.C7	Columbia Co.
157.C73	Conemaugh River and Valley
	Conestoga Creek and Valley, *see F157.L2*
157.C75	Conewago Creek and Valley
157.C76	Cook Forest Park
157.C77	Crawford Co.
	Including Conneaut Lake
157.C8	Cumberland Co.
	Including Old Cumberland Co. (Formed 1750)
157.C85	Cumberland Road. National Road
	Cf. HE356.C8, Traffic engineering
157.C9	Cumberland (Kittochtinny) Valley
	Including Cumberland and Franklin Counties
	For Franklin County only, see F157.F8
157.D2	Dauphin Co.
157.D28	Delaware and Lehigh National Heritage Corridor
157.D3	Delaware Co.
157.D4	Delaware River and Valley (General, and Pa.)
	Cf. F127.D4, New York
	Cf. F142.D4, New Jersey
	Cf. F172.D4, Delaware
157.D5	Delaware Water Gap
157.E4	Elk Co.
157.E45	Endless Mountains
157.E6	Erie Co.
	Including Lake Erie region, Pa.
	Cf. F555, Lake Erie (General)
157.F2	Fayette Co. (Formed 1783)
	Cf. F157.W5, Old Westmoreland Co.
157.F65	Forbes Road
157.F7	Forest Co.

	Pennsylvania
157.A-.Z	**Regions, counties, etc., A-Z — Continued**
157.F8	Franklin Co.
	Including Cumberland Valley (the part in Franklin Co.), Conococheague Creek and Valley
	Cf. F157.C9, Cumberland Valley (General, and Cumberland Co.)
	Cf. F187.W3, Conococheague Creek, Md.
157.F9	Fulton Co.
157.G8	Greene Co. (Formed 1796)
	Cf. F157.W5 , Old Westmoreland Co.
157.H9	Huntingdon Co.
	Independence National Historical Park, *see* F158.65.I3
157.I3	Indiana Co.
157.J4	Jefferson Co.
157.J6	Juniata Co.
157.J7	Juniata River and Valley
157.L15	Lackawanna Co.
157.L17	Lackawanna River and Valley
157.L2	Lancaster Co.
	Including Conestoga Creek, Mill Creek and Valley, Pequea Creek
157.L3	Lawrence Co.
	League Island, *see* F158.68.L4
157.L4	Lebanon Co.
157.L5	Lehigh Co.
157.L6	Lehigh River and Valley
157.L8	Luzerne Co.
157.L9	Lycoming Co.
157.M2	McKean Co.
157.M3	Mahoning River and Valley, Pa.
	Cf. F497.M2 , General, and Ohio
	Mason and Dixon's line, *see* F157.B7
157.M5	Mercer Co.
157.M55	Mifflin Co.
	Mill Creek and Valley, *see* F157.L2
157.M58	Monongahela River and Valley (General, and Pa.)
	Cf. F247.M6, West Virginia
157.M6	Monroe Co.
	Including Pocono Mountains, etc.
	For Delaware Water Gap, see F157.D5
157.M7	Montgomery Co.
	Including Perkiomen River and Valley, etc.
157.M8	Montour Co.
157.N7	Northampton Co.
157.N8	Northumberland Co.
157.O26	Octoraro Creek and Valley (General and Pennsylvania)
	Cf. F187.O27, Maryland
	Ohio River and Valley, *see* F157.B2
	Oley Valley, *see* F157.B3
157.P44	Pennsylvania Dutch Country
	Cf. F157.L2, Pennsylvania Dutch in Lancaster County
157.P5	Perry Co.
157.P56	Philadelphia Co.
	Cf. F158.44 , Consolidation Act merging the county into the city in 1854
157.P6	Pike Co.
157.P63	Pine Creek (Potter County-Lycoming County)
157.P64	Pine Creek Gorge Natural Area
157.P8	Potter Co.
157.S3	Schuylkill Co.
157.S33	Schuylkill River and Valley
157.S47	Shenango River and Valley
157.S49	Sinnamahoning Creek

	Pennsylvania
157.A-.Z	**Regions, counties, etc., A-Z — Continued**
157.S5	Snyder Co.
157.S6	Somerset Co.
157.S67	Sullivan Co.
	Including Eagle's Mere
157.S7	Susquehanna Co.
157.S8	Susquehanna River and Valley (General, and Pa.)
	Cf. F127.S96, New York
	Cf. F187.S8, Maryland
157.S9	West Branch of the Susquehanna
157.T5	Tioga Co.
157.U5	Union Co.
	Including Buffalo Creek and Valley
157.V4	Venango Co.
157.W2	Warren Co.
157.W3	Washington Co. (Formed 1781)
	Cf. F157.W5, Old Westmoreland Co.
157.W35	Wayne Co.
157.W5	Westmoreland Co.
	Including Old Westmoreland County, formed 1773 (present-day Westmoreland, Washington, Fayette, and Greene Counties); boundary disputes with Virginia until 1784 over land south and east of the Ohio River (Virginia's so-called District of West Augusta: counties of Monongalia, Yohogania, and Ohio)
	Cf. F157.W9, Connecticut's old county of Westmoreland
	Cf. F247.M7, Monongalia Co., W. Va.
	Cf. F247.O3, Ohio Co., W. Va.
157.W8	Wyoming Co.
157.W9	Wyoming Valley
	Including Connecticut claims, Susquehanna Company, "Connecticut Gore," Connecticut town and county of Westmoreland
157.Y6	York Co.
	For Conewago Creek and Valley, see F157.C75
157.Y7	York Road
157.Y72	Youghiogheny River and Valley (General, and Pennsylvania)
	Cf. F187.Y68, Maryland
	Cf. F247.Y68, West Virginia
158	**Philadelphia**
158.1	Periodicals. Societies. Collections
158.15	Museums. Exhibitions, exhibits
	For Centennial Exposition, 1876, see T825
	For Sesquicentennial International Exposition, 1926, see T826.3
158.18	Guidebooks
158.25	Biography (Collective). Genealogy (Collective)
158.27	Historiography
158.29	Study and teaching
158.3	General works. Histories
158.33	Juvenile works
	Pamphlets, addresses, essays, etc.
158.35	General
158.36	Anecdotes, legends, pageants, etc.
158.37	Historic monuments. Illustrative material
158.39	Antiquities (Non-Indian)
	By period
158.4	Early to 1775
158.44	1775-1865
	Including merging of the county of Philadelphia into the city; burning of the Orphan Asylum, 1822; riots of 1831, 1838, 1844
	Cf. E233, Howe's occupation in 1777
158.5	1865-1950

	Pennsylvania
158	**Philadelphia**
	By period — Continued
	1951-
158.52	General works
	Biography
158.53	Collective
158.54.A-.54.Z	Individual, A-Z
	GALE NOTE *See note at the head of Table F5 at the end of the text for further instructions on how to subdivide this number*
	Sections. Localities. Districts, etc.
158.6	General works
158.61.A-.61.Z	Cemeteries
158.61.A1	General works
158.61.M8	Monument Cemetery
158.62.A-.62.Z	Churches
158.62.A1	General works
158.62.C5	Christ Church
158.62.F5	First Presbyterian Church
158.625	Hotels, taverns, etc.
158.627	Places of amusement
158.63	Harbor
158.64.A-.64.Z	Monuments. Statues
	GALE NOTE *The cutter number(s) listed below have been given only as examples by the Library of Congress*
158.64.A1	General works
158.64.G3	Garfield Memorial
158.64.M2	McKinley Statue
158.64.P4	Pennypacker Memorial
158.64.W3	Washington monuments
158.65.A-.65.Z	Parks. Squares. Circles
	GALE NOTE *The cutter number(s) listed below have been given only as examples by the Library of Congress*
158.65.A1	General works
158.65.F2	Fairmount Park
158.65.I3	Independence National Historical Park
	For Independence Hall alone, see F158.8.I3
158.67.A-.67.Z	Streets. Bridges. Railroads
	GALE NOTE *The cutter number(s) listed below have been given only as examples by the Library of Congress*
158.67.A1	General works
158.67.F17	Fairmount Parkway
158.67.I33	Independence Square
158.67.M34	Market Street
158.68.A-.68.Z	Suburbs. Sections of the city. Rivers, etc.
	GALE NOTE *The cutter number(s) listed below have been given only as examples by the Library of Congress*
158.68.A1	General works
158.68.E4	Elmwood
158.68.F2	Falls of Schuylkill
	Germantown, *see* F159.G3
158.68.L4	League Island
158.68.N8	North Penn Village
158.68.N9	Northern Liberties
158.68.O8	Oxford Township
158.68.P8	Port Royal Farm
158.68.S6	Southwark
158.68.W5	West Philadelphia
158.68.W7	Windmill Island
158.68.W8	Wissahickon Creek

	Pennsylvania
158	**Philadelphia**
	Sections. Localities. Districts, etc. — Continued
158.69	Wards
	Buildings
158.7	General works. Collective
158.8.A-.8.Z	Individual, A-Z
	GALE NOTE *The cutter number(s) listed below have been given only as examples by the Library of Congress*
158.8.A7	Arsenal, Frankford
158.8.C2	Carpenters' Hall
158.8.C5	City Hall
158.8.C7	Congress Hall
158.8.I3	Independence Hall
	Including Liberty bell
158.8.P4	Pennsylvania Hall
158.8.S8	Strawberry Mansion
158.8.W3	Washington Mansion
	Elements in the population
158.9.A1	General works
158.9.A2-.9.Z	Individual elements
	For a list of racial, ethnic, and religious elements (with cutter numbers), see E184.A+
159.A-.Z	**Other cities, towns, etc., A-Z**
	GALE NOTE *The cutter number(s) listed below have been given only as examples by the Library of Congress*
159.C4	Chambersburg
159.E7	Erie
159.G3	Germantown
159.H3	Harrisburg
	Jim Thorpe, *see* F159.M4
159.J7	Johnstown
159.M4	Mauch Chunk. Jim Thorpe
159.P6	Pittsburgh
	Subarrange by Table F2 at the end of the text
159.R2	Reading
159.S4	Scranton
159.W6	Wilkes-Barre
	Elements in the population
160.A1	General works
160.A2-.Z	Individual elements
	For a list of racial, ethnic, and religious elements (with cutter numbers), see E184.A+
	Delaware
161	**Periodicals. Societies. Collections**
161.5	**Museums. Exhibitions, exhibits**
162	**Gazetteers. Dictionaries. Geographic names**
162.3	**Guidebooks**
163	**Biography (Collective). Genealogy (Collective)**
163.2	**Historiography**
	Historians, *see* E175.5.A+
163.5	**Study and teaching**
164	**General works. Histories**
164.3	**Juvenile works**
	Pamphlets, addresses, essays, etc.
164.5	General
164.6	Anecdotes, legends, pageants, etc.
165	**Historic monuments (General). Illustrative material**
166	**Antiquities (Non-Indian)**

	Delaware — Continued
	By period
167	Early to 1775
	Including Swedish settlements on the Delaware River; New Sweden; Dutch conquest, 1655;
	English conquest, 1664; part of Penn's grant, 1681; the "Lower Counties on the Delaware"
	Including biography: Johan Classon Rising, etc.
168	1775-1865
	Including biography: Jacob Broom, etc.
	Cf. E263.D3, Delaware in the Revolution (General)
	Cf. E230+, Military operations and battles in the Revolution
	Cf. E500+, Civil War, 1861-1865 (General)
169	1865-1950
	Including biography: John Edward Addicks, Edward Woodward Gilpin, etc.
	Cf. D570.85.D4+, World War I, 1914-1918
	Cf. D769.85.D4+, World War II, 1939-1945
	1951-
170	General works
	Biography
170.3	Collective
170.4.A-.4.Z	Individual, A-Z
	GALE NOTE *See note at the head of Table F5 at the end of the text for further*
	instructions on how to subdivide this number
172.A-.Z	**Regions, counties, etc., A-Z**
172.A15	Counties
172.A16	Mountains
172.A17	Rivers
172.A18	Lakes
172.A19	Islands
172.B7	Boundaries
	Cf. F157.B7, Pennsylvania boundary; Mason and Dixon's line
	Cf. F187.B7, Maryland boundary
172.B78	Brandywine Creek and Valley
	Cf. F157.B77, General and Pennsylvania
172.D3	Delaware Bay and region
	Including General, and Delaware (State)
	Cf. F142.D3, New Jersey
172.D4	Delaware River and Valley, Del.
	Cf. F127.D4, New York
	Cf.F142.D4, New Jersey
	Cf. F157.D4, General, and Pennsylvania
	Delmarva Peninsula, *see* F187.E2
172.K3	Kent Co.
172.N35	Nanticoke River and Valley (General and Delaware)
	Cf. F187.N35, Maryland
172.N5	New Castle Co.
	Including Christina River (Creek)
	For Bohemia Manor, see F187.C3
172.S8	Sussex Co.
174.A-.Z	**Cities, towns, etc., A-Z**
	GALE NOTE *The cutter number(s) listed below have been given only as examples by the Library*
	of Congress
174.D74	Dover
174.W7	Wilmington
	Subarrange by Table F2 at the end of the text
	Elements in the population
175.A1	General works
175.A2-.Z	Individual elements
	For a list of racial, ethnic, and religious elements (with cutter numbers), see E184.A+
	Maryland
176	**Periodicals. Societies. Collections**

	Maryland — Continued
178	**Museums. Exhibitions, exhibits**
179	**Gazetteers. Dictionaries. Geographic names**
179.3	**Guidebooks**
180	**Biography (Collective). Genealogy (Collective)**
180.2	**Historiography**
	Historians, *see* E175.5.A+
180.5	**Study and teaching**
181	**General works. Histories**
181.3	**Juvenile works**
	Pamphlets, addresses, essays, etc.
181.5	General
181.6	Anecdotes, legends, pageants, etc.
181.8	**Geography**
182	**Historic monuments (General). Illustrative material**
183	**Antiquities (Non-Indian)**
	By period
184	Early to 1775
	Including the Calverts, proprietors of Maryland; Kent Island and Claiborne; toleration in Maryland
	Including biography: George Calvert, 1st Baron of Baltimore; Cecilius Calvert, 2d Baron of Baltimore; William Claiborne; etc.
	Cf. E199, French and Indian Wars, 1755-1763
	Cf. F157.B7, Mason and Dixon's line
185	1775-1865
	Including biography: Enoch Louis Lowe, John Van Lear McMahon, etc.
	Cf. E263.M3, Maryland in the Revolution (General)
	Cf. E230+, Military operations and battles in the Revolution
	Cf. E359.5.M2, War of 1812 (General)
	Cf. E355+, Military operations and battles in the War of 1812
	Cf. F189.B1, Baltimore Riot, 1812
	Cf. E409.5.M2, War with Mexico, 1845-1848
	Cf. E512.1+, Civil War, 1861-1865 (General)
	Cf. E470.2+, E471+, Military operations and battles in the Civil War, 1861-1865
	Cf. E566.1+, As a Confederate state
186	1865-1950
	Including Reconstruction, 1865-1877
	Including biography: Aloysius Leo Knott, Charles Edward Phelps
	Cf. D570.85.M3+ , World War I, 1914-1918
	Cf. D769.85.M3+ , World War II, 1939-1945
	1951-
186.2	General works
	Biography
186.3	Collective
186.35.A-.35.Z	Individual, A-Z
	GALE NOTE *See note at the head of Table F5 at the end of the text for further instructions on how to subdivide this number*
186.9	**Western Maryland**
187.A-.Z	**Regions, counties, etc., A-Z**
187.A15	Counties
187.A16	Mountains
187.A17	Rivers
187.A18	Lakes
187.A19	Islands
187.A4	Allegany Co.
187.A6	Anne Arundel Co.
	Including Severn River and Valley, St. Anne's Parish, St. James' Parish
	Assateague Island National Seashore, *see* F187.W7
187.B2	Baltimore Co.
	Including Patapsco Neck and River, Hampton National Historic Site

	Maryland
187.A-.Z	**Regions, counties, etc., A-Z — Continued**
187.B7	Boundaries
	Cf. F157.B7, Pennsylvania boundary; Mason and Dixon's line
	Cf. F202.B7, District of Columbia boundary
187.C15	Calvert Co.
	Including Christ Church Parish, Solomons Island
187.C2	Caroline Co.
187.C25	Carroll Co.
	Catoctin Mountain, *see F187.F8*
187.C3	Cecil Co.
	Including St. Mary Anne's Parish, Bohemia Manor, Worsell Manor
187.C4	Charles Co.
187.C47	Chesapeake and Ohio Canal area
187.C5	Chesapeake Bay region (General, and Md.)
	Including Kent Island, Magothy River and Valley, Smith Island
	Cf. F187.E2, Eastern Shore, Md.
	Cf. F232.C43, Virginia
	Cf. F232.E2, Eastern Shore, Va.
187.C6	Cobb Island
187.D6	Dorchester Co.
	Including Blackwater River and Valley, Elliott Island
187.E2	Eastern Shore of Maryland. Delmarva Peninsula
	Including Pocomoke River, etc.
	Elliott Island, *see F187.D6*
187.F8	Frederick Co.
	Including Catoctin Mountain, Prince George's Parish, Sugar Loaf Mountain
187.G2	Garrett Co.
	Great Falls of the Potomac, *see F187.M7*
	Hampton National Historic Site, *see F187.B2*
187.H2	Harford Co.
	Including Deer Creek, St. George's Parish
187.H8	Howard Co.
187.K3	Kent Co.
	Including Chester Parish
	Kent Island, *see F187.C5*
	Magothy River and Valley, *see F187.C5*
	Maryland Heights, *see F187.W3*
	Mason and Dixon's line, *see F157.B7*
187.M7	Montgomery Co.
	Including Great Falls of the Potomac, Prince George's Parish
187.N35	Nanticoke River and Valley
	Cf. F172.N35, General and Delaware
187.O27	Octoraro Creek and Valley
	Cf. F157.O26, General and Pennsylvania
	Patapsco Neck and River, *see F187.B2*
187.P38	Patuxent River and Valley
187.P56	Piscataway Park
	Pocomoke River, *see F187.E2*
187.P8	Potomac River and Valley (General, and Md.)
	Cf. F202.P8, District of Columbia
	Cf. F232.P8, Virginia
	Cf. F247.P8, West Virginia
	For Great Falls, see F187.M7
187.P9	Prince Georges Co.
	Including King George's Parish, Queen Anne's Parish, etc.
187.Q3	Queen Annes Co.
187.S2	St. Marys Co.
	Severn River and Valley, *see F187.A6*
	Smith Island, *see F187.C5*

	Maryland
187.A-.Z	**Regions, counties, etc., A-Z — Continued**
	Solomons Island, *see* F187.C15
187.S7	Somerset Co.
	Sugar Loaf Mountain, *see* F187.F8
187.S8	Susquehanna River and Valley, Md.
	Cf. F127.S96, New York
	Cf. F157.S8, General, and Pennsylvania
187.T2	Talbot Co.
187.W3	Washington Co.
	Including Antietam Creek, Conococheague Creek and Valley, Md., Maryland Heights
	Cf. F157.F8, Conococheague Creek and Valley, Pennsylvania
187.W5	Wicomico Co.
187.W7	Worcester Co.
	Including Assateague Island National Seashore
187.Y68	Youghiogheny River and Valley
	Cf. F157.Y72, General, and Pennsylvania
	Cf. F247.Y68, West Virginia
189.A-.Z	**Cities, towns, etc., A-Z**
	GALE NOTE *The cutter number(s) listed below have been given only as examples by the Library of Congress*
189.A6	Annapolis
	Subarrange by Table F2 at the end of the text
189.B1	Baltimore
	Subarrange by Table F2 at the end of the text
	Elements in the population
190.A1	General works
190.A2-.Z	Individual elements
	For a list of racial, ethnic, and religious elements (with cutter numbers), see E184.A+
	District of Columbia. Washington
191	**Periodicals. Societies. Collections**
191.5	**Museums. Exhibitions, exhibits**
192	**Gazetteers. Dictionaries. Geographic names**
192.3	**Guidebooks**
193	**Biography (Collective). Genealogy (Collective)**
193.2	**Historiography**
	Historians, *see* E175.5.A+
193.5	**Study and teaching**
194	**General works. Histories**
194.3	**Juvenile works**
	Pamphlets, addresses, essays, etc.
194.5	General
194.6	Anecdotes, legends, pageants, etc.
195	**Historic monuments. Illustrative material**
	Including location of national capital, L'Enfant and his plan, retrocession
195.5	**Antiquities (Non-Indian)**
196	**Political and social life**
	By period
	Including Inauguration ceremonies, 1801-
197	Early to 1815
	Cf. E356.W3, Capture by the British, 1814
198	1815-1878
	Including biography: William Albert Bradley, Joseph Gales, Walter Lenox, Alexander Robey Shepherd, etc.
	Cf. E396, Explosion of frigate Princeton, 1844
	Cf. E409.5.D6, War with Mexico, 1845-1848
	Cf. E501.1+, Civil War, 1861-1865 (General)
	Cf. E470.2+, E471+, Military operations and battles in the Civil War, 1861-1865
	Cf. F195, Retrocession of Alexandria County to Virginia, 1846

District of Columbia. Washington
By period — Continued

199	1878-1950
	Including Bonus Expeditionary Force, 1932, 1933, etc.
	Cf. D570.85.D6, World War I, 1914-1918
	Cf. D769.85.D6, World War II, 1939-1945
	1951-1980
200	General works
	Biography and memoirs
200.2	Collective
200.3.A-.3.Z	Individual, A-Z
	GALE NOTE *See note at the head of Table F5 at the end of the text for further instructions on how to subdivide this number*
	1981-
201	General works
	Biography and memoirs
201.2	Collective
201.3.A-.3.Z	Individual, A-Z
	GALE NOTE *See note at the head of Table F5 at the end of the text for further instructions on how to subdivide this number*
202.A-.Z	**Regions, suburbs, etc., A-Z**
202.A5	Anacostia River and Valley
202.B7	Boundaries
	Cf. F195, Retrocession of Alexandria County to Virginia, 1846
202.B8	Brightwood
202.B9	Brookland
	For West Brookland, see F202.W5
202.C2	Capitol Hill
202.C46	Chinatown
202.C6	Columbia Heights
202.G3	Georgetown
202.L4	Le Droit Park
202.M9	Mount Pleasant
202.N5	Northeast Washington
202.N7	Northwest Washington
202.P8	Potomac River and Valley, D.C
	Cf. F187.P8, General, and Maryland
	Cf. F203.3, Washington Harbor
	Cf. F232.P8, Virginia
	Cf. F247.P8, West Virginia
202.S6	Southeast Washington
202.S7	Southwest Washington
202.T4	Temple Heights
202.T43	Tenleytown
	Theodore Roosevelt (Analostan) Island, *see F203.4.T5*
202.W5	West Brookland
203	**Localities, etc.**
203.1.A-.1.Z	Cemeteries
	Cf. RA626+, Management, laying-out, etc., of cemeteries
	GALE NOTE *The cutter number(s) listed below have been given only as examples by the Library of Congress*
203.1.A1	General works
	Arlington National Cemetery, *see F234.A7*
203.1.C7	Congressional Cemetery
203.1.G5	Glenwood Cemetery
203.1.O12	Oak Hill Cemetery
203.2.A-.2.Z	Churches
	GALE NOTE *The cutter number(s) listed below have been given only as examples by the Library of Congress*
203.2.A1	General works

District of Columbia. Washington

203	**Localities, etc.**
203.2.A-.2.Z	Churches — Continued
203.2.N4	New York Avenue Presbyterian Church
203.2.S14	St. John's Church, Georgetown
203.3	Harbor
203.35	Hotels, taverns, etc.
203.4.A-.4.Z	Monuments. Statues. Memorials
	GALE NOTE *The cutter number(s) listed below have been given only as examples by the Library of Congress*
203.4.A1	General works
	Cf. F204.C2, The Capitol, Statuary Hall
203.4.B7	Braddock's Rock
203.4.C7	Columbus Monument
203.4.E6	Ericsson Monument
203.4.G2	Garfield Statue
203.4.G7	Grant Memorial
203.4.J4	Jefferson Memorial
203.4.L73	Lincoln Memorial
203.4.M5	Meade Monument
203.4.T5	Theodore Roosevelt Island
203.4.W3	Washington Monument
203.5.A-.5.Z	Parks. Squares. Circles
	GALE NOTE *The cutter number(s) listed below have been given only as examples by the Library of Congress*
203.5.A1	General works
203.5.C2	Capitol Grounds
203.5.L2	Lafayette Park
203.5.M2	The Mall
203.5.P86	Potomac Park
203.5.R6	Rock Creek Park
203.7.A-.7.Z	Streets. Bridges. Railroads
	GALE NOTE *The cutter number(s) listed below have been given only as examples by the Library of Congress*
203.7.A1	General works
203.7.A6	Arlington Memorial Bridge
203.7.C7	Constitution Avenue
203.7.F7	Fourteenth Street
203.7.L8	Long Bridge
203.7.P4	Pennsylvania Avenue
203.7.S6	Sixteenth Street
203.9	Wards
204.A-.Z	**Buildings**
	GALE NOTE *The cutter number(s) listed below have been given only as examples by the Library of Congress*
204.A1	General works
204.B5	Blair House
204.C2	Capitol
204.C3	Cathedral of St. Peter and Paul
204.C5	City Hall
204.D43	Department of Commerce Building
204.F6	Ford Theatre
204.H8	House Office Building
204.M5	Memorial Continental Hall
204.N23	National Theatre
204.O2	Octagon House
204.P47	Petersen House
204.S9	Supreme Court Building
204.U5	Union Railroad Station
204.W5	White House

	District of Columbia. Washington — Continued
	Elements in the population
205.A1	General works
205.A2-.Z	Individual elements
	For a list of racial, ethnic, and religious elements (with cutter numbers), see E184.A+
	The South. South Atlantic States
	Region south of Mason and Dixon's line and Ohio River
	Cf. E440.92+, Slavery in the United States
206	**Periodicals. Societies. Collections**
206.5	**Museums. Exhibitions, exhibits**
207	**Gazetteers. Dictionaries. Geographic names**
207.3	**Guidebooks**
207.7	**Dictionaries and encyclopedias of history**
208	**Biography (Collective). Genealogy (Collective)**
208.2	**Historiography**
	Historians, *see* E175.5.A+
208.5	**Study and teaching**
209	**General works. Histories**
209.3	**Juvenile works**
	Pamphlets, addresses, essays, etc.
209.5	General
209.6	Anecdotes, legends, pageants, etc.
209.8	**Geography**
210	**Historic monuments (General). Illustrative material**
	Including life and conditions of Appalachian people (General)
211	**Antiquities (Non-Indian)**
	By period
212	Early to 1775
	Cf. F229, Early grants of Virginia, Raleigh's colonies, etc.
	1775-1865
213	General works
	Including plantation life, etc.
	Cf. E230+, Campaigns of the Revolution
	Cf. E423, Southern Convention, Nashville 1850
	Cf. E440.92+, Slavery
214	Period of the Civil War
	Including description and travel
	Cf. E468+, Civil War, 1861-1865 (General)
	Cf. E482+, Confederate States of America
	1865-1951
215	General works
216	1865-1877. Reconstruction
	Including Northern societies formed to ameliorate conditions in the South, etc.
	Cf. E668 , Histories of reconstruction
216.2	1951-
217.A-.Z	**Regions, A-Z**
217.A15	Counties
217.A16	Mountains
217.A17	Rivers
217.A18	Lakes
217.A19	Islands
217.A3	Allegheny (Alleghany) Mountains
217.A65	Appalachian Mountains, Southern
	Atlantic Coast, *see* F106
217.B6	Blue Ridge Mountains
	Cf. F232.S48, Shenandoah National Park (Va.)
	Cf. F262.B6, North Carolina
217.C45	Chattooga River and Valley
	Chesapeake Bay region, *see* F187.C5
	Gulf Coast, *see* F296

	The South. South Atlantic States
217.A-.Z	**Regions, A-Z — Continued**
217.N37	Natchez Trace
	Ohio River and Valley, *see* F516+
	Old Southwest, Lower Mississippi Valley, *see* F396
	Pickwick Landing Reservoir, *see* F217.T3
217.P53	Piedmont Region
	Potomac River and Valley, *see* F187.P8
217.T3	Tennessee River and Valley
	Including Pickwick Landing Reservoir
	Cf. F332.T2, Alabama
	Cf. F443.T3, Tennessee
	Cf. F457.T3, Kentucky
217.W57	Wiregrass Country
	Elements in the population
220.A1A-.A1Z	General works
220.A2-.Z	Individual elements, A-Z
	For list of racial, ethnic and religious elements (with cutter numbers), see E184.A+
	Virginia
221	**Periodicals. Societies. Collections**
223	**Museums. Exhibitions, exhibits**
224	**Gazetteers. Dictionaries. Geographic names**
224.3	**Guidebooks**
225	**Biography (Collective). Genealogy (Collective)**
225.2	**Historiography**
	Historians, *see* E175.5.A+
225.5	**Study and teaching**
226	**General works. Histories**
226.3	**Juvenile works**
	Pamphlets, addresses, essays, etc.
226.5	General
226.6	Anecdotes, legends, pageants, etc.
227	**Historic monuments (General). Illustrative material**
228	**Antiquities (Non-Indian)**
	By period
229	Early to 1775
	Including Raleigh's explorations and colonies, 1584-1590; Virginia Company of London; Jamestown settlement; Indian massacres; Bacon's Rebellion, 1676; the Parsons' Cause, 1763; etc.
	Including biography: William Claiborne, Virginia Dare, Nicolas Martiau, John Smith, Alexander Spotswood, etc.
	Cf. E83.759, Cherokee War, 1759-1761
	Cf. E83.76, Pontiac's Conspiracy, 1763-1765
	Cf. E83.77, Dunmore's War, 1774; Battle of Point Pleasant
	Cf. E99.P85, Pocahontas
	Cf. E199, French and Indian War, 1755-1763
	Cf. F517, Explorations in Ohio Valley
230	1775-1865
	Including biography: Archibald Cary, John Floyd, Edmund Pendleton, John Howe Peyton, Edmund Ruffin, etc.
	For Kentucky County and District, see F454
	Cf. E263.V8, Virginia in the Revolution (General)
	Cf. E230+, Military operations and battles in the Revolution
	Cf. E234, Clark's conquest of the Northwest
	Cf. E309, F483, Cession of territory north of Ohio River
	Cf. E328, Virginia Resolutions, 1798
	Cf. E359.5.V8, War of 1812 (General)
	Cf. E355+, Military operations and battles in the War of 1812
	Cf. E451, John Brown at Harper's Ferry
	Cf. E581.1+, Civil War, 1861-1865 (General)
	Cf. E534.1+, Union history, Civil War, 1861-1865

	Virginia
	By period
230	1775-1865 — Continued
	Cf. E471+, Military operations and battles in the Civil War, 1861-1865
	Cf. F232.S7, Nat Turner's Insurrection, 1831
	Cf. F241, Separation of West Virginia
	Cf. F454, Final withdrawal of claims to Kentucky
231	1865-1950. Reconstruction
	Including biography: William Mahone, John Edward Massey
	Cf. D570.85.V8+, World War I, 1914-1918
	Cf. D769.85.V8, World War II, 1939-1945
	Cf. F241, Controversies with West Virginia
	1951-
231.2	General works
	Biography
231.3.A2A-.3.A2Z	Collective
231.3.A3-.3.Z	Individual, A-Z
	GALE NOTE *See note at the head of Table F5 at the end of the text for further instructions on how to subdivide this number*
232.A-.Z	**Regions, counties, etc., A-Z**
232.A15	Counties
232.A16	Mountains
232.A17	Rivers
232.A18	Lakes
232.A19	Islands
232.A2	Accomac (Accomack) Co.
	Including Chincoteague Island
	Cf. F232.E2, Eastern Shore of Virginia
232.A3	Albemarle Co.
232.A35	Albemarle Parish
232.A4	Alexandria Co. (To June 6, 1920). Arlington Co. (Since June 6, 1920)
	For retrocession from the District of Columbia, see F195
	Cf. F202.B7, District of Columbia boundary
232.A5	Alleghany Co.
232.A54	Amelia Co.
232.A55	Amherst Co.
232.A6	Appomattox Co.
	Arlington Co., *see F232.A4*
	Arlington National Cemetery, *see F234.A7*
	Assateague Island National Seashore, *see F187.W7*
232.A9	Augusta Co.
	Including Weyer's (Wier's) Cave
232.B24	Back Creek and Valley (General, and Virginia)
	Cf. F247.B14 , West Virginia
232.B3	Bath Co.
232.B4	Bedford Co.
	Blacks Run and Valley, *see F232.R7*
232.B5	Bland Co.
232.B55	Blissland (Blisland) Parish
232.B6	Botetourt Co.
232.B7	Boundaries
	For Mason and Dixon's line, see F157.B7
	Cf. F187.B7, Maryland boundary
	Cf. F202.B7, District of Columbia boundary
232.B8	Bristol Parish
232.B9	Brunswick Co.
232.B94	Buchanan Co.
232.B96	Buckingham Co.
	Cabell Co., *see F247.C2*

	Virginia
232.A-.Z	**Regions, counties, etc., A-Z — Continued**
232.C15	Campbell Co.
	Including Timber Lake
232.C2	Caroline Co.
232.C27	Carroll Co.
232.C3	Charles City Co.
232.C4	Charlotte Co.
232.C43	Chesapeake Bay region, Va.
	Including Governor's Land Archaeological District
	Cf. F187.C5, General, and Maryland
232.C52	Chesterfield Co.
	Chincoteague Island, *see* F232.A2
	Clark Mountain, *see* F232.O6
232.C59	Clarke Co.
	Including Cunningham Chapel Parish, Frederick Parish
232.C65	Clinch River and Valley (General, and Virginia)
	Cf. F443.C57, Tennessee
232.C7	Colonial National Historical Park
232.C8	Craig Co.
232.C9	Culpepper Co.
	Cf. F232.S2, St. Mark's Parish
232.C93	Cumberland Co.
232.C94	Cumberland Parish
	Dean Mountain, *see* F232.S48
	Delmarva Peninsula, *see* F187.E2
232.D2	Dickenson Co.
232.D6	Dinwiddie Co.
232.D7	Dismal Swamp. Lake Drummond
	Cf. F262.D7, North Carolina
232.E2	Eastern Shore of Virginia
	Cf. F187.E2, Maryland
232.E5	Elizabeth City Co.
232.E6	Elizabeth City Parish
	Endless Caverns, *see* F232.S47
232.E7	Essex Co.
	Including Rappahannock Co. (1656-1692)
232.F2	Fairfax Co.
232.F3	Fauquier Co.
232.F38	Fincastle Co.
232.F4	Floyd Co.
232.F6	Fluvanna Co.
232.F7	Franklin Co.
232.F75	Frederick Co.
	Frederick Parish, *see* F232.C59
232.F76	Fredericksville Parish
232.G38	George Washington Memorial Parkway. Mount Vernon Memorial Highway
232.G4	Giles Co.
	Including Mountain Lake
232.G6	Gloucester Co.
	Cf. F232.K54, Kingston Parish
	Cf. F232.P45, Petsworth Parish
232.G65	Goochland Co.
	Governor's Land Archaeological District, *see* F232.C43
232.G7	Grayson Co.
	Great Falls of the Potomac, *see* F187.M7
232.G8	Greene Co.
232.G85	Greensville Co.
	Gwynn Island, *see* F232.M3
232.H17	Halifax Co.

	Virginia
232.A-.Z	**Regions, counties, etc., A-Z — Continued**
232.H2	Hamilton Parish
232.H23	Hampton Roads
	Cf. F232.J2, James River and Valley
232.H3	Hanover Co.
232.H4	Henrico Co.
232.H5	Henrico Parish
232.H6	Henry Co.
232.H8	Highland Co.
	Holmans Creek, *see* F232.S47
	Hungary Mother Creek and Valley, *see* F232.S6
232.I8	Isle of Wight Co.
232.J13	Jackson River and Valley (General, and Virginia)
	Cf. F247.J22, West Virginia
232.J15	James City Co.
	Cf. F232.B55, Blissland Parish
232.J2	James River and Valley
	Including Mulberry Island, etc.
	Cf. F232.H23, Hampton Roads
	Jones Mountain, *see* F232.S48
	Kentucky County and District, *see* F454
232.K4	King and Queen Co.
232.K45	King George Co.
232.K5	King William Co.
232.K54	Kingston Parish
232.L2	Lancaster Co.
232.L4	Lee Co.
	Lewis Mountain *see* F232.S48
232.L8	Loudoun Co.
	Including Lowes area
232.L85	Louisa Co.
232.L9	Lunenburg Co.
	Luray Caverns, *see* F232.P2
232.M2	Madison Co.
232.M3	Mathews Co.
	Including Gwynn Island, etc.
	Cf. F232.K54, Kingston Parish
232.M4	Mecklenburg Co.
232.M6	Middlesex Co.
	Monongalia Co., *see* F247.M7
232.M7	Montgomery Co.
	Mount Vernon Memorial Highway, *see* F232.G38
	Mulberry Island, *see* F232.J2
232.N2	Nansemond Co.
	Natural Bridge, *see* F232.R68
232.N25	Nelson Co.
232.N3	New Kent Co.
	Including St. Peter's Parish
	Cf. F232.B55, Blissland Parish
	New Market Endless Caverns, *see* F232.S47
232.N5	New River and Valley, Va.
	Cf. F247.N5, General, and West Virginia
	Cf. F262.N6, North Carolina
232.N8	Norfolk Co.
232.N85	Northampton Co.
	Cf. F232.E2 , Eastern Shore of Virginia
232.N86	Northern Neck
232.N87	Northumberland Co.
232.N9	Nottoway Co.

	Virginia
232.A-.Z	**Regions, counties, etc., A-Z — Continued**
	Ohio Co., *see* F247.O3
232.O6	Orange Co.
	Including Clark Mountain
232.O85	Otter, Peaks of
232.O9	Overwharton Parish
232.P2	Page Co.
	Including Luray Caverns
232.P25	Pamunkey River and Valley
232.P3	Patrick Co.
232.P45	Petsworth Parish
232.P7	Pittsylvania Co.
232.P8	Potomac River and Valley, Va.
	For Great Falls, see F187.M7
	Cf. F187.P8, General, and Maryland
	Cf. F202.P8, District of Columbia
	Cf. F247.P8, West Virginia
232.P816	Powell River and Valley (General, and Virginia)
	Cf. F443.P78, Tennessee
232.P82	Powhatan Co.
232.P83	Prince Edward Co.
232.P85	Prince George Co.
232.P86	Prince William Co.
	Including Prince William Forest Park
232.P87	Princess Anne Co.
	Including Lynnhaven Parish
232.P9	Pulaski Co.
232.R18	Rapidan River and Valley
232.R2	Rappahannock Co.
	Cf. F232.E7, Rappahannock Co. (1656-1692)
232.R4	Richmond Co.
232.R6	Roanoke Co.
232.R63	Roanoke River and Valley, Va.
	Cf. F262.R5, General, and North Carolina
232.R68	Rockbridge Co.
	Including Natural Bridge
232.R7	Rockingham Co.
	Including Blacks Run and Valley
232.R9	Russell Co.
232.S15	St. George's Parish
232.S2	St. Mark's Parish
232.S3	Scott Co.
232.S47	Shenandoah Co.
	Including Endless Caverns, Holmans Creek
232.S48	Shenandoah National Park
	Including Dean Mountain, Jones Mountain, Lewis Mountain
232.S5	Shenandoah River and Valley (Valley of Virginia)
	For individual caves, see the county
	Cf. F247.S5, West Virginia
232.S6	Smyth Co.
	Including Hungary Mother Creek and Valley
232.S7	Southampton Co.
	Including Southampton Insurrection, 1831 (Nat Turner's Insurrection, Turner's Negro Insurrection)
232.S8	Spotsylvania Co.
	Cf. F232.S15, St. George's Parish
232.S86	Stafford Co.
	Cf. F232.O9, Overwharton Parish

	Virginia
232.A-.Z	**Regions, counties, etc., A-Z — Continued**
232.S9	Surry Co.
	Cf. F232.A35, Albemarle Parish
232.S96	Sussex Co.
	Cf. F232.A35, Albemarle Parish
232.T15	Tangier Island
232.T2	Tazewell Co.
232.T54	Tidewater Region
	Timber Lake, *see F232.C15*
232.T8	Truro Parish
	Valley of Virginia, *see F232.S5*
232.W25	Warren Co.
232.W27	Warwick Co.
	Including Lake Maury
232.W3	Washington Co.
	West Augusta District, *see F157.W5*
232.W4	Westmoreland Co.
232.W8	Wise Co.
	Wood Co., *see F247.W8*
232.W9	Wythe Co.
	Yohogania Co., *see F157.W5*
232.Y6	York Co.
234.A-.Z	**Cities, towns, etc., A-Z**
	GALE NOTE *The cutter number(s) listed below have been given only as examples by the Library of Congress*
234.A3	Alexandria
234.A7	Arlington
	Including Arlington National Cemetery, Lee Mansion
234.F8	Fredericksburg
234.J3	Jamestown
	Monticello, *see E332.74*
	Mount Vernon, *see E312.5*
234.N48	New Market
	For Endless Caverns, see F232.S47
234.N8	Norfolk
234.R5	Richmond
	Subarrange by Table F2 at the end of the text
234.S865	Stratford Hall, Albemarle Co.
234.W7	Williamsburg
234.Y6	Yorktown
	Cf. F232.C7, Colonial National Historical Park
	Elements in the population
235.A1	General works
235.A2-.Z	Individual elements
	For a list of racial, ethnic, and religious elements (with cutter numbers), see E184.A+
	West Virginia
236	**Periodicals. Societies. Collections**
238	**Museums. Exhibitions, exhibits**
239	**Gazetteers. Dictionaries. Geographic names**
239.3	**Guidebooks**
240	**Biography (Collective). Genealogy (Collective)**
240.2	**Historiography**
	Historians, *see E175.5.A+*
240.5	**Study and teaching**
241	**General works. Histories**
	Including by period (Early to 1950) as well as general
	For 1951 and later, see F245
	Including controversies between Virginia and West Virginia growing out of separation; admission as a state, June 20, 1863; etc.

	West Virginia
241	**General works. Histories — Continued**
	Including biography: Anne Bailey
	Cf. D570.85.W4+ , World War I, 1914-1918
	Cf. D769.85.W4+, World War II, 1939-1945
	Cf. E536.1+, West Virginia in the Civil War and organization of the state (General)
	Cf. E470.3, E471+, Military operations and battles in the Civil War
	Cf. E534.1+, Union government of Virginia
	Cf. E536.1+, Civil War history of West Virginia
	Cf. F582.1+, Confederate history
	Cf. F229-230, Virginia (Early to 1865)
241.3	**Juvenile works**
	Pamphlets, addresses, essays, etc.
241.5	General
241.6	Anecdotes, legends, pageants, etc.
242	**Historic monuments (General). Illustrative material**
243	**Antiquities (Non-Indian)**
	By period
(244)	Early to 1950, *see* F229-230 , F241
	1951-
245	General works
	Biography
245.4	Collective
245.42.A-.42.Z	Individual, A-Z
	GALE NOTE *See note at the head of Table F5 at the end of the text for further instructions on how to subdivide this number*
247.A-.Z	**Regions, counties, etc., A-Z**
247.A15	Counties
247.A16	Mountains
247.A17	Rivers
247.A18	Lakes
247.A19	Islands
247.B14	Back Creek and Valley
	Cf. F232.B24, General, and Virginia
247.B2	Barbour Co.
247.B5	Berkeley Co.
247.B54	Big Coal River and Valley
247.B56	Blennerhassett Island
247.B6	Boone Co.
	Including Turtle Creek and Valley
247.B7	Boundaries
	Cf. F187.B7, Maryland and old Maryland-Virginia boundary
	Cf. F497.B7, Ohio boundary
247.B8	Braxton Co.
247.B9	Brooke Co.
247.C2	Cabell Co.
247.C24	Cacapon River and Valley
247.C3	Calhoun Co.
	Campbell's Creek and Valley, *see* F247.K2
	Canaan Valley, *see* F247.T8
	Cheat Mountain, *see* F247.R2
247.C5	Clay Co.
247.D6	Doddridge Co.
247.D79	Dry Fork River and region
247.E4	Elk River and Valley
247.F2	Fayette Co.
247.G5	Gilmer Co.
247.G67	Grant Co.
	Great Kanawha River and Valley, *see* F247.K3
247.G7	Greenbrier Co.

	West Virginia
247.A-.Z	**Regions, counties, etc., A-Z — Continued**
247.G73	Greenbrier River Trail
247.H17	Hacker's Creek and Valley
247.H2	Hampshire Co.
247.H24	Hancock Co.
	Including Tomlinson Run, Tomlinson Run State Park
247.H28	Hardy Co.
247.H3	Harrison Co.
	Indian Creek and Valley (Ritchie County), *see* F247.R6
247.J2	Jackson Co.
247.J22	Jackson River and Valley
	Cf. F232.J13 , General, and Virginia
247.J4	Jefferson Co.
247.K2	Kanawha Co.
	Including Campbell's Creek and Valley
247.K3	Kanawha River and Valley
247.L6	Lewis Co.
247.L7	Lincoln Co.
247.L8	Logan Co.
247.M2	McDowell Co.
247.M26	Marion Co.
247.M3	Marshall Co.
247.M4	Mason Co.
247.M5	Mercer Co.
247.M55	Mineral Co.
247.M57	Mingo Co.
247.M59	Monongahela National Forest
247.M6	Monongahela River and Valley, W. Va.
	Cf. F157.M58, General, and Pennsylvania
247.M7	Monongalia Co.
247.M75	Monroe Co.
247.M8	Morgan Co.
247.N5	New River and Valley (General, and W. Va.)
	Cf. F232.N5, Virginia
	Cf. F262.N6, North Carolina
247.N6	Nicholas Co.
247.O3	Ohio Co.
247.O4	Ohio River and Valley, W. Va.
	Cf. F516+, General
247.P3	Pendleton Co.
247.P5	Pleasants Co.
247.P7	Pocahontas Co.
247.P8	Potomac River and Valley, W. Va.
	Cf. F187.P8, General, and Maryland
	Cf. F202.P8, District of Columbia
	Cf. F232.P8, Virginia
247.P9	Preston Co.
247.P95	Putnam Co.
247.R15	Raleigh Co.
247.R2	Randolph Co.
	Including Cave of Dry Fork of Cheat River, Cheat Mountain
247.R6	Ritchie Co.
	Including Indian Creek and Valley
247.R8	Roane Co.
247.S5	Shenandoah River and Valley, W. Va.
	Cf. F232.S5, General, and Virginia
247.S9	Summers Co.
247.T3	Taylor Co.
247.T4	Tenmile Creek and Valley

	West Virginia
247.A-.Z	**Regions, counties, etc., A-Z — Continued**
	Tomlinson Run, *see* F247.H24
	Tomlinson Run State Park, *see* F247.H24
247.T8	Tucker Co.
	Including Canaan Valley
	Turtle Creek and Valley, *see* F247.B6
247.T9	Tyler Co.
247.U6	Upshur Co.
247.W3	Wayne Co.
247.W37	Webster Co.
247.W5	Wetzel Co.
247.W6	Wirt Co.
247.W8	Wood Co.
247.W9	Wyoming Co.
247.Y68	Youghiogheny River and Valley
	Cf. F157.Y72, General, and Pennsylvania
	Cf. F187.Y68, Maryland
249.A-.Z	**Cities, towns, etc., A-Z**
	GALE NOTE *The cutter number(s) listed below have been given only as examples by the Library of Congress*
249.C4	Charleston
249.H2	Harpers Ferry
249.H95	Huntington
249.W5	Wheeling
249.W6	White Sulphur Springs
	Elements in the population
250.A1	General works
250.A2-.Z	Individual elements
	For a list of racial, ethnic, and religious elements (with cutter numbers), see E184.A+
	North Carolina
251	**Periodicals. Societies. Collections**
251.5	**Museums. Exhibitions, exhibits**
252	**Gazetteers. Dictionaries. Geographic names**
252.3	**Guidebooks**
253	**Biography (Collective). Genealogy (Collective)**
253.2	**Historiography**
	Historians, *see* E175.5.A+
253.5	**Study and teaching**
254	**General works. Histories**
254.3	**Juvenile works**
	Pamphlets, addresses, essays, etc.
254.5	General
254.6	Anecdotes, legends, pageants, etc.
254.8	**Geography**
255	**Historic monuments (General). Illustrative material**
256	**Antiquities (Non-Indian)**
	By period
257	Early to 1775
	Including grant of Carolina to eight proprietors, 1663; Albemarle and Clarendon settlements; Royal province; Regulator Insurrection, 1766-1771
	Including biography: George Burrington, Sir Richard Everard, William Tryon, etc.
	Cf. E83.71, Tuscarora War, 1711-1713
	Cf. E83.759, Cherokee War, 1759-1761
	Cf. E197, Queen Anne's War, 1702-1713
	Cf. F229, Raleigh's Roanoke colonies, 1584-1590
	Cf. F272, The original grant of Carolina, before the division
	Cf. F314, War with Spaniards of Florida, 1740
258	1775-1865
	Including biography: Charles Manly, John Motley Morehead, Thomas Ruffin, Benjamin Smith

	North Carolina
	By period
258	1775-1865 — Continued
	Cf. E263.N8, North Carolina in the Revolution (General)
	Cf. E230+, Military operations and battles in the Revolution
	Cf. E215.9, Mecklenburg Resolves, 1775
	Cf. E309, North Carolina cessions of 1784 and 1790
	Cf. E359.5.N7, War of 1812
	Cf. E524.1+, E526.1+, E573.1+, Civil War, 1861-1865 (General)
	Cf. E470.6, E471+, Military operations and battles in the Civil War, 1861-1865
259	1865-1950. Reconstruction
	Including biography: Charles Brantley Aycock, William Woods Holden, Jonathan Worth
	Cf. D570.85.N8+, World War I, 1914-1918
	Cf. D769.85.N8+, World War II, 1939-1945
	Cf. E726.N8, War of 1898 (Spanish-American War)
	1951-
260	General works
	Biography
260.4	Collective
260.42.A-.42.Z	Individual, A-Z
	GALE NOTE *See note at the head of Table F5 at the end of the text for further instructions on how to subdivide this number*
261	**Western North Carolina**
262.A-.Z	**Regions, counties, etc., A-Z**
262.A15	Counties
262.A16	Mountains
262.A17	Rivers
262.A18	Lakes
262.A19	Islands
262.A3	Alamance Co.
262.A33	Albemarle region (Northeast coast region)
262.A4	Alexander Co.
262.A45	Alleghany Co.
262.A5	Anson Co.
262.A7	Ashe Co.
	Including Pond Mountain
262.A84	Atlantic Coast
262.A9	Avery Co.
	Including North Toe River and Valley
	Bald Head Island, *see* F262.B9
262.B3	Bald Mountains
	Including Big Bald Mountain
	Cf. F443.B3, General, and Tennessee
262.B37	Beaufort Co.
262.B38	Bertie Co.
	Big Bald Mountain, *see* F262.B3
	Big Pine Creek and Valley, *see* F262.M25
262.B4	Black Mountains
	Including Mount Mitchell
262.B45	Bladen Co.
262.B6	Blue Ridge Mountains, N.C.
	Including Grandfather Mountain
	Cf. F217.B6, General
	Bogue Banks, *see* F262.C23
262.B7	Boundaries
	Cf. F232.B7, Virginia boundary
	Cf. F292.B7, Georgia boundary
262.B89	Broad River and Valley, North Carolina
	Cf. F277.B73, General, and South Carolina

	North Carolina
262.A-.Z	**Regions, counties, etc., A-Z — Continued**
262.B9	Brunswick Co.
	Including Cape Fear, Smith Island, Bald Head Island
262.B94	Buncombe Co.
262.B96	Burke Co.
262.B97	Bute Co.
262.C12	Cabarrus Co.
262.C15	Caldwell Co.
262.C17	Camden Co.
	Cape Fear, *see* F262.B9
262.C2	Cape Fear River and Valley
	Cape Hatteras National Seashore, *see* F262.O96
262.C23	Carteret Co.
	Including Bogue Banks, Harkers Island, Portsmouth Island
262.C26	Caswell Co.
262.C28	Catawba Co.
262.C3	Catawba River and Valley, N.C.
	Cf. F277.C3, South Carolina
	Charlotte and Mecklenburg County, *see* F264.C4
262.C4	Chatham Co.
262.C43	Cherokee Co.
262.C44	Chowan Co.
262.C47	Clay Co.
262.C5	Cleveland Co.
262.C6	Columbus Co.
262.C8	Craven Co.
262.C9	Cumberland Co.
262.C95	Currituck Co.
262.D2	Dare Co.
	Cf. F262.R4 , Roanoke Island
262.D3	Davidson Co.
262.D4	Davie Co.
262.D7	Dismal Swamp, N.C.
	Cf. F232.D7, General, and Virginia
262.D77	Duplin Co.
262.D8	Durham Co.
262.E2	Edgecombe Co.
262.F7	Forsyth Co. Wachovia
	Including Tanglewood Park
262.F8	Franklin Co.
262.F85	French Broad River and Valley
	Cf. F443.F8, General, and Tennessee
262.G2	Gaston Co.
262.G3	Gates Co.
	Goose Creek Island, *see* F262.P2
262.G8	Graham Co.
	Grandfather Mountain, *see* F262.B6
262.G85	Granville Co.
	Great Smoky Mountains, *see* F443.G7
262.G86	Greene Co.
262.G9	Guilford Co.
262.H2	Halifax Co.
	Harkers Island, *see* F262.C23
262.H3	Harnett Co.
262.H35	Haywood Co.
	Hazel Creek and Valley, *see* F262.S95
262.H47	Henderson Co.
262.H5	Hertford Co.
262.H7	Hoke Co.

	North Carolina
262.A-.Z	**Regions, counties, etc., A-Z — Continued**
262.H9	Hyde Co.
	Including Ocracoke Island
262.I7	Iredell Co.
262.J2	Jackson Co.
	Including Whiteside Cove
262.J6	Johnston Co.
262.J7	Jones Co.
262.L4	Lee Co.
262.L5	Lenoir Co.
262.L6	Lincoln Co.
262.L64	Little Laurel Creek and Valley
262.M15	McDowell Co.
262.M2	Macon Co.
	Including Tellico Creek and Valley
262.M25	Madison Co.
	Including Big Pine Creek and Valley, Shelton Laurel Creek and Valley
262.M3	Martin Co.
262.M4	Mecklenburg Co.
	Mitchell, Mount, *see* F262.B4
262.M5	Mitchell Co.
262.M6	Montgomery Co.
262.M7	Moore Co.
262.N2	Nash Co.
262.N48	Neuse River and Valley
262.N5	New Hanover Co.
	New River and Valley (Onslow Co.), *see* F262.O5
262.N6	New River and Valley (Watauga Co.)
	Including Ingles Ferry
	Cf. F232.N5, Virginia
	Cf. F247.N5, General, and West Virginia
262.N67	Norman, Lake
	North Toe River and Valley, *see* F262.A9
262.N7	Northampton Co.
	Ocracoke Island, *see* F262.H9
262.O5	Onslow Co.
	Including New River and Valley, Topsail Island
262.O7	Orange Co.
262.O96	Outer Banks (General)
	Including Cape Hatteras National Seashore
262.P2	Pamlico Co.
	Including Goose Creek Island
262.P25	Pasquotank Co.
	Pee Dee (Pedee) River and Valley, *see* F262.Y2, F277.P3
262.P35	Peltier Creek and Valley
262.P37	Pender Co.
262.P4	Perquimans Co.
262.P5	Person Co.
262.P6	Pitt Co.
262.P65	Polk Co.
	Pond Mountain (Ashe County), *see* F262.A7
	Portsmouth Island, *see* F262.C23
	Raleigh's Roanoke Colonies, 1584-1590, *see* F229
262.R2	Randolph Co.
262.R25	Reed Gold Mine State Historic Site
262.R3	Richmond Co.
262.R39	Roan Mountain (General, and N.C.)
	Cf. F443.R49, Tennessee

	North Carolina
262.A-.Z	**Regions, counties, etc., A-Z — Continued**
262.R4	Roanoke Island
	Including Fort Raleigh National Historic Site
	For Raleigh's Roanoke Colonies, 1584-1590, see F229
262.R5	Roanoke River and Valley (General, and N.C.)
	Cf. F232.R63, Virginia
262.R6	Robeson Co.
262.R7	Rockingham Co.
262.R8	Rowan Co.
262.R9	Rutherford Co.
262.S3	Sampson Co.
262.S34	Sandhills (General, and N.C.)
	Cf. F277.S27, South Carolina
	Cf. F292.S25, Georgia
262.S4	Scotland Co.
	For Smoky Mountains (The Smokies), see F443.G7
	Shelton Laurel Creek and Valley, *see F262.M25*
	Smith Island, *see F262.B9*
262.S7	Stanly Co.
262.S8	Stokes Co.
262.S9	Surry Co.
262.S95	Swain Co.
	Including Hazel Creek and Valley
	Tanglewood Park, *see F262.F7*
	Tellico Creek and Valley, *see F262.M2*
	Topsail Island, *see F262.O5*
262.T7	Transylvania Co.
	Tryon Co. (To 1778), *see F262.L6 and F262.R9*
262.T9	Tyrrell Co.
262.U5	Union Co.
262.V3	Vance Co.
262.W18	Waccamaw River and Valley
	Cf. F277.W33 , General, and South Carolina
	Wachovia, *see F262.F7*
262.W2	Wake Co.
262.W27	Warren Co.
262.W3	Washington Co.
262.W34	Watauga Co.
	For New River and Valley, see F262.N6
262.W4	Wayne Co.
	Western North Carolina, *see F261*
	Whiteside Cove, *see F262.J2*
262.W6	Wilkes Co.
262.W7	Wilson Co.
262.Y19	Yadkin Co.
262.Y2	Yadkin (Pee Dee) River and Valley
	Cf. F277.P3, Pee Dee River of South Carolina
262.Y3	Yancey Co.
264.A-.Z	**Cities, towns, etc., A-Z**
	GALE NOTE *The cutter number(s) listed below have been given only as examples by the Library of Congress*
264.A8	Asheville
264.C4	Charlotte
264.R1	Raleigh
264.W8	Winston-Salem
	Elements in the population
265.A1	General works
265.A2-.Z	Individual elements
	For a list of racial, ethnic, and religious elements (with cutter numbers), see E184.A+

	South Carolina
266	**Periodicals. Societies. Collections**
266.5	**Museums. Exhibitions, exhibits**
267	**Gazetteers. Dictionaries. Geographic names**
267.3	**Guidebooks**
268	**Biography (Collective). Genealogy (Collective)**
268.2	**Historiography**
	Historians, *see* E175.5.A+
268.5	**Study and teaching**
269	**General works. Histories**
269.3	**Juvenile works**
	Pamphlets, addresses, essays, etc.
269.5	General
269.6	Anecdotes, legends, pageants, etc.
269.8	**Geography**
270	**Historic monuments (General). Illustrative material**
271	**Antiquities (Non-Indian)**
	By period
272	Early to 1775

> *Including The "Carolana" grant of 1629; province of Carolina (1663-1712); Charleston settlement; Locke's Fundamental constitutions; Spanish attack from Florida in 1680; separation of the two Carolinas*
> *Including biography: Eliza (Lucas) Pinckney, etc.*
> *Cf. E83.759, Cherokee War, 1759-1761*
> *Cf. E197, Queen Anne's War, 1702-1713*
> *Cf. F257, North Carolina settlement*
> *Cf. F289, George settlement, Montgomery's Margravate of Azilia*
> *Cf. F314, Huguenot colony at Port Royal, 1562; St. Augustine Expedition, 1740*

273	1775-1865

> *Including dispute with Massachusetts over the latter's Afro-American citizens, 1845; secession*
> *Including biography: James Henry Hammond, Thomas Lee, James Louis Petigru, Robert Barnwell Rhett*
> *Cf. E263.S7, South Carolina in the Revolution (General)*
> *Cf. E230+, Military operations and battles in the Revolution*
> *Cf. E384.3, Nullification*
> *Cf. E409.5.S7, War with Mexico, 1845-1849*
> *Cf. E577.1+, Civil War, 1861-1865 (General)*
> *Cf. E470.6, E471+, Military operations and battles in the Civil War, 1861-1865*
> *Cf. E529.1+, Union history, Civil War, 1861-1865*
> *Cf. E185.93.S7, Afro-Americans in the Sea Islands, Port Royal mission*
> *Cf. F292.B7, South Carolina's cession of 1787*
> *Cf. HF1754, Tariff of 1828*

274	1865-1950. Reconstruction

> *Including biography: David Henry Chamberlain, Benjamin Franklin Perry, Frederick Adolphus Sawyer, etc.*
> *Cf. D570.85.S6+, World War I, 1914-1918*
> *Cf. D769.85.S6+, World War II, 1939-1945*

	1951-
275	General works
	Biography
275.4	Collective
275.42.A-.42.Z	Individual, A-Z
	GALE NOTE *See note at the head of Table F5 at the end of the text for further instructions on how to subdivide this number*
277.A-.Z	**Regions, counties, etc., A-Z**
277.A15	Counties
277.A16	Mountains
277.A17	Rivers
277.A18	Lakes

	South Carolina
277.A-.Z	**Regions, counties, etc., A-Z — Continued**
277.A19	Islands
277.A2	Abbeville Co.
277.A3	Aiken Co.
277.A4	Allendale Co.
277.A5	Anderson Co.
277.A84	Ashley River and Valley
277.A86	Atlantic coast
277.B2	Bamberg Co.
277.B25	Barnwell Co.
277.B3	Beaufort Co. Sea Islands, S.C.

Including Hilton Head Island, Hunting Island, Kiawah Island, Parris Island, St. Helena Island, Edisto Island

Cf. E185.93.S7, Afro-Americans in the Sea Islands District

277.B5	Berkeley Co. Craven Co.

Including Cooper River

277.B7	Boundaries

Cf. F262.B7, North Carolina boundary

For South Carolina cession south of Tennessee, see F292.B7

277.B73	Broad River and Valley (General, and South Carolina)

Cf. F262.B89, North Carolina

Bullock Creek and Valley, *see F277.Y6*

277.C2	Calhoun Co.
277.C22	Camden District
277.C3	Catawba River and Valley, S.C.

Cf. F262.C3, North Carolina

277.C4	Charleston Co.

Including Folly Island, Hampton Plantation State Park, Tea Farm Park, Jehossee Island, Wadmalaw Island, Seabrook Island

For Sea Islands, S.C., see F277.B3

277.C5	Cherokee Co.
277.C55	Chester Co.
277.C57	Chesterfield Co.
277.C7	Clarendon Co.
277.C8	Colleton Co.
277.C85	Congaree Swamp and Region
	Cooper River, *see F277.B5*
	Craven Co., *see F277.B5*
277.D2	Darlington Co.
277.D5	Dillon Co.
277.D6	Dorchester Co.
277.E2	Edgefield Co.
	Edisto Island, *see F277.B3*
277.F3	Fairfield Co.
277.F5	Florence Co.
	Folly Island, *see F277.C4*
277.G35	Georgetown Co.

Including Pawleys Island

277.G6	Greenville Co.
277.G7	Greenwood Co.
277.H3	Hampton Co.
	Hampton Plantation State Park, *see F277.C4*
	Hilton Head Island, *see F277.B3*
277.H6	Horry Co.
	Hunting Island, *see F277.B3*
277.J3	Jasper Co.
	Jehossee Island, *see F277.C4*
277.K3	Kershaw Co.
	Kiawah Island, *see F277.B3*

	South Carolina
277.A-.Z	**Regions, counties, etc., A-Z — Continued**
277.K5	Kings Mountain National Military Park
277.L2	Lancaster Co.
277.L3	Laurens Co.
	Including Rosemont Plantation
277.L4	Lee Co.
277.L5	Lexington Co.
277.M15	McCormick Co.
277.M2	Marion Co.
277.M3	Marlboro Co.
277.M87	Murray, Lake, and Region
277.N5	Newberry Co. Newberry District
277.N6	Ninety-Six (District)
277.O3	Oconee Co.
277.O5	Orangeburg Co.
277.O6	Orangeburgh District
	Parris Island, *see* F277.B3
277.P3	Pee Dee region. Pee Dee River and Valley (Great Pedee and Little Pedee Rivers)
	Cf. F262.Y2, North Carolina
277.P35	Pendleton Co. Pendleton District
277.P5	Pickens Co.
277.P95	Prince Frederick Parish
277.P97	Prince William's Parish
277.R49	Richard B. Russell Lake, S.C.
	Cf. F292.R49, General, and Georgia
277.R5	Richland Co.
	St. Helena Island, *see* F277.B3
277.S2	St. Mark's Parish
277.S24	St. Thomas and St. Denis Parish
277.S26	Saluda Co.
277.S27	Sandhills, S.C.
	Cf. F262.S34, General, and North Carolina
	Cf. F292.S25, Georgia
277.S28	Santee River. Santee River system
277.S3	Savannah River and Valley, S.C.
	Including Argyle Island
	Cf. F292.S3, General, and Georgia
	Sea Islands, S.C., *see* F277.B3
	Seabrook Island, *see* F277.C4
277.S7	Spartanburg Co.
277.S77	Sullivans Island
277.S8	Sumter Co.
	Tea Farm Park, *see* F277.C4
277.U5	Union Co.
277.W33	Waccamaw River and Valley (General, and South Carolina)
	Cf. F262.W18, North Carolina
	Wadmalaw Island, *see* F277.C4
277.W7	Williamsburg Co.
277.Y6	York Co.
	Including Bullock Creek and Valley
277.Y62	York District
279.A-.Z	**Cities, towns, etc., A-Z**
	GALE NOTE *The cutter number(s) listed below have been given only as examples by the Library of Congress*
279.C4	Charleston
	Subarrange by Table F2 at the end of the text
279.C7	Columbia
279.G79	Greenville
279.S7	Spartanburg

South Carolina — Continued

Elements in the population

280.A1	General works
280.A2-.Z	Individual elements
	For a list of racial, ethnic, and religious elements (with cutter numbers), see E184.A+

Georgia

281	**Periodicals. Societies. Collections**
283	**Museums. Exhibitions, exhibits**
284	**Gazetteers. Dictionaries. Geographic names**
284.3	**Guidebooks**
285	**Biography (Collective). Genealogy (Collective)**
285.2	**Historiography**
	Historians, *see* E175.5.A+
285.5	**Study and teaching**
286	**General works. Histories**
286.3	**Juvenile works**
	Pamphlets, addresses, essays, etc.
286.5	General
286.6	Anecdotes, legends, pageants, etc.
287	**Historic monuments (General). Illustrative material**
288	**Antiquities (Non-Indian)**
	By period
289	Early to 1775
	Including Indian affairs; Spanish claims and attacks; Montgomery's Margravate of Azilia; Trustees for establishing the colony of Georgia in America; Royal province
	Including biography: James Edward Oglethorpe, etc.
	Cf. E197, Queen Anne's War, 1702-1713
	Cf. F295.S1, Salzburger immigration
	Cf. F314, St. Augustine Expedition, 1740
290	1775-1865
	Including cession of western lands to United States, 1802
	Including biography: Elijah Clarke, Howell Cobb, Herschel Vespasian Johnson, Charles James McDonald, Thomas Spalding, Linton Stephens, etc.
	Cf. E83.813, First Creek War, 1813-1814
	Cf. E83.817, First Seminole War, 1817-1818
	Cf. E83.836, Second Creek War, 1836
	Cf. E99.C5, Cherokee troubles
	Cf. E263.G3, Georgia in the Revolution (General)
	Cf. E230+, Military operations and battles in the Revolution
	Cf. E359.5.G4, War of 1812
	Cf. E559.1+, Civil War, 1861-1865 (General)
	Cf. E470.6, E471+, Military operations and battles in the Civil War, 1861-1865
	Cf. E503.1+, Union history, Civil War, 1861-1865
	Cf. F296, F321-350, Western lands ceded to the United States (General)
	Cf. F341, Yazoo land companies, Yazoo fraud
291	1865-1950. Reconstruction
	Including biography: Rufus Brown Bullock, William Harrell Felton, Charles Jones Jenkins, Eugene Talmadge, etc.
	Cf. D570.85.G4+, World War I, 1914-1918
	Cf. D769.85.G4+, World War II, 1939-1945
	1951-
291.2	General works
	Biography
291.3.A2A-.3.A2Z	Collective
291.3.A3-.3.Z	Individual, A-Z
	GALE NOTE *See note at the head of Table F5 at the end of the text for further instructions on how to subdivide this number*
291.7	**North Georgia**
291.8	**South Georgia**

	Georgia — Continued
292.A-.Z	**Regions, counties, etc., A-Z**
292.A15	Counties
292.A16	Mountains
292.A17	Rivers
292.A18	Lakes
292.A19	Islands
292.A6	Appling Co.
	Argyle Island, *see* F292.S3
292.A7	Atkinson Co.
292.A74	Atlantic Coast
292.B13	Bacon Co.
292.B14	Baker Co.
292.B15	Baldwin Co.
292.B2	Banks Co.
292.B27	Barrow Co.
292.B3	Bartow Co.
292.B4	Ben Hill Co.
292.B45	Berrien Co.
292.B5	Bibb Co.
	Billys Island, *see* F292.O5
292.B6	Bleckley Co.
292.B7	Boundaries. South Carolina cession south of Tennessee
	Cf. *F277.B7 , South Carolina boundary*
	Cf. *F317.B7 , Florida boundary*
	Cf. *F443.B7 , Tennessee boundary*
292.B8	Brantley Co.
292.B83	Brooks Co.
292.B85	Bryan Co.
292.B9	Bulloch Co.
292.B95	Burke Co.
292.B97	Butts Co.
292.C15	Calhoun Co.
292.C17	Camden Co.
	Including Kings Bay
	Campbell County, *see* F292.F9
292.C18	Candler Co.
292.C19	Carroll Co.
292.C2	Catoosa Co.
292.C3	Charlton Co.
292.C36	Chatham Co.
292.C39	Chattahoochee Co.
292.C4	Chattahoochee River and Valley (General, and Ga.)
	Cf. *F317.J2, Florida*
	Cf. *F332.C4, Alabama*
292.C43	Chattooga Co.
292.C47	Cherokee Co.
292.C5	Clarke Co.
292.C53	Clay Co.
292.C54	Clayton Co.
292.C55	Clinch Co.
292.C6	Cobb Co.
292.C63	Coffee Co.
	Colonel's Island, *see* F292.G5
292.C7	Colquitt Co.
292.C73	Columbia Co.
292.C76	Cook Co.
292.C8	Coweta Co.
292.C85	Crawford Co.
292.C93	Crisp Co.

	Georgia
292.A-.Z	**Regions, counties, etc., A-Z — Continued**
292.C94	Cumberland Island. Cumberland Island National Seashore
292.D15	Dade Co.
292.D2	Dawson Co.
292.D27	Decatur Co.
292.D3	De Kalb Co.
292.D5	Dodge Co.
292.D55	Dooly Co.
292.D6	Dougherty Co.
292.D65	Douglas Co.
292.E2	Early Co.
292.E25	Echols Co.
292.E3	Effingham Co.
292.E4	Elbert Co.
292.E5	Emanuel Co.
292.E9	Evans Co.
292.F2	Fannin Co.
292.F3	Fayette Co.
292.F6	Floyd Co.
292.F67	Forsyth Co.
292.F7	Fort Frederica National Monument
292.F8	Franklin Co.
292.F9	Fulton Co.
	Including Campbell County, Milton County
292.G3	Gilmer Co.
292.G4	Glascock Co.
292.G5	Glynn Co.
	Including Colonel's Island
	For Fort Frederica National Monument, see F292.F7
292.G58	Golden Isles
	Including Jekyl Island, St. Simon's Island
292.G6	Gordon Co.
292.G66	Grady Co.
292.G7	Greene Co.
292.G9	Gwinnett Co.
292.H2	Habersham Co.
292.H25	Hall Co.
292.H3	Hancock Co.
292.H5	Haralson Co.
292.H55	Harris Co.
292.H6	Hart Co.
292.H7	Heard Co.
292.H73	Henry Co.
292.H8	Houston Co.
292.I67	Irwin Co.
292.J13	Jackson Co.
292.J2	Jasper Co.
292.J25	Jeff Davis Co.
292.J28	Jefferson Co.
	Jekyl Island, *see* F292.G58
292.J4	Jenkins Co.
292.J6	Johnson Co.
292.J7	Jones Co.
	Kings Bay, *see* F292.C17
292.L2	Lamar Co.
	Lanier, Lake, *see* F292.S53
292.L25	Lanier Co.
292.L3	Laurens Co.
292.L4	Lee Co.

	Georgia
292.A-.Z	**Regions, counties, etc., A-Z — Continued**
292.L6	Liberty Co.
292.L63	Lincoln Co.
	Little Tennessee River and Valley, *see* F443.L64
292.L66	Long Co.
	Lookout Mountain, *see* F443.L8
292.L7	Lowndes Co.
292.L8	Lumpkin Co.
292.M13	McDuffie Co.
292.M15	McIntosh Co.
	Including Sapelo Island
292.M17	Macon Co.
292.M2	Madison Co.
292.M25	Marion Co.
292.M5	Meriwether Co.
292.M6	Miller Co.
	Milton County, *see* F292.F9
292.M65	Mitchell Co.
292.M7	Monroe Co.
292.M73	Montgomery Co.
292.M76	Morgan Co.
292.M8	Murray Co.
292.M9	Muscogee Co.
292.N4	Newton Co.
292.O27	Ocmulgee River
292.O3	Oconee Co.
292.O33	Oconee River and Valley
292.O38	Ogeechee River and Valley
292.O4	Oglethorpe Co.
292.O5	Okefenokee Swamp
	Including Billys Island
292.P3	Paulding Co.
292.P4	Peach Co.
292.P57	Pickens Co.
292.P61	Pierce Co.
292.P65	Pike Co.
292.P7	Polk Co.
292.P85	Pulaski Co.
292.P9	Putnam Co.
292.Q5	Quitman Co.
292.R3	Rabun Co.
292.R35	Randolph Co.
292.R49	Richard B. Russell Lake and region (General, and Georgia)
	Cf. F277.R49, South Carolina
292.R5	Richmond Co.
292.R6	Rockdale Co.
292.S2	St. Marys River and Valley, Ga.
	Cf. F317.S3, General, and Florida
	St. Simon's Island, *see* F292.G58
292.S25	Sandhills, Ga.
	Cf. F262.S34, General, and North Carolina
	Cf. F277.S27, South Carolina
	Sapelo Island, *see* F292.M15
292.S3	Savannah River and Valley (General, and Ga.)
	Including Argyle Island
	Cf. F277.S3, South Carolina
292.S33	Schley Co.
292.S35	Screven Co.
292.S4	Seminole Co.

	Georgia
292.A-.Z	**Regions, counties, etc., A-Z — Continued**
292.S53	Sidney Lanier, Lake
292.S6	Spalding Co.
292.S7	Stephens Co.
292.S8	Stewart Co.
292.S85	Stone Mountain Memorial
292.S9	Sumter Co.
292.T2	Talbot Co.
292.T23	Taliaferro Co.
292.T27	Tattnall Co.
292.T3	Taylor Co.
292.T35	Telfair Co.
292.T37	Terrell Co.
292.T4	Thomas Co.
292.T5	Tift Co.
292.T6	Toombs Co.
292.T65	Towns Co.
292.T7	Treutlen Co.
292.T75	Troup Co.
292.T8	Turner Co.
292.T9	Twiggs Co.
292.U5	Union Co.
292.U6	Upson Co.
292.W16	Walker Co.
292.W17	Walton Co.
292.W2	Ware Co.
292.W23	Warren Co.
292.W25	Washington Co.
292.W3	Wayne Co.
292.W35	Webster Co.
292.W45	Wheeler Co.
292.W48	White Co.
292.W5	Whitfield Co.
292.W65	Wilcox Co.
292.W7	Wilkes Co.
292.W75	Wilkinson Co.
292.W9	Worth Co.
294.A-.Z	**Cities, towns, etc., A-Z**
	GALE NOTE *The cutter number(s) listed below have been given only as examples by the Library of Congress*
294.A8	Atlanta
	Subarrange by Table F2 at the end of the text
294.A9	Augusta
294.C7	Columbus
294.M2	Macon
294.S2	Savannah
	Elements in the population
295.A1	General works
295.A2-.Z	Individual elements
	For a list of racial, ethnic, and religious elements (with cutter numbers), see E184.A+
295.S1	Salzburgers
296	**Gulf States**
	Including Gulf coast after 1803; Gulf of Mexico
	For Gulf coast early to 1803, see F372
	For Lower Mississippi Valley, see F396
	For Mississippi Territory (1798), see F336+
	For South Atlantic States, see F206+
	For West Florida, see F301
	Cf. F332.G9 , Gulf coast of Alabama

296	**Gulf States — Continued**
	Cf. F392.G9 , Gulf coast of Texas; etc.
301	**West Florida**
	Cf. F317.W5 , Pensacola District after 1819
	Cf. F334.M6, Mobile
	Cf. F341, Natchez District
	Cf. F377.B7, Louisiana boundary
	Cf. F377.F6, Florida parishes of Louisiana, Baton Rouge District since 1812
	Florida
306	**Periodicals. Societies. Collections**
308	**Museums. Exhibitions, exhibits**
309	**Gazetteers. Dictionaries. Geographic names**
309.3	**Guidebooks**
310	**Biography (Collective). Genealogy (Collective)**
310.2	**Historiography**
	Historians, *see* E175.5.A+
310.5	**Study and teaching**
311	**General works. Histories**
311.3	**Juvenile works**
	Pamphlets, addresses, essays, etc.
311.5	General
311.6	Anecdotes, legends, pageants, etc.
311.8	**Geography**
312	**Historic monuments (General). Illustrative material**
313	**Antiquities (Non-Indian)**
	By period
314	Early to 1821
	Including French Huguenot colonies, 1562-1565; Spanish Colony, 1565-1763, 1783-1821; St. Augustine expeditions, 1740, 1743; East Florida; English Colony, 1763-1783; "Republic of Florida," 1812-1816; MacGregor at Amelia Island, 1817; Treaty of Washington, 1819 (with Spain); Spanish Florida claims (General)
	Including biography: Dominique de Gourgues, René Goulaine de Laudonnière, Pedro Menéndez de Avilés, Jean Ribaut (Ribault), etc.
	For West Florida, see F301
	Cf. E83.813, First Creek War, 1813-1814
	Cf. E83.817, First Seminole War, 1817-1818; execution of Arbuthnot and Ambrister
	Cf. E359.5.F6, War of 1812
	Cf. F319.S2, St. Augustine
	Cf. F372, Gulf coast before 1763
	Cf. F1410, Spaniards in North America (General)
315	1821-1865
	Including Andrew Jackson's administration as governor; admission as a state, 1845
	Cf. E83.835, Second Seminole War, 1835-1842
	Cf. E83.855, Third Seminole War, 1855-1858
	Cf. E558.1+, Civil War, 1861-1865 (General)
	Cf. E470.7, E471+, Military operations and battles in the Civil War, 1861-1865
	Cf. E502.1+, Union history, Civil War, 1861-1865
316	1865-1950
	Including Reconstruction; hurricane disasters, 1926, 1927
	Cf. D769.85.F5+, World War II, 1939-1945
	Cf. E726.F6, War of 1898 (Spanish-American War)
	1951-
316.2	General works
	Biography
316.22	Collective
316.23.A-.23.Z	Individual, A-Z
	GALE NOTE *See note at the head of Table F5 at the end of the text for further instructions on how to subdivide this number*
317.A-.Z	**Regions, counties, etc., A-Z**
317.A15	Counties

	Florida
317.A-.Z	**Regions, counties, etc., A-Z — Continued**
317.A16	Mountains
317.A17	Rivers
317.A18	Lakes
317.A19	Islands
317.A4	Alachua Co.
	Including Paynes Prairie
	Amelia Island, *see* F317.N3
317.A6	Apalachicola River and Valley
317.A74	Atlantic Coast
317.B2	Baker Co.
317.B3	Bay Co.
317.B54	Big Bend Region
	Biscayne Bay, *see* F317.D2
317.B7	Boundaries
	Cf. F332.B7 , Alabama boundary
317.B75	Bradford Co.
317.B8	Brevard Co.
	Including Cape Canaveral, Indian River
317.B85	Broward Co.
317.C3	Calhoun Co.
	Cape Canaveral, *see* F317.B8
317.C4	Charlotte Co.
	Chattahoochee River and Valley, Fla., *see* F317.J2
317.C5	Citrus Co.
317.C6	Clay Co.
317.C7	Collier Co.
317.C75	Columbia Co.
317.D2	Dade Co.
	Including Biscayne Bay, Lake Worth
	For Everglades, see F317.E9
317.D4	De Soto Co.
317.D5	Dixie Co.
317.D9	Duval Co.
317.E7	Escambia Co.
	For Perdido River and Valley, see F317.P4
317.E9	Everglades
	Including Everglades National Park
317.F6	Flagler Co.
	Florida Keys, *see* F317.M7
	Fort Jefferson National Monument, *see* F317.M7
317.F7	Franklin Co.
317.G2	Gadsden Co.
317.G5	Gilchrist Co.
317.G6	Glades Co.
317.G8	Gulf coast of Florida
	Including Gulf Islands National Seashore (General, and Florida)
	Cf. F347.G9, Gulf Islands National Seashore (Mississippi)
317.G9	Gulf Co.
	Gulf Islands National Seashore, *see* F317.G8
317.H2	Hamilton Co.
317.H3	Hardee Co.
317.H4	Hendry Co.
317.H5	Hernando Co.
317.H54	Highlands Co.
317.H6	Hillsborough Co.
317.H7	Holmes Co.
317.H73	Holmes Creek and Valley (General, and Florida)
	Cf. F332.H56, Alabama

	Florida
317.A-.Z	**Regions, counties, etc., A-Z — Continued**
	Indian River, *see* F317.B8
317.I5	Indian River Co.
317.J2	Jackson Co.
	Including Chattahoochee River and Valley, Fla.
	Cf. F292.C4, General, and Georgia
	Cf. F332.C4, Alabama, etc.
	Cf. F317.A6, Apalachicola River and Valley
317.J4	Jefferson Co.
317.K57	Kissimmee River and Valley
317.L15	Lafayette Co.
317.L2	Lake Co.
317.L3	Lee Co.
	Including Pine Island
	For Everglades, see F317.E9
317.L5	Leon Co.
317.L6	Levy Co.
317.L7	Liberty Co.
317.M15	Madison Co.
317.M2	Manatee Co.
	Including Manatee River
317.M3	Marion Co.
	Including Lake Weir
317.M35	Martin Co.
317.M7	Monroe Co.
	Including Florida Keys, Fort Jefferson National Monument
	For Everglades, see F317.E9
317.M92	Myakka River State Park
317.N3	Nassau Co.
	Including Amelia Island
	Cf. F314, History before 1819
317.O3	Okaloosa Co.
317.O4	Lake Okeechobee
317.O43	Okeechobee Co.
	Okefenokee Swamp, *see* F292.O5
317.O46	Oklawaha River and Valley
317.O6	Orange Co.
317.O7	Osceola Co.
317.P2	Palm Beach Co.
317.P3	Pasco Co.
	Paynes Prairie, *see* F317.A4
317.P4	Perdido River and Valley, Fla.
	Cf. F332.P4, General, and Alabama
	Pine Island, *see* F317.L3
317.P6	Pinellas Co.
317.P7	Polk Co.
317.P8	Putnam Co.
317.R43	Red Hills
317.S18	Saint Johns Co.
317.S2	Saint Johns River and Valley
	Including Timucuan Ecological and Historic Preserve
317.S27	Saint Lucie Co.
317.S3	Saint Mary's River and Valley (General, and Fla.)
	Cf. F292.S2, Georgia
317.S37	Sanibel Island
317.S4	Santa Rosa Co.
317.S45	Sarasota Co.
317.S5	Seminole Co.
317.S75	Sumter Co.

Florida

317.A-.Z	**Regions, counties, etc., A-Z — Continued**
317.S78	Suwannee Co.
317.S8	Suwannee River and Valley
317.T3	Taylor Co.
	Timucuan Ecological and Historic Preserve, *see* F317.S2
	Tomoka River, *see* F317.V7
317.U5	Union Co.
317.V7	Volusia Co.
	Including Tomoka River
317.W23	Wakulla Co.
317.W24	Walton Co.
317.W3	Washington Co.
	Including St. Andrews Bay
317.W5	West Florida region
	Including The Pensacola District after 1819
	For the Pensacola district, early to 1819, see F301
319.A-.Z	**Cities, towns, etc., A-Z**
	GALE NOTE *The cutter number(s) listed below have been given only as examples by the Library of Congress*
319.J1	Jacksonville
319.K4	Key West
319.M6	Miami
319.P4	Pensacola
319.S2	St. Augustine
319.S24	St. Petersburg
319.T14	Tallahassee
319.T2	Tampa
	Elements in the population
320.A1	General works
320.A2-.Z	Individual elements
	For a list of racial, ethnic, and religious elements (with cutter numbers), see E184.A+

Alabama

321	**Periodicals. Societies. Collections**
323	**Museums. Exhibitions, exhibits**
324	**Gazetteers. Dictionaries. Geographic names**
324.3	**Guidebooks**
325	**Biography (Collective). Genealogy (Collective)**
325.2	**Historiography**
	Historians, *see* E175.5.A+
325.5	**Study and teaching**
326	**General works. Histories**
	Including admission as a state, December 14, 1819
	Including by period (Early to 1950)
	Including secession; Reconstruction; Ku-Klux Klan
	Including biography: John Hollis Bankhead, William Parish Chilton, Thomas Erby Kilby, Thomas Hill Watts, etc.
	For West Florida, see F301
	Cf. D570.85.A2+, World War I, 1914-1918
	Cf. D769.85.A2+, World War II, 1939-1945
	Cf. E83.813, First Creek War, 1813-1814
	Cf. E83.836, Second Creek War, 1836
	Cf. E99.C5, Cherokee Indians
	Cf. E551.1+, Civil War, 1861-1865 (General)
	Cf. E470.7, E471+, Military operations and battles in the Civil War, 1861-1865
	Cf. E495.1+, Union history, Civil War, 1861-1865
	Cf. E726.A3, War of 1898 (Spanish-American War)
	Cf. F292.B7, South Carolina cession south of Tennessee
	Cf. F341, Mississippi Territory
	Cf. F372, Early French settlements on the coast (Louisiana)

	Alabama — Continued
326.3	**Juvenile works**
	Pamphlets, addresses, essays, etc.
326.5	General
326.6	Anecdotes, legends, pageants, etc.
327	**Historic monuments (General). Illustrative material**
328	**Antiquities (Non-Indian)**
	By period
(329)	Early to 1950, *see* F326
	1951-
330	General works
	Biography
330.2	Collective
330.3.A-.3.Z	Individual, A-Z

> GALE NOTE *See note at the head of Table F5 at the end of the text for further*
> *instructions on how to subdivide this number*

332.A-.Z	**Regions, counties, etc., A-Z**
332.A15	Counties
332.A16	Mountains
332.A17	Rivers
332.A18	Lakes
332.A19	Islands
332.A8	Autauga Co.
332.B2	Baldwin Co.
	For Mobile Bay, see F332.M58
	For Perdido River and Valley, see F332.P4
332.B3	Barbour Co.
332.B5	Bibb Co.
332.B6	Blount Co.
	Including Garfield Colony, Rickwood Caverns State Park
332.B7	Boundaries
	Cf. F443.B7, Tennessee boundary
332.B8	Bullock Co.
332.B9	Butler Co.
332.C25	Calhoun Co.
332.C35	Chambers Co.
332.C4	Chattahoochee River and Valley, Ala
	Cf. F292.C4, General, and Georgia
	Cf. F317.J2, Florida
332.C44	Cherokee Co.
332.C46	Chilton Co.
332.C48	Choctaw Co.
332.C6	Clarke Co.
332.C62	Clay Co.
332.C63	Cleburne Co.
332.C65	Coffee Co.
332.C68	Colbert Co.
332.C7	Conecuh Co.
332.C74	Coosa Co.
332.C75	Coosa River and Valley
332.C8	Covington Co.
332.C85	Crenshaw Co.
332.C9	Cullman Co.
332.D17	Dale Co.
332.D3	Dallas Co.
	Dauphin Island, *see* F332.M6
332.D4	De Kalb Co.
332.E4	Elmore Co.
332.E7	Escambia Co.
332.E8	Etowah Co.

	Alabama
332.A-.Z	**Regions, counties, etc., A-Z — Continued**
332.F4	Fayette Co.
332.F83	Franklin Co.
332.G4	Geneva Co.
332.G7	Greene Co.
332.G9	Gulf coast of Alabama
	For Mobile Bay, see F332.M58
	Cf. F296, Gulf coast (General)
332.H3	Hale Co.
332.H4	Henry Co.
332.H56	Holmes Creek and Valley
	Cf. F317.H73, General, and Florida
332.H6	Houston (Huston) Co.
332.J2	Jackson Co.
332.J4	Jefferson Co.
	Including Rouges Creek and Valley
332.L2	Lamar Co.
332.L3	Lauderdale Co.
332.L4	Lawrence Co.
332.L5	Lee Co.
332.L6	Limestone Co.
332.L7	Lowndes Co.
332.M2	Macon Co.
332.M3	Madison Co.
332.M35	Marengo Co.
332.M37	Marion Co.
332.M4	Marshall Co.
332.M58	Mobile Bay
332.M6	Mobile Co.
	Including Dauphin Island
332.M7	Monroe Co.
332.M73	Montgomery Co.
332.M8	Morgan Co.
	Muscle Shoals, *see* F332.T2
	Oliver Dam, *see* F332.T9
332.P34	Paint Rock River (General, and Alabama)
	Cf. F443.P34, Tennessee
332.P37	Pea River and Valley
332.P4	Perdido River and Valley (General, and Ala.)
	Cf. F317.P4, Florida
332.P45	Perry Co.
332.P5	Pickens Co.
332.P55	Pike Co.
332.R3	Randolph Co.
	Rickwood Caverns State Park, *see* F332.B6
	Rouges Creek and Valley, *see* F332.J4
332.R87	Russell Co.
332.S2	St. Clair Co.
332.S5	Shelby Co.
332.S8	Sumter Co.
332.T14	Talladega Co.
332.T15	Tallapoosa Co.
332.T17	Tannehill Historical State Park
332.T2	Tennessee River and Valley, Ala
	Including Muscle Shoals (Topography)
	Cf. F217.T3, General
332.T6	Tombigbee River and Valley (General, and Ala.)
	Cf. F347.T6, Mississippi

	Alabama
332.A-.Z	**Regions, counties, etc., A-Z — Continued**
332.T9	Tuscaloosa Co.
	Including Oliver Dam
332.W3	Walker Co.
332.W4	Washington Co.
332.W48	Wheeler Lake and region
332.W5	Wilcox Co.
332.W54	William B. Bankhead National Forest
332.W6	Winston Co.
334.A-.Z	**Cities, towns, etc., A-Z**
	GALE NOTE *The cutter number(s) listed below have been given only as examples by the Library of Congress*
334.B6	Birmingham
	Subarrange by Table F2 at the end of the text
334.M6	Mobile
334.M7	Montgomery
	Subarrange by Table F2 at the end of the text
334.T9	Tuscaloosa
	Elements in the population
335.A1	General works
335.A2-.Z	Individual elements
	For a list of racial, ethnic, and religious elements (with cutter numbers), see E184.A+
	Mississippi
336	**Periodicals. Societies. Collections**
338	**Museums. Exhibitions, exhibits, etc.**
339	**Gazetteers. Dictionaries. Geographic names**
339.3	**Guidebooks**
340	**Biography (Collective). Genealogy (Collective)**
340.2	**Historiography**
	Historians, *see* E175.5.A+
340.5	**Study and teaching**
341	**General works. Histories**
	Including admission as a state, December 10, 1817
	Including by period (Early to 1950) as well as general
	For 1951 and later, see F345
	Including secession; Reconstruction; Yazoo land companies; etc.
	Including Natchez District of West Florida
	Including biography: Albert Gallatin Brown, Winthrop Sargent, etc.
	For West Florida, Mobile District before 1812, see F301
	Cf. D769.85.M7+, World War II, 1939-1945
	Cf. E83.813, First Creek War, 1813-1814
	Cf. E99.N2, Natchez Indians
	Cf. E568.1+, Civil War (General)
	Cf. E470.7, E471+, Military operations and battles in the Civil War
	Cf. E516.1+, Union history, Civil War, 1861-1865
	Cf. F292.B7, South Carolina cession south of Tennessee
341.3	**Juvenile works**
	Pamphlets, addresses, essays, etc.
341.5	General
341.6	Anecdotes, legends, pageants, etc.
342	**Historic monuments (General). Illustrative material**
343	**Antiquities (Non-Indian)**
	By period
(344)	Early to 1950, *see* F341
	1951-
345	General works
	Biography
345.2	Collective

Mississippi

By period

1951-

Biography — Continued

345.3.A-.3.Z	Individual, A-Z
	Subarrange each by Table F5 at the end of the text
347.A-.Z	**Regions, counties, etc., A-Z**
347.A15	Counties
347.A16	Mountains
347.A17	Rivers
347.A18	Lakes
347.A19	Islands
	Ackia Battleground National Monument, *see* F347.L45
347.A2	Adams Co.
347.A4	Alcorn Co.
347.A5	Amite Co.
347.A7	Attala Co.
347.B4	Benton Co.
347.B6	Bolivar Co.
347.B7	Boundaries
	Cf. F332.B7, Alabama boundary
	Cf. F377.B7, Louisiana boundary
	Cf. F443.B7, Tennessee boundary
347.C2	Calhoun Co.
347.C3	Carroll Co.
347.C4	Chickasaw Co.
347.C45	Choctaw Co.
347.C5	Claiborne Co.
	Including Grand Gulf State Military Park
347.C55	Clarke Co.
347.C6	Clay Co.
347.C7	Coahoma Co.
347.C75	Copiah Co.
347.C8	Covington Co.
347.D4	De Soto Co.
347.F6	Forrest Co.
347.F7	Franklin Co.
347.G4	George Co.
	Grand Gulf State Military Park, *see* F347.C5
347.G65	Greene Co.
347.G7	Grenada Co.
347.G9	Gulf coast of Mississippi
	Including Gulf Islands National Seashore
	Cf. F296, Gulf coast (General)
	Cf. F317.G8, Gulf Islands National Seashore (General, and Florida)
	Gulf Islands National Seashore, *see* F347.G9
347.H2	Hancock Co.
347.H3	Harrison Co.
	Including Ship Island
347.H5	Hinds Co.
347.H6	Holmes Co.
347.H8	Humphreys Co.
347.I7	Issaquena Co.
347.I8	Itawamba Co.
347.J3	Jackson Co.
347.J4	Jasper Co.
347.J48	Jefferson Co.
347.J5	Jefferson Davis Co.
347.J6	Jones Co.
347.K3	Kemper Co.

	Mississippi
347.A-.Z	**Regions, counties, etc., A-Z — Continued**
347.L2	Lafayette Co.
347.L25	Lamar Co.
347.L3	Lauderdale Co.
347.L35	Lawrence Co.
347.L4	Leake Co.
347.L45	Lee Co.
	Including Ackia Battleground National Monument
347.L47	Leflore Co.
347.L6	Lincoln Co.
347.L8	Lowndes Co.
347.M15	Madison Co.
347.M25	Marion Co.
347.M3	Marshall Co.
347.M6	Mississippi River and Valley, Miss.
	Cf. F350.5+, General
	Cf. F396, Lower Mississippi Valley
347.M7	Monroe Co.
347.M75	Montgomery Co.
347.N4	Neshoba Co.
347.N48	Newton Co.
347.N6	Noxubee Co.
347.O4	Oktibbeha Co.
347.P2	Panola Co.
347.P3	Pearl River and Valley (General, and Miss.)
	Cf. F377.P3, Louisiana
347.P33	Pearl River Co.
347.P4	Perry Co.
347.P6	Pike Co.
347.P63	Piney Woods
347.P7	Pontotoc Co.
347.P8	Prentiss Co.
347.Q5	Quitman Co.
347.R3	Rankin Co.
347.S3	Scott Co.
347.S45	Sharkey Co.
347.S5	Simpson Co.
347.S6	Smith Co.
347.S8 .	Stone Co.
347.S9	Sunflower Co.
347.T3	Tallahatchie Co.
347.T35	Tate Co.
347.T45	Tippah Co.
347.T5	Tishomingo Co.
347.T6	Tombigbee River and Valley, Miss.
	Cf. F332.T6, General, and Alabama
347.T8	Tunica Co.
347.U5	Union Co.
347.W24	Walthall Co.
347.W29	Warren Co.
347.W35	Washington Co.
347.W4	Wayne Co.
347.W45	Webster Co.
347.W65	Wilkinson Co.
347.W7	Winston Co.
347.Y15	Yalobusha Co.
347.Y2	Yazoo Co.
347.Y3	Yazoo River and Valley

	Mississippi — Continued
349.A-.Z	**Cities, towns, etc., A-Z**
	GALE NOTE *The cutter number(s) listed below have been given only as examples by the Library of Congress*
349.B5	Biloxi
349.J13	Jackson
349.M5	Meridian
349.N2	Natchez
349.V6	Vicksburg
	Elements in the population
350.A1	General works
350.A2-.Z	Individual elements
	For a list of racial, ethnic, and religious elements (with cutter numbers), see E184.A+
350.3-358.2	**Mississippi River and Valley. Middle West**
350.5	**Biography (Collective). Genealogy (Collective)**
350.8	**Antiquities (Non-Indian)**
351	**General works**
	Including the Mississippi Valley under Spain, France, Great Britain, and the United States. History; description, exploration, and travel; manners and customs
	Including periodicals, societies, collections, collective biography, etc.
	For Louisiana purchase (Diplomatic and political aspects), see E333
	Cf. F347.B7, Mississippi-Arkansas boundary
	Cf. F366+, Louisiana
	Cf. F377.B7, Mississippi-Louisiana boundary
	Cf. F396, Lower Mississippi River and Valley
	Cf. F516+, Ohio River and Valley
	Cf. F547.I2, Illinois River and Valley
	Cf. F597, Upper Mississippi River and Valley
	Cf. F598, Missouri River and Valley
	By period
352	Early to 1803
	Including early explorations and discoveries, by Hennepin, La Salle, Marquette
	Cf. E125.S7, Soto's explorations (General)
	Cf. E234, Clark's Expedition
	Cf. E333, Purchase of Louisiana by the United States (Diplomatic and political aspects)
	Cf. F372-373, Louisiana (French and Spanish)
	Cf. F597, Carver's explorations (Upper Mississippi Valley)
	Cf. F1030, New France
	Cf. F1030.2, Marquette's explorations (General)
	Cf. F1030.3, Joliet's explorations (General)
	Cf. F1030.4, Hennepin's explorations (General)
	Cf. F1030.5, La Salle's explorations (General)
	Cf. HG6007, Law's Mississippi Scheme
353	1803-1865
	Cf. E83.83, Black Hawk War, 1832
	Cf. E334, Burr's Conspiracy, 1805-1807
	Cf. E471+, Civil War, 1861-1865 (History and campaigns)
	Cf. F592, Lewis and Clark Expedition, 1804-1806; Pike's Expedition, 1805-1807
354	1865-1950
	Including individual floods, cruises down the river
	Cf. TC425.M65, Jetties of the Mississippi
355	1951-
	Elements in the population
358	General works
358.2.A-.2.Z	Individual elements
	For a list of individual racial, ethnic and religious elements (with cutter numbers), see E184.A+
	Louisiana
366	**Periodicals. Societies. Collections**
366.5	**Museums. Exhibitions, exhibits**

	Louisiana — Continued
367	**Gazetteers. Dictionaries. Geographic names**
367.3	**Guidebooks**
367.5	**Directories**
368	**Biography (Collective). Genealogy (Collective)**
368.2	**Historiography**
	Historians, *see* E175.5.A+
368.5	**Study and teaching**
369	**General works. Histories**
369.3	**Juvenile works**
	Pamphlets, addresses, essays, etc.
369.5	General
369.6	Anecdotes, legends, pageants, etc.
370	**Historic monuments (General). Illustrative material**
371	**Antiquities (Non-Indian)**
	By period
372	Early to 1803

Including French Louisiana; Settlement of 1698; Crozat's Grant, 1712-1717; Cession to Spain, 1763

Including biography: Jean Baptiste Le Moyne de Bienville, Pierre Le Moyne d'Iberville, etc.

Cf. E83.739, Chickasaw War, 1739-1740

Cf. F334.M6, Mobile, Ala

Cf. F352, Mississippi Valley

Cf. HG6007, Law's Mississippi scheme, 1717-1720

373   1764-1803

Including Spanish Louisiana; right of navigation of the Mississippi; retrocession to France, 1800-1801

Including biography: Esteban Miró, etc.

For purchase of Louisiana by the United States, see E333

For Spaniards in North America (General), see F1410

374   1803-1865

Including admission as a state, April 30, 1812

Including Province of Louisiana, 1803-1804; Territory of Orleans, 1804-1812; boundary disputes with Spain

Including biography: William Charles Cole Claiborne, Thomas Jefferson Durant, Charles Étienne Arthur Gayarré, Jean Lafitte, Alexander Porter, etc.

Cf. E334, Burr's Conspiracy, 1805-1807

Cf. E355, War of 1812 (Military operations)

Cf. E565.1+, Civil War (General)

Cf. E470.7, E471+, Military operations and battles in the Civil War

Cf. F301, West Florida

Cf. F314, Spanish Treaty of 1819

Cf. F592, Lewis and Clark Expedition

Cf. F697, The "Indian country"

375   1865-1950. Reconstruction

Including Carpetbag misrule; Committee of Seventy; Ku-Klux Klan

Including biography: Edgar Howard Farrar, Samuel Douglas McEnery, etc.

Cf. D769.85.L6+, World War II, 1939-1945

1951-

376   General works

Biography and memoirs

376.2   Collective

376.3.A-.3.Z   Individual, A-Z

GALE NOTE *See note at the head of Table F5 at the end of the text for further instructions on how to subdivide this number*

377.A-.Z   **Regions, parishes, etc., A-Z**

377.A15   Counties

377.A16   Mountains

377.A17   Rivers

377.A18   Lakes

	Louisiana
	Regions, parishes, etc., A-Z — Continued
377.A19	Islands
377.A2	Acadia Parish
377.A4	Allen Parish
377.A7	Ascension Parish
377.A75	Assumption Parish
377.A78	Atchafalaya River and Swamp
	Including Bayou Chene and other bayous in the region
377.A8	Attakapas District
	Avery Island, *see* F377.F57
377.A9	Avoyelles Parish
377.B37	Bartholomew Bayou
	Class here works limited to the part of the Bartholomew Bayou located in Louisiana
	For general works on the Bartholomew Bayou and works limited to the part located in
	Arkansas, see F417.B27
	Bayou Lafourche, *see* F377.L24
	Bayou Teche, *see* F377.T4
377.B4	Beauregard Parish
377.B5	Bienville Parish
377.B6	Bossier Parish
377.B7	Boundaries
	Cf. F377.F6 , Florida parishes
	Caddo Lake, *see* F377.C15
377.C15	Caddo Parish
	Including Caddo Lake
	Cf. F392.C17 , General, and Texas
377.C2	Calcasieu Parish
377.C23	Caldwell Parish
377.C25	Cameron Parish
	Cane River Lake, *see* F377.N4
377.C3	Catahoula Parish
	Chalmette National Historical Park, *see* E356.N5
377.C5	Claiborne Parish
377.C7	Concordia Parish
377.D4	Delta region
377.D45	De Soto Parish
377.E17	East Baton Rouge Parish
377.E2	East Carroll Parish
377.E3	East Feliciana Parish
377.E8	Evangeline Parish
377.F57	Five Islands
	Including Avery Island
377.F6	Florida parishes. Baton Rouge district of West Florida since 1812 (between Pearl and Mississippi rivers)
	For early to 1812, see F301
377.F7	Franklin Parish
	Grand Isle, *see* F377.J4
377.G7	Grant Parish
377.G9	Gulf coast of Louisiana
	Cf. F296, Gulf coast (General)
377.I15	Iberia Parish
377.I2	Iberville Parish
377.J2	Jackson Parish
377.J4	Jefferson Parish
	Including Grand Isle
377.J43	Jefferson Davis Parish
377.L2	Lafayette Parish
377.L24	Lafourche Bayou
377.L25	Lafourche Parish

	Louisiana
377.A-.Z	**Regions, parishes, etc., A-Z — Continued**
377.L3	La Salle Parish
377.L5	Lincoln Parish
377.L6	Livingston Parish
377.M2	Madison Parish
377.M6	Mississippi River and Valley, La.
	Cf. F350.5+, General
	Cf. F396, Lower Mississippi Valley
377.M7	Morehouse Parish
	Murphys Lake, *see* F377.N4
377.N4	Natchitoches Parish
	Including Murphys Lake and Cane River Lake
377.O7	Orleans Parish
377.O78	Ouachita Parish
377.O8	Ouachita River and Valley (General, and La.)
	Cf. F417.O83, Arkansas
377.P3	Pearl River and Valley (General, and La.)
	Cf. F347.P3, General, and Mississippi
377.P45	Plaquemines Parish
377.P55	Pointe Coupee Parish
377.P6	Lake Pontchartrain
377.R25	Rapides Parish
	Including Cotile Lake
377.R3	Red River and Valley (General, and La.)
	Cf. F392.R3, Texas
	Cf. F417.R3, Arkansas
	Cf. F702.R3, Oklahoma
	Cf. F802.R36, New Mexico
377.R32	Red River Parish
377.R5	Richland Parish
377.R58	River Road
377.S115	Sabine Parish
377.S116	Sabine River and Valley (General, and La.)
	Cf. F392.S12, Texas
377.S12	St. Bernard Parish
377.S124	St. Charles Parish
377.S13	St. Helena Parish
377.S134	St. James Parish
377.S135	St. John the Baptist Parish
377.S14	St. Landry Parish
377.S16	St. Martin Parish
377.S2	St. Mary Parish
377.S3	St. Tammany Parish
377.T3	Tangipahoa Parish
377.T4	Bayou Teche
377.T45	Tensas Parish
377.T5	Terrebonne Parish
377.T6	Toledo Bend Reservoir. Toledo Bend region
377.U5	Union Parish
377.V5	Vermilion Parish
377.V6	Vernon Parish
377.W3	Washington Parish
377.W4	Webster Parish
377.W45	West Baton Rouge Parish
377.W47	West Carroll Parish
377.W5	West Feliciana Parish
377.W6	Winn Parish

	Texas
	By period
	1846- — Continued
	1951-
391.2	General works
	Biography
391.3	Collective
391.4.A-.4.Z	Individual, A-Z

GALE NOTE *See note at the head of Table F5 at the end of the text for further instructions on how to subdivide this number*

392.A-.Z	**Regions, counties, etc., A-Z**
392.A15	Counties
392.A16	Mountains
392.A17	Rivers
392.A18	Lakes
392.A19	Islands
392.A2	Anderson Co.
392.A25	Andrews Co.
392.A3	Angelina Co.
392.A6	Aransas Co.
392.A65	Archer Co.
	Armand Bayou Park and Nature Center, *see* F392.H38
392.A7	Armstrong Co.
392.A8	Atacosa Co.
392.A9	Austin Co.
392.B15	Bailey Co.
392.B17	Balcones Canyonlands National Wildlife Refuge
392.B2	Bandera Co.
392.B23	Bastrop Co.
392.B25	Baylor Co.
392.B3	Bee Co.
392.B34	Bell Co.
	Including Tennessee Valley
392.B5	Bexar Co.
392.B53	Big Bend National Park
392.B54	Big Bend region
	Big Thicket, *see* F392.H37
392.B55	Blanco Co.
392.B57	Bolivar Peninsula
392.B58	Borden Co.
392.B6	Bosque Co.
392.B7	Boundaries
	For International boundary, see F786
	Cf. F377.B7, Louisiana boundary
392.B74	Bowie Co.
392.B82	Brazoria Co.
392.B84	Brazos Co.
392.B842	Brazos River and Valley
	Including South Bend Reservoir
392.B85	Brewster Co.
	For Big Bend National Park, see F392.B53
392.B86	Briscoe Co.
392.B88	Brooks Co.
392.B89	Brown Co.
392.B95	Burleson Co.
392.B97	Burnet Co.
392.C17	Caddo Lake (General, and Texas)
	Cf. F377.C15, Louisiana
392.C2	Caldwell Co.
392.C22	Calhoun Co.

Texas

392.A-.Z	**Regions, counties, etc., A-Z — Continued**
392.C23	Callahan Co.
392.C25	Cameron Co.
392.C26	Camp Co.
392.C27	Canadian River and Valley, Tex.
	Cf. F702.C2, General, and Oklahoma
392.C28	Carson Co.
392.C287	Casa Blanca Land Grant
392.C29	Cass Co.
392.C3	Castro Co.
392.C4	Chambers Co.
392.C44	Cherokee Co.
392.C45	Childress Co.
	Choke Canyon Reservoir, *see* F392.F92
392.C5	Clay Co.
392.C517	Coastal Bend
392.C52	Cochino Bayou and Valley
392.C53	Cochran Co.
392.C54	Coke Co.
392.C55	Coleman Co.
392.C56	Collin Co.
392.C57	Collingsworth Co.
392.C58	Colorado Co.
392.C6	Colorado River and Valley
392.C7	Comal Co.
392.C75	Comanche Co.
392.C77	Concho Co.
392.C773	Concho River and Valley
392.C78	Cooke Co.
392.C79	Cooper Lake
392.C8	Coryell Co.
	Including Mother Neff State Park
392.C82	Cottle Co.
392.C83	Crane Co.
392.C84	Crockett Co.
392.C85	Crosby Co.
392.C9	Culberson Co.
392.D13	Dallam Co.
392.D14	Dallas Co.
392.D25	Dawson Co.
392.D3	Deaf Smith Co.
392.D35	Delta Co.
392.D4	Denton Co.
	Including Green Valley
392.D5	De Witt Co.
392.D6	Dickens Co.
392.D65	Dimmit Co.
392.D7	Donley Co.
392.D9	Duval Co.
392.E16	Eastland Co.
	Ecleto Creek and Valley, *see* F392.W7
392.E25	Ector Co.
392.E3	Edwards Co.
392.E33	Edwards Plateau
392.E4	Ellis Co.
392.E45	El Paso Co.
392.E64	Enchanted Rock State Natural Area
392.E7	Erath Co.
392.F15	Falls Co.

	Texas
392.A-.Z	**Regions, counties, etc., A-Z — Continued**
392.F17	Fannin Co.
392.F2	Fayette Co.
392.F4	Fisher Co.
392.F6	Floyd Co.
392.F65	Foard Co.
392.F7	Fort Bend Co.
	Fort Leaton State Park, *see* F392.P7
392.F8	Franklin Co.
392.F85	Freestone Co.
392.F9	Frio Co.
392.F92	Frio River and Valley
	Including Choke Canyon Reservoir
392.G2	Gaines Co.
392.G25	Galveston Co.
392.G3	Garza Co.
392.G5	Gillespie Co.
392.G55	Glasscock Co.
392.G6	Goliad Co.
	Including Goliad State Park
392.G65	Gonzales Co.
392.G68	Gray Co.
392.G7	Grayson Co.
392.G73	Gregg Co.
392.G75	Grimes Co.
392.G85	Guadalupe Co.
392.G86	Guadalupe Mountains, Texas. Guadalupe Mountains National Park
	Cf. F802.G93, General, and New Mexico
392.G9	Gulf coast of Texas
	For Padre Island, see F392.P14
	Cf. F296, Gulf coast (General)
392.H3	Hale Co.
392.H33	Hall Co.
392.H34	Hamilton Co.
392.H35	Hansford Co.
392.H36	Hardeman Co.
392.H37	Hardin Co.
	Including Big Thicket
392.H38	Harris Co.
	Including Armand Bayou Park and Nature Center
392.H39	Harrison Co.
392.H4	Hartley Co.
392.H43	Haskell Co.
392.H46	Hays Co.
392.H5	Hemphill Co.
392.H54	Henderson Co.
392.H56	Hidalgo Co.
392.H57	Hill Co.
392.H6	Hockley Co.
392.H65	Hood Co.
392.H67	Hopkins Co.
392.H7	Houston Co.
392.H75	Howard Co.
392.H8	Hudspeth Co.
392.H82	Hueco Mountains (General, and Texas)
	Cf. F802.H84, New Mexico
392.H9	Hunt Co.
392.H95	Hutchinson Co.
	Including Lake Meredith National Recreation Area

	Texas
392.A-.Z	**Regions, counties, etc., A-Z — Continued**
392.I6	Irion Co.
392.J22	Jack Co.
392.J24	Jackson Co.
392.J27	Jasper Co.
392.J3	Jeff Davis Co.
392.J33	Jefferson Co.
	Including Sabine Pass Battlefield State Historical Park
392.J48	Jim Hogg Co.
392.J5	Jim Wells Co.
392.J6	Johnson Co.
392.J7	Jones Co.
392.K2	Karnes Co.
392.K25	Kaufman Co.
392.K3	Kendall Co.
392.K32	Kenedy Co.
392.K33	Kent Co.
392.K35	Kerr Co.
392.K4	Kimble Co.
392.K45	King Co.
392.K47	King Ranch
392.K5	Kinney Co.
392.K6	Kleberg Co.
392.K7	Knox Co.
392.L33	La Junta de los Rios
	Lake Meredith National Recreation Area, *see* F392.H95
392.L36	Lamar Co.
392.L37	Lamb Co.
392.L38	Lampasas Co.
392.L4	La Salle Co.
392.L42	Lavaca Co.
392.L45	Lee Co.
392.L46	Leon Co.
392.L5	Liberty Co.
392.L54	Limestone Co.
392.L55	Lipscomb Co.
392.L58	Live Oak Co.
392.L6	Llano Co.
392.L62	Llano Estacado (Staked Plain)
392.L66	Long Cove
392.L7	Loving Co.
392.L8	Lubbock Co.
392.L87	Lyndon B. Johnson Historical Park
392.L9	Lynn Co.
392.M15	McCulloch Co.
392.M2	McLennan Co.
392.M23	McMullen Co.
392.M25	Madison Co.
392.M3	Marion Co.
392.M33	Martin Co.
392.M36	Mason Co.
392.M4	Matagorda Co.
	Including Matagorda Bay
392.M43	Maverick Co.
392.M44	Medina Co.
392.M45	Menard Co.
	Meredith, Lake, National Recreation Area, *see* F392.H95
392.M5	Midland Co.
392.M54	Milam Co.

	Texas
392.A-.Z	**Regions, counties, etc., A-Z — Continued**
392.M56	Mills Co.
392.M6	Mitchell Co.
392.M67	Montague Co.
392.M7	Montgomery Co.
392.M75	Moore Co.
392.M8	Morris Co.
	Mother Neff State Park, *see* F392.C8
392.M85	Motley Co.
	Mustang Island State Park, *see* F392.N8
392.N2	Nacogdoches Co.
392.N24	Nacogdoches District
392.N3	Navarro Co.
392.N35	Neches River and Valley
392.N4	Newton Co.
392.N6	Nolan Co.
392.N8	Nueces Co.
392.N82	Nueces River and Valley
392.O2	Ochiltree Co.
392.O4	Oldham Co.
392.O7	Orange Co.
392.P14	Padre Island
392.P16	Palo Duro State Park. Palo Duro Canyon
392.P165	Palo Pinto Co.
392.P168	Panhandle
392.P17	Panola Co.
392.P2	Parker Co.
392.P24	Parmer Co.
392.P28	Pecos Co.
392.P3	Pecos River and Valley (General, and Tex.)
	Cf. F802.P3, New Mexico
392.P55	Polk Co.
392.P6	Potter Co.
392.P7	Presidio Co.
	Including Fort Leaton State Park
392.R15	Rains Co.
392.R2	Randall Co.
392.R22	Ray Roberts Lake
392.R25	Reagan Co.
392.R26	Real Co.
392.R3	Red River and Valley, Tex.
	Cf. F377.R3 , General, and Louisiana
392.R33	Red River Co.
392.R4	Reeves Co.
392.R45	Refugio Co.
392.R48	Richland Creek and Valley
	Including Richland-Chambers Dam and Reservoir
392.R5	Rio Grande (General, and Tex.)
	Including Rio Grande Valley
	For Big Bend National Park, see F392.B53
	Cf. F802.R5, New Mexico
	Cf. F1334, Mexico
392.R6	Roberts Co.
392.R63	Robertson Co.
392.R64	Rocking Chair Ranche
392.R65	Rockwell Co.
392.R75	Runnels Co.
392.R8	Rusk Co.
392.S11	Sabine Co.

	Texas
392.A-.Z	**Regions, counties, etc., A-Z — Continued**
	Sabine Pass Battlefield State Historical Park, *see* F392.J33
392.S12	Sabine River and Valley, Tex.
	Cf. F377.S116, General, and Louisiana
392.S19	San Antonio River and Valley
392.S23	San Augustine Co.
392.S234	San Gabriel River and Valley
392.S235	San Jacinto Co.
392.S237	San Patricio Co.
392.S24	San Saba Co.
392.S35	Schleicher Co.
392.S4	Scurry Co.
392.S46	Shackelford Co.
392.S5	Shelby Co.
392.S52	Sherman Co.
392.S55	Smith Co.
392.S65	Somervell Co.
	South Bend Reservoir, *see* F392.B842
	Staked Plain, *see* F392.L62
392.S75	Starr Co.
392.S78	Stephens Co.
392.S8	Sterling Co.
392.S85	Stonewall Co.
392.S9	Sutton Co.
392.S95	Swisher Co.
392.T25	Tarrant Co.
392.T3	Taylor Co.
	Tennessee Valley, *see* F392.B34
392.T4	Terrell Co.
392.T45	Terry Co.
392.T47	Texas Hill Country
392.T5	Throckmorton Co.
392.T55	Titus Co.
	Toledo Bend Reservoir and Toledo Bend region, *see* F377.T6
392.T6	Tom Green Co.
392.T7	Travis Co.
392.T8	Trinity Co.
392.T83	Trinity River and Valley
392.T9	Tyler Co.
392.U5	Upshur Co.
392.U6	Upton Co.
392.U9	Uvalde Co.
392.V17	Val Verde Co.
392.V2	Van Zandt Co.
392.V5	Victoria Co.
392.W24	Walker Co.
392.W25	Waller Co.
392.W27	Ward Co.
392.W3	Washington Co.
392.W33	Washita River and Valley (General, and Texas)
	Cf. F702.W36, Oklahoma
392.W4	Webb Co.
392.W45	Wharton Co.
392.W47	Wheeler Co.
392.W55	Wichita Co.
392.W6	Wilbarger Co.
392.W64	Willacy Co.
392.W66	Williamson Co.

	Texas
392.A-.Z	**Regions, counties, etc., A-Z — Continued**
392.W7	Wilson Co.
	Including Ecleto Creek
392.W75	Winkler Co.
392.W8	Wise Co.
392.W9	Wood Co.
392.X2	XIT Ranch
392.Y6	Yoakum Co.
392.Y7	Young Co.
392.Z3	Zapata Co.
392.Z4	Zavala Co.
394.A-.Z	**Cities, towns, etc, A-Z**
	GALE NOTE *The cutter number(s) listed below have been given only as examples by the Library of Congress*
394.A4	Amarillo
394.A9	Austin
	Subarrange by Table F2 at the end of the text
394.B3	Beaumont
394.C78	Corpus Christi
394.D21	Dallas
	Subarrange by Table F2 at the end of the text
394.E4	El Paso
394.F7	Fort Worth
394.G2	Galveston
394.H8	Houston
	Subarrange by Table F2 at the end of the text
394.S211	San Antonio
	Subarrange by Table F2 at the end of the text
394.W12	Waco
	Elements in the population
395.A1	General works
395.A2-.Z	Individual elements
	For a list of racial, ethnic, and religious elements (with cutter numbers), see E184.A+
396	**Old Southwest. Lower Mississippi Valley**
	Including biography: John A. Murrell
	Cf. E78.S8, Indians of the Old Southwest
	Cf. E334, Burr's Conspiracy
	Cf. F296, Gulf coast
	Cf. F350.5+, Mississippi River and Valley
	Cf. F366+, Louisiana
	Cf. F377.R3, Red River, La.
	Cf. F392.B7, Texas boundaries (United States)
	Cf. F417.O9, Ozark Mountain region
	Cf. F786, Mexican boundaries (United States)
	Arkansas
406	**Periodicals. Societies. Collections**
408	**Museums. Exhibitions, exhibits**
409	**Gazetteers. Dictionaries. Geographic names**
409.3	**Guidebooks**
410	**Biography (Collective). Genealogy (Collective)**
410.2	**Historiography**
	Historians, *see* E175.5.A+
410.5	**Study and teaching**
411	**General works. Histories**
	Admission as a state, June 15, 1836
	Including by period (Early to 1950) as well as general
	For 1951 and later, see F415+
	Including Reconstruction
	Including biography: Thomas Chipman McRae, etc.

Arkansas

411   **General works. Histories — Continued**

Cf. D769.85.A8+, World War II, 1939-1945

Cf. E553.1+, Civil War, 1861-1865 (General)

Cf. E470.4+, E471+, Military operations and battles in the Civil War, 1861-1865

Cf. E496.1+ , Union history, Civil War, 1861-1865

411.3   **Juvenile works**

    Pamphlets, addresses, essays, etc.

411.5   General

411.6   Anecdotes, legends, pageants, etc.

412   **Historic monuments (General). Illustrative material**

413   **Antiquities (Non-Indian)**

    By period

    Early to 1950, *see* F411

    1951-

415   General works

    Biography and memoirs

415.2   Collective

415.3.A-.3.Z   Individual, A-Z

    GALE NOTE *See note at the head of Table F5 at the end of the text for further instructions on how to subdivide this number*

417.A-.Z   **Regions, counties, etc., A-Z**

417.A15   Counties

427.A16   Mountains

417.A17   Rivers

417.A18   Lakes

417.A19   Islands

417.A65   Arkansas Co.

417.A67   Arkansas Delta

417.A7   Arkansas River and Valley (General, and Ark.)

Cf. F687.A7, Kansas

Cf. F702.A7, Oklahoma

Cf. F782.A7, Colorado

417.A8   Ashley Co.

417.B27   Bartholomew Bayou

Class here general works on the Bartholomew Bayou, and works limited to the part located in Arkansas

For works limited to the part of the Bartholomew Bayou located in Louisiana, see F377.B37

417.B3   Baxter Co.

417.B4   Benton Co.

    Blue Mountain Lake, *see* F417.L75

417.B6   Boone Co.

417.B7   Boundaries

Cf. F347.B7, Mississippi boundary

417.B8   Bradley Co.

417.B85   Buffalo River and Valley

417.B86   Bull Shoals Lake and region (General, and Arkansas)

Cf. F472.B94, Missouri

417.C27   Cadron Creek and Valley

417.C3   Calhoun Co.

Including Sparta Mine

417.C4   Carroll Co.

417.C45   Chicot Co.

417.C5   Clamorgan land grant (Arkansas and Missouri)

417.C53   Clark Co.

417.C54   Clay Co.

417.C55   Cleburne Co.

417.C56   Cleveland Co.

417.C6   Columbia Co.

	Arkansas
417.A-.Z	**Regions, counties, etc., A-Z — Continued**
417.C7	Conway Co.
	Including Cypress Creek and Valley
417.C8	Craighead Co.
	Crater of Diamonds State Park, *see* F417.P5
417.C87	Crawford Co.
417.C9	Crittenden Co.
417.C95	Cross Co.
	Cypress Creek and Valley, *see* F417.C7
417.D3	Dallas Co.
417.D4	Desha Co.
417.D7	Drew Co.
417.F3	Faulkner Co.
417.F7	Franklin Co.
417.F8	Fulton Co.
417.G3	Garland Co.
417.G7	Grant Co.
417.G8	Greene Co.
417.H4	Hempstead Co.
417.H6	Hot Spring Co.
417.H7	Howard Co.
417.I5	Independence Co.
417.I9	Izard Co.
417.J3	Jackson Co.
417.J4	Jefferson Co.
417.J6	Johnson Co.
417.L2	Lafayette Co.
417.L4	Lawrence Co.
417.L45	Lee Co.
417.L6	Lincoln Co.
417.L64	Little River and Valley, Ark.
	Cf. F702.L55, General and Oklahoma
417.L65	Little River Co.
417.L75	Logan Co.
	Including Blue Mountain Lake
417.L8	Lonoke Co.
417.M3	Madison Co.
417.M35	Marion Co.
417.M5	Miller Co.
417.M58	Mississippi Co.
417.M6	Mississippi River and Valley, Ark.
	Cf. F350.5+, General
	Cf. F396, Lower Mississippi Valley
417.M7	Monroe Co.
417.M75	Montgomery Co.
417.N4	Nevada Co.
417.N5	Newton Co.
417.N56	Nimrod Lake and Region
417.O75	Ouachita Co.
417.O77	Ouachita Mountains
	Cf. F702.O9, General, and Oklahoma
417.O8	Ouachita National Forest (Arkansas National Forest)
417.O83	Ouachita River and Valley, Ark.
	Cf. F377.O8, General, and Louisiana
417.O9	Ozark Mountains (General, and Ark.)
	Cf. F472.O9, Missouri
417.P4	Perry Co.
417.P43	Petit Jean Mountain
417.P45	Phillips Co.

	Arkansas
417.A-.Z	**Regions, counties, etc., A-Z — Continued**
417.P5	Pike Co.
	Including Crater of Diamonds State Park
417.P65	Poinsett Co.
417.P7	Polk Co.
417.P75	Pope Co.
417.P85	Prairie Co.
417.P98	Pulaski Co.
417.R2	Randolph Co.
417.R3	Red River and Valley, Ark.
	Cf. F377.R3, General, and Louisiana
417.S15	St. Francis Co.
417.S2	St. Francis River and Valley (General, and Ark.)
	Cf. F472.S25, Missouri
417.S23	Saline Co.
417.S25	Scott Co.
417.S3	Searcy Co.
417.S33	Sebastian Co.
417.S4	Sevier Co.
417.S5	Sharp Co.
	Sparta Mine, *see* F417.C3
417.S8	Stone Co.
417.U5	Union Co.
417.V3	Van Buren Co.
417.V55	Village Creek and Valley
417.W3	Washington Co.
417.W4	White Co.
417.W5	White River and Valley (General, and Ark.)
	Cf. F472.W5, Missouri
417.W6	Woodruff Co.
417.Y4	Yell Co.
	For Blue Mountain Lake, see F417.L75
419.A-.Z	**Cities, towns, etc., A-Z**
	GALE NOTE *The cutter number(s) listed below have been given only as examples by the Library of Congress*
419.H8	Hot Springs
419.L7	Little Rock
	Elements in the population
420.A1	General works
420.A2-.Z	Individual elements
	For a list of racial, ethnic, and religious elements (with cutter numbers), see E184.A+
	Tennessee
431	**Periodicals. Societies. Collections**
433	**Museums. Exhibitions, exhibits**
434	**Gazetteers. Dictionaries. Geographic names**
434.3	**Guidebooks**
435	**Biography (Collective). Genealogy (Collective)**
435.2	**Historiography**
	Historians, *see* E175.5.A+
435.5	**Study and teaching**
436	**General works. Histories**
	Including the state of Franklin, 1784-1788; admission as a state June 1, 1796
	Including by period (Early to 1950) as well as general
	For 1951 and later, see F440
	Including Pioneer days; Secession and Reconstruction; etc.
	Including biography: David Crockett, Jefferson Dillard Goodpasture, Austin Peay, Archibald Roane, James Robertson, William Tatham, Alfred Alexander Taylor, Robert Love Taylor, etc.
	Cf. D570.85.T2+, World War I, 1914-1918
	Cf. D769.85.T2+, World War II, 1939-1945

	Tennessee
436	**General works. Histories — Continued**
	Cf. E83.813, First Creek War, 1813-1814
	Cf. E263.T4, Tennessee in the Revolution, 1775-1783
	Cf. E309, North Carolina cessions of 1784 and 1790
	Cf. E409.5.T4, War with Mexico, 1845-1848
	Cf. E579.1+, Civil War, 1861-1865 (General)
	Cf. E470.4-.5, E471+, Military operations and battles in the Civil War, 1861-1865
	Cf. E531, Union history
	Cf. E726.T4, War of 1898 (Spanish-American War)
436.3	**Juvenile works**
	Pamphlets, addresses, essays, etc.
436.5	General
436.6	Anecdotes, legends, pageants, etc.
437	**Historic monuments (General). Illustrative material**
438	**Antiquities (Non-Indian)**
	By period
	Early to 1950, *see* F436
	1951-
440	General works
	Biography and memoirs
440.2	Collective
440.22.A-.22.Z	Individual, A-Z
	GALE NOTE *See note at the head of Table F5 at the end of the text for further instructions on how to subdivide this number*
442.1	**East Tennessee**
	Including Association of the Territorial Company of Philadelphia, Ocoee District
	Cf. F210, Mountain whites of the South
442.2	**Middle Tennessee. Cumberland Valley**
	Cf. F457.C9, Cumberland Valley, Ky
442.3	**West Tennessee**
	Cf. F443.M6, Mississippi Valley, Tenn.
443.A-.Z	**Regions, counties, etc., A-Z**
443.A15	Counties
443.A16	Mountains
443.A17	Rivers
443.A18	Lakes
443.A19	Islands
443.A5	Anderson Co.
443.B3	Bald Mountains (General, and Tennessee)
	Including Big Bald Mountain
	Cf. F262.B3 , North Carolina
443.B35	Bedford Co.
	Including Liberty Gap
443.B4	Benton Co.
	Big Bald Mountain, *see* F443.B3
443.B55	Bledsoe Co.
443.B6	Blount Co.
443.B7	Boundaries
	Cf. F262.B7, North Carolina boundary
	Cf. F457.B7, Kentucky boundary
	For South Carolina cession south of Tennessee, see F292.B7
443.B74	Boyd's Creek and Valley
443.B8	Bradley Co.
	Including Chatata Creek and Valley
443.C3	Campbell Co.
443.C313	Cannon Co.
443.C316	Carroll Co.
443.C32	Carter Co.
	Including Lost Cove

	Tennessee
443.A-.Z	**Regions, counties, etc., A-Z — Continued**
	Chatata Creek and Valley, *see* F443.B8
443.C4	Cheatham Co.
443.C45	Chester Co.
443.C47	Chickamauga Lake and region
443.C5	Claiborne Co.
443.C55	Clay Co.
443.C56	Clear Fork River and Valley
	Cf. F457.C58, General, and Kentucky
443.C57	Clinch River and Valley
443.C6	Cocke Co.
443.C65	Coffee Co.
443.C7	Crockett Co.
	Cumberland Caverns, *see* F443.W2
443.C78	Cumberland Co.
	Cumberland River and Valley, *see* F442.2
443.D2	Davidson Co.
443.D25	Decatur Co.
443.D3	De Kalb Co.
443.D5	Dickson Co.
443.D9	Dyer Co.
443.F3	Fayette Co.
443.F34	Fentress Co.
	Fort Loudoun Lake, *see* F443.L9
	Fort Pillow State Park, *see* F443.L35
443.F7	Franklin Co.
443.F8	French Broad River and Valley (General, and Tennessee)
	Cf. F262.F85, North Carolina
443.G35	Gibson Co.
443.G4	Giles Co.
443.G65	Grainger Co.
443.G7	Great Smoky Mountains
	Including Great Smoky Mountains National Park
443.G75	Greene Co.
443.G85	Grundy Co.
	Hales Bar Dam Region, *see* F443.M32
443.H17	Hamblen Co.
443.H19	Hamilton Co.
443.H24	Hancock Co.
443.H28	Hardeman Co.
443.H3	Hardin Co.
443.H37	Hawkins Co.
443.H4	Haywood Co.
443.H45	Henderson Co.
443.H5	Henry Co.
443.H6	Hickman Co.
443.H7	Holston River and Valley
443.H75	Houston Co.
443.H8	Humphreys Co.
443.J3	Jackson Co.
443.J35	James Co.
443.J5	Jefferson Co.
443.J7	Johnson Co.
443.K6	Knox Co.
443.L25	Lake Co.
443.L35	Lauderdale Co.
	Including Fort Pillow State Park
443.L4	Lawrence Co.
	LeConte, Mount, *see* F443.S45

	Tennessee
443.A-.Z	**Regions, counties, etc., A-Z — Continued**
443.L5	Lewis Co.
	Liberty Gap, *see* F443.B35
443.L6	Lincoln Co.
443.L63	Little River and Valley
443.L64	Little Tennessee River and Valley
443.L8	Lookout Mountain
	Lost Cove (Carter County), *see* F443.C32
443.L9	Loudon Co.
	Including Fort Loudoun Lake
443.M15	McMinn Co.
443.M2	McNairy Co.
443.M23	Macon Co.
443.M25	Madison Co.
443.M32	Marion Co.
	Including Hale's Bar Dam Region
443.M35	Marshall Co.
443.M4	Maury Co.
443.M5	Meigs Co.
443.M6	Mississippi River and Valley, Tenn.
	Cf. F350.5+, General
	Cf. F396, Lower Mississippi Valley
443.M7	Monroe Co.
	Including Fort Loudoun
443.M8	Montgomery Co.
443.M83	Moore Co.
443.M85	Morgan Co.
443.N67	Norris Lake
443.O2	Obion Co.
443.O9	Overton Co.
443.P34	Paint Rock River
	Cf. F332.P34, General, and Alabama
443.P4	Perry Co.
443.P5	Pickett Co.
443.P7	Polk Co.
443.P75	Possum Trot Hollow
443.P78	Powell River and Valley
443.P9	Putnam Co.
443.R34	Reelfoot Lake and Region
443.R4	Rhea Co.
443.R49	Roan Mountain
	Cf. F262.R39, General, and North Carolina
443.R5	Roane Co.
443.R55	Robertson Co.
443.R8	Rutherford Co.
443.S2	Scott Co.
443.S35	Sequatchie Co.
443.S36	Sequatchie River and Valley
443.S45	Sevier Co.
	Including Mount LeConte, Sugarlands
443.S5	Shelby Co.
443.S6	Smith Co.
	Smoky Mountains (The Smokies), *see* F443.G7
443.S7	Stewart Co.
	Sugarlands, *see* F443.S45
443.S8	Sullivan Co.
443.S9	Sumner Co.
443.S97	Sweetwater Valley

	Tennessee
443.A-.Z	Regions, counties, etc., A-Z — Continued
443.T3	Tennessee River and Valley, Tenn.
	Cf. F217.T3, General
443.T5	Tipton Co.
443.T7	Trousdale Co.
443.U5	Unicoi Co.
443.U6	Union Co.
443.V3	Van Buren Co.
443.W2	Warren Co.
	Including Cumberland Caverns, etc.
443.W3	Washington Co.
443.W33	Watts Bar Reservoir and region
443.W4	Wayne Co.
443.W5	Weakley Co.
443.W6	White Co.
443.W7	Williamson Co.
443.W75	Wilson Co.
444.A-.Z	**Cities, towns, etc., A-Z**
	GALE NOTE *The cutter number(s) listed below have been given only as examples by the Library of Congress*
444.C4	Chattanooga
	Subarrange by Table F2 at the end of the text
444.K7	Knoxville
	Lookout Mountain, *see* F443.L8
444.M5	Memphis
	Subarrange by Table F2 at the end of the text
444.N2	Nashville
	Subarrange by Table F2 at the end of the text
444.O3	Oak Ridge
	Elements in the population
445.A1	General works
445.A2-.Z	Individual elements
	For a list of racial, ethnic, and religious elements (with cutter numbers), see E184.A1+
	Kentucky
446	**Periodicals. Societies. Collections**
448	**Museums. Exhibitions, exhibits**
449	**Gazetteers. Dictionaries. Geographic names**
449.3	**Guidebooks**
450	**Biography (Collective). Genealogy (Collective)**
450.2	**Historiography**
	Historians, *see* E175.5.A+
450.5	**Study and teaching**
451	**General works. Histories**
451.3	**Juvenile works**
	Pamphlets, addresses, essays, etc.
451.5	General
451.6	Anecdotes, legends, pageants, etc.
452	**Historic monuments (General). Illustrative material**
453	**Antiquities (Non-Indian)**
	By period
454	Early to 1792
	Including Transylvania; County and District of Kentucky; etc.
	Including biography: Daniel Boone, James Harrod, Richard Henderson, etc.
	Cf. E83.79, Wars with northwestern Indians, 1790-1795
	Cf. F517, Early explorations on Ohio River
455	1792-1865
	Including admission as a state, June 1, 1792
	Including biography: George Michael Bedinger, Joseph Hamilton Daveiss, Harry Innes, Benjamin Sebastian, Isaac Shelby, etc.

	Kentucky
	By period
455	1792-1865 — Continued
	Cf. E328, Kentucky and Virginia Resolutions, 1798
	Cf. E359.5.K5, War of 1812
	Cf. E409.5.K4, War with Mexico, 1845-1848
	Cf. E509.1+, Civil War, 1861-1865 (General)
	Cf. E470.4+, E471+, Military operations and battles in the Civil War, 1861-1865
	Cf. E564.1+, Confederate history, Civil War
	Cf. F210, Mountain whites of the South
456	1865-1950
	Including biography: William Goebel, etc.
	Cf. D570.85.K4+, World War I, 1914-1918
	Cf. D769.85.K4+, World War II, 1939-1945
	Cf. E726.K37, War of 1898 (Spanish-American War)
	1951-
456.2	General works
	Biography and memoirs
456.25	Collective
456.26.A-.26.Z	Individual, A-Z
	GALE NOTE *See note at the head of Table F5 at the end of the text for further instructions on how to subdivide this number*
457.A-.Z	**Regions, counties, etc., A-Z**
457.A15	Counties
457.A16	Mountains
457.A17	Rivers
457.A18	Lakes
457.A19	Islands
457.A3	Adair Co.
457.A5	Allen Co.
457.A6	Anderson Co.
457.B16	Ballard Co.
457.B2	Barren Co.
	Including Diamond Cave, Great Onyx Cave
457.B23	Bath Co.
457.B4	Bell Co.
	Big Bone Lick, *see F457.B65*
457.B5	Big Sandy River and Valley
457.B6	Bluegrass region
457.B65	Boone Co.
	Including Big Bone Lick
457.B7	Boundaries
457.B8	Bourbon Co.
457.B82	Boyd Co.
457.B83	Boyle Co.
457.B84	Bracken Co.
457.B85	Breathitt Co.
457.B9	Breckinridge Co.
457.B92	Bullitt Co.
457.B95	Butler Co.
457.C15	Caldwell Co.
457.C17	Calloway Co.
457.C2	Campbell Co.
457.C25	Carlisle Co.
457.C3	Carroll Co.
457.C35	Carter Co.
457.C37	Casey Co.
457.C55	Christian Co.
457.C56	Clark Co.
457.C57	Clay Co.

	Kentucky
457.A-.Z	**Regions, counties, etc., A-Z — Continued**
457.C58	Clear Fork River and Valley (General, and Kentucky)
	Cf. F443.C56, Tennessee
457.C6	Clinton Co.
457.C66	Crittenden Co.
457.C7	Cumberland Co.
457.C77	Cumberland Gap National Historical Park
457.C8	Cumberland Mountains
	Cf. F210, Mountain whites of the South
457.C9	Cumberland River and Valley, Ky.
	Cf. F442.2, Tennessee
	Cypress Creek and Valley, *see* F457.U5
457.D3	Daviess Co.
	Diamond Cave, *see* F457.B2
457.E2	Edmonson Co.
	For Mammoth Cave, see F457.M2
457.E4	Elliott Co.
457.E7	Estill Co.
457.F2	Fayette Co.
457.F4	Fleming Co.
457.F6	Floyd Co.
457.F8	Franklin Co.
457.F9	Fulton Co.
457.G16	Gallatin Co.
457.G2	Garrard Co.
457.G6	Grant Co.
457.G77	Graves Co.
457.G78	Grayson Co.
	Great Onyx Cave, *see* F457.B2
457.G82	Green Co.
457.G85	Green River and Valley
457.G86	Greenup Co.
457.H16	Hancock Co.
457.H2	Hardin Co.
457.H3	Harlan Co.
457.H4	Harrison Co.
457.H43	Hart Co.
457.H5	Henderson Co.
457.H6	Henry Co.
457.H7	Hickman Co.
457.H8	Hopkins Co.
457.J2	Jackson Co.
457.J23	Jackson Purchase region
457.J4	Jefferson Co.
457.J5	Jessamine Co.
457.J7	Johnson Co.
457.K28	Kenton Co.
457.K29	Kentucky Lake
457.K3	Kentucky River and Valley
457.K5	Knott Co.
457.K6	Knox Co.
457.L2	Larue Co.
457.L25	Laurel Co.
457.L27	Lawrence Co.
457.L45	Lee Co.
457.L47	Leslie Co.
457.L48	Letcher Co.
457.L5	Lewis Co.
457.L6	Lincoln Co.

	Kentucky
457.A-.Z	**Regions, counties, etc., A-Z — Continued**
457.L7	Livingston Co.
457.L8	Logan Co.
457.L9	Lyon Co.
457.M14	McCracken Co.
457.M15	McCreary Co.
457.M16	McLean Co.
457.M17	Madison Co.
457.M18	Magoffin Co.
457.M2	Mammoth Cave
	Including Mammoth Cave National Park
457.M3	Marion Co.
457.M34	Marshall Co.
457.M36	Martin Co.
457.M4	Mason Co.
457.M5	Meade Co.
457.M54	Menifee Co.
457.M56	Mercer Co.
457.M57	Metcalfe Co.
457.M6	Mississippi River and Valley, Ky.
	Cf. F350.5+, General
457.M7	Monroe Co.
457.M74	Montgomery Co.
457.M8	Morgan Co.
457.M9	Muhlenberg Co.
457.N2	Nelson Co.
457.N5	Nicholas Co.
457.O2	Ohio Co.
457.O3	Ohio River and Valley, Ky.
	Cf. F516+, General
457.O4	Oldham Co.
457.O97	Owen Co.
457.O98	Owsley Co.
	Payne Hollow, *see* F457.T65
457.P3	Pendleton Co.
457.P4	Perry Co.
457.P6	Pike Co.
457.P7	Powell Co.
457.P8	Pulaski Co.
457.R4	Red River and Valley
	Including Red River Gorge
457.R6	Robertson Co.
457.R65	Rockcastle Co.
457.R7	Rowan Co.
457.R8	Russell Co.
457.S24	Salt Lick Creek and Valley
457.S3	Scott Co.
457.S4	Shelby Co.
457.S5	Simpson Co.
457.S7	Spencer Co.
457.T25	Taylor Co.
457.T3	Tennessee River and Valley, Ky.
	Cf. F217.T3, General
	For Kentucky Lake, see F457.K29
457.T5	Todd Co.
457.T6	Trigg Co.
457.T65	Trimble Co.
	Including Payne Hollow

	Kentucky
457.A-.Z	**Regions, counties, etc., A-Z — Continued**
457.U5	Union Co.
	Including Cypress Creek and Valley
457.W2	Warren Co.
457.W3	Washington Co.
457.W4	Wayne Co.
457.W5	Webster Co.
457.W6	Whitley Co.
457.W7	Wolfe Co.
457.W8	Woodford Co.
459.A-.Z	**Cities, towns, etc., A-Z**
	GALE NOTE *The cutter number(s) listed below have been given only as examples by the Library of Congress*
459.C8	Covington
459.F8	Frankfort
459.L6	Lexington
459.L8	Louisville
	Subarrange by Table F2 at the end of the text
	Elements in the population
460.A1	General works
460.A2-.Z	Individual elements
	For a list of racial, ethnic, and religious elements (with cutter numbers), see E184.A+
	Missouri
461	**Periodicals. Societies. Collections**
463	**Museums. Exhibitions, exhibits**
464	**Gazetteers. Dictionaries. Geographic names**
464.3	**Guidebooks**
465	**Biography (Collective). Genealogy (Collective)**
465.2	**Historiography**
	Historians, *see* E175.5.A+
465.5	**Study and teaching**
466	**General works. Histories**
	Admission as a state, August 10, 1821
	Including by period (Early to 1950) as well as general
	For 1951 and later, see F470
	Including The Platt Purchase
	Including biography: Frederick Bates, Joseph Wingate Folk, etc.
	For local guidebooks, see Class F, e.g. F444.C4, Chattanooga
	Cf. D570.85.M8+, World War I, 1914-1918
	Cf. D769.85.M8+, World War II, 1939-1945
	Cf. E373, Missouri Compromise, 1820
	Cf. E571.1+, Civil War, 1861-1865 (General)
	Cf. E470.4+, E470.9, Military operations and battles in the Civil War, 1861-1865
	Cf. E569.1+, Confederate history, Civil War
	Cf. E726.M8, War of 1898 (Spanish-American War)
	Cf. F685, Kansas troubles, 1854-1859
466.3	**Juvenile works**
	Pamphlets, addresses, essays, etc.
466.5	General
466.6	Anecdotes, legends, pageants, etc.
467	**Historic monuments (General). Illustrative material**
468	**Antiquities (Non-Indian)**
	By period
(469)	Early to 1950, *see* F466
470	1951-
472.A-.Z	**Regions, counties, etc., A-Z**
472.A15	Counties
472.A16	Mountains
472.A17	Rivers

	Missouri
472.A-.Z	**Regions, counties, etc., A-Z — Continued**
472.A18	Lakes
472.A19	Islands
472.A2	Adair Co.
472.A5	Andrew Co.
472.A8	Atchison Co.
472.A9	Audrain Co.
472.B27	Barry Co.
472.B28	Barton Co.
472.B3	Bates Co.
472.B38	Bellevue Valley
472.B4	Benton Co.
	Including Harry S. Truman Dam and Reservoir
472.B57	Bollinger Co.
472.B6	Boone Co.
472.B7	Boundaries
472.B9	Buchanan Co.
472.B94	Bull Shoals Lake and region, Mo.
	Cf. F417.B86 , General, and Arkansas
472.B96	Butler Co.
472.C2	Caldwell Co.
472.C3	Callaway Co.
472.C32	Camden Co.
472.C33	Cape Girardeau Co.
472.C35	Carroll Co.
472.C36	Carter Co.
472.C37	Cass Co.
472.C4	Cedar Co.
472.C44	Chariton Co.
472.C45	Christian Co.
	Clamorgan land grant, *see* F417.C5
472.C47	Clarence Cannon Reservoir
472.C48	Clark Co.
472.C5	Clay Co.
472.C53	Clinton Co.
472.C65	Cole Co.
472.C7	Copper Co.
472.C8	Crawford Co.
472.C9	Current River and Valley (General, and Mo.)
472.D15	Dade Co.
472.D2	Dallas Co.
472.D25	Daviess Co.
472.D3	De Kalb Co.
472.D35	Dent Co.
472.D4	Des Moines River and Valley, Mo.
	Cf. F627.D43, General, and Iowa
472.D6	Douglas Co.
472.D9	Dunklin Co.
472.E4	Eleven Point Wild and Scenic River
472.F6	Franklin Co.
472.G3	Gasconade Co.
472.G4	Gentry Co.
472.G8	Greene Co.
472.G88	Grundy Co.
472.H3	Harrison Co.
	Harry S. Truman Dam and Reservoir, *see* F472.B4
472.H6	Henry Co. Rives Co.
472.H65	Hickory Co.
	For Harry S. Truman Dam and Reservoir, see F472.B4

	Missouri
472.A-.Z	**Regions, counties, etc., A-Z — Continued**
472.H7	Holt Co.
472.H8	Howard Co.
472.H9	Howell Co.
472.I7	Iron Co.
472.J2	Jackson Co.
472.J3	Jasper Co.
	Including Prosperity Lake and region
472.J4	Jefferson Co.
472.J6	Johnson Co.
472.K6	Knox Co.
472.L15	Laclede Co.
472.L2	Lafayette Co.
472.L4	Lawrence Co.
472.L6	Lewis Co.
472.L7	Lincoln Co.
472.L8	Linn Co.
472.L85	Livingston Co.
472.L88	Loess Hills
	Cf. F627.L76 , General and Iowa
	Long Branch Lake and region, *see* F472.M2
472.M13	McDonald Co.
	Including Jacob's Cavern, etc.
472.M2	Macon Co.
	Including Long Branch Lake and region
472.M23	Madison Co.
472.M29	Maries Co.
472.M3	Marion Co.
472.M4	Mercer Co.
472.M45	Miller Co.
	Including Bone Cave
472.M55	Mississippi Co.
472.M6	Mississippi River and Valley, Mo.
	Cf. F350.5+, General
472.M7	Missouri River and Valley, Mo.
	Cf. F598, General
472.M75	Moniteau Co.
472.M76	Monroe Co.
472.M77	Montgomery Co.
472.M8	Morgan Co.
472.N4	New Madrid Co.
472.N5	Newton Co.
472.N7	Nodaway Co.
472.O6	Oregon Co.
472.O7	Osage Co.
472.O74	Osage River and Valley
472.O85	Ozark Co.
472.O9	Ozark Mountains, Mo.
	Cf. F417.O9, General, and Arkansas
472.P3	Pemiscot Co.
472.P4	Perry Co.
	Including Tower Rock
472.P5	Pettis Co.
472.P55	Phelps Co.
472.P6	Pike Co.
472.P64	Pine Ford Dam and Reservoir
472.P7	Platte Co.
472.P8	Polk Co.
	Prosperity Lake and region, *see* F472.J3

	Missouri
472.A-.Z	**Regions, counties, etc., A-Z — Continued**
472.P9	Pulaski Co.
472.P95	Putnam Co.
472.R14	Ralls Co.
472.R15	Randolph Co.
472.R2	Ray Co.
472.R4	Reynolds Co.
472.R6	Ripley Co.
	Rives Co., *see* F472.H6
472.S2	St. Charles Co.
472.S23	St. Clair Co.
472.S25	St. Francis River and Valley, Mo.
	Cf. F417.S2, General, and Arkansas
472.S28	St Francois Co.
472.S3	St. Louis Co.
472.S33	Ste. Genevieve Co.
472.S35	Saline Co.
472.S4	Schuyler Co.
472.S42	Scotland Co.
472.S43	Scott Co.
472.S48	Shannon Co.
472.S5	Shelby Co.
472.S65	Stoddard Co.
472.S7	Stone Co.
472.S8	Sullivan Co.
472.T16	Taney Co.
472.T4	Texas Co.
472.V4	Vernon Co.
472.W17	Warren Co.
472.W2	Washington Co.
472.W3	Wayne Co.
472.W4	Webster Co.
472.W5	White River and Valley, Mo.
	Cf. F417.W5, General, and Arkansas
472.W6	Worth Co.
472.W7	Wright Co.
474.A-.Z	**Cities, towns, etc., A-Z**
	GALE NOTE *The cutter number(s) listed below have been given only as examples by the Library of Congress*
474.J4	Jefferson City
474.K2	Kansas City
	Subarrange by Table F2 at the end of the text
474.S18	St. Joseph
474.S2	St. Louis
	Subarrange by Table F2 at the end of the text
474.S7	Springfield
	Elements in the population
475.A1	General works
475.A2-.Z	Individual elements
	For a list of racial, ethnic, and religious elements (with cutter numbers), see E184.A+
476-485	**Old Northwest. Northwest Territory**
	Region between the Ohio and Mississippi Rivers and the Great Lakes
	Cf. F366+, Louisiana
	Cf. F516+, Ohio Valley
	Cf. F597, Upper Mississippi Valley
476	**Periodicals. Societies. Collections**
476.5	**Museums. Exhibitions, exhibits**
477	**Gazetteers. Dictionaries. Geographic names**
477.3	**Guidebooks**

476-485	**Old Northwest. Northwest Territory — Continued**
478	**Biography (Collective). Genealogy (Collective)**
478.2	**Historiography**
	Historians, *see* E175.5.A+
478.5	**Study and teaching**
479	**General works. Histories**
	Cf. E78.N76, Indians of the Old Northwest
479.3	**Juvenile works**
	Pamphlets, addresses, essays, etc.
479.5	General
479.6	Anecdotes, legends, pageants, etc.
480	**Historic monuments (General). Illustrative material**
481	**Antiquities (Non-Indian)**
	By period
482	Early to 1763
	Cf. E199, French and Indian War, 1755-1763
	Cf. F517, Ohio Company, 1749
	Cf. F544, Illinois country
	Cf. F572.M16, Mackinac region
	Cf. F574.D4, Detroit, 1701
	Cf. F1030, New France
483	1763-1803
	Including cessions by Virginia and other states, 1781-1786; settlement; Virginia military lands (Chillicothe); the Seven Ranges; Ohio Company, 1786-1795 (Marietta); American and French Scioto companies (Gallipolis); the Miami or Symmes Purchase (Cincinnati)
	Including biography: Manasseh Cutler, Nathaniel Massie, Rufus Putnam, Arthur St. Clair
	Cf. E83.76, Pontiac's Conspiracy, 1763-1765
	Cf. E83.775, Indian wars, 1775-1783
	Cf. E83.79, Indian wars, 1790-1795
	Cf. E83.794, Wayne's Campaign, 1793-1795
	Cf. E263.N84, Old Northwest in the Revolution
	Cf. E234, E237, Clark's campaigns
	Cf. E309, Northwest Ordinance of 1787
	Cf. F230, Virginia
	Cf. F497.W5, Western Reserve of Connecticut
	Cf. F534.V7, Vincennes
	Cf. F1032, Province of Quebec (Canada); Quebec Act
484.3	1803-1865
	Cf. E83.81, Tippecanoe Campaign, 1811
	Cf. E355, War of 1812 (Military operations)
484.5	1865-1950
484.6	1951-
	Elements in the population
485.A1	General works
485.A2-.Z	Individual elements
	For a list of racial, ethnic, and religious elements (with cutter numbers), see E184.A+
	Ohio
486	**Periodicals. Societies. Collections**
488	**Museums. Exhibitions, exhibits**
489	**Gazetteers. Dictionaries. Geographic names**
489.3	**Guidebooks**
490	**Biography (Collective). Genealogy (Collective)**
490.2	**Historiography**
	Historians, *see* E175.5.A+
490.5	**Study and teaching**
491	**General works. Histories**
491.3	**Juvenile works**
	Pamphlets, addresses, essays, etc.
491.5	General
491.6	Anecdotes, legends, pageants, etc.

	Ohio — Continued
491.8	**Geography**
492	**Historic monuments (General). Illustrative material**
493	**Antiquities (Non-Indian)**
	By period
495	Early to 1865

Including admission as a state, February 19, 1803

Including biography: Jacob Burnet, Alfred Kelley, Edward Tiffin, Allen Trimble, Thomas Worthington, etc.

    Cf. E83.81, Tippecanoe Campaign, 1811

    Cf. E359.5.O2, War of 1812 (General)

    Cf. E355+, Military operations, War of 1812

    Cf. E409.5.O3, War with Mexico, 1845-1848

    Cf. E525.1+, Civil War, 1861-1865 (General)

    Cf. E470.4+, Military operations and battles in the Civil War, 1861-1865

    Cf. F483, History before 1803 (Old Northwest)

    Cf. F497.B7, Toledo War, 1836

| 496 | 1865-1950 |

Including biography: William Allen, Asa Smith Bushnell, George Barnsdale Cox, Donn Piatt, Tom Loftin Johnson, Charles Reemelin, etc.

    Cf. D570.85.O3+, World War I, 1914-1918

    Cf. D769.85.O3+, World War II, 1939-1945

    Cf. E726.O3, War of 1898 (Spanish-American War)

	1951-
496.2	General works
	Biography
496.3	Collective
496.4.A-.4.Z	Individual, A-Z
497.A-.Z	**Regions, counties, etc., A-Z**
497.A15	Counties
497.A16	Mountains
497.A17	Rivers
497.A18	Lakes
497.A19	Islands
497.A2	Adams Co.
497.A4	Allen Co.
497.A7	Ashland Co.
497.A73	Ashtabula Co.
497.A8	Athens Co.
497.A9	Auglaize Co.
	Bass Islands, *see* F497.O8
497.B3	Bean Creek and Valley (General, and Ohio)
	Cf. F572.B36, Michigan
497.B4	Belmont Co.
	Including Raven Rocks
	Blennerhassett Island, *see* F247.B56
497.B7	Boundaries
	Including Toledo War, 1836 (Ohio-Michigan boundary)
497.B8	Brown Co.
497.B86	Buckeye Lake
497.B9	Butler Co.
497.C2	Carroll Co.
497.C4	Champaign Co.
497.C5	Clark Co.
	Including George Rogers Clark Memorial Park
497.C53	Clermont Co.
497.C55	Clinton Co.
497.C6	Columbiana Co.
	Including Sandy Beaver Canal
	Connecticut Reserve, *see* F497.W5

	Ohio
497.A-.Z	**Regions, counties, etc., A-Z — Continued**
497.C7	Coshocton Co.
497.C8	Crawford Co.
497.C9	Cuyahoga Co.
497.C95	Cuyahoga River and Valley
	Including Tinkers Creek and Valley
497.D2	Darke Co.
497.D25	Defiance Co.
497.D3	Delaware Co.
497.E5	Erie Co.
	Including Kelleys Island
	For Firelands, see F497.W5
497.E6	Lake Erie region, Ohio
	For Bass Islands, see F497.O8
	For Kelleys Island, see F497.E5
	For Put-in Bay, see F497.O8
	For Sandusky Bay, see F497.S23
	Cf. F555, General
497.F15	Fairfield Co.
497.F2	Fayette Co.
	Firelands, *see F497.W5*
497.F8	Franklin Co.
497.F9	Fulton Co.
497.G15	Gallia Co.
497.G2	Geauga Co.
	George Rogers Clark Memorial Park, *see F497.C5*
497.G7	Greene Co.
497.G93	Guernsey Co.
497.H2	Hamilton Co.
	Including Duck Creek, Mill Creek
497.H3	Hancock Co.
497.H35	Hanging Rock iron region
497.H4	Hardin Co.
497.H5	Harrison Co.
497.H55	Henry Co.
497.H6	Highland Co.
497.H68	Hocking Co.
497.H7	Hocking River and Valley
497.H74	Holmes Co.
497.H8	Huron Co.
	For Firelands, see F497.W5
497.J2	Jackson Co.
497.J4	Jefferson Co.
	Including Yellow Creek
	Kelleys Island, *see F497.E5*
497.K7	Knox Co.
497.L2	Lake Co.
497.L3	Lawrence Co.
497.L4	Leatherwood Creek and Valley
497.L6	Licking Co.
497.L7	Little Miami River and Valley
	Cf. F497.M64, Miami (Great Miami) River and Valley
497.L8	Logan Co.
497.L86	Lorain Co.
497.L9	Lucas Co.
497.M14	Madison Co.
497.M18	Mahoning Co.
497.M2	Mahoning River and Valley (General, and Ohio)
	Cf. F157.M3, Pennsylvania

Ohio

497.A-.Z	**Regions, counties, etc., A-Z — Continued**
497.M3	Marion Co.
497.M4	Maumee River and Valley (General, and Ohio)
	Cf. F532.M62, Indiana
497.M5	Medina Co.
497.M53	Meigs Co.
497.M56	Mercer Co.
497.M6	Miami Co.
497.M64	Miami (Great Miami) River and Valley
	Cf. F497.L7 , Little Miami River and Valley
497.M67	Monroe Co.
497.M7	Montgomery Co.
	Including Twin Valley
497.M76	Morgan Co.
497.M8	Morrow Co.
497.M9	Muskingum Co.
497.M92	Muskingum River and Valley
497.N6	Noble Co.
497.O3	Ohio River and Valley, Ohio
	Cf. F516+, General
497.O8	Ottawa Co.
	Including Bass Islands, Put-in Bay
497.P2	Paulding Co.
497.P4	Perry Co.
497.P5	Pickaway Co.
497.P55	Pike Co.
497.P8	Portage Co.
497.P9	Preble Co.
	Put-in Bay, *see* F497.O8
497.P96	Putnam Co.
	Raven Rocks, *see* F497.B4
497.R5	Richland Co.
497.R7	Rocky River and Valley
497.R8	Ross Co.
497.S2	Sandusky Co.
497.S23	Sandusky River and Valley. Sandusky Bay
	Sandy Beaver Canal, *see* F497.C6
497.S3	Scioto Co.
497.S32	Scioto River and Valley
497.S4	Seneca Co.
497.S54	Shelby Co.
497.S7	Stark Co.
497.S9	Summit Co.
	Including Portage Path
	Tiffin River and Valley, *see* F497.B3
	Tinkers Creek and Valley, *see* F497.C95
497.T8	Trumbull Co.
497.T9	Tuscarawas Co.
497.T93	Tuscarawas River and Valley
497.U5	Union Co.
497.V2	Van Wert Co.
497.V5	Vinton Co.
497.W13	Wabash and Erie Canal
	Cf. F532.W16, General, and Indiana
497.W2	Warren Co.
497.W3	Washington Co.
	For Blennerhassett Island, see F247.B56
497.W4	Wayne Co.
497.W5	Western Reserve (Connecticut Reserve). Firelands

	Ohio
497.A-.Z	**Regions, counties, etc., A-Z — Continued**
497.W7	Williams Co.
497.W8	Wood Co.
497.W9	Wyandot Co.
499.A-.Z	**Cities, towns, etc., A-Z**
	GALE NOTE *The cutter number(s) listed below have been given only as examples by the Library of Congress*
499.A3	Akron
499.C2	Canton
499.C4	Chillicothe
499.C5	Cincinnati
	Subarrange by Table F2 at the end of the text
499.C6	Cleveland
	Subarrange by Table F2 at the end of the text
499.C7	Columbus
	Subarrange by Table F2 at the end of the text
499.D2	Dayton
	Subarrange by Table F2 at the end of the text
499.M3	Marietta
499.S7	Springfield
499.T6	Toledo
499.Y8	Youngstown
	Elements in the population
500.A1	General works
500.A2-.Z	Individual elements
	For a list of racial, ethnic, and religious elements (with cutter numbers), see E184.A+
	Ohio River and Valley
	Cf. E78.O4, Indians of the Ohio Valley
	Cf. F157.B2, Pennsylvania
	Cf. F350.5+, Mississippi River and Valley
	Cf. F457.O3, Kentucky
	Cf. F497.O3, Ohio
	Cf. F532.O4, Indiana
516	**General works**
	Including periodicals, societies, collections, biography, etc.
	By period
517	Early to 1795
	Including Celoron's Expedition, 1749; Ohio Company, 1747-1779
	Including biography: Michael Cresap, Simon Girty, Simon Kenton, Lewis Wetzel
	Cf. E83.79, Wars with northwestern Indians, 1790-1795
	Cf. E199, French and Indian War, 1755-1763
	Cf. E234, Clark's Campaign, 1778
	Cf. F372, Louisiana before 1803
	Cf. F534.V7, Vincennes
	Cf. F1030, New France
518	1795-1865
	Cf. E470.4+, Civil War, 1861-1865 (General)
519	1865-1950
	Including floods, 1884, 1913
520	1951-
	Elements in the population
520.5	General works
520.6.A-.6.Z	Individual elements, A-Z
	For a list of racial, ethnic, and religious elements (with cutter numbers), see E184.A+
	Indiana
521	**Periodicals. Societies. Collections**
523	**Museums. Exhibitions, exhibits**
524	**Gazetteers. Dictionaries. Geographic names**
524.3	**Guidebooks**

Indiana — Continued

525	**Biography (Collective). Genealogy (Collective)**
525.2	**Historiography**
	Historians, *see* E175.5.A+
525.5	**Study and teaching**
526	**General works. Histories**
	Including admission as a state, December 11, 1816
	Including biography: James Franklin Doughty Lanier, etc.
	For 1951 and later, see F530
	Cf. D570.85.I6+, World War I, 1914-1918
	Cf. D769.85.I6+, World War II, 1939-1945
	Cf. E83.81, Tippecanoe Campaign, 1811
	Cf. E355, War of 1812 (Military operations)
	Cf. E409.5.I7, War with Mexico, 1845-1848
	Cf. E506.1+, Civil War, 1861-1865 (General)
	Cf. E470.4+, Military operations in the Civil War, 1861-1865
	Cf. E726.I3, War of 1898 (Spanish-American War)
526.3	**Juvenile works**
	Pamphlets, addresses, essays, etc.
526.5	General
526.6	Anecdotes, legends, pageants, etc.
527	**Historic monuments (General). Illustrative material**
528	**Antiquities (Non-Indian)**
	By period
	Early to 1950, *see* F526
	1951-
530	General works
	Biography and memoirs
530.2	Collective
530.22.A-.22.Z	Individual, A-Z
	GALE NOTE *See note at the head of Table F5 at the end of the text for further instructions on how to subdivide this number*
532.A-.Z	**Regions, counties, etc., A-Z**
532.A15	Counties
532.A16	Mountains
532.A17	Rivers
532.A18	Lakes
532.A19	Islands
532.A2	Adams Co.
532.A4	Allen Co.
	For Maumee River, see F532.M62
532.B2	Bartholomew Co.
532.B4	Benton Co.
532.B5	Blackford Co.
532.B6	Boone Co.
532.B7	Boundaries
532.B76	Brown Co.
	Calumet region, *see* F532.L2
532.C3	Carroll Co.
532.C4	Cass Co.
532.C5	Clark Co.
532.C6	Clay Co.
	Clifty Falls State Park, *see* F532.J5
532.C65	Clinton Co.
532.C8	Crawford Co.
	Including Wyandotte Cave
532.D17	Daviess Co.
532.D18	Dearborn Co.
532.D2	Decatur Co.
532.D25	De Kalb Co.

	Indiana
532.A-.Z	**Regions, counties, etc., A-Z — Continued**
532.D3	Delaware Co.
532.D8	Dubois Co.
	Dune region, *see* F532.M67
	Dunes State Park, *see* F532.I5
532.E4	Elkhart Co.
532.F2	Fayette Co.
532.F6	Floyd Co.
532.F77	Fountain Co.
532.F8	Franklin Co.
532.F9	Fulton Co.
532.G4	Gibson Co.
532.G7	Grant Co.
532.G75	Greene Co.
532.H2	Hamilton Co.
532.H3	Hancock Co.
532.H4	Harrison Co.
532.H5	Hendricks Co.
532.H6	Henry Co.
532.H75	Hoosier National Forest
532.H8	Howard Co.
532.H9	Huntington Co.
532.I5	Indiana Dunes State Park
532.J14	Jackson Co.
532.J3	Jasper Co.
532.J4	Jay Co.
532.J5	Jefferson Co.
	Including Clifty Falls State Park
532.J53	Jennings Co.
532.J6	Johnson Co.
	Kankakee-St. Joseph portage, *see* F532.S2
532.K2	Kankakee River and Valley (General, and Ind.)
	Cf. F547.K27, Illinois
532.K6	Knox Co.
532.K8	Kosciusko Co.
532.L17	Lagrange Co.
532.L2	Lake Co.
	Including Calumet region, Ind.
	Cf. F547.C7, Illinois
532.L3	La Porte Co.
532.L4	Lawrence Co.
	Including Spring Mill State Park
	Lost River and Valley, *see* F532.O63
532.M2	Madison Co.
532.M4	Marion Co.
532.M6	Marshall Co.
532.M613	Martin Co.
532.M62	Maumee River and Valley, Ind.
	Cf. F497.M4, General, and Ohio
532.M65	Miami Co.
532.M67	Lake Michigan region, Ind.
	Including the dunes of Indiana
	For Indiana Dunes State Park, see F532.I5
	Cf. F553, General
532.M7	Monroe Co.
532.M75	Montgomery Co.
532.M8	Morgan Co.
532.N5	Newton Co.
	Including Beaver Lake

Indiana

532.A-.Z	**Regions, counties, etc., A-Z — Continued**
532.N6	Noble Co.
532.O3	Ohio Co.
532.O4	Ohio River and Valley, Ind.
	Cf. F516+, General
532.O63	Orange Co.
	Including Lost River and Valley
532.O9	Owen Co.
532.P2	Parke Co.
	Including Turkey Run State Park
532.P4	Perry Co.
532.P6	Pike Co.
	Pokagon State Park, *see* F532.S8
532.P8	Porter Co.
532.P85	Posey Co.
532.P88	Pulaski Co.
532.P9	Putnam Co.
532.R3	Randolph Co.
532.R5	Ripley Co.
532.R95	Rush Co.
532.S2	St. Joseph Co.
	Including St. Joseph-Kankakee portage
	Cf. F572.S43, St. Joseph River and Valley, Mich.
532.S3	St. Joseph River and Valley (General, and Ind.)
	Cf. F572.S43, Michigan
532.S35	Scott Co.
532.S47	Shakamak State Park
532.S5	Shelby Co.
532.S6	Spencer Co.
	Including Lincoln Boyhood National Memorial and Nancy Hanks Lincoln Memorial
	Spring Mill State Park, *see* F532.L4
532.S7	Starke Co.
532.S8	Steuben Co.
	Including Pokagon State Park
532.S9	Sullivan Co.
532.S97	Switzerland Co.
532.T6	Tippecanoe Co.
532.T63	Tipton Co.
	Turkey Run State Park, *see* F532.P2
532.U5	Union Co.
532.V2	Vanderburgh Co.
532.V5	Vermillion Co.
532.V7	Vigo Co.
532.W16	Wabash and Erie Canal (General, and Indiana)
	Cf. F497.W13, Ohio
532.W18	Wabash Co.
532.W2	Wabash River and Valley (General, and Ind.)
	Cf. F547.W14, Illinois
532.W3	Warren Co.
532.W4	Warrick Co.
532.W45	Washington Co.
532.W5	Wayne Co.
532.W55	Wells Co.
532.W58	White Co.
532.W59	Whitewater (White Water) River and Valley
532.W6	Whitley Co.
534.A-.Z	**Cities, towns, etc., A-Z**
	GALE NOTE *The cutter number(s) listed below have been given only as examples by the Library of Congress*

	Illinois
	By period
	1951-
	Biography — Continued
546.4.A-.4.Z	Individual, A-Z
	GALE NOTE *See note at the head of Table F5 at the end of the text for further instructions on how to subdivide this number*
547.A-.Z	**Regions, counties, etc., A-Z**
547.A15	Counties
547.A16	Mountains
547.A17	Rivers
547.A18	Lakes
547.A19	Islands
547.A2	Adams Co.
547.A3	Alexander Co.
	Including Horseshoe Lake
547.B6	Bond Co.
547.B65	Boone Co.
547.B7	Boundaries
547.B75	Brown Co.
547.B8	Bureau Co.
547.C13	Cache River and Valley
547.C15	Calhoun Co.
	Calumet region, *see* F547.C7
547.C2	Carroll Co.
547.C3	Cass Co.
547.C4	Champaign Co.
547.C45	Chicago River
547.C5	Christian Co.
547.C53	Clark Co.
547.C55	Clay Co.
547.C57	Clinton Co.
547.C6	Coles Co.
547.C7	Cook Co.
	Including Calumet region, Ill.
	Cf. F532.L2, Indiana
547.C8	Crawford Co.
547.C9	Cumberland Co.
547.D3	De Kalb Co.
547.D4	Des Plaines River and Valley, Ill.
547.D5	De Witt Co.
547.D7	Douglas Co.
547.D9	Du Page Co.
	Dunes of Illinois, *see* F547.M56
547.E25	Edgar Co.
547.E3	Edwards Co.
	Including English settlement
547.E4	Effingham Co.
547.F35	Fayette Co.
547.F7	Ford Co.
547.F77	Fox River and Valley, Ill.
	Cf. F587.F7 , Wisconsin
547.F78	Franklin Co.
547.F8	Fulton Co.
547.G3	Gallatin Co.
547.G7	Greene Co.
547.G8	Grundy Co.
547.H17	Hamilton Co.
547.H2	Hancock Co.
547.H3	Hardin Co.

	Illinois
547.A-.Z	**Regions, counties, etc., A-Z — Continued**
547.H4	Henderson Co.
547.H52	Henry Co.
	Horseshoe Lake, *see* F547.A3
547.I13	Illinois and Michigan Canal National Heritage Corridor
547.I2	Illinois River and Valley
547.I7	Iroquois Co.
547.J2	Jackson Co.
547.J3	Jasper Co.
547.J4	Jefferson Co.
547.J5	Jersey Co.
547.J6	Jo Daviess Co.
547.J8	Johnson Co.
	Jubilee College State Park, *see* F547.P4
547.K2	Kane Co.
547.K25	Kankakee Co.
547.K27	Kankakee River and Valley, Ill.
	Including Willow Creek and Valley
	Cf. F532.K2 , General, and Indiana
547.K4	Kendall Co.
547.K7	Knox Co.
547.L2	Lake Co.
547.L3	La Salle Co.
	Including Starved Rock State Park
547.L4	Lawrence Co.
547.L5	Lee Co.
547.L78	Livingston Co.
547.L8	Logan Co.
547.M13	McDonough Co.
547.M14	McHenry Co.
547.M16	McLean Co.
547.M17	Macon Co.
547.M18	Macoupin Co.
547.M2	Madison Co.
547.M3	Marion Co.
547.M34	Marshall Co.
547.M37	Mason Co.
547.M4	Massac Co.
547.M5	Menard Co.
547.M55	Mercer Co.
547.M56	Lake Michigan region, Ill.
	Including the dunes of Illinois
	Cf. F553, General
547.M6	Military lands between the Mississippi and Illinois Rivers
	Cf. E359.4, Military bounties (War of 1812)
547.M65	Mississippi River and Valley, Ill.
	Cf. F350.5+ , General
	Cf. F597 , Upper Mississippi Valley
547.M68	Monroe Co.
547.M7	Montgomery Co.
547.M8	Morgan Co.
547.M9	Moultrie Co.
547.O3	Ogle Co.
547.O4	Ohio River and Valley, Ill.
	Cf. F516+, General
547.P4	Peoria Co.
	Including Jubilee College State Park, etc.
547.P45	Perry Co.
	Including White Walnut Creek and Valley

Illinois

547.A-.Z	**Regions, counties, etc., A-Z — Continued**
547.P5	Piatt Co.
547.P6	Pike Co.
547.P7	Pope Co.
547.P78	Pulaski Co.
547.P8	Putnam Co.
547.R2	Randolph Co.
547.R5	Richland Co.
547.R6	Rock Island Co.
547.R7	Rock River and Valley (General, and Ill.)
	Cf. F587.R63, Wisconsin
547.S2	St. Clair Co.
547.S24	Saline Co.
547.S3	Sangamon Co.
547.S33	Sangamon River and Valley
547.S4	Schuyler Co.
547.S45	Scott Co.
547.S6	Shelby Co.
547.S65	Spoon River and Valley
547.S7	Stark Co.
	Starved Rock State Park, *see* F547.L3
547.S8	Stephenson Co.
547.S94	Sugar Creek and Valley, Macoupin County and Sangamon County
547.T2	Tazewell Co.
547.U5	Union Co.
547.V2	Vermilion Co.
547.W12	Wabash Co.
547.W14	Wabash River and Valley, Ill.
	Cf. F532.W2, General, and Indiana
547.W2	Warren Co.
547.W23	Washington Co.
547.W25	Wayne Co.
547.W3	White Co.
	White Walnut Creek and Valley, *see* F547.P45
547.W4	Whiteside Co.
547.W5	Will Co.
547.W6	Williamson Co.
	Willow Creek and Valley, *see* F547.K27
547.W7	Winnebago Co.
547.W8	Woodford Co.

Chicago

548.1	Periodicals. Societies. Collections
548.15	Museums. Exhibitions, exhibits
	Cf. T500, World's Columbian Exposition, 1893
	Cf. T501, Century of Progress International Exposition, 1933-1934
548.18	Guidebooks
548.25	Biography (Collective). Genealogy (Collective)
548.27	Historiography
548.29	Study and teaching
548.3	General works. Histories
548.33	Juvenile works
	Pamphlets, addresses, essays, etc.
548.35	General
548.36	Anecdotes, legends, pageants, etc.
548.37	Historic monuments. Illustrative material
548.39	Antiquities (Non-Indian)
	By period
	Early to 1875
	Cf. E356.C53, Fort Dearborn Massacre, 1812

	Illinois
	Chicago
	By period
	Early to 1875 — Continued
548.4	General works
548.42	1865-1875
	Including the great fire of 1871
548.45	1875-1892
	Cf. T500, World's Columbian Exposition, 1893
548.5	1892-1950
	1951-
548.52	General works
	Biography
548.53	Collective
548.54.A-.54.Z	Individual, A-Z
	GALE NOTE *See note at the head of Table F5 at the end of the text for further instructions on how to subdivide this number*
	Sections. Localities. Districts, etc.
548.6	General works
	Cemeteries
548.61	General works
548.612.A-.612.Z	Individual, A-Z
548.612.G72	Graceland Cemetery
548.62	Churches
548.625	Hotels, taverns, etc.
548.627	Places of amusement
548.63	Harbor
548.64	Monuments. Statues
	GALE NOTE *The cutter number(s) listed below have been given only as examples by the Library of Congress*
548.64.A1	General works
548.64.G4	George Washington-Robert Morris-Haym Salomon Monument
548.65	Parks. Squares. Circles
	GALE NOTE *The cutter number(s) listed below have been given only as examples by the Library of Congress*
548.65.A1	General works
548.65.D2	Dearborn Park
548.65.L7	Lincoln Park
548.65.S7	South Park
548.67	Streets. Bridges. Railroads
	GALE NOTE *The cutter number(s) listed below have been given only as examples by the Library of Congress*
548.67.A1	General works
548.67.M75	Monroe Street
548.68	Suburbs. Sections of the city. Rivers, etc.
	GALE NOTE *The cutter number(s) listed below have been given only as examples by the Library of Congress*
548.68.A1	General works
548.68.I7	Irving Park
548.68.N7	North Shore
548.68.R8	Roseland
548.68.S7	South Shore
548.68.W8	Wolf's Point
548.68.W82	Woodlawn
548.69	Wards
	Buildings
548.7	General works. Collective
548.8.A-.8.Z	Individual, A-Z
	GALE NOTE *The cutter number(s) listed below have been given only as examples by the Library of Congress*

	Illinois
	Chicago
	Buildings
548.8.A-.8.Z	Individual, A-Z — Continued
548.8.A9	Auditorium Building
548.8.C9	Custom House
548.8.G7	Grand Central Passenger Station
548.8.P17	Palmer House
	Elements in the population
548.9.A1	General works
548.9.A2-.9.Z	Individual elements
549.A-.Z	**Other cities, towns, etc., A-Z**
	GALE NOTE *The cutter number(s) listed below have been given only as examples by the Library*
	of Congress
549.A4	Alton
549.B65	Bloomington
549.C44	Champaign
549.C56	Cicero
549.D3	Decatur
549.E2	East St. Louis
549.E8	Evanston
549.J7	Joliet
549.O13	Oak Park
549.P4	Peoria
549.Q6	Quincy
549.R6	Rock Island
549.R7	Rockford
549.S7	Springfield
	Elements in the population
550.A1	General works
550.A2-.Z	Individual elements
	For a list of racial, ethnic, and religious elements (with cutter numbers), see E184.A+
	The Lake region. Great Lakes
	The portion of the northern boundary of the United States between the St. Lawrence River and the
	Lake of the Woods; early French explorations; British posts
	Cf. F1030, New France
	Cf. GB1627, Physical geography
550.5	**Biography (Collective). Genealogy (Collective)**
551	**General works**
552	**Lake Superior**
	Cf. F572.S9, Lake Superior region, Mich.
	Cf. F587.A8, Apostle Islands and Chequamegon Bay
	Cf. F587.S9, Lake Superior region, Wis.
	Cf. F612.S9, Lake Superior region, Minn.
	Cf. F1059.S9, Lake Superior region, Ontario
	Cf. F1059.T5, Thunder Bay region, Ontario
553	**Lake Michigan**
	Cf. F532.M67, Lake Michigan region, Ind.
	Cf. F547.M56, Lake Michigan region, Ill.
	Cf. F572.M16, Mackinac Straits and region
	Cf. F572.M57, Lake Michigan region, Mich.
	Cf. F587.G6, Green Bay
	Cf. F587.M57, Lake Michigan region, Wis.
554	**Lake Huron**
	Cf. F572.H92, Lake Huron region, Mich.
	Cf. F572.S15, Saginaw Bay
	Cf. F572.S34, Lake St. Clair
	Cf. F1059.G3, Georgian Bay
	Cf. F1059.H95, Lake Huron region, Ontario

	Michigan
572.A-.Z	**Regions, counties, etc., A-Z — Continued**
572.A18	Lakes
572.A19	Islands
572.A2	Alcona Co.
572.A25	Alger Co.
572.A3	Allegan Co.
572.A4	Alpena Co.
	Including Thunder Bay
572.A5	Antrim Co.
572.A7	Arenac Co.
	Including Point Lookout
572.B15	Baraga Co.
572.B2	Barry Co.
572.B3	Bay Co.
	Including Tobico Marsh
572.B36	Bean Creek and Valley
	Cf. F497.B3, General, and Ohio
572.B38	Beaver Island
572.B4	Benzie Co.
	Including Crystal Lake, Herring Lake
572.B5	Berrien Co.
	Including Paw Paw Lake
572.B7	Boundaries
	For Toledo War, 1836 (Michigan-Ohio boundary), see F497.B7
	Cf. F497.B7, Ohio boundary
	Cf. F532.B7, Indiana boundary
572.B8	Branch Co.
572.B86	Brule River and Valley (General, and Michigan)
	Cf. F587.B85, Wisconsin
572.C2	Calhoun Co.
572.C3	Cass Co.
572.C4	Charlevoix Co.
	For Beaver Island, see F572.B38
572.C5	Cheboygan Co.
	Including Douglas Lake
	Cheneaux Islands, *see F572.L57*
572.C54	Chippewa Co.
	For Drummond Island, see F572.D88
572.C65	Clare Co.
572.C7	Clinton Co.
572.C9	Crawford Co.
	Crystal Lake, *see F572.B4*
572.D4	Delta Co.
572.D46	Detroit River and Valley (General, and Mich.)
	Cf. F1059.D46, Ontario
	Devils Lake (Lenawee County), *see F572.L5*
572.D5	Dickinson Co.
	Douglas Lake, *see F572.C5*
572.D88	Drummond Island
572.E2	Eaton Co.
572.E5	Emmet Co.
	Fox Islands, *see F572.L45*
572.G3	Genesee Co.
572.G38	Gladwin Co.
572.G44	Gogebic Co.
572.G45	Grand Island
572.G46	Grand River and Valley
572.G5	Grand Traverse Bay region. The Traverse region
	Including Power Island

	Michigan
572.A-.Z	**Regions, counties, etc., A-Z**
572.G5	Grand Traverse Bay region. The Traverse region — Continued
	Cf. F572.L7, Little Traverse Bay region
572.G6	Grand Traverse Co.
572.G8	Gratiot Co.
572.G87	Green Bay region, Mich.
	Cf. F587.G6, General, and Wisconsin
572.H6	Hillsdale Co.
572.H8	Houghton Co.
	Houghton Lake, *see* F572.R6
572.H9	Huron Co.
	Huron Mountains, *see* F572.M33
572.H92	Lake Huron region, Mich.
	Cf. F554, General
572.H93	Huron-Manistee National Forests
572.I5	Ingham Co.
572.I6	Ionia Co.
	Including Long Lake
572.I63	Iosco Co.
572.I66	Iron Co.
572.I7	Isabella Co.
572.I8	Isle Royale
572.J2	Jackson Co.
572.K2	Kalamazoo Co.
572.K22	Kalamazoo River and Valley
572.K23	Kalkaska Co.
572.K3	Kent Co.
572.K4	Keweenaw Co.
	For Isle Royale, see F572.I8
572.K43	Keweenaw Peninsula
572.L2	Lake Co.
572.L3	Lapeer Co.
572.L45	Leelanau Co.
	Including Fox Islands
572.L5	Lenawee Co.
	Including Devils Lake
572.L57	Les Cheneaux Islands (The Snows)
572.L7	Little Traverse Bay region
	Cf. F572.G5 , Grand Traverse Bay region
572.L8	Livingston Co.
	Long Lake (Ionia County), *see* F572.I6
	Lookout, Point (Arenac Co.), *see* F572.A7
572.L9	Luce Co.
572.M14	Mackinac (Mackinaw) Co. Mackinac region. Straits of Mackinac, etc.
	For Les Cheneaux Islands, see F572.L57
572.M16	Mackinac Island. Mackinac Island (City)
572.M2	Macomb Co.
572.M3	Manistee Co.
572.M33	Marquette Co.
	Including Huron Mountains
572.M36	Mason Co.
572.M4	Mecosta Co.
572.M5	Menominee Co.
572.M516	Menominee Range (General, and Michigan)
	Cf. F587.M49, Wisconsin
572.M52	Menominee River and Valley (General, and Mich.)
	Cf. F587.M5, Wisconsin
572.M57	Lake Michigan region, Mich
	Cf. F553, General

	Michigan
572.A-.Z	**Regions, counties, etc., A–Z — Continued**
	Michilimackinac, *see* F572.M16
572.M6	Midland Co.
572.M65	Missaukee Co.
572.M7	Monroe Co.
572.M8	Montcalm Co.
572.M83	Montmorency Co.
572.M9	Muskegon Co.
572.N5	Newaygo Co.
572.N7	Northern Michigan (Northern part of Lower Peninsula)
572.N8	Northern (Upper) Peninsula
572.O2	Oakland Co.
572.O3	Oceana Co.
572.O4	Ogemaw Co.
572.O6	Ontonagon Co.
572.O62	Ontonagon River and Valley
572.O7	Osceola Co.
572.O73	Oscoda Co.
572.O78	Otsego Co.
572.O8	Ottawa Co.
	Paw Paw Lake, *see* F572.B5
572.P38	Paw Paw River and Valley
572.P46	Pere Marquette River and Valley
572.P5	Pictured Rocks National Lakeshore
572.P53	Pigeon River and Valley. Pigeon River Country State Forest, etc.
	Point Lookout (Arenac Co.), *see* F572.A7
	Power Island, *see* F572.G5
572.P7	Presque Isle Co.
572.R6	Roscommon Co.
	Including Houghton Lake
572.S15	Saginaw Bay region
	Including Fort Saginaw
572.S17	Saginaw Co.
572.S2	Saginaw River and Valley
572.S3	St. Clair Co.
572.S34	Lake St. Clair, Mich.
	Cf. F1059.S3, Ontario
572.S4	St. Joseph Co.
572.S43	St. Joseph River and Valley, Mich.
	Cf. F532.S3, General, and Indiana
572.S5	Sanilac Co.
572.S6	Schoolcraft Co.
572.S7	Shiawassee Co.
572.S8	Sleeping Bear Dunes National Lakeshore
	The Snows (Islands), *see* F572.L57
572.S86	South Manitou Island
572.S9	Lake Superior region, Mich.
	Cf. F552, General
572.T58	Thumb District. Thumb Area
	Thunder Bay, *see* F572.A4
	Tiffin River and Valley, *see* F572.B36
	Tobico Marsh, *see* F572.B3
	Traverse region, *see* F572.G5
572.T9	Tuscola Co.
	Upper Peninsula, *see* F572.N8
572.V3	Van Buren Co.
572.W24	Walloon Lake
572.W3	Washtenaw Co.
572.W4	Wayne Co.

	Michigan
572.A-.Z	**Regions, counties, etc., A-Z — Continued**
572.W5	Wexford Co.
574.A-.Z	**Cities, towns, etc., A-Z**
	GALE NOTE *The cutter number(s) listed below have been given only as examples by the Library*
	of Congress
574.A6	Ann Arbor
574.B3	Bay City
574.D2	Dearborn
	For Edison Institute (Henry Ford Museum and Greenfield Village), Dearborn, Mich., see E161
574.D4	Detroit
	Subarrange by Table F2 at the end of the text
574.G7	Grand Rapids
574.K1	Kalamazoo
574.L2	Lansing
	Mackinac Island (City), *see* F572.M16
574.M17	Mackinaw
574.M9	Muskegon
574.S15	Saginaw
574.S3	Sault Ste. Marie
	Elements in the population
575.A1	General works
575.A2-.Z	Individual elements
	For a list of racial, ethnic, and religious elements (with cutter numbers), see E184.A+
	Wisconsin
576	**Periodicals. Societies. Collections**
578	**Museums. Exhibitions, exhibits**
579	**Gazetteers. Dictionaries. Geographic names**
579.3	**Guidebooks**
580	**Biography (Collective). Genealogy (Collective)**
580.2	**Historiography**
	Historians, *see* E175.5.A+
580.5	**Study and teaching**
581	**General works. Histories**
581.3	**Juvenile works**
	Pamphlets, addresses, essays, etc.
581.5	General
581.6	Anecdotes, legends, pageants, etc.
581.8	**Geography**
582	**Historic monuments (General). Illustrative material**
583	**Antiquities (Non-Indian)**
	By period
584	Early to 1848
	For biography: Thomas Pendleton Burnett, etc.
585	1836-1848. Wisconsin Territory
586	1848-1950
	Admission as a state, May 29, 1848
	Including biography: Benjamin Franklin Hopkins, Morgan Lewis Martin, Cadwallader Colden
	Washburn, etc.
	Cf. D570.85.W6+, World War I, 1914-1918
	Cf. D769.85.W6+, World War II, 1939-1945
	Cf. E537.1+, Civil War, 1861-1865 (General)
	Cf. E470.4+, Military operations and battles in the Civil War, 1861-1865
	Cf. E726.W6, War of 1898 (Spanish-American War)
	1951-
586.2	General works
	Biography
586.4	Collective

	Wisconsin
	By period
	1951-
	Biography — Continued
586.42.A-.42.Z	Individual, A-Z
	GALE NOTE *See note at the head of Table F5 at the end of the text for further instructions on how to subdivide this number*
587.A-.Z	**Regions, counties, etc., A-Z**
587.A15	Counties
587.A16	Mountains
587.A17	Rivers
587.A18	Lakes
587.A19	Islands
587.A2	Adams Co.
	Apostle Islands, *see* F587.A8
587.A8	Ashland Co.
	Including Apostle Islands, Chequamegon Bay, Madeline Island
587.B25	Barron Co.
587.B3	Bayfield Co.
	For Chequamegon Bay, see F587.A8
587.B55	Black River and Valley
587.B7	Boundaries
	Cf. F547.B7, Illinois boundary
	Cf. F612.B7, Minnesota boundary
587.B8	Brown Co.
587.B85	Brule River and Valley, Wis.
	Cf. F572.B86, General and Michigan
587.B9	Buffalo Co.
587.B95	Burnett Co.
587.C2	Calumet Co.
	Chain O' Lakes, *see* F587.W3
	Chequamegon Bay, *see* F587.A8
587.C48	Chippewa Co.
587.C5	Chippewa River and Valley
587.C6	Clark Co.
587.C7	Columbia Co.
587.C8	Crawford Co.
	Dalles of the Wisconsin, *see* F587.W8
587.D3	Dane Co.
	Including Cave of the Mounds, Lake Mendota
	Dells of the Wisconsin, *see* F587.W8
587.D6	Dodge Co.
587.D7	Door Co.
	Including Rock Island, Washington Island
587.D8	Douglas Co.
587.D9	Dunn Co.
587.E2	Eau Claire Co.
587.F5	Florence Co.
587.F6	Fond du Lac Co.
587.F65	Forest Co.
587.F7	Fox River and Valley (General, and Waukesha Co., Wisconsin)
	Cf. F547.F77, Illinois
587.F72	Fox River and Valley (Columbia Co.-Brown Co.)
	Lake Geneva, *see* F587.W18
587.G5	Grant Co.
587.G6	Green Bay region (General, and Wis.)
	Cf. F572.G87, Michigan
587.G7	Green Co.
587.G74	Green Lake Co.
587.I6	Iowa Co.

Wisconsin

587.A-.Z	**Regions, counties, etc., A-Z — Continued**
587.I7	Iron Co.
587.J2	Jackson Co.
587.J4	Jefferson Co.
587.J9	Juneau Co.
587.K3	Kenosha Co.
587.K35	Kewaunee Co.
587.K4	Kickapoo River and Valley, Wisc.
587.L14	La Crosse Co.
587.L2	Lafayette Co.
587.L3	Langlade Co.
587.L5	Lincoln Co.
	Madeline Island, *see* F587.A8
587.M2	Manitowoc Co.
587.M3	Marathon Co.
587.M35	Marinette Co.
587.M4	Marquette Co.
587.M49	Menominee Range
	Cf. F572.M516, General, and Michigan
587.M5	Menominee River and Valley, Wis.
	Cf. F572.M52, General, and Michigan
587.M57	Lake Michigan region, Wis.
	Cf. F553, General
587.M6	Milwaukee Co.
587.M63	Mississippi River and Valley, Wis.
	Cf. F350.5, General
	Cf. F597, Upper Mississippi Valley
587.M7	Monroe Co.
587.O2	Oconto Co.
587.O5	Oneida Co.
587.O93	Outagamie Co.
587.O98	Ozaukee Co.
587.P4	Pepin Co.
587.P6	Pierce Co.
587.P7	Polk Co.
587.P8	Portage Co.
587.P83	Porte des Morts Strait
587.P9	Price Co.
587.R2	Racine Co.
587.R4	Richland Co.
587.R6	Rock Co.
	Rock Island, *see* F587.D7
587.R63	Rock River and Valley (Sinnissippi Valley), Wis.
	Cf. F547.R7, General, and Illinois
587.R8	Rusk Co.
587.S13	St. Croix Co.
587.S14	St. Croix River and Valley (General, and Wis.)
	Cf. F612.S2, Minnesota
587.S2	Sauk Co.
	Including Devil's Island, Durward's Glen
587.S3	Sawyer Co.
587.S45	Shawano Co.
587.S5	Sheboygan Co.
587.S9	Lake Superior region, Wis.
	Cf. F552, General
587.T3	Taylor Co.
587.T79	Trempealeau Co.
587.V5	Vernon Co.
587.V6	Vilas Co.

	Wisconsin
587.A-.Z	**Regions, counties, etc., A-Z — Continued**
587.W18	Walworth Co.
	Including Lake Geneva
587.W185	Washburn Co.
587.W19	Washington Co.
	Washington Island, *see* F587.D7
587.W2	Waukesha Co.
587.W3	Waupaca Co.
	Including Chain O' Lakes
587.W35	Waushara Co.
587.W5	Winnebago Co.
587.W8	Wisconsin River and Valley
	Including Dells (Dalles) of the Wisconsin
587.W86	Wolf River. Wolf National Scenic Riverway
587.W9	Wood Co.
589.A-.Z	**Cities, towns, etc., A-Z**
	GALE NOTE *The cutter number(s) listed below have been given only as examples by the Library of Congress*
589.G7	Green Bay
589.K3	Kenosha
589.L1	La Crosse
589.M1	Madison
	Subarrange by Table F2 at the end of the text
589.M6	Milwaukee
	Subarrange by Table F2 at the end of the text
589.O8	Oshkosh
589.P8	Prairie du Chien
589.R2	Racine
589.S95	Superior
	Elements in the population
590.A1	General works
590.A2-.Z	Individual elements
	For a list of racial, ethnic, and religious elements (with cutter numbers), see E184.A+
	The West. Trans-Mississippi Region. Great Plains
	For The "Indian country," 1803-1854, see F697
	For Louisiana (Province), see F374
	For Middle West, see F350.5+
	For Mississippi River and Valley, see F350.5+
	For Missouri River and Valley, see F598
	For The Northwest (Upper Mississippi Valley), see F597
	For Pacific coast, see F851
	For Pacific Northwest, see F852
	For Rocky Mountains, see F721
	For The Southwest, see F786
	Cf. E81+, Indian wars (General)
590.3	**Guidebooks**
590.5	**Biography (Collective). Genealogy (Collective)**
590.6	**Geography**
590.7	**Historic monuments (General). Illustrative material**
591	**General works. Histories**
	Cf. E78.W5, Indians of the West
	By period
592	Early to 1848
	Including United States exploring expeditions: Fremont, Lewis and Clark, Pike
	Including biography: James Bridger, Christopher Carson, John Colter, Zebulon Montgomery Pike, Jedediah Strong Smith, William Sherley Williams, etc.
	For California, see F864
	For the "Indian country," 1821-1854, see F697
	For New Mexico (Spanish and Mexican), see F800-801

The West. Trans-Mississippi Region. Great Plains
By period

592   Early to 1848 — Continued
For Texas, see F390
Cf. E123+, Spanish discoveries
Cf. E401+, War with Mexico, 1845-1848
Cf. E408; F786, Mexican cession of 1848
Cf. F799, Cibola, Quivira
Cf. F868.N5, Donner party
Cf. F880, Oregon question
Lewis and Clark Expedition, 1804-1806
592.3   President Jefferson's message and accompanying documents
Subarrange by date of edition
592.4   Authentic history of the expedition. Lewis and Clark journals
Subarrange by date of edition
592.5   Journals of other members of the expedition. By author
Subarrange by date of edition
592.6   Spurious publications
Subarrange by date of edition
592.7   Other works about the expedition and its members
Subarrange by author or biographee as the case may be
593   1848-1860
Including later United States expeditions; overland journeys to the Pacific
Including biography: Edward Fitzgerald Beale, William Gilpin, etc.
Cf. E83.84, Wars with Pacific coast Indians, 1847-1865
Cf. E83.857, Spirit Lake Massacre, 1857
Cf. E83.858, Mill Creek War, 1857-1865
Cf. F786, Gadsden Purchase, 1853
Cf. F801 , Texas cession of 1850
594   1860-1880
Including biography: Martha Canary ("Calamity Jane"); William Frederick Cody, ("Buffalo Bill"); James Butler Hickok ("Wild Bill Hickok"); Jesse James; Moses Embree Milner ("California Joe"); Cole Younger; etc.
Cf. E83.86, Dakota Indian War, 1862-1863
Cf. E83.863, Indian wars, 1863-1865
Cf. E83.866, Indian wars, 1866-1898
595   1880-1950
Including biography: George Le Roy Parker ("Butch Cassidy")
Cf. E83.866, Indian wars, 1866-1898
595.2   1951-1980
595.3   1981-
596   **Frontier and pioneer life. Ranch life, cowboys, cattle trails, etc.**
Elements in the population
596.2   General works
596.3.A-.3.Z   Individual elements
For a list of individual elements, see E184.A+
597   **The Northwest**
Including Upper Mississippi Valley; sources of the Mississippi; northern boundary of the United States (from Lake of the Woods to Rocky Mountains), including works on region between Great Lakes and Pacific Ocean, the Oregon Trail, and the Overland Trail
Including biography: Jonathan Carver
For Canadian Northwest, see F1060+
For Pacific Northwest, see F851.72+
Cf. E78.N8 , Indians of the Northwestern States
Cf. F612.I8 , Lake Itasca and park
598   **Missouri River and Valley**
Cf. F472.M7 , Missouri
Cf. F627.M66, Iowa
Cf. F642.M6, North Dakota
Cf. F657.M7, South Dakota

598	**Missouri River and Valley — Continued**
	Cf. F672.M6, Nebraska
	Cf. F687.M6, Kansas
	Cf. F737.M7, Montana
	Minnesota
601	**Periodicals. Societies. Collections**
603	**Museums. Exhibitions, exhibits**
604	**Gazetteers. Dictionaries. Geographic names**
604.3	**Guidebooks**
605	**Biography (Collective). Genealogy (Collective)**
605.2	**Historiography**
	Historians, *see* E175.5.A+
605.5	**Study and teaching**
606	**General works. Histories**
	Including admission as a state, May 11, 1858
	For 1951 and later, see F610
	Including biography: Willis Arnold Gorman, John Albert Johnson, Floyd Bjönsterne Olson,
	Henry Hastings Sibley, etc.
	Cf. D570.85.M6+, World War I, 1914-1918
	Cf. D769.85.M6+, World War II, 1939-1945
	Cf. E83.86, Dakota Indian War, 1862-1863
	Cf. E515.1+, Civil War, 1861-1865 (General)
	Cf. E726.M7, War of 1898 (Spanish-American War)
606.3	**Juvenile works**
	Pamphlets, addresses, essays, etc.
606.5	General
606.6	Anecdotes, legends, pageants, etc.
607	**Historic monuments (General). Illustrative material**
608	**Antiquities (Non-Indian)**
	By period
	Early through 1950, *see* F606
	1951-
610	General works
	Biography
610.2	Collective
610.3.A-.3.Z	Individual, A-Z
	GALE NOTE *See note at the head of Table F5 at the end of the text for further*
	instructions on how to subdivide this number
612.A-.Z	**Regions, counties, etc., A-Z**
612.A15	Counties
612.A16	Mountains
612.A17	Rivers
612.A18	Lakes
612.A19	Islands
612.A3	Aitkin Co.
612.A6	Anoka Co.
612.B39	Becker Co.
612.B43	Beltrami Co.
	Including Star Island
612.B45	Benton Co.
	Big Fork River and Valley, *see* F612.K7
612.B5	Big Stone Co.
612.B6	Blue Earth Co.
612.B7	Boundaries
	For International boundary, see F597
612.B73	Boundary Waters Canoe Area
612.B8	Brown Co.
612.C15	Carlton Co.
612.C2	Carver Co.
612.C25	Cass Co.

	Minnesota
612.A-.Z	**Regions, counties, etc., A-Z — Continued**
612.C4	Chippewa Co.
612.C45	Chisago Co.
612.C6	Clay Co.
612.C63	Clearwater Co.
	For Itasca State Park, see F612.I8
612.C65	Cook Co.
612.C67	Cottonwood Co.
	Crane Island, *see F612.H5*
612.C7	Crow Wing Co.
612.D2	Dakota Co.
612.D6	Dodge Co.
612.D7	Douglas Co.
612.F2	Faribault Co.
612.F25	Father Hennepin State Park
612.F4	Fillmore Co.
	Including Forestville State Park
	Forestville State Park, *see F612.F4*
612.F7	Freeborn Co.
612.G6	Goodhue Co.
	Gooseberry Falls State Park, *see F612.L3*
612.G7	Grant Co.
612.H5	Hennepin Co.
	Including Lake Minnetonka, Crane Island
612.H8	Houston Co.
612.H9	Hubbard Co.
612.I6	Isanti Co.
612.I7	Itasca Co.
612.I8	Itasca Lake. Itasca State Park
612.J2	Jackson Co.
612.K17	Kanabec Co.
612.K2	Kandiyohi Co.
	Including Monogalia Co.
612.K5	Kittson Co.
612.K7	Koochiching Co.
	Including Big Fork River and Valley
612.L2	Lac qui Parle Co.
612.L3	Lake Co.
	Including Gooseberry Falls State Park
612.L4	Lake of the Woods Co.
	Including Northwest Angle
612.L5	Le Sueur Co.
612.L6	Lincoln Co.
612.L9	Lyon Co.
612.M25	McLeod Co.
612.M26	Mahnomen Co.
612.M266	Mankahta Co.
612.M27	Marshall Co.
612.M28	Martin Co.
612.M3	Meeker Co.
612.M36	Mesaba (Mesabi) range
612.M38	Mille Lacs Co.
612.M4	Minnesota River and Valley
612.M5	Mississippi River and Valley, Minn.
	Cf. F350.5+, General
	Cf. F597, Upper Mississippi Valley
	Monogalia Co., *see F612.K2*
612.M88	Morrison Co.
612.M9	Mower Co.

	Minnesota
612.A-.Z	**Regions, counties, etc., A-Z — Continued**
612.M95	Murray Co.
612.N5	Nicollet Co.
612.N7	Nobles Co.
612.N8	Norman Co.
	Northwest Angle, *see* F612.L4
612.O5	Olmsted Co.
612.O9	Otter Tail Co.
	Including Pelican Lake
	Pelican Lake, *see* F612.O9
612.P4	Pennington Co.
612.P42	Pepin, Lake
612.P5	Pine Co.
612.P55	Pipestone Co.
612.P7	Polk Co.
612.P8	Pope Co.
612.R18	Rainy River region
612.R2	Ramsey Co.
612.R25	Red Lake Co.
612.R27	Red River of the North and Valley, Minn.
	Cf. F642.R3, North Dakota
	Cf. F1064.R3, Manitoba
612.R3	Redwood Co.
612.R42	Renville Co.
612.R5	Rice Co.
612.R7	Rock Co.
612.R8	Roseau Co.
612.S2	St. Croix River and Valley, Minn.
	Cf. F587.S14, General, and Wisconsin
612.S25	St. Louis Co.
	Including Side Lake
612.S3	Scott Co.
612.S4	Sherburne Co.
612.S5	Sibley Co.
	Side Lake, *see* F612.S25
612.S64	Split Rock Creek and Valley, Minn.
	Cf. F657.S73, General and South Dakota
	Star Island, *see* F612.B43
612.S75	Stearns Co.
612.S8	Steele Co.
612.S84	Stevens Co.
612.S86	Straight River and Valley (Steele and Rice Counties)
612.S9	Lake Superior region, Minn.
	Cf. F552, General
612.S95	Superior National Forest
612.S98	Swift Co.
612.T6	Todd Co.
612.T7	Traverse Co.
612.V6	Voyageurs National Park
612.W12	Wabasha Co.
612.W14	Wadena Co.
612.W15	Wadsworth Trail
612.W17	Waseca Co.
612.W2	Washington Co.
612.W35	Watonwan Co.
612.W65	Wilkin Co.
612.W7	Winona Co.
	Including Rush Creek Valley
612.W9	Wright Co.

	Minnesota
612.A-.Z	**Regions, counties, etc., A-Z — Continued**
612.Y4	Yellow Medicine Co.
614.A-.Z	**Cities, towns, etc., A-Z**
	GALE NOTE *The cutter number(s) listed below have been given only as examples by the Library of Congress*
614.D8	Duluth
614.F7	Fort Snelling
614.M5	Minneapolis
	Subarrange by Table F2 at the end of the text
614.M6	Minneapolis and St. Paul. "The Twin Cities"
614.R6	Rochester
614.S25	St. Cloud
614.S4	St. Paul
614.W7	Winona
	Elements in the population
615.A1	General works
615.A2-.Z	Individual elements
	For a list of racial, ethnic, and religious elements (with cutter numbers), see E184.A+
	Iowa
616	**Periodicals. Societies. Collections**
618	**Museums. Exhibitions, exhibits**
619	**Gazetteers. Dictionaries. Geographic names**
619.3	**Guidebooks**
620	**Biography (Collective). Genealogy (Collective)**
620.2	**Historiography**
	Historians, *see* E175.5.A+
620.5	**Study and teaching**
621	**General works. Histories**
	Including admission as a state, December 28, 1846
	Including by period (Early to 1950) as well as general
	For 1951 and later, see F625+
	Including biography: John Chambers, Augustus Caesar Dodge, Robert Lucas, etc.
	Cf. D570.85.18+, World War I, 1914-1918
	Cf. D769.85.18+, World War II, 1939-1945
	Cf. E83.857, Spirit Lake Massacre, 1857
	Cf. E409.5.172, War with Mexico, 1845-1848
	Cf. E507.1+, Civil War, 1861-1865 (General)
	Cf. E726.14, War of 1898 (Spanish-American War)
621.3	**Juvenile works**
	Pamphlets, addresses, essays, etc.
621.5	General
621.6	Anecdotes, legends, pageants, etc.
622	**Historic monuments (General). Illustrative material**
623	**Antiquities (Non-Indian)**
	By period
(624)	Early to 1950, *see* F621
	1951-
625	General works
	Biography
625.4	Collective
625.42.A-.42.Z	Individual, A-Z
	GALE NOTE *See note at the head of Table F5 at the end of the text for further instructions on how to subdivide this number*
627.A-.Z	**Regions, counties, etc., A-Z**
627.A15	Counties
627.A16	Mountains
627.A17	Rivers
627.A18	Lakes
627.A19	Islands

	Iowa
627.A-.Z	**Regions, counties, etc., A-Z — Continued**
627.A2	Adair Co.
627.A3	Adams Co.
627.A5	Allamakee Co.
627.A6	Appanoose Co.
627.A8	Audubon Co.
627.B4	Benton Co.
627.B5	Big Sioux River and Valley, Iowa
	Cf. F657.B5, General, and South Dakota
627.B6	Black Hawk Co.
627.B67	Boone Co.
627.B7	Boundaries
	Cf. F472.B7, Missouri boundary
627.B8	Bremer Co.
627.B85	Buchanan Co.
627.B87	Buena Vista Co.
627.B9	Butler Co.
627.C2	Calhoun Co.
627.C25	Carroll Co.
627.C3	Cass Co.
627.C4	Cedar Co.
627.C44	Cerro Gordo Co.
627.C47	Cherokee Co.
627.C5	Chickasaw Co.
627.C53	Clarke Co.
627.C54	Clay Co.
627.C56	Clayton Co.
627.C6	Clinton Co.
627.C8	Crawford Co.
627.D14	Dallas Co.
627.D2	Davis Co.
627.D26	Decatur Co.
627.D3	Delaware Co.
627.D4	Des Moines Co.
627.D43	Des Moines River and Valley (General, and Iowa)
	Cf. F472.D4, Missouri
627.D5	Dickinson Co.
	Including Okoboji Lake, Spirit Lake
	Cf. E83.857, Spirit Lake Massacre, 1857
627.D8	Dubuque Co.
627.E5	Emmet Co.
627.F2	Fayette Co.
627.F5	Floyd Co.
627.F78	Franklin Co.
627.F8	Fremont Co.
	Including Waubonsie State Park
	Geode State Park, *see F627.H5*
627.G7	Greene Co.
627.G75	Grundy Co.
627.G8	Guthrie Co.
627.H2	Hamilton Co.
627.H25	Hancock Co.
627.H3	Hardin Co.
627.H4	Harrison Co.
627.H5	Henry Co.
	Including Geode State Park
627.H7	Howard Co.
627.H8	Humboldt Co.
627.I2	Ida Co.

Iowa

627.A-.Z	**Regions, counties, etc., A-Z — Continued**
627.I6	Iowa Co.
627.J2	Jackson Co.
627.J3	Jasper Co.
627.J4	Jefferson Co.
627.J6	Johnson Co.
627.J7	Jones Co.
627.K3	Keokuk Co.
627.K6	Kossuth Co.
627.L4	Lee Co.
627.L7	Linn Co.
627.L76	Loess Hills (General and Iowa)
	Cf. F472.L88, Missouri
627.L8	Louisa Co.
627.L85	Lucas Co.
627.L9	Lyon Co.
627.M18	Madison Co.
627.M2	Mahaska Co.
627.M3	Marion Co.
627.M4	Marshall Co.
627.M6	Mills Co.
627.M64	Mississippi River and Valley, Iowa
	Cf. F350.5+, General
	Cf. F597, Upper Mississippi Valley
627.M66	Missouri River and Valley, Iowa
	Cf. F598, General
627.M7	Mitchell Co.
627.M75	Monona Co.
627.M8	Monroe Co.
627.M83	Montgomery Co.
627.M9	Muscatine Co.
627.O2	O'Brien Co.
	Okoboji Lakes, *see* F627.D5
627.O8	Osceola Co.
627.P2	Page Co.
627.P3	Palo Alto Co.
627.P5	Plymouth Co.
627.P6	Pocahontas Co.
627.P7	Polk Co.
627.P8	Pottawattamie Co.
627.P88	Poweshiek Co.
627.R5	Ringgold Co.
627.S2	Sac Co.
627.S4	Scott Co.
627.S5	Shelby Co.
627.S55	Sioux Co.
	Spirit Lake, *see* F627.D5
627.S8	Story Co.
627.T3	Tama Co.
627.T5	Taylor Co.
627.U5	Union Co.
627.V2	Van Buren Co.
627.W2	Wapello Co.
627.W25	Warren Co.
627.W26	Washington Co.
627.W28	Wayne Co.
627.W3	Webster Co.
627.W65	Winnebago Co.
627.W7	Winneshiek Co.

	Iowa
627.A-.Z	**Regions, counties, etc., A-Z — Continued**
627.W8	Woodbury Co.
627.W86	Worth Co.
627.W9	Wright Co.
629.A-.Z	**Cities, towns, etc., A-Z**
	GALE NOTE *The cutter number(s) listed below have been given only as examples by the Library of Congress*
629.B9	Burlington
629.C3	Cedar Rapids
629.C8	Council Bluffs
629.D2	Davenport
629.D4	Des Moines
629.D8	Dubuque
629.M9	Muscatine
629.S6	Sioux City
	Elements in the population
630.A1	General works
630.A2-.Z	Individual elements
	For a list of racial, ethnic, and religious elements (with cutter numbers), see E184.A+
	North Dakota
631	**Periodicals. Societies. Collections**
633	**Museums. Exhibitions, exhibits**
634	**Gazetteers. Dictionaries. Geographic names**
634.3	**Guidebooks**
635	**Biography (Collective). Genealogy (Collective)**
635.2	**Historiography**
	Historians, *see* E175.5.A+
635.5	**Study and teaching**
636	**General works. Histories**
	Admission as a state, November 2, 1889
	Including by period (Early to 1950) as well as general
	For early to 1889, see F655
	For 1951 and later, see F640
	Cf. D769.85.N9+, World War II, 1939-1945
636.3	**Juvenile works**
	Pamphlets, addresses, essays, etc.
636.5	General
636.6	Anecdotes, legends, pageants, etc.
637	**Historic monuments (General). Illustrative material**
638	**Antiquities (Non-Indian)**
	By period
(639)	Early to 1950, *see* F636 , F655
	1951-
640	General
	Biography
641.A2A-.A2Z	Collective
641.A3-.Z	Individual
	GALE NOTE *See note at the head of Table F5 at the end of the text for further instructions on how to subdivide this number*
642.A-.Z	**Regions, counties, etc., A-Z**
642.A15	Counties
642.A16	Mountains
642.A17	Rivers
642.A18	Lakes
642.A19	Islands
642.A2	Adams Co.
642.B3	Barnes Co.
642.B4	Benson Co.
	For Devils Lake, see F642.D5

	North Dakota
642.A-.Z	**Regions, counties, etc., A-Z — Continued**
642.B5	Billings Co.
642.B6	Bottineau Co.
642.B7	Boundaries
	For International boundary, see F597
642.B75	Bowman Co.
642.B85	Burke Co.
642.B9	Burleigh Co.
642.C34	Cass Co.
642.C4	Cavalier Co.
	Coteau du Missouri, *see F642.M26*
642.D5	Devils Lake
642.D6	Dickey Co.
642.D7	Divide Co.
642.D9	Dunn Co.
	Including Killdeer Mountains, Killdeer Mountain Park
642.E2	Eddy Co.
642.E5	Emmons Co.
642.F6	Foster Co.
642.G6	Golden Valley Co.
642.G7	Grand Forks Co.
642.G75	Grant Co.
642.G8	Griggs Co.
642.H4	Hettinger Co.
642.K5	Kidder Co.
	Kildeer Mountains, *see F642.D9*
642.K54	Knife River and Valley
642.L3	La Moure Co.
642.L5	Little Missouri Badlands
	For Theodore Roosevelt National Memorial Park, see F642.T5
642.L6	Logan Co.
642.M2	McHenry Co.
642.M26	McIntosh Co.
	Including Coteau du Missouri
642.M28	McKenzie Co.
	Including Yellowstone River and Valley
	Cf. F737.Y4 , General, and Montana
642.M29	McLean Co.
642.M5	Mercer Co.
642.M6	Missouri River and Valley, N. Dak.
	Cf. F598, General
642.M7	Morton Co.
642.M8	Mountrail Co.
642.N4	Nelson Co.
642.O4	Oliver Co.
642.P4	Pembina Co.
642.P5	Pierce Co.
642.R17	Ramsey Co.
	For Devils Lake, see F642.D5
642.R2	Ransom Co.
642.R3	Red River of the North and Valley, N. Dak.
	Cf. F612.R27, Minnesota
	Cf. F1064.R3, Manitoba
642.R4	Renville Co.
642.R5	Richland Co.
642.R6	Rolette Co.
642.S2	Sargent Co.
642.S5	Sheridan Co.
642.S55	Sioux Co.

	North Dakota
642.A-.Z	**Regions, counties, etc., A-Z — Continued**
642.S6	Slope Co.
642.S68	Souris River and Valley
	Cf. F1064.S6, Manitoba
	Cf. F1074.S67, General, and Saskatchewan
642.S7	Stark Co.
642.S75	Steele Co.
642.S8	Stutsman Co.
642.T5	Theodore Roosevelt National Memorial Park
642.T6	Towner Co.
642.T7	Traill Co.
642.W3	Walsh Co.
642.W35	Ward Co.
642.W45	Wells Co.
642.W6	Williams Co.
644.A-.Z	**Cities, towns, etc., A-Z**
	GALE NOTE *The cutter number(s) listed below have been given only as examples by the Library of Congress*
644.B6	Bismarck
644.F2	Fargo
644.G8	Grand Forks
	Elements in the population
645.A1	General works
645.A2-.Z	Individual elements
	For a list of racial, ethnic, and religious elements (with cutter numbers), see E184.A+
	South Dakota
	Including works covering both North and South Dakota
646	**Periodicals. Societies. Collections**
648	**Museums. Exhibitions, exhibits**
649	**Gazetteers. Dictionaries. Geographic names**
649.3	**Guidebooks**
650	**Biography (Collective). Genealogy (Collective)**
650.2	**Historiography**
	Historians, *see E175.5.A+*
650.5	**Study and teaching**
651	**General works. Histories**
651.3	**Juvenile works**
	Pamphlets, addresses, essays, etc.
651.5	General
651.6	Anecdotes, legends, pageants, etc.
651.8	**Geography**
652	**Historic monuments (General). Illustrative material**
653	**Antiquities (Non-Indian)**
	By period
655	Early to 1889
	Including the Dakota region before 1861, Dakota Territory, 1861-1889
	Cf. E83.863, Indian wars, 1863-1865
656	1889-1950
	Including admission as a state, November 2, 1889
	Including biography: Peter Norbeck
	Cf. D570.85.S7+, World War I, 1914-1918
	Cf. D769.85.S7+, World War II, 1939-1945
	Cf. E83.89, Dakota Indian War, 1890-1891
	1951-
656.2	General works
	Biography
656.3	Collective

	South Dakota
	By period
	1951-
	Biography — Continued
656.4.A-.4.Z	Individual, A-Z
	GALE NOTE *See note at the head of Table F5 at the end of the text for further instructions on how to subdivide this number*
657.A-.Z	**Regions, counties, etc., A-Z**
657.A15	Counties
657.A16	Mountains
657.A17	Rivers
657.A18	Lakes
657.A19	Islands
657.A6	Armstrong Co.
657.A8	Aurora Co.
657.B24	Badlands
657.B3	Beadle Co.
657.B4	Bennett Co.
657.B5	Big Sioux River and Valley (General, and S. Dak.)
	Cf. F627.B5, Iowa
657.B6	Black Hills
	For Custer State Park, see F657.C92
	For Mount Rushmore National Memorial, see F657.R8
	For Wind Cave National Park, see F657.W7
657.B65	Bon Homme Co.
657.B7	Boundaries
657.B75	Brookings Co.
657.B76	Brown Co.
657.B77	Brule Co.
657.B8	Buffalo Co.
657.B9	Butte Co.
657.C25	Campbell Co.
657.C4	Charles Mix Co.
657.C55	Clark Co.
657.C6	Clay Co.
657.C8	Codington Co.
657.C83	Corson Co.
657.C9	Custer Co.
	For Wind Cave, see F657.W7
657.C92	Custer State Park
657.D25	Davison Co.
657.D3	Day Co.
657.D4	Deuel Co.
657.D45	Dewey Co.
657.D7	Douglas Co.
657.E2	Edmunds Co.
657.F3	Fall River Co.
657.F4	Faulk Co.
	Fort Sisseton State Park, *see F657.R6*
657.G7	Grant Co.
657.G8	Gregory Co.
657.H2	Haakon Co.
657.H3	Hamlin Co.
657.H35	Hand Co.
657.H4	Hanson Co.
657.H45	Harding Co.
657.H8	Hughes Co.
657.H85	Hutchinson Co.
657.H9	Hyde Co.
657.J2	Jackson Co.

	South Dakota
657.A-.Z	**Regions, counties, etc., A-Z — Continued**
657.J4	Jerauld Co.
657.J6	Jones Co.
657.K5	Kingsbury Co.
657.L3	Lake Co.
657.L4	Lawrence Co.
657.L6	Lincoln Co.
657.L9	Lyman Co.
657.M15	McCook Co.
657.M2	McPherson Co.
657.M3	Marshall Co.
657.M4	Meade Co.
	Including Bear Butte
657.M45	Mellette Co.
657.M55	Miner Co.
657.M6	Minnehaha Co.
657.M7	Missouri River and Valley, S. Dak.
	Cf. F598, General
657.M8	Moody Co.
657.P4	Pennington Co.
	For Mount Rushmore National Memorial, see F657.R8
657.P5	Perkins Co.
657.P8	Potter Co.
657.R6	Roberts Co.
	Including Fort Sisseton State Park
657.R8	Mount Rushmore National Memorial
657.S3	Sanborn Co.
657.S5	Shannon Co.
657.S7	Spink Co.
657.S73	Split Rock Creek and Valley (General and South Dakota)
	Cf. F612.S64, Minnesota
657.S8	Stanley Co.
657.S9	Sully Co.
657.T6	Todd Co.
657.T7	Tripp Co.
657.T8	Turner Co.
657.U5	Union Co.
657.W2	Walworth Co.
657.W3	Washabaugh Co.
657.W4	Washington Co.
	In 1944, combined with Shannon County
657.W7	Wind Cave. Wind Cave National Park
657.Y2	Yankton Co.
657.Z5	Ziebach Co.
659.A-.Z	**Cities, towns, etc., A-Z**
	GALE NOTE *The cutter number(s) listed below have been given only as examples by the Library of Congress*
659.A14	Aberdeen
659.P6	Pierre
659.R2	Rapid City
659.S6	Sioux Falls
	Elements in the population
660.A1	General works
660.A2-.Z	Individual elements
	For a list of racial, ethnic, and religious elements (with cutter numbers), see E184.A+
	Nebraska
661	**Periodicals. Societies. Collections**
663	**Museums. Exhibitions, exhibits**
664	**Gazetteers. Dictionaries. Geographic names**

Nebraska — Continued
664.3	**Guidebooks**
665	**Biography (Collective). Genealogy (Collective)**
665.2	**Historiography**
	Historians, *see* E175.5.A+
665.5	**Study and teaching**
666	**General works. Histories**
	Including admission as a state, March 1, 1867
	Including by period (Early to 1950) as well as general
	For 1951 and later, see F670
	Including biography: Jules Ami Sandoz, Thomas Clark White
	Cf. D570.85.N19+, World War I, 1914-1918
	Cf. D769.85.N19+, World War II, 1939-1945
	Cf. E433, Kansas-Nebraska Bill, 1854
666.3	**Juvenile works**
	Pamphlets, addresses, essays, etc.
666.5	General
666.6	Anecdotes, legends, pageants, etc.
667	**Historic monuments (General). Illustrative material**
668	**Antiquities (Non-Indian)**
	By period
	Early to 1950, *see* F666
	1951-
670	General works
	Biography
670.3	Collective
670.4	Individual, A-Z
672.A-.Z	**Regions, counties, etc., A-Z**
672.A15	Counties
672.A16	Mountains
672.A17	Rivers
672.A18	Lakes
672.A19	Islands
672.A2	Adams Co.
	Agate Fossil Beds National Monument, *see* F672.S6
672.A6	Antelope Co.
672.A7	Arthur Co.
672.B3	Banner Co.
672.B5	Blaine Co.
672.B6	Boone Co.
672.B7	Boundaries
672.B75	Box Butte Co.
672.B77	Boyd Co.
672.B8	Brown Co.
672.B85	Buffalo Co.
672.B87	Burt Co.
672.B9	Butler Co.
672.C3	Cass Co.
672.C35	Cedar Co.
672.C4	Chase Co.
672.C45	Cherry Co.
672.C5	Cheyenne Co.
	Chimney Rock National Historic Site, *see* F672.M7
672.C6	Clay Co.
672.C7	Colfax Co.
672.C8	Cuming Co.
672.C9	Custer Co.
672.D2	Dakota Co.
672.D3	Dawes Co.
672.D35	Dawson Co.

	Nebraska
672.A-.Z	**Regions, counties, etc., A-Z — Continued**
672.D4	Deuel Co.
672.D58	Dixon Co.
672.D6	Dodge Co.
672.D7	Douglas Co.
672.D8	Dundy Co.
672.F48	Fillmore Co.
672.F7	Franklin Co.
672.F8	Frontier Co.
672.F9	Furnas Co.
672.G13	Gage Co.
672.G2	Garden Co.
672.G3	Garfield Co.
672.G5	Gosper Co.
672.G6	Grant Co.
672.G7	Greeley Co.
672.H2	Hall Co.
672.H25	Hamilton Co.
672.H3	Harlan Co.
672.H4	Hayes Co.
672.H5	Hitchcock Co.
672.H6	Holt Co.
672.H7	Hooker Co.
672.H8	Howard Co.
672.J4	Jefferson Co.
672.J6	Johnson Co.
672.K4	Kearney Co.
672.K45	Keith Co.
672.K5	Keya Paha Co.
672.K6	Kimball Co.
672.K7	Knox Co.
672.L2	Lancaster Co.
672.L4	Lincoln Co.
672.L6	Logan Co.
672.L7	Loup Co.
672.L8	Loup River and Valley
672.M2	McPherson Co.
672.M3	Madison Co.
672.M4	Merrick Co.
672.M6	Missouri River and Valley, Nebr.
	Cf. F598, General
672.M7	Morrill Co.
	Including Chimney Rock National Historic Site
672.N3	Nance Co.
672.N4	Nemaha Co.
672.N56	Niobrara River and Valley (General, and Nebraska)
	Cf. F767.N52, Wyoming
672.N8	North Platte River and Valley (General, and Nebr.)
	Cf. F767.N8, Wyoming
672.N9	Nuckolls Co.
672.O8	Otoe Co.
672.P3	Pawnee Co.
672.P4	Perkins Co.
672.P5	Phelps Co.
672.P54	Pierce Co.
672.P58	Platte Co.
672.P6	Platte River and Valley
672.P7	Polk Co.
672.R4	Red Willow Co.

Nebraska

672.A-.Z	**Regions, counties, etc., A-Z — Continued**
672.R5	Richardson Co.
672.R6	Rock Co.
672.S15	Saline Co.
672.S17	Sandhills
672.S2	Sarpy Co.
672.S24	Saunders Co.
672.S3	Scotts Bluff Co.
672.S5	Seward Co.
672.S53	Sheridan Co.
672.S54	Sherman Co.
672.S6	Sioux Co.

Including Agate Fossil Beds National Monument

672.S7	South Platte River and Valley (General, and Nebr.)

Cf. F782.S7, Colorado

672.S8	Stanton Co.
672.T3	Thayer Co.
672.T4	Thomas Co.
672.T5	Thurston Co.
672.V3	Valley Co.
672.W3	Washington Co.
672.W35	Wayne Co.
672.W4	Webster Co.
672.W5	Wheeler Co.
672.Y62	York Co.
674.A-.Z	**Cities, towns, etc., A-Z**

GALE NOTE *The cutter number(s) listed below have been given only as examples by the Library of Congress*

674.B4	Bellevue
674.G7	Grand Island
674.H3	Hastings
674.L7	Lincoln
674.O5	Omaha

Subarrange by Table F2 at the end of the text

	Elements in the population
675.A1	General works
675.A2-.Z	Individual elements

For a list of racial, ethnic, and religious elements (with cutter numbers), see E184.A+

Kansas

676	**Periodicals. Societies. Collections**
678	**Museums. Exhibitions, exhibits**
679	**Gazetteers. Dictionaries. Geographic names**
679.3	**Guidebooks**
680	**Biography (Collective). Genealogy (Collective)**
680.2	**Historiography**

Historians, *see* E175.5.A+

680.5	**Study and teaching**
681	**General works. Histories**
681.3	**Juvenile works**
	Pamphlets, addresses, essays, etc.
681.5	General
681.6	Anecdotes, legends, pageants, etc.
682	**Historic monuments (General). Illustrative material**
683	**Antiquities (Non-Indian)**
	By period
685	Early to 1861

Including struggle between proslavery and anti-slavery parties; New England Emigrant Aid Company; armed bands from Missouri; Battle of Osawatomie, 1856; Lecompton Constitution

Including biography: James Henry Lane, Charles Robinson, etc.

	Kansas
	By period
685	Early to 1861 — Continued
	Cf. E433, Kansas-Nebraska Bill, 1854
	Cf. F799, Quivira
686	1861-1950
	Including admission as a state, January 29, 1861
	Including biography: Alfred Mossman Landon, etc.
	Cf. D570.85.K2+, World War I, 1914-1918
	Cf. D769.85.K2+, World War II, 1939-1945
	Cf. E508.1+, Civil War, 1861-1865 (General)
	Cf. E470.9, Campaigns and battles of the Civil War, 1861-1865
	Cf. E474.97, Quantrill's Raid, 1863
	Cf. E726.K2, War of 1898 (Spanish-American War)
	1951-
686.2	General works
	Biography
686.3	Collective
686.4.A-.4.Z	Individual, A-Z
	GALE NOTE *See note at the head of Table F5 at the end of the text for further instructions on how to subdivide this number*
687.A-.Z	**Regions, counties, etc., A-Z**
687.A15	Counties
687.A16	Mountains
687.A17	Rivers
687.A18	Lakes
687.A19	Islands
687.A4	Allen Co.
687.A5	Anderson Co.
687.A7	Arkansas River and Valley, Kans.
	Cf. F417.A7, General, and Arkansas
687.A8	Atchison Co.
687.B18	Barber Co.
687.B2	Barton Co.
687.B6	Big Blue River. Blue Valley
687.B7	Boundaries
687.B73	Bourbon Co.
687.B8	Brown Co.
687.B9	Butler Co.
	Including El Dorado Lake
	Cedar Point Lake, *see* F687.C35
687.C35	Chase Co.
	Including Cedar Point Lake
687.C36	Chautauqua Co.
687.C38	Cherokee Co.
687.C5	Cheyenne Co.
687.C53	Clark Co.
687.C55	Clay Co.
	Clinton Lake, *see* F687.W4
687.C6	Cloud Co.
687.C7	Coffey Co.
687.C75	Comanche Co.
687.C8	Cowley Co.
687.C9	Crawford Co.
	Davis Co., *see* F687.G3
687.D4	Decatur Co.
687.D5	Dickinson Co.
687.D6	Doniphan Co.
687.D7	Douglas Co.
687.E2	Edwards Co.

	Kansas
687.A-.Z	**Regions, counties, etc., A-Z — Continued**
	El Dorado Lake, *see* F687.B9
687.E28	Elk Co.
687.E3	Ellis Co.
687.E4	Ellsworth Co.
687.F5	Finney Co.
687.F55	Flint Hills (General, and Kansas)
	Cf. F702.F55 , Oklahoma
687.F6	Ford Co.
687.F8	Franklin Co.
687.G3	Geary Co.
	Formerly Davis County
687.G72	Gove Co.
687.G74	Graham Co.
687.G75	Grant Co.
687.G78	Gray Co.
687.G8	Greeley Co.
687.G85	Greenwood Co.
687.H3	Hamilton Co.
687.H4	Harper Co.
687.H45	Harvey Co.
687.H5	Haskell Co.
687.H8	Hodgeman Co.
687.J2	Jackson Co.
687.J3	Jefferson Co.
687.J4	Jewell Co.
687.J6	Johnson Co.
687.K3	Kansas River and Valley
687.K4	Kearny Co.
687.K53	Kingman Co.
687.K6	Kiowa Co.
687.L2	Labette Co.
687.L3	Lane Co.
687.L4	Leavenworth Co.
687.L7	Lincoln Co.
687.L75	Linn Co.
687.L8	Logan Co.
687.L9	Lyon Co.
687.M2	McPherson Co.
687.M3	Marion Co.
	For Cedar Point Lake, see F687.C35
687.M35	Marshall Co.
687.M48	Meade Co.
687.M55	Miami Co.
687.M6	Missouri River and Valley, Kans.
	Cf. F598, General
687.M65	Mitchell Co.
687.M7	Montgomery Co.
687.M75	Morris Co.
687.M8	Morton Co.
687.N3	Nemaha Co.
687.N4	Neosho Co.
687.N43	Ness Co.
687.N8	Norton Co.
687.O6	Osage Co.
687.O7	Osborne Co.
687.O8	Ottawa Co.
687.P3	Pawnee Co.
687.P5	Phillips Co.

	Kansas
687.A-.Z	**Regions, counties, etc., A-Z — Continued**
687.P8	Pottawatomie Co.
687.P9	Pratt Co.
687.R25	Rawlins Co.
687.R3	Reno Co.
687.R4	Republic Co.
687.R45	Rice Co.
687.R5	Riley Co.
687.R7	Rooks Co.
687.R8	Rush Co.
687.R9	Russell Co.
687.S16	Saline Co.
687.S3	Scott Co.
687.S4	Sedgwick Co.
687.S45	Seward Co.
687.S5	Shawnee Co.
687.S55	Sheridan Co.
687.S6	Sherman Co.
687.S8	Smith Co.
687.S84	Smoky Hill River and Valley (General, and Kansas)
	Cf. F782.S53, Colorado
687.S85	Solomon River and Valley
687.S86	Stafford Co.
687.S87	Stanton Co.
687.S88	Stevens Co.
687.S9	Sumner Co.
687.T34	Tallgrass Prairie National Preserve
687.T4	Thomas Co.
687.T7	Trego Co.
687.W2	Wabaunsee River and Valley
687.W4	Wakarusa River and Valley
	Including Clinton Lake
687.W43	Wallace Co.
687.W45	Washington Co.
687.W6	Wichita Co.
687.W7	Wilson Co.
687.W73	Wilson Lake
687.W8	Woodson Co.
687.W97	Wyandotte Co.
689.A-.Z	**Cities, towns, etc., A-Z**
	GALE NOTE *The cutter number(s) listed below have been given only as examples by the Library of Congress*
689.H9	Hutchinson
689.K2	Kansas City
689.L4	Lawrence
689.L5	Leavenworth
689.T6	Topeka
689.W6	Wichita
	Elements in the population
690.A1	General works
690.A2-.Z	Individual elements
	For a list of racial, ethnic, and religious elements (with cutter numbers), see E184.A+
	Oklahoma
691	**Periodicals. Societies. Collections**
691.5	**Museums. Exhibitions, exhibits**
692	**Gazetteers. Dictionaries. Geographic names**
692.3	**Guidebooks**
693	**Biography (Collective). Genealogy (Collective)**

	Oklahoma — Continued
693.2	**Historiography**
	Historians, *see* E175.5.A+
693.5	**Study and teaching**
694	**General works. Histories**
694.3	**Juvenile works**
	Pamphlets, addresses, essays, etc.
694.5	General
694.6	Anecdotes, legends, pageants, etc.
694.8	**Geography**
695	**Historic monuments (General). Illustrative material**
696	**Antiquities (Non-Indian)**
	By period
697	Early to 1890
	Including the "Indian country," that part of the Louisiana purchase west of Arkansas, Missouri, and the Missouri River, Indian Territory before division in 1890
	Including biography: Davis Lewis Payne
	1890-1907
698	Indian Territory
699	Oklahoma Territory
700	1907-1950
	Including admission as a state, November 16, 1907
	Including biography: William Henry Murray
	Cf. D570.85.O5+, World War I, 1914-1918
	Cf. D769.85.O5+, World War II, 1939-1945
701	1951-
702.A-.Z	**Regions, counties, etc., A-Z**
702.A15	Counties
702.A16	Mountains
702.A17	Rivers
702.A18	Lakes
702.A19	Islands
702.A3	Adair Co.
702.A4	Alfalfa Co.
702.A7	Arkansas River and Valley, Okla.
	Cf. F417.A7, General, and Arkansas
702.A8	Atoka Co.
702.B4	Beaver Co.
702.B45	Beckham Co.
702.B5	Blaine Co.
702.B7	Boundaries
	Cf. F392.B7, Texas boundary
	Cf. F782.B7, Colorado boundary
702.B8	Bryan Co.
702.C15	Caddo Co.
702.C17	Camp Creek and Valley
702.C18	Canadian Co.
702.C2	Canadian River and Valley (General, and Okla.)
	Cf. F392.C27, Texas
	Cf. F802.C2, New Mexico
702.C3	Carter Co.
702.C4	Cherokee Co.
702.C42	Cherokee Outlet
	Chickasaw National Recreation Area, *see* F702.M84
702.C45	Choctaw Co.
702.C5	Cimarron Co.
702.C53	Cimarron River and Valley
702.C6	Cleveland Co.
702.C65	Coal Co.
702.C7	Comanche Co.

Oklahoma

702.A-.Z	**Regions, counties, etc., A-Z — Continued**
702.C75	Cotton Co.
702.C8	Craig Co.
702.C85	Creek Co.
702.C9	Custer Co.
702.D4	Delaware Co.
702.D5	Dewey Co.
702.E4	Ellis Co.
702.F55	Flint Hills
	Cf. F687.F55, General, and Kansas
702.G25	Garfield Co.
702.G3	Garvin Co.
702.G7	Grady Co.
702.G75	Grant Co.
702.G8	Greer Co.
702.H3	Harmon Co.
702.H35	Harper Co.
702.H4	Haskell Co.
702.H9	Hughes Co.
702.J3	Jackson Co.
702.J4	Jefferson Co.
702.J6	Johnston Co.
702.K23	Kay Co.
702.K4	Kingfisher Co.
702.K5	Kiowa Co.
702.L3	Latimer Co.
702.L4	Le Flore Co.
702.L5	Lincoln Co.
	Including Robinson Creek and Valley, etc.
702.L55	Little River and Valley (General, and Oklahoma)
	Cf. F417.L64, Arkansas
702.L6	Logan Co.
702.L7	Love Co.
702.M2	McClain Co.
702.M3	McCurtain Co.
702.M35	McIntosh Co.
702.M4	Major Co.
702.M5	Marshall Co.
702.M55	Mayes Co.
702.M84	Murray Co.
	Including Chickasaw National Recreation Area
	For Platt National Park, see F702.P7
702.M9	Muskogee Co.
702.N6	No Man's Land. Oklahoma Panhandle
702.N8	Noble Co.
702.N9	Nowata Co.
702.O5	Okfuskee Co.
702.O55	Oklahoma Co.
	Oklahoma Panhandle, *see* F702.N6
702.O6	Okmulgee Co.
702.O7	Osage Co.
	Including Salt Creek and Valley
702.O8	Ottawa Co.
702.O9	Ouachita Mountains (General, and Oklahoma)
	Cf. F417.O77, Arkansas
	Panhandle, *see* F702.N6
702.P35	Pawnee Co.
	For Camp Creek and Valley, see F702.C17

	Oklahoma
702.A-.Z	**Regions, counties, etc., A-Z — Continued**
702.P4	Payne Co.
	For Camp Creek and Valley, see F702.C17
702.P6	Pittsburg Co.
702.P7	Platt National Park
702.P74	Pontotoc Co.
702.P75	Pottawatomie Co.
702.P9	Pushmataha Co.
702.R3	Red River and Valley, Okla.
	Cf. F377.R3, General, and Louisiana
	Robinson Creek and Valley, *see* F702.L5
702.R6	Roger Mills Co.
702.R7	Rogers Co.
	Salt Creek and Valley, *see* F702.O7
702.S35	Seminole Co.
702.S4	Sequoyah Co.
702.S8	Stephens Co.
702.T4	Texas Co.
702.T5	Tillman Co.
702.T8	Tulsa Co.
702.W2	Wagoner Co.
702.W3	Washington Co.
702.W35	Washita Co.
702.W36	Washita River and Valley
	Cf. F392.W33, General, and Texas
702.W55	Wichita Mountains and region
702.W7	Woods Co.
702.W8	Woodward Co.
704.A-.Z	**Cities, towns, etc., A-Z**
	GALE NOTE *The cutter number(s) listed below have been given only as examples by the Library of Congress*
704.E6	Enid
704.G9	Guthrie
704.M9	Muskogee
704.N6	Norman
704.O41	Oklahoma City
704.T92	Tulsa
	Elements in the population
705.A1	General works
705.A2-.Z	Individual elements
	For a list of racial, ethnic, and religious elements (with cutter numbers), see E184.A+
	Rocky Mountains. Rocky Mountains in the United States
	Cf. F782.26, Rocky Mountain region of Colorado, etc.
	Cf. F1090, Rocky Mountain region of Canada
721	**General works**
722	**Yellowstone National Park**
	Including boundaries
	Cf. F737.Y4, Yellowstone River and Valley
	Montana
726	**Periodicals. Societies. Collections**
728	**Museums. Exhibitions, exhibits**
729	**Gazetteers. Dictionaries. Geographic names**
729.3	**Guidebooks**
730	**Biography (Collective). Genealogy (Collective)**
730.2	**Historiography**
	Historians, *see* E175.5.A+
730.5	**Study and teaching**
731	**General works. Histories**
	Including admission as a state, November 2, 1889

	Montana
731	**General works. Histories — Continued**
	Including by period (Early to 1950) as well as general
	For 1951 and later, see F735
	Including biography: Granville Stuart
	Cf. D570.85.M9+, World War I, 1914-1918
	Cf. D769.85.M9+, World War II, 1939-1945
	Cf. E83.876, Dakota Indian War, 1876
	Cf. E83.877, Nez Perce War, 1877
731.3	**Juvenile works**
	Pamphlets, addresses, essays, etc.
731.5	General
731.6	Anecdotes, legends, pageants, etc.
731.8	**Geography**
732	**Historic monuments (General). Illustrative material**
733	**Antiquities (Non-Indian)**
	By period
(734)	Early to 1950, *see* F731
735	1951-
	Biography
735.2.A2A-.2.A2Z	Collective
735.2.A3-.2.Z	Individual, A-Z
	GALE NOTE *See note at the head of Table F5 at the end of the text for further*
	instructions on how to subdivide this number
737.A-.Z	**Regions, counties, etc., A-Z**
737.A15	Counties
737.A16	Mountains
737.A17	Rivers
737.A18	Lakes
737.A19	Islands
737.A3	Absaroka National Forest
737.B35	Beartooth Mountains (General and Montana)
737.B38	Beaverhead Co.
737.B48	Big Hole River and Valley
737.B49	Big Horn Canyon National Recreation Area
737.B5	Big Horn Co.
737.B53	Big Horn Mountains
	Cf. F767.B37, General, and Wyoming
	Bird-Truax Trail, *see* F752.B64
737.B6	Bitter Root River and Valley
737.B62	Blackfoot River and Valley
737.B63	Blaine Co.
737.B66	Bob Marshall Wilderness
737.B7	Boundaries
	For International boundary, see F597
	For Yellowstone National Park boundary, see F722
	Cf. F752.B7, Idaho boundary
737.B8	Broadwater Co.
737.C14	Cabinet National Forest
	Camas Prairie, *see* F737.M6
737.C25	Carbon Co.
737.C3	Carter Co.
737.C33	Cascade Co.
737.C5	Chouteau Co.
737.C55	Clark Fork and Valley (General, and Montana)
	Cf. F752.C57, Idaho
737.C9	Custer Co.
737.D3	Daniels Co.
737.D4	Dawson Co.
737.D5	Deer Lodge Co.

	Montana
737.A-.Z	**Regions, counties, etc., A-Z — Continued**
737.F2	Fallon Co.
737.F3	Fergus Co.
737.F58	Flathead Co.
	Including Tobacco Plains
737.F6	Flathead Lake and Valley
737.G18	Gallatin Co.
737.G2	Gallatin Valley. East and West Gallatin Rivers
737.G3	Garfield Co.
737.G45	Glacier Co.
737.G5	Glacier National Park
	Including Lake McDonald
737.G6	Golden Valley Co.
737.G7	Granite Co.
	Grant-Kohrs Ranch National Historic Site, *see* F737.P88
737.H55	Hi-Line Region
737.H6	Hill Co.
737.J4	Jefferson Co.
	For Lewis and Clark Cavern State Park, see F737.L65
	Jocko or Flathead Indian Reservation, *see* E99.S2
737.J8	Judith Basin Co.
737.J83	Judith River and Valley
737.L3	Lake Co.
	Including St. Ignatius Mission
	For Flathead Lake, see F737.F6
737.L65	Lewis and Clark Cavern State Park
	Including Morrison Cave
737.L67	Lewis and Clark Co.
737.L7	Liberty Co.
737.L8	Lincoln Co.
737.M13	McCone Co.
737.M2	Madison Co.
737.M24	Madison River and Valley, Montana
	Cf. F767.M34 , General, and Wyoming
737.M4	Meagher Co.
737.M48	Milk River and Valley
	Cf. F1079.M54, General and Alberta
737.M5	Mineral Co.
737.M6	Missoula Co.
	Including Camas Prairie
737.M7	Missouri River and Valley, Mont.
	Cf. F598, General
	Morrison Cave, *see* F737.L65
737.M9	Musselshell Co.
737.P23	Park Co.
737.P4	Petroleum Co.
737.P5	Phillips Co.
737.P6	Pondera Co.
737.P8	Powder River Co.
737.P88	Powell Co.
	Including Grant-Kohrs Ranch National Historic Site
737.P9	Prairie Co.
737.P93	Prickly Pear Creek and Valley
737.R3	Ravalli Co.
737.R5	Richland Co.
737.R8	Rocky Mountain region, Mont.
	Including Marias Pass
	Cf. F721, General
737.R9	Roosevelt Co.

	Montana
737.A-.Z	**Regions, counties, etc., A-Z — Continued**
737.R95	Rosebud Co.
737.R96	Rosebud Creek and Valley
737.S3	Sanders Co.
737.S4	Sheridan Co.
737.S5	Silver Bow Co.
737.S8	Stillwater Co.
737.S84	Sun River and Valley
737.S9	Sweet Grass Co.
	Including West Boulder River and Valley
	Sweet Grass Hills, *see* F737.T6
737.T4	Teton Co.
737.T55	Tongue River and Valley
	Cf. F767.T65, Wyoming
737.T6	Toole Co.
	Including Sweet Grass Hills
737.T7	Treasure Co.
737.V3	Valley Co.
737.W4	Wheatland Co.
737.W5	Wibaux Co.
737.Y3	Yellowstone Co.
	Yellowstone National Park, *see* F722
737.Y4	Yellowstone River and Valley (General, and Montana)
	Including Fort Custer
	Cf. F642.M28, North Dakota
	Cf. F767.Y44, Wyoming
739.A-.Z	**Cities, towns, etc., A-Z**
	GALE NOTE *The cutter number(s) listed below have been given only as examples by the Library of Congress*
739.B5	Billings
739.B8	Butte
739.G7	Great Falls
739.H4	Helena
739.M7	Missoula
	Elements in the population
740.A1	General works
740.A2-.Z	Individual elements
	For a list of racial, ethnic, and religious elements (with cutter numbers), see E184.A+
	Idaho
741	**Periodicals. Societies. Collections**
743	**Museums. Exhibitions, exhibits**
744	**Gazetteers. Dictionaries. Geographic names**
744.3	**Guidebooks**
745	**Biography (Collective). Genealogy (Collective)**
745.2	**Historiography**
	Historians, *see* E175.5.A+
745.5	**Study and teaching**
746	**General works. Histories**
	Including admission as a state, July 3, 1890
	Including biography: Frank Steunenberg
	Including by period (Early to 1950) as well as general
	For 1951 and later, see F750+
	Cf. D769.85.I2+, World War II, 1939-1945
	Cf. E83.877, Nez Perce War, 1877
746.3	**Juvenile works**
	Pamphlets, addresses, essays, etc.
746.5	General
746.6	Anecdotes, legends, pageants, etc.
747	**Historic monuments (General). Illustrative material**

	Idaho — Continued
748	**Antiquities (Non-Indian)**
	By period
	Early to 1950, *see* F746
	1951-
750	General works
	Biography
750.2	Collective
750.22.A-.22.Z	Individual, A-Z
	GALE NOTE *See note at the head of Table F5 at the end of the text for further instructions on how to subdivide this number*
752.A-.Z	**Regions, counties, etc., A-Z**
752.A15	Counties
752.A16	Mountains
752.A17	Rivers
752.A18	Lakes
752.A19	Islands
752.A3	Ada Co.
752.A4	Adams Co.
752.A55	Albeni Falls Dam and Region
752.A6	Alturas Co. (1864-1895)
752.B2	Bannock Co.
752.B3	Bear Lake Co.
752.B4	Benewah Co.
752.B55	Big Wood River and Valley
752.B6	Bingham Co.
752.B63	Birch Creek Valley
752.B64	Bird-Truax Trail
752.B65	Blaine Co.
	Including Sawtooth Mountains and Valley
752.B67	Boise Co.
752.B673	Boise River and Valley
752.B677	Bonner Co.
	Including Priest Lake and Region
752.B68	Bonneville Co.
752.B7	Boundaries
	For International boundary, see F597, F854, F880
	For Yellowstone National Park boundary, see F722
	Cf. F897.B7, Washington boundary
752.B73	Boundary Co.
	Bruneau River and Valley, *see* F752.O97
752.B9	Butte Co.
752.C17	Camas Co.
752.C2	Canyon Co.
752.C3	Caribou Co.
	Including Gem Valley
752.C35	Cassia Co.
	Including City of Rocks National Reserve
	City of Rocks National Reserve, *see* F752.C35
752.C55	Clark Co.
752.C57	Clark Fork and Valley
	Cf. F737.C55, General, and Montana
752.C6	Clearwater Co.
752.C62	Clearwater River and Valley
	Coeur d'Alene mining district, *see* F752.S5
752.C65	Coeur d'Alene River and Valley
752.C7	Craters of the Moon National Monument
752.C9	Custer Co.
752.E4	Elmore Co.
752.F7	Franklin Co.

	Idaho
752.A-.Z	**Regions, counties, etc., A-Z — Continued**
752.F8	Fremont Co.
752.G4	Gem Co.
	Gem Valley, *see* F752.C3
	Gilmore Ranch, *see* F752.I2
752.G6	Gooding Co.
	Hagerman Fossil Beds National Monument, *see* F752.T8
752.H44	Hells Canyon National Recreation Area
	Cf. F882.H44, General and Oregon
752.I2	Idaho Co.
	Including Gilmore Ranch, Joseph Plains, Lochea River and Valley
752.I7	Island Park region
752.J4	Jefferson Co.
752.J5	Jerome Co.
752.K8	Kootenai Co.
	For Coeur d'Alene mining district, see F752.S5
752.L3	Latah Co.
752.L4	Lemhi Co.
752.L45	Lewis Co.
752.L5	Lincoln Co.
	Lochea River and Valley, *see* F752.I2
752.M3	Madison Co.
	Mann Creek and Valley, *see* F752.W3
752.M5	Minidoka Co.
752.N57	Nez Perce Co.
752.O5	Oneida Co.
752.O97	Owyhee Co. Owyhee Mountains region
	Including Bruneau River and Valley
752.O98	Owyhee River and Valley
	Cf. F882.O98, General, and Oregon
752.P23	Pahsimeroi River and Valley
752.P25	Palouse River and Valley (General, and Idaho)
	Cf. F897.P24, Washington
752.P3	Payette Co.
752.P33	Payette River and Valley
752.P6	Power Co.
	Priest Lake and Region, *see* F752.B677
752.S28	Saint Maries River and Valley
752.S35	Salmon River and Valley
752.S37	Salt Valley
	Cf. F767.S37, General, and Wyoming
	Sawtooth Mountains and Valley, *see* F752.B65
752.S5	Shoshone Co.
	Including Coeur d'Alene mining district
752.S7	Snake River and Valley (General, and Idaho)
	Cf. F882.S6, Oregon
	Cf. F897.S6, Washington
752.S74	St. Joe River and Valley
752.T4	Teton Co.
752.T5	Teton River and Valley
752.T8	Twin Falls Co.
	Including Hagerman Fossil Beds National Monument
752.V3	Valley Co.
752.W27	Wasatch Range
	Class here works limited to the part of the Wasatch Range located in Idaho
	For general works on the Wasatch Range, as well as works limited to the part located in Utah, see F832.W22
752.W3	Washington Co.
	Including Mann Creek and Valley

Idaho

752.A-.Z	**Regions, counties, etc., A-Z — Continued**
	Yellowstone National Park, *see* F722
754.A-.Z	**Cities, towns, etc., A-Z**
	GALE NOTE *The cutter number(s) listed below have been given only as examples by the Library*
	of Congress
754.B65	Boise
754.I2	Idaho Falls
754.L6	Lewiston
754.P7	Pocatello
754.T97	Twin Falls
	Elements in the population
755.A1	General works
755.A2-.Z	Individual elements
	For a list of racial, ethnic, and religious elements (with cutter numbers), see E184.A+

Wyoming

756	**Periodicals. Societies. Collections**
758	**Museums. Exhibitions, exhibits**
759	**Gazetteers. Dictionaries. Geographic names**
759.3	**Guidebooks**
760	**Biography (Collective). Genealogy (Collective)**
760.2	**Historiography**
	Historians, *see* E175.5.A+
760.5	**Study and teaching**
761	**General works. Histories**
	Including admission as a state, July 10, 1890
	Including by period (Early to 1950) as well as general
	For 1951 and later, see F765
	Cf. D769.85.W8+, World War II, 1939-1945
	Cf. E83.879, Ute War, 1879
761.3	**Juvenile works**
	Pamphlets, addresses, essays, etc.
761.5	General
761.6	Anecdotes, legends, pageants, etc.
762	**Historic monuments (General). Illustrative material**
763	**Antiquities (Non-Indian)**
	By period
	Early to 1950, *see* F761
	1951-
765	General works
	Biography
765.2	Collective
765.22.A-.22.Z	Individual, A-Z
767.A-.Z	**Regions, counties, etc., A-Z**
767.A15	Counties
767.A16	Mountains
767.A17	Rivers
767.A18	Lakes
767.A19	Islands
767.A3	Albany Co.
767.B23	Beartooth Mountains
	Cf. F737.B35, General, and Montana
	Big Horn Canyon National Recreation Area, *see* F737.B49
767.B35	Big Horn Co.
767.B37	Big Horn Mountains (General, and Wyoming)
	Cf. F737.B53 , Montana
767.B4	Big Horn River and Valley, Wyo.
767.B7	Boundaries
	For Yellowstone National Park boundary, see F722
	Bridger Pass Overland Trail, *see* F767.O94

	Wyoming
767.A-.Z	**Regions, counties, etc., A-Z — Continued**
767.C16	Campbell Co.
767.C2	Carbon Co.
	Casper Mountain, *see* F767.N2
767.C55	Clear Creek and Valley (Big Horn County-Sheridan County)
767.C6	Converse Co.
767.C7	Crook Co.
767.D47	Devils Tower National Monument
	Eden Valley, *see* F767.S9
767.F5	Flaming Gorge National Recreation Area (General, and Wyoming)
	Cf. F832.F52, Utah
767.F8	Fremont Co.
767.F88	Front Range
	Cf. F782.F88, General, and Colorado
	Gibbon Falls, *see* F767.Y44
767.G6	Goshen Co.
	Grand Teton National Park, *see* F767.T3
767.G7	Green River and Valley
	Including Brown's Park
767.H6	Hot Springs Co.
767.I38	Independence Rock
	Jackson Hole, *see* F767.T28
767.J3	Jackson Hole National Monument (1943-1950)
	Included (1950) in Grand Teton National Park, Teton National Forest, and Jackson Hole Wildlife Park
	Jackson Lake, *see* F767.T3
	Jenny Lake, *see* F767.T3
767.J8	Johnson Co.
767.L3	Laramie Co.
767.L5	Lincoln Co.
767.M34	Madison River and Valley (General, and Wyoming)
	Cf. F737.M24, Montana
767.M42	Medicine Bow Mountains
	Cf. F782.M43, General, and Colorado
767.M43	Medicine Bow National Forest
767.N2	Natrona Co.
	Including Casper Mountain
	For Independence Rock, see F767.I38
767.N5	Niobrara Co.
767.N52	Niobrara River and Valley, Wyoming
	Cf. F672.N56, General, and Nebraska
767.N8	North Platte River and Valley, Wyo.
	Cf. F672.N8, General, and Nebraska
767.O94	Overland Trail (General, and Wyoming)
	Including Bridger Pass Overland Trail
	Cf. F597, Overland Trails (Northwest)
	Cf. F782.O94, Colorado
767.P3	Park Co.
767.P5	Platte Co.
767.P6	Powder River and Valley, Wyo.
767.S37	Salt Valley (General, and Wyoming)
	Cf. F752.S37, Idaho
767.S55	Sheridan Co.
767.S57	Shoshone National Forest
767.S58	Shoshone River and Valley
	String Lake, *see* F767.T3
767.S8	Sublette Co.
767.S9	Sweetwater Co.
	Including Eden Valley

	Wyoming
767.A-.Z	**Regions, counties, etc., A-Z — Continued**
767.T28	Teton Co.
	Including Jackson Hole
	Teton Mountains
767.T29	General
767.T3	Grand Teton National Park
	Including Jackson Lake, String Lake, Jenny Lake
767.T65	Tongue River and Valley
	Cf. F737.T55, General, and Montana
767.U3	Uinta Co.
767.U33	Uinta Mountains
	Cf. F832.U39, General, and Utah
767.W3	Washakie Co.
767.W4	Weston Co.
767.W5	Wind River and Valley. Wind River Range
	Yellowstone National Park, *see* F722
767.Y44	Yellowstone River and Valley
	Including Gibbon Falls
	Cf. F737.Y4, General, and Montana
769.A-.Z	**Cities, towns, etc., A-Z**
	GALE NOTE *The cutter number(s) listed below have been given only as examples by the Library of Congress*
769.C3	Casper
769.C5	Cheyenne
769.L2	Laramie
	Elements in the population
770.A1	General works
770.A2-.Z	Individual elements
	For a list of racial, ethnic, and religious elements (with cutter numbers), see E184.A+
	Colorado
771	**Periodicals. Societies. Collections**
773	**Museums. Exhibitions, exhibits**
774	**Gazetteers. Dictionaries. Geographic names**
774.3	**Guidebooks**
775	**Biography (Collective). Genealogy (Collective)**
775.2	**Historiography**
	Historians, *see* E175.5.A+
775.5	**Study and teaching**
776	**General works. Histories**
776.3	**Juvenile works**
	Pamphlets, addresses, essays, etc.
776.5	General
776.6	Anecdotes, legends, pageants, etc.
777	**Historic monuments (General). Illustrative material**
778	**Antiquities (Non-Indian)**
	By period
780	Early to 1876
	Including biography: John Evans, Benjamin Franklin Hall, etc.
	Cf. E83.868, Battle of Beecher Island, 1868
	Cf. E333, Louisiana Purchase, 1803
	Cf. F786, Mexican Cession of 1848
	Cf. F801, Purchase of Northwest Texas by United States, 1850
781	1876-1950
	Including admission as a state, August 1, 1876
	Including biography: Robert Wilbur Steele, Davis Hanson Waite, etc.
	Cf. D570.85.C6+, World War I, 1914-1918
	Cf. D769.85.C6+, World War II, 1939-1945
	Cf. E83.879, Ute Indian War, 1879
781.2	1951-1980

	Colorado
	By period — Continued
781.3	1981-
782.A-.Z	**Regions, counties, etc., A-Z**
782.A15	Counties
782.A16	Mountains
782.A17	Rivers
782.A18	Lakes
782.A19	Islands
782.A2	Adams Co.
782.A4	Alamosa Co.
782.A5	Arapahoe Co.
782.A6	Archuleta Co.
782.A7	Arkansas River and Valley, Colo.

Including Bent's Old Fort National Historic Site
For Royal Gorge, see F782.F8
Cf. F417.A7, General, and Arkansas

782.B2	Baca Co.
782.B33	Battlement National Forest
	Beaver Creek and Valley, *see* F782.E15
782.B4	Bent Co.
	Bent's Old Fort National Historic Site, *see* F782.A7
782.B45	Big Thompson River and Valley

Including Big Thompson Canyon

782.B5	Black Canyon of the Gunnison National Monument
782.B6	Boulder Co.

For Longs Peak, see F782.L83

782.B7	Boundaries
	Bridger Pass Overland Trail, *see* F782.O94
782.C5	Chaffee Co.

Including Chalk Creek

782.C55	Cheyenne Co.
	Cheyenne Mountain, *see* F782.E3
782.C59	Clear Creek and Valley
782.C6	Clear Creek Co.
782.C66	Cochetopa National Forest
	Colorado National Monument, *see* F782.M5
782.C7	Colorado River and Valley, Colo.

Formerly Grand River, Colo.
Cf. F788, General

782.C75	Conejos Co.
782.C8	Costilla Co.

Including Sangre de Cristo Grant (Costilla and Trinchera estates)

782.C9	Crowley Co.
782.C95	Custer Co.
782.D4	Delta Co.

Including Surface Creek and Valley

782.D45	Denver Co.
	Dinosaur National Monument, *see* F832.D5
782.D57	Disappointment Creek and Valley
782.D7	Dolores Co.
782.D8	Douglas Co.
782.E15	Eagle Co.

Including Beaver Creek and Valley

782.E25	Elbert Co.
782.E3	El Paso Co.

Including Cave of the Winds, Cheyenne Mountain, Crystal Park, Garden of the Gods
For Pikes Peak, see F782.P63

782.E82	Escalante Canyon
	Estes Park region, *see* F782.L2

	Colorado
782.A-.Z	**Regions, counties, etc., A-Z — Continued**
782.F8	Fremont Co.
	Including Royal Gorge (Grand Canyon of the Arkansas)
782.F88	Front Range (General, and Colorado)
	Cf. F767.F88, Wyoming
	Garden of the Gods, *see* F782.E3
782.G3	Garfield Co.
	Including Glenwood Canyon
782.G4	Gilpin Co.
	Glenwood Canyon, *see* F782.G3
	Grand Canyon of the Arkansas, *see* F782.F8
782.G7	Grand Co.
	Including Grand Lake (Lake)
782.G73	Grand Mesa
	Grand River and Valley, Colo., *see* F782.C7
782.G78	Great Sand Dunes National Monument
782.G9	Gunnison Co.
782.H5	Hinsdale Co.
782.H6	Holy Cross, Mount of the
782.H8	Huerfano Co.
782.J3	Jackson Co.
	Including North Park
782.J4	Jefferson Co.
782.K4	Kiowa Co.
782.K5	Kit Carson Co.
782.L15	Lake Co.
782.L18	La Plata Co.
782.L2	Larimer Co.
	Including Estes Park region
782.L3	Las Animas Co.
	Including Pinon Canyon
782.L4	Leadville National Forest
	Lime Creek and Valley, *see* F782.S18
782.L6	Lincoln Co.
	Lodore, Canyon of, *see* F782.M65
782.L8	Logan Co.
782.L83	Longs Peak
	Manti La Sal National Forest, *see* F832.M3
	Maxwell Land Grant, *see* F802.M38
782.M43	Medicine Bow Mountains (General, and Colorado)
	Cf. F767.M42, Wyoming
782.M5	Mesa Co.
	Including Colorado National Monument
782.M52	Mesa Verde National Park
	Cf. E99.P9, Pueblo Indian antiquities
782.M6	Mineral Co.
782.M65	Moffat Co.
	Including Canyon of Lodore
	For Dinosaur National Monument, see F832.D5
782.M7	Montezuma Co.
	Including Mancos River and Valley, Colo.
782.M8	Montrose Co.
	For Uncompahgre Valley, see F782.U5
782.M9	Morgan Co.
	North Park, *see* F782.J3
782.O8	Otero Co.
782.O9	Ouray Co.
782.O94	Overland Trail
	Including Bridger Pass Overland Trail

	Colorado
782.A-.Z	**Regions, counties, etc., A-Z**
782.O94	Overland Trail — Continued
	Cf. F597, Overland Trails (Northwest)
	Cf. F767.O94, Bridger Pass Overland Trail (General, and Wyoming)
782.P3	Park Co.
782.P37	Peak-to-Peak Highway
782.P5	Phillips Co.
782.P52	Piceance Creek and watershed
782.P63	Pikes Peak
	Including Pike National Forest
	Pinon Canyon, *see* F782.L3
782.P7	Pitkin Co.
782.P8	Prowers Co.
782.P9	Pueblo Co.
782.R36	Red Mountain Mining District
782.R4	Rio Blanco Co.
	Including White River and Valley (General, and Colorado)
	Cf. F832.U4, White River and Valley, Utah
782.R45	Rio Grande Co.
782.R46	Rio Grande National Forest
782.R52	Roaring Fork Valley
782.R59	Rocky Mountain National Park
	For Estes Park region, see F782.L2
	For Longs Peak, see F782.L83
782.R6	Rocky Mountain region, Colo.
	Including Colorado Trail
	For Pikes Peak, see F782.P63
	Cf. F721, General
782.R7	Routt Co.
782.R8	Routt National Forest
	Royal Gorge, *see* F782.F8
782.S14	Saguache Co.
782.S15	St. Vrain Creek and Valley
782.S17	San Juan Co.
782.S18	San Juan Mountains
	Including Lime Creek and Valley
782.S19	San Juan region
782.S2	San Luis Park (Valley)
	Cf. F782.C8, Sangre de Cristo Grant
782.S23	San Miguel Co.
	Sangre de Cristo Grant, *see* F782.C8
782.S26	Sangre de Cristo Mountains
	Cf. F802.S32, General, and New Mexico
782.S4	Sedgwick Co.
782.S53	Smoky Hill River and Valley
	Cf. F687.S84, General, and Kansas
782.S6	South Park (Region)
782.S7	South Platte River and Valley, Colo.
	Cf. F672.S7, General, and Nebraska
782.S76	Spanish Peaks
782.S95	Summit Co.
	Surface Creek and Valley, *see* F782.D4
782.T37	Tarryall Mountains
782.T4	Teller Co.
782.U5	Uncompahgre Valley
	Including Uncompahgre National Forest
782.U8	Ute Pass
782.W3	Washington Co.
782.W4	Weld Co.

	Colorado
782.A-.Z	**Regions, counties, etc., A-Z — Continued**
782.W46	West Elk Loop Scenic and Historic Byway
	White River and Valley (General, and Colorado), *see* F782.R4
782.Y8	Yuma Co.
784.A-.Z	**Cities, towns, etc., A-Z**
	GALE NOTE *The cutter number(s) listed below have been given only as examples by the Library of Congress*
784.A7	Aspen
784.C4	Central City
784.C7	Colorado Springs
784.C8	Cripple Creek
784.D4	Denver
	Subarrange by Table F2 at the end of the text
784.G7	Greeley
784.L4	Leadville
784.M3	Manitou
784.P9	Pueblo
	Elements in the population
785.A1	General works
785.A2-.Z	Individual elements
	For a list of racial, ethnic, and religious elements (with cutter numbers), see E184.A+
	The New Southwest. Southwestern States
785.3	**Guidebooks**
785.5	**Biography (Collective). Genealogy (Collective)**
786	**1848-1950**
	Including the region of the Mexican Cession of 1848, the Texas Purchase of 1850, and the Gadsden Purchase
	Including Mexican boundary; Santa Fe Trail; frontier troubles with Mexico; Gadsden Purchase, 1853
	Including biography: William H. Bonney (Billy the Kid), etc.
	Cf. E78.S7, Indians of the New Southwest
	Cf. E401+, War with Mexico, 1845-1848
	Cf. E470.9, Civil War, 1861-1865 (Military operations)
	Cf. F799+, Southwest before 1848
	Cf. F1232, Mexican frontier troubles (General)
787	**1951-**
788	**Colorado River, Canyon, and Valley**
	Including Grand Canyon National Park and Lake Mead National Recreation Area
788.5	**Four Corners Region**
789	**Great Basin**
	Elements in the population
790.A1	General works
790.A2-.Z	Individual elements
	For a list of racial, ethnic, and religious elements (with cutter numbers), see E184.A+
	New Mexico
791	**Periodicals. Societies. Collections**
793	**Museums. Exhibitions, exhibits**
794	**Gazetteers. Dictionaries. Geographic names**
794.3	**Guidebooks**
795	**Biography (Collective). Genealogy (Collective)**
795.2	**Historiography**
	Historians, *see* E175.5.A+
795.5	**Study and teaching**
796	**General works. Histories**
796.3	**Juvenile works**
	Pamphlets, addresses, essays, etc.
796.5	General
796.6	Anecdotes, legends, pageants, etc.
797	**Historic monuments (General). Illustrative material**

	New Mexico — Continued
798	**Antiquities (Non-Indian)**
	By period
799	Early to 1822
	Including Spanish discoveries and settlements in the Southwest between the Mississippi River and California; seven cities of Cibola; Quivira; Spanish province; Pimería Alta
	Including biography: Eusebio Francisco Kino, Diego Dionisio de Peñalosa, etc.
	Cf. F1410, Spaniards in North America (General)
800	1822-1848
	Including Mexican state, region between Texas and California
	Cf. E405.2, Conquest by United States Troops, War with Mexico, 1845-1848
	Cf. F389, Texas
	Cf. F390, Texan Santa Fe Expedition, 1841
	Cf. F786, Santa Fe Trail
	Cf. F826, Utah
801	1848-1950
	Including admission as a state, January 6, 1912
	Including purchase of northwest Texas by United States, 1850
	Including biography: Octaviano Ambrosio Larrazola, Antonio Miguel Otero, etc.
	Cf. D769.85.M33+, World War II, 1939-1945
	Cf. E83.88, Apache War, 1883-1886
	Cf. E423, Compromise of 1850
	Cf. E522.1+, Civil War, 1861-1865 (General)
	Cf. E470.9, Military operations in the Civil War, 1861-1865
	Cf. E571.1+, Confederate history
	Cf. F786, Gadsden Purchase, 1853
	1951-
801.2	General works
	Biography
801.3	Collective
801.4.A-.4.Z	Individual, A-Z
802.A-.Z	**Regions, counties, etc., A-Z**
802.A15	Counties
802.A16	Mountains
802.A17	Rivers
802.A18	Lakes
802.A19	Islands
	Aztec Ruins National Monument, *see E99.P9*
802.B25	Bandelier National Monument
	Including Frijoles Canyon
802.B5	Bernalillo Co.
802.B58	Bisti
802.B63	Black Range
802.B7	Boundaries
	For International boundary, see F786
	Cf. F392.B7, Texas boundary
	Cf. F782.B7, Colorado boundary
802.C2	Canadian River and Valley, N. Mex.
	Cf. F702.C2, General, and Oklahoma
	Capulin Volcano National Monument, *see F802.U5*
802.C28	Carlsbad Caverns
	Including Carlsbad Caverns National Park
802.C3	Catron Co.
802.C4	Chaco Canyon
	Including Chaco Canyon National Monument
802.C45	Chama Valley
	Including Rio Chama
802.C5	Chaves Co.
802.C52	Chihuahuan Desert

New Mexico

802.A-.Z	**Regions, counties, etc., A-Z — Continued**
802.C54	Cibola Co.
	Including El Malpais National Monument, El Malpais National Conservation Area
802.C7	Colfax Co.
	Including Moreno Creek and Valley
802.C8	Curry Co.
802.D4	De Baca Co.
802.D6	Dona Ana Co.
	For Mesilla Valley, see F802.M4
802.E2	Eddy Co.
	For Carlsbad Caverns, see F802.C28
	El Malpais National Conservation Area, *see F802.C54*
	El Malpais National Monument, *see F802.C54*
802.E5	El Morro National Monument
802.E8	Española Valley
	Frijoles Canyon, *see F802.B25*
	Gadsden Purchase, *see F786*
802.G54	Gila River and Valley
	Cf. F817.G52, General, and Arizona
802.G62	Gobermador Canyon
802.G7	Grant Co.
	Including Mimbres River and Valley
802.G9	Guadalupe Co.
	Including Leonard Wood Co. (1903-1904), Santa Rosa Lake and Region
802.G93	Guadalupe Mountains (General, and New Mexico)
	Cf. F392.G86, Texas
802.H3	Harding Co.
802.H5	Hidalgo Co.
802.H84	Hueco Mountains
	Cf. F392.H82, General, and Texas
	Jemez Mountains, *see F802.S3*
	Jornada del Muerto Road, *see F802.J67*
802.J67	Jornada del Muerto Wilderness. Jornada del Muerto Road
802.L4	Lea Co.
	Leonard Wood Co. (1903-1904), *see F802.G9*
802.L7	Lincoln Co.
802.L84	Los Alamos Co.
802.L9	Luna Co.
802.M2	McKinley Co.
802.M34	Manzano Mountains
802.M38	Maxwell Land Grant
802.M4	Mesilla Valley
	For Gadsden Purchase, see F786
	Mimbres River and Valley, *see F802.G7*
802.M6	Mora Co.
	Moreno Creek and Valley, *see F802.C7*
802.O7	Otero Co.
802.P25	Pajarito Plateau
802.P3	Pecos River and Valley, N. Mex.
	Cf. F392.P3, General, and Texas
802.P5	Pine Lawn Valley
802.P83	Puerco River and Valley (General, and New Mexico)
802.Q2	Quay Co.
	Red River, *see F802.T2*
802.R36	Red River and Valley
	Cf. F377.R3, General, and Louisiana
802.R4	Rio Arriba Co.
	Rio Chama, *see F802.C45*

	New Mexico
802.A-.Z	**Regions, counties, etc., A-Z — Continued**
802.R5	Rio Grande and Valley, N. Mex.
	Cf. F392.R5, General, and Texas
802.R68	Rocky Mountain region, N. Mex.
	Cf. F721, General
802.R7	Roosevelt Co.
802.S13	Salinas National Monument
802.S15	San Andres Mountains
802.S18	San Juan Co.
	San Mateo Mountains, *see* F802.V3
802.S2	San Miguel Co.
802.S28	Sandia Mountains
802.S3	Sandoval Co.
	Including Jemez Mountains
	For Frijoles Canyon, see F802.B25
	For Sangre de Cristo Grant, see F782.C8
802.S32	Sangre de Cristo Mountains (General, and New Mexico)
	Cf. F782.S26, Colorado
802.S4	Santa Fe Co.
	Santa Rosa Lake and Region, *see* F802.G9
802.S5	Sierra Co.
802.S6	Socorro Co.
802.T2	Taos Co.
	Including Red River
	Cf. F782.C8 , Sangre de Cristo Grant
802.T47	Tewa Basin
802.T6	Torrance Co.
802.U5	Union Co.
	Including Capulin Volcano National Monument
802.V3	Valencia Co.
	Including San Mateo Mountains
	For Leonard Wood Co. (1903-1904), see F802.G9
802.W44	White Sands Missile Range
802.W45	White Sands National Monument
804.A-.Z	**Cities, towns, etc., A-Z**
	GALE NOTE *The cutter number(s) listed below have been given only as examples by the Library of Congress*
804.A3	Albuquerque
804.L6	Los Alamos
804.S2	Santa Fe
	Subarrange by Table F2 at the end of the text
804.T2	Taos
	Elements in the population
805.A1	General works
805.A2-.Z	Individual elements
	For a list of racial, ethnic, and religious elements (with cutter numbers), see E184.A+
	Arizona
806	**Periodicals. Societies. Collections**
808	**Museums. Exhibitions, exhibits**
809	**Gazetteers. Dictionaries. Geographic names**
809.3	**Guidebooks**
810	**Biography (Collective). Genealogy (Collective)**
810.2	**Historiography**
	Historians, *see* E175.5.A+
810.5	**Study and teaching**
811	**General works. Histories**
	Including admission as a state, February 14, 1912
	Including by period (Early to 1950) as well as general
	For 1951 and later, see F815

	Arizona
811	**General works. Histories — Continued**
	Cf. D769.85.A7+, World War II, 1939-1945
	Cf. E83.88, Apache War, 1883-1886
	Cf. E470.9, E472.3, E473.4, E474.1, Civil War, 1861-1865
	Cf. F786, Mexican Cession of 1848; Gadsden Purchase of 1853
811.3	**Juvenile works**
	Pamphlets, addresses, essays
811.5	General
811.6	Anecdotes, legends, pageants, etc.
812	**Historic monuments (General). Illustrative material**
813	**Antiquities (Non-Indian)**
	By period
	Early to 1950, *see* F811
	1951-
815	General works
	Biography
815.2	Collective
815.3.A-.3.Z	Individual, A-Z
	GALE NOTE *See note at the head of Table F5 at the end of the text for further instructions on how to subdivide this number*
817.A-.Z	**Regions, counties, etc., A-Z**
817.A15	Counties
817.A16	Mountains
817.A17	Rivers
817.A18	Lakes
817.A19	Islands
817.A6	Apache Co.
817.A73	Aravaipa Canyon
817.A75	Arizona Strip
817.B5	Big Sandy River and region
	Bonita Creek and Valley, *see* F817.G7
817.B7	Boundaries
	For International boundary, see F786
817.C3	Canyon de Chelly National Monument
817.C35	Casa Grande National Monument
	Chiricahua National Monument, *see* F817.C5
817.C5	Cochise Co.
	Including Chiricahua National Monument, Coronado National Memorial, Sulphur Springs Valley
817.C6	Coconino Co.
	Including Sunset Crater Volcano National Monument
817.C7	Colorado River and Valley, Ariz.
	For Grand Canyon, see F788
	Cf. F788, General
	Gadsden Purchase, *see* F786
817.G5	Gila Co.
	Including Pleasant Valley
817.G52	Gila River and Valley (General, and Arizona)
	Cf. F802.G54, New Mexico
	Glen Canyon National Recreation Area, *see* F832.G5
817.G7	Graham Co.
	Including Bonita Creek and Valley
	Grand Canyon National Park, *see* F788
817.G8	Greenlee Co.
	Havasu Canyon, *see* F788
817.L5	Little Colorado River and Valley
817.M3	Maricopa Co.
	Lake Mead National Recreation Area, *see* F788
817.M5	Mohave Co.
	Including Pipe Spring National Monument

	Arizona
817.A-.Z	**Regions, counties, etc., A-Z — Continued**
	Mohawk Valley, *see* F817.Y9
817.M57	Montezuma Castle National Monument
817.M6	Monument Valley
817.N3	Navajo Co.
817.O7	Organ Pipe Cactus National Monument
817.P2	Painted Desert
817.P4	Petrified Forest National Monument
817.P5	Pima Co.
	Including Quijotoa Mountains
	For Santa Catalina Mountains, see F817.S28
817.P6	Pinal Co.
	Pipe Spring National Monument, *see* F817.M5
	Pleasant Valley, *see* F817.G5
	Powell, Lake, *see* F832.G5
817.S18	Saguaro National Park
817.S2	Salt River and Valley
817.S25	San Pedro River and Valley (General and Arizona)
	Cf. F1346, Mexico
817.S28	Santa Catalina Mountains
817.S3	Santa Cruz Co.
817.S33	Santa Cruz River and Valley
	Sulphur Springs Valley, *see* F817.C5
	Sunset Crater Volcano National Monument, *see* F817.C6
817.S9	Superstition Mountains
817.T66	Tonto River and Valley
817.T8	Tumacacori National Monument
817.V37	Verde River and Valley
817.W47	Wet Beaver Creek and Valley
817.W8	Wupatki National Monument
817.Y3	Yavapai Co.
817.Y9	Yuma Co.
	Including Lechuguilla Desert, Mohawk Valley
819.A-.Z	**Cities, towns, etc., A-Z**
	GALE NOTE *The cutter number(s) listed below have been given only as examples by the Library of Congress*
819.G5	Globe
819.P57	Phoenix
819.T6	Tombstone
819.T9	Tucson
	Subarrange by Table F2 at the end of the text
	Elements in the population
820.A1	General works
820.A2-.Z	Individual elements
	For a list of racial, ethnic, and religious elements (with cutter numbers), see E184.A+
	Utah
821	**Periodicals. Societies. Collections**
823	**Museums. Exhibitions, exhibits**
824	**Gazetteers. Dictionaries. Geographic names**
824.3	**Guidebooks**
825	**Biography (Collective). Genealogy (Collective)**
825.2	**Historiography**
	Historians, *see* E175.5.A+
825.5	**Study and teaching**
826	**General works. Histories**
	Including admission as a state, January 4, 1896
	Including by period (Early to 1950) as well as general
	For 1951 and later, see F830

	Utah
826	**General works. Histories — Continued**
	Including Mormon settlement; State of Deseret; Mountain Meadows Massacre, 1857; Mormon Rebellion, 1857-1859
	Including biography: Jacob Hamblin, John Doyle Lee, etc.
	Cf. BX8601-8695, Mormons (Church of Jesus Christ of Latter Day Saints)
	Cf. D570.85.U8+, World War I, 1914-1918
	Cf. D769.85.U8+, World War II, 1939-1945
	Cf. E423, Compromise of 1850
826.3	**Juvenile works**
	Pamphlets, addresses, essays, etc.
826.5	General
826.6	Anecdotes, legends, pageants, etc.
827	**Historic monuments (General). Illustrative material**
828	**Antiquities (Non-Indian)**
	By period
	Early to 1950, *see* F826
	1951-
830	General works
	Biography
830.2	Collective
830.3.A-.Z	Individual, A-Z
	GALE NOTE *See note at the head of Table F5 at the end of the text for further instructions on how to subdivide this number*
832.A-.Z	**Regions, counties, etc., A-Z**
832.A15	Counties
832.A16	Mountains
832.A17	Rivers
832.A18	Lakes
832.A19	Islands
832.A7	Arches National Park
832.B3	Bear River and Valley
832.B35	Beaver Co.
832.B6	Lake Bonneville
832.B7	Boundaries
832.B8	Box Elder Co.
	For Bear River and Valley, see F832.B3
	Brown's Park, *see* F767.G7
832.B9	Bryce Canyon National Park
832.C3	Cache Co.
	Including Cache Valley
832.C35	Cache National Forest
832.C37	Canyonlands National Park
	Capitol Reef National Park, *see* F832.W27
832.C4	Carbon Co.
	Cedar Breaks National Monument, *see* F832.I6
	Cedar Mesa, *see* F832.S4
832.C7	Colorado River and Valley, Utah
	Formerly Grand River, Utah
	Cf. F788, General
832.D2	Daggett Co.
832.D3	Davis Co.
832.D5	Dinosaur National Monument
	For Canyon of Lodore, see F782.M65
832.D8	Duchesne Co.
832.E5	Emery Co.
832.F52	Flaming Gorge National Recreation Area
	Cf. F767.F5, General, and Wyoming
832.G3	Garfield Co.

	Utah
832.A-.Z	**Regions, counties, etc., A-Z — Continued**
832.G5	Glen Canyon National Recreation Area
	Including Lake Powell
832.G65	Grand Co.
	Grand River and Valley, Utah, *see* F832.C7
832.G66	Grand Staircase-Escalante National Monument
832.G7	Great Salt Lake and region
	Including Great Salt Desert
	Green River and Valley, *see* F767.G7
832.I6	Iron Co.
	Including Cedar Breaks National Monument
832.J8	Juab Co.
832.K3	Kane Co.
	Manti Canyon, *see* F832.S42
832.M3	Manti La Sal National Forest
832.M5	Millard Co.
	Monument Valley, *see* F817.M6
832.M6	Morgan Co.
832.N55	Nine Mile Canyon
	Parley's Canyon, *see* F832.S2
832.P5	Piute Co.
	Powell, Lake, *see* F832.G5
832.R3	Rainbow Bridge. Rainbow Bridge National Monument
832.R5	Rich Co.
832.S2	Salt Lake Co.
	Including Parley's Canyon
832.S4	San Juan Co.
	Including Cedar Mesa
832.S415	San Rafael River and Valley. San Rafael Swell
	San Rafael Swell, *see* F832.S415
832.S42	Sanpete Co.
	Including Manti Canyon
832.S6	Sevier Co.
832.S9	Summit Co.
832.T6	Tooele Co.
832.U39	Uinta Mountains (General, and Utah)
	Cf. F676.U33, Wyoming
832.U4	Uintah Co.
	Including Uintah Basin, White River and Valley, Utah
	Cf. F782.R4, White River and Valley (General, and Colorado)
	Uncompahgre Indian Reservation, *see* E99.U8
832.U8	Utah Co.
	Utah National Park, *see* F832.B9
832.W2	Wasatch Co.
832.W22	Wasatch Range
	Class here general works on the Wasatch Range, as well as works limited to the part located in Utah
	For works limited to the part of the Wasatch Range located in Idaho, see F752.W27
832.W24	Washington Co.
832.W27	Wayne Co.
	Including Capitol Reef National Park
832.W3	Weber Co.
	Including Ben Lomond
	White River and Valley, Utah, *see* F832.U4
832.Z8	Zion National Park
834.A-.Z	**Cities, towns, etc., A-Z**
	GALE NOTE *The cutter number(s) listed below have been given only as examples by the Library of Congress*
834.L8	Logan

	Nevada
847.A-.Z	**Regions, counties, etc., A-Z — Continued**
847.E8	Eureka Co.
847.F6	Fort Churchill Historic State Monument
847.G32	Gabbs Valley
847.G7	Grass Valley
847.G73	Great Basin National Park
847.H8	Humboldt Co.
	Including Paradise Valley
847.H85	Humboldt River and Valley
847.L3	Lander Co.
847.L5	Lincoln Co.
847.L9	Lyon Co.
	Lake Mead National Recreation Area, *see F788*
847.M5	Mineral Co.
	Including Walker River and Valley
	Moapa River and Valley, *see F847.C5*
847.N9	Nye Co.
	Including Ellsworth Canyon
847.O6	Ormsby Co.
	Owyhee Mountains region, *see F752.O97*
847.O98	Owyhee River and Valley
	Cf. F882.O98, General, and Oregon
	Paradise Valley, *see F847.H8*
847.P4	Pershing Co.
847.R33	Rainbow Canyon
	Red Rock Canyon National Conservation Area, *see F847.C5*
847.S8	Storey Co.
	Lake Tahoe, *see F868.T2*
	Valley of Fire, *see F847.C5*
	Walker River and Valley, *see F847.M5*
847.W3	Washoe Co.
847.W5	White Pine Co.
849.A-.Z	**Cities, towns, etc., A-Z**
	GALE NOTE *The cutter number(s) listed below have been given only as examples by the Library of Congress*
849.A9	Austin
849.C3	Carson City
	Comstock Lode, *see F849.V8*
849.L35	Las Vegas
849.R4	Reno
849.V8	Virginia City. Comstock Lode
	Elements in the population
850.A1	General works
850.A2-.Z	Individual elements
	For a list of racial, ethnic, and religious elements (with cutter numbers), see E184.A+
	The Pacific States
	Including Pacific coast of North America, works on the coast of America (North and South), Pacific Northwest
	Cf. E78.P2, Indians of the Pacific States
	Cf. E83.84, Wars with the Pacific coast Indians, 1847-1865
850.5	**Biography (Collective). Genealogy (Collective)**
851	**General works**
851.5	**Exploring expeditions to the Pacific coast before 1800**
	For California explorations since 1800, see F864
	For Oregon explorations since 1800, see F880
	For Alaska explorations since 1800, see F907
	For British Columbia explorations since 1800, see F1088
851.7	**Cascade Range**
	Cf. F882.C3, Cascade Range in Oregon

	The Pacific States
851.7	**Cascade Range — Continued**
	Cf. F897.C3, Cascade Range in Washington (State)
	The Pacific Northwest
	Including Washington, Oregon, Idaho, Montana, British Columbia
	By period
	Early to 1769, *see* F851.5
	1769-1859, *see* F880
852	1859-1950
	Cf. E78.N77, Indians of the Pacific Northwest
852.2	1951-1980
852.3	1981-
853	Columbia River and Valley
	Cf. F882.C63, Oregon
	Cf. F897.C7, Washington
854	Northwest boundary of the United States, 1846-
	Including Rocky Mountains to the Pacific
	Boundary controversy before 1846, *see* F880
	Elements in the population
855	General works
855.2.A-.2.Z	Individual elements, A-Z
	For a list of racial, ethnic, and religious elements (with cutter numbers), see E184.A+
	California
856	**Periodicals. Societies. Collections**
858	**Museums. Exhibitions, exhibits**
859	**Gazetteers. Dictionaries. Geographic names**
859.3	**Guidebooks**
860	**Biography (Collective). Genealogy (Collective)**
860.2	**Historiography**
	Historians, *see* E175.5.A+
860.5	**Study and teaching**
861	**General works. Histories**
861.3	**Juvenile works**
861.5	**Pamphlets, addresses, essays, etc.**
861.6	**Anecdotes, legends, pageants, etc.**
861.8	**Geography**
862	**Historic monuments (General). Illustrative material**
	Including Spanish mission buildings (General)
863	**Antiquities (Non-Indian)**
	By period
864	Early to 1869
	Admission as a state, September 9, 1850
	Including Spanish explorers after 1769; Spanish California, including Lower and Upper California; Indian missions; American and European intrigues before 1846; Fremont in California, 1846; Bear Flag War, 1846
	Including biography: John Bidwell, William Brown Ide, Peter Lassen, Junípero Serra, David Smith Terry, Mariano Guadalupe Vallejo, George Calvert Yount, Augustín Juan Vicente Zamorano, etc.
	Cf. E83.84, Wars with Pacific coast Indians, 1847-1865
	Cf. E83.858, Mill Creek War, 1857-1865
	Cf. E405.2, American military conquest, 1846
	Cf. E423, Compromise of 1850
	Cf. E497.1+, Civil War, 1861-1865 (General)
	Cf. F786, Mexican cession of 1848
	Cf. F1089.N8, Nootka Sound Controversy, 1789-1790
	Cf. F1246+, Lower California
	For explorations before 1769, see F851.5
865	1848-1856
	Including gold discoveries; Argonauts; voyages to California by the Cape Horn or Central American isthmus routes; vigilance committees

	California
	By period
864	Early to 1869
865	1848-1856— Continued

<table>
<tr><td></td><td>Including biography: William Tell Coleman, James Wilson Marshall, John Marsh, Joaquin
Murrieta, John Augustus Sutter, etc.</td></tr>
<tr><td></td><td>Cf. F593, Overland journeys from the East</td></tr>
<tr><td>866</td><td>1869-1950</td></tr>
<tr><td></td><td>Cf. D570.85.C2+, World War I, 1914-1918</td></tr>
<tr><td></td><td>Cf. D769.85.C2+, World War II, 1939-1945</td></tr>
<tr><td></td><td>Cf. E83.87, Modoc War, 1872-1873</td></tr>
<tr><td></td><td>Cf. E726.C1, War of 1898 (Spanish-American War)</td></tr>
<tr><td></td><td>1951-</td></tr>
<tr><td>866.2</td><td>General works</td></tr>
<tr><td></td><td>Biography</td></tr>
<tr><td>866.3</td><td>Collective</td></tr>
<tr><td>866.4.A-.4.Z</td><td>Individual, A-Z</td></tr>
<tr><td></td><td>GALE NOTE See note at the head of Table F5 at the end of the text for further
instructions on how to subdivide this number</td></tr>
<tr><td>867</td><td>Southern California</td></tr>
<tr><td></td><td>Cf. F864, Early Spanish missions</td></tr>
<tr><td>867.5</td><td>Northern California</td></tr>
<tr><td>868.A-.Z</td><td>Regions, counties, etc., A-Z</td></tr>
<tr><td>868.A15</td><td>Counties</td></tr>
<tr><td>868.A16</td><td>Mountains</td></tr>
<tr><td>868.A17</td><td>Rivers</td></tr>
<tr><td>868.A18</td><td>Lakes</td></tr>
<tr><td>868.A19</td><td>Islands</td></tr>
<tr><td>868.A3</td><td>Alameda Co.</td></tr>
<tr><td></td><td>Including Livermore Valley</td></tr>
<tr><td></td><td>Alcatraz Island, see F868.S156</td></tr>
<tr><td></td><td>Algodones Dunes, see F868.I2</td></tr>
<tr><td>868.A35</td><td>Alpine Co.</td></tr>
<tr><td>868.A4</td><td>Amador Co.</td></tr>
<tr><td>868.A44</td><td>American River and Valley</td></tr>
<tr><td></td><td>Anacapa Island, see F868.V5</td></tr>
<tr><td></td><td>Anderson Valley, see F868.M5</td></tr>
<tr><td>868.A5</td><td>Angeles National Forest</td></tr>
<tr><td></td><td>Annadel State Park, see F868.S7</td></tr>
<tr><td></td><td>Anza-Borrego Desert State Park, see F868.S15</td></tr>
<tr><td></td><td>Ashurst Colony, see F868.S13</td></tr>
<tr><td></td><td>Balboa Island, see F868.O6</td></tr>
<tr><td></td><td>Barona Valley, see F868.S15</td></tr>
<tr><td></td><td>Beckworth Trail, see F868.S5</td></tr>
<tr><td></td><td>Big Creek Lake, see F868.S14</td></tr>
<tr><td>868.B5</td><td>Big Oak Flat Road</td></tr>
<tr><td>868.B7</td><td>Boundaries</td></tr>
<tr><td>868.B8</td><td>Butte Co.</td></tr>
<tr><td>868.C14</td><td>Calaveras Big Tree National Forest</td></tr>
<tr><td>868.C15</td><td>Calaveras Big Trees State Park</td></tr>
<tr><td>868.C16</td><td>Calaveras Co.</td></tr>
<tr><td></td><td>For Calaveras Big Trees State Park, see F868.C15</td></tr>
<tr><td></td><td>California Redwood Park (Santa Cruz Co.), see F868.S3</td></tr>
<tr><td></td><td>Capay Valley, see F868.Y5</td></tr>
<tr><td></td><td>Cape Horn, see F868.S5</td></tr>
<tr><td></td><td>Carquinez Strait, see F868.S156</td></tr>
<tr><td></td><td>Catalina Island, see F868.L8</td></tr>
<tr><td>868.C45</td><td>Central Valley</td></tr>
<tr><td></td><td>Channel Islands, see F868.S232</td></tr>
<tr><td></td><td>Chocolate Mountains, see F868.I2</td></tr>
</table>

	California
868.A-.Z	**Regions, counties, etc., A-Z — Continued**
	Coachella Valley, *see* F868.R6
	Colorado Desert, *see* F868.I2
868.C6	Colorado River and Valley, Calif.
	Cf. F788, General
868.C7	Colusa Co.
868.C74	Conejo Valley
868.C76	Contra Costa Co.
	Including Winter Island, Mount Diablo State Park
	Crane Valley Dam and Lake, *see* F868.M2
868.D2	Death Valley
	Including Death Valley National Monument, Scotty's Castle
868.D4	Del Norte Co.
868.D45	Delta Region
	Donner Lake, *see* F868.N5
	Eagle Lake, *see* F868.L33
868.E22	East Bay
868.E25	Eel River and Valley
868.E28	El Camino Real
868.E3	El Dorado Co.
	Including Wrights Lake
	Emerald Bay and region, *see* F868.O6
	Emigrant Trail, *see* F868.S5
	Empire Mine State Historic Park, *see* F868.N5
868.F24	Farallon Islands (Farallones)
868.F3	Feather River, Canyon, and Valley
	Forest of Nisene Marks State Park, *see* F868.S3
868.F8	Fresno Co.
	Including Shaver Lake
	For San Joaquin Valley, see F868.S173
868.G39	Gazos Creek and Valley
	General Grant National Park, *see* F868.K48
868.G5	Glenn Co.
	Goat Island, *see* F869.S3
	Golden Gate National Recreation Area, *see* F868.S156
	Guenoc Valley, *see* F868.L2
	Hearst-San Simeon State Historical Monument, *see* F868.S18
	Huichica Creek and Valley, *see* F868.N2
868.H8	Humboldt Co.
	Including Humboldt Bay, Humboldt Redwoods State Park, Shelter Cove
868.I2	Imperial Co.
	Including Chocolate Mountains, Colorado Desert, Imperial Valley, Algodones Dunes
	Indian Wells Valley, *see* F868.K3
868.I6	Inyo Co.
	Including Manzanar National Historic Site
	For Death Valley, see F868.D2
	Irvine Park, *see* F868.O6
	Jalama Beach Park, *see* F868.S23
	John Muir Trail, *see* F868.S5
868.J6	Joshua Tree National Monument
868.K3	Kern Co.
	Including Indian Wells Valley, Tejon Ranch
868.K48	Kings Canyon National Park
	Including General Grant Grove area (General Grant National Park until 1940)
868.K5	Kings Co.
868.K55	Klamath River and Valley
868.L2	Lake Co.
	Including Guenoc Valley
	Lake Elsinore and region, *see* F868.R6

868.A-.Z	**California** **Regions, counties, etc., A-Z — Continued**
868.L33	Lassen Co.
	Including Eagle Lake
868.L34	Lassen Peak. Lassen Volcanic National Park
868.L38	Lava Beds National Monument
868.L8	Los Angeles Co.
	Including Mount Lowe, Rustic Canyon, San Fernando Valley, San Gabriel Valley, Santa Catalina Island, Santa Clarita Valley, Santa Monica Bay region, Santa Monica Canyon, Los Angeles River
	For Channel Islands, see F868.S232
	Los Angeles River, *see* F868.L8
868.L83	Los Padres National Forest
	Lytle Creek Canyon, *see* F868.S14
868.M2	Madera Co.
	Including Crane Valley Dam and Lake
	Malakoff Diggins State Historic Park, *see* F868.N5
	Manzanar National Historic Site, *see* F868.I6
868.M3	Marin Co.
	Including Marin Peninsula, Mount Tamalpais State Park, Muir Woods National Monument
868.M4	Mariposa Co.
	Including Fremont Land Grant (Mariposa estate), etc.
868.M5	Mendocino Co.
	Including Anderson Valley, Mendocino Headlands State Park, and Round Valley
868.M55	Merced Co.
	Mineral King Valley, *see* F868.T8
868.M6	Modoc Co.
	Including Surprise Valley
868.M65	Mohave (Mojave) Desert
868.M67	Mono Co.
	Including Mono Lake
	Mono Lake, *see* F868.M67
	Monterey Bay, *see* F868.M7
868.M7	Monterey Co.
	Including Point Lobos, Monterey Bay, Pfeiffer Big Sur State Park
	Moreno Valley, *see* F868.R6
	Mount Diablo State Park, *see* F868.C76
	Muir Trail, *see* F868.S5
	Muir Woods National Monument, *see* F868.M3
868.N16	Nacimiento River and Valley
868.N2	Napa Co.
	Including Huichica Creek and Valley
868.N5	Nevada Co.
	Including Donner Lake, Donner Party Expedition, Empire Mine State Historic Park, Malakoff Diggins State Historic Park
868.N52	New Melones Lake and region
	Nobles Trail, *see* F868.S5
	Ojai Valley, *see* F868.V5
	Old Emigrant Trail, *see* F868.S5
	Ontario Colony, *see* F869.O5
868.O6	Orange Co.
	Including Balboa Island, Emerald Bay and region, Irvine Park
868.O9	Owens River and Valley
	Pajaro River and Valey, *see* F868.S3
868.P33	Pacific Coast
	Pfeiffer Big Sur State Park, *see* F868.M7
868.P7	Placer Co.
868.P85	Plumas Co.
868.P9	Point Reyes
868.R4	Redwood National Park (Humboldt and Del Norte Counties)

	California
868.A-.Z	**Regions, counties, etc., A-Z — Continued**
	Redwood Park (Santa Cruz Co.), *see* F868.S3
868.R6	Riverside Co.
	Including Coachella Valley, Lake Elsinore and regions, Moreno Valley, San Jacinto River and Valley, Temecula Creek and Valley
	Roosevelt-Sequoia National Park (Proposed), *see* F868.S4
	Round Valley, *see* F868.M5
868.R9	Russian River and Valley
	Rustic Canyon, *see* F868.L8
868.S12	Sacramento Co.
868.S13	Sacramento River and Valley
	Including Ashurst Colony
868.S132	Saint Helena, Mount
868.S133	Salinas River and Valley
868.S136	San Benito Co.
	Including San Juan Valley
868.S14	San Bernardino Co.
	Including Lytle Creek Canyon, San Bernardino Valley, Bear Valley, Big Bear Valley, Big Bear Lake
	For Ontario Colony, see F869.O5
868.S144	San Bernardino National Forest
868.S15	San Diego Co.
	Including Anza-Borrego Desert State Park, Barona Valley, Borrego Valley, Escondido Valley, Palomar Mountain, San Pasqual Valley, San Vicente Valley
	For Imperial Valley, see F868.I2
	San Fernando Valley, *see* F868.L8
868.S156	San Francisco Bay region
	Including Alcatraz Island, Carquinez Strait, Golden Gate National Recreation Area
868.S157	San Francisco Co.
	Cf. F869.S3, San Francisco (City)
	For Farallon Islands, see F868.F24
	San Gabriel Valley, *see* F868.L8
	San Jacinto River and Valley, *see* F868.R6
868.S17	San Joaquin Co.
868.S173	San Joaquin River and Valley
	Including Tulare Lake and region
	San Juan Valley, *see* F868.S136
868.S18	San Luis Obispo Co.
	Including Morro Bay, Hearst-San Simeon State Historical Monument
	For Santa Maria River and Valley, see F868.S23
868.S19	San Mateo Co.
	San Miguel Island, *see* F868.S23
	San Pasqual Valley, *see* F868.S15
868.S2	San Ramon Valley
	San Vicente Valley, *see* F868.S15
868.S21	Santa Ana Mountains
868.S22	Santa Ana River and Valley
868.S23	Santa Barbara Co.
	Including Jalama Beach Park, San Miguel Island, Santa Barbara Valley, Santa Cruz Island, Santa Maria River and Valley, Santa Rosa Island, Santa Ynez River and Valley, Zaca Lake
	Cf. F868.S232, Santa Barbara Islands
868.S232	Santa Barbara (Channel) Islands (General)
	For individual islands, see the counties (Santa Barbara, Ventura, and Los Angeles) to which they belong
	Santa Catalina Island, *see* F868.L8
868.S25	Santa Clara Co.
	Including Santa Clara Valley
	For San Juan Valley, see F868.S136
	Santa Clarita Valley, *see* F868.L8

	California
868.A-.Z	**Regions, counties, etc., A-Z — Continued**
868.S3	Santa Cruz Co.
	Including California Redwood Park, Forest of Nisene Marks State Park, Pajaro River and Valley
	Santa Cruz Island, *see F868.S23*
868.S33	Santa Cruz Mountains
	Including Montara Mountain
868.S34	Santa Margarita River and Valley
	Including Rancho Santa Margarita
	Santa Maria River and Valley, *see F868.S23*
	Santa Monica Canyon, *see F868.L8*
868.S355	Santa Monica Mountains National Recreation Area
	Santa Rosa Island, *see F868.S23*
	Santa Ynez River and Valley, *see F868.S23*
868.S37	Searles Valley
	Seiad Creek and Valley, *see F868.S6*
868.S4	Sequoia National Park. Sequoia National Forest
	Mount Shasta, *see F868.S6*
868.S49	Shasta Co.
	Including Whiskeytown-Shasta-Trinity National Recreation Area
	For Lassen Peak, see F868.L34
868.S495	Shasta Mountains
	Shaver Lake, *see F868.F8*
	Shelter Cove, *see F868.H8*
868.S497	Sierra Co.
868.S5	Sierra Nevada Mountains (The Sierras)
	Including Beckworth Trail, Cape Horn, John Muir Trail, Old Emigrant Trail, Squaw Valley
	For Donner Party Expedition, see F868.N5
	For Kings Canyon National Park, see F868.K48
	For Lassen Peak, see F868.L34
	For Mount Whitney, see F868.W6
	For Sequoia National Park, see F868.S4
	For Yosemite Valley, see F868.Y6
868.S6	Siskiyou Co.
	Including Butte Valley, Mount Shasta, Seiad Creek and Valley, Tule Lake
868.S66	Solano Co.
868.S7	Sonoma Co.
	Including Annadel State Park, Arroyo de San Antonio (Estate), Lake Sonoma
	Squaw Valley, *see F868.S5*
868.S8	Stanislaus Co.
	Surprise Valley, *see F868.M6*
868.S9	Sutter Co.
868.T2	Lake Tahoe
	Including Tahoe National Forest
	Mount Tamalpais State Park, *see F868.M3*
868.T3	Tehama Co.
	Temecula Creek and Valley, *see F868.R6*
868.T58	Trinity Alps
868.T6	Trinity Co.
868.T8	Tulare Co.
	For Mt. Whitney, see F868.W6
	For Sequoia National Park, see F868.S4
	Tulare Lake and region, *see F868.S173*
	Tule Lake, *see F868.S6*
868.T9	Tuolumne Co.
	For Calaveras Big Trees State Park, see F868.C15
	For Calaveras Grove, see F868.C14
868.T92	Tuolumne River and Valley

	California
868.A-.Z	**Regions, counties, etc., A-Z — Continued**
868.V5	Ventura Co.
	Including Anacapa Island, Ojai Valley
	Whiskeytown-Shasta-Trinity National Recreation Area, *see F868.S49*
868.W6	Mount Whitney
	Winter Island, *see F868.C76*
	Wrights Lake, *see F868.E3*
	Yerba Buena (Goat) Island, *see F869.S3*
868.Y5	Yolo Co.
	Including Capay Valley
868.Y6	Yosemite Valley. Yosemite National Park
	Including Half Dome
868.Y8	Yuba Co.
	Zaca Lake, *see F868.S23*
869.A-.Z	**Cities, towns, etc., A-Z**
	GALE NOTE *The cutter number(s) listed below have been given only as examples by the Library of Congress*
869.A15	General
869.B5	Berkeley
869.C27	Carmel
869.G5	Glendale
	Including Forest Lawn Memorial Park
869.H74	Hollywood
869.L7	Long Beach
869.L8	Los Angeles
	Subarrange by Table F2 at the end of the text
869.O2	Oakland
869.O5	Ontario
	Including Ontario Colony
869.P3	Pasadena
869.S12	Sacramento
869.S22	San Diego
869.S3	San Francisco
	Subarrange by Table F2 at the end of the text
	Including Yerba Buena (Goat) Island
	For Farallon Islands, see F868.F24
	Cf. F868.S157, San Francisco Co.
	Elements in the population
870.A1	General works
870.A2-.Z	Individual elements
	For a list of racial, ethnic, and religious elements (with cutter numbers), see E184.A+
	Oregon
871	**Periodicals. Societies. Collections**
873	**Museums. Exhibitions, exhibits**
874	**Gazetteers. Dictionaries. Geographic names**
874.3	**Guidebooks**
875	**Biography (Collective). Genealogy (Collective)**
875.2	**Historiography**
	Historians, *see E175.5.A+*
875.5	**Study and teaching**
876	**General works. Histories**
876.3	**Juvenile works**
	Pamphlets, addresses, essays
876.5	General
876.6	Anecdotes, legends, pageants, etc.
877	**Historic monuments (General). Illustrative material**
878	**Antiquities (Non-Indian)**

	Oregon — Continued
	By period
879	Early to 1792
	Cf. F851.5, Exploring expeditions to the Pacific coast before 1800
	Cf. F1060.7, Explorations in the Canadian Northwest before 1821
	Cf. F1089.N8, Nootka Sound Controversy, 1789-1790
880	1792-1859
	Including the Oregon country; "joint occupation" by Great Britain and the United States, 1818-1846; the Oregon question; Northwest boundary to 1846; Oregon Trail
	Including biography: Jesse Applegate, Jason Lee, John McLoughlin, Joseph L. Meek, Isaac Ingalls Stevens, Marcus Whitman, etc.
	Cf. E83.84, Wars with the Pacific coast Indians, 1847-1865
	Cf. F592.3+, Lewis and Clark Expedition
	Cf. F854, International boundary since 1846
	Cf. F1060+, Hudson Bay Company
	Cf. F1086+, British Columbia, the northern part of the Oregon country since 1846
881	1859-1950
	Including admission as a state, February 14, 1859
	Including biography: Harry Lane, Alfred Benjamin Meacham, etc.
	Cf. D570.85.O8+, World War I, 1914-1918
	Cf. D769.85.O8+, World War II, 1939-1945
	Cf. E83.84, Wars with Pacific coast Indians, 1847-1865
	Cf. E83.87, Modoc War, 1872-1873
	Cf. E83.877, Nez Percé War, 1877
	Cf. E526.1+, Civil War, 1861-1865 (General)
	1951-
881.2	General works
	Biography
881.3	Collective
881.35.A-.35.Z	Individual, A-Z
	GALE NOTE *See note at the head of Table F5 at the end of the text for further instructions on how to subdivide this number*
882.A-.Z	**Regions, counties, etc., A-Z**
882.A15	Counties
882.A16	Mountains
882.A17	Rivers
882.A18	Lakes
882.A19	Islands
882.A65	Applegate River and Valley
882.B2	Baker Co.
882.B4	Benton Co.
882.B7	Boundaries
	Including Sand Island controversy
	For International boundary, see F854, F880
	Calapooia River and Valley, *see F882.L7*
882.C3	Cascade Range
	Including Spencer Butte
882.C5	Clackamas Co.
	For Mount Hood, see F882.H85
882.C53	Clatsop Co.
	Including Fort Clatsop National Memorial
882.C6	Columbia Co.
	For Sauvies Island, see F882.S3
882.C63	Columbia River and Valley, Oreg.
	Including Columbia River Highway
	For Sand Island controversy, see F882.B7
	For Sauvies Island, see F882.S3
	Cf. F853 , General
882.C7	Coos Co.
	Including Coos Bay

	Oregon
882.A-.Z	**Regions, counties, etc., A-Z — Continued**
	Cow Creek and Valley (Douglas County), *see* F882.D7
882.C8	Crater Lake. Crater Lake National Park
	Including Mount Mazama
882.C83	Crater National Forest
882.C9	Crook Co.
882.C95	Curry Co.
882.D4	Deschutes Co.
	Including Newberry National Volcanic Monument, Paulina Lake
882.D43	Deschutes National Forest
882.D45	Deschutes River and Valley
882.D7	Douglas Co.
	Including Cow Creek and Valley
	Fort Clatsop National Memorial, *see* F882.C53
	Fort Rock Valley, *see* F882.L15
	French Prairie, *see* F882.W6
882.G5	Gilliam Co.
882.G7	Grant Co.
882.H37	Harney Co.
882.H44	Hells Canyon National Recreation Area
	Cf. F752.H44, Idaho
882.H85	Mount Hood
	Including Timberline Lodge
882.H9	Hood River Co.
	Including Hood River and Valley
882.J14	Jackson Co.
882.J4	Jefferson Co.
882.J73	Joaquin Miller Trail
882.J76	John Day River and Valley
882.J8	Josephine Co.
882.K5	Klamath Co.
	For Crater Lake, see F882.C8
882.L15	Lake Co.
	Including Fort Rock Valley
882.L2	Lane Co.
882.L6	Lincoln Co.
882.L7	Linn Co.
	Including Calapooia River and Valley
882.L78	Long Tom River and Valley
882.M2	Malheur Co.
882.M3	Marion Co.
882.M8	Morrow Co.
882.M9	Multnomah Co.
	For Sauvies Island, see F882.S3
	Newberry National Volcanic Monument, *see* F882.D4
882.O16	Ochoco National Forest
	Owyhee Mountains region, *see* F752.O97
882.O98	Owyhee River and Valley (General, and Oregon)
	Cf. F752.O98, Idaho
	Cf. F847.O98, Nevada
882.P34	Pacific Coast
882.P7	Polk Co.
882.R6	Rogue River and Valley
882.S18	Salmon River and Valley
	Sand Island controversy, *see* F882.B7
882.S2	Santiam National Forest
882.S3	Sauvies Island
882.S5	Sherman Co.
882.S56	Siskiyou Mountains

Oregon

882.A-.Z	**Regions, counties, etc., A-Z — Continued**
882.S58	Siuslaw National Forest
882.S6	Snake River and Valley, Oreg.
	Cf. F752.S7, General, and Idaho
	Spencer Butte, *see* F882.C3
882.T5	Tillamook Co.
882.U4	Umatilla Co.
882.U43	Umpqua Co.
882.U5	Union Co.
882.W2	Wallowa Co.
	Including Wallowa Lake
882.W25	Wallowa National Forest
882.W3	Wasco Co.
	Including Mosier Hills
882.W4	Washington Co.
882.W5	Wheeler Co.
882.W6	Willamette River and Valley
	Including French Prairie
882.Y2	Yamhill Co.
882.Y24	Yaquina River and Valley
884.A-.Z	**Cities, towns, etc., A-Z**
	GALE NOTE *The cutter number(s) listed below have been given only as examples by the Library of Congress*
884.A8	Astoria
884.E9	Eugene
884.K62	Klamath Falls
884.P39	Pendleton
884.P8	Portland
	Subarrange by Table F2 at the end of the text
884.S2	Salem
	Elements in the population
885.A1	General works
885.A2-.Z	Individual elements
	For a list of racial, ethnic, and religious elements (with cutter numbers), see E184.A+

Washington

886	**Periodicals. Societies. Collections**
888	**Museums. Exhibitions, exhibits**
889	**Gazetteers. Dictionaries. Geographic names**
889.3	**Guidebooks**
890	**Biography (Collective). Genealogy (Collective)**
890.2	**Historiography**
	Historians, *see* E175.5.A+
890.5	**Study and teaching**
890.5.A1-.5.Z8	General works
890.5.Z9A-.5.Z9Z	Catalogs of audiovisual materials
891	**General works. Histories**
	Including admission as a state, November 11, 1889
	Including by period (Early to 1950) as well as general
	For 1951 and later, see F895+
	Cf. D570.85.W3+, World War I, 1914-1918
	Cf. D769.85.W3+, World War II, 1939-1945
	Cf. E83.84, Wars with Pacific coast Indians, 1847-1865
891.3	**Juvenile works**
	Pamphlets, addresses, essays
891.5	General
891.6	Anecdotes, legends, pageants, etc.
892	**Historic monuments (General). Illustrative material**
893	**Antiquities (Non-Indian)**

	Washington — Continued
	By period
(894)	Early to 1950, *see* F891
	1951-
895	General works
	Biography
895.2	Collective
895.22.A-.22.Z	Individual, A-Z
	GALE NOTE *See note at the head of Table F5 at the end of the text for further*
	instructions on how to subdivide this number
897.A-.Z	**Regions, counties, etc., A-Z**
897.A15	Counties
897.A16	Mountains
897.A17	Rivers
897.A18	Lakes
897.A19	Islands
	Adams, Mount, *see* F897.K6
897.A2	Adams Co.
897.A7	Asotin Co.
	Bainbridge Island, *see* F897.K5
	Mount Baker, *see* F897.W57
897.B4	Benton Co.
897.B7	Boundaries
	For International boundary, see F854, F880
	Cf. F882.B7, Oregon boundary and Sand Island controversy
897.C3	Cascade Range
	Including North Cascades National Park, Stevens Pass
	Chambers Creek, *see* F897.P6
	Chehalis Co., *see* F897.G84
897.C4	Chelan Co.
897.C52	Clallam Co.
	Including Mount Angeles
	For Olympic National Park, see F897.O5
897.C6	Clark Co. (Clarke Co. to 1925)
	For Sauvies Island, see F882.S3
	Clover Creek, *see* F897.P6
897.C68	Columbia Co.
897.C7	Columbia River and Valley, Wash.
	Including Grand Coulee Dam region
	For Sand Island controversy, see F882.B7
	For Sauvies Island, see F882.S3
	Cf. F853, General
897.C8	Columbia National Forest
	Colville River and Valley, *see* F897.S9
897.C85	Cowlitz Co.
897.D7	Douglas Co.
	Ebey's Landing National Historical Preserve, *see* F897.I7
897.F4	Ferry Co.
897.F8	Franklin Co.
897.G3	Garfield Co.
	Ginkgo Petrified Forest State Park, *see* F897.K53
	Grand Coulee Dam region, *see* F897.C7
897.G75	Grant Co.
897.G84	Grays Harbor Co. (Chehalis Co., 1854-1915)
	Including Grays Harbor
	Hartstene Island, *see* F897.M4
897.H63	Hoh River and Valley
	Hood Canal, *see* F897.P9
897.I7	Island Co.
	Including Ebey's Landing National Historical Preserve, Whidbey Island

	Washington
897.A-.Z	**Regions, counties, etc., A-Z — Continued**
897.J4	Jefferson Co.
	Including Marrowstone Island, Protection Island
897.J9	Juan de Fuca Strait region
	Cf. F897.P9, Puget Sound region
	Cf. F1089.V3, Vancouver Island
897.K3	Kettle River and Valley
	Cf. F1089.K57, General, and British Columbia
897.K4	King Co.
	Including Lake Washington, Vashon Island
897.K5	Kitsap Co.
	Including Bainbridge Island
897.K53	Kittitas Co.
	Including Ginkgo Petrified Forest State Park
897.K6	Klickitat Co.
	Including Mount Adams
897.L35	Lake Roosevelt National Recreation Area
	Lake Washington, *see* F897.K4
897.L6	Lewis Co.
897.L7	Lincoln Co.
	Marrowstone Island, *see* F897.J4
897.M4	Mason Co.
	Including Hartstene Island
	Naches River and Valley, *see* F897.Y18
	Nile Creek and Valley, *see* F897.Y18
	North Cascades National Park, *see* F897.C3
897.O4	Okanogan Co.
	Including Methow River and Valley
897.O5	Olympic Mountains. Olympic National Park
	For Mount Angeles, see F897.C52
897.P2	Pacific Co.
897.P24	Palouse River and Valley, Washington
	Cf. F752.P25, General, and Idaho
897.P4	Pend Oreille Co.
897.P6	Pierce Co.
	Including Chambers Creek, Clover Creek
	For Mount Rainier (Tacoma), see F897.R2
897.P65	Point Roberts
	Protection Island, *see* F897.J4
897.P9	Puget Sound region
	Including Fort Nisqualli, Hood Canal
	Cf. F897.J9, Juan de Fuca Strait region
897.R2	Mount Rainier (Tacoma). Mount Rainier National Park
897.S17	Saint Helens, Mount
897.S2	San Juan Co.
	Including San Juan Islands (San Juan, Orcas, Lopez, and Waldron)
	Sand Island, *see* F882.B7
	Sauvies Island, *see* F882.S3
897.S48	Similkameen River and Valley
	Cf. F1089.S48, General, and British Columbia
897.S5	Skagit Co.
897.S52	Skagit River and Valley
897.S53	Skamania Co.
897.S54	Skokomish River and Valley
897.S6	Snake River and Valley, Wash.
	Cf. F752.S7, General, and Idaho
897.S66	Snohomish Co.
	Including Mount Pilchuck, Three Fingers Mountain
897.S67	Snoqualmie River and Valley

	Washington
897.A-.Z	**Regions, counties, etc., A-Z — Continued**
897.S7	Spokane Co.
	Including Medical Lake, Spokane River and Valley
897.S9	Stevens Co.
	Including Colville River and Valley
	Stevens Pass, *see* F897.C3
	Mount Tacoma, *see* F897.R2
	Three Fingers Mountain, *see* F897.S66
897.T5	Thurston Co.
	Vancouver Island, *see* F1089.V3
	Vashon Island, *see* F897.K4
897.W15	Wahkiakum Co.
897.W18	Walla Walla Co.
897.W2	Walla Walla River and Valley
897.W57	Whatcom Co.
	Including Mount Baker
	Whidbey Island, *see* F897.I7
897.W6	Whitman Co.
897.W65	Whitman National Monument. Whitman Mission National Historic Site
897.Y18	Yakima Co.
	Including Naches River and Valley, Nile Creek and Valley
897.Y2	Yakima River and Valley
899.A-.Z	**Cities, towns, etc., A-Z**
	GALE NOTE *The cutter number(s) listed below have been given only as examples by the Library of Congress*
899.O5	Olympia
899.P8	Port Angeles
899.S4	Seattle
	Subarrange by Table F2 at the end of the text
899.S7	Spokane
899.T2	Tacoma
899.V2	Vancouver
899.Y15	Yakima
	Elements in the population
900.A1	General works
900.A2-.Z	Individual elements
	For a list of racial, ethnic, and religious elements (with cutter numbers), see E184.A+
	Alaska
901	**Periodicals. Societies. Collections**
901.5	**Museums. Exhibitions, exhibits**
902	**Gazetteers. Dictionaries. Geographic names**
902.3	**Guidebooks**
903	**Biography (Collective). Genealogy (Collective)**
903.2	**Historiography**
	Historians, *see* E175.5.A+
903.5	**Study and teaching**
903.5.A1-5.Z8	General works
903.5.Z9	Catalogs of audiovisual materials
904	**General works. Histories**
904.3	**Juvenile works**
	Pamphlets, addresses, essays
904.5	General
904.6	Anecdotes, legends, pageants, etc.
904.8	**Geography**
905	**Historic monuments (General). Illustrative material**
906	**Antiquities (Non-Indian)**

	Alaska — Continued
	By period
907	Early to 1867

Including exploration; settlement by the Russians; purchase by the United States, 1867 (E669); Rossiĭsko-Amerikanskai͡a kompanii͡a

Including biography: Aleksandr Andreevich Baranov, etc.

Cf. F851.5, Early voyages to Northwest

Cf. G600+, Polar voyages

908	1867-1896
909	1896-1959
910	1959-1981

Admission as a state, January 3, 1959

	1981-
910.5	General works
	Biography
910.6	Collective
910.7.A-.7.Z	Individual, A-Z

GALE NOTE *See note at the head of Table F5 at the end of the text for further instructions on how to subdivide this number*

912.A-.Z	**Regions, etc., A-Z**
912.A15	Counties
912.A16	Mountains
912.A17	Rivers
912.A18	Lakes
912.A19	Islands
912.A43	Alaska, Gulf of
	Aleutian Islands, *see* F951
912.A54	Aniakchak National Monument and Preserve
912.B14	Baranof Island
912.B2	Point Barrow
912.B24	Beaufort Sea
	Bering Sea, *see* F951
912.B57	Bird Creek and Valley (Anchorage Borough)
912.B7	Boundaries
912.B74	Bristol Bay
912.B75	Brooks Range
912.C34	Cape Krusenstern National Monument
912.C43	Chandler River and Valley
912.C47	Clark Lake
	Including Clark Lake National Park and Preserve
912.C6	Cook Inlet region
	Including Turnagain Arm
912.C7	Copper River region
912.D58	Deadfish Lake Region
912.D6	Mount Deborah
	Denali National Park and Preserve, *see* F912.M23
912.D65	Denali State Park
912.F2	Mount Fairweather
912.G36	Gates of the Arctic National Park and Preserve
912.G5	Glacier Bay. Glacier Bay National Monument
912.G64	Gold Creek and Valley
912.H37	Hatcher Pass
912.H8	Mount Huntington
912.I56	Inside Passage
	Cf. F1089.I5, General, and British Columbia
912.K26	Kachemak Bay State Park. Kachemak Bay State Wilderness Park
912.K3	Katmai National Monument
912.K4	Kenai Peninsula
	Including Kenai Fjords National Park
912.K56	Klondike Gold Rush National Historical Park

	Alaska
912.A-.Z	**Regions, etc., A-Z — Continued**
	Klondike River and Valley, *see* F1095.K5
912.K58	Knik Arm
912.K6	Kobuk River and Valley
912.K62	Kodiak Island
912.K66	Kotzebue Sound and region
912.K67	Koyukuk River and Valley
	Krusenstern, Cape, National Monument, *see* F912.C34
912.K85	Kuskokwim River and Valley
	Lake Clark National Park and Preserve, *see* F912.C47
912.L57	Lituya Bay
912.L65	Long Island (Prince of Wales-Outer Ketchikan Census Area)
912.M2	McKinley, Mount (Denali)
912.M23	McKinley, Mount, National Park (Denali National Park and Preserve)
912.M3	Matanuska River and Valley
912.M55	Minook Creek and Valley
	Mount McKinley, *see* F912.M2
912.M9	Muir Glacier
912.N45	Nenana River and Valley
912.N6	Noatak National Preserve
912.N7	Cape Nome region
912.N73	Nome-Taylor Highway
912.N75	Norton Sound and region
912.P9	Pribilof Islands
	Including Alaska Commercial Company, 1868-1940
912.P95	Prince of Wales Island
912.P97	Prince William Sound region
912.R48	Revillagigedo Island
912.S15	Mount St. Elias
912.S2	Saint Lawrence Island
912.S27	Sergief Island
912.S3	Seward Peninsula
912.S38	Shuyak Island State Park
912.S85	Stikine River and Valley
	Cf. F1089.S85, General, and British Columbia
912.S95	Susitna River and Valley
912.T32	Taku River and Valley
	Cf. F1089.T14, General and British Columbia
912.T4	Thomas Bay
912.T64	Tongass National Forest
	Turnagain Arm, *see* F912.C6
912.T85	Twin Lakes region
912.W56	Willow Creek State Recreation Area
912.W64	Wood-Tikchik State Park
912.W72	Wrangell Mountains
912.W74	Wrangell-Saint Elias National Park and Preserve
912.Y2	Yakutat Bay
912.Y9	Yukon River and Valley (General, and Alaska)
	Cf. F1095.Y9, Yukon Territory
914.A-.Z	**Cities, towns, etc., A-Z**
	GALE NOTE *The cutter number(s) listed below have been given only as examples by the Library of Congress*
914.A5	Anchorage
914.F16	Fairbanks
914.J9	Juneau
914.K4	Ketchikan
914.N6	Nome
914.S6	Sitka
914.S7	Skagway

	Alaska
914.A-.Z	**Cities, towns, etc., A-Z — Continued**
914.W8	Wrangell
	Elements in the population
915.A1	General works
915.A2-.Z	Individual elements

     For a list of racial, ethnic, and religious elements (with cutter numbers), see E184.A+

    Klondike River and Valley, *see* F1095.K5

951	**Bering Sea and Aleutian Islands**

     Including discovery and exploration; antiquities

      Cf. D769.87.A4, Aleutian Islands in World War II, 1939-1945

      Cf. F912.P9, Pribilof Islands

965	**The territories of the United States (General)**

     Including since 1912, Alaska, Hawaii, Puerto Rico

970	**Insular possessions of the United States (General)**

     Individual possessions are classified according to location: Guam, see DU647; *Hawaii, see* DU620+;
      Puerto Rico, see F1951+; *American Samoa, see* DU810+; *Virgin Islands of the United States, see*
      F2136

975	**Central American, West Indian, and other countries protected by and having close political**
	affiliations with the United States (General)

     For Cuba, see F1751+

     For Dominican Republic, see F1931+

     For Haiti, see F1912+

     For Liberia, see DT621+

     For Nicaragua, see F1521+

     For Republic of Panama, see F1561+

	Canada
1001	**Periodicals. Societies. Collections (Serial)**
	For Canadian geographical societies, see G4
1003	**Collections (nonserial). Collected works**
1003.5	**Museums. Collections of Canadiana. Exhibitions, exhibits**
1004	**Gazetteers. Geographic names**
1004.7	**Directories**
	Biography
1005	Collective
	Individual, *see* F1024.6.A+, F1029.92+
1006	**Dictionaries and encyclopedias**
	Including chronological tables
1008	**General works**
	For New France, see F1030
1008.2	**Juvenile works**
	Pamphlets, addresses, essays
1008.3	General
1008.4	Anecdotes, legends, pageants, etc.
	Cf. GR113+, Folklore
	Cf. Class P, Literature
1009	**Guidebooks. Handbooks**
1010	**Historic monuments (General)**
1011	**Parks of Canada (Collective descriptive works)**
	For works on individual parks including theory, management and description, see the subject or local division
	For works on theory, management and history, etc., of Canadian parks and public reservations in general, see SB484.C2
1011.3	**Geography**
	Description and travel. Views
1012	General works
	Early to 1762, *see* F1030
1013	1763-1866
1015	1867-1950
1016	1951-1980
1017	1981-
1019	**Antiquities (Non-Indian)**
	For Indians of Canada, see E78.C2 , E92
	For individual Indian tribes, see E99.A+
	Social life and customs. Civilization. Intellectual life
	Including national characteristics
	For New France, see F1030
1021	General works
	By period
	Early to 1945, *see* F1021
1021.2	1945-
	Elements in the population, *see* F1027, F1035.A+
	History
	For New France, see F1030
1022	Periodicals. Yearbooks
	Chronological tables, *see* F1006
	Historiography
1024	General works
	Biography of historians
1024.5	Collective
1024.6.A-.6.Z	Individual, A-Z
	GALE NOTE *See note at the head of Table F5 at the end of the text for further instructions on how to subdivide this number*
1025	Study and teaching
1026	General works
	Including political history

           Canada
           History — Continued

1026.4	Comic and satirical works
1026.6	Addresses, essays, lectures, etc.
	General special
1027	French Canadians. French Canadian question

If the pertinent number provides for an A-Z arrangement for elements in the population, assign ".F83"

For works on French Canadians in Quebec (Province), see F1052.92+

For works on French Canadians in other provinces, cities, or towns, see the province, city, or town

1027.5	Historical geography

Including general works on boundaries, territorial expansion, geopolitics

1028	Military history
1028.5	Naval history
	Diplomatic history. Foreign and general relations
1029	General works

Class general works on the diplomatic history of a period with the period, e.g. F1034.2, Foreign relations after 1945

For works on relations with a specific country regardless of period, see F1029.5.A+

1029.5.A-.5.Z	Relations with individual countries, A-Z
1029.9	Other (not A-Z)
	By period
	Early to 1603, *see* E101+

         For Jacques Cartier, see E133.C3

1030	1603-1763. New France

Including history and description. English conquest of 1629; Company of New France, 1629-1663; Royal Province, 1663; Company of the West Indies, 1665-1674; French explorers before 1760

Including biography: François Bigot; Pierre Boucher; Louis de Buade, comte de Frontenac; Pierre Jacques de Taffanel, marquis de La Jonquière; François Xavier de Laval de Montmorency; Pierre du Guast, sieur de Monts; Jean Talon, comte d'Orsainville; Philippe de Rigaud, marquis de Vaudreuil; Jean Baptiste Bissot, sieur de Vincennes; etc.

Cf. E81+, Indian wars

Cf. E195+, Intercolonial wars

Cf. F350.5+, Mississippi River and Valley

Cf. F366+, Louisiana

Cf. F544, The Illinois country

Cf. F1036+, Acadia, Nova Scotia

Cf. F1060+, Hudson's Bay Company and Rupert's Land

	Writings of Francis Parkman
1030.P24	Collected works. By date
1030.P245	Partial collections. Selections. By date
1030.P247	Battle for North America
	California and Oregon trail, *see* F592
	Conspiracy of Pontiac, *see* E83.76
1030.P25	France and England in North America. By date
	Selections, *see* F1030.P245
1030.P252-.P268	Individual works

         Under each (using successive cutter numbers):

           1   English editions

           2   Translations

1030.P261-.P262	Pioneers of France

         Subarrange by table below F1030.P252-.P268

         Jesuits in North America, *see* F1030.7+

         LaSalle and the discovery of the Great West, *see* F1030.5

1030.P264-.P265	Old régime in Canada

         Subarrange by table below F1030.P252-.P268

	Canada
	History
	By period
1030	1603-1763. New France
	Writings of Francis Parkman
1030.P25	France and England in North America. By date
1030.P252-.P268	Individual works — Continued
1030.P267-.P268	Count Frontenac and New France under Louis XIV
	Subarrange by table below F1030.P252-.P268
	Montcalm and Wolfe, *see* E199
	Half century of conflict, *see* E198
1030.1	Champlain, Samuel de
	Including Champlain Tercentenary, 1908
	For Lake Champlain Tercentenary, 1909, see F127.C6
1030.13	Brulé, Étienne
1030.15	Nicolet, Jean
1030.2	Marquette, Jacques
	Cf. F352, Exploration of the Mississippi
1030.3	Joliet, Louis
	Cf. F352, Exploration of the Mississippi
1030.4	Hennepin, Louis
	Cf. F352, Exploration of the Mississippi
1030.5	La Salle, Robert Cavelier, sieur de
	Cf. F352, Exploration of the Mississippi
	Jesuits in New France
	Including adjacent regions
1030.7.A-.7.Z5	General works
	Jesuit relations
1030.7.Z6-.7.Z9	Collective
1030.8	Individual relations and other writings
	Including works about individual missionaries
1030.9	1754-1763
	Including last years of French rule; the English conquest
	Cf. E199, French and Indian War, 1755-1763; Quebec Campaign, 1759
	1763-
1031	General works
1031.5	19th century
1032	1763-1867
	Including Province of Quebec, 1760; its expansion by Quebec Act of 1774; its division in 1791 and reunion in 1841; Canadian Rebellion, 1837-1838; burning of the "Caroline," 1837; Fenian Raids, 1866-1870; Union of British North American provinces, 1867
	Including biography: George Brown, 1818-1880; Joseph Frederick Wallet Des Barres; Lord Dorchester (Guy Carleton); Sir Alexander Tilloch Galt; Sir Frederick Haldimand; Sir Francis Hincks; Sir Louis Hippolyte La Fontaine; Thomas D'Arcy McGee; William Lyon Mackenzie; Louis Joseph Papineau; Lord Sydenham (Charles Edward Poulett Thomson); etc.
	Cf. E201+, American Revolution
	Cf. E263.C2, E263.N9, British North America
	Cf. E231, Quebec Campaign, 1775-1776
	Cf. E277+; F1036+ ,F1041+ ,F1056+, American loyalists in Canada
	Cf. E359.85, War of 1812
	Cf. E355+, Military operations, War of 1812
	Cf. E470.95, Confederates in Canada, St. Albans Raid, 1864
1033	1867- . Dominion of Canada
	Including annexation question; Fenian invasion of 1870-1871
	Including biography: Richard Belford Bennett; Sir George Étienne Cartier; Sir George Eulas Foster; Sir Sam Hughes; William Lyon Mackenzie King; Sir Wilfrid Laurier; Sir John Alexander MacDonald; David Mills; Sir Clifford Sifton; Lord Strathcona and Mount Royal (Donald Alexander Smith); Sir John Sparrow David Thompson; Sir Charles Tupper; etc.

	Canada
	History
	By period
	1763-
1033	1867- . Dominion of Canada — Continued
	Cf. DT930+, South African War, 1899-1902
	Cf. F1060.9, Purchase of Northwest Territories, 1869; Riel Rebellion, 1885
	Cf. F1063, Red River Rebellion, 1869-1870
1034	1914-1945
	Including New Dominion status, 1926; Statute of Westminster, 1931
	Including biography: Pierre Edouard Blondin, Henri Bourassa, etc.
	Cf. D501+, World War I, 1914-1918
	Cf. D731+, World War II, 1939-1945
	Cf. F1123, Newfoundland with Labrador established as a province, 1949
	1945-
	Cf. DT407.43, Somalia Affair, 1992-1997
1034.2	General works
	Biography
1034.3.A2	Collective
1034.3.A3-.3.Z	Individual
	GALE NOTE *See note at the head of Table F5 at the end of the text for further instructions on how to subdivide this number; the cutter number(s) listed below have been given only as examples by the Library of Congress*
1034.3.D5	Diefenbaker, John George
1034.3.P4	Pearson, Lester B.
1035.A-.Z	**Elements in the population**
	The cutter numbers are intended to be used as a guide for the best distribution of numbers and not to be used as a fixed standard or to affect numbers already assigned
	Including racial and ethnic groups and religious bodies which have significance in the history of Canada
	For elements in individual regions, provinces, cities, etc., see the region, province, city, etc.
1035.A1	General works
	Including foreign elements (General), minorities, etc.
	For race conflicts and problems, see F1027
	Acadians, *see* F1027
1035.A5	Americans
1035.A7	Arabs
1035.A74	Armenians
	Asians, South, *see* F1035.S66
1035.A87	Assyrians
1035.A94	Austrians
1035.B3	Basques
1035.B4	Belgians
	Blacks, *see* F1035.N3
1035.B7	British
	Cf. F1035.E53, Canadians, English-speaking
	Cf. F1035.I6, Irish
	Cf. F1035.S4, Scotch. Scots
1035.B84	Bulgarians
1035.C27	Cambodians
1035.C3	Catholics
1035.C4	Celts
1035.C48	Chileans
1035.C5	Chinese
1035.C64	Cornish
1035.C7	Croats
1035.C9	Czechs
1035.D3	Danes
1035.D76	Dukhobors

Canada

1035.A-.Z   **Elements in the population — Continued**

1035.D8   Dutch

1035.E28   East Europeans

1035.E3   East Indians

1035.E53   English-speaking Canadians

            Use only for English speakers in predominantly French-speaking areas, i.e., Quebec

1035.E85   Estonians

1035.E89   Ethiopians

1035.F48   Filipinos

1035.F5   Finns

1035.F8   French

         French Canadians (General), *see* F1027

            For works on French Canadians in Quebec (Province), see F1053

1035.G3   Germans

1035.G7   Greeks

1035.H34   Haitians

1035.H36   Hawaiians

1035.H54   Hindus

1035.H76   Huguenots

1035.H8   Hungarians

1035.I2   Icelanders

         Indians, *see* E78.A+

1035.I55   Indochinese

1035.I58   Iranians

1035.I6   Irish

1035.I8   Italians

1035.J3   Japanese

1035.J5   Jews

1035.K36   Kashubes

1035.K65   Koreans

1035.L27   Latin Americans

1035.L3   Latvians

1035.L43   Lebanese

1035.L5   Lithuanians

1035.M33   Macedonians

1035.M35   Maltese

1035.M45   Mennonites

1035.M67   Mormons

1035.M87   Muslims

1035.N3   Negroes. Blacks

1035.N52   Nigerians

1035.N6   Norwegians

1035.O6   Orientals

            For Japanese, see F1035.J3

1035.P34   Pakistanis

1035.P36   Palatines

1035.P6   Poles

1035.P65   Portuguese

1035.R65   Romanians

1035.R79   Russian Germans

1035.R8   Russians

         Ruthenians, *see* F1035.U5

1035.S3   Scandinavians

            For Danes, see F1035.D3

            For Norwegians, see F1035.N6

            For Swedes, see F1035.S9

1035.S4   Scotch. Scots

1035.S47   Serbs

1035.S54   Sikhs

	Canada
1035.A-.Z	**Elements in the population — Continued**
1035.S6	Slavs
1035.S63	Slovaks
1035.S64	Slovenes
1035.S65	Somalis
1035.S66	South Asians
1035.S68	Spaniards
1035.S88	Swabians
1035.S9	Swedes
1035.S94	Swiss
1035.T85	Tunisians
1035.U5	Ukrainians
1035.W44	Welsh
1035.W47	West Indians
1035.W5	White Russians

	Regions, provinces, territories
1035.8	Maritime provinces

> *Including Atlantic coast of Canada*
> *Cf. F106, Atlantic coast of North America*

Nova Scotia. Acadia

1036	Periodicals. Societies. Collections
1036.4	Gazetteers. Dictionaries. Geographic names
1036.5	Directories
	Biography
1036.8	Collective
	Individual, *see* F1038
1037	General works

> *Including description and travel, social life and customs*

1037.4	Juvenile works
	Pamphlets, addresses, essays, etc.
1037.5	General
1037.6	Anecdotes, legends, pageants, etc.

> *Cf. GR113+, Folklore*
> *Cf. Class P, Literature*

1037.7	Guidebooks. Handbooks
1037.8	Historic monuments (General). Illustrative material
1037.9	Antiquities (Non-Indian)

> *For Indians, see E78.A+ , E99.A+*

1038	History

> *Including French beginnings; English conquest; Winslow's Expedition, 1755; removal of*
>   *Acadians; settlement by New Englanders, 1760-1761*
> *Including biography: Thomas Chandler Haliburton; Sir Brenton Halliburton; Joseph*
>   *Howe; Charles Amador de Saint-Étienne de la Tour; Sir William Alexander, Earl of*
>   *Stirling (Cf. PR2369.S5); etc.*
> *Cf. E78.C2, Indians in Canada*
> *Cf. E78.N9, Indians in Nova Scotia*
> *Cf. E83.72, Wars with eastern Indians, 1722-1726*
> *Cf. E184.A2, Acadians in the United States*
> *Cf. E263.N9, American Revolution, 1775-1783*
> *Cf. E277+, American loyalists (General)*
> *Cf. F16+, Maine*
> *Cf. F27.W3, Washington County, including St. Croix Island*
> *Cf. F380, Acadians in Louisiana*
> *Cf. F1030, New France, 1603-1763*

1039.A-.Z	Regions, counties, etc., A-Z
1039.A2	Annapolis Co.
	Including Fort Anne Park
1039.A25	Antigonish Co.
1039.A74	Atlantic Coast

Canada

Regions, provinces, territories

Nova Scotia. Acadia

1039.A-.Z	Regions, counties, etc., A-Z — Continued
1039.B7	Boundaries
	Including old boundaries of Acadia, etc.
	For International boundary since 1783, see E398
	Brier Island, *see* F1039.F9
	Cabot Trail, *see* F1039.C2
1039.C15	Cape Breton Co.
1039.C2	Cape Breton Island (Île Royale)
	Including Cabot Trail
	Cf. F1039.C15, Cape Breton Co.
	Cf. F1039.I5, Inverness Co.
	Cf. F1039.R5, Richmond Co.
	Cf. F1039.V5, Victoria Co.
1039.C3	Cape Sable Island
	Chezzetcook Inlet, *see* F1039.H3
1039.C5	Chignecto Isthmus
	Including Fort Lawrence
1039.C6	Colchester Co.
1039.C8	Cumberland Co.
1039.D5	Digby Co.
1039.F9	Bay of Fundy
	Including Brier Island
1039.G8	Guysborough Co.
1039.H3	Halifax Co.
	Including Chezzetcook Inlet, McNabs Island, etc.
1039.H4	Hants Co.
	Île Royale, *see* F1039.C2
1039.I5	Inverness Co.
1039.J43	Jeddore Harbour
1039.K43	Kejimkujik Lake and region
1039.K44	Kejimkujik National Park
1039.K5	Kings Co.
1039.L9	Lunenburg Co.
	McNabs Island, *see* F1039.H3
1039.O35	Oak Island
1039.P6	Pictou Co.
	Including Pictou Island
	Prince Edward Island, *see* F1046+
1039.Q3	Queens Co.
1039.R5	Richmond Co.
1039.S13	Sable Island
1039.S18	Saint Ann's Bay and region
	Gulf of St. Lawrence, *see* F1050
1039.S19	Saint Margaret's Bay and Region
1039.S20	Saint Mary's Bay and region
1039.S5	Shelburne Co.
1039.S55	Shubenacadie River and Valley
	Surette's Island, *see* F1039.Y3
1039.T35	Tancook Island. Big Tancook Island
1039.V5	Victoria Co.
1039.Y3	Yarmouth Co.
	Including Surette's Island
1039.5.A-.5.Z	Cities, towns, etc., A-Z
	GALE NOTE *The cutter number(s) listed below have been given only as examples by the Library of Congress*
1039.5.A16	Annapolis Royal
1039.5.D3	Dartmouth

                                       Canada

                                          Regions, provinces, territories

                                            Nova Scotia. Acadia

1039.5.A-.5.Z	Cities, towns, etc., A-Z — Continued
1039.5.G5	Glace Bay
1039.5.H17	Halifax
1039.5.L8	Louisburg
	Including Fortress of Louisbourg National Historic Park
	For Capture of Louisburg, 1745, see E198
	For Capture of Louisburg, 1758, see E199
1039.5.S9	Sydney
1039.5.Y3	Yarmouth
	Elements in the population
1040.A1	General works
1040.A2-.Z	Individual elements
	For a list of racial, ethnic, and religious elements, (with cutter numbers), see F1035.A+
	New Brunswick
1041	Periodicals. Societies. Collections
1041.4	Gazetteers. Dictionaries. Geographic names
1041.5	Directories
	Biography
1041.8	Collective
	Individual, *see F1043-1044.5*
1042	General works
	Including description and travel, social life and customs
1042.4	Juvenile works
	Pamphlets, addresses, essays
1042.5	General
1042.6	Anecdotes, legends, pageants, etc.
	Cf. GR113+, Folklore
	Cf. Class P, Literature
1042.8	Historic monuments (General). Illustrative material
1042.9	Antiquities (Non-Indian)
	For Indians, see E78.A+
1043	History
	Entered the Dominion of Canada, 1867
	Cf. E263.N9, American Revolution, 1775-1783
	Cf. E277+, Loyalists, American Revolution, 1775-1783
	Cf. E398, Boundary troubles with the United States
1044.A-.Z	Regions, counties, etc., A-Z
1044.A4	Albert Co.
1044.A7	Aroostook River and Valley, N.B.
	Cf. F27.A7, General, and Maine
1044.B7	Boundaries
	For International boundary since 1783 and Aroostook War, see E398
1044.C2	Campobello Island
1044.C3	Carleton Co.
1044.C4	Chaleur Bay
1044.C5	Charlotte Co.
	For Campobello Island, see F1044.C2
	For Deer Island, see F1044.D3
	For Grand Manan Island, see F1044.G7
	Chignecto Isthmus, *see F1039.C5*
1044.D3	Deer Island
1044.F6	Fort Beauséjour National Park
	Fundy, Bay of, *see F1039.F9*
1044.F86	Fundy National Park
	Gaspé Peninsula, *see F1054.G2*
1044.G7	Grand Manan Island

             Canada

              Regions, provinces, territories

                New Brunswick

1044.A-.Z	Regions, counties, etc., A-Z — Continued
1044.K5	Kings Co.
1044.K53	Kingston Peninsula
1044.L35	Lamèque Island
1044.M3	Madawaska Co.
1044.M5	Miramichi River and Valley
1044.N7	Nepisiguit River and Valley
1044.N83	Northwest Miramichi River and Valley
1044.P3	Passamaquoddy Bay region, N.B
	Cf. F27.P3, Maine
1044.S17	St. Croix River and Valley, N.B
	Cf. F27.S2 , General, and Maine
1044.S2	St. John River and Valley (General, and New Brunswick)
	Cf. F27.S3 , Maine
	Gulf of St. Lawrence, *see* F1050
1044.S9	Sugarloaf Provincial Park
1044.T6	Tobique River and Valley
1044.Y65	York County
1044.5.A-.5.Z	Cities, towns, etc., A-Z
	GALE NOTE *The cutter number(s) listed below have been given only as examples by the Library of Congress*
1044.5.F8	Fredericton
1044.5.M7	Moncton
1044.5.S14	St. John
	Elements in the population
1045.A1	General works
1045.A2-.Z	Individual elements
	For a list of racial, ethnic, and religious elements, (with cutter numbers), see F1035.A+

            Prince Edward Island

1046	Periodicals. Societies. Collections
1046.4	Gazetteers. Dictionaries. Geographic names
1046.5	Directories
	Biography
1046.8	Collective
	Individual, *see* F1048-1049.5
1047	General works
	Including description and travel, social life and customs
1047.4	Juvenile works
	Pamphlets, addresses, essays
1047.5	General
1047.6	Anecdotes, legends, pageants, etc.
	Cf. GR113+, Folklore
	Cf. Class P, Literature
1047.7	Guidebooks. Handbooks
1047.8	Historic monuments (General). Illustrative material
1047.9	Antiquities (Non-Indian)
	For Indians, see E78.A+, E99.A+
1048	History
	Including separating from Nova Scotia, 1769
1049.A-.Z	Regions, counties, etc., A-Z
1049.K5	Kings Co.
1049.P7	Prince Co.
1049.Q6	Queens Co.
1049.5.A-.5.Z	Cities, towns, etc., A-Z
	GALE NOTE *The cutter number(s) listed below have been given only as examples by the Library of Congress*

           Canada
               Regions, provinces, territories
                  Prince Edward Island

1049.5.A-.5.Z	Cities, towns, etc., A-Z — Continued
1049.5.C5	Charlottetown
1049.5.S8	Summerside
	Elements in the population
1049.7.A1	General works
1049.7.A2-.7.Z	Individual elements

                      For a list of racial, ethnic, and religious elements (with cutter numbers), see F1035.A+

1050	St. Lawrence Gulf, River, and Valley (General)

                    Cf. F127.S23, St. Lawrence Valley, N.Y.
                    Cf. F127.T5, Thousand Islands
                    Cf. F1054.A6, Anticosti Island
                    Cf. F1054.O7, Isle of Orleans
                    Cf. F1054.S26, St. Helen's Island
                    Cf. F1054.S3, St. Lawrence Valley, Quebec
                    Cf. F1059.S4, St. Lawrence Valley, Ontario
                    Cf. F1121+, Newfoundland
                    Cf. F1170, Saint Pierre and Miquelon
                Quebec

1051	Periodicals. Societies. Collections
1051.4	Gazetteers. Dictionaries. Geographic names
1051.5	Directories
	Biography
1051.8	Collective
	Individual, *see* F1052.96-1054.5.A+
1052	General works

                    Including description and travel, social life and customs, etc.

1052.4	Juvenile works
	Pamphlets, addresses, essays
1052.5	General
1052.6	Anecdotes, legends, pageants, etc.

                      Cf. GR113+, Folklore
                      Cf. Class P, Literature

1052.7	Guidebooks. Handbooks
1052.8	Historic monuments (General). Illustrative material
1052.9	Antiquities (Non-Indian)
	Indians, *see* E78.A+, E99.A+
	History
1052.92	Study and teaching
1052.95	General works
	By period
	Through 1791, *see* F1030
1053	1791-1960

                      Including biography: Pierre Stanislas Bedard; René Edouard Caron; Earl of
                          Dalhousie (George Ramsay); Honoré Mercier; etc.
                      Cf. E184.F85, French Canadians in the United States
                    Cf. E231, Quebec Campaign
                    Cf. E263.C2, American Revolution, 1775-1783
                    Cf. E277+, F1058, American loyalists
                    Cf. E355+, Military operations (War of 1812)
                    Cf. E359.85, Canadian participation (War of 1812)
                    Cf. F1027, French Canadians (General)

	1960-
1053.2	General works
	Biography
1053.24	Collective

	Canada
	Regions, provinces, territories
	Quebec
	History
	By period
	1960-
	Biography — Continued
1053.25.A-.25.Z	Individual, A-Z

GALE NOTE *See note at the head of Table F5 at the end of the text for further instructions on how to subdivide this number*

1054.A-.Z	Regions, counties, seigniories, etc., A-Z
1054.A3	Abitibi Co. Abitibi (region)
1054.A6	Anticosti Island
1054.A67	Argenteuil Co.
1054.A7	Arthabaska Co.
	Including Bois-Francs, etc.
1054.B35	Baie Saint-Paul region
1054.B36	Bas-Saint-Láurent
1054.B38	Beauce Co.
1054.B45	Bellechasse Co.
1054.B54	Berthier Co.
1054.B58	Bizard Island
	Bois-Francs, *see* F1054.A7
1054.B6	Bonaventure Co.
1054.B63	Bonaventure Island
1054.B7	Boundaries
	For International boundary since 1783, see E398
	Cf. F42.B7, New Hampshire boundary
	Cf. F127.B7, New York boundary
1054.B8	Brome Co.
	Including Missisquoi River and Valley, Quebec, etc.
	Cf. F57.M7, Vermont
1054.C22	Caplan River and Valley
1054.C4	Cent-Iles
	Chaleur Bay, *see* F1044.C4
1054.C44	Chambly Co.
	Including Fort Chambly National Historic Park
1054.C445	Charlevoix Region
1054.C45	Chateauguay Co.
1054.C49	Chicoutimi Co.
1054.C7	Compton Co.
1054.C75	Côte de Beaupré (Seigniory)
	Côte-du-Sud, *see* F1054.S3
	Côte Nord, *see* F1054.S3
1054.C8	Crane Island (Île aux Grues)
1054.D4	Deux Montagnes Co.
1054.D6	Dorchester Co.
1054.D9	Drummond Co.
1054.E13	Eastern Townships
	For Bois-Francs, see F1054.A7
1054.G2	Gaspé Peninsula. Gaspé District
	Including Île Percée
	For Chaleur Bay, see F1044.C4
1054.G26	Gatineau River and Valley
	Grosse Île, *see* F1054.S3
	Hudson Strait, *see* F1103
1054.H9	Huntington Co.
1054.I3	Île aux Coudres
1054.I35	Île aux Noix
	Including Fort Lennox

	Canada
	Regions, provinces, territories
	Quebec
1054.A-.Z	Regions, counties, seigniories, etc., A-Z — Continued
1054.I5	Île Verte
	James Bay region, *see* F1059.J3
1054.J47	Jesus Island
1054.K2	Kamouraska Co.
1054.L17	Lanaudière
1054.L2	L'Assomption Co.
	Laurentian Mountains, *see* F1054.S3
1054.L3	Levis Co.
1054.L57	L'Islet Co.
1054.M18	Magdalen Islands (Îles Madeleine)
1054.M2	Mantawa River and Valley
1054.M35	Massue (Seigniory)
1054.M4	Matane Co.
1054.M42	Matapédia River and Valley
1054.M45	Megantic Co.
	For Bois-Francs, *see* F1054.A7
1054.M5	Lake Memphremagog region, Quebec
	Cf. F57.M5, Vermont
1054.M59	Mingan Islands
1054.M6	Missisquoi Co.
1054.M79	Montmagny Co.
1054.M8	Montmorency Co.
1054.M83	Montreal District
1054.N5	New Quebec (Ungava) District
	Ungava was created as district of Northwest Territories in 1895; in 1912 was annexed to the province of Quebec as New Quebec
	North Shore, *see* F1054.S3
1054.N93	Nunavik
1054.O7	Isle of Orleans
1054.O9	Ottawa River and Valley (General, and Quebec)
	Cf. F1059.O91, Ontario
1054.O94	Outaouais region
1054.P36	Parc de la Jacques-Cartier
1054.P365	Parc de Plaisance
1054.P367	Parc des Hautes-Gorges-de-la-Rivière-Malbaie
1054.P37	Parc du Mont-Orford
1054.P54	Piémont des Appalaches
1054.P8	Pontiac Co.
1054.P83	Port Burwell (Island)
1054.P85	Portneuf Co.
1054.Q4	Quebec Co.
1054.Q5	Quebec District
1054.R5	Richelieu River and Valley
1054.R615	Rivière-du-Loup Co. and region
1054.R87	Rupert River and Valley
1054.S13	Saguenay Co.
	For New Quebec District, *see* F1054.N5
1054.S14	Saguenay River and Valley
	Cf. F1054.S267, Lake St. John
1054.S254	Saint Francis River and Valley
1054.S26	St. Helen's Island
1054.S264	St. Hyacinthe Co.
1054.S267	Lake St. John
1054.S3	St. Lawrence Gulf, River, and Valley, Quebec
	Including Côte-du-Sud, Laurentian Mountains, North Shore, Grosse Île
	Cf. F1050 , General

	Canada
	Regions, provinces, territories
	Quebec
1054.A-.Z	Regions, counties, seigniories, etc., A-Z — Continued
1054.S33	Saint Maurice River and Valley
1054.S34	Saint-Ours (Seigniory)
1054.S48	Shefford Co.
1054.S7	Stanstead Co.
	Lake Tamiscamingue, *see* F1054.T6
	Témiscamingue Co., *see* F1054.T6
1054.T29	Temiscouata Co.
1054.T4	Terrebonne Co.
	Thousand Islands, *see* F127.T5
1054.T5	Three Rivers District
1054.T6	Timiskaming (region). Témiscamingue Co.
	Including Lake Timiskaming
	Trois Rivières Co., *see* F1054.T5
	Two Mountains Co., *see* F1054.D4
	Ungava, *see* F1054.N5
1054.V3	Varennes (Seigniory)
1054.V47	Verchères Co.
1054.Y3	Yamaska Co.
1054.5.A-.5.Z	Cities, towns, etc., A-Z
	GALE NOTE *The cutter number(s) listed below have been given only as examples by the Library of Congress*
1054.5.H8	Hull
1054.5.M8	Montreal
	Subarrange by Table F2 at the end of the text
1054.5.Q3	Quebec
1054.5.S55	Sherbrooke
1054.5.T53	Three Rivers
1054.5.Y2	Yamachiche (Village and parish)
	Elements in the population
1055.A1	General works
1055.A2-.Z	Individual elements
	For a list of racial, ethnic, and religious elements (with cutter numbers), see F1035.A+
	Ontario
1056	Periodicals. Societies. Collections
1056.4	Gazetteers. Dictionaries. Geographic names
1056.5	Directories
	Biography
1056.8	Collective
	Individual, *see* F1058-1059.5.A+
1057	General works
	Including description and travel, social life and customs
1057.4	Juvenile works
	Pamphlets, addresses, essays
1057.5	General
1057.6	Anecdotes, legends, pageants, etc.
	Cf. GR113+, Folklore
	Cf. Class P, Literature
1057.7	Guidebooks. Handbooks
1057.8	Historic monuments (General). Illustrative material
1057.9	Antiquities (Non-Indian)
	For Indians, see E78.O5, E99.A+
1058	History
	For early history to 1791, see F1030, F1053
	Including United empire loyalists from the United States; political history

	Canada
	Regions, provinces, territories
	Ontario
1058	History — Continued
	Including biography: Richard Cartwright, Sir Oliver Mowat, Sir John Beverley Robinson, John Graves Simcoe, etc.
	Cf. E78.C2,E78.O5, Indians
	Cf. E277+, American loyalists (General)
	Cf. E359.85, War of 1812
	Cf. E355+, Military operations, War of 1812
	Cf. F1032, Canadian Rebellion, 1837
1059.A-.Z	Regions, counties, etc., A-Z
	Addington Co., *see* F1059.L5
1059.A3	Algoma District
	Cf. F1059.T5, Thunder Bay District
1059.A4	Algonquin Provincial Park
	Including Opeongo Lake
1059.A44	Almaguin Highlands
1059.B36	Bathurst District
1059.B53	Blackstone Harbour Provincial Park
1059.B64	Bon Echo Provincial Park
1059.B7	Boundaries
	For International boundary, see F550.5
	Cf. F1054.B7, Quebec boundary
1059.B82	Brant Co.
1059.B95	Bruce Co.
1059.C3	Carleton Co.
1059.C53	Charleston, Lake and region
1059.C7	Credit River and Valley
1059.D46	Detroit River and Valley
	Cf. F572.D46, General, and Mich
	Cf. F1059.Y6, Don River and Valley
1059.D88	Dufferin Co.
1059.D9	Dundas Co.
1059.D93	Durham Co.
1059.E4	Elgin Co.
1059.E46	Lake Eloida region, Ont.
1059.E6	Lake Erie region, Ont.
	Cf. F555, General
1059.E7	Essex Co.
1059.F3	Fathom Five Provincial Park
1059.F85	French River and Valley
1059.F9	Frontenac Co. Frontenac Provincial Park
1059.G3	Georgian Bay region
1059.G5	Glengarry Co.
1059.G78	Grand River and Valley
1059.G84	Grey Co.
1059.H27	Haliburton Co.
1059.H3	Hastings Co.
1059.H9	Humber River and Valley
1059.H92	Huron Co.
1059.H95	Lake Huron region, Ont.
	Cf. F554, General
1059.J3	James Bay region
	Joseph, Lake, *see* F1059.M9
1059.K2	Kawartha Lakes
1059.K3	Kent Co.
1059.K5	Killarney Provincial Park
1059.K52	Killbear Provincial Park

	Canada
	Regions, provinces, territories
	Ontario
1059.A-.Z	Regions, counties, etc., A-Z — Continued
1059.L2	Lake of the Woods region (General, and Ont.)
	Cf. F1064.L2, Manitoba
1059.L23	Lambton Co.
1059.L3	Lanark Co.
1059.L4	Leeds Co.
1059.L5	Lennox and Addington Co.
1059.L8	Long Point
1059.M27	Manitoulin Island
1059.M6	Middlesex Co.
1059.M65	Mississippi River and Valley
1059.M9	Muskoka District. Muskoka Lake region
	Including Lake Joseph, Peninsula Lake
	Niagara Falls, *see* F127.N8
1059.N5	Niagara Peninsula
	Cf. F127.N6, Niagara River region (General, and New York)
	Cf. F1059.Q3, Queen Victoria Niagara Falls Park
	Cf. F1059.S58, Short Hills Provincial Park
1059.N55	Nipissing District
1059.N6	Norfolk Co.
	For Long Point, see F1059.L8
1059.N65	Northumberland Co.
	Nym Lake and region, *see* F1059.T5
1059.O5	Ontario Co.
1059.O6	Lake Ontario region, Ont.
	Including Toronto Islands, etc.
	Cf. F556, General
	Opeongo Lake, *see* F1059.A4
1059.O91	Ottawa River and Valley, Ont.
	Cf. F1054.O9, General, and Quebec
1059.O98	Oxford Co.
1059.P25	Peel Co.
	Peninsula Lake (Muskoka), *see* F1059.M9
1059.P3	Perth Co.
1059.P4	Peterborough Co.
	Including Stony Lake
1059.P65	Polar Bear Provincial Park
1059.P75	Prince Edward
1059.Q3	Queen Victoria Niagara Falls Park
	Cf. F127.N8, Niagara Falls
1059.Q4	Quetico Provincial Park
1059.Q6	Bay of Quinte
1059.R4	Renfrew Co.
1059.R46	Rideau River and Valley
1059.S3	Lake St. Clair region, Ont.
	Cf. F572.S34, Michigan
1059.S33	St. Joseph Island
1059.S4	St. Lawrence River and Valley, Ont.
	Cf. F1050, General
1059.S49	Severn River and Valley
	Severn-Trent Waterway, *see* F1059.T7
1059.S58	Short Hills Provincial Park
1059.S59	Simcoe, Lake
1059.S6	Simcoe Co.
1059.S65	Sparrow Lake (Muskoka District and Simcoe County)
	Stony Lake, *see* F1059.P4

	Canada
	Regions, provinces, territories
	Ontario
1059.A-.Z	Regions, counties, etc., A-Z — Continued
1059.S89	Stormont, Dundas and Glengarry
	Cf. F1059.D9, Dundas Co.
	Cf. F1059.G5, Glengarry Co.
1059.S9	Lake Superior region, Ont.
	Cf. F552, General
1059.T34	Talbot Settlement
1059.T5	Thunder Bay District and region
	Including Nym Lake and region
	Cf. F1059.A3, Algoma District
1059.T53	Timagani Lake and region
1059.T56	Timiskaming
	Toronto Islands, *see* F1059.O6
1059.T7	Trent River and Valley. Trent-Severn Waterway
	Trent-Severn Waterway, *see* F1059.T7
1059.W32	Waterloo Co.
1059.W34	Wawa Lake and region
1059.W36	Welland Co.
	Including Navy Island
1059.W37	Wellington Co.
1059.W4	Wentworth Co.
1059.W63	Woodland Caribou Provincial Park
1059.Y6	York Co. York Regional Municipality
	Including Don River and Valley
1059.5.A-.5.Z	Cities, towns, etc., A-Z
	GALE NOTE *The cutter number(s) listed below have been given only as examples by the Library of Congress*
1059.5.H2	Hamilton
1059.5.L6	London
1059.5.N5	Niagara
	Present name: Niagara-on-the-Lake
1059.5.N55	Niagara Falls
	Cf. F127.N8, New York
	Cf. F1059.Q3, Queen Victoria Niagara Falls Park
1059.5.O9	Ottawa
1059.5.T68	Toronto
	Subarrange by Table F2 at the end of the text
1059.5.W5	Windsor
	Elements in the population
1059.7.A1	General works
1059.7.A2-.7.Z	Individual elements
	For a list of racial, ethnic, and religious elements (with cutter numbers), see F1035.A+
	Canadian Northwest. Northwest Territories
	Including region to the west and northwest of ancient New France
	Including Hudson Bay, Hudson's Bay Company, Rupert's Land, Northwest Company of Canada
	For boundaries, see F597, F854, F880, United States; F912.B7, Alaska; F1059.B7, Ontario
	Cf. F1060.9, Purchase of Northwest Territories, 1869
	Cf. F1090, Canadian Rocky Mountains
	Cf. G575+, Polar regions
	Cf. G640+, Northwest Passage
1060.A1	Periodicals. Societies. Collections
1060.A2-.Z	General works
	Including history, description and travel
1060.1	Gazetteers. Dictionaries. Geographic names
1060.15	Museums. Exhibitions, exhibits
1060.2	Directories

Canada

Regions, provinces, territories

Canadian Northwest. Northwest Territories — Continued

Biography

1060.3	Collective
	Individual, *see* F1060.7+
1060.35	Juvenile works
	Pamphlets, addresses, essays
1060.37	General
1060.38	Anecdotes, legends, pageants, etc.

         Cf. GR113+, Folklore

         Cf. Class P, Literature

1060.4	Guidebooks. Handbooks
1060.5	Historic monuments (General). Illustrative material
1060.6	Antiquities (Non-Indian)

         For Eskimos, see E99.E7

         For Indians, see E78.A+ , E99.A+

By period

     Including history, explorations, description and travel

1060.7	Early to 1821

         Including biography: Médard Chouart, sieur des Groseilliers; Matthew Cocking; Daniel Williams Harmon; Samuel Hearne; Alexander Henry, 1739-1824; Pierre Gautier de Varennes, sieur de La Vérendrye; Sir Alexander Mackenzie; Pierre Esprit Radisson; David Thompson; etc.

         Cf. F1030, New France and early French explorations (General)

         Cf. F1063, Red River Settlement, 1815-1816

         Cf. F1089.N8, Nootka Sound Controversy, 1789-1790

1060.8	1821-1867

         Including biography: John McLeod, Sir George Simpson, Thomas Simpson, etc.

         Cf. F880, Oregon question and international boundary

         Cf. F1086+, British Columbia

         Cf. F1089.V3, Vancouver Island

1060.9	1867-1945

         Including Purchase from the old Hudson's Bay Company, 1869; Riel Rebellion, 1885; Alaska Highway

         Cf. F1061+, Manitoba

         Cf. F1070+, Saskatchewan

         Cf. F1075+, Alberta

         Cf. F1086+, British Columbia

         Cf. F1091+, Yukon

         Cf. F1096+, Mackenzie

         Cf. F1101+, Franklin

         Cf. F1106+, Keewatin

1060.92	1945-
1060.94	Frontier and pioneer life. Ranch life, cowboys, cattle trails, etc.
	Elements in the population
1060.96	General works
1060.97.A-.97.Z	Individual elements, A-Z

         For a list of racial, ethnic, and religious elements (with cutter numbers), see F1035.A+

Manitoba

1061	Periodicals. Societies. Collections
1061.4	Gazetteers. Dictionaries. Geographic names
1061.5	Directories
	Biography
1061.8	Collective
	Individual, *see* F1063-1064.5
1062	General works

     Including description and travel, social life and customs

1062.4	Juvenile works

	Canada
	Regions, provinces, territories
	Manitoba — Continued
	Pamphlets, addresses, essays
1062.5	General
1062.6	Anecdotes, legends, pageants, etc.
	Cf. GR113+, Folklore
	Cf. Class P, Literature
1062.7	Guidebooks. Handbooks
1062.8	Historic monuments (General). Illustrative material
1062.9	Antiquities (Non-Indian)
	For Indians, see E78.A+, E99.A+
	Cf. E73, Mound builders in Manitoba
1063	History
	Including admission as a province, 1870
	Including Red River Settlement; Red River Rebellion, 1869-1870
	Including biography: Thomas Douglas, 5th earl of Selkirk
	Cf. F1033, Fenian Raid, 1870-1871
	Cf. F1060+, Hudson Bay Company; Rupert's Land
	Cf. F1060.9, Riel and his rebellion, 1885
1064.A-.Z	Regions, etc., A-Z
1064.B7	Boundaries
	For International boundary, see F597
	Cf. F1059.B7, Ontario boundary
1064.C58	Churchill River and Valley, Manitoba
	Cf. F1074.C58, General, and Saskatchewan
1064.D8	Duck Mountain Provincial Park
1064.G22	Fort Garry (Lower)
1064.H42	Hecla Provincial Park
1064.L2	Lake of the Woods region, Manitoba
	Cf. F1059.L2, General, and Ontario
1064.M5	Minnedosa River and Valley
1064.M67	Morris River and Valley
1064.Q34	Qu'Appelle River and Valley (Manitoba)
	Cf. F1074.Q34, General, and Saskatchewan
1064.R3	Red River of the North and Red River Valley, Manitoba
	Cf. F612.R27, Minnesota
	Cf. F642.R3, North Dakota
1064.S6	Souris (Mouse) River and Valley, Manitoba
	Cf. F642.S68, North Dakota
	Cf. F1074.S67, General, and Saskatchewan
1064.S79	Stuartburn
1064.S9	Swan River and Valley
	Cf. F1074.S9, General, and Saskatchewan
1064.W47	Whiteshell Provincial Park
1064.W5	Lake Winnipeg region
1064.5.A-.5.Z	Cities, towns, etc., A-Z
	GALE NOTE *The cutter number(s) listed below have been given only as examples by the Library of Congress*
1064.5.B73	Brandon
1064.5.S13	Saint Boniface
1064.5.W7	Winnipeg
	Elements in the population
1065.A1	General works
1065.A2-.Z	Individual elements
	For a list of racial, ethnic, and religious elements, (with cutter numbers), see F1035.A+
1067	Assiniboia
	Became part of province of Saskatchewan, September 1, 1905

                    Canada
                      Regions, provinces, territories — Continued

	Saskatchewan
1070	Periodicals. Societies. Collections
1070.4	Gazetteers. Dictionaries. Geographic names
1070.5	Directories
	Biography
1070.8	Collective
	Individual, *see* F1074.5.A+
1071	General works
	Including description and travel, social life and customs
1071.4	Juvenile works
	Pamphlets, addresses, essays
1071.5	General
1071.6	Anecdotes, legends, pageants, etc.
	Cf. GR113+, Folklore
	Cf. Class P, Literature
1071.8	Historic monuments (General). Illustrative material
1071.9	Antiquities (Non-Indian)
	For Indians, see E78.A+, E99.A+
1072	History
	Province created in 1905
1074.A-.Z	Regions, counties, etc., A-Z
	Assiniboia, *see* F1067
1074.A75	Athabasca Sand Dunes Provincial Wilderness Park
	Battle Valley, *see* F1079.B55
1074.B7	Boundaries
	For international boundary, see F597
	Cf. F1064.B7, Manitoba boundary
1074.C58	Churchill River and Valley (General, and Saskatchewan)
	Cf. F1064.C58, Manitoba
	Cypress Hills, *see* F1079.C9
1074.C92	Cypress Hills Provincial Park
1074.G72	Grasslands National Park
1074.G74	Greenwater Lake Provincial Park
1074.L5	Little Pipestone Creek and Valley
1074.L65	Lovering Lake and region
1074.M4	Meadow Lake Provincial Park
1074.M66	Moose Mountain Provincial Park
	Motherwell Farmstead National Historic Park, *see* F1074.W28
1074.P7	Prince Albert National Park
1074.Q34	Qu'Appelle River and Valley (General, and Saskatchewan)
	Cf. F1064.Q34, Manitoba
	Red Deer River and Valley, *see* F1079.R4
1074.R8	Russell Lake region
1074.S3	Saskatchewan River and Valley (General, and Saskatchewan)
1074.S67	Souris (Mouse) River and Valley (General, and Saskatchewan)
	Cf. F642.S68, North Dakota
	Cf. F1064.S6, Manitoba
1074.S9	Swan River and Valley (General, and Saskatchewan)
	Cf. F1064.S9, Manitoba
1074.W28	W.R. Motherwell Farmstead National Historic Park
1074.W65	Wood Mountain (Region)
1074.5.A-.5.Z	Cities, towns, etc., A-Z
	GALE NOTE *The cutter number(s) listed below have been given only as examples by the Library of Congress*
1074.5.R3	Regina
1074.5.S3	Saskatoon
	Elements in the population
1074.7.A1	General works

	Canada
	Regions, provinces, territories
	Saskatchewan
	Elements in the population — Continued
1074.7.A2-.7.Z	Individual elements
	For a list of racial, ethnic, and religious elements (with cutter numbers), see F1035.A+
	Alberta
1075	Periodicals. Societies. Collections
1075.4	Gazetteers. Dictionaries. Geographic names
1075.5	Directories
	Biography
1075.8	Collective
	Individual, *see F1078-1079.5.A+*
1076	General works
	Including description and travel, social life and customs, etc.
1076.4	Juvenile works
	Pamphlets, addresses, essays
1076.5	General
1076.6	Anecdotes, legends, pageants, etc.
	Cf. GR113+, Folklore
	Cf. Class P, Literature
1076.8	Historic monuments (General). Illustrative material
1076.9	Antiquities (Non-Indian)
	For Indians, see E78.A+, E99.A+
	History
	Class here works on the province formed in 1905
1078	General works
	By period
	Early to 1970, *see F1078*
	1971-
1078.2	General works
	Biography
1078.24	Collective
1078.25.A-.25.Z	Individual, A-Z
	GALE NOTE *See note at the head of Table F5 at the end of the text for further instructions on how to subdivide this number*
1079.A-.Z	Regions, counties, etc., A-Z
1079.A8	Athabasca region
1079.B5	Banff National Park
	Including Mount Castleguard
1079.B55	Battle Valley
1079.B7	Boundaries
	For International boundary, see F597
	Cf. F1074.B7, Saskatchewan boundary
1079.B8	Buffalo Hill region
	Castleguard, Mount, *see F1079.B5*
1079.C57	Cooking Lake-Blackfoot Grazing, Wildlife, and Provincial Recreation Area
1079.C6	Coyote Flats
1079.C76	Crowsnest Pass. Crowsnest River and Valley (General, and Alberta)
	Cf. F1089.C77, British Columbia
1079.C9	Cypress Hills
1079.E24	Eagle Creek and Valley
1079.E5	Elk Island National Park
1079.F67	Forty Mile Coulee and Valley
	Including Forty Mile Coulee Reservoir
1079.J27	James River and Valley
1079.J3	Jasper National Park
	Including Maligne Lake
1079.K34	Kananaskis Country

	Canada
	Regions, provinces, territories
	Alberta
1079.A-.Z	Regions, counties, etc., A-Z — Continued
1079.L47	Lesser Slave Lake
1079.L8	Lake Louise
	Maligne Lake and region, *see* F1079.J3
1079.M54	Milk River and Valley (General, and Alberta)
	Cf. F737.M48, Montana
1079.P3	Peace River District
	Cf. F1089.P3, Peace River and Valley, B.C.
1079.P36	Pembina River and Valley
1079.R4	Red Deer River and Valley
1079.R53	Rife
1079.R66	Rosebud River and Valley
1079.S7	Strathcona
1079.T3	Tail Creek region
1079.T8	Twin Butte region
1079.W3	Waterton Lakes National Park
1079.W6	Wood Buffalo National Park
1079.W74	Writing-on-Stone Provincial Park
	Including Writing-on-Stone Northwest Mounted Police Post
1079.Y4	Yellowhead Pass
1079.5.A-.5.Z	Cities, towns, etc., A-Z
	GALE NOTE *The cutter number(s) listed below have been given only as examples by the Library of Congress*
1079.5.C35	Calgary
1079.5.E3	Edmonton
1079.5.L5	Lethbridge
1079.5.M4	Medicine Hat
	Elements in the population
1080.A1	General works
1080.A2-.Z	Individual elements
	For a list of racial, ethnic, and religious elements (with cutter numbers), see F1035.A+
	British Columbia
1086	Periodicals. Societies. Collections
1086.4	Gazetteers. Dictionaries. Geographic names
1086.5	Directories
	Biography
1086.8	Collective
	Individual, *see* F1088-1089.5.A+
1087	General works
	Including description and travel, social life and customs
	Cf. F851, Pacific coast of North America
1087.4	Juvenile works
	Pamphlets, addresses, essays
1087.5	General
1087.6	Anecdotes, legends, pageants, etc.
	Cf. GR113+, Folklore
	Cf. Class P, Literature
1087.7	Guidebooks. Handbooks
1087.8	Historic monuments (General). Illustrative material
1087.9	Antiquities (Non-Indian)
	For Indians, see E78.A+ , E99.A+
1088	History
	Joined the Dominion of Canada in 1871
	Including biography: Sir James Douglas, etc.
	Cf. E78.B9, Indians in British Columbia
	Cf. E78.C2, Indians in Canada

Canada

Regions, provinces, territories

British Columbia

1088 History — Continued

Cf. F851.5 , Exploring expeditions before 1800

Cf. F879-880 , Northwest coast between Alaska and New Spain (California), 1769-1846,
including the Oregon question

Cf. F1060+, Hudson's Bay and Northwest companies

1089.A-.Z Regions, etc., A-Z

1089.A4 Alberni region

1089.B43 Bella Coola/Chilcotin Road

1089.B44 Bella Coola River and Valley

1089.B7 Boundaries

For international boundary, see F854, F880

Cf. F912.B7, Alaska boundary

Cf. F1079.B7, Alberta boundary

1089.B74 Bowen Island

1089.B8 Bridge River and Valley

1089.B9 Bulkley River and Valley

1089.C3 Cariboo District

Including Chilako River and Valley, Deka Lake, Mitchell Lake

1089.C35 Cassiar District

Chilako River and Valley, see F1089.C3

1089.C42 Chilcotin River and Valley

1089.C45 Chilliwack River and Valley

1089.C47 Christina Lake and region

Clayoquot Sound, see F1089.V3

1089.C7 Coast Range

Mount Waddington (Mount George Dawson, Mystery Mountain)

Comox Valley, see F1089.V3

1089.C73 Cowichan Lake and region

1089.C75 Creston Valley

1089.C77 Crowsnest Pass. Crowsnest River and Valley, British Columbia

Cf. F1079.C76, General, and Alberta

Deka Lake, see F1089.C3

1089.D45 Denman Island

1089.E38 Elk River and Valley

1089.F5 Finlay River and Valley

1089.F54 Fintry Provincial Park

1089.F7 Fraser River and Valley

1089.G3 Garibaldi Provincial Park

1089.G44 Georgia, Strait of, Region

1089.G55 Glacier National Park

1089.G8 Gulf Islands

1089.H6 Hope region

1089.H63 Hornby Island

1089.I5 Inside Passage (General, and B.C.)

Cf. F912.I56, Alaska

1089.J43 Jedediah Island

Juan de Fuca Strait region, see F897.J9

1089.K4 Kamloops District

1089.K57 Kettle River and Valley (General, and B.C.)

Cf. F897.K3, Washington

1089.K7 Kootenay (Kootenai) River and Valley, B.C. Kootenay District

1089.L3 Lac La Hache region

1089.L7 Lillooet District

1089.L75 Lonesome Lake and region

1089.M3 Manning Provincial Park

Metchosin District, see F1089.V3

Mitchell Lake, see F1089.C3

	Canada
	Regions, provinces, territories
	British Columbia
1089.A-.Z	Regions, etc., A-Z — Continued
1089.N52	Nicola River and Valley
1089.N8	Nootka Sound
	Including Nootka Sound controversy, 1789-1790
1089.O5	Okanagan River and Valley, B.C
1089.O55	Omineca River and Valley
1089.P2	Pacific Coast
	Pacific Rim National Park, *see* F1089.V3
1089.P3	Peace River and Valley, B.C
	Cf. F1079.P3, Peace River District, Alberta
1089.P4	Pemberton Valley
1089.P5	Pitt Lake and region
1089.P77	Princess Louisa Inlet and region
1089.P8	Purcell Range
	Quadra Island, *see* F1089.V3
1089.Q3	Queen Charlotte Islands
1089.R62	Robson River and Valley
1089.S2	Saltspring (Salt Spring) Island
	San Juan Islands, *see* F897.S2
1089.S4	Selkirk Range
	Including Nakimu Caves
1089.S46	Shuswap Lake
1089.S48	Similkameen River and Valley (General, and British Columbia)
	Cf. F897.S48, Washington (State)
1089.S5	Skeena River and Valley
1089.S77	Stein River and Valley
1089.S85	Stikine River and Valley (General, and British Columbia)
1089.S88	Stuart Lake and region
1089.S94	Sunshine Coast
1089.T14	Taku River and Valley (General, and British Columbia)
	Cf. F912.T32, Alaska
1089.T17	Tatlayoko Lake
1089.T18	Tatshenshini River and Valley
1089.T2	Telkwa River and Valley
1089.T25	Teslin River and Valley
	Cf. F1095.T47, General and Yukon
1089.T3	Texada Island
1089.T48	Thompson River and Valley
1089.T85	Tweedsmuir Provincial Park
1089.V3	Vancouver Island
	Including Clayoquot Sound, Metchosin District, Pacific Rim National Park, Quadra Island, Comox Valley
	For Juan de Fuca Strait region, see F897.J9
1089.W44	Wells Gray Provincial Park
1089.W55	Windermere Lake
1089.Y4	Yale District
	Yellowhead Pass, *see* F1079.Y4
1089.5.A-.5.Z	Cities, towns, etc., A-Z
	GALE NOTE *The cutter number(s) listed below have been given only as examples by the Library of Congress*
1089.5.P7	Prince George
1089.5.V22	Vancouver
1089.5.V6	Victoria
	Elements in the population
1089.7.A1	General works

	Canada
	Regions, provinces, territories
	British Columbia
	Elements in the population — Continued
1089.7.A2-.7.Z	Individual elements
	For a list of racial, ethnic, and religious elements (with cutter numbers), see F1035.A+
1090	Rocky Mountains of Canada
	Cf. F721, General, and in the United States
	Cf. F1011, Canadian national parks (General)
1090.5	Northern regions of Canada (General). Arctic regions
	Yukon
	District created in 1897; made a territory in 1898
	Cf. G770, Arctic regions
1091.A1	Periodicals. Societies. Collections
1091.A2-.Z	General works
	Including description and travel
	For Inuit, see E99.E7
	For Indians, see E78.Y8 or individual tribes in E99.A+
1091.4	Juvenile works
1092	Gazetteers. Dictionaries. Geographic names
	Biography
1092.8	Collective
	Individual, *see* F1093, F1095.A+, F1095.5.A+
1093	History
1095.A-.Z	Regions, etc., A-Z
1095.B7	Boundaries
	Cf. F912.B7, Alaska boundary
	Cf. F1089.B7, British Columbia boundary
1095.F7	Frances Lake
1095.K5	Klondike River and Valley
1095.T47	Teslin River and Valley (General, and Yukon)
	Cf. F1089.T25, British Columbia
1095.Y9	Yukon River and Valley
	Cf. F912.Y9, Alaska
1095.5.A-.5.Z	Cities, towns, etc., A-Z
	GALE NOTE *The cutter number(s) listed below have been given only as examples by the Library of Congress*
1095.5.D3	Dawson
1095.5.W5	Whitehorse
	Mackenzie
	District created in 1895; boundaries redefined in 1918
	Cf. G770, Arctic regions
1096.A1	Periodicals. Societies. Collections
1096.A2-.Z	General works
	Including description and travel
	For Eskimos, see E99.E7
	For Indians, see E99.A+
1098	History
1100.A-.Z	Regions, etc., A-Z
1100.B33	Back River and Valley (General, and Mackenzie)
	Cf. F1110.B33, Keewatin
1100.B7	Boundaries
	Cf. F1074.B7, Saskatchewan boundary
	Cf. F1079.B7, Alberta boundary
	Cf. F1089.B7, British Columbia boundary
	Cf. F1095.B7, Yukon boundary
	Cf. F1110.B7, Keewatin boundary
1100.F7	Franklin Mountains
1100.G7	Great Bear Lake

	Canada
	Regions, provinces, territories
	Mackenzie
1100.A-.Z	Regions, etc., A-Z — Continued
1100.G8	Great Slave Lake
1100.K39	Kazan River and Valley (General, and Mackenzie)
	Cf. F1110.K39, Keewatin
1100.M3	Mackenzie River and Valley
1100.S6	South Nahanni River and Valley
1100.T54	Thelon River and Valley (General, and Mackenzie)
	Cf. F1110.T54, Keewatin
	Wood Buffalo National Park, *see* F1079.W6
1100.5.A-.5.Z	Cities, towns, etc., A-Z
	GALE NOTE *The cutter number(s) listed below have been given only as examples by the Library of Congress*
1100.5.A4	Aklavik
1100.5.F6	Fort Smith
1100.5.N6	Norman Wells
	Franklin
	District formed in 1895; boundaries redefined in 1897 and 1918; area made a game preserve in 1926
	Cf. G770, Arctic regions
1101.A1	Periodicals. Societies. Collections
1101.A2-.Z	General works
	Including description and travel
	For Eskimos, see E99.E7
	For Indians, see E78.A+, E99.A+
1103	History
1105.A-.Z	Regions, etc., A-Z
	GALE NOTE *The cutter number(s) listed below have been given only as examples by the Library of Congress*
1105.A89	Auyuittuq National Park
1105.B3	Baffin Island
	Formerly Baffin Land
1105.B7	Boundaries
	Cf. F1100.B7, Mackenzie boundary
	Cf. F1110.B7, Keewatin boundary
1105.F74	Frobisher Bay
1105.G7	Grinnell Land
1105.K5	King William Island
1105.Q44	Queen Elizabeth Islands
1105.S8	Sverdrup Islands
1105.5.A-.5.Z	Cities, towns, etc., A-Z
	GALE NOTE *The cutter number(s) listed below have been given only as examples by the Library of Congress*
1105.5.A7	Arctic Bay (Trading post)
1105.5.F6	Fort Ross (Trading post)
1105.7	Hudson Strait
	Keewatin
	District created in 1876; boundaries redefined in 1912
	Cf. G770, Arctic regions
1106.A1	Periodicals. Societies. Collections
1106.A2-.Z	General works
	Including description and travel, etc.
	For Eskimos, see E99.E7
	For Indians, see E78.A+, E99.A+
1108	History
1110.A-.Z	Regions, etc., A-Z
1110.B33	Back River and Valley
	Cf. F1100.B33, General, and Mackenzie

	Canada
	Regions, provinces, territories
	Keewatin
1110.A-.Z	Regions, etc., A-Z — Continued
1110.B7	Boundaries
	Cf. F1054.B7, Quebec
	Cf. F1064.B7, Manitoba
1110.K39	Kazan River and Valley
	Cf. F1100.K39, General, and Mackenzie
1110.M5	Melville Peninsula
1110.S6	Southampton Island
1110.T54	Thelon River and Valley
	Cf. F1100.T54, General, and Mackenzie
1110.5.A-.5.Z	Cities, towns, etc., A-Z
	GALE NOTE *The cutter number(s) listed below have been given only as examples by the Library of Congress*
1110.5.B3	Baker Lake (Trading post)
1110.5.C5	Chesterfield Inlet (Trading post)
(1111)	Ungava, *see* F1054.N5
	Newfoundland
1121	Periodicals. Societies. Collections
1121.4	Gazetteers. Dictionaries. Geographic names
1121.5	Directories
	Biography
1121.8	Collective
	Individual, *see* F1123-1124.5.A+
1122	General works
	Including description and travel, social life and customs
1122.4	Juvenile works
	Pamphlets, addresses, essays
1122.5	General
1122.6	Anecdotes, legends, pageants, etc.
	Cf. GR113+, Folklore
	Cf. Class P, Literature
1122.7	Guidebooks. Handbooks
1122.8	Historic monuments (General). Illustrative material
1122.9	Antiquities (Non-Indian)
	For Indians, see E78.A+, E99.A+
1123	History
	Province created in 1949, including Labrador
	Including Baltimore colony of Avalon, political history
	Including biography: Philippe de Pastour, sieur de Costebelle; etc.
1124.A-.Z	Regions, counties, etc., A-Z
	GALE NOTE *The cutter number(s) listed below have been given only as examples by the Library of Congress*
1124.B7	Boundaries
	Cf. F1138.B7, Labrador boundary
1124.F6	Fogo Island
1124.F9	Funk Island
	Gulf of St. Lawrence, *see* F1050
	Labrador, *see* F1136
1124.5.A-.5.Z	Cities, towns, etc., A-Z
	GALE NOTE *The cutter number(s) listed below have been given only as examples by the Library of Congress*
1124.5.C6	Corner Brook
1124.5.G3	Gander
1124.5.G7	Grand Falls
1124.5.S14	Saint John's
	Elements in the population
1125.A1	General works

          Canada
            Regions, provinces, territories
               Newfoundland
                 Elements in the population — Continued

1125.A2-.Z	Individual elements
	For a list of racial, ethnic, and religious elements (with cutter numbers), see F1035.A+
	Labrador
1135	Periodicals. Societies. Collections
1135.4	Gazetteers. Dictionaries. Geographic names
1135.5	Directories
	Biography
1135.8	Collective
	Individual, *see* F1137-1138.A+
1136	General works
	Including description and travel, social life and customs
	For Indians, see E78.A+, E99.A+
1137	History
	Annexed to Newfoundland in 1876
	Including biography: Sir William Thomason Grenfell, etc.
1138.A-.Z	Regions, etc., A-Z
	GALE NOTE *The cutter number(s) listed below have been given only as examples by the Library of Congress*
1138.B7	Boundaries
	Cf. F1054.B7, Quebec boundary
1138.G7	Grand Falls
1139	Cities, towns, etc., A-Z
	GALE NOTE *The cutter number(s) listed below have been given only as examples by the Library of Congress*
1139.B3	Battle Harbour (Fishing port)
1139.C3	Cartwright (Fishing port)
1139.H6	Hopedale (Fishing port)
1140	The Labrador Peninsula
	Cf. F1051+, Quebec
	Cf. F1135+, Labrador (Newfoundland)
	Nunavut
1141	Periodicals. Societies. Collections
1141.4	Gazetteers. Dictionaries. Geographic names
1141.5	Directories
	Biography
1141.8	Collective
	Individual, *see* F1143, F1144.A+, F1144.5.A+
1142	General works
	Including description and travel, social life and customs
1142.4	Juvenile works
	Pamphlets, addresses, essays
1142.5	General works
1142.6	Anecdotes, legends, pageants, etc.
	Cf. GR113+, Folklore
	Cf. Class P, Literature
1142.8	Historic monuments (General). Illustrative material
1142.9	Antiquities (non-Indian)
	For Indians (General), see E78.A+
	For Indians (Specific tribes), see E99.A+
	For Eskimos, see E99.E7
1143	History
1144.A-.Z	Regions, counties, etc., A-Z
1144.E44	Ellesmere Island
1144.5.A-.5.Z	Cities, towns, etc., A-Z

Canada
    Regions, provinces, territories
        Nunavut — Continued
            Elements in the population

1145	General works
1145.2.A-.2.Z	Individual elements, A-Z

                    For a list of racial, ethnic, and religious elements (with cutter numbers), see F1035.A+

Other British America
    For Bahamas, see F1650+
    For Bermudas, see F1630+
    For British East and West Florida, 1763-1783, see F301, F314
    For British Guiana, see F2361+
    For British Honduras, see F1441+
    For British West Indies, see F2131
    For Falkland Islands, see F3031+
    For thirteen North American colonies before 1776, see E186+

Colony in Brazil, 1625-1661, *see* F2532
Dutch Guiana, *see* F2401+
Dutch West Indies, *see* F2141
New Netherlands to 1664, *see* F122.1
New Sweden (Dutch possession, 1655-1664), *see* F167

1170	**Saint Pierre and Miquelon**
	Including overseas territory of the French union; local autonomy since 1935
	Other French America
	For Colony in Brazil, 1555-1567, see F2529
	For Colony in Florida, 1562-1565, see F314
	For French Guiana, see F2441+
	For French West Indies, see F2151
	For Louisiana, 1698-1803, see F372
	For New France and Acadia, 1600-1763, see F1030, F1038

For General, see salem F1401+
For Saint Pierre and Miquelon, see F1170
For New Spain (Viceroyalty), see F1231

Mexico

1201	**Periodicals. Societies**
	For Mexican geographical societies, see G5
1202	**Congresses**
1203	**Collections. Collected works**
	Museums. Exhibitions, exhibits
1203.49	General works
1203.5.A-.5.Z	Special institutions. By place, A-Z
	GALE NOTE *The cutter number(s) listed below have been given only as examples by the Library of Congress*
1203.5.M43	Mexico (City). Galería de Historia - La Lucha del Pueblo Mexicano por su Libertad
1204	**Gazetteers. Dictionaries. Geographic names**
1204.5	**Directories**
	Biography
1205	Collective
	Individual, *see* F1225.A+
1208	**General works**
	Cf. F851, Pacific coast of North America
	Cf. F1410, Spaniards in North America
1208.5	**Juvenile works**
	Minor works, *see* F1227
	Anecdotes, legends, pageants, etc., *see* F1227.2
1209	**Guidebooks. Handbooks**
1209.5	**Historic monuments (General)**
	Cf. F1218.5+, Indian antiquities
1210	**Social life and customs. Civilization. Intellectual life**
	Including national characteristics
	Elements in the population, other than Indian, *see* F1392.A+
	Indians, *see* F1218.5+
1210.5	**Mexicans in foreign countries (General)**
1210.9	**Geography**
	Description and travel. Views
1211	1516-1809
	For early discoveries, see E101+
1213	1810-1866
1215	1867-1950
	Including Inter-American Highway
1216	1951-1980
1216.5	1981-
	Antiquities. Indians
1218.5	Museums. Exhibitions
1218.6	Encyclopedias
1219	General works
1219.1.A-.1.Z	Local (Pre-Columbian and Modern), A-Z
	Unless otherwise provided for, class individual sites with the state in which they are located
	For Mayan sites, see F1435.1.A+
	Cf. F799, Cibola, N. Mex.
	GALE NOTE *The cutter number(s) listed below have been given only as examples by the Library of Congress*
1219.1.C25	Campeche (State)
1219.1.C3	Casas Grandes
1219.1.C35	Cerro de las Mesas
1219.1.C4	Chametla (Sinaloa)
1219.1.M5	Mexico City
1219.1.M55	Michoacán (State)
	Including Apatzingan (District)

	Mexico
	Antiquities. Indians
1219.1.A-.1.Z	Local (Pre-Columbian and Modern), A-Z— Continued
1219.1.M6	Mitla
	Officially: San Pablo Villa de Mitla
1219.1.O11	Oaxaca (State)
	Including Monte Albán
1219.1.Q5	Quintana Roo
1219.1.S22	San Luis Potosí (State)
1219.1.T13	Tabasco (State)
	Including La Venta
1219.1.T24	Tenayuca San Bartolo (Pyramid)
1219.1.T27	Teotihuacán (San Juan Teotihuacán)
1219.1.T43	Ticomán
	Including El Arbolillo
1219.1.T7	Tres Zapotes
1219.1.T8	Tula de Allende
	Including Tula Site
1219.1.U8	Usumacinta Valley
1219.1.V47	Veracruz (Vera Cruz) (State)
	Including Isla de Sacrificios
1219.1.Y8	Yucatan
1219.3.A-.3.Z	Special topics (Pre-Columbian and Modern), A-Z
	Class here general works on specific topics only
	For works on specific topics pertaining to specific peoples, see the people in F1219.7 or F1221
	For works on special topics pertaining to specific localities, see the locality in F1219.1.A+
1219.3.A35	Agriculture
1219.3.A42	Alcohol use
1219.3.A5	Anthropometry
1219.3.A6	Architecture
1219.3.A7	Art
1219.3.A85	Astronomy
1219.3.B4	Beadwork
1219.3.B6	Bone carving
1219.3.C2	Calendar. Chronology
1219.3.C4	Census
1219.3.C45	Children
	Codices, *see* F1219.5+
1219.3.C6	Commerce
1219.3.C65	Cosmogony. Cosmology
1219.3.C75	Costume
1219.3.C8	Craniology
1219.3.C85	Cultural assimilation
	Culture, *see* F1219
1219.3.D2	Dances
1219.3.D3	Dentistry
1219.3.D5	Diseases
1219.3.D8	Drama
1219.3.D83	Drug use
1219.3.D9	Dwellings
1219.3.E2	Economic conditions
1219.3.E3	Education
1219.3.E79	Ethnic identity
1219.3.E82	Ethnobotany
1219.3.E83	Ethnozoology
1219.3.F57	Fishing
1219.3.F6	Folklore. Legends
1219.3.F64	Food

	Mexico
	Antiquities. Indians
1219.3.A-.3.Z	Special topics (Pre-Columbian and Modern), A-Z — Continued
1219.3.F85	Funeral customs and rites
1219.3.G3	Games
1219.3.G57	Goldwork
1219.3.G59	Gourds
1219.3.G6	Government relations
1219.3.H56	Historiography
1219.3.I4	Implements
1219.3.I5	Industries
1219.3.I56	Intellectual life
1219.3.I77	Irrigation
1219.3.J48	Jewelry
1219.3.K55	Kings and rulers
1219.3.L34	Land tenure
1219.3.L4	Law
1219.3.M34	Magic
1219.3.M38	Marriage customs and rites
1219.3.M4	Masks
1219.3.M42	Material culture
1219.3.M43	Mathematics
1219.3.M5	Medicine. Surgery
1219.3.M52	Metalwork
1219.3.M54	Migrations
1219.3.M55	Military science
1219.3.M58	Mines and mining. Mineralogy
1219.3.M59	Missions
1219.3.M597	Money
1219.3.M6	Monuments
1219.3.N9	Numeral systems
1219.3.P25	Painting
1219.3.P3	Paper and paper making
1219.3.P46	Petroglyphs. Rock paintings
1219.3.P5	Philosophy
1219.3.P55	Physical characteristics
1219.3.P7	Politics and government
1219.3.P73	Population
1219.3.P8	Pottery
1219.3.P84	Psychology
1219.3.P87	Public opinion
1219.3.P9	Pyramids
1219.3.R38	Religion and mythology
1219.3.R56	Rites and ceremonies
	Rock paintings, *see* F1219.3.P46
1219.3.S38	Sculpture
1219.3.S45	Sexual behavior
1219.3.S5	Slavery
1219.3.S57	Social conditions
1219.3.S6	Social life and customs
1219.3.S64	Societies
1219.3.S7	Statistics
1219.3.T3	Taxation
1219.3.T4	Textile industry and fabrics
1219.3.T73	Transatlantic influences
1219.3.W37	Wars
1219.3.W6	Women
1219.3.W65	Wood carving
1219.3.W94	Writing

	Mexico
	Antiquities. Indians — Continued
	Codices
1219.5	General works
1219.54.A-.54.Z	Special. By people, A-Z
	GALE NOTE *The cutter number(s) listed below have been given only as examples by the Library of Congress*
1219.54.A98	Aztec
	Mayas, *see* F1435.3.W75
1219.54.M59	Mixtec
1219.56.A-.56.Z	Individual. By name, A-Z
	Under each:
	GALE NOTE *".x" represents the cutter number for the name of the codex*
	.x Texts. By date
	Including translations
	.x2 Commentaries
1219.56.A52	Anales de Tecamachalco
1219.56.B53	Biblioteca nazionale centrale di Firenze. Manuscript. Magl. XIII, 3
1219.56.B56	Bibliothèque National de France. Manuscript 210
1219.56.B58	Bibliothèque nationale (France). Manuscript. Mexicain 40
1219.56.B65	Codex Borgianus
1219.56.B67	Códice Boturini
1219.56.B74	British Library. Manuscript. Egerton 2895
1219.56.C38	Codex Azcatitlan
1219.56.C43	Codex Borbonicus
1219.56.C45	Codex Cempoallan
1219.56.C62	Codex Chimalpopocatl
1219.56.C6215	Codex Dresdensis Maya
1219.56.C622	Codex en croix
1219.56.C623	Codex Fejérváry-Mayer
1219.56.C624	Codex Laud
1219.56.C6244	Codex Lopez Ruiz
1219.56.C625	Codex Mendoza
1219.56.C6253	Codex Nuttall
1219.56.C626	Codex Ramírez
1219.56.C627	Codex Telleriano-Remensis
1219.56.C628	Codex Tro-Cortesianus
1219.56.C629	Codex Tulane
1219.56.C633	Codex Vaticanus Lat. 3773
1219.56.C634	Codex Veytia
1219.56.C636	Codex Vindobonensis Mexicanus
1219.56.C64	Codex Xolotl
1219.56.C66	Códice Azoyu 1
1219.56.C68	Códice Baranda
1219.56.C717	Códice Chapultepec
1219.56.C718	Códice Colombino
1219.56.C72	Códice Cospi
1219.56.C725	Códice Cozcatzin
1219.56.C73	Códice Cuauhtinchan
1219.56.C74	Códice de Huamantla
1219.56.C743	Códice de Jilotepec
1219.56.C746	Códice de Metepec
1219.56.C7467	Codice de San Antonio Techialoyan
1219.56.C747	Códice de Santa María Asunción
1219.56.C748	Códice de Tlatelolco
1219.56.C7486	Códice de Xicotepec
1219.56.C749	Códice de Yanhuitlan
1219.56.C75	Códice Fernández Leal
1219.56.C764	Códice Kingsborough

	Mexico
	Antiquities. Indians
	Codices
1219.56.A-.56.Z	Individual. By name, A-Z — Continued
1219.56.C767	Códice Muro
1219.56.C77	Códice Osuna
1219.56.C78	Códice Sierra
1219.56.C787	Códice Techialoyan de Huixquilucan
1219.56.C788	Códice Techialoyan de San Pedro Tototepec
1219.56.C79	Códice Techialoyan García Granados
1219.56.C82	Códice Xiquipilco-Temoaya
1219.56.G46	Genealogía de Zolín
1219.56.H83	Huexotzinco codex
1219.56.H84	Códice de Huichapan
1219.56.L48	Lienzo de Parapan
1219.56.L52	Lienzo de Tepetícpac
1219.56.L525	Lienzo de Tiltepec
1219.56.L53	Lienzo de Tlaxcala
1219.56.L54	Lienzo of Petlacala
1219.56.L55	Lienzo Totomixtlahuaca
1219.56.L57	Lienzos de Acaxochitlán
1219.56.M33	Mapa de Cuauhtinchan núm. 3
1219.56.M36	Mapa de Santiago Guevea
1219.56.M37	Matrícula de tributos
1219.56.O73	Ordenanza del Senor Cuauhtemoc
1219.56.O84	Österreichische Nationalbibliothek. Manuscript. Mexicanus 1
1219.56.P33	Padrones de Tlaxcala del siglo XVI
1219.56.P56	Plano en papel maguey
1219.56.R56	Codex Rios
1219.56.T46	Mapa de Tepechpan
1219.56.T66	Tonalámatl de Aubin
1219.56.T86	Códice Tudela
	Pre-Columbian peoples
	Class here works on the pre-Columbian period only
	For works limited to the post-contact period, as well as comprehensive works on individual peoples existing during both periods, see F1221.A+
	For works on local archaeological sites, see F1219.1.A+, except for Mayan sites, see F1435.1.A+
1219.7	General works
	Aztecs
	Including works on the Nahua peoples (General)
1219.73	General works
	Biography
1219.74	Collective
1219.75	Individual, A-Z
	GALE NOTE *See note at the head of Table F5 at the end of the text for further instructions on how to subdivide this number; the cutter number(s) listed below have been given only as examples by the Library of Congress*
1219.75.C83	Cuauhtemoc, Emperor of Mexico, 1495-1525
1219.75.M75	Montezuma I, Emperor of Mexico, ca. 1398-1468
	Montezuma II, *see F1230*
1219.75.N49	Nezahualcóyotl, King of Texcoco, *fl.* 1400-1470
	For works on Nezahualcóyotl as a poet, see PM4068
1219.76.A-.76.Z	Special topics, A-Z
1219.76.A57	Agriculture
1219.76.A59	Alcohol use
1219.76.A62	Anthropometry
1219.76.A74	Architecture
1219.76.A78	Art
1219.76.A83	Astrology

	Mexico
	Antiquities. Indians
	Pre-Columbian peoples
	Aztecs
1219.76.A-.76.Z	Special topics, A-Z — Continued
1219.76.A84	Astronomy
1219.76.B48	Beverages
1219.76.C35	Calendar. Chronology
1219.76.C37	Cartography
1219.76.C45	Census
1219.76.C53	Chalchihuitl
1219.76.C56	Children
1219.76.C59	City planning
1219.76.C65	Commerce
1219.76.C68	Costume and adornment
	Customs, *see* F1219.76.S64
1219.76.D35	Dance
1219.76.D64	Dolls
1219.76.D76	Drug use
1219.76.E36	Economic conditions
1219.76.E38	Education
1219.76.E47	Employment
1219.76.E83	Ethnobotany
1219.76.F65	Folklore. Legends
1219.76.F67	Food
1219.76.G35	Games
1219.76.G64	Goldwork
	Government, *see* F1219.76.P75
1219.76.H57	Historiography
1219.76.I53	Industries
1219.76.K53	Kings and rulers
1219.76.K55	Kinship
1219.76.L35	Land tenure
	Legends, *see* F1219.76.F65
1219.76.M35	Magic
1219.76.M37	Material culture
1219.76.M38	Mathematics
1219.76.M43	Medicine
	Mythology, *see* F1219.76.R45
1219.76.N35	Names
1219.76.P35	Painting
1219.76.P37	Paper making
1219.76.P55	Philosophy
1219.76.P75	Politics and government
1219.76.P78	Pottery
1219.76.R45	Religion and mythology
1219.76.R57	Rites and ceremonies
1219.76.S35	Sculpture
1219.76.S53	Slavery
1219.76.S63	Social conditions
1219.76.S64	Social life and customs
1219.76.T39	Taxation
1219.76.U74	Urban residence
1219.76.W37	Wars
1219.76.W44	Weights and measures
1219.76.W75	Women
1219.76.W85	Writing
	For works limited to the Aztec codices, see F1219.54.A98
1219.8.A-.8.Z	Other individual Pre-Columbian peoples or cultures, A-Z
1219.8.A33	Acaxee

	Mexico
	Antiquities. Indians
	Pre-Columbian peoples
1219.8.A-.8.Z	Other individual Pre-Columbian peoples or cultures, A-Z — Continued
1219.8.C55	Chichimec
1219.8.H83	Huastec
1219.8.M38	Matlatzinca
	Mayas, *see* F1435+
1219.8.M59	Mixtec
	Nahua, *see* F1219.73+
1219.8.O56	Olmec
1219.8.O87	Otomi
1219.8.T37	Tarasco
1219.8.T43	Teco
1219.8.T47	Tepanec
1219.8.T49	Tezcucan
1219.8.T52	Tlahuica
1219.8.T53	Tlaxcalan
1219.8.T65	Toltec
1219.8.T68	Totonac
1219.8.Z37	Zapotec
	Modern Indian peoples
	For works on peoples in both Mexico and the United States, see E99.A+
1220	General works
1221.A-.Z	Individual peoples, A-Z
1221.A4	Akwa'ala
1221.A58	Amuzgo
1221.C3	Cahita
1221.C38	Cazcan
	Chañabal, *see* F1221.T58
1221.C47	Chatino
1221.C5	Chiapanec
1221.C53	Chichimeca-Jonaz
1221.C56	Chinantec
1221.C567	Chocho
1221.C57	Chol
1221.C58	Chontal
1221.C585	Chuj
1221.C6	Cora
1221.C84	Cuicatec
1221.G79	Guachichile
1221.G82	Guarijío
1221.H8	Huastec
1221.H85	Huave
1221.H9	Huichol
	Jacalteca, *see* F1465.2.J3
1221.K35	Kamia
1221.K5	Kiliwa
1221.L2	Lacandon
	Mam, *see* F1465.2.M3
1221.M27	Matlatzinca
	Mayas, *see* F1435+
1221.M3	Mayo
1221.M33	Mazahua
1221.M35	Mazatec
1221.M67	Mixe
1221.M7	Mixtec
1221.M74	Motozintlec
1221.N3	Nahua
1221.O6	Opata

        Mexico

          Antiquities. Indians

            Modern Indian peoples

1221.A-.Z	Individual peoples, A-Z — Continued
1221.O86	Otomi
1221.P3	Pame
1221.P35	Patarabueye
1221.P6	Popoloca
1221.P62	Popoluca (Vera Cruz)
1221.S43	Seri
1221.T25	Tarahumara
1221.T3	Tarasco
1221.T33	Tecuexe
1221.T37	Tepecano
1221.T39	Tepehua
1221.T4	Tepehuan
1221.T5	Tlahuica
1221.T53	Tlapanec
1221.T56	Tlaxcalan
1221.T58	Tojolabal. Chañabal
1221.T6	Totonac
1221.T7	Trique
1221.T8	Tzeltal
1221.T9	Tzotzil
1221.Y3	Yaqui
1221.Y64	Yopi
1221.Z3	Zapotec
1221.Z6	Zoque

       History

1223	Chronological tables. Outlines, syllabi, etc. Questions and answers, etc.
	Historiography
1224	General works
	Biography of historians
1225.A2	Collective
1225.A3-.Z	Individual

                GALE NOTE *See note at the head of Table F5 at the end of the text for further instructions on how to subdivide this number*

1225.5	Study and teaching
1226	General works
	Including political history
	Pamphlets, addresses, essays, etc.
1227	General
1227.2	Anecdotes, legends, pageants, etc.
	Cf. GR115+, Folklore
	Cf. Class P, Literature
	General special
1227.5	Military and naval history
	Diplomatic history (General). Foreign and general relations
1228	General works
1228.5.A-.5.Z	Relations with individual countries, A-Z
1228.9	Other (not A-Z)
	By period
	Pre-Columbian period, *see* F1219.1.A+, F1435.1.A+
1228.98	1492-1519
	1519-1824
1229	General works

                Including End of Spanish rule, 1824

                Cf. E123+, Post-Columbian explorers and explorations (Early to 1607)

                Cf. E141+, Early descriptive works on America

	Mexico
	History
	By period
	1519-1824 — Continued
1230	1519-1535
	Including the Spanish conquest; Cortés and his companions; Bernal Díaz del Castillo; Montezuma II
1231	1535-1810. New Spain (Viceroyalty)
	Including period of the viceroys; church and state; expulsion of the Jesuits
	Including biography: Luis de Carvajal; José de Iturrigaray y Aróstegui; Guillén Lombardo; Antonio de Mendoza, conde de Tendilla; Juan de Palafox y Mendoza; Melchor de Talamantes Salvador y Baeza; etc.
	1810-
1231.5	General works
1232	1810-1849
	Including Wars of Independence, 1810-1821; Empire of Iturbide; troubles with France, 1838-1839
	Including biography: Lucas Alamán; Ignacio José Allende y Unzaga; Nicolás Bravo; Félix María Calleja, Conde de Calderón; Miguel Hidalgo y Costilla; Augustín de Iturbide; José María Teclo Morelos y Pavón; Antonio López de Santa Anna; etc.
	Cf. E401+, War with United States; loss of New Mexico and California
	Cf. F390, Revolt and independence of Texas; Texan Mier Expedition, 1842
	Cf. F1438, Annexation and secession of Central America
	Cf. F1466.4, Annexation and secession of El Salvador
1232.5	1849-1858/1861
	Including revolutions; state and church; Constitution of 1857; Raousset-Boulbon and Walker Sonora Expeditions
	Including biography: Juan Álvarez; Mariano Arista; Ignacio Comonfort; Gaston Raoux, comte Raousset-Boulbon; etc.
1233	1849/1861-1867
	Including European intervention, 1861-1867; French army in Mexico; Empire of Maximilian, 1864-1867
	Including biography: Charlotte, consort of Maximilian; Mariana Escobedo; Benito Pablo Juárez; Maximilian, Emperor of Mexico; etc.
	For Gadsden Treaty, sale of territory south of the Gila to the United States, see F786
1233.5	1867-1910
	Including biography: Porfirio Díaz. etc.
	For Apache War, 1883-1886, see E83.88
1234	1910-1946. Mexican Revolution (1910-)
	Including frontier troubles with the United States; American occupation of Veracruz, 1914; Pershing's expedition to capture Villa, 1916; Constitution of 1917
	Including biography: Plutarco Elías Calles, Manual Ávila Camacho, Lázaro Cárdenas, Venustiano Carranza, Victoriano Huerta, Francisco Indalecio Madero, Álvaro Obregón, Francisco Villa, Emiliano Zapata, etc.
	Cf. D501+, World War I, 1914-1918
	Cf. D731+, World War II, 1939-1945
	Cf. DU950.C5, Clipperton Island dispute
	1946-1970
1235	General works
	Biography
1235.5.A2	Collective
1235.5.A3-.5.Z	Individual
	GALE NOTE See note at the head of Table F5 at the end of the text for further instructions on how to subdivide this number; the cutter number(s) listed below have been given only as examples by the Library of Congress
1235.5.E25	Echeverría, Luis, 1922-
1235.5.L6	López Mateos, Adolfo
1235.5.L65	López Portillo, José

              Mexico
              History
                By period
                  1810-
                    1946-1970
                      Biography

1235.5.A3-.5.Z   Individual — Continued
1235.5.R8   Ruiz Cortines, Adolfo
                  1970-
1236   General works
                  Biography
1236.5   Collective
1236.6.A-.6.Z   Individual, A-Z
                      GALE NOTE *See note at the head of Table F5 at the end of the text for further instructions on how to subdivide this number*
             Regions, states, territories, etc.
                Including the ecclesiastical subdivisions of New Spain, bishoprics, etc., as well as the provinces of the religious orders which are to be classed with provinces of same name even if they are not identical as to extent
                For Indian local history and antiquities, see F1219.1.A+
1240   Islands of Mexico (General)
1241   Aguascalientes
               Baja California
                  Including Baja California (Territory)
                  Cf. F788, Colorado River
                  Cf. F864, California before 1869
1246   General works
1246.2   Baja California (State)
1246.3   Baja California Sur
1246.6   Bajío Region
1247   Balsas River
1249   Boundaries
                Including Guatemala boundary
                Cf. F392.B7, Republic of Texas boundary
                Cf. F392.R5, Rio Grande (General, and Texas)
                Cf. F786, United States boundary
                Cf. F1449.B7, Belize boundary
                For Gadsden Purchase, 1853, see F786
                For Nootka Sound Controversy with Great Britain, 1789-1790, see F1089.N8
                For western boundary of the Louisiana Purchase, see F374
               California (Spanish and Mexican province to 1848), *see F864*
1250   California, Gulf of
1251   Campeche
1254   Lake Chapala
1256   Chiapas
                Formed one of the Central American states under the Audiencia of Guatemala during colonial period
                Cf. DU950.C5, Clipperton Island
                Cf. F1437, Central America before 1821
1261   Chihuahua
                Province of Nueva Viscaya in colonial period
                Including Papigochic River and Valley
                Cf. F392.R5, Rio Grande (General, and Texas)
                Cf. F786, International boundary
1262   Chihuahuan Desert
1266   Coahuila
                Including Laguna (Region)
                Cf. F1234, Frontier troubles
                Cf. F392.R5, Rio Grande (General, and Texas)
                Cf. F786, International boundary

Mexico
     Regions, states, territories, etc. — Continued

1271	Colima
1272	Cozumel Island
1276	Durango
1279	Grijalva River
1281	Guanajuato
1286	Guerrero
1291	Hidalgo
	Including Ixmiquilpan, Metztitlán, and Pachuca Districts; Mezquital Valley
1294	Huasteca (Region)
1296	Jalisco
	Including Nueva Galicia (Audiencia de Guadalajara) covering not only the present states of Jalisco and Zacatecas but the provinces to the north
	Laguna Region, *see* F1266
	Lower California, *see* F1246+
	Mexico (State). Mexico (Archdiocese)
1301	General
	Mexico (Federal District and City), *see* F1386
1302	Mexico, Valley of
	Including Federal District and parts of states of Mexico, Hidalgo, and Tlaxcala
1306	Michoacán
	Including Coalcomán and Jiquilpan Districts
1311	Morelos
1313	Nayarit
	In early colonial days the area was part of Nueva Galicia (F1296)
1314	North Mexico
	Nueva Galicia, *see* F1296
1316	Nuevo León
	In colonial times called "Nuevo Reino de León"
	Cf. F391+, F1234, Frontier troubles
	Cf. F392.R5, Rio Grande (General, and Texas)
	Cf. F786, International boundary
	Nuevo Mexico (Spanish and Mexican province to 1848), *see* F799
1321	Oaxaca
	Cf. F1359, Isthmus of Tehuantepec
1322	Occidente (State)
	Cf. F1341, Sinaloa after 1831
	Cf. F1346, Sonora after 1831
1323	Pánuco (Province)
	Papigochic River and Valley, *see* F1261
1325	Popocatepetl (Volcano)
	Cf. QE523.P8, Geology
1326	Puebla
	Including Sierra Norte de Puebla
	For Popocatepetl, see F1325
1331	Querétaro
1333	Quintana Roo
	Cf. F1272, Cozumel Island
	Cf. F1449.B7, Belize boundary
1333.5	Revilla Gigedo Islands
1334	Rio Grande, Mexico
	Including Rio Grande Valley
	Cf. F392.R5 , General, and Texas
1335	San Juan de Ulúa Island
1336	San Luis Potosí
1339	Sierra Gorda
1340	Sierra Madre
	Including Copper Canyon
1341	Sinaloa

	Mexico
	Regions, states, territories, etc. — Continued
1346	Sonora
	Including San Pedro River and Valley, Mexico, and Yaqui River
	Cf. F817.S25, San Pedro River and Valley (General and Arizona)
1348	Southeast Mexico
1351	Tabasco
1356	Tamaulipas
	Includes Nuevo Santander in colonial times
	Cf. F391+, F1234, Frontier troubles
	Cf. F392.R5, Rio Grande (General, and Texas)
	Cf. F786, International boundary
1359	Isthmus of Tehuantepec
1361	Tepic (Territory)
	Texas (Mexican province to 1836), *see* F389
1366	Tlaxcala
1368	Tres Marias Islands
1371	Veracruz (Vera Cruz)
	Including cantons: Córdoba, Jalapa (Xalapa), Orizaba, Tuxpan
	For Veracruz (Vera Cruz) (City), see F1391.V4
1376	Yucatán Peninsula. Yucatán (State)
	Cf. F1449.B7, Belize border
	For Indian history and antiquities, see F1219.1.Y8
	For local Mayan antiquities, see F1435.1.A+
1381	Zacatecas
	In colonial times part of Nueva Galicia (F1296)
	Cities, towns, etc.
	For Indian local history and antiquities, see F1219.1.A+
1386	Mexico (Federal District and City)
	Subarrange by Table F1 at the end of the text
1391.A-.Z	Other, A-Z
	GALE NOTE *The cutter number(s) listed below have been given only as examples by the Library of Congress*
1391.G9	Guadalajara
1391.G98	Guanajuato
1391.J2	Jalapa (Xalapa)
1391.M5	Mérida
1391.M7	Monterrey
	Subarrange by Table F2 at the end of the text
1391.M8	Morelia
1391.O12	Oaxaca
1391.P6	Puebla
1391.Q4	Querétaro
1391.S19	San Luis Potosí
1391.T2	Tampico
1391.T23	Taxco
1391.T3	Tepoztlán
1391.T6	Toluca
1391.V4	Veracruz (Vera Cruz)
	Xalapa, *see* F1391.J2
1391.Z2	Zacatecas
1392.A-.Z	**Elements in the population, A-Z**
	Racial and ethnic groups including religious bodies which have significance in the history of Mexico
	Elements in individual regions, states, cities, etc., are classed with the region, state, city, etc.
1392.A1	General works
	Including foreign elements (General), minorities, race conflicts and problems
1392.A5	Americans
1392.A7	Arabs

	Mexico
1392.A-.Z	**Elements in the population, A-Z — Continued**
1392.B3	Basques
1392.B55	Blacks
1392.C28	Cantabrians
1392.C3	Catalans
1392.C45	Chinese
1392.C8	Cubans
1392.C93	Czechs
1392.E5	English
1392.F8	French
1392.G4	Germans
	Indians, *see* F1218.5+
1392.I82	Italians
1392.J3	Japanese
1392.J4	Jews
1392.K65	Koreans
1392.L4	Lebanese
1392.M6	Mormons
	Negroes, *see* F1392.B55
1392.P6	Poles
1392.S7	Spaniards
1392.V45	Venezuelans
	Latin America (General)
	Cf. F301,F314, Florida before 1819
	Cf. F373, Louisiana, 1764-1803
	Cf. F799+, New Mexico to 1848
	Cf. F864, California to 1848
	Cf. F1201+, Mexico
	Cf. F1421+, Central America
	Cf. F1601+, West Indies
	Cf. F2201+, South America
	Periodicals. Societies. Collections
1401	General
	For geographical societies, see G5
1402	Organization of American States
	Publications on special subjects are to be classed with the subjects in Classes B-Z
	Documents
1402.A1-.A29	Serial
	Nonserial
1402.A3	By the organization as a whole. By date
1402.A4A-.A4Z	By subordinate bodies, departments, etc., A-Z
	For Inter-American Council for Education, Science, and Culture, see F1408.4
1402.A5-.Z	Nonofficial publications
	Including official publications by individual countries of the Organization
	Pan American Union
	Formerly Bureau of the American Republics, and International Bureau of American Republics
	Official publications
1403	By the organization as a whole
1403.3	By subordinate bodies, departments, etc.
1403.5	Nonofficial publications
	Including works about the organization, addresses, essays, etc.
	Congresses
1403.9	General works
	Pan-American conferences
1404	Early congresses: American Congress, Panama, 1826

	Latin America (General)
	Congresses
	Pan-American conferences — Continued
1405	International American Conference, 1889-1948
	Continued as Inter-American Conference, 1954-
	All conferences subarranged like that of the first conference, 1889
	Under each:
	.A1-.A7 Official publications
	.A8-.Z4 Reports of delegations from participating countries
	Arranged alphabetically by country
	.Z5 Works about the conference
1405.3	Inter-American Conference for the Maintenance of Peace, Buenos Aires, 1936
1405.5	Meeting of Consultation of Ministers of Foreign Affairs of American States. By date
1405.9.A-.9.Z	Other conferences, congresses, etc., A-Z
	GALE NOTE *The cutter number(s) listed below have been given only as examples by the Library of Congress*
1405.9.I5	Inter-American Conference for the Maintenance of Continental Peace and Security, Rio de Janeiro, 1947
1406	**Gazetteers. Dictionaries. Geographic names**
1406.5	**Directories**
	Collected works
1406.7	Several authors
1406.8	Individual authors
	Including collected papers, addresses, essays, etc.
	Biography
1407	Collective
	Individual, *see* F1228.96+, F1411+, etc.
1408	**General works**
1408.2	**Juvenile works**
	Pamphlets, addresses, essays, etc.
1408.25	General
1408.27	Anecdotes, legends, pageants, etc.
1408.29	**Guidebooks. Handbooks**
	Social life and customs. Civilization. Intellectual life
1408.3	General
	Including characteristics of the people
	For specific periods, see the period
1408.4	Inter-American Council for Education, Science, and Culture
	Formerly Inter-American Cultural Council
1408.5	**Historic monuments (General)**
	Cf. F1409.5, Antiquities
1408.8	**Historical geography**
1408.9	**Geography**
	Description and travel. Views
	Early to 1810, *see* E141+
1409	1811-1950
	Including Inter-American Highway
	Cf. F865, Voyages to the Pacific coast following discovery of gold
1409.2	1951-1980
1409.3	1981-
1409.5	**Antiquities (Non-Indian)**
	For Indians of Latin America, see E65
	History
1409.6	Chronological tables. Outlines, syllabi, etc. Questions and answers, etc.
	Historiography
1409.7	General works
	Biography of historians
1409.8.A2	Collective

	Latin America (General)
	History
	Historiography
	Biography of historians — Continued
1409.8.A3-.8.Z	Individual
	GALE NOTE *See note at the head of Table F5 at the end of the text for further*
	instructions on how to subdivide this number
	Study and teaching
1409.9.A-.9.Z8	General works
1409.9.Z9	Audio-visual materials catalogs
1409.95.A-.95.Z	By region or country, A-Z
	Subarranged by author
1410	General works
	Including Spain's government of her American colonies
	Including political history
1410.5	Military history
1410.6	Naval history
	By period
1411	Early to 1601
	Including colonization, treatment of Indians, Las Casas tracts
	For biography of Las Casas, see E125.C4
	Cf. E141+, Early accounts of America
1412	1601-1830. Wars of independence, 1806-1830
1413	1830-1898
	20th century. 1898-
1414	General works
1414.2	1948-
	Diplomatic history. Foreign and general relations
1415	General works
	Including relations with several countries
1416.A-.Z	Relations with individual countries, A-Z
	For United States, see F1418
1418	Relations with the United States
	Including relations of United States with Latin America
	Cf. E18.85, Twentieth century America
	Cf. F975, Central American, West Indian, and other countries protected by and having close
	political affiliations with the United States
	Cf. F1403+, Pan American Union, Pan-American Conferences
	Cf. JZ1482, Monroe Doctrine
	Elements in the population
	For interpretation, see F1392.A+
1419.A1	General works
	Including foreign elements (General), minorities, race conflicts and problems, etc.
1419.A2-.Z	Individual, A-Z
1419.A84	Asians
1419.A87	Asturians
1419.B37	Basques
	Blacks, *see F1419.N4*
1419.C26	Canary Islanders
1419.C3	Cantabrians
1419.C94	Czechs
1419.E87	Europeans
1419.G2	Gallegans
1419.G3	Germans
	Indians, *see E65*
1419.I8	Italians
1419.J3	Japanese
1419.J4	Jews
1419.M45	Mennonites
1419.M87	Muslims

Latin America (General)
    Elements in the population

1419.A2-.Z	Individual, A-Z — Continued
1419.N38	Navarrese
1419.N4	Negroes. Blacks
1419.P65	Poles
1419.S5	Slavs
1419.S63	Spaniards

    Central America

1421	**Periodicals. Societies. Collections**
	For Central American geographical societies, see G5
1422	**Congresses**
	Collected works
1423	Several authors
1423.5	Individual authors
	Including collected papers, addresses, essays, etc.
1424	**Gazetteers. Dictionaries**
1425	**Directories**
	Biography
1426	Collective
	Individual, *see* F1435.6.A2+, F1436.92+
1428	**General works**
1428.5	**Juvenile works**
	Pamphlets, addresses, essays, etc.
1428.7	General
1428.8	Anecdotes, legends, pageants, etc.
	Cf. GR117+, Folklore
	Cf. Class P, Literature
1429	**Guidebooks. Handbooks**
1430	**Social life and customs. Civilization. Intellectual life**
	Description and travel. Views
1431	Early to 1820
	Cf. E101+; F1230, Earliest voyages and explorations
1432	1821-1950
	Including voyages to the Pacific coast following discovery of gold
1433	1951-1980
1433.2	1981-
	Antiquities. Indians (Ancient and modern)
1434	General works
1434.2.A-.2.Z	Topics, A-Z
1434.2.A37	Agriculture
1434.2.A55	Anthropometry
1434.2.A7	Art
1434.2.C58	Civil rights
1434.2.C65	Commerce
1434.2.E38	Education
1434.2.F6	Folklore. Legends
1434.2.G6	Goldwork
1434.2.G68	Government relations
1434.2.H85	Hunting
1434.2.L35	Land tenure
1434.2.M4	Metalwork
1434.2.M6	Missions
1434.2.P76	Politics and government
1434.2.P8	Pottery
1434.2.R3	Religion and mythology
1434.2.S38	Sculpture
1434.2.S62	Social conditions
1434.2.S63	Social life and customs
1434.2.W37	Wars

	Central America
	Antiquities. Indians (Ancient and modern)
1434.2.A-.2.Z	Topics, A-Z — Continued
1434.2.W65	Women
1434.3.A-.3.Z	Tribes (other than Mayas), A-Z
	For guidance in classification, see note under F2230.2.A+
	For Aztecs, see F1219.1.A+
	Mayas
	Cf. F1445+, British Honduras
	Cf. F1465+, Guatemala
1435	General works
1435.A1-.A4	Periodicals. Societies
1435.1.A-.1.Z	Local, A-Z
1435.1.A34	Abaj Takalik
1435.1.A35	Acanceh
1435.1.A36	Agua Tibia
1435.1.A38	Alta Verapaz
1435.1.A4	Altar de Sacrificios
1435.1.A57	Altun Ha
1435.1.B35	Balberta
1435.1.B4	Becan
1435.1.B6	Bonampak
1435.1.C32	Cacaxtla
1435.1.C33	Cahal Pech
1435.1.C34	Calakmul
1435.1.C35	Campeche
1435.1.C37	Caracol
1435.1.C38	Cayo
1435.1.C39	Ceren Site
1435.1.C43	Cerros Site
1435.1.C44	Chaguite Site
1435.1.C47	Chan Kom
1435.1.C49	Chiapa de Corso Site
1435.1.C494	Chicanná Site
1435.1.C5	Chichén Itzá
1435.1.C54	Chinkultic
1435.1.C56	Cimientos Site
1435.1.C63	Cobá
1435.1.C65	Colha
1435.1.C67	Comalcalco Site
1435.1.C7	Copan
1435.1.C76	Cozumel Island
1435.1.C84	Cuello
1435.1.D67	Dos Pilas
1435.1.D85	Dzibilchaltún
1435.1.D87	Dzibilnocac Site
1435.1.E32	Ecab
1435.1.E37	Edzná Site
1435.1.F45	Felipe Carrillo Puerto
1435.1.H7	Holmul
1435.1.K3	Kaminaljuyu
1435.1.K64	Kohunlich
1435.1.L2	Labná
1435.1.L23	Laguna de On Site
1435.1.L24	Lagunita
1435.1.L64	Loltun Cave
1435.1.L83	Lubaantun
1435.1.M22	Macanché Island
1435.1.M26	Marco Gonzalez Site
1435.1.M32	Meco Site

                       Central America
                          Antiquities. Indians (Ancient and modern)
                            Mayas

1435.1.A-.1.Z	Local, A-Z — Continued
1435.1.M64	Mojarra
1435.1.M84	Mul-Chic
1435.1.N35	Naj Tunich
1435.1.N37	Naranjo
1435.1.N55	Nim Li Punit Site
1435.1.N64	Nohmul
1435.1.O94	Oxkintok
1435.1.P2	Palenque
1435.1.P25	Pataxte
1435.1.P38	Paxil
1435.1.P47	Petén
1435.1.P53	Pilar Site
1435.1.P55	Planchon de las Figuras
1435.1.P88	Puuc Region
1435.1.Q78	Quintana Roo
1435.1.Q8	Quirigua
1435.1.R56	Rio Azul Site
1435.1.R67	Rosario Valley
1435.1.S26	San Gervasio Site
1435.1.S29	Sayil
1435.1.S44	Seibal
1435.1.S92	Sumidero
1435.1.T48	Tihosuco
1435.1.T5	Tikal
1435.1.T65	Tonina
1435.1.T67	Topoxté
1435.1.T8	Tulum
1435.1.T96	Tzutzuculi Site
1435.1.U2	Uaxactun
1435.1.U65	Utatlan Site
1435.1.U7	Uxmal
1435.1.X26	Xamanhá Site
1435.1.X32	Xcan Cave
1435.1.X35	Xcaret
1435.1.X7	Xkichmook
1435.1.X77	Xtacumbilxunaan Cave
1435.1.X82	Xunantunich
1435.1.Y3	Yaxchilán
1435.1.Y89	Yucatán (State)
1435.1.Z3	Zaculeu
1435.3.A-.3.Z	Topics, A-Z
1435.3.A37	Agriculture
1435.3.A56	Anthropometry
1435.3.A6	Architecture
1435.3.A7	Art
1435.3.A8	Astrology
1435.3.B37	Basket making
1435.3.C14	Calendar. Chronology. Astronomy
1435.3.C47	Children
1435.3.C49	Chinese influences
1435.3.C57	City planning
1435.3.C58	Civil rights
	Codices, *see* F1435.3.W75
1435.3.C6	Commerce
1435.3.C69	Costume and adornment
1435.3.D34	Dances

	Central America
	Antiquities. Indians (Ancient and modern)
	Mayas
1435.3.A-.3.Z	Topics, A-Z — Continued
1435.3.D4	Dentistry
1435.3.D84	Dwellings
1435.3.E27	Economic conditions
1435.3.E37	Education
1435.3.E52	Embroidery
1435.3.E72	Ethnic identity
1475.3.E73	Ethnobiology
1435.3.E74	Ethnobotany
1435.3.E76	Ethnozoology
1435.3.E87	Extraterrestrial influences
1435.3.F57	Fishing
1435.3.F6	Folklore. Legends
1435.3.F7	Food
	Government, *see* F1435.3.P7
1435.3.H85	Hunting
1435.3.I46	Implements
1435.3.I53	Industries
1435.3.J48	Jewelry
1435.3.K55	Kings and rulers
1435.3.K57	Kinship
1435.3.L35	Land tenure
	Legends, *see* F1435.3.F6
1435.3.M3	Masks
1435.3.M32	Material culture
1435.3.M35	Mathematics. Numeration
1435.3.M4	Medicine. Hygiene
1435.3.M53	Missions
1435.3.M6	Mortuary customs
	Mythology, *see* F1435.3.R3
(1435.3.N8)	Numeration, *see* F1435.3.M35
1435.3.O73	Origin
1435.3.P34	Painting
1435.3.P44	Petroglyphs. Rock paintings
1435.3.P5	Philosophy
1435.3.P7	Politics and government
1435.3.P75	Population
1435.3.P8	Pottery
1435.3.R3	Religion and mythology
1435.3.R56	Rites and ceremonies
1435.3.R6	Roads and trails
	Rock painting, *see* F1435.3.P44
1435.3.S24	Salt
1435.3.S32	Science
1435.3.S34	Sculpture
1435.3.S5	Sisal hemp
1435.3.S68	Social conditions
1435.3.S7	Social life and customs
1435.3.T48	Textile industry and fabrics
1435.3.T63	Tobacco use
1435.3.W2	Wars
1435.3.W55	Women
1435.3.W6	Wood carving
1435.3.W75	Writing. Codices
	History
1435.4	Chronological tables. Outlines, syllabi, etc. Questions and answers, etc.

               Central America
                  History — Continued
                     Historiography

1435.5	General works
	Biography of historians
1435.6.A2	Collective
1435.6.A3-.6.Z	Individual
	GALE NOTE *See note at the head of Table F5 at the end of the text for further instructions on how to subdivide this number*
1435.8	Study and teaching
1436	General works
	Including political history
	General special
1436.5	Military and naval history
	Diplomatic history. Foreign and general relations
1436.7	General works
1436.8.A-.8.Z	Relations with individual countries, A-Z
	By period
	Pre-Columbian period, *see* F1434+
1437	1502-1821
	Including Spanish period; Audiencia of Guatemala, 1542-1821
	Including biography: Pedro de Alvarado, Pedro Arias de Avila, Juan Vázquez de Coronado, etc.
	Cf. E101+, Early explorations and discoveries
	Cf. F1232, Mexican wars of independence, 1810-1821
	Cf. F1256, Chiapas
	Cf. F1441+, F1529.M9, English aggressions on the coast
1438	1821-1950
	Including annexation to and separation from Mexico, 1822-1823; Confederación de Centro América, 1823-1838/1842; other attempts at Central American unity; Clayton-Bulwer Treaty of 1850; Filibuster wars, 1855-1860; Zeledon-Wyke Treaty of 1860; Hay-Pauncefote Treaty of 1901
	Including biography: Manuel José Arce, José Francisco Barrundia, José Simeón Cañas y Villacorta, Francisco Morazán, Rafael Heliodoro Valle, etc.
	Cf. F1526.27, Walker in Nicaragua
1439	1951-1979
	Including Organization of Central American States (Charter of Salvador, 1951)
1439.5	1979-
	Elements in the population
	Including foreign elements (General), minorities, race conflicts and problems, etc.
	For interpretation, see F1392.A+
1440.A1	General works
1440.A2-.Z	Individual elements, A-Z
1440.A54	Americans
1440.B55	Blacks
1440.G3	Germans
	Indians, *see* F1434+
1440.J48	Jews
	Negroes, *see* F1440.B55
1440.P34	Palestinian Arabs
1440.S7	Spaniards
	British Honduras. Belize (Belice)
1441	Periodicals. Societies. Collections
1441.3	Congresses
	Collected works
1441.5	Several authors
1441.6	Individual authors
	Including collected papers, addresses, essays
1441.8	Museums. Exhibitions, exhibits

Central America
British Honduras. Belize (Belice) — Continued

1442	Gazetteers. Dictionaries. Geographic names
1442.3	Directories
	Biography
1442.7	Collective
	Individual, *see* F1445.7, F1446.92+
1443	General works
1443.2	Juvenile works
	Pamphlets, addresses, essays, etc.
1443.3	General
1443.4	Anecdotes, legends, pageants, etc.
	Cf. GR117+, Folklore
	Cf. Class P, Literature
1443.5	Guidebooks. Handbooks
1443.7	Historic monuments (General)
	For Indian antiquities, see F1445+
1443.8	Social life and customs. Civilization. Intellectual life
	Including national characteristics
	Description and travel. Views
1444	Early to 1950
1444.2	1951-1980
1444.3	1981-
	Antiquities. Indians (Ancient and modern)
	Including Mayas
1445	General works
1445.1.A-.1.Z	Local, A-Z
	For individual Mayan archaeological sites, see F1435.1.A+
1445.2.A-.2.Z	Tribes, A-Z
	Black Carib Indians, *see* F1505.2.C3
	Kekchi, *see* F1465.2.K5
	Mayas, *see* F1445+
1445.3.A-.3.Z	Topics, A-Z
	For topics pertaining to the Mayas only, see F1435.3.A+
	GALE NOTE *The cutter number(s) listed below have been given only as examples by the Library of Congress*
1445.3.P6	Pottery
	History
1445.5	Chronological tables. Outlines, syllabi, etc. Questions and answers, etc.
	Historiography
1445.6	General works
	Biography of historians
1445.7.A2	Collective
1445.7.A3-.7.Z	Individual
	GALE NOTE *See note at the head of Table F5 at the end of the text for further instructions on how to subdivide this number*
1445.8	Study and teaching
1446	General works
	Including political history
	General special
1446.3	General
	Diplomatic history. Foreign and general relations
1446.4	General works
1446.5.A-.5.Z	Relations with individual countries, A-Z
	By period
	Pre-Columbian period, *see* F1445+
1447	1506-1884
	Including self-governing British settlement, 1638-1786; colony with lieutenant governor under governor of Jamaica, 1862-1884; Crown Colony, 1871; separation from Jamaica, 1884

Central America
British Honduras. Belize (Belice)

         History
           By period

1447   1506-1884 — Continued
                    For disputes over claims of Spain, Guatemala, and Mexico, see F1449.B7

1447.5   1884-1945
1448   1945-
                    For dispute over claim of Guatemala, see F1449.B7G1+

1449.A-.Z   Regions, districts, etc., A-Z
1449.A53   Ambergris Cay
1449.B4   Belize
                Including Turneffe Island
          Boundaries
1449.B7A1-.B7A9   General works
1449.B7G1-.B7G9   Guatemala
1449.B7M1-.B7M9   Mexico
1449.B7S1-.B7S9   Spain
1449.S24   Saint George's Cay
1449.T6   Toledo
         Turneffe Island, *see F1449.B4*
1456.A-.Z   Cities, towns, etc., A-Z
         Cf. F1445.1.A+, Indian local history and antiquities
         GALE NOTE *The cutter number(s) listed below have been given only as examples by the Library of Congress*
1456.B4   Belize
        Elements in the population
         Including foreign elements (General), minorities, race conflicts and problems, etc.
         For interpretation, see F1392.A+
1457.A1   General works
1457.A2-.Z   Individual elements, A-Z
1457.B4   Belgians
1457.B55   Blacks
         Indians, *see F1445+*
1457.M45   Mennonites
         Negroes, *see F1457.B55*

Guatemala

         For Audiencia or captain-generalcy of Guatemala before 1821, see F1437
1461   Periodicals. Societies. Collections
        Collected works
1461.5   Several authors
1461.6   Individual authors
         Including collected papers, addresses, essays
1461.8   Museums. Exhibitions, exhibits
1462   Gazetteers. Dictionaries. Geographic names
1462.3   Directories
        Biography
1462.7   Collective
         Individual, *see F1465.7.A+, F1466.4+*
1463   General works
1463.2   Juvenile works
        Pamphlets, addresses, essays, etc.
1463.3   General
1463.4   Anecdotes, legends, pageants, etc.
         Cf. GR117+, Folklore
         Cf. Class P, Literature
1463.5   Social life and customs. Civilization. Intellectual life
         Including national characteristics
1463.6   Guidebooks. Handbooks

	Central America
	Guatemala — Continued
1463.7	Historic monuments (General)
	For Indian antiquities, see F1465+
	Description and travel. Views
1464	Early to 1950
1464.2	1951-1980
1464.3	1981-
	Antiquities. Indians (Ancient and modern)
1465	General
	Including Mayas
1465.P8	Popul vuh
	Class translations and studies of the contents here
	For original text and linguistic studies, see PM4231.Z6
1465.1.A-.1.Z	Local, A-Z
	For individual Mayan archaeological sites, see F1435.1.A+
	GALE NOTE *The cutter number(s) listed below have been given only as examples by the Library of Congress*
1465.1.A8	Atitlán, Lake
1465.1.C5	Chinautla
1465.2.A-.2.Z	Tribes, A-Z
1465.2.A34	Akatek
	Black Carib, *see* F1505.2.C3
1465.2.C3	Cakchikel
1465.2.C5	Chorti
1465.2.I87	Itza
1465.2.I95	Ixil
1465.2.J3	Jacalteca
1465.2.K36	Kanjobal
1465.2.K5	Kekchi
	Lacandon, *see* F1221.L2
1465.2.M3	Mam
1465.2.M65	Mopan
	Pipil, *see* F1485.2.P5
1465.2.P6	Pokomam
1465.2.Q5	Quichés
1465.2.R32	Rabinal Achi
1465.2.T9	Tzutuhil
1465.2.X5	Xinca
1465.3.A-.3.Z	Topics, A-Z
	For topics pertaining to the Mayas only, see F1435.3.A+
1465.3.A37	Agriculture
1465.3.A7	Art
1465.3.C58	Civil rights
1465.3.C77	Commerce
1465.3.C8	Costume and adornment
1465.3.D3	Dances
1465.3.E2	Economic conditions
1465.3.E84	Ethnic identity
1465.3.F6	Folklore. Legends
1465.3.G6	Government relations
1465.3.I5	Industries
1465.3.M36	Masks
1465.3.M4	Medicine
1465.3.M57	Missions
1465.3.P64	Politics and government
1465.3.P68	Pottery
1465.3.R4	Religion and mythology
1465.3.R44	Removal
1465.3.S6	Social conditions

	Central America
	Guatemala
	Antiquities. Indians (Ancient and modern)
1465.3.A-.3.Z	Topics, A-Z — Continued
1465.3.S62	Social life and customs
1465.3.T3	Taxation
1465.3.T4	Textiles
1465.3.W37	Wars
	History
1465.5	Chronological tables. Outlines, syllabi, etc. Questions and answers, etc.
	Historiography
1465.6	General works
	Biography of historians
1465.7.A2	Collective
1465.7.A3-.7.Z	Individual
	GALE NOTE *See note at the head of Table F5 at the end of the text for further instructions on how to subdivide this number*
1465.8	Study and teaching
1466	General works
	Including political history
	General special
1466.1	Military and naval history
	Diplomatic history. Foreign and general relations
	Cf. F1469.B7, Boundaries
1466.2	General works
1466.3.A-.3.Z	Relations with individual countries, A-Z
1466.35	Other (not A-Z)
	By period
	Pre-Columbian period, *see* F1465+
1466.4	1523-1838
	Including end of Spanish rule, 1821; annexation to and separation from Mexico, 1822-1823; Confederación de Centro América, 1823-1838/1842; earthquake of 1773
1466.45	1838-1945
	Including establishment as a republic, April 17, 1839; era of despots; wars with El Salvador; revolutions of 1898, 1906, 1920, 1930, 1944, etc.; epidemic of cholera, 1837; earthquakes of 1902, 1917, 1918
	Including biography: Justo Rufino Barrios, Rafael Carrera, Lázaro Chacón, Manuel Estrada Cabrera, Miguel García Granados, Jorge Ubico, etc.
	Cf. D731+, World War II, 1939-1945
	Cf. F1507.5, Wars with Honduras
1466.5	1945-1985
	Including Revolution of 1954
	Including biography: Jacobo Arbenz Guzmán, Juan José Arévalo, Carlos Castillo Armas, etc.
1466.7	1985-
1469.A-.Z	Regions, departments, etc., A-Z
	Alta Vera Paz, *see* F1469.V3
	Baja Vera Paz, *see* F1469.V4
1469.B7	Boundaries
1469.B7A1-.B7A5	General
	British Honduras, *see* F1449.B7
1469.B7A6-.B7Z	Honduras
	Mexico, *see* F1249
	El Salvador, *see* F1489.B7
1469.G9	Guatemala
1469.H8	Huehuetenango
1469.I9	Izabal
	Cf. F1469.S2, Santo Tomas (District)
1469.J8	Jutiapa (Dept.)
1469.M68	Motagua River

Central America
  Guatemala

1469.A-.Z	Regions, departments, etc., A-Z — Continued
1469.P4	Petén
	Including Usumacinta River
1469.Q5	Quezaltenango
1469.S13	Sacatepéquez
1469.S17	San Marcos
1469.S2	Santo Tomas (District)
1469.S64	Sololá
	Including Lake Atitlán
1469.T7	Totonicapán
1469.V3	Vera Paz, Alta
1469.V4	Vera Paz, Baja
	Including former department of Vera Paz
1469.Z3	Zacapa
1476.A-.Z	Cities, towns, etc., A-Z
	Cf. F1465.1.A+, Indian local history and antiquities
	GALE NOTE *The cutter number(s) listed below have been given only as examples by the Library of Congress*
1476.A5	Antigua
1476.G9	Guatemala (City)
1476.P8	Puerto Barrios
1476.Q8	Quezaltenango
	Elements in the population
	For interpretation, see F1392.A+
1477.A1	General works
	Including foreign elements (General), minorities, race conflicts and problems, etc.
1477.A2-.Z	Individual elements
	GALE NOTE *The cutter number(s) listed below have been given only as examples by the Library of Congress*
1477.G3	Germans
	Indians, *see* F1465+

  Salvador (El Salvador)

1481	Periodicals. Societies. Collections
	Collected works
1481.5	Several authors
1481.6	Individual authors
	Including collected papers, addresses, essays, etc.
1481.8	Museums. Exhibitions, exhibits
1482	Gazetteers. Dictionaries. Geographic names
1482.3	Directories
	Biography
1482.7	Collective
	Individual, *see* F1485.7
1483	General works
1483.2	Juvenile works
	Pamphlets, addresses, essays, etc.
1483.3	General
1483.4	Anecdotes, legends, pageants, etc.
	Cf. GR117+, Folklore
	Cf. Class P, Literature
1483.5	Guidebooks. Handbooks
1483.7	Historic monuments (General)
	For Indian antiquities, see F1485+
1483.8	Social life and customs. Civilization. Intellectual life
	Including national characteristics
	Description and travel. Views
1484	Early to 1950
1484.2	1951-1980

	Central America
	Salvador (El Salvador)
	Description and travel. Views — Continued
1484.3	1981-
	Antiquities. Indians (Ancient and modern)
1485	General works
1485.1.A-.1.Z	Local, A-Z
1485.1.C8	Cuscatlán
1485.2.A-.2.Z	Tribes, A-Z

GALE NOTE *The cutter number(s) listed below have been given only as examples by the Library of Congress*

	Matagalpa, *see* F1525.2.M3
1485.2.P5	Pipil
1485.3.A-.3.Z	Topics, A-Z
	For topics pertaining to the Mayas only, see F1435.3.A+
	Government, *see* F1485.3.P7
1485.3.N35	Names
1485.3.P7	Politics and government
1485.3.P8	Pottery
1485.3.S6	Social conditions
	History
1485.5	Chronological tables. Outlines, syllabi, etc. Questions and answers, etc.
	Historiography
1485.6	General works
	Biography of historians
1485.7.A2	Collective
1485.7.A3-.7.Z	Individual

GALE NOTE *See note at the head of Table F5 at the end of the text for further instructions on how to subdivide this number*

1485.8	Study and teaching
1486	General works
	Including political history
	General special
1486.1	Military and naval history
	Diplomatic history. Foreign and general relations
	Cf. F1489.B7, Boundaries
1486.2	General works
1486.3.A-.3.Z	Relations with individual countries, A-Z
1486.9	Other (A-Z)
	By period
	Pre-Columbian period, *see* F1485+
1487	1524-1838
	Including end of Spanish rule, 1821; appeal to United States for annexation, 1822; Mexican rule, 1822-1823; Confederación de Centro América, 1823-1838/1842
	Including biography: José Matías Delgado, etc.
1487.5	1838-1944. Martínez regime, 1931-1944
	Including period of internal struggles and changing constitution; wars with Guatemala; conflicts with Honduras; Revolt of 1944
	Including biography: Manuel Enrique Araujo, Maximiliano Hernández Martínez, Alfonso Quiñónez Molina, Pío Romero Bosque, etc.
1488	1944-1979
	Including earthquake of May 6, 1951
	Including biography: Salvador Castañeda Castro, Oscar Osorio, etc.
	1979-1992
1488.3	General works
	Biography
1488.4	Collective
1488.42.A-.42.Z	Individual, A-Z

GALE NOTE *See note at the head of Table F5 at the end of the text for further instructions on how to subdivide this number*

	Central America
	Salvador (El Salvador)
	History
	By period — Continued
	1992-
1488.5	General works
	Biography
1488.52	Collective
1488.53.A-.53.Z	Individual, A-Z
	GALE NOTE *See note at the head of Table F5 at the end of the text for further instructions on how to subdivide this number*
1489.A-.Z	Regions, departments, etc., A-Z
	GALE NOTE *The cutter number(s) listed below have been given only as examples by the Library of Congress*
	Boundaries
1489.B7A1-.B7A9	General
1489.B7G1-.B7G9	Guatemala
1489.B7H1-.B7H9	Honduras
1489.C8	Cuscatlán
1489.L3	La Unión
1489.M46	Metapán (District)
1489.S2	San Salvador
	Unión, *see* F1489.L3
1489.U8	Usulután
1496.A-.Z	Cities, towns, etc., A-Z
	Cf. F1485.1.A+, Indian local history and antiquities
1496.S2	San Salvador
	Including Fire of August 8, 1951
1496.S35	Santa Ana
	Elements in the population
	Including foreign elements (General), minorities, race conflicts and problems, etc.
	For interpretation, see F1392.A+
1497.A1	General works
1497.A2-.Z	Individual elements, A-Z
1497.B55	Blacks
	Indians, *see* F1485+
	Negroes, *see* F1497.B55
	Honduras
1501	Periodicals. Societies. Collections
	Collected works
1501.5	Several authors
1501.6	Individual authors
	Including collected papers, addresses, essays, etc.
1501.8	Museums. Exhibitions, exhibits
1502	Gazetteers. Dictionaries. Geographic names
1502.3	Directories
	Biography
1502.7	Collective
	Individual, *see* F1505.7
1503	General works
1503.2	Juvenile works
	Pamphlets, addresses, essays, etc.
1503.3	General
1503.4	Anecdotes, legends, pageants, etc.
	Cf. GR117+, Folklore
	Cf. Class P, Literature
1503.5	Guidebooks. Handbooks
1503.7	Historic monuments (General)
	For Indian antiquities, see F1505+

<table>
</table>

	Central America
	Honduras — Continued
1503.8	Social life and customs. Civilization. Intellectual life
	Including national characteristics
1504	Description and travel. Views
	Antiquities. Indians (Ancient and modern)
1504.5	Museums. Exhibitions
1505	General works
1505.1.A-.1.Z	Local, A-Z
	GALE NOTE *The cutter number(s) listed below have been given only as examples by the Library of Congress*
1505.1.T2	Tenampua
1505.2.A-.2.Z	Tribes, A-Z
	GALE NOTE *The cutter number(s) listed below have been given only as examples by the Library of Congress*
1505.2.C3	Carib (Black)
1505.2.L4	Lenca
	Matagalpa, *see* F1525.2.M3
	Miskito, *see* F1529.M9
1505.2.P3	Paya
	Sumo, *see* F1525.2.S8
1505.2.X5	Xicaque
1505.3.A-.3.Z	Topics, A-Z
	For topics pertaining to the Mayas only, see F1435.3.A+
1505.3.A72	Architecture
1505.3.P57	Population
1505.3.P6	Pottery
1505.3.S63	Social life and customs
	History
1505.5	Chronological tables. Outlines, syllabi, etc. Questions and answers, etc.
	Historiography
1505.6	General works
	Biography of historians
1505.7.A2	Collective
1505.7.A3-.7.Z	Individual
	GALE NOTE *See note at the head of Table F5 at the end of the text for further instructions on how to subdivide this number*
1505.8	Study and teaching
1506	General works
	Including political history
	General special
1506.2	Military and naval history
	Diplomatic history. Foreign and general relations
	Cf. F1509.B7, Boundaries
1506.3	General works
1506.4.A-.4.Z	Relations with individual countries, A-Z
1506.9	Other (not A-Z)
	By period
	Pre-Columbian period, *see* F1505+
1507	1502-1838
	Including end of Spanish rule, 1821; Mexican rule, 1822-1823; Confederación de Centro America, 1823-1838/1842
1507.5	1838-1933
	Including establishment as republic, October 26, 1838; winning of Bay Islands and Mosquito coast, 1859; Walker's filibustering expedition, 1860; Insurrection of Amapala, 1910; wars with Guatemala and El Salvador; United States intervention, 1911, 1913, etc.
	Including biography: Manuel Bonilla, Policarpo Bonilla, Juan Nepomuceno Fernández Lindo y Zelaya, Marco Aurelio Soto, Vicente Tosta, etc.

	Central America
	Honduras
	History
	By period — Continued
	1933-1982
1508	General works
	Biography
1508.2	Collective
1508.22.A-.22.Z	Individual, A-Z
	GALE NOTE *See note at the head of Table F5 at the end of the text for further instructions on how to subdivide this number*
	1982-
1508.3	General works
	Biography
1508.32	Collective
1508.33.A-.33.Z	Individual, A-Z
	GALE NOTE *See note at the head of Table F5 at the end of the text for further instructions on how to subdivide this number*
1509.A-.Z	Regions, departments, etc., A-Z
1509.B3	Bay Islands (Department)
	Including Swan Islands (Islas del Cisne)
1509.B7	Boundaries
1509.B7A1-.B7A5	General
	Guatemala, *see* F1469.B7
1509.B7A6-.B7Z	Nicaragua
	El Salvador, *see* F1489.B7
1509.C4	Choluteca
	Cisne, Islas del, *see* F1509.B3
1509.C6	Colón
	Cf. F1509.M9, Mosquitia (District)
1509.M9	Mosquitia (District)
	Cf. F1529.M9, Mosquito Coast of Nicaragua
1509.O4	Olancho
	Swan Islands, *see* F1509.B3
1509.T2	Tegucigalpa (Province)
1509.U4	Ulua (Lua) River and Valley
1509.V2	Valle
	Including Tigre Island
1509.Y6	Yoro
1516.A-.Z	Cities, towns, etc., A-Z
	Cf. F1505.1.A+, Indian local history and antiquities
	GALE NOTE *The cutter number(s) listed below have been given only as examples by the Library of Congress*
1516.C72	Comayagua
1516.G7	Gracias
1516.S3	San Pedro Sula
1516.T4	Tegucigalpa
	Elements in the population
	Including foreign elements (General), minorities, race conflicts and problems, etc.
	For interpretation, see F1392.A+
1517.A1	General works
1517.A2-.Z	Individual elements, A-Z
1517.A73	Arabs
1517.B55	Blacks
	Indians, *see* F1505+
	Negroes, *see* F1517.B55
	Nicaragua
1521	Periodicals. Societies. Collections
	Collected works
1521.5	Several authors

	Central America
	Nicaragua
	Collected works — Continued
1521.6	Individual authors
	Including collected papers, addresses, essays, etc.
1521.8	Museums. Exhibitions, exhibits
1522	Gazetteers. Dictionaries. Geographic names
1522.3	Directories
	Biography
1522.7	Collective
	Individual, *see* F1525.7
1523	General works
1523.2	Juvenile works
	Pamphlets, addresses, essays, etc.
1523.3	General
1523.4	Anecdotes, legends, pageants, etc.
	Cf. GR117+, Folklore
	Cf. Class P, Literature
1523.5	Guidebooks. Handbooks
1523.7	Historic monuments (General)
	For Indian antiquities, see F1525+
1523.8	Social life and customs. Civilization. Intellectual life
	Including national characteristics
	Description and travel. Views
1524	Through 1980
1524.3	1981-
	Antiquities. Indians (Ancient and modern)
1525	General works
1525.1.A-.1.Z	Local, A-Z
	GALE NOTE *The cutter number(s) listed below have been given only as examples by the Library of Congress*
1525.1.Z3	Zapatera Island
1525.2.A-.2.Z	Tribes, A-Z
	Carib (Black), *see* F1505.2.C3
	Chiapanec, *see* F1221.C5
	Lenca, *see* F1505.2.L4
1525.2.M3	Matagalpa
	Miskito, *see* F1529.M9
1525.2.N5	Nicarao
1525.2.R3	Rama
1525.2.S7	Subtiaba
1525.2.S8	Sumo
(1525.2.T4)	Terraba, *see* F1545.2.T4
1525.2.U4	Ulva
1525.3.A-.3.Z	Topics, A-Z
1525.3.A7	Art
1525.3.C84	Cultural assimilation
1525.3.E38	Education
1525.3.E74	Ethnic identity
1525.3.E76	Ethnobiology
1525.3.G68	Government relations
1525.3.L35	Land tenure
1525.3.M43	Medicine
1525.3.M57	Missions
	Mythology and religion, *see* F1525.3.R44
1525.3.N35	Names
1525.3.P6	Pottery
1525.3.R44	Religion and mythology
1525.3.S38	Sculpture
1525.3.S63	Social conditions

	Central America
	Nicaragua — Continued
	History
1525.5	Chronological tables. Outlines, syllabi, etc. Questions and answers, etc.
	Historiography
1525.6	General works
	Biography of historians
1525.7.A2	Collective
1525.7.A3-.7.Z	Individual

GALE NOTE *See note at the head of Table F5 at the end of the text for further instructions on how to subdivide this number*

1525.8	Study and teaching
1526	General works
	Including political history
	General special
1526.1	Military and naval history
	Diplomatic history. Foreign and general relations
	Cf. F1529.B7, Boundaries
1526.2	General works
1526.22.A-.22.Z	Relations with individual countries, A-Z
1526.24	Other (not A-Z)
	By period
	Pre-Columbian period, *see F1525+*
1526.25	1522-1838

Including end of Spanish rule, 1821; Mexican rule, 1822-1823; Confederación de Centro América, 1823-1838/1842; rivalry between León and Granada; English invasion, 1780-1781

1526.27	1838-1909

Including foreign intervention, 1848- ; Filibuster War, 1855-1860 (Battle of Rivas, 1856); transfer of Mosquito Territory by Great Britain, 1893; Nicaragua Canal (Cf. TC784)

Including biography: Pedro Joaquín Chamorro, Roberto Sacasa, William Walker, José Santos Zelaya, etc.

Cf. F1438, Filibusters in Central America

Cf. F1529.M9, Mosquito coast and the English protectorate

Cf. F1536.S2, Bombardment of Greytown, 1854

1526.3	1909-1937

Including revolts and revolutions of 1909-1910, 1912, 1916, 1926-1929, etc.; United States intervention, 1909-1933; Bryan-Chamorro Treaty, 1916

Including biography: Emiliano Chamorro, Adolfo Díaz, Juan Bautista Sacasa, Augusto César Sandino, etc.

1527	1937-1979

Including invasion from El Salvador, 1944; Inter-American Highway

Including biography: Anastasio Somoza, etc.

Cf. D731+, World War II, 1939-1945

	1979-
1528	General works
	Biography
1528.2	Collective
1528.22.A-.22.Z	Individual, A-Z

GALE NOTE *See note at the head of Table F5 at the end of the text for further instructions on how to subdivide this number*

1529.A-.Z	Regions, departments, etc., A-Z
	Atlantic Coast, *see F1529.M9*
1529.B7	Boundaries
1529.B7A1-.B7A5	General
1529.B7A6-.B7Z	Costa Rica
	Honduras, *see F1509.B7*
	Saint Andrews Island, *see F2281.S15*
1529.C53	Chontales

	Central America
	Nicaragua
1529.A-.Z	Regions, departments, etc., A-Z — Continued
1529.J4	Jinotega
1529.M9	Mosquitia (Mosquito Coast). Atlantic Coast, etc.
	Including Mosquito Reservation and Miskito Indians
	Cf. F1509.M9 , Mosquitia (District) of Honduras
	Cf. F1526.27, Transfer of Mosquito Territory by Great Britain, 1893
1529.N5	Lake Nicaragua region
1529.S35	San Juan River and Valley
	Cf. F1549.S17, Costa Rica
1529.Z4	Zelaya
	Cf. F1529.M9, Mosquitia
1536.A-.Z	Cities, towns, etc., A-Z
	Cf. F1525.1.A+, Indian local history and antiquities
	GALE NOTE *The cutter number(s) listed below have been given only as examples by the Library of Congress*
1536.D5	Diriamba
1536.G72	Granada
	Cf. F1526.25, Early history
1536.L4	León
	Cf. F1526.25, Early history
1536.M26	Managua
1536.S2	San Juan del Norte. Greytown
	Elements in the population
	Including foreign elements (General), minorities, race conflicts and problems, etc.
	For interpretation, see F1392.A+
1537.A1	General works
1537.A2-.Z	Individual elements, A-Z
1537.A5	Americans
1537.B55	Blacks
1537.G47	Germans
	Indians, *see* F1525+
	Negroes, *see* F1537.B55
	Costa Rica
1541	Periodicals. Societies. Collections
	Collected works
1541.5	Several authors
1541.6	Individual authors
	Including collected papers, addresses, essays, etc.
1541.8	Museums. Exhibitions, exhibits
1542	Gazetteers. Dictionaries. Geographic names
1542.3	Directories
	Biography
1542.7	Collective
	Individual, *see* F1545.7
1543	General works
1543.2	Juvenile works
	Pamphlets, addresses, essays, etc.
1543.3	General
1543.4	Anecdotes, legends, pageants, etc.
	Cf. GR117+, Folklore
	Cf. Class P, Literature
1543.5	Guidebooks. Handbooks
1543.7	Historic monuments (General)
	For Indian antiquities, see F1545+
1543.8	Social life and customs. Civilization. Intellectual life
	Including national characteristics
1543.9	Geography
1544	Description and travel. Views

	Central America
	Costa Rica — Continued
	Antiquities. Indians (Ancient and modern)
1545	General works
1545.1.A-.1.Z	Local, A-Z
	GALE NOTE *The cutter number(s) listed below have been given only as examples by the Library of Congress*
1545.1.V6	Volcán Irazú
1545.15	Museums. Exhibitions
1545.2.A-.2.Z	Tribes, A-Z
1545.2.B6	Boruca
1545.2.B7	Bribri
1545.2.C33	Cabecar
1545.2.C48	Chorotega
1545.2.G77	Guatuso
	Guaymi, *see* F1565.2.G8
1545.2.G8	Guetar
1545.2.M3	Mangue
1545.2.T4	Terraba
1545.3.A-.3.Z	Topics, A-Z
1545.3.A7	Art
1545.3.F6	Folklore. Legends
1545.3.G65	Goldwork
1545.3.J48	Jewelry
1545.3.L34	Land tenure
1545.3.P57	Politics and government
1545.3.P6	Pottery
1545.3.R4	Religion and mythology
1545.3.R44	Reservations
1545.3.S35	Sculpture
1545.3.W2	Warfare
	History
1545.5	Chronological tables. Outlines, syllabi, etc. Questions and answers, etc.
	Historiography
1545.6	General works
	Biography of historians
1545.7.A2	Collective
1545.7.A3-.7.Z	Individual
	GALE NOTE *See note at the head of Table F5 at the end of the text for further instructions on how to subdivide this number*
1545.8	Study and teaching
1546	General works
	Including political history
	General special
1546.2	Military and naval history
	Diplomatic history. Foreign and general relations
	For boundary disputes, see F1549.B7
1546.3	General works
1546.4.A-.4.Z	Relations with individual countries, A-Z
1546.9	Other (not A-Z)
	By period
	Pre-Columbian period, *see* F1545+
1547	1502-1838
	Including end of Spanish rule, 1821; Mexican rule, 1822-1823; Confederación de Centro América, 1823-1838/1842
1547.5	1838-1948
	Including revolutions of 1917, 1919, 1948; Inter-American Highway
	Including biography: Tomás Guardia, Rafael Iglesias, Ricardo Jiménez, Juan Rafael Mora, Teodoro Picado Michalski, Bernardo Soto, etc.

	Central America
	Costa Rica
	History
	By period — Continued
1548	1948-1986
	Including biography: José Figueres, Otilio Ulate Blanco, etc.
	1986-
1548.2	General works
	Biography
1548.22	Collective
1548.23.A-.23.Z	Individual, A-Z

GALE NOTE *See note at the head of Table F5 at the end of the text for further instructions on how to subdivide this number*

1549.A-.Z	Regions, provinces, cantons, etc., A-Z
1549.B7	Boundaries
1549.B7A1-.B7A29	General
	Nicaragua, *see* F1529.B7
1549.B7A3-.B7Z	Panama
	Including ancient Costa Rica-Columbia boundary
1549.C6	Cocos Island
1549.D8	Golfo Dulce (Osa Gulf)
1549.G9	Guanacaste
1549.H5	Heredia
1549.I7	Irazú Volcano
1549.L55	Limón (Province)
1549.N5	Nicoya Peninsula
	Osa Gulf, *see* F1549.D8
1549.O83	Osa Peninsula
1549.R5	Rio Grande de Térraba
1549.S15	San José
1549.S17	San Juan River and Valley
	Cf. F1529.S35, Nicaragua
1549.T13	Talamanca (District)
	Térraba River and Valley, *see* F1549.R5
1556.A-.Z	Cities, towns, etc., A-Z
	Cf. F1545.1.A+, Indian local history and antiquities

GALE NOTE *The cutter number(s) listed below have been given only as examples by the Library of Congress*

1556.A6	Alajuela
1556.C3	Cartago
	Including earthquake of 1910
1556.L5	Limón
1556.S2	San José
	Elements in the population
	For interpretation, see F1392.A+
1557.A1	General works
1557.A2-.Z	Individual elements, A-Z
1557.B55	Blacks
1557.C66	Colombians
1557.G3	Germans
	Indians, *see* F1545+
1557.J4	Jews
1557.L42	Lebanese
	Negroes, *see* F1557.B55
1557.N5	Nicaraguans
1557.S7	Spaniards
	Panama
1561	Periodicals. Societies. Collections
	Collected works
1561.5	Several authors

	Central America
	Panama
	Collected works — Continued
1561.6	Individual authors
	Including collected papers, addresses, essays, etc.
1561.8	Museums. Exhibitions, exhibits
1562	Gazetteers. Dictionaries. Geographic names
1562.3	Directories
	Biography
1562.7	Collective
	Individual, *see* F1565.7
1563	General works
	Cf. F1569.C2, Canal Zone
1563.2	Juvenile works
	Pamphlets, addresses, essays, etc.
1563.3	General
1563.4	Anecdotes, legends, pageants, etc.
	Cf. GR117+, Folklore
	Cf. Class P, Literature
1563.5	Guidebooks. Handbooks
1563.7	Historic monuments (General)
	For Indian antiquities, see F1565+
1563.8	Social life and customs. Civilization. Intellectual life
	Including national characteristics
	Description and travel. Views
1564	Early to 1950
1564.2	1951-1980
1564.3	1981-
	Antiquities. Indians (Ancient and modern)
1565	General works
1565.1.A-.1.Z	Local, A-Z
	GALE NOTE *The cutter number(s) listed below have been given only as examples by the Library of Congress*
1565.1.C6	Coclé
1565.1.D26	Darien
1565.1.V47	Veraguas
1565.2.A-.2.Z	Tribes, A-Z
	Boruca, *see* F1545.2.B6
1565.2.C77	Cueva
1565.2.C8	Cuna
1565.2.D6	Dorask
1565.2.G8	Guaymi
	Terraba, *see* F1545.2.T4
1565.3.A-.3.Z	Topics, A-Z
1565.3.A7	Art
1565.3.F64	Folklore
1565.3.G68	Government relations
1565.3.I54	Industries
	Music, *see* M1685.P2+; ML3572
1565.3.P45	Philosophy
1565.3.T49	Textile industry and fabrics
	History
1565.5	Chronological tables. Outlines, syllabi, etc. Questions and answers, etc.
	Historiography
1565.6	General works
	Biography of historians
1565.7.A2	Collective
1565.7.A3-.7.Z	Individual
	GALE NOTE *See note at the head of Table F5 at the end of the text for further instructions on how to subdivide this number*

	Central America
	Panama
	History — Continued
1565.8	Study and teaching
1566	General works
	Including political history
	For boundary disputes, see F1569.B7
	General special
1566.2	Military history
	Diplomatic history. Foreign and general relations
	Cf. F1569.B7, Boundaries
1566.3	General works
1566.4.A-.4.Z	Relations with individual countries, A-Z
1566.44	Other (not A-Z)
	By period
	Pre-Columbian period, *see F1565+*
1566.45	1501-1903
	Including end of Spanish rule, 1821; part of Greater Colombia (Colombian Federation), 1821-1831; under New Granada (later Colombia), 1831-1903; independent in 1841 and 1857; secessionist revolts in 1830, 1831, 1840, 1895, 1898-1903; Massacre of 1856; Panama expeditions, 1741, 1875, 1885
1566.5	1903-1952
	Including secession from Colombia, 1903; Hay-Bunau-Varilla Treaty of 1903; Hay-Herrán Treaty of 1903; under protection of the United States, 1903-1936; revolutions of 1931, 1951
	Including biography: Manuel Amador Guerrero; Arnulfo Arias Madrid; Pablo Arosemena; Belisario Porras; etc.
1567	1952-
	Including biography: José Antonio Remón, etc.
1569.A-.Z	Regions, provinces, etc., A-Z
1569.B6	Bocas del Toro
	Including Laguna de Chiriqui
1569.B7	Boundaries
1569.B7A1-.B7A5	General
1569.B7A6-.B7A7	Canal Zone
1569.B7A8-.B7Z	Colombia
	Costa Rica, *see F1549.B7*
	Caledonia (Scots' Colony), *see F2281.D2*
1569.C2	Canal Zone. Panama Canal
	Including Chagres River
	Cf. F1569.B7, Panama boundary
	Cf. TC774+, Panama Canal (Construction and maintenance)
	Chagres River, *see F1569.C2*
1569.C5	Chiriquí
	For Laguna de Chiriqui, see F1569.B6
1569.C6	Coclé
1569.C7	Colón
1569.D3	Darien
	Cf. F2281.D2 , Scots' Colony of Darien
	Morro Island, *see F1569.P3*
1569.P3	Panama
	Including Isla Taboga (Morro Island), Pearl Islands
	For Darién Province, see F1569.D3
1569.P35	Panama Bay. Gulf of Panama
	Pearl Islands (Islas de las Perlas), *see F1569.P3*
1569.S3	San Blas coast
	Scots' Colony of Darien, *see F2281.D2*
	Isla Taboga, *see F1569.P3*
1569.V4	Veraguas (Veragua)

Central America

Panama — Continued

1576.A-.Z	Cities, towns, etc., A-Z
	Cf. F1565.1.A+, Indian local history and antiquities
	GALE NOTE *The cutter number(s) listed below have been given only as examples by the*
	Library of Congress
1576.C7	Colón
1576.P2	Panama
	Elements in the population
	Including foreign elements (General), minorities, race conflicts and problems, etc.
	For interpretation, see F1392.A+
1577.A1	General works
1577.A2-.Z	Individual elements, A-Z
1577.B55	Blacks
1577.C48	Chinese
	Indians, *see* F1565.1.A+
1577.J4	Jews
	Negroes, *see* F1577.B55
	Caribbean area, *see* **F2155+**
	West Indies
1601	**Periodicals. Societies. Collections**
	Including conferences, congresses, etc.
	Collected works
1602	Several authors
1603	Individual authors
	Including collected papers, addresses, essays, etc.
1604	**Gazetteers. Dictionaries. Geographic names**
1606	**Directories**
	Biography
1607	Collective
	Individual, *see* F1620.5.A2+, F1621, F1623
1608	**General works**
1608.3	**Juvenile works**
	Pamphlets, addresses, essays, etc.
1608.5	General
1608.7	Anecdotes, legends, pageants, etc.
	Cf. GR120+, Folklore
	Cf. Class P, Literature
1609	**Guidebooks. Handbooks**
1609.3	**Historic monuments (General)**
	For Indian antiquities, see F1619+
1609.5	**Social life and customs. Civilization. Intellectual life**
	Including characteristics of the people
	Description and travel. Views
1610	Early to 1809
	Cf. E141+, Descriptive accounts of America to 1810
1611	1810-1950
1612	1951-1980
1613	1981-
	Antiquities. Indians (Ancient and modern)
	Works on the aborigines and antiquities of a group of islands or an individual island are classed
	with the group of islands or the individual island
1619	General works
1619.2.A-.2.Z	Tribes, A-Z
	GALE NOTE *The cutter number(s) listed below have been given only as examples by the*
	Library of Congress
	Arawak Indians, *see* F2230.2.A7
	Carib Indians, *see* F2001
	Lucayan Indians, *see* F1655
1619.2.T3	Taino

	West Indies
	Antiquities. Indians (Ancient and modern) — Continued
1619.3.A-.3.Z	Topics, A-Z
1619.3.C65	Commerce
1619.3.E83	Ethnic identity. Ethnicity
	Ethnicity, *see* F1619.3.E83
1619.3.F6	Folklore. Legends
1619.3.G68	Government relations
1619.3.I6	Implements (Celts, axes, etc.)
1619.3.P6	Pottery
1619.3.S38	Sculpture
	History
1620	Chronological tables. Outlines, syllabi, etc. Questions and answers, etc.
	Historiography
1620.3	General works
	Biography of historians
1620.5.A2	Collective
1620.5.A3-.5.Z	Individual
	GALE NOTE *See note at the head of Table F5 at the end of the text for further instructions on how to subdivide this number*
1620.7	Study and teaching
1621	General works
	Including general histories and histories of the Spanish West Indies to 1898; naval operations in West Indian waters; Audiencia of Santo Domingo; military and naval history; English West Indian expeditions of 1654-1655, and 1695; George Brydges Rodney and other commanders in the Seven Years' War, 1756-1763; expeditions and campaigns of 1793-1815
	Cf. E101+, Early discoveries
	Cf. E263.W5, E271+, Naval operations in the American Revolution
	Cf. F1411+, Spanish America in general
	Cf. F1566.45, Panama Expedition, 1741
	Cf. F1781, Capture of Havana, 1762
	Cf. F1783, Spanish West Indies in the nineteenth century
	Cf. F2041, Ruyter's attack on Barbados, 1655
	Cf. F2081, English capture of Martinique, 1809
	Cf. F2097, Rodney at St. Eustatius, 1781
	Cf. F2161, Buccaneers and pirates in the West Indies
	Cf. F2272.5, English West Indian Expedition, 1739-1742
	General special
	Military and naval history, *see* F1621
	Diplomatic history. Foreign and general relations
1621.5	General works
1622	Relations with the United States
1622.5.A-.5.Z	Relations with other countries, A-Z
	By period
	Early to 1898, *see* F1621
1623	1898-
	Cf. F1783, Spanish West Indies, 1810-1898
	Elements in the population
	Including minorities, race conflicts, problems, etc.
	For interpretation, see F1392.A+
1628.8	General works
1629.A-.Z	Individual elements, A-Z
1629.B55	Blacks
	Cf. HT1071+, Slavery
	Indians, *see* F1619+
	Negroes, *see* F1629.B55
	Bermudas. Somers Islands
1630	Periodicals. Societies. Collections
	Collected works
1630.4	Several authors

	West Indies
	Bermudas. Somers Islands
	Collected works — Continued
1630.5	Individual authors
	Including collected papers, addresses, essays, etc.
1630.6	Museums. Exhibitions, exhibits
1630.7	Gazetteers. Dictionaries. Geographic names
1630.8	Directories
	Biography
1630.9	Collective
	Individual, *see* F1635.6, F1636, F1639.A+
1631	General works. Description and travel. Views
1631.2	Juvenile works
	Pamphlets, addresses, essays, etc.
1631.3	General
1631.4	Anecdotes, legends, pageants, etc.
	Cf. GR120+, Folklore
	Cf. Class P, Literature
1632	Guidebooks. Handbooks
1632.5	Historic monuments (General)
1633	Social life and customs. Civilization. Intellectual life
	Including characteristics of the people
	Description and travel, *see* F1631
1634	Antiquities
	History
1635	Chronological tables. Outlines, syllabi, etc. Questions and answers, etc.
	Historiography
1635.5	General works
	Biography of historians
1635.6.A2	Collective
1635.6.A3-.6.Z	Individual
	GALE NOTE *See note at the head of Table F5 at the end of the text for further instructions on how to subdivide this number*
1635.7	Study and teaching
1636	General works
	Including political history
1637	General special
1639.A-.Z	Islands, cities, etc., A-Z
	GALE NOTE *The cutter number(s) listed below have been given only as examples by the Library of Congress*
1639.H3	Hamilton
1639.S3	St. George Island
	Elements in the population
	Including foreign elements (General), minorities, race conflicts and problems, etc.
	For interpretation, see F1392.A+
1640.A1	General works
1640.A2-.Z	Individual elements, A-Z
1640.B55	Blacks
	Negroes, *see* F1640.B55
1640.P67	Portuguese
	Bahamas. Bahama Islands. Lucayos
1650	Periodicals. Societies. Collections
	Collected works
1650.4	Several authors
1650.5	Individual authors
	Including collected papers, addresses, essays, etc.
1650.6	Museums. Exhibitions, exhibits
1650.7	Gazetteers. Dictionaries. Geographic names
1650.8	Directories

	West Indies
	Bahamas. Bahama Islands. Lucayos — Continued
	Biography
1650.9	Collective
	Individual, *see* F1656
1651	General works. Description and travel. Views
1651.2	Juvenile works
	Pamphlets, addresses, essays, etc.
1651.3	General
1651.4	Anecdotes, legends, pageants, etc.
	Cf. GR120+, Folklore
	Cf. Class P, Literature
1652	Guidebooks. Handbooks
1653	Historic monuments (General)
1654	Social life and customs. Civilization. Intellectual life
	Including characteristics of the people
	Description and travel, *see* F1651
1655	Antiquities. Indians
	Including Lucayan Indians (now extinct)
	For Taino Indians, see F1619.2.T3
	History
1655.3	Chronological tables. Outlines, syllabi, etc. Questions and answers, etc.
	Historiography
1655.5	General works
	Biography of historians
1655.6.A2	Collective
1655.6.A3-.6.Z	Individual
	GALE NOTE *See note at the head of Table F5 at the end of the text for further instructions on how to subdivide this number*
1655.7	Study and teaching
1656	General works
	Including political history
1657	General special
	By period
	Early to 1973, *see* F1656
1657.2	1973-
1659.A-.Z	Islands, cities, etc., A-Z
	GALE NOTE *The cutter number(s) listed below have been given only as examples by the Library of Congress*
1659.C37	Cat Island (Cat Cay)
1659.N3	Nassau
1659.T9	Turks and Caicos Islands
	Elements in the population
	Including foreign elements (General), minorities, race conflicts and problems, etc.
	For interpretation, see F1392.A+
1660.A1	General works
1660.A2-.Z	Individual elements, A-Z
1660.B55	Blacks
	Indians, *see* F1655
	Negroes, *see* F1660.B55
	Greater Antilles
	Including Cuba, Haiti, Puerto Rico, Jamaica, and outlying islands. The Windward Passage
1741	General works
	Including description and travel, history, antiquities
	Cuba
1751	Periodicals. Societies. Collections
	Collected works
1752	Several authors
1753	Individual authors
	Including collected papers, addresses, essays, etc.

	West Indies
	Greater Antilles
	Cuba — Continued
1753.5	Museums. Exhibitions, exhibits
1754	Gazetteers. Dictionaries. Geographic names
1754.5	Directories
1754.7	Guidebooks. Handbooks
	Biography
1755	Collective
1758	General works
1758.5	Juvenile works
	Pamphlets, addresses, essays, etc.
1759	General
1759.5	Anecdotes, legends, pageants, etc.
	Cf. GR120+, Folklore
	Cf. Class P, Literature
1759.7	Historic monuments
	For Indian antiquities, see F1769
1760	Social life and customs. Civilization. Intellectual life
	Including national characteristics
1760.9	Geography
	Description and travel. Views
1761	Early to 1810
1763	1811-1897
1765	1898-1951
1765.2	1951-1980
1765.3	1981-
1769	Antiquities. Indians
	Including inscriptions, monuments, Ciboney Indians, etc.
	For Taino Indians, see F1619.2.T3
	History
1772	Chronological tables. Outlines, syllabi, etc. Questions and answers, etc.
	Historiography
1773	General works
	Biography of historians
1774.A2	Collective
1774.A3-.Z	Individual
	GALE NOTE *See note at the head of Table F5 at the end of the text for further instructions on how to subdivide this number*
1774.S3	Saco, José Antonio
1775	Study and teaching
1776	General works
	Including political history
	General special
1776.1	Military and naval history
	Diplomatic history. Foreign and general relations
1776.2	General works
1776.3.A-.3.Z	Relations with individual countries, A-Z
1778	Other (not A-Z)
	By period
	Pre-Columbian period, *see F1769*
	1492-1810
1779	General
	Including Age of buccaneers (16th century); Sir Charles Knowles; Edward Vernon; capture of Spanish silver-fleet in Matanzas Bay, 1628; period of internal development (18th century)
	For discovery and exploration, see E101+
1781	1762-1763
	Including Siege of Havana; English occupation, 1762-1763
	Cf. DA505+,DS674.8, Anglo-Spanish War, 1762-1763

	West Indies
	Greater Antilles
	Cuba
	History
	By period
	1492-1810
1781	1762-1763 — Continued
	Cf. E199, French and Indian War, 1755-1763
	1810-1898
1783	General

Including general works on the Spanish West Indies; question of annexation to the United States; Black Eagle Conspiracy, 1830; Black Conspiracy, 1844

Including biography: Gaspar Betancourt Cisneros; Calixto García; Máximo Gómez y Báez; José Cipriano de la Luz y Caballero; Jose Marti (Cf. PQ7389.M2); Félix Varela y Morales; etc.

Cf. E431, Ostend Manifesto, 1854

Cf. PQ7389.M2, José Martí

| 1784 | Insurrection, 1849-1851. López |

Including filibusters and individual biography, e.g. Narciso López

| 1785 | 1868-1895 |

Including Ten Years' War, 1868-1878; Treaty of Zanjon, 1878; the Virginius; the "Little War," 1879-1880

Including biography: Ignacio Agramonte y Loinaz, Francisco Vicente Aguilera, Carlos Manuel de Céspedes y del Castillo

| 1786 | 1895-1898 |

Including Revolution of 1895-1898; question of intervention to February 15, 1898

Including biography: Pedro Estanislao Betancourt y Dávalos, Antonio Maceo, Bartolomé Masó

| 1787 | 1898-1933 |

Including Cuban Republic, 1902- ; Platt Amendment; Revolution of 1906; American occupation, 1906-1909

Including biography: Antonio Sánchez de Bustamante y Sirvén, Tomás Estrada Palma, Juan Gualberto Gómez, Gerardo Machado y Morales, Mario García Menocal, Gonzalo de Quesada, Cosme de la Torriente y Peraza, Alfredo Zayas y Alfonso

1787.5	1933-1959
	1959- . Communist regime
	Cf. E841+, Cuban missile crisis
1788	General works
1788.2	Addresses, essays, lectures
	Biography
1788.22.A2	Collective
1788.22.A3-.22.Z	Individual

GALE NOTE See note at the head of Table F5 at the end of the text for further instructions on how to subdivide this number; the cutter number(s) listed below have been given only as examples by the Library of Congress

1788.22.C3	Castro, Fidel
	Elements in the population
	For interpretation, see F1392.A+
1789.A1	General works
1789.A2-.Z	Individual elements, A-Z
1789.A45	Americans
1789.A7	Asturians
	Blacks, see F1789.N3
1789.C3	Catalans
1789.C53	Chinese
1789.F7	French
1789.G3	Gallegans
	Indians, see F1769

	West Indies
	Greater Antilles
	Cuba
	Elements in the population
1789.A2-.Z	Individual elements, A-Z — Continued
1789.J3	Japanese
1789.J4	Jews
1789.N3	Negroes. Blacks
1789.S7	Spaniards
	Cf. F1789.A7, Asturians
	Cf. F1789.G3, Gallegans
1789.Y6	Yoruba
	Provinces
	Cf. F1769, Indian history and antiquities
	Camagüey, *see* F1831+
	Havana (Province)
1791	General works
1795	History
1799.A-.Z	Cities, towns, etc., A-Z
	GALE NOTE *The cutter number(s) listed below have been given only as examples by the Library of Congress*
1799.G8	Guanabacoa
1799.H3	Havana (City)
	Subarrange by Table F2 at the end of the text
1799.I8	Isle of Pines
1799.S2	San Antonio de los Baños
	Las Villas, *see* F1821+
	Oriente, *see* F1841+
	Pinar del Rio
1801	General works
1805	History
1809.A-.Z	Cities, towns, etc., A-Z
	GALE NOTE *The cutter number(s) listed below have been given only as examples by the Library of Congress*
1809.M4	Mantua
1809.P5	Pinar del Rio (City)
	Matanzas
1811	General works
1815	History
1819.A-.Z	Cities, towns, etc., A-Z
	GALE NOTE *The cutter number(s) listed below have been given only as examples by the Library of Congress*
1819.B4	Bellamar Cave
1819.C3	Cárdenas
1819.M4	Matanzas (City)
	Las Villas
	Formerly Santa Clara
1821	General works
1825	History
1829.A-.Z	Cities, towns, etc., A-Z
	GALE NOTE *The cutter number(s) listed below have been given only as examples by the Library of Congress*
1829.C5	Cienfuegos
1829.R4	Remedios
1829.S12	Sagua la Grande
1829.S2	Sancti-Spiritus
1829.S3	Santa Clara
1829.T8	Trinidad
	Camagüey
	Formerly Puerto Principe

	West Indies
	Greater Antilles
	Cuba
	Provinces
	Camagüey — Continued
1831	General works
1835	History
1839.A-.Z	Cities, towns, etc., A-Z

GALE NOTE *The cutter number(s) listed below have been given only as examples by the Library of Congress*

1839.C3	Camagüey (City)
1839.G8	Guáimaro
1839.N9	Nuevitas
	Puerto Principe (City), *see* F1839.C3
1839.S23	Santa Cruz del Sur
	Oriente
	Formerly Santiago de Cuba
1841	General works
1845	History
1849.A-.Z	Cities, towns, etc., A-Z

GALE NOTE *The cutter number(s) listed below have been given only as examples by the Library of Congress*

1849.B2	Baracoa
1849.B3	Bayamo
1849.G5	Gibara
1849.H6	Holguín
1849.S3	Santiago de Cuba
1849.T62	Toa River
1849.V5	Victoria de las Tunas
	Guantanamo
1850	General works
1850.5	History
1850.9.A-.9.Z	Cities, towns, etc., A-Z
	Ciego de Avila
1851	General works
1851.5	History
1851.9.A-.9.Z	Cities, towns, etc., A-Z
	Cienfuegos
1852	General works
1852.5	History
1852.9.A-.9.Z	Cities, towns, etc., A-Z
	Sancti Spíritus
1853	General works
1853.5	History
1853.9.A-.9.Z	Cities, towns, etc., A-Z
	Holguín Province
1854	General works
1854.5	History
1854.9.A-.9.Z	Cities, towns, etc., A-Z
	Jamaica
1861	Periodicals. Societies. Collections
	Collected works
1862	Several authors
1863	Individual authors
	Including collected papers, addresses, essays, etc.
1863.5	Museums. Exhibitions, exhibits
1864	Gazetteers. Dictionaries. Geographic names
1864.5	Directories
	Biography
1865	Collective

	West Indies
	Greater Antilles
	Jamaica
	Biography — Continued
	Individual, *see* F1879.5
1868	General works
1868.2	Juvenile works
	Pamphlets, addresses, essays, etc.
1868.3	General
1868.4	Anecdotes, legends, pageants, etc.
	Cf. GR120+, Folklore
	Cf. Class P, Literature
1869	Guidebooks. Handbooks
1869.5	Historic monuments (General)
	For Indian antiquities, see F1875
	Description and travel. Views
1870	Early to 1810
1871	1811-1950
1872	1951-1980
1872.2	1981-
1874	Social life and customs. Civilization. Intellectual life
	Including characteristics of the people
1875	Antiquities. Indians
	History
1878	Chronological tables. Outlines, syllabi, etc. Questions and answers, etc.
	Historiography
1879	General works
	Biography of historians
1879.5.A2	Collective
1879.5.A3-.5.Z	Individual
	GALE NOTE *See note at the head of Table F5 at the end of the text for further instructions on how to subdivide this number*
1880	Study and teaching
1881	General works
	Including political history
	General special
1882	General
	Diplomatic history. Foreign and general relations
1882.2	General works
1882.3.A-.3.Z	Relations with individual countries, A-Z
1882.4	Other (not A-Z)
	By period
	Pre-Columbian period, *see* F1875
1884	1494-1810
	Including Spanish rule, 1494-1655; British conquests of 1596, 1643, 1655; Treaty of Madrid, 1670; attempted invasion by France and Spain, 1694, by France alone, 1782, 1806; Maroon War, 1795-1796; Earthquake of 1692
	Including biography: Sir Thomas Lynch, etc.
	Cf. F2272.5, Admiral Vernon and the English West Indian Expedition of 1739-1742
	Cf. F1526.25, British expedition from Jamaica against Nicaragua, 1780-1781
1886	1810-1962
	Including Negro insurrection, 1831; Morant Bay Rebellion, 1865-1866; reorganization of Colony, 1844, 1866; earthquake of 1907; hurricanes, 1944, 1951; move toward British West-Indian federation
	Including biography: Sir John Peter Grant, Edward John Eyre, etc.
	Cf. D501+, World War I, 1914-1918
	Cf. D731+, World War II, 1939-1945
	Cf. F1447 , British Honduras under governor of Jamaica, 1862-1884
1887	1962-

          West Indies
            Greater Antilles
              Jamaica — Continued

1891.A-.Z	Regions, parishes, etc., A-Z
	GALE NOTE *The cutter number(s) listed below have been given only as examples by the Library of Congress*
(1891.C5)	Cayman Islands, *see* F2048.5
1891.H2	Hanover Parish
1891.S14	St. James Parish
1891.S2	St. Mary Parish
	For Turks and Caicos Islands, see F1659.T9
1895.A-.Z	Cities, towns, etc., A-Z
	Cf. F1875, Indian local history and antiquities
	GALE NOTE *The cutter number(s) listed below have been given only as examples by the Library of Congress*
1895.K5	Kingston
	Including earthquake of 1907
1895.M6	Montego Bay
1895.P6	Port Royal
	Including earthquake of 1692; hurricanes of 1712, 1714, 1722
1895.S7	Spanish Town
	Elements in the population
	For interpretation, see F1392.A+
1896.A1	General works
	Including race conflicts and problems, etc.
1896.A2-.Z	Individual elements, A-Z
	Blacks, *see* F1896.N4
1896.C5	Chinese
1896.E2	East Indians
	Indians, *see* F1875
1896.I6	Irish
1896.J48	Jews
1896.N4	Negroes. Blacks
	Cf. HT1096+, Slavery
	Haiti (Island). Hispaniola
1900	Periodicals. Societies. Collections
1901	General works
	Including description and travel of the whole island
1909	Antiquities. Indians
1911	History (of the island). Spanish Colony, 1492-1795
	Spanish Colony of Santo Domingo, 1808-1822, *see* F1938.3
	Union of the whole island, 1822-1844, *see* F1924
	Haiti (Republic)
1912	Periodicals. Societies. Collections, etc.
	Collected works
1912.5	Several authors
1912.6	Individual authors
	Including collected papers, addresses, essays, etc.
1912.8	Museums. Exhibitions, exhibits
1913	Gazetteers. Dictionaries. Geographic names
1913.5	Directories
	Biography
1914	Collective
	Individual, *see* F1920
1915	General works
1915.2	Juvenile works
	Pamphlets, addresses, essays, etc.
1915.3	General
1915.4	Anecdotes, legends, pageants, etc.
	Cf. GR120+, Folklore

	West Indies
	Greater Antilles
	Haiti (Island). Hispaniola
	Haiti (Republic)
	Pamphlets, addresses, essays, etc.
1915.4	Anecdotes, legends, pageants, etc. — Continued
	Cf. Class P, Literature
1915.5	Guidebooks. Handbooks
1915.7	Historic monuments (General)
	For Indian antiquities, see F1909
1916	Social life and customs. Civilization. Intellectual life
	Including national characteristics
1917	Description and travel. Views
	Antiquities, Indians, *see* F1909
	History
1918	Chronological tables. Outlines, syllabi, etc. Questions and answers, etc.
	Historiography
1919	General works
	Biography of historians
1920.A2	Collective
1920.A3-.Z	Individual
	GALE NOTE *See note at the head of Table F5 at the end of the text for further instructions on how to subdivide this number*
1920.5	Study and teaching
1921	General works
	Including political history
	General special
1921.5	Military and naval history
	Diplomatic history. Foreign and general relations
1922	General works
1922.5.A-.5.Z	Relations with individual countries, A-Z
1922.9	Other (not A-Z)
	By period
	Pre-Columbian period, *see* F1909
1923	1492-1803
	For period of Spanish control, see F1911
	Including French settlement, 1630-1677; Colony of Saint Domingue, 1677-1803; Treaty of Ryswick, 1697; Revolution of 1791-1803; English invasion, 1793-1798; withdrawal of Spain from island, 1795
	Including biography: François Dominique Toussaint Louverture, etc.
1924	1804-1843
	Including proclamation of independent nation, January 1, 1804; Republic, 1806; separate north and south states, 1806-1820; annexation of Santo Domingo, 1822; Revolution of 1843
	Including biography: Jean Pierre Boyer; Henri Christophe (Henri I); Jean Jacques Dessalines; Alexandre Sabès Pétion; etc.
	Cf. F1938.3 , Revival of Spanish Colony in the east, 1808-1822
1926	1843-1915
	Including loss of Santo Domingo, 1844; period of tumult
	Including biography: Fabre Nicolas Geffrard; Pierre Nord Alexis; Louis Étienne Félicité Salomon; Faustino Soulouque (Faustino I, Emperor); etc.
1927	1915-1950
	Including United States intervention (Military occupation, 1915-1934; fiscal control ended, 1947); Revolt of 1946
	Including biography: Louis Borno, Sudre Dartiguenave, Dumarsais Estimé, Élie Lescot, Sténio Vincent, etc.
1928	1950-1986
	Including constitution of 1946 abrogated
	Including biography: Paul Eugène Magloire, etc.

	West Indies
	Greater Antilles
	Haiti (Island). Hispaniola
	Haiti (Republic)
	History
	By period — Continued
	1986-
1928.2	General works
	Biography
1928.22	Collective
1928.23.A-.23.Z	Individual, A-Z

GALE NOTE *See note at the head of Table F5 at the end of the text for further instructions on how to subdivide this number*

1929.A-.Z	Regions, departments, cities, etc., A-Z

        Cf. F1909, Indian local history and antiquities

GALE NOTE *The cutter number(s) listed below have been given only as examples by the Library of Congress*

1929.B7	Boundaries
	Including boundary between Haiti and Dominican Republic
1929.C3	Cap-Haïtien
1929.C8	Cul de Sac
1929.G6	Gonave Island
1929.P8	Port-au-Prince
	Elements in the population
	Including foreign elements (General), minorities, race conflicts and problems, etc.
	For interpretation, see F1392.A+
1930.A1	General works
1930.A2-.Z	Individual elements, A-Z
1930.B55	Blacks
1930.F7	French
	Indians, *see* F1909
	Negroes, *see* F1930.B55
1930.P64	Poles
	Dominican Republic. Santo Domingo
1931	Periodicals. Societies. Collections
	Collected works
1931.5	Several authors
1931.6	Individual authors
	Including collected papers, addresses, essays, etc.
1931.7	Museums. Exhibitions, exhibits
1932	Gazetteers. Dictionaries. Geographic names
1932.5	Directories
	Biography
1933	Collective
	Individual, *see* F1937.6
1934	General works
1934.2	Juvenile works
	Pamphlets, addresses, essays, etc.
1934.3	General
1934.4	Anecdotes, legends, pageants, etc.
	Cf. GR120+, Folklore
	Cf. Class P, Literature
1934.5	Guidebooks. Handbooks
1934.7	Historic monuments (General)
	For Indian antiquities, see F1909
1935	Social life and customs. Civilization. Intellectual life
	Including national characteristics
1935.5	Geography
	Description and travel. Views
1936	Early to 1951

	West Indies
	Greater Antilles
	Haiti (Island). Hispaniola
	Dominican Republic. Santo Domingo
	Description and travel. Views — Continued
1936.2	1951-1980
1936.3	1981-
	Antiquities, Indians, *see* F1909
	History
1937	Chronological tables. Outlines, syllabi, etc. Questions and answers, etc.
	Historiography
1937.5	General works
	Biography of historians
1937.6.A2	Collective
1937.6.A3-.6.Z	Individual
	GALE NOTE *See note at the head of Table F5 at the end of the text for further instructions on how to subdivide this number*
1937.8	Study and teaching
1938	General works
	Including political history
	General special
1938.1	Military and naval history
	Diplomatic history. Foreign and general relations
1938.2	General works
1938.25.A-.25.Z	Relations with individual countries, A-Z
1938.29	Other (not A-Z)
	By period
	Pre-Columbian period, *see* F1909
1938.3	1492-1844
	For Spanish colony, 1492-1795, see F1911
	Including period under French or Haitian control, 1795-1808; Spanish colony, 1808-1822; union with Haiti, 1822-1844
	1844-1930
1938.4	General
	Including establishment of republic, 1844; Spanish regime, 1861-1865; period of revolutions
	Including biography: Buenaventura Báez, Juan Pablo Duarte, Ulises Heureaux, Gregorio Luperón, Adolfo Alejandro Nouel y Bobadilla, Francisco del Rosario Sánchez, Pedro Santana, etc.
1938.45	1916-1924
	Including period of United States military occupation
1938.5	1930-1961
	Including biography: Rafael Leónidas Trujillo Molina, etc.
	1961-
1938.55	General works
	Biography
1938.57	Collective
1938.58.A-.58.Z	Individual, A-Z
	GALE NOTE *See note at the head of Table F5 at the end of the text for further instructions on how to subdivide this number*
1939.A-.Z	Regions, provinces, cities, etc., A-Z
	Cf. F1909, Indian local history and antiquity
	GALE NOTE *The cutter number(s) listed below have been given only as examples by the Library of Congress*
1939.A4	Alta Vela (Island). Isla Alto Velo
	Boundaries, *see* F1929.B7
	Ciudad Trujillo, *see* F1939.S4
1939.C67	Cotuí (Town)
	Disitrito Nacional, *see* F1939.S4

West Indies
  Greater Antilles
    Haiti (Island). Hispaniola
      Dominican Republic. Santo Domingo

1939.A-.Z	Regions, provinces, cities, etc., A-Z — Continued
1939.I8	Isabela
	Ruined town, founded in 1493 by Columbus
	La Isabela, *see* F1939.I8
1939.L3	La Vega (City). Concepción de la Vega
1939.M6	Monte Plata (Town)
	Monte Tina, *see* F1939.T5
	National District, *see* F1939.S4
1939.P9	Puerto Plata (City). San Felipe de Puerto Plata
1939.S15	Salcedo (Province)
1939.S18	Samaná (Town). Santa Bárbara de Samaná
1939.S4	Santo Domingo (National District and City)
	Subarrange by Table F2 at the end of the text
	Formerly Ciudad Trujillo from 1936 to 1961
1939.T5	Tina (Mountain peak) Monte Tina or Loma Tina
	Trujillo (City), *see* F1939.S4
1939.Y38	Yaque del Norte River
	Elements in the population
	Including foreign elements (General), minorities, race conflicts and problems, etc.
	For interpretation, see F1392.A+
1941.A1	General works
1941.A2-.Z	Individual elements, A-Z
1941.A73	Arabs
1941.B55	Blacks
1941.C37	Catalans
1941.F5	Flemings
1941.H3	Haitians
	Indians, *see* F1909
1941.J3	Japanese
1941.J4	Jews
	Negroes, *see* F1941.B55
1941.S7	Spaniards
	Puerto Rico. Boriquén
1951	Periodicals. Societies. Collections
	Collected works
1952	Several authors
1953	Individual authors
	Including collected papers, addresses, essays
1953.5	Museums. Exhibitions, exhibits
1954	Gazetteers. Dictionaries. Geographic names
1954.5	Directories
	Biography
1955	Collective
	Individual, *see* F1970.6
1958	General works
1958.3	Juvenile works
	Pamphlets, addresses, essays, etc.
1958.5	General
1958.7	Anecdotes, legends, pageants, etc.
	Cf. GR120+, Folklore
	Cf. Class P, Literature
1959	Guidebooks. Handbooks
1959.5	Historic monuments (General)
	For Indian antiquities, see F1969
1960	Social life and customs. Civilization. Intellectual life
	Including national characteristics

	West Indies
	Greater Antilles
	Puerto Rico. Boriquén — Continued
	Description and travel. Views
1961	Early to 1897
1965	1898-1950
1965.2	1951-1980
1965.3	1981-
1969	Antiquities. Indians
	Including the Borinque ño Indians (now extinct)
	History
1970	Chronological tables. Outlines, syllabi, etc. Questions and answers, etc.
	Historiography
1970.5	General works
	Biography of historians
1970.6.A2	Collective
1970.6.A3-.6.Z	Individual

> GALE NOTE *See note at the head of Table F5 at the end of the text for further instructions on how to subdivide this number; the cutter number(s) listed below have been given only as examples by the Library of Congress*

1970.6.T3	Tapia y Rivera, Alejandro
1970.8	Study and teaching
1971	General works
	Including political history
1972	General special
	By period
	Pre-Columbian period, *see* F1969
1973	1493-1898

> *Including period of Spanish rule; attacks by British in 1595, 1598, 1791; attack by Dutch, 1625; revolts against Spain in 1812, 1867; autonomous regime, 1897*
> *Including biography: Eugenio Mar ía de Hostos y Bonilla, etc.*
> Cf. E717.3, *Spanish-American War, 1898*
> Cf. F1783, *Spanish West Indies, 1810-1898*

1975	1898-1952

> *United States possession, 1898; United States Territory (Organized but unincorporated), 1917-1952; hurricanes of 1899, 1928, 1932; etc.*
> *Known as Porto Rico, 1898-1932*
> *Including biography: Jes ús T. Pi ñero, etc.*

	1952-
1976	General works
	Biography
1976.2	Collective
1976.3.A-.3.Z	Individual, A-Z

> GALE NOTE *See note at the head of Table F5 at the end of the text for further instructions on how to subdivide this number*

1981	Regions, departments, cities, etc., A-Z
	Cf. F1969 , *Indian local history and antiquities*

> GALE NOTE *The cutter number(s) listed below have been given only as examples by the Library of Congress*

1981.A26	Aguada
1981.A6	Arecibo (City)
1981.C24	Caguas
1981.C9	Culebra Island
1981.G7	Guayama
1981.M4	Mayagüez (City)
1981.P7	Ponce
1981.R5	Río Piedras
1981.S2	San Juan
	Including La Fortaleza (Government house), San Juan National Monument, etc.
1981.U8	Utuado

	West Indies
	Greater Antilles
	Puerto Rico. Boriquén
1981	Regions, departments, cities, etc., A-Z — Continued
1981.V5	Vieques Island. Crab Island
	Elements in the population
	Including foreign elements (General), minorities, race conflicts and problems, etc.
	For interpretation, see F1392.A+
1983.A1	General works
1983.A2-.Z	Individual elements, A-Z
	Blacks, *see* F1983.N4
1983.C83	Cubans
1983.D65	Dominicans
	Indians, *see* F1969
1983.N4	Negroes. Blacks
1983.S64	Spaniards
	Other islands
1991	Navassa
	Lesser Antilles. Caribbees
2001	General works. Cariban Indians
	Cf. F2161, The Caribbean Sea with coasts and adjoining islands
	Groups of islands, by geographical distribution
	For groups by political allegiance, see F2130+
	For individual islands, see F2033+
2006	Leeward Islands
	Including Anguilla, Antigua, Barbuda, Désirade, Dominica, Guadeloupe, Les Saintes, Marie Galante, Montserrat, Nevis, Redonda, Saba, Saint Bartholomew, Saint Christopher, Saint Croix, Saint Eustatius, Saint John, Saint Martin, Saint Thomas, Virgin Islands
2011	Windward Islands
	Including Barbados, Grenada, The Grenadines, Martinique, Saint Lucia, Saint Vincent
2016	Islands along the Venezuela coast
	Including Aruba, Bonaire, Curaçao, Tobago, Trinidad
	For islands belonging to Venezuela, see F2331.A2
	Individual islands (alphabetically)
2033	Anguilla (British)
2035	Antigua and Barbuda
2038	Aruba (Dutch)
2041	Barbados (British)
	Including Ruyter's attack on Barbados, 1655
	Barbuda, *see* F2035
	Basse-Terre Island, *see* F2066
2048	Bonaire. Buen Ayre (Dutch)
2048.5	Cayman Islands (British)
2049	Curaçao (Dutch)
2050	Désirade (French)
2051	Dominica (British)
2056	Grenada (British)
	Subarrange by Table F3 at the end of the text
2061	The Grenadines
	For Saint Vincent and the Grenadines, see F2106+
2066	Guadeloupe (French)
2070	Les Saintes (French)
2076	Marie Galante (French)
2081	Martinique (French)
	Subarrange by Table F3 at the end of the text
2082	Montserrat (British)
2084	Nevis (British). Saint Kitts-Nevis
	Redonda, *see* F2035
2088	Saba (Dutch)
2089	Saint Bartholomew. Saint Barthélemy (French)

	West Indies
	Lesser Antilles. Caribbees
	Individual islands (alphabetically) — Continued
2091	Saint Christopher. Saint Kitts (British)
	For Saint Kitts-Nevis, see F2084
2096	Saint Croix (United States, formerly Danish)
2097	Saint Eustatius (Dutch)
2098	Saint John (United States, formerly Danish)
2100	Saint Lucia (British)
2103	Saint Martin (Dutch and French)
2105	Saint Thomas (United States, formerly Danish)
	Saint Vincent. Saint Vincent and the Grenadines
2106	General works
2110.A-.Z	Local, A-Z
2116	Tobago
	For Trinidad and Tobago, see F2119+
	Trinidad. Trinidad and Tobago
2119	General works
	By period
2120	Early to 1888
2121	1888-1962
2122	1962-
2123.A-.Z	Local, A-Z
2129	Virgin Islands (British)
	Class individual islands here
	Groups of islands. By political allegiance or national language
2130	English-speaking Caribbean
2131	British West Indies (Commonwealth Caribbean)
	Including Bahamas, Bermudas, Cayman Islands, Jamaica, the Leeward Islands (Anguilla, Antigua, Barbuda, Dominica, Montserrat, Nevis, Redonda, Saint Christopher), Tobago, Trinidad, the Windward Islands (Barbados, Grenada, The Grenadines, Saint Lucia, Saint Vincent)
	For individual groups of islands (geographical distribution) or individual islands, see F1630+, F1650+, F1861+
	Cf. E162, E188, English colonies in America before 1775 (General)
	Cf. E263.W5, West Indies in the American Revolution, 1775-1783
	Cf. F1529.M9, British Protectorate of Mosquito coast
	Cf. HT1091+, Slavery
2132	Travel and description, 1951-
2133	History, 1943-
2134	West Indies Federation
	Came into effect January 1958. Consists of 10 colonies embracing 13 islands: Antigua, Barbados, Dominica, Grenada, Jamaica, Montserrat, Saint Christopher, Nevis, Anguilla, Saint Lucia, Saint Vincent, Trinidad, and Tobago
2136	Virgin Islands of the United States
	Danish West Indies before 1917
	For individual islands (Saint Croix), see F2096
	For individual islands (Saint John), see F2098
	For individual islands (Saint Thomas), see F2105
	Cf. E669, Proposed annexation to United States, 1867-1869
	Cf. E756, Proposed annexation to United States, 1902
	Cf. E768, Purchase by United States, 1917
2141	Netherlands West Indies. Dutch West Indies
	Including Aruba, Bonaire, Curaçao, Saba, Saint Eustatius, Saint Martin
	For individual islands, see F2038-2103
2151	French West Indies
	Leeward Islands (Guadeloupe, Marie Galante, Saint Bartholomew, part of Saint Martin); Martinique (Windward Islands); Les Saintes
	For individual islands, see F2066-2103
	Saint Domingue (French colony, Haiti), *see F1923*
	Spanish West Indies, *see F1601-1623*

West Indies — Continued
    Caribbean area. Caribbean Sea
        Including the West Indies and coasts of the Caribbean Sea, the Gulf of Mexico, and Spanish Main

2155	Periodicals. Societies. Collections
2155.3	Congresses
	Collected works
2156	Several authors
2157	Individual authors
	Including collected papers, addresses, essays
2158	Gazetteers. Dictionaries. Geographic names
	Biography
2160	Collective
	Individual, *see* F2161, F2180.2+
2161	General works
	Including pirates and buccaneers
2161.5	Juvenile works
2165	Guidebooks. Handbooks
2169	Social life and customs. Civilization. Intellectual life
	Including national characteristics
	For specific periods after 1810, see F2181
	Description and travel. Views
2171	Early through 1950
2171.2	1951-1980
2171.3	1981-
2172	Antiquities. Indians
	History
2173	Study and teaching
2175	General works
2176	General special
	Diplomatic history. Foreign and general relations
2177	General works
2178.A-.Z	Relations with individual countries, A-Z
	By period
	Early through 1810, *see* F2161
	1811-
2181	General
2183	1945-
	Elements in the population
	For interpretation, see F1392.A+
2190	General works
2191.A-.Z	Individual elements, A-Z
2191.B55	Blacks
2191.C35	Canary Islanders
2191.E27	East Indians
	South America
2201	**Periodicals. Societies. Collections**
	For South American geographic societies, see G5
2204	**Gazetteers. Dictionaries. Geographic names**
	Biography
2205	Collective
	Individual, *see* F2230.5, F2232.92+
2208	**General works**
2208.5	**Juvenile works**
	Pamphlets, addresses, essays, etc.
2209	General
2209.5	Anecdotes, legends, pageants, etc.
	Cf. GR130+, Folklore
	Cf. Class P, Literature

	South America — Continued
2210	**Social life and customs. Civilization. Intellectual life**
	Cf. F2239, Elements in the population
2211	**Guidebooks. Handbooks**
	Regions
2212	Andes Mountains (General). Altiplano (General)
	For the Andes or Altiplano in individual countries, see the region of the country, e.g. F2851, Andes in Argentina
2213	Pacific coast
	For Galápagos Islands, see F3741.G2
2214	Atlantic coast
2215	Islands of South America (General)
2216	Northern South America
	Including Brazil, Colombia, Ecuador, Guiana, Peru and Venezuela
	For Amazon River, see F2546
	For Spanish Main, see F2161
2217	Southern South America
	Including Argentina, Bolivia, Brazil (South), Chile, Paraguay, Peru and Uruguay
	Including Gauchos (General)
	For Gran Chaco, see F2876
	For gauchos in individual countries, see F2621, Brazil; F2682.9, Paraguay; F2722.9, Uruguay; F2926, Argentina
	For La Plata region, see F2801+
	For Falkland Islands, see F3031+
	Description and travel (General). Views
2221	Early to 1810
2223	1811-1950
	Cf. F865, Voyages to the Pacific coast following discovery of gold
2224	1951-1980
2225	1981-
	Antiquities. Indians
2229	General works
2230	Modern Indians (General)
2230.1.A-.1.Z	Topics (Ancient and modern), A-Z
2230.1.A3	Agriculture
2230.1.A4	Anthropometry
2230.1.A5	Architecture
2230.1.A6	Arms and armor
2230.1.A7	Art
2230.1.A85	Astronomy
2230.1.B6	Boats. Canoes
2230.1.B7	Botany (Economics). Ethnobotany
2230.1.C5	Children
2230.1.C75	Commerce
2230.1.C8	Costume and adornment
2230.1.C9	Culture
2230.1.D35	Dance
2230.1.D65	Domestic animals
2230.1.D75	Drinking vessels. Queros
2230.1.D78	Drug use
2230.1.E25	Economic conditions
2230.1.E37	Education
2230.1.E84	Ethnic identity
	Ethnobotany, *see* F2230.1.B7
2230.1.E87	Ethnozoology
2230.1.F2	Feather work
2230.1.F56	Folk literature
2230.1.F6	Folklore. Legends
2230.1.G2	Games
2230.1.G64	Goldwork

	South America
	Antiquities. Indians
2230.1.A-.1.Z	Topics (Ancient and modern), A-Z — Continued
2230.1.G68	Government relations
2230.1.H84	Hunting
2230.1.I4	Implements
2230.1.I42	Industries
2230.1.I77	Irrigation
2230.1.K5	Kinship
2230.1.L35	Land tenure
2230.1.M24	Magic
2230.1.M28	Marriage customs and rites
2230.1.M3	Masks
2230.1.M34	Material culture
2230.1.M4	Medicine
2230.1.M43	Metalwork
2230.1.M47	Migrations
2230.1.M5	Missions
	Including biography of missionaries
2230.1.M54	Mixed descent
2230.1.M6	Mortuary customs
	Music, *see* ML3575.A2A+
2230.1.N37	Narcotics
2230.1.P48	Petroglyphs. Rock paintings
2230.1.P53	Philosophy
2230.1.P65	Politics and government
2230.1.P8	Pottery
	Queros, *see* F2230.1.D75
2230.1.R3	Religion and mythology
2230.1.R6	Roads. Trails
	Rock paintings, *see* F2230.1.P48
2230.1.S37	Sculpture
2230.1.S44	Semitic influences
2230.1.S54	Shell beads. Shell engraving. Shell jewelry
2230.1.S68	Social conditions
2230.1.S7	Social life and customs
2230.1.T3	Textile industry and fabrics
2230.1.T63	Tobacco use
	Trails, *see* F2230.1.R6
2230.1.T7	Treatment of Indians
2230.1.W37	Wars
2230.1.W6	Women
2230.1.W7	Writing
2230.2.A-.2.Z	Tribes (Ancient and modern), A-Z
	Class here tribes which do not live or are not identified with one particular country
	Tribes which live or before extinction have lived in one country or are usually identified with one country, although they may occupy or have occupied areas of one or more adjacent countries, are classed with the individual country
2230.2.A68	Araona Indians
2230.2.A7	Arawak
2230.2.A78	Ashluslay
2230.2.A82	Avachiripá
2230.2.A9	Aymara
2230.2.C3	Caingua
	Carib, *see* F2001
2230.2.C5	Chamacoco
(2230.2.C64)	Cofán, *see* F3722.1.C67
2230.2.G72	Guarani
2230.2.G75	Guayana
2230.2.G78	Guaycuruan. Guaycuru

	South America
	Antiquities. Indians
2230.2.A-.2.Z	Tribes (Ancient and modern), A-Z — Continued
2230.2.J58	Jivaran
2230.2.K4	Kechua. Quechua
2230.2.O8	Oyana. Wayana
	Quechua, *see* F2230.2.K4
2230.2.T84	Tupi
	Wayana, *see* F2230.2.O8
	History
2230.3	Chronological tables. Outlines, syllabi, etc. Questions and answers, etc.
	Historiography
2230.4	General works
	Biography of historians
2230.5.A2	Collective
2230.5.A3-.5.Z	Individual
	GALE NOTE *See note at the head of Table F5 at the end of the text for further instructions on how to subdivide this number*
2230.6	Study and teaching
2231	General works
	General special
2231.5	General
2231.7	Military history
2231.8	Naval history
	Diplomatic history. Foreign and general relations
2232	General works
2232.2.A-.2.Z	Relations with individual countries, A-Z
	By period
	Pre-Columbian period, *see* F2229+
2233	1498-1806
	Including Colonial period
	Cf. E101+, Early discoveries
	1806-1830. Wars of independence
2235	General works
2235.3	Bolívar, Simón
	Including life and works
2235.36	Guayaquil meeting, 1822
2235.4	San Martín, José de
	Including life and correspondence
2235.5.A-.5.Z	Other liberators, A-Z
2235.5.R6	Rodríguez, Simón
2235.5.S9	Sucre, Antonio José de
2235.5.U7	Urdaneta, Rafael
	1830-
2236	General works
2237	1939-
	Cf. D731+, World War II, 1939-1945
	Elements in the population
	Including foreign elements (General), minorities, race conflicts and problems
	For interpretation, see F1392.A+
2239.A1	General works
2239.A2-.Z	Individual elements, A-Z
2239.A7	Arabs
2239.B3	Basques
2239.B55	Blacks
2239.B8	British
2239.B9	Bulgarians
2239.C48	Chinese
2239.C76	Croats
2239.D8	Dutch

South America
    Elements in the population

2239.A2-.Z	Individual elements, A-Z — Continued
2239.G3	Germans
2239.G74	Greeks
2239.H85	Hungarians
	Indians, *see* F2229+
2239.I8	Italians
2239.J3	Japanese
2239.J5	Jews
2239.K65	Kongo
2239.K67	Koreans
2239.L7	Lithuanians
	Negroes, *see* F2239.B55
2239.N6	Norwegians
2239.P6	Poles
2239.P67	Portuguese
2239.S8	Swedes
2239.S9	Swiss
2239.Y83	Yugoslavs

Colombia

2251	Periodicals. Societies. Collections
	Collected works
2252	Several authors
2253	Individual authors
	Including collected papers, addresses, essays
2253.5	Museums. Exhibitions, exhibits
2254	Gazetteers. Dictionaries. Geographic names
2254.5	Directories
	Biography
2255	Collective
	Individual, *see* F2270.6, F2272-2279.22
2258	General works
2258.5	Juvenile works
	Pamphlets, addresses, essays, etc.
2259	General
2259.3	Anecdotes, legends, pageants, etc.
	Cf. GR130+, Folklore
	Cf. Class P, Literature
2259.5	Guidebooks. Handbooks
2259.7	Historic monuments (General)
2260	Social life and customs. Civilization. Intellectual life
	Including national characteristics
	For race conflicts and problems, see F2299
2260.9	Geography
	Description and travel. Views
2261	Early to 1809
2263	1810-1950
2264	1951-1980
2264.2	1981-
	Antiquities. Indians
2269	General works
2269.1.A-.1.Z	Local (Ancient and modern), A-Z
	GALE NOTE *The cutter number(s) listed below have been given only as examples by the Library of Congress*
2269.1.A28	Aburrá Valley
2269.1.C95	Cundinamarca
2269.1.P66	Popayán (Province)
2269.1.S24	San Agustin
2269.1.S25	Santa Marta Lagoon region

South America
    Colombia
        Antiquities. Indians

2269.1.A-.1.Z	Local (Ancient and modern), A-Z — Continued
2269.1.T54	Tierra Adentro
2269.1.V35	Valle del Cauca
2270	Modern Indians (General)
2270.1.A-.1.Z	Topics (Ancient and modern), A-Z
2270.1.A47	Agriculture
2270.1.A58	Anthropometry
2270.1.A7	Art
2270.1.C4	Census
2270.1.C58	Civil rights
2270.1.E3	Economic conditions
2270.1.E36	Education
2270.1.E84	Ethnic identity
2270.1.E86	Ethnobotany
2270.1.F6	Folklore. Legends
2270.1.F85	Funeral customs and rites
2270.1.G57	Goldwork
2270.1.G6	Government relations
	Including reservations (General)
2270.1.K55	Kinship
2270.1.L3	Land tenure
	Legends, *see* F2270.1.F6
2270.1.M43	Medicine
2270.1.M5	Missions
2270.1.N35	Narcotics. Drugs
2270.1.P4	Petroglyphs. Rock paintings
2270.1.P63	Politics and government
2270.1.P65	Pottery
2270.1.R4	Religion and mythology
	Rock paintings, *see* F2270.1.P4
2270.1.S63	Social conditions
2270.1.S64	Social life and customs
2270.1.T38	Taxation
2270.1.T48	Textile industry and fabrics
2270.2.A-.2.Z	Tribes and cultures (Ancient and modern), A-Z
2270.2.A3	Achagua
2270.2.A6	Andaqui
2270.2.A63	Anserma
	Arawak, *see* F2230.2.A7
2270.2.A67	Arhuaco
	Aruac, *see* F2270.2.A67
	Baniva, *see* F2520.1.B35
2270.2.B27	Barasana
2270.2.B3	Barbacoa
2270.2.B6	Bora
2270.2.C22	Cabiyari
2270.2.C24	Calima culture
2270.2.C25	Camsa
2270.2.C26	Carapana
2270.2.C27	Carijona
2270.2.C3	Catio
2270.2.C34	Cenu
2270.2.C37	Chamí
2270.2.C4	Chibcha
2270.2.C5	Chimila
2270.2.C6	Choco
2270.2.C63	Churoya

	South America
	Colombia
	Antiquities. Indians
2270.2.A-.2.Z	Tribes and cultures (Ancient and modern), A-Z — Continued
	Cobaría, *see* F2270.2.T8
2270.2.C65	Coconuco
2270.2.C67	Colima
2270.2.C68	Coyaima
	Cuaiquer, *see* F3722.1.C83
2270.2.C8	Cubeo
	Cuna, *see* F1565.2.C8
2270.2.C87	Curripaco
2270.2.D4	Desana
2270.2.E43	Embera
2270.2.E53	Epena Saija
2270.2.G6	Goajiro
	Guahibo, *see* F2319.2.G8
2270.2.G8	Guane
2270.2.G83	Guarino
	Ijca, *see* F2270.2.A67
2270.2.I53	Ingano
2270.2.K3	Kagaba
	Macu, *see* F2520.1.M2
2270.2.M33	Macuna
2270.2.M5	Mocoa
2270.2.M6	Moguex
	Motilon, *see* F2319.2.M6
2270.2.M75	Muinane
2270.2.M8	Muzo
2270.2.N8	Nukak
2270.2.P3	Paez
	Panare, *see* F2319.2.P34
2270.2.P4	Paniquita
2270.2.P44	Pasto
	Peban, *see* F3430.1.P4
2270.2.P64	Pijao
2270.2.P8	Puinave
2270.2.Q54	Quillacinga
2270.2.Q8	Quimbaya
	Saliva, *see* F2319.2.S3
2270.2.S35	San Agustin culture
2270.2.T3	Tairona
2270.2.T32	Taiwano
2270.2.T34	Tanimuca-Retuama
	Timote, *see* F2319.2.T5
	Tucano, *see* F2520.1.T9
	Tucuna, *see* F2520.1.T925
2270.2.T77	Tukanoan
2270.2.T8	Tunebo
2270.2.W5	Witoto
2270.2.W54	Wiwa
2270.2.Y3	Yakalamarure
2270.2.Y42	Yebamasa
2270.2.Y87	Yucuna
2270.2.Y9	Yuko
	Yupa, *see* F2319.2.Y8
	History
	Including political history
2270.3	Chronological tables. Outlines, syllabi, etc. Questions and answers, etc.

South America
Colombia
History — Continued
Historiography
2270.4	General works
	Biography of historians
2270.5	Collective
2270.6.A-.6.Z	Individual, A-Z

> GALE NOTE *See note at the head of Table F5 at the end of the text for further instructions on how to subdivide this number*

2270.7	Study and teaching
2271	General works

> *Including political history*

General special
2271.4	Military and naval history
	Diplomatic history. Foreign and general relations
2271.5	General works
2271.52.A-.52.Z	Relations with individual countries, A-Z
2271.9	Other (not A-Z)

By period
Pre-Columbian period, *see* F2269+
1499-1810
2272	General works

> *Including Viceroyalty and Audiencia of New Granada; conquest of Chibcha Indians, 1536-1538; Siege of Cartagena, 1585, 1697; Insurrection of the Comuneros, 1781*
> *Including biography: Gonzalo Jiménez de Quesada, etc.*
> *Cf. E135.G3, The Welsers, 1529-1556*
> *Cf. F2272.5, Siege of Cartagena 1741*
> *Cf. F2281.D2, Scot's Colony, 1698-1700*

2272.5	1739-1742. English West Indian Expedition

> *Including siege of Cartagena, 1741*
> *Cf. F2272, Siege of Cartagena, 1585 and 1697*
> *Cf. F1621, English West Indian Expedition, 1654-1655, 1695*

1810-
2273	General works

> *Including biography: Francisco de Paula Santander, etc.*

2274	1810-1822. War of Independence

> *Republic of Colombia formed by union of New Granada, Venezuela, and Ecuador, 1819-1822*
> *Including Battle of Boyacá, 1819*
> *Including biography: José María Córdoba, José Fernandez Madrid, Antonio Nariño, Antonio Ricaurte y Lozano, etc.*

2275	1822-1832

> *After Venezuela and Ecuador became independent, the name "State of New Granada" was adopted (Law of 1831 and Constitution of 1832)*
> *Including separatist movements, 1829-1830; Battle of Portete de Tarqui, 1829*

2276	1832-1886

> *In modification of Constitution of 1842 and 1843, the name changed to "Republic of New Granada"; under Constitution of 1858, name changed to "Confederation of Granada"; in Pact of 1861 and Constitution of 1863, name changed to "United States of Colombia"*
> *Including biography: Pascual Bravo, Pedro Alcántara Herrán, José Hilario López, Tomás Cipriano de Mosquera, Rafael Núñez, etc.*

2276.5	1886-1903

> *Under the Constitution of 1886, name changed to "Republic of Colombia"*
> *Including Revolution of 1899-1903; Secession of Panama, 1903*
> *Cf. F1566.5, Hay-Herrán Treaty, 1903*
> *Including biography: José Manuel Marroquín, Próspero Pinzón, Manuel Antonio Sanclemente, etc.*

	South America
	Colombia
	History
	By period
	1810- — Continued
2277	1904-1946
	Including Conservative rule, 1904-1930; the liberals, 1930-1946; Thomson-Urrutia Treaty, 1914
	Including biography: Miguel Antonio Caro, Alfonso López, Enrique Olaya Herrera, Pedro Nel Ospina, Rafael Reyes, Eduardo Santos, etc.
	Cf. D501+, World War I, 1914-1918
	Cf. D731+, World War II, 1939-1945
	Cf. F2281.B7P1+, Leticia Dispute, 1932-1934
2278	1946-1974
	Including conservative restoration, 1946; etc.
	Including biography: Laureano Gómez, Mariano Ospina Pérez, Gustavo Rojas Pinilla, etc.
	1974-
2279	General works
	Biography
2279.2	Collective
2279.22.A-.22.Z	Individual, A-Z
	GALE NOTE *See note at the head of Table F5 at the end of the text for further instructions on how to subdivide this number*
2281.A-.Z	Regions, departments, etc., A-Z
	GALE NOTE *The cutter number(s) listed below have been given only as examples by the Library of Congress*
2281.A4	Amazon River and Valley, Colombia
	Cf. F2546, General, and Brazil
2281.A5	Andes Mountains, Colombia
	Cf. F2212, General
2281.A6	Antioquia
2281.A7	Arauca (Dept.)
2281.A79	Atlantic Coast
2281.A8	Atlántico
	Bogotá River, *see F2281.C9*
2281.B6	Bolívar
	Including Barú Island, Rosario Islands, Tierra Bomba Island, San Jorge River, and Sinú River
	Boundaries
2281.B7A1-.B7A9	General
	Brazil, *see F2554.C7*
	Costa Rica (Ancient boundary), *see F1549.B7*
2281.B7E1-.B7E9	Ecuador
	Panama, *see F1569.B7*
2281.B7P1-.B7P9	Peru
	Including Leticia question
	Saint Andrews Island, *see F2281.S15*
2281.B7V1-.B7V9	Venezuela
2281.B8	Boyacá
2281.C25	Caldas
2281.C26	Caquetá
2281.C27	Cartagena (Province)
2281.C3	Cauca
	For Patía River, see F2281.P37
2281.C32	Cauca River and Valley
2281.C4	César
2281.C5	Chocó
2281.C9	Cundinamarca
	Including Bogotá River

	South America
	Colombia
2281.A-.Z	Regions, departments, etc., A-Z
2281.C9	Cundinamarca — Continued
	For San Martín (Territory), see F2281.M49
2281.D2	Darien. Scots' Colony (Caledonia)
	For modern Darien, see F1569.D3
2281.G8	Goajira (Territory). La Guajira (Dept.)
	Including Goajira peninsula
2281.H8	Huila
	La Guajira (Dept.), *see* F2281.G8
	Leticia question, *see* F2281.B7P1+
2281.L52	Llanos Orientales
	Cf. F2331.O7, Orinoco River and Valley
2281.M2	Magdalena (Dept.). Santa Marta (Province)
	Including Sierra Nevada de Santa Marta
2281.M23	Magdalena River and Valley
2281.M3	Malpelo Island
2281.M49	Meta (Dept.). San Martín (Territory)
	Including Ariari River
2281.M5	Meta River and Valley
	Morrosquillo, Gulf of, *see* F2281.S82
2281.N3	Nariño
	For Patía River, see F2281.P37
2281.N5	Neiva (Province)
2281.N6	Norte de Santander
2281.P23	Pacific Coast
2281.P3	Pamplona (Province)
2281.P37	Patía River and Valley
2281.P4	Sierra de Perijá
	Cf. F2331.P4, Perijá (District) of Venezuela
2281.P8	Popayán (Province)
2281.P9	Putumayo (Dept.)
	Including Putumayo River and Valley, Colombia, and Sibundoy Valley
	Cf. F3451.P94, General, and Peru
2281.Q55	Quindío (Province)
2281.S15	San Andrés y Providencia (Territory)
	Including Saint Andrews Island, Providence Island
	San Martín (Territory), *see* F2281.M49
	Santa Marta (Province), *see* F2281.M2
	Santa Marta, Sierra Nevada de, *see* P2281.M2
2281.S3	Santander
	Sierra de Perijá, *see* P2281.P4
2281.S82	Sucre (Dept.)
	Including Gulf of Morrosquillo
2281.S86	Sumapaz Region
2281.T6	Tolima
2281.T8	Tunja (Province)
2281.U7	Urabá (Province)
2281.V3	Valle del Cauca
2291.A-.Z	Cities, towns, etc., A-Z
	GALE NOTE *The cutter number(s) listed below have been given only as examples by the Library of Congress*
2291.B3	Barranquilla
2291.B6	Bogotá
	Subarrange by Table F2 at the end of the text
2291.B77	Bucaramanga
2291.B8	Buga
2291.C15	Cali

                                   South America
                                     Colombia

2291.A-.Z	Cities, towns, etc., A-Z — Continued
2291.C3	Cartagena
	For Siege of 1697, see F2272
2291.M4	Medellín
2291.P28	Pasto
2291.T8	Tunja
	Elements in the population
	Including foreign elements (General), minorities, race conflicts and problems
	For interpretation, see F1392.A+
2299.A1	General works
2299.A2-.Z	Individual elements
2299.B37	Basques
2299.B55	Blacks
2299.G3	Germans
	Indians, *see F2269+*
2299.J3	Japanese
2299.J5	Jews
2299.L42	Lebanese
	Negroes, *see F2299.B55*
	Venezuela
2301	Periodicals. Societies. Collections
2301.5	Sources and documents
	Collected works
2302	Several authors
2303	Individual authors
	Including collected papers, addresses, essays, etc.
2303.5	Museums. Exhibitions, exhibits
2304	Gazetteers. Dictionaries. Geographic names
2304.5	Directories
	Biography
2305	Collective
	Individual, *see F2320.6, F2322-2328.52*
2308	General works
2308.5	Juvenile works
	Pamphlets, addresses, essays, etc.
2309	General
2309.3	Anecdotes, legends, pageants, etc.
	Cf. GR130+, Folklore
	Cf. Class P, Literature
2309.5	Guidebooks. Handbooks
2309.7	Historic monuments (General)
2310	Social life and customs. Civilization. Intellectual life
	Including national characteristics
	For race conflicts and problems, see F2349.A+
2310.9	Geography
	Description and travel. Views
2311	Early to 1809
2313	1810-1950
2314	1951-1980
2315	1981-
	Antiquities. Indians
2318	Museums. Exhibitions
2319	General works
2319.1.A-.1.Z	Local (Ancient and modern), A-Z
	GALE NOTE *The cutter number(s) listed below have been given only as examples by the Library of Congress*
2319.1.M3	Maracay
2319.1.S8	Sucre (State)

	South America
	Venezuela
	Antiquities. Indians — Continued
2319.2.A-.2.Z	Tribes (Ancient and modern), A-Z
	Arawak, *see* F2230.2 A7
	Arecuna, *see* F2380.1.A7
2319.2.A73	Arekena
	Baniva, *see* F2520.1.B35
	Baré, *see* F2520.1.B4
	Betoya, *see* F2270.2.T77
2319.2.C28	Caquetio
	Carib, *see* F2460.1.C37
	Cariban, *see* F2001
	Churoya, *see* F2270.2.C63
2319.2.C78	Cuiva
2319.2.C8	Cumana
	Goajiro, *see* F2270.2.G6
2319.2.G8	Guahibo
2319.2.I7	Irapa
	Macu, *see* F2520.1.M2
	Macusi, *see* F2380.1.M3
2319.2.M3	Maipure
2319.2.M6	Motilone
2319.2.O8	Otomaco
2319.2.P3	Palenque
2319.2.P34	Panare
2319.2.P37	Paraujano
2319.2.P45	Pemon
2319.2.P5	Piaroa
2319.2.S3	Saliva
2319.2.S52	Sicuane
2319.2.T25	Tamanca
	Taurepan, *see* F2380.1.A7
2319.2.T4	Teque
2319.2.T5	Timote
	Waica, *see* F2520.1.W3
2319.2.W3	Warao
	Yanomamo, *see* F2520.1.Y3
2319.2.Y3	Yaruro
2319.2.Y4	Yecuana
2319.2.Y8	Yupa
2319.3.A-.3.Z	Topics (Ancient and modern), A-Z
2319.3.A37	Agriculture
2319.3.A5	Anthropometry
2319.3.A7	Art
2319.3.B37	Baskets
2319.3.C4	Census
2319.3.E26	Economic conditions
2319.3.E46	Employment
(2319.3.F58)	Folk literature, *see* F2319.3.F6
2319.3.F6	Folklore. Legends
2319.3.G6	Government relations
2319.3.L35	Land tenure
2319.3.M5	Missions
2319.3.N35	Names
2319.3.P4	Petroglyphs. Rock paintings
2319.3.P6	Pottery
	Rock paintings, *see* F2319.3.P4
2319.3.S6	Social conditions
2319.3.S62	Social life and customs

South America
Venezuela
Antiquities. Indians

	Topics (Ancient and modern), A-Z — Continued
2319.3.A-.3.Z	
2319.3.T43	Teenagers
	History
2319.5	Chronological tables. Outlines, syllabi, etc. Questions and answers, etc.
	Historiography
2320	General works
	Biography of historians
2320.5	Collective
2320.6.A-.6.Z	Individual, A-Z

GALE NOTE *See note at the head of Table F5 at the end of the text for further instructions on how to subdivide this number*

2320.7	Study and teaching
2321	General works
	Including political history
	General special
2321.1	Military and naval history
	Diplomatic history. Foreign and general relations
2321.2	General works
2321.3.A-.3.Z	Relations with individual countries, A-Z
2321.9	Other (not A-Z)
	By period
	Pre-Columbian period, *see* F2318+
2322	1498-1806/1810

Including early settlement; German occupation to 1556; pillage and attacks by English and French, 1595-1798; separation from Viceroyalty of Peru, 1731. In 1777, Captain-Generalcy of Caracas established; in 1786, Audiencia of Caracas created
Including biography: Alonso Andrea de Ledesma

	1806/1810-
2322.8	General works

Including biography: José Antonio Páez, etc.

2323	1806-1812

Including Francisco de Miranda's attempts at independence and his biography; Treaty of San Mateo, 1812

2324	1810-1830. War of Independence, 1810-1823

Including earthquake of 1812; Battle of Carabobo, 1821. Province of Republic of Colombia, 1822-1829
Including biography: José Antonio Anzoátegui, José Tomás Boves, Pedro Luis Brión, Pablo Morillo y Morillo, José Félix Ribas, etc.

2325	1830-1935

Including Republic of Venezuela formed in 1830; era of civil wars, 1848-1870; Revolution, 1902-1903; Anglo-German-Italian Blockade, 1902; Dutch Blockade, 1908
Including biography: Cipriano Castro, Joaquín Crespo, Juan Vicente Gómez, Antonio Guzmán Blanco, Santos Michelena, José Tadeo Monagas, Juan Pietri, Arístides Rojas, José María Vargas

2326	1935-1958

Including movement toward democracy, 1935-1948; Revolution of 1945
Including biography: Rómulo Betancourt, Carlos Delgado Chalband, Eleazar López Contreras, Isaías Medina Angarita, Marcos Pérez Jiménez, etc.
Cf. D731+, World War II, 1939-1945

	1958-1974
2327	General works
	Biography
2327.5	Collective

        South America
         Venezuela
          History
           By period
            1806/1810-
             1958-1974
              Biography — Continued

2327.52.A-.52.Z	Individual, A-Z

GALE NOTE *See note at the head of Table F5 at the end of the text for further instructions on how to subdivide this number*

             1974-1999

2328	General works
	Biography
2328.5	Collective
2328.52.A-.52.Z	Individual, A-Z

GALE NOTE *See note at the head of Table F5 at the end of the text for further instructions on how to subdivide this number*

             1999-

2329	General works
	Biography
2329.2	Collective
2329.22.A-.22.Z	Individual, A-Z

GALE NOTE *See note at the head of Table F5 at the end of the text for further instructions on how to subdivide this number*

2331.A-.Z	Regions, states, etc., A-Z
2331.A2	Islands along the Venezuela coast (General)
	For islands off the coast, belonging to other countries, see F2016
2331.A3	Amazonas (Territory)
2331.A5	Andes Mountains, Venezuela
	Cf. F2212, General
2331.A55	Anzoátegui
2331.A65	Apure
2331.A7	Aragua
2331.A9	Aves Islands
2331.A93	Avila Mountain
2331.B3	Barinas (Sur de Occidente, Zamora)
2331.B6	Bolívar
	Including Great Savannah
	Boundaries
2331.B7	General
	Brazil, *see* F2554.V4
2331.B72	British Guiana. Guyana
	Colombia, *see* F2281.B7
	Guyana, *see* F2331.B72
2331.B75	Bruzual
2331.C3	Carabobo
2331.C5	Chacao (Caracas) Valley
2331.C6	Cojedes
2331.C7	Cubagua Island
2331.D44	Delta Amacuro
2331.F2	Falcón
	Including Paraguaná Peninsula
	Goajira (Guajira) peninsula, *see* F2281.G8
	Great Savannah, *see* F2331.B6
2331.G8	Guárico
2331.G83	Guayana Region
	Isla de Patos, *see* F2331.P3
2331.J82	Juan José Mora
	Lake Maracaibo Region, *see* F2331.M27
	Lake Valencia, *see* F2331.V3

South America

Venezuela

2331.A-.Z	Regions, states, etc., A-Z— Continued
2331.L3	Lara
2331.M27	Maracaibo Lake Region
2331.M3	Margarita (Island)
2331.M5	Mérida
2331.M52	Mérida, Cordillera de (Sierra Nevada de Mérida)
2331.M6	Miranda
2331.M7	Monagas
2331.N8	Nueva Esparta
	For Margarita Island, see F2331.M3
2331.O7	Orinoco River and Valley
	Cf. F2281.L52, Llanos Orientales
	Paraguaná Peninsula, *see F2331.F2*
2331.P3	Isla de Patos
2331.P4	Perijá (District)
	Cf. F2281.P4, Sierra de Perijá, Colombia
2331.P6	Portuguesa
	Roraima, Mount, *see F2609*
2331.S8	Sucre
	Sur de Occidente, *see F2331.B3*
2331.T2	Táchira
2331.T7	Trujillo
2331.V3	Lake Valencia
2331.V35	Vargas
2331.Y3	Yaracuy
	Zamora, *see F2331.B3*
2331.Z9	Zulia
	For Perijá (District), see F2331.P4
2341.A-.Z	Cities, towns, etc., A-Z
	GALE NOTE *The cutter number(s) listed below have been given only as examples by the Library of Congress*
2341.A2	Collective
2341.B3	Barquisimeto
2341.C2	Caracas
	Subarrange by Table F2 at the end of the text
2341.C8	Cumaná
2341.M2	Maracaibó
2341.M25	Maracay
2341.M5	Mérida
2341.S13	San Cristóbal
2341.V25	Valencia
	Elements in the population
	For interpretation, see F1392.A+
2349.A1	General works
2349.A2-.Z	Individual, A-Z
2349.A5	Americans (U.S.)
2349.B3	Basques
2349.B55	Blacks
	Cf. HT1151+, Slavery
2349.C35	Canary Islanders
2349.C64	Colombians
2349.C83	Cubans
2349.D8	Dutch
2349.F73	French
2349.G24	Gallegans
2349.G3	Germans
	Indians, *see F2318+*
2349.I8	Italians

South America
  Venezuela
    Elements in the population

2349.A2-.Z	Individual, A-Z — Continued
2349.J48	Jews
2349.L43	Lebanese
2349.P6	Portuguese
2349.S36	Scotch. Scots
	Scots, *see* F2349.S36
2349.S7	Spaniards

  Guiana
Region between the Amazon and Orinoco although at present usually restricted to British, Dutch, and French Guiana

2351	General works
	Cf. E111+, Early voyages
2354	Antiquities. Indians
	Guyana. British Guiana
2361	Periodicals. Societies. Collections
	Collected works
2362	Several authors
2363	Individual authors
	Including collected papers, addresses, essays, etc.
2363.5	Museums. Exhibitions, exhibits
2364	Gazetteers. Dictionaries. Geographic names
2364.5	Directories
	Biography
2365	Collective
	Individual, *see* F2380.6, F2383-2385
2368	General works
2368.5	Juvenile works
	Pamphlets, essays
2369	General
2369.3	Anecdotes, legends, pageants
	Cf. GR130, Folklore
	Cf. Class P, Literature
2369.5	Guidebooks. Handbooks
2369.7	Historic monuments (General)
2369.8	Social life and customs. Civilization. Intellectual life
	Including national characteristics
	For race conflicts and problems, see F2391
2369.9	Geography
	Description and travel. Views
2370	Early to 1802
2371	1803-1950
2372	1951-1980
2373	1981-
	Antiquities. Indians
2379	General works
2380	Modern Indians (General)
	Including local (not A-Z)
2380.1.A-.1.Z	Tribes (Ancient and modern), A-Z
	GALE NOTE *The cutter number(s) listed below have been given only as examples by the Library of Congress*
2380.1.A2	Accawai
	Arawak, *see* F2230.2.A7
2380.1.A7	Arecuna
	Carib, *see* F2001
2380.1.M3	Macusi
2380.1.P3	Paramona
2380.1.T3	Taruma

	South America
	Guiana
	Guyana. British Guiana
	Antiquities. Indians
2380.1.A-.1.Z	Tribes (Ancient and modern), A-Z — Continued
	Trio, *see* F2420.1.T7
2380.1.W25	Waiwai
2380.1.W3	Wapisiana
2380.2.A-.2.Z	Topics (Ancient and modern), A-Z
2380.2.A7	Art
2380.2.F6	Folklore. Legends
2380.2.G3	Games
2380.2.G68	Government relations
2380.2.M44	Medicine
2380.2.M57	Missions
2380.2.S63	Social life and customs
2380.2.S7	String figures
2380.2.W7	Writing
	History
2380.3	Chronological tables. Outlines, syllabi, etc. Questions and answers, etc.
	Historiography
2380.4	General works
	Biography of historians
2380.5	Collective
2380.6.A-.6.Z	Individual, A-Z
	GALE NOTE *See note at the head of Table F5 at the end of the text for further instructions on how to subdivide this number*
2380.7	Study and teaching
2381	General works
	Including political history
2382	General special
	Diplomatic history. Foreign and general relations
2382.3	General works
2382.4.A-.4.Z	Relations with individual countries, A-Z
	By period
	Pre-Columbian period, *see* F2379+
2383	1580-1803
	Including Dutch colonies of Essequibo, Demerara, and Berbice; English conquests; French conquest, 1782
	Cf. E129.R2, Raleigh's explorations, 1595-1617
	Cf. F2423, English in Dutch Guiana
	Cf. F2462, English in French Guiana
2384	1803-1966
	Including Great Britain given permanent title by Convention of London, 1814; union of three colonies to form British Guiana, 1831
	Including biography: John Smith, 1790-1824; etc.
	For boundary disputes with Venezuela, see F2331.B7
	For boundary disputes with Brazil, see F2554.B8
	Cf. D731+, World War II, 1939-1945
2385	1966-
2387.A-.Z	Regions, counties, etc., A-Z
2387.B4	Berbice
2387.B7	Boundaries
2387.B7A1-.B7A5	General
	Brazil, *see* F2554.B8
2387.B7A6-.B7Z	Surinam. Netherlands or Dutch Guiana
	Venezuela, *see* F2331.B72
2387.D4	Demerara
2387.E8	Essequibo
	Including Kaieteur Falls

	South America
	Guiana
	Guyana. British Guiana
2387.A-.Z	Regions, counties, etc., A-Z — Continued
	Roraima, Mount, *see* F2609
2389.A-.Z	Cities, towns, etc., A-Z
	GALE NOTE *The cutter number(s) listed below have been given only as examples by the Library of Congress*
2389.B3	Bartica
2389.G3	Georgetown
2389.N4	New Amsterdam
	Formerly Berbice
	Elements in the population
	For interpretation, see F1392.A+
2391.A1	General works
	Including foreign elements (General), minorities, race conflicts and problems
2391.A2-.Z	Individual elements
	GALE NOTE *The cutter number(s) listed below have been given only as examples by the Library of Congress*
2391.C5	Chinese
2391.E2	East Indians
	Indians, *see* F2379+
2391.N4	Negroes
	Cf. HT1139+, Slavery
	Suriname. Netherlands or Dutch Guiana
2401	Periodicals. Societies. Collections
	Collected works
2402	Several authors
2403	Individual authors
	Including collected papers, addresses, essays
2403.5	Museums. Exhibitions, exhibits
2404	Gazetteers. Dictionaries. Geographic names
2404.5	Directories
	Biography
2405	Collective
	Individual, *see* F2423-2429
2408	General works
2408.5	Juvenile works
	Pamphlets, addresses, essays
2409	General
2409.4	Anecdotes, legends, pageants
	Cf. GR130+, Folklore
	Cf. Class P, Literature
2409.5	Guidebooks. Handbooks
2409.6	Historic monuments (General)
2409.8	Social life and customs. Civilization. Intellectual life
	Including national characteristics
	For race conflicts and problems, see F2431
	Description and travel. Views
2410	Early to 1813
2411	1814-1950
2412	1951-1980
2413	1981-
	Antiquities. Indians
2419	General works
2420	Modern Indians (General)
	Including local (not A-Z)
2420.1.A-.1.Z	Tribes (Ancient and modern), A-Z
2420.1.A35	Akurio
	Arawak, *see* F2230.2.A7

	South America
	Guiana
	Suriname. Netherlands or Dutch Guiana
	Antiquities. Indians
2420.1.A-.1.Z	Tribes (Ancient and modern), A-Z — Continued
	Cariban, *see* F2001
	Galibi, *see* F2460.1.C37
2420.1.O8	Oyaricoulet
2420.1.T7	Trio
	Warrau, *see* F2319.2.W3
	Wayana, *see* F2230.2.O8
2420.2.A-.2.Z	Topics (Ancient and modern), A-Z
2420.2.A7	Art
2420.2.P64	Politics and government
	History
2420.3	Chronological tables. Outlines, syllabi, etc. Questions and answers, etc.
	Historiography
2420.4	General works
	Biography of historians
2420.5	Collective
2420.6.A-.6.Z	Individual, A-Z
	GALE NOTE *See note at the head of Table F5 at the end of the text for further instructions on how to subdivide this number*
2420.7	Study and teaching
2421	General works
	Including political history
2422	General special
	By period
2423	1604-1814
	Including early English settlements; Willoughby and Hyde's Grant, 1663; Dutch West India Company, 1621-1791; etc.
	Includes general works on the four Dutch colonies (Essequibo, Demerara, Berbice, and Surinam), 1667-1803
	Including biography: Cornelis van Aerssen, heer van Sommelsdijk; Abraham Crijnssen; Jan Jacob Mauricius; etc.
	Cf. E129.R2, Raleigh's explorations, 1595-1617
	Cf. F2381-2383, Essequibo, Dememrara, and Berbice (Former Dutch colonies)
2424	1814-1950
	Including Dutch given permanent title by Treaty of Paris, 1814; member of Dutch American Union, 1828-1845
	Cf. D731+, World War II, 1939-1945
2425	1950-1975
	As of January 10, 1950, became autonomous within the Dutch Empire
	1975-
2425.2	General works
	Biography
2425.22	Collective
2425.23.A-.23.Z	Individual, A-Z
	GALE NOTE *See note at the head of Table F5 at the end of the text for further instructions on how to subdivide this number*
2427.A-.Z	Regions, districts, etc., A-Z
2427.B7	Boundaries
2427.B7A1-.B7A5	General
	Brazil, *see* F2554.D8
	British Guiana, *see* F2387.B7
2427.B7A6-.B7Z	French Guiana
2427.M3	Maroni River and Valley, Surinam
	Cf. F2467.M3, General, and French Guiana

	South America
	Guiana
	Suriname. Netherlands or Dutch Guiana — Continued
2429.A-.Z	Cities, towns, etc., A-Z
	GALE NOTE *The cutter number(s) listed below have been given only as examples by the Library of Congress*
2429.N5	Nieuw Nickerie
2429.P3	Paramaribo
	Elements in the population
	For interpretation, see F1392.A+
2431.A1	General works
	Including foreign elements (General), minorities, race conflicts and problems
2431.A2-.Z	Individual elements
2431.B64	Boni
2431.E2	East Indians
	Indians, *see* F2419+
2431.J3	Javanese
2431.J4	Jews
2431.N3	Negroes. Blacks
	Cf. HT1141+, Slavery
2431.S27	Saramacca
	French Guiana
2441	Periodicals. Societies. Collections
	Collected works
2442	Several authors
2443	Individual authors
	Including collected papers, addresses, essays, etc.
2443.5	Museums. Exhibitions, exhibits
2444	Gazetteers. Dictionaries. Geographic names
2444.5	Directories
	Biography
2445	Collective
	Individual, *see* F2460.6, F2462-2464
2448	General works
2448.5	Juvenile works
	Pamphlets, addresses, essays
2449	General
2449.3	Anecdotes, legends, pageants
	Cf. GR130+, Folklore
	Cf. Class P, Literature
2449.5	Guidebooks. Handbooks
2449.7	Historic monuments (General)
2449.8	Social life and customs. Civilization. Intellectual life
	Including national characteristics
	For race conflicts and problems, see F2471
	Description and travel. Views
2450	Early to 1813
2451	1814-1950
2452	1951-
	Antiquities. Indians
2459	General works
2460	Modern Indians (General)
	Including local (not A-Z)
2460.1.A-.1.Z	Tribes (Ancient and modern), A-Z
	Arawak, *see* F2230.2.A7
2460.1.C37	Carib (Galibi)
	Cariban, *see* F2001
2460.1.E5	Emerillon
(2460.1.G3)	Galibi, *see* F2460.1.C37
2460.1.O9	Oyampi. Wayampi

	South America
	Guiana
	French Guiana
	Antiquities. Indians
2460.1.A-.1.Z	Tribes (Ancient and modern), A-Z — Continued
2460.1.P3	Palicur
	Wayampi, *see* F2460.1.O9
	Wayana, *see* F2230.2.O8
2460.2.A-.2.Z	Topics (Ancient and modern), A-Z
2460.2.A37	Agriculture
2460.2.E38	Education
2460.2.F64	Folklore. Legends
2460.2.G68	Government relations
	Legends, *see* F2460.2.F64
2460.2.P6	Pottery
	History
2460.3	Chronological tables. Outlines, syllabi, etc. Questions and answers, etc.
	Historiography
2460.4	General works
	Biography of historians
2460.5	Collective
2460.6.A-.6.Z	Individual, A-Z
	GALE NOTE *See note at the head of Table F5 at the end of the text for further instructions on how to subdivide this number*
2460.7	Study and teaching
2461	General works
	Including political history
	By period
	Pre-Columbian period, *see* F2459+
2462	1626-1814
	Including early English settlements on the Oyapok; first French settlement, 1643; expedition of Kourou, 1763-1765; Portuguese (from Brazil) occupation, 1809-1817
	Cf. E129.R2, Raleigh's explorations, 1595-1617
	Cf. F2383, French in British Guiana
2463	1814-1946
	Including French given permanent title by Treaty of Paris, 1814
	For boundary disputes with Brazil, see F2554.F8
	For use as a penal colony, see HV8955+
	Cf. D731+, World War II, 1939-1945
2464	1947-
	As of January 1, 1947, became a department of Metropolitan France
2467.A-.Z	Regions, districts, etc., A-Z
2467.B7	Boundaries
	Brazil, *see* F2554.F8
	Surinam (Dutch Guiana), *see* F2427.B7
2467.I4	Îles du Salut (Devil's Island)
	As penal colony, see HV8947.A+
2467.I5	Inine (Territory)
2467.M25	Mana River and Valley
2467.M3	Maroni River and Valley (General, and French Guiana)
	Cf. F2427.M3, Surinam
2467.T9	Tumuc-Humac Mountains
2469.A-.Z	Cities, towns, etc., A-Z
	GALE NOTE *The cutter number(s) listed below have been given only as examples by the Library of Congress*
2469.C3	Cayenne
2469.S3	Saint-Georges (Saint-Georges-de-l'Oyapock)
2469.S5	Saint-Laurent (Saint-Laurent-du-Maroni)
	Elements in the population
	Including foreign elements (General), minorities, race conflicts and problems

	South America
	Guiana
	French Guiana
	Elements in the population — Continued
	For interpretation, see F1392.A+
2471.A1	General works
2471.A2-.Z	Individual elements, A-Z
2471.B55	Blacks
2471.H56	Hmong (Asian people)
	Indians, *see* F2459+
	Negroes, *see* F2471.B55
	Brazil
2501	Periodicals. Societies. Serials
2501.5	Congresses
	Collected works (Nonserial)
2502	Several authors
2503	Individual authors
	Including collected papers, addresses, essays, etc.
2503.5	Museums. Exhibitions, exhibits
2504	Gazetteers. Dictionaries. Geographic names
2504.5	Directories
	Biography
2505	Collective
	Individual, *see* F2520.6, F2524-2538.5
2508	General works
2508.5	Juvenile works
	Pamphlets, addresses, essays, etc.
2509	General
2509.3	Anecdotes, legends, pageants, etc.
	Cf. GR130+, Folklore
	Cf. Class P, Literature
2509.5	Guidebooks. Handbooks
2509.7	Historic monuments (General)
2510	Social life and customs. Civilization. Intellectual life
	Including national characteristics
	For race conflicts and problems, see F2659
2510.5	Brazilians in foreign countries (General)
	For Brazilians in a particular country, see the country
2510.9	Geography
	Description and travel. Views
2511	Early to 1821
2513	1822-1889
2515	1890-1950
2516	1951-1980
2517	1981-
	Antiquities. Indians
2518.5	Museums. Exhibitions
2519	General works
2519.1.A-.1.Z	Local (Ancient and modern), A-Z
	GALE NOTE *The cutter number(s) listed below have been given only as examples by the*
	Library of Congress
2519.1.A6	Amazon Valley
2519.1.B3	Bahia (State)
2519.1.G68	Goiás (State). Goyaz (State)
2519.1.L3	Lagoa Santa
2519.1.M37	Maranhão (State)
2519.1.M4	Matto Grosso (State)
2519.1.P2	Pará (State)
2519.1.P3	Paraná (State)
2519.1.P8	Purus River

	South America
	Brazil
	Antiquities. Indians
2519.1.A-.1.Z	Local (Ancient and modern), A-Z — Continued
2519.1.R5	Rio de Janeiro (State)
2519.1.R6	Rio Grande do Sul (State)
2519.1.S2	São Paulo (State)
2519.1.U3	Uaupés Valley
2519.1.X56	Xingu Valley
2519.3.A-.3.Z	Topics (Ancient and modern), A-Z
	Adornment, *see* F2519.3.C68
2519.3.A5	Anthropometry
2519.3.A7	Art
2519.3.A84	Astronomy
2519.3.B36	Basket making
2519.3.B5	Boats
2519.3.B6	Bows and arrows
2519.3.C3	Cannibalism
2519.3.C65	Communication
2519.3.C68	Costume and adornment
2519.3.C85	Cultural assimilation
2519.3.D2	Dances
2519.3.D84	Dwellings
2519.3.E2	Education
2519.3.E83	Ethnic identity
2519.3.F4	Feather work
2519.3.F6	Folklore. Legends
2519.3.F63	Food
2519.3.G3	Games
	Government, *see* F2519.3.P58
2519.3.G6	Government relations
2519.3.H85	Hunting
2519.3.I4	Implements
2519.3.I5	Industries
2519.3.K53	Kings and rulers
2519.3.K55	Kinship
2519.3.L36	Land tenure
2519.3.M37	Mathematics
2519.3.M43	Medicine
2519.3.M5	Missions
2519.3.N35	Names
2519.3.P58	Politics and government
2519.3.P6	Pottery
2519.3.R3	Religion. Mythology
2519.3.S58	Social conditions
2519.3.S6	Social life and customs
2519.3.S94	Suicidal behavior
2519.3.W37	Wars
2519.3.W66	Women
2519.3.W7	Writing
2520	Modern Indians (General)
2520.1.A-.1.Z	Tribes (Ancient and modern), A-Z
2520.1.A4	Akwĕ-Shavante. Xavante
	Amahuaca, *see* F3430.1.A5
2520.1.A6	Apalai
2520.1.A63	Apalakiri
2520.1.A632	Apapocuva
2520.1.A64	Apiacá
2520.1.A65	Apinagé
2520.1.A7	Arara

South America
Brazil
Antiquities. Indians

	Tribes (Ancient and modern), A-Z — Continued
2520.1.A-.1.Z	
2520.1.A75	Araua
	Arawak, *see* F2230.2.A7
2520.1.A77	Araweté
	Arecuna, *see* F2380.1.A7
2520.1.A84	Asurini
2520.1.A93	Ava-Canoeiro
2520.1.B3	Bakairi
2520.1.B35	Baniva
2520.1.B4	Baré
	Betoya, *see* F2270.2.T77
	Boro, *see* F2270.2.B6
2520.1.B75	Bororo
2520.1.B76	Botocudo
2520.1.C3	Cadioeo
	Caingua, *see* F2230.2.C3
2520.1.C32	Canella
	Canoeiro, *see* F2520.1.R53
2520.1.C35	Caraja
	Carib, *see* F2001
2520.1.C37	Caripuna
2520.1.C38	Cashinawa
2520.1.C4	Catoquina
2520.1.C45	Cayapo
	Chamacoco, *see* F3320.2.C5
	Chapacura, *see* F3320.2.C38
	Charrua, *see* F2719.2.C5
	Chavante, *see* F2520.1.A4
(2520.1.C6)	Chipaya, *see* F3320.2.C388
	Chiquito, *see* F3320.2.C3
2520.1.C64	Cinta Larga
2520.1.C67	Craho. Kraho
2520.1.C7	Crichaná
2520.1.C84	Culina
2520.1.D47	Desana
2520.1.F8	Fulnio
2520.1.G37	Gaviões
2520.1.G4	Ge
2520.1.G6	Goyataca
2520.1.G68	Guaharibo
2520.1.G69	Guajá
	Guajajara, *see* F2520.1.T4
2520.1.G718	Guana
2520.1.G72	Guanano
	Guarani, *see* F2230.2.G72
2520.1.G75	Guató
	Guayana, *see* F2230.2.G75
	Guayaqui, *see* F2679.2.G9
	Guaycuru, *see* F2230.2.G78
2520.1.H48	Heta
2520.1.I6	Ipurucotó
2520.1.I7	Iranxe
2520.1.J8	Juruna. Yuruna
2520.1.K3	Kaingang. Kaingangue
2520.1.K35	Kamaiurá
2520.1.K4	Kariri
	Kashinaua, *see* F2520.1.C38

South America

Brazil

Antiquities. Indians

2520.1.A-.1.Z	Tribes (Ancient and modern), A-Z — Continued
2520.1.K45	Kayabi
	Kraho, *see* F2520.1.C67
2520.1.K7	Kreen-Akarore
2520.1.M2	Macu
	Macusi, *see* F2380.1.M3
2520.1.M24	Mamaindê
2520.1.M26	Maruba
2520.1.M27	Masacali
2520.1.M3	Maue
	Mayoruna, *see* F3430.1.M45
	Mbaya, *see* F2679.2.M3
2520.1.M44	Mehinacu
2520.1.M45	Mekranoti
	Mojo, *see* F3320.2.M55
2520.1.M8	Mundurucu
2520.1.M9	Mura
	Including Pirahá Indians
2520.1.N3	Nambicuara
	Omagua, *see* F3430.1.O5
2520.1.O63	Opaye
	Pacaguara, *see* F3320.2.P3
	Painguá, *see* F2230.2.C3
2520.1.P32	Pakaa Nova
	Palicur, *see* F2460.1.P3
2520.1.P35	Pancararu
	Pano, *see* F3430.1.P3
	Panoan Indians, *see* F3430.1.P33
2520.1.P38	Parakaña
2520.1.P4	Parintintin
2520.1.P43	Patashó
2520.1.P45	Pauishana
	Peban, *see* F3430.1.P4
	Pirahá, *see* F2520.1.M9
	Piro, *see* F3430.1.P5
2520.1.P68	Potiguara
2520.1.P8	Puri
2520.1.R53	Rikbaktsa. Canoeiro (Mato Grosso)
2520.1.S24	Saluma
2520.1.S3	Sanavirona
	Sapuya, *see* F2520.1.K4
2520.1.S47	Sherente
2520.1.S5	Shokleng
2520.1.S86	Surui
2520.1.S89	Suya
2520.1.T2	Tapajo
2520.1.T25	Tapirapé
2520.1.T3	Tapuya
2520.1.T32	Tariana
2520.1.T4	Tenetehara
2520.1.T43	Teremembe
2520.1.T45	Terena. Tereno
2520.1.T5	Timbira
	Trio, *see* F2420.1.T7
2520.1.T7	Trumai
2520.1.T9	Tucano
2520.1.T925	Tucuna

	South America
	Brazil
	Antiquities. Indians
2520.1.A-.1.Z	Tribes (Ancient and modern), A-Z — Continued
	Tukanoan, *see* F2270.2.T77
2520.1.T933	Tupari
	Tupi, *see* F2230.2.T84
2520.1.T94	Tupinamba
2520.1.T97	Tuxá
2520.1.U3	Uaboi
2520.1.U5	Umotina
2520.1.U7	Urubu Kaapor
2520.1.U74	Uruewawau
2520.1.W3	Waica
2520.1.W34	Waimiri
	Waiwai, *see* F2380.1.W25
	Wapisiana, *see* F2380.1.W3
2520.1.W38	Waura
	Wayampi, *see* F2460.1.O9
	Wayana, *see* F2230.2.O8
2520.1.X33	Xacriaba
	Xavante, *see* F2520.1.A4
2520.1.X5	Xikrin
2520.1.Y3	Yanomamo
	Yuruna, *see* F2520.1.J8
2520.1.Z65	Zoró
2520.1.Z87	Zuruahá
	History
2520.3	Chronological tables. Outlines, syllabi, etc. Questions and answers, etc.
	Historiography
2520.4	General works
	Biography of historians
2520.5	Collective
2520.6.A-.6.Z	Individual, A-Z
	GALE NOTE *See note at the head of Table F5 at the end of the text for further instructions on how to subdivide this number; the cutter number(s) listed below have been given only as examples by the Library of Congress*
2520.6.A2	Abreu, João Capistrano de
2520.6.P4	Pereira da Costa, Francisco Augusto
2520.7	Study and teaching
2521	General works
	Including political history
	General special
2522	Military and naval history
	Diplomatic history. Foreign and general relations
2523	General works
2523.5.A-.5.Z	Relations with individual countries, A-Z
	United States, *see* E183.8.A+
2523.9	Other (not A-Z)
	By period
	Pre-Columbian period, *see* F2518.5+
	1500-1821
2524	General works
2526	1500-1548
	Including discovery, exploration, and colonization by Portuguese
	Cf. E123, Demarkation line of Alexander VI
	1549-1762
2528	General works
	Including Bandeiras (General; if limited to a state, class with state); expulsion of Jesuits

South America

Brazil

History

By period

1500-1821

1549-1762

2528   General works — Continued

Including biography: José de Anchieta; Salvador Correia de Sá e Benavides; Mem de Sá; Antônio Vieira, etc.

Cf. BX4705.V55, Vieira as religious figure

Cf. F2684, Jesuit missions of Paraguay, War of the Seven Reductions (Guarani War), 1754-1756

Cf. F2723, Portuguese settlement at Colonia, Uruguay

2529   French colony at Rio de Janeiro, 1555-1567

Including biography: Nicolas Durand de Villegagnon

2530   Spanish control, 1580-1640

2532   Dutch conquest, 1624-1654

Including capture of Bahia, 1625; battles at Guararapes, 1648 and 1649; capture of Olinda, 1630

Including biography: Henrique Dias, Joao Fernandes Vieira, etc.

2534   1763-1821

Including Portuguese court in Brazil, 1808-1821; revolt in Pernambuco, 1817

Including biography: Joaquim José da Silva Xavier (Tiradentes), etc.

Cf. DP650, João VI, king of Portugal

Cf. F2461, French Guiana

Cf. F2723, Expulsion of Brazilians from Colonia

         1822-

2535   General works

2536   Empire, 1822-1889

Including Pedro I, 1822-1831; Regency, 1831-1841; Pedro II, 1841-1889

Including Brazil declared independent of Portugal on September 7, 1822; Empire established on October 12, 1822; Revolution of 1842; separatist movement in Rio Grande do Sul, 1845

Including biography: José Bonifacio de Andrada e Silva (Cf. PQ9697 , as author); Benjamin Constant Botelho Magalhães; Luiz Alves de Lima e Silva, duque de Caxias; Marcilio Dias; Diogo Antonio Feijo; Giuseppe Garibaldi (Cf. DG558.2.G2, as Italian patriot); Irineo Evangelista de Souza, visconde de Maua; Joaquim Nabuco; Joaquim Marques Lisbôa, marques de Tamandare

Cf. F2687, Paraguayan War, 1865-1870

Cf. F2725, War with Argentina over Uruguay, 1825-1828

Cf. F2846.3, War with Argentina, 1849-1852

2537   Republic, 1889-

Including Brazil declared a republic, November 15, 1889

Including special period, 1889-1930; naval revolt of 1893-1894; Conselheiro Insurrection, 1897; military revolution of 1924-1925; etc.

Including biography: Ruy Barbosa; Manuel Ferraz de Campos Salles; Manuel Deodoro da Fonseca; Antonio Vicente Mendes Maciel; Manuel de Oliveira Lima; Floriano Peixoto; José Gomes Pinheiro Machado; José Maria da Silva Paranhos, barão do Rio Branco; etc.

Cf. D501+, World War I, 1914-1918

2538   1930-1954. Period of Vargas

Including Revolution of 1930; Communist Revolution of 1935; Integralist Revolt of 1938

Including biography: Eurico Gaspar Dutra, Getulio Vargas, etc.

Cf. D731+, World War II, 1939-1945

         1954-1964

Including administrations of Kubitschek, Quadros, and Goulart

2538.2   General works

         Biography

2538.22.A2   Collective

	South America
	Brazil
	History
	By period
	1822-
	1954-1964
	Biography — Continued
2538.22.A3-.22.Z	Individual
	GALE NOTE *See note at the head of Table F5 at the end of the text for further instructions on how to subdivide this number; the cutter number(s) listed below have been given only as examples by the Library of Congress*
2538.22.G6	Goulart, João Belchior Marques
2538.22.K8	Kubitschek, Juscelino
	1964-1985
2538.25	General works
	Biography and memoirs
2538.26	Collective
2538.27.A-.27.Z	Individual, A-Z
	GALE NOTE *See note at the head of Table F5 at the end of the text for further instructions on how to subdivide this number; the cutter number(s) listed below have been given only as examples by the Library of Congress*
2538.27.F53	Figueiredo, João Baptista de Oliveira, 1918-
2538.27.G44	Geisel, Ernesto
2538.27.P38	Paula, Francisco Julião Arruda de, 1915-
	1985-
2538.3	General works
	Biography
2538.4	Collective
2538.5.A-.5.Z	Individual, A-Z
	GALE NOTE *See note at the head of Table F5 at the end of the text for further instructions on how to subdivide this number*
	Regions, states, etc.
2539	Islands of Brazil (General)
2540	Acre (Territory)
	Cf. F2546, Amazonas boundary
2541	Alagoas
2543	Amapá (Territory)
2546	Amazonas
	Including Amazon River and Valley; Içá River; Japurá (Yapurá) River; Javarí (Yavarí) River; Jurua River; Jutaí (Jutahy) River; Purus River; Rio Negro
	Cf. F2281.A4, Amazon River and Valley, Colombia
	Cf. F3451.A4, Amazonas (Peru)
	Cf. F3451.L8, Amazon River and Valley, Peru
2548	Atlantic Coast
2551	Bahia (Baía)
	Including Jacuípe River and Valley, and Diamantina Plateau
	Cf. F2601, Pernambuco boundary
	Cf. F2636, Sergipe boundary
2554	Boundaries
2554.A1-.A8	General
2554.A82	Argentina
	For Misiones question, see F2916
2554.B6	Bolivia
	Cf. F2540, Acre (Territory)
2554.B8	British Guiana
2554.C7	Colombia
2554.D8	Dutch Guiana. Surinam
2554.F8	French Guiana
2554.P3	Paraguay

	South America
	Brazil
	Regions, states, etc.
2554	Boundaries — Continued
2554.P4	Peru
2554.U8	Uruguay
2554.V4	Venezuela
2556	Ceará
2557	Central West Brazil
2558	Counani
	Contested territory awarded to Brazil
	Distrito Federal, *see* F2646
2561	Espírito Santo
	Including colonies of Germans, Poles, Swedes, Tyrolese
2564	Fernando de Noronha Island (Territory)
2566	Goyaz (Goías, Goiaz)
	Including Araguaya River, Tocantins River
2567	Guanabara
	Guaporé (Territory), *see* F2624
	Guartelá (Region), *see* F2596
2567.3	Ibiapaba
2567.9	Mar Mountains
2568	Marajó (Island)
	Including French Colony, 1612-1618
2571	Maranhão
	Including Gurupy River, Parnahyba (Parnaíba) River, etc.
2576	Mato Grosso
	Including Araguaya River, Garças River, Xingú River
	Cf. F2566, Goyaz boundary
	Cf. F2684, Jesuit missions of Paraguay
2578	Mato Grosso do Sul
2581	Minas Geraes (Minas Gerais)
	Including Jequitinhonha River, Mucury Colony, and Paraibuna River
2582	North Brazil
2583	Northeast Brazil
2585	Pantanal
2586	Pará
	Including Rivers: Araguaya, Capim, Gurupy (Gurupi), Tapajos, Tocantins, Pará, Xingú
	For Marajó Island, see F2568
	Cf. F2546, Amazonas boundary
2591	Parahyba (Paraíba)
2596	Paraná
	Including Assunguy Colony, Guartelá (Region), Guayra Falls, Iguazú River and Falls, Paraná River, etc.
	Cf. F2909, Argentina
	Cf. F2684, Jesuit missions of Paraguay
2601	Pernambuco
	Including Itamaracá Island
2606	Piauhy (Piauí)
	Including Parnahyba (Parnaíba) River
	Cf. F2571, Maranhão boundary
2609	Rio Branco (Territory). Roraima
	Including Mount Roraima
2611	Rio de Janeiro (State)
	Including Parahyba (Paraíba) do Sul River and Valley, Grande Island Bay
	For Rio de Janeiro (Federal District and City), see F2646
2616	Rio Grande do Norte
	Cf. F2556, Ceará boundary

	South America
	Brazil
	Regions, states, etc. — Continued
2621	Rio Grande do Sul
	Including German colonies; Revolution of the Farrapos, 1835-1845; Taquari-Antes River and Valley; gauchos in Brazil
	Cf. F2217, Gauchos (General)
	Cf. F2684, Jesuit missions; War of the Seven Reductions, 1754-1756
2624	Rondônia (Territory). Rondônia (State)
	Including Madeira River
	Roraima, *see F2609*
2626	Santa Catharina (Santa Catarina)
	Including Santa Catarina Island
	Part of Misiones awarded to Brazil
	Including German colonies, e.g. Blumenau; Itajahy (Itajaí) River and Valley
	Cf. F2596, Paraná boundary
	Cf. F2916, Misiones award (General)
	Cf. F2916, Misiones Territory of Argentina
2629	São Francisco River and Valley
2631	São Paulo
	Including Bandeiras; Revolution of 1932; etc.; Rivers: Aguapehy (Aguapeí), Juquiá, Paraná, Peixe, Piracicaba, Ribeira de Iguape, Tietê
	Cf. F2581, Minas Geraes boundary
	Cf. F2684, Jesuit missions of Paraguay; War of the Seven Reductions, 1754-1756
2636	Sergipe
2638	Sinos River and Valley
2639	South Brazil
2640	Tocantins State
2641	Vargem Alegre (District)
	Cities, towns, etc., A-Z
2646	Rio de Janeiro (City; and Federal District until April 21, 1960)
	Subarrange by Table F1 at the end of the text
2647	Brasilia (City; and Federal District, April 21, 1960-)
	Subarrange by Table F1 at the end of the text
2651.A-.Z	Other, A-Z
	GALE NOTE *The cutter number(s) listed below have been given only as examples by the Library of Congress*
	Bahia, *see F2651.S13*
2651.B4	Belém
2651.B42	Belo Horizonte
2651.C83	Curitiba
2651.F6	Fortaleza
2651.N5	Niterói (Nictheroy)
2651.O9	Ouro Preto
2651.P15	Palmares
	Pará, *see F2651.B4*
	Pernambuco, *see F2651.R4*
2651.P8	Porto Alegre
2651.R4	Recife
	Subarrange by Table F2 at the end of the text
2651.S13	Salvador
	Subarrange by Table F2 at the end of the text
2651.S15	Santos
2651.S2	São Paulo
	Subarrange by Table F2 at the end of the text
	Elements in the population
	For interpretation, see F1392.A+
2659.A1	General works
	Including foreign elements (General), minorities, race conflicts and problems

	South America
	Brazil
	Elements in the population — Continued
2659.A2-.Z	Individual elements, A-Z
2659.A5	Americans
2659.A7	Arabs
2659.A75	Armenians
2659.A84	Asians
2659.A9	Austrians
2659.B4	Belgians
	Blacks, *see* F2659.N4
2659.B7	British
2659.C32	Caboclos
2659.D7	Dutch
2659.E8	Estonians
2659.E95	Europeans
2659.F8	French
2659.G3	Germans
2659.H85	Hungarians
	Indians, *see* F2518.5+
2659.I8	Italians
2659.J3	Japanese
2659.J5	Jews
2659.L38	Latvians
2659.L42	Lebanese
2659.L5	Lithuanians
2659.M69	Mozambicans
2659.N4	Negroes. Blacks
	Cf. HT1126+, Slavery
2659.P7	Poles
2659.P8	Portuguese
2659.S45	Slovenes
2659.S63	Spaniards
2659.U4	Ukrainians
	Paraguay
2661	Periodicals. Societies. Collections
2661.5	Congresses
	Collected works
2662	Several authors
2663	Individual authors
	Including collected papers, addresses, essays
2663.5	Museums. Exhibitions, exhibits
2664	Gazetteers. Dictionaries. Geographic names
2664.5	Directories
	Biography
2665	Collective
	Individual, *see* F2679.6, F2683-2689.23
2668	General works
2668.5	Juvenile works
	Pamphlets, addresses, essays, etc.
2669	General
2669.3	Anecdotes, legends, pageants, etc.
	Cf. GR130+, Folklore
	Cf. Class P, Literature
2669.5	Guidebooks. Handbooks
2669.7	Historic monuments (General)
2670	Social life and customs. Civilization. Intellectual life
	Including national characteristics
	For race conflicts and problems, see F2699
2670.9	Geography

	South America
	Paraguay — Continued
	Description and travel. Views
2671	Early to 1810
2675	1810-1950
2676	1951-
	Antiquities. Indians
2678	Museums. Exhibitions.
2679	General works
2679.1	Modern Indians (General)
2679.15.A-.15.Z	Local (Ancient and modern), A-Z
	GALE NOTE *The cutter number(s) listed below have been given only as examples by the Library of Congress*
2679.15.C48	Chaco Region
2679.15.M35	Marcelina Kue Site
2679.2.A-.2.Z	Tribes (Ancient and modern), A-Z
2679.2.A2	Abipon Indians
	Arawak, *see* F2230.2.A7
	Caingua, *see* F2230.2.C3
	Chamacoco, *see* F2230.2.C5
	Chiquito, *see* F3320.2.C39
2679.2.C5	Chiripá Indians
	Guarani, *see* F2230.2.G72
2679.2.G9	Guayaki Indians
	Guaycuru, *see* F2230.2.G78
2679.2.L4	Lengua
2679.2.M25	Maca
2679.2.M3	Mbaya
2679.2.M34	Mbya
	Mocobi, *see* F2823.M6
2679.2.M6	Moro Indians
2679.2.P3	Payagua
	Pilaga, *see* F2823.P5
	Tereno, *see* F2520.1.T45
	Toba, *see* F2823.T7
2679.2.T65	Tomaráxo
2679.3.A-.3.Z	Topics (Ancient and modern), A-Z
2679.3.A77	Art
2679.3.C64	Colonization
2679.3.E38	Education
2679.3.F42	Featherwork
2679.3.F64	Folklore. Legends
2679.3.G67	Government relations
	Health and hygiene, *see* RA475+
2679.3.I53	Industries
2679.3.L35	Land tenure
	Legends, *see* F2679.3.F64
2679.3.M5	Missions
2679.3.P64	Politics and government
2679.3.P66	Population
2679.3.R44	Religion and mythology
2679.3.S65	Social conditions
	History
2679.35	Chronological tables. Outlines, syllabi, etc. Questions and answers, etc.
	Historiography
2679.4	General works
	Biography of historians
2679.5	Collective

	South America
	Paraguay
	History
	Historiography
	Biography of historians — Continued
2679.6.A-.6.Z	Individual, A-Z
	GALE NOTE *See note at the head of Table F5 at the end of the text for further instructions on how to subdivide this number*
2679.7	Study and teaching
2681	General works
	Including political history
	General special
2681.5	Military history
	Diplomatic history. Foreign and general relations
2682	General works
2682.5.A-.5.Z	Relations with individual countries, A-Z
2682.9	Other (not A-Z)
	Cf. F2217, Gauchos (General)
	By period
	Pre-Columbian period, *see F2678+*
	1527-1811
	Including before 1620, part of La Plata region; in 1620, Province of Paraguay established under jurisdiction of viceroy at Lima; in 1776, transferred to viceroy at Buenos Aires
	Including War of Independence, 1810-1811
2683	General works
2684	Jesuit province. Missions or reductions, 1609-1769
	Including Treaty of Madrid, 1750; War of the Seven Reductions (Guarani War), 1754-1756
	Cf. F2621, F2723, F2891, F2916, Regions occupied by the missions
	1811-1870. Era of three dictators
	Including independence from Buenos Aires viceroyalty , 1813; United States Paraguay Expedition, 1858-1859
	Including biography: José Gaspar Rodríguez Francia, Carlos Antonio López, Francisco Solano López, etc.
2686	General works
2687	Paraguayan War, 1865-1870
	Also called "War of the Triple Alliance"
	Including battles at Campo Grande, 1869; Curupaity, 1866; Riachuelo, 1865; Tuyuty, 1866; Yatayty-Corá, 1866
	1870-1938
	Including biography: Eusebio Ayala, Rafael Franco, Eduardo Schaerer
	Cf. D501+, World War I, 1914-1918
2688	General works
2688.5	Chaco War, 1932-1935
	Including Chaco Peace Conference at Buenos Aires, 1935-1939; Treaty of Peace, 1938
	Cf. F2691.C4 , Chaco Boreal
2689	1938-1989
	Including political revolts; Colorados, communists, Franquistas, Tiempistas
	Including biography: José Félix Estigarribia, Higinio Moríñingo Martínez, etc.
	Cf. D731+, World War II, 1939-1945
	1989-
2689.2	General works
	Biography
2689.22	Collective
2689.23.A-.23.Z	Individual, A-Z
	GALE NOTE *See note at the head of Table F5 at the end of the text for further instructions on how to subdivide this number*

South America

Paraguay — Continued

2691.A-.Z	Regions, departments, etc., A-Z
	GALE NOTE *The cutter number(s) listed below have been given only as examples by the Library of Congress*
2691.A4	Alto Paraná
	Including Colonia Mayntzhusen
	Boundaries
2691.B7A1-.B7A5	General
	Argentina, *see* F2857.P2
2691.B7A6-.B7Z	Bolivia
	Chaco Boreal dispute, see F2691.C4
	Brazil, *see* F2554.P3
2691.C4	Chaco Boreal. Paraguayan Chaco. Western Paraguay
	Including territory between the Paraguay and Pilcomayo rivers
	Cf. F2688.5, Chaco War, 1932-1935
	Cf. F2876, El Gran Chaco (General, and Argentina)
	Cf. F3341.C4, Bolivian Chaco
2691.C6	Concepción
2691.P3	Paraguay River and Valley
2695.A-.Z	Cities, towns, etc., A-Z
	GALE NOTE *The cutter number(s) listed below have been given only as examples by the Library of Congress*
2695.A8	Asunción
2695.C7	Concepción
2695.C8	Coronel Oviedo
2695.C9	Curuguaty
2695.E5	Encarnación
	Including Tornado of 1926
2695.H7	Hohenau
2695.T6	Tobatí
2695.V5	Villarrica
	Elements in the population
	Including foreign elements (General), minorities, race conflicts and problems
	For interpretation, see F1392.A+
2699.A1	General works
2699.A2-.Z	Individual elements, A-Z
2699.A72	Arabs
2699.A87	Australians
2699.B67	Brazilians
2699.B7	British
2699.D34	Danes
2699.F7	French
2699.G3	Germans
	Indians, *see* F2678+
2699.I8	Italians
2699.J35	Japanese
2699.J4	Jews
2699.M44	Mennonites
2699.R8	Russians

Uruguay

2701	Periodicals. Societies. Collections
	Collected works
2702	Several authors
2703	Individual authors
	Including collected papers, addresses, essays
2703.5	Museums. Exhibitions, exhibits, etc.
2704	Gazetteers. Dictionaries. Geographic names
2704.5	Directories

	South America
	Uruguay — Continued
	Biography
2705	Collective
	Individual, *see* F2720.6, F2723-2729.52
2708	General works
2708.5	Juvenile works
	Pamphlets, addresses, essays
2709	General
2709.3	Anecdotes, legends, pageants
	Cf. GR130+, Folklore
	Cf. Class P, Literature
2709.5	Guidebooks. Handbooks
2709.7	Historic monuments (General)
2710	Social life and customs. Civilization. Intellectual life
	Including national characteristics
	For race conflicts and problems, see F2799
	Description and travel. Views
2711	Early to 1810
2713	1811-1950
2714	1951-1980
2715	1981-
	Antiquities. Indians
2719	General works
2719.1.A-.1.Z	Local (Ancient and modern), A-Z
2719.1.C65	Colonia (Dept.)
2719.1.S24	Salto Grand Dept
2719.1.T7	Treinta y Tres (Dept.)
2719.2.A-.2.Z	Tribes (Ancient and modern), A-Z
	Chané, *see* F3320.2.C37
2719.2.C5	Charrua
	Guarani, *see* F2230.2.G72
2719.2.G84	Güenoa
2719.3.A-.3.Z	Topics (Ancient and modern), A-Z
	GALE NOTE *The cutter number(s) listed below have been given only as examples by the Library of Congress*
2719.3.P6	Pottery
2719.3.T6	Tobacco pipes
	History
2720	Chronological tables. Outlines, syllabi, etc. Questions and answers, etc.
	Historiography
2720.3	General works
	Biography of historians
2720.5	Collective
2720.6.A-.6.Z	Individual, A-Z
	GALE NOTE *See note at the head of Table F5 at the end of the text for further instructions on how to subdivide this number*
2720.7	Study and teaching
2721	General works
	Including political history
	General special
2721.5	Military and naval history
	Diplomatic history. Foreign and general relations
2722	General works
2722.5.A-.5.Z	Relations with individual countries, A-Z
2722.9	Other (not A-Z)
	Including gauchos in Uruguay
	Cf. F2217 , Gauchos (General)
	By period
	Pre-Columbian period, *see* F2719+

	South America
	Uruguay
	History
	By period — Continued
2723	1516-1811
	Known as the "Banda Oriental." In 1776 placed under the viceroy in Buenos Aires
	Including contests over Colonia; Treaty of San Ildefonso, 1777
	Cf. F2684, Jesuit missions; War of the Seven Reductions, 1754-1756
	Cf. F2845, English invasion of the La Plata, 1806-1807
	1811-
2724	General works
2725	1811-1830
	In 1821, incorporated in Brazil as Cisplatine Province; declared itself independent, 1825; recognized as independent, 1828
	Including wars of independence; Argentine-Brazilian War, 1825-1828 (battles at Sarandi, 1825; Ituzaingó, 1827)
	Including biography: José Gervasio Artigas, etc.
2726	1830-1904
	Formally constituted as a republic, 1830
	Including civil wars between Blancos and Colorados; foreign intervention; Siege of Montevideo, 1843-1851
	Including biography: Juan Lindolfo Cuestas, Juan Carlos Gómez, Julio Herrera y Obes; Juan Idiarte Borda, Lorenzo Latorre, Manuel Oribe, José Fructuoso Rivera, Máximo Santos, Aparicio Saravia, etc.
	Cf. F2687, Paraguayan War, 1865-1870
	Cf. F2846.3, War against Rosas, 1849-1852
2728	1904-1973. Era of Batlle, 1903-1929
	Including Revolution of 1904; Battle of Tupambaé, 1904; Revolution of 1910
	Including biography: Juan José Améraga, José Batlle y Ordóñez, Baltasar Brum, Luis Alberto de Herrera, Andrés Martínez Trueba, José Serrato, Gabriel Terra, etc.
	Cf. D501+, World War I, 1914-1918
	Cf. D731+, World War II, 1939-1945
	Cf. D772.G7, Admiral Graf Spee (Battleship)
	1973-
2729	General works
	Biography
2729.5	Collective
2729.52.A-.52.Z	Individual, A-Z
	GALE NOTE *See note at the head of Table F5 at the end of the text for further instructions on how to subdivide this number*
2731.A-.Z	Regions, departments, etc., A-Z
2731.A7	Artigas
2731.A84	Atlantic Coast
2731.B7	Boundaries (General)
	For Argentina, see F2857.U7
	For Brazil, see F2554.U8
2731.C22	Canelones
2731.C4	Cerro Largo
2731.C7	Colonia
	For Portuguese settlement at Colonia, see F2723
2731.D8	Durazno
2731.F5	Flores
2731.F55	Florida
2731.L3	Lavalleja
2731.M2	Maldonado
	Including Punta Ballema
	Montevideo, *see F2781*
2731.P3	Paysandú
2731.R4	Río Negro

	South America
	Uruguay
2731.A-.Z	Regions, departments, etc., A-Z — Continued
2731.R5	Rivera
2731.R6	Rocha
2731.S2	Salto
2731.S3	San José
2731.S6	Soriano
2731.T3	Tacuarembó
2731.T6	Treinta y Tres
2731.U7	Uruguay River
	Cities, towns, etc.
2781	Montevideo
	Subarrange by Table F1 at the end of the text
2791.A-.Z	Other, A-Z
	GALE NOTE *The cutter number(s) listed below have been given only as examples by the Library of Congress*
2791.M3	Maldonado
2791.M55	Mercedes
2791.P34	Paysandú
2791.S2	Salto
	Elements in the population
	Including foreign elements (General), minorities, race conflicts and problems
	For interpretation, see F1392.A+
2799.A1	General works
2799.A2-.Z	Individual elements, A-Z
2799.B2	Basques
	Blacks, *see* F2799.N3
2799.B7	Brazilians
2799.F7	French
2799.G3	Germans
2799.G74	Greeks
	Indians, *see* F2719+
2799.I8	Italians
2799.J36	Japanese
2799.J4	Jews
2799.L4	Lebanese
2799.N3	Negroes. Blacks
2799.S6	Spaniards
2799.S9	Swiss
	Argentina. La Plata region
2801	Periodicals. Societies. Collections
2801.5	Congresses
	Collected works
2802	Several authors
2803	Individual authors
	Including collected papers, addresses, essays
2803.5	Museums. Exhibitions, exhibits, etc.
2804	Gazetteers. Dictionaries. Geographic names
2804.5	Directories
	Biography
2805	Collective
	Individual, *see* F2829.6, F2841-2849.22
2808	General works
2808.2	Juvenile works
	Pamphlets, addresses, essays
2808.3	General
2808.4	Anecdotes, legends, pageants, etc.
	Cf. GR130+, Folklore
	Cf. Class P, Literature

South America
    Argentina. La Plata region — Continued

2808.5	Guidebooks. Handbooks
2809	Historic monuments (General)
2810	Social life and customs. Civilization. Intellectual life
	Including national characteristics
	For race conflicts and problems, see F3021.A+
2810.9	Geography
	Description and travel. Views
2811	Early to 1805
2815	1806-1950
2816	1951-1980
2817	1981-
	Antiquities. Indians
2819	Study and teaching
2820	Museums. Exhibitions
2821	General works
2821.1.A-.1.Z	Local (Ancient and modern), A-Z
	GALE NOTE *The cutter number(s) listed below have been given only as examples by the*
	Library of Congress
2821.1.A3	Andalgala
2821.1.B8	Buenos Aires (Province)
2821.1.C3	Catamarca (Province)
2821.1.C5	Chubut (Territory)
2821.1.C7	Córdoba (Province)
2821.1.E5	Entre Rios (Province)
2821.1.J9	Jujuy (Province)
2821.1.N4	Neuquén (Province)
2821.1.P22	Paraná Valley
2821.1.P29	Patagonia
2821.1.R58	La Rioja (Province)
2821.1.S15	Salta (Province)
2821.1.S23	Santiago del Estero (Province)
2821.1.T89	Tucumán (Province)
2821.3.A-.3.Z	Topics (Ancient and modern), A-Z
2821.3.A3	Agriculture
2821.3.A78	Architecture
2821.3.A8	Art
2821.3.B6	Bolas
2821.3.C4	Census
2821.3.C73	Craniology
2821.3.D4	Dentistry
	Including dental mutilation
2821.3.D5	Diseases
2821.3.E84	Ethnic identity
2821.3.F57	First contact with Europeans
2821.3.F6	Folklore. Legends
2821.3.F7	Food
2821.3.G65	Government relations
2821.3.H8	Hunting
2821.3.I5	Implements
2821.3.I6	Industries
2821.3.L35	Land tenure
2821.3.M4	Medicine
2821.3.M5	Missions
2821.3.M6	Mortuary customs
2821.3.N3	Names
2821.3.P6	Petroglyphs. Rock paintings
2821.3.P66	Philosophy
2821.3.P8	Pottery

	South America
	Argentina. La Plata region
	Antiquities. Indians
2821.3.A-.3.Z	Topics (Ancient and modern), A-Z — Continued
2821.3.R4	Religion and mythology
	Rock paintings, *see* F2821.3.P6
2821.3.S54	Silverwork
2821.3.T6	Tobacco pipes
2821.3.T65	Tombs
2821.3.U7	Urns
	Wars, *see* F2822
2822	Modern tribes (General)
	Including Indian wars
2823.A-.Z	Tribes (Ancient and modern), A-Z
	Abipone, *see* F2679.2.A2
	Alacaluf, *see* F2986
	Araucanian, *see* F3126
	Ashluslay, *see* F2230.2.A78
	Aymara, *see* F2230.2.A9
	Caingua, *see* F2230.2.C3
2823.C2	Calchaqui
2823.C4	Catamarca
	Chamacoco, *see* F2230.2.C5
	Chané, *see* F3320.2.C37
	Charrua, *see* F2719.2.C5
	Choroti, *see* F3320.2.C5
2823.C5	Comechingone
2823.D5	Diaguita
	Cf. F3070.1.D5, Chile
	Fuegian, *see* F2986
	Guarani, *see* F2230.2.G72
2823.G8	Guarpe
	Kaingangue, *see* F2520.1.K3
	Lengua, *see* F2679.2.L4
2823.L8	Lule
2823.M3	Mataco
2823.M6	Mocobi
2823.O34	Ocloya
	Ona, *see* F2986
2823.P3	Pampean
	Payagua, *see* F2679.2.P3
2823.P5	Pilaga
2823.P8	Puelche
2823.Q4	Querandi
2823.R2	Ranqueles
2823.T7	Toba
2823.T8	Tonocote
	Tzoneca, *see* F2936
2823.V5	Vilela
	Yahgan, *see* F2986
	History
2827	Chronological tables. Outlines, syllabi, etc. Questions and answers, etc.
	Historiography
2829	General works
	Biography of historians
2829.5	Collective
2829.6.A-.6.Z	Individual, A-Z
	GALE NOTE *See note at the head of Table F5 at the end of the text for further instructions on how to subdivide this number*
2830	Study and teaching

	South America
	Argentina. La Plata region
	History — Continued
2831	General works
	Including political history
	General special
2832	Military and naval history
	Diplomatic history. Foreign and general relations
2833	General works
	Cf. F2857, Boundaries
2833.5.A-.5.Z	Relations with individual countries, A-Z
2834	Other (not A-Z)
	By period
	Pre-Columbian period, *see* F2821+
2841	1516-1810

Including period of discovery, exploration, and settlement. Colonial period. In 1617, Buenos Aires separated from Asunción, became the province of Rio de la Plata under the viceroy of Peru; in 1776, Viceroyalty of La Plata was formed including Argentina, Uruguay, Paraguay, and Bolivia

Including biography: Hernando Arias de Saavedra (Hernandarias); Francisco de Céspedes; Juan de Garay; Domingo Martínez de Irala; Juan de San Martín; Rafael de Sobremonte, marqués de Sobremonte; etc.

Cf. F2683, Paraguay before 1811

Cf. F2684, Jesuit province; War of the Seven Reductions (Guarani War), 1754-1756

Cf. F2723, Brazil's claims to Colonia

Cf. F3301+, Upper Peru and the Audiencia of Charcas

| 2843 | 1810- |

On May 25, 1810, declared independence from Spain

| 2845 | 1806-1817 |

Including English invasions, 1806-1807; War of Independence, 1810-1817

Including biography: Manuel Belgrano; Guillermo Brown; Martín Miguel Güemes; Santiago Antonio María de Liniers y Bremond, conde de Buenos Aires; Bernardo Monteagudo; Mariano Morena; Juan Martín de Pueyrredón; Cornelio de Saavedra; etc.

| | 1817-1861. Civil wars |

Including unitarism versus federalism; secession and return of province of Buenos Aires; battles at Cepeda (1859), Pavón (1861)

Including biography: Manuel Dorrego, Esteban Echeverría, Juan Galo de Lavalle, José María Paz, Juan Facundo Quiroga, Bernardino Rivadavia, Domingo Faustino Sarmiento, Justo José de Urquiza, Dalmacio Vélez Sársfield, etc.

Cf. F2725, War with Brazil over Uruguay, 1825-1828

| 2846 | General works |
| 2846.3 | 1829-1852. Period of Rosas |

Including English and French blockades of Argentine coast, 1838, and of Río de la Plata, 1845-1847; War with Brazil (War against Rosas), 1849-1852; battles at Angaco (1841), Obligado (1845)

Including biography: Juan Manuel José Domingo Ortiz de Rosas

| 2847 | 1861-1910 |

Including League of Córdoba; Civil War, 1880; oligarchy in control, 1890-1910

Including biography: Nicolás Avellaneda, Bartolomé Mitre, Carlos Pellegrini, Julio Argentino Roca, Roque Sáenz Peña, etc.

Cf. F2687, Paraguayan War, 1865-1870

Cf. F2822, Conquista del desierto, 1879-1880

Cf. F2916, Misiones award, 1894

| 2848 | 1910-1943 |

Including radicals in control, 1910-1930; Revolution of 1930; oligarchy in control, 1930-1943

	South America
	Argentina. La Plata region
	History
	By period
2843	1810-
2848	1910-1943 — Continued
	Including biography: Marcelo Torcuato de Alvear, Joaquín Víctor Gonzáles, Hipólito Irigoyen, Juan Bautista Justo, Lisandro de la Torre, José Félix Uriburu
	Cf. D501+, World War I, 1914-1918
2849	1943-1955
	Including the "G.O.U." Coup, 1943; Perón regime, 1943-1955; fascism
	Including biography: Juan Domingo Perón, etc.
	Cf. D731+, World War II, 1939-1945
	1955-2002
2849.2	General works
	Biography
2849.22.A2	Collective
2849.22.A3-.22.Z	Individual, A-Z
	GALE NOTE *See note at the head of Table F5 at the end of the text for further instructions on how to subdivide this number*
	2002-
2849.3	General works
	Biography
2849.33.A2	Collective
2849.33.A3-.33.Z	Individual, A-Z
	GALE NOTE *See note at the head of Table F5 at the end of the text for further instructions on how to subdivide this number*
2850-2991	Regions, provinces, etc.
	Class an individual department or partido with the province of which it is a part
2850	Territories (General)
2850.4	Aconquija Mountains
2851	Andes Mountains
	Including Chilean boundary question
2853	Los Andes (Territory)
	Before 1910 was Bolivian territory of Atacama; in 1943, departments were assigned to the provinces of Jujuy, Salta, and Catamarca
2857	Boundaries
2857.A2	General
2857.B6	Bolivia
	Cf. F2853, Former Bolivian territory of Atacama
	Brazil, *see* F2554.A82, F2916
	Chaco Boreal dispute, *see* F2688.5
	Chile, *see* F2851, F2853
2857.P2	Paraguay
2857.U7	Uruguay
	Buenos Aires (Federal District and City), *see* F3001
2861	Buenos Aires (Province)
	Including Avellaneda (Partido); Lechiguanas Islands
	For Martin Garcia (Island), see F2909
	Cf. F2846, Battles of Cepeda, 1859; Pavón, 1861
	Cf. F2886, Córdoba boundary
2871	Catamarca
2876	Chaco. Chaco Austral. El Gran Chaco (General, and Argentina)
	Became a province, August 8, 1951
	For Bolivian Chaco, see F3341.C4
	For Chaco Boreal (Paraguayan Chaco), see F2691.C4
	For Chaco Central, see F2901
	For Chaco War, 1932-1935, see F2688.5

South America
Argentina. La Plata region

2850-2991	Regions, provinces, etc. — Continued
2881	Chubut (Territory)
	For Comodoro Rivadavia, see F2884
2884	Comodoro Rivadavia
	Including military zone carved out of Chubut and Santa Cruz Territories in 1946
2886	Córdoba
2891	Corrientes
	Including battle of Caá Guazú, 1841
	Cf. F2916, Misiones boundary
	Cuyo, *see F2911*
2896	Entre Rios
	For Lechiguanas Islands, see F2861
	Cf. F2861, Buenos Aires (Province) boundary
2901	Formosa (Territory). Chaco Central
2906	Jujuy
2909	La Plata River and Valley (Rio de La Plata). Paraná River
	Including Iguazú Falls, Martín Garcia (Island)
	Cf. F2596 , Paraná River in Brazil
2911	Mendoza
	Including the ancient Chilean governación of Cuyo
	Including Malargüe (District); Tupungato (Department)
	Cf. F2961, San Juan boundary
2916	Misiones
	Became a province, December 9, 1953
	Including Parque nacional del Iguazú
	Cf. F2554.A82, Brazil-Argentina boundary dispute
	Cf. F2626, Santa Catarina, Brazil (Part of Misiones awarded to Brazil)
	Cf. F2684, Jesuit missions of Paraguay
2921	Neuquén (Territory)
	Including Neuquén River, Parque nacional "Lanín"
2921.5	Northeast Argentina
	Including Chaco, Corrientes, Formosa Misiones, and northern Sante Fe
2922	Northwest Argentina
	Including Calchaqui River
2924	La Pampa
	Became a province, August 8, 1951
2926	Pampas (Region)
	Including region south of Mendoza and San Luis, and west of Buenos Aires, extending to Patagonia (about 40 degrees)
	Cf. F2217, Gauchos (General)
2936	Patagonia
	Including collective works on Patagonia, Falkland Islands, Tierra del Fuego, Strait of Magellan, Cape Horn, etc.; Tzoneca Indians
	Argentine Patagonia is now subdivided into the territories of Chubut, Neuquén, Río Negro, Santa Cruz, and Tierra del Fuego
	Chilean Patagonia covers the Chilean provinces of Chiloé and Magallanes
	Cf. F2986, Tierra del Fuego
	Cf. F3031+, Falkland Islands
	Cf. F3191, Strait of Magellan
2951	Río Negro (Territory)
	Including Nahuel Huapí (Lake), Parque nacional de Nahuel Huapí
2956	La Rioja
2957	Salado River and Valley
	In provinces of Salta, Santiago del Estero, and Santa Fé
2958	Salta
2961	San Juan
2966	San Luis
	Cf. F2886, Córdoba boundary

	South America
	Argentina. La Plata region
2850-2991	Regions, provinces, etc. — Continued
2971	Santa Cruz (Territory)
	For Comodoro Rivadavia, see F2884
2976	Santa Fé
2981	Santiago del Estero
2986	Tierra del Fuego (Territory and island)
	The western part of the island forms part of the Chilean territory of Magallanes
	Including Fuegians: The Alacaluf, Ona, and Yahgan
2991	Tucumán (Province)
	In colonial times was the gobernación of Tucumán, part of Upper Peru
	Cities, towns, etc.
3001	Buenos Aires (Federal District and City)
	Subarrange by Table F1 at the end of the text
3011.A-.Z	Other, A-Z
	GALE NOTE *The cutter number(s) listed below have been given only as examples by the Library of Congress*
3011.A9	Avellaneda
	Formerly Barrácas al Sud
3011.B3	Bahia Blancha
3011.C7	Córdoba
3011.L4	La Plata
3011.L45	La Rioja
	Including earthquake of 1894, etc.
3011.L8	Luján
3011.M29	Mar del Plata
3011.M45	Mendoza
	Including earthquake of 1861, etc.
3011.R7	Rosario
3011.S2	Salta
3011.S218	San Juan
	Formerly San Juan de la Frontera
	Including earthquake of 1944, etc.
	San Miguel de Tucumán, *see F3011.T89*
3011.S26	Santa Fé
3011.T89	Tucumán
	Elements in the population
	Including foreign elements (General), minorities, race conflicts and problems
	For interpretation, see F1392.A+
3021.A1	General works
3021.A2-.Z	Individual elements, A-Z
3021.A5	Americans
3021.A59	Arabs
3021.A64	Armenians
3021.B2	Basques
3021.B55	Blacks
3021.B65	Bolivians
3021.B86	British
3021.B93	Bulgarians
3021.C3	Catalans
3021.C7	Croats
3021.D2	Danes
3021.D87	Dutch
3021.F56	Finns
3021.F8	French
3021.G2	Gallegans
3021.G3	Germans
	Indians, *see F2821+*
3021.I6	Irish

	South America
	Argentina. La Plata region
	Elements in the population
3021.A2-.Z	Individual elements, A-Z — Continued
3021.I8	Italians
3021.J36	Japanese
3021.J5	Jews
	Negroes, *see* F3021.B55
3021.P6	Poles
3021.P8	Portuguese
3021.R87	Russian Germans
3021.S6	Slovaks
3021.S62	Slovenes
3021.S7	Spaniards
3021.S86	Swedes
3021.S88	Swiss
3021.U5	Ukrainians
3021.U7	Uruguayans
3021.Y7	Yugoslavs
3030	**South Atlantic region**
3030.3	Ascension Island
	Falkland Islands. Islas Malvinas
	Including dependencies: Graham Land (Palmer Peninsula), South Georgia, South Orkneys, South Sheltands, South Sandwich Island
	Cf. G890.P3, Palmer Peninsula (Graham Land)
3031	General works
3031.5	Falkland Islands War, 1982
	St. Helena, Tristan da Cunha, etc., *see* DT669+
	Chile
3051	Periodicals. Societies. Collections
	Collected works
3052	Several authors
3053	Individual authors
	Including collected papers, addresses, essays
3053.5	Museums. Exhibitions, exhibits, etc.
3054	Gazetteers. Dictionaries. Geographic names
3054.5	Directories
	Biography
3055	Collective
	Individual, *see* F3076, F3091-3101
3058	General works
3058.5	Juvenile works
	Pamphlets, addresses, essays, etc.
3059	General
3059.3	Anecdotes, legends, pageants, etc.
	Cf. GR130+, Folklore
	Cf. Class P, Literature
3059.5	Guidebooks. Handbooks
3059.8	Historic monuments (General)
3060	Social life and customs. Civilization. Intellectual life
	Including national characteristics
	For race conflicts and problems, see F3285
3060.9	Geography
	Description and travel. Views
3061	Early to 1809
3063	1810-1950
3064	1951-1980
3065	1981-
	Antiquities. Indians
3069	General works

	South America
	Chile
	Antiquities. Indians — Continued
3069.1.A-.1.Z	Local (Ancient and modern), A-Z
	GALE NOTE *The cutter number(s) listed below have been given only as examples by the Library of Congress*
	Araucania, *see* F3126
3069.1.A8	Atacama (Province)
3069.1.H8	Huasco (Province)
3069.1.L5	Llaima (Department)
3069.1.L6	Rio Loa region
3069.1.M25	Malloa
3069.1.M6	Molle
3069.1.P5	Pichilemu
3069.1.Q6	Quilpué
3069.3.A-.3.Z	Topics (Ancient and modern), A-Z
3069.3.A3	Agriculture
3069.3.A7	Art
3069.3.C66	Commerce
3069.3.E2	Economic conditions
3069.3.E38	Education
3069.3.E46	Employment
3069.3.F64	Folklore. Legends
3069.3.G6	Government relations
	Legends, *see* F3069.3.F64
3069.3.M4	Metalwork
3069.3.M5	Missions
3069.3.M55	Mixed bloods
3069.3.P76	Population
3069.3.P8	Pottery
3069.3.R44	Religion and mythology
3069.3.T4	Textile industry and fabrics
3069.3.W37	Wars
3070	Modern Indians (General)
3070.1.A-.1.Z	Tribes (Ancient and modern), A-Z
	Araucanians (Chilote, Huilliche, Mapuche, Pehuenche, and Picunche), *see* F3126
3070.1.A7	Atacameno
3070.1.C5	Chango
3070.1.C6	Chono
3070.1.D5	Diaguita
	Cf. F2823.D5, Argentina
	Fuegian (Alacaluf, Yahgan), *see* F2986
3072	Ciudad de los Césares
	History
3073	Chronological tables. Outlines, syllabi, etc. Questions and answers, etc.
	Historiography
3074	General works
	Biography of historians
3075	Collective
3076.A-.Z	Individual, A-Z
	GALE NOTE *See note at the head of Table F5 at the end of the text for further instructions on how to subdivide this number*
3076.B3	Barros Arana, Diego
3077	Study and teaching
3081	General works
	Including political history
	General special
3082	Military and naval history
	Diplomatic history. Foreign and general relations
3083	General works

	South America
	Chile
	History
	General special
	Diplomatic history. Foreign and general relations — Continued
3083.5.A-.5.Z	Relations with individual countries, A-Z
3083.9	Other (not A-Z)
	By period
	Pre-Columbian period, *see* F3069+
3091	1535-1810

> *Including conquest of the Araucanian Indians; history as a Spanish colony*
> *Including biography: Pedro de Valdivia, etc.*

	1810-

> *Declared independence from Spain, July 16, 1810*

3093	General works
3094	1810-1824. War of Independence

> *Including battles of Rancagua (1814), Chacabuco (1817), Maipo (1818)*
> *Including biography: Jose Miguel Carrera, Juan Mackenna, Bernardo O'Higgins,*
> *etc.*

	1824-1920

> *Including domination of the conservatives, 1830-1861; War with Spain, 1865-1866;*
> *bombardment of Valparaiso, 1866; civil wars*
> *Including biography: Manuel Francisco Antonio Julián Montt, Diego José Víctor*
> *Portales, Benjamín Vicuña Mackenna, etc.*
> *Cf. D501+, World War I, 1914-1918*
> *Cf. F3447, War with Spain, 1865-1866*

3095	General works
	War of the Pacific, 1879-1884
3097	General works
3097.3	Territorial questions growing out of the war

> *Including Tacna-Arica question (Controversial topic until 1929); Treaty of*
> *Ancón, 1883; Treaty of Valparaiso, 1884*

3098	Revolution of 1891

> *Including biography: José Manuel Balmaceda, etc.*

	1921-

> *Including restoration of presidential power, 1921-1938; Popular Front, 1938-1942;*
> *earthquake of 1938*
> *Including biography: Pedro Aguirre Cerda, Arturo Alessandri, Carlos Ibáñez del*
> *Campo, etc.*
> *Cf. D731+, World War II, 1939-1945*

3099	General works
	1970-
3100	General works
	Biography
3101.A2	Collective
3101.A3-.Z	Individual, A-Z

> GALE NOTE *See note at the head of Table F5 at the end of the text for further*
> *instructions on how to subdivide this number*

3101.A4	Allende, Salvador
	Regions, provinces, etc.
3105	Islands of Chile (General)
3106	Aconcagua
	Aisén, *see* F3134
3111	Andes Mountains in Chile

> *Cf. F2212, South America*
> *Cf. F2851, Argentina*

3116	Antofagasta

> *Formerly Bolivian territory of Atacama*
> *For Taltal (Department), see F3238*

	South America
	Chile
	Regions, provinces, etc. — Continued
3126	Arauco

                Including ancient and modern Mapuche Indians (Araucanian) and ancient and modern Araucanian Indians in Chile and adjacent areas of Argentina

                For Malleco, formerly part of Arauco, see F3196

         Arica (Department), *see* F3231

3131   Atacama (Desert and Province)

                Including the islands: Gonzalez; Saint Ambrose (San Ambrosio); Saint Felix (San Félix), Huasco River

3134   Aysén (Aisén)

                Including Baker River

         Baker River, *see* F3134

3136   Bío-Bío

                Including Antuco (Volcano)

         Boundaries

3139.A1-.A4   General

            Argentina, *see* F2851, F2853

3139.A5-.Z   Bolivia

                Cf. F3097.3, Tacna and Arica question

                Cf. F3116, Former Bolivian territory of Atacama

            Peru, *see* F3451.B73

         Cape Horn, *see* F3186

3141   Cautín

                Including Llaima (Department)

3146   Chiloé

                A province of Chilean Patagonia

                Cf. F2936, Patagonia

                Including wreck of the Wager (Ship)

3151   Colchagua

                Including Tinguiririca (Volcano)

3156   Concepción

3161   Coquimbo

                Including Guayacán Bay

3166   Curicó

         Cuyo (Transferred to Viceroyalty of La Plata, 1776), *see* F2911

3169   Easter Island

                Including Isla de Pascua, L'ile de Pâques, Rapa Nui, Te Pito te Henua

3170   El Loa

3171   Juan Fernández Islands

                Including earthquake of 1835

3174   Laja River and Valley

3176   Linares

         Llaima (Department), *see* F3141

3181   Llanquihue

                Including Llanquihue Lake, Reloncaví Bay, Rio Cisnes, Rio Puelo

         Loa, *see* F3170

3186   Magallanes y Antártica Chilena

                Name of Region XII created in 1974 by the union of the former province of Magallanes (western part of the island of Tierra del Fuego, formed as a province of Chilean Patagonia, 1929) and the former Territorio Antártico Chileno (formally claimed by Chile in Nov. 1940)

                Including Cape Horn, etc.

                For Ultima Esperanza (Department), see F3244

                Cf. F2936, Patagonia

                Cf. F2986, Tierra del Fuego (Island)

3191   Strait of Magellan

                Cf. G286.M2, Life and travels of Fernão de Magalhães (Ferdinand Magellan)

                Cf. G420.M2, First circumnavigation of the globe by Magellan and crew

      South America
        Chile
          Regions, provinces, etc. — Continued

3196	Malleco
	Including Tolhuaca and Lonquimay Volcanoes
	Formerly a part of the Province of Arauco; formed as a separate province, 1887
3201	Maule
3205	North Chile
3206	Ñuble
	Including earthquake of 1939
3211	O'Higgins
3214	Pisagua (Department)
3218	Region de los Lagos
3221	Santiago
	Cf. F3271, Santiago de Chile (City)
3231	Tacna (Department). Arica (Department)
	Between 1883 and 1929, Tacna belonged to Chile; in 1929, became a department of Peru
	Before 1883, Arica belonged to Peru
	Cf. F3097.3 , Territorial questions arising from war with Peru and Bolivia, 1879-1884
3236	Talca
3238	Taltal (Department)
3241	Tarapacá
	Before 1883, belonged to Peru
	For departments of Tacna and Arica, see F3231
	For Pisagua (Department), see F3214
	Cf. F3097.3, Territorial questions arising from war with Peru and Bolivia, 1879-1884
	Tierra del Fuego (Chilean part of island), *see F3186*
3244	Ultima Esperanza (Department)
3246	Valdivia
3251	Valparaiso
	For Easter Island, see F3169
	For Juan Fernández Island, see F3171

          Cities, towns, etc.

3271	Santiago de Chile (City)
	Subarrange by Table F1 at the end of the text
3281.A-.Z	Other, A-Z
3281.A45	Antofagasta
3281.A6	Arica
3281.C46	Chillán
3281.C5	Concepción
3281.I6	Iquique
3281.T17	Talca
3281.T2	Talcahuano
3281.T4	Temuco
3281.V15	Valdivia
3281.V2	Valparaiso
3281.V6	Viña del Mar

         Elements in the population
            For interpretation, see F1392.A+

3285.A1	General works
	Including foreign elements (General), minorities, race conflicts and problems
3285.A2-.Z	Individual elements, A-Z
3285.A5	Americans
3285.A7	Arabs
3285.B3	Basques
3285.B53	Blacks
3285.B7	British
3285.C94	Czechs
3285.F8	French
3285.G25	Galicians (Spain)

	South America
	Chile
	Elements in the population
3285.A2-.Z	Individual elements, A-Z — Continued
3285.G3	Germans
	Indians, *see* F3069+
3285.I8	Italians
3285.J4	Jews
3285.P4	Peruvians
3285.S7	Spaniards
3285.S9	Swiss
3285.Y8	Yugoslavs
	Bolivia
3301	Periodicals. Societies. Collections
	Collected works
3302	Several authors
3303	Individual authors
	Including collected papers, addresses, essays
3303.5	Museums. Exhibitions, exhibits
3304	Gazetteers. Dictionaries. Geographic names
3304.5	Directories
	Biography
3305	Collective
	Individual, *see* F3320.6, F3322-3341
3308	General works
3308.5	Juvenile works
	Pamphlets, addresses, essays, etc.
3309	General
3309.4	Anecdotes, legends, pageants, etc.
	Cf. GR130+, Folklore
	Cf. Class P, Literature
3309.5	Guidebooks. Handbooks
3309.7	Historic monuments (General)
3310	Social life and customs. Civilization. Intellectual life
	Including national characteristics
3310.9	Geography
	Description and travel. Views
3311	Early to 1808
3313	1809-1950
3314	1951-1980
3315	1981-
	Antiquities. Indians
3319	General works
3319.1.A-.1.Z	Local (Ancient and modern), A-Z
	GALE NOTE *The cutter number(s) listed below have been given only as examples by the Library of Congress*
3319.1.C4	Chaco (Bolivian)
3319.1.C6	Cochabamba (Department)
3319.1.P6	Potosí
3319.1.S2	Samaypata
3319.1.T55	Tiahuanaco (Tiwanaku, Tiahuanacu)
	Including the Tiwanaku Valley and the Tiwanaku culture
3320	Modern Indians (General)
3320.1.A-.1.Z	Topics (Ancient and modern), A-Z
3320.1.A47	Agriculture
3320.1.A68	Architecture
3320.1.A7	Art
3320.1.C45	Census
3320.1.C57	Civil rights
3320.1.C6	Colonization

South America
  Bolivia
    Antiquities. Indians

3320.1.A-.1.Z	Topics (Ancient and modern), A-Z — Continued
3320.1.C64	Costume and adornment
3320.1.D35	Dance
3320.1.D83	Dwellings
3320.1.E4	Education
3320.1.E84	Ethnic identity
3320.1.F6	Folklore. Legends
3320.1.F64	Food
3320.1.G35	Games
3320.1.G6	Government relations
3320.1.I45	Implements
3320.1.I54	Industries
3320.1.L35	Land tenure
3320.1.M37	Marriage customs
3320.1.M38	Masks
3320.1.M4	Medicine
3320.1.M43	Metalwork
3320.1.M47	Missions
3320.1.M5	Mixed bloods
3320.1.N37	Narcotics
3320.1.P53	Philosophy
3320.1.P56	Politics and government
3320.1.P6	Pottery
3320.1.P8	Psychology
3320.1.R3	Religion. Mythology
3320.1.S38	Sculpture
3320.1.S62	Social conditions
3320.1.T38	Taxation
3320.1.T48	Textile industry and fabrics
3320.1.W37	Wars
3320.1.W65	Women
3320.2.A-.2.Z	Tribes (Ancient and modern), A-Z
3320.2.A6	Apolista
3320.2.A7	Arauna
	Arawak, *see* F2230.2.A7
	Aymara, *see* F2230.2.A9
3320.2.C3	Callahuaya
3320.2.C33	Canichana
	Caripuna, *see* F2520.1.C37
3320.2.C34	Cavineño
3320.2.C35	Cayubaba
3320.2.C36	Chacobo
	Chamacoco, *see* F2230.2.C5
3320.2.C37	Chané
3320.2.C38	Chapacura
3320.2.C387	Chimane
3320.2.C388	Chipaya
3320.2.C39	Chiquito
3320.2.C4	Chiriguano
3320.2.C5	Choroti
3320.2.C62	Churumata
	Colla, *see* F3430.1.C6
3320.2.G8	Guarayo
	Guaycuru, *see* F2230.2.G78
3320.2.I8	Itene
3320.2.J84	Jukumani
	Kechua, *see* F2230.2.K4

	South America
	Bolivia
	Antiquities. Indians
3320.2.A-.2.Z	Tribes (Ancient and modern), A-Z — Continued
	Lengua, *see* F2679.2.L4
3320.2.M26	Manacica
	Mataco, *see* F2823.M3
3320.2.M55	Mojo
3320.2.M57	Mollo culture
3320.2.M6	Moseten
	Moxo, *see* F3320.2.M55
3320.2.O3	Ocorona
3320.2.O8	Otuquis
3320.2.P3	Pacaguara
	Pano, *see* F3430.1.P3
	Panoan Indians, *see* F3430.1.P33
3320.2.P37	Pauserna
	Pilaga, *see* F2823.P5
	Puquina, *see* F3430.1.P8
	Quechua, *see* F2230.2.K4
3320.2.S3	Samucu
3320.2.S5	Siriono
3320.2.T3	Tacana
	Toba, *see* F2823.T7
3320.2.T6	Toromona
	Tucuna, *see* F2520.1.T925
3320.2.U78	Uru
3320.2.Y78	Yuqui
3320.2.Y8	Yurucari
3320.2.Z3	Zamucoan
	History
3320.3	Chronological tables. Outlines, syllabi, etc. Questions and answers
	Historiography
3320.4	General works
	Biography of historians
3320.5	Collective
3320.6.A-.6.Z	Individual, A-Z
	GALE NOTE *See note at the head of Table F5 at the end of the text for further instructions on how to subdivide this number*
3320.7	Study and teaching
3321	General works
	Including political history
	General special
3321.1	Military history
	Diplomatic history. Foreign and general relations
3321.2	General works
3321.3.A-.3.Z	Relations with individual countries, A-Z
3321.9	Other (not A-Z)
	By period
	Pre-Columbian period, *see* F3319+
3322	1538-1809. Upper Peru
	In colonial times, Bolivia was the southern part of Upper Peru; formed Audiencia of Charcas under viceroy of Peru, 1559-1776 (Cf. F3444, Colonial Peru); under viceroy of Buenos Aires (La Plata), 1776-1810
	Cf. F2841, Argentina, 1516-1810
	Cf. F2991, Ancient gobernación of Tucumán
	Cf. F3444, Insurrection of Tupac Amaru, 1780-1781
3323	1809-1825. Wars of independence

	South America
	Bolivia
	History
	By period — Continued
3324	1825-1884
	Including independence from Peru declared August 6, 1825. Period of civil wars and conflicts with neighboring countries
	For loss of southern Chaco to Argentina, 1878, see F2876
	For war with Chile (War of the Pacific), 1879-1884, see F3097
	Including biography: Mariano Melgarejo, Andrés Santa-Cruz, etc.
	Cf. F3447, Confederación Perú-Boliviana
3325	1884-1938
	Including conflicts between the civil and the military; rule of dictators; etc.
	Including biography: Mariano Baptista, Ismael Montes, etc.
	For loss of Acre District to Brazil (Treaty of Petropolis, 1903), see F2540
	For Chaco War, 1932-1935 and Treaty of peace, 1938, see F2688.5
3326	1938-1982
	Including biography: Victor Paz Estenssoro, Enrique Peñaranda Castillo, etc.
	Cf. D731+, World War II, 1939-1945
3327	1982-
3341.A-.Z	Regions, departments, etc., A-Z
3341.A1	Collective
	Acre Territory, see F2540
3341.A5	Andes Mountains
	Cf. F2212, General
	Atacama, see F2853, Argentine territory of Los Andes; F3116, Chilean province of Antofagasta
3341.A9	Azero (Province)
3341.B4	Beni
3341.B7	Boundaries (General)
	For Argentina, see F2857.B6
	For Brazil, see F2554.B6
	For Chaco Boreal dispute, see F2691.C4
	For Chile, see F3139.A1+
	For Paraguay, see F2691.B7A+
	For Peru, see F3451.B71
3341.C27	Capinota (Province)
3341.C3	Caupolican (Province)
3341.C4	Chaco (Bolivian)
	For Chaco War, 1932-1935, see F2688.5
	Cf. F2691.C4, Chaco Boreal, Paraguay
	Cf. F2876, El Gran Chaco (General, and Argentina)
3341.C5	Chiquitos (Province)
3341.C6	Chuquisaca
	For Azero (Province), see F3341.A9
3341.C7	Cochabamba
3341.C75	Cordillera (Province)
3341.I25	Ichilo (Province)
3341.L3	La Paz
	For Acre Territory, see F2540
	For Caupolican (Province), see F3341.C3
	For Lake Titicaca, see F3341.T6
	For Nor Yungas (Province), see F3341.N67
3341.L35	Larecaja (Province)
3341.M58	Mizque (Province)
3341.M9	Moxos (Province)
3341.N67	Nor Yungas (Province)
3341.O5	Omasuyos (Province)
3341.O6	Oriente
3341.O7	Oruro
3341.P3	Pando

South America

Bolivia

3341.A-.Z	Regions, departments, etc., A-Z — Continued
	Piray River and Valley, *see* F3341.S2
3341.P7	Potosí
3341.S2	Santa Cruz
	Including Piray River and Valley
	Cf. F2691.C4, Chaco Boreal dispute
3341.S9	Sud Chichas
3341.T2	Tarija
	Cf. F2691.C4, Chaco Boreal dispute
3341.T3	Territorio Nacional de Colonias
3341.T6	Lake Titicaca region (General, and Bolivia)
	Including Titicaca Island
	Cf. F3451.P9, Peru
3351.A-.Z	Cities, towns, etc., A-Z
	GALE NOTE *The cutter number(s) listed below have been given only as examples by the Library of Congress*
3351.C67	Cochabamba
3351.L2	La Paz
	Subarrange by Table F2 at the end of the text
3351.O7	Oruro
3351.P85	Potosí
3351.S3	Santa Cruz
3351.S94	Sucre
	Formerly known as Charcas, Chuquisaca, and La Plata
	Elements in the population
	For interpretation, see F1392.A+
3359.A1	General works
	Including foreign elements (General), minorities, race conflicts and problems
3359.A2-.Z	Individual elements, A-Z
3359.B55	Blacks
3359.B73	Brazilians
3359.G3	Germans
	Indians, *see* F3319+
3359.J3	Japanese
3359.J47	Jews

Peru

3401	Periodicals. Societies. Collections
	Collected works
3402	Several authors
3403	Individual authors
	Including collected papers, addresses, essays
3403.5	Museums. Exhibitions, exhibits
3404	Gazetteers. Dictionaries. Geographic names
3404.5	Directories
	Biography
3405	Collective
	Individual, *see* F3430.6, F3442-3448.4
3408	General works
3408.5	Juvenile works
	Pamphlets, addresses, essays
3409	General
3409.3	Anecdotes, legends, pageants, etc.
	Cf. Class P, Literature
3409.5	Guidebooks. Handbooks
3409.7	Historic monuments (General)
3410	Social life and customs. Civilization. Intellectual life
	Including national characteristics
	For race conflicts and problems, see F3619

	South America
	Peru — Continued
3410.4	Geography
	Description and travel. Views
3410.5	History of travel
3411	Early to 1819
3423	1820-1950
3424	1951-1980
3425	1981-
	Antiquities. Indians
3429	General works
	Including Incas
3429.1.A-1.Z	Local (Ancient and modern), A-Z
	GALE NOTE *The cutter number(s) listed below have been given only as examples by the Library of Congress*
3429.1.A45	Ancachs (Department)
3429.1.A5	Ancón
3429.1.A7	Arequipa (Department)
3429.1.C3	Callejón de Huaylas
3429.1.C47	Chancay Valley
	Including Chancay culture
3429.1.C48	Chavín
	Including Chavín culture
3429.1.C5	Choqquequirau
3429.1.C8	Cuelap
3429.1.C9	Cuzco
3429.1.E7	Espiritu Pampa
3429.1.H8	Huamachuco
3429.1.H828	Huari
3429.1.L7	Lima (Department)
3429.1.M3	Machu Picchu
3429.1.M35	Maranga
3429.1.N3	Nazca
	Including Nazca culture
3429.1.N5	Nievería
3429.1.P2	Pachacamac
3429.1.P25	Paracas
3429.1.P28	Paramonga
3429.1.P8	Puno (Department)
3429.1.P86	Putumayo Valley
3429.1.R55	Rimac Valley
3429.1.T8	Trujillo (Province)
3429.1.V45	Vicús
	Including Vicús culture
3429.1.V77	Virú Valley
3429.1.V8	Vitcos
3429.3.A-.3.Z	Topics (Ancient and modern), A-Z
3429.3.A37	Aged
3429.3.A4	Agriculture
3429.3.A45	Alcohol use
3429.3.A5	Anthropometry
3429.3.A65	Architecture
3429.3.A7	Art
3429.3.A76	Astronomy
3429.3.A9	Axes
3429.3.B63	Boats
	Burial customs, *see* F3429.3.M7
3429.3.C14	Calendar. Chronology. Astronomy
3429.3.C4	Census
	Ceremonies, *see* F3429.3.R3

	South America
	Peru
	Antiquities. Indians
3429.3.A-.3.Z	Topics (Ancient and modern), A-Z — Continued
3429.3.C56	Civil rights
3429.3.C59	Commerce
3429.3.C594	Communication
3429.3.C6	Consanguinity
3429.3.C74	Cosmology
3429.3.C8	Costume and adornment
3429.3.C85	Craniology
3429.3.D6	Diseases
3429.3.D69	Domestic animals
3429.3.D72	Domestic relations
3429.3.D77	Drinking vessels
3429.3.D79	Drug use
3429.3.E2	Economic conditions
3429.3.E3	Education
3429.3.E35	Egyptian influences
3429.3.E45	Employment
3429.3.E84	Ethnic identity
3429.3.E86	Ethnobotany
3429.3.F55	First contact with Europeans
3429.3.F57	Fishing
3429.3.F6	Folklore. Legends
3429.3.F65	Food
3429.3.F85	Funeral customs and rites
3429.3.G3	Games
3429.3.G4	Genealogy
3429.3.G5	Goldwork
	Government, *see* F3429.3.P65
3429.3.G6	Government relations
3429.3.H5	Historiography
3429.3.I53	Industries
3429.3.I77	Irrigation
3429.3.J8	Judiciary
3429.3.K53	Kings and rulers
3429.3.K55	Kinship
3429.3.L3	Land tenure
3429.3.L45	Law and legislation
	Legends, *see* F3429.3.F6
3429.3.L5	Litters
3429.3.M3	Magic
3429.3.M34	Marriage customs
3429.3.M35	Masks (Sculpture)
3429.3.M36	Mathematics
	For works limited to Quipu, see F3429.3.Q6
3429.3.M4	Medicine
3429.3.M42	Metalwork
3429.3.M6	Missions
3429.3.M63	Mixed bloods
3429.3.M7	Mortuary customs
3429.3.M8	Mummies
3429.3.P34	Painting
3429.3.P47	Petroglyphs. Rock paintings
3429.3.P55	Philosophy
3429.3.P65	Politics and government
3429.3.P68	Population
3429.3.P69	Portraits, Indian
3429.3.P7	Postal service

	South America
	Peru
	Antiquities. Indians
3429.3.A-.3.Z	Topics (Ancient and modern), A-Z — Continued
3429.3.P8	Pottery
3429.3.P85	Psychology
3429.3.Q6	Quipu
3429.3.R27	Relations with Blacks
3429.3.R3	Religion. Mythology
3429.3.R58	Rites and ceremonies
3429.3.R6	Roads and trails
	Rock paintings, *see* F3429.3.P47
3429.3.S39	Sculpture
3429.3.S45	Sexual behavior
3429.3.S54	Silverwork
3429.3.S59	Social conditions
3429.3.S6	Social life and customs
3429.3.T2	Tattooing
3429.3.T28	Taxation. Tribute
3429.3.T29	Teeth
3429.3.T3	Textile industry and fabrics
3429.3.T7	Trephining
	Tribute, *see* F3429.3.T28
3429.3.W2	Warfare
3429.3.W27	Wars
3429.3.W4	Weights and measures
3429.3.W65	Women
3429.3.W7	Writing
3430	Modern Indians (General)
3430.1.A-.1.Z	Tribes (Ancient and modern), A-Z
	Achuale, *see* F3430.1.A25
3430.1.A25	Achuar. Achuale
3430.1.A35	Aguaruna
3430.1.A5	Amahuaca
3430.1.A54	Amuesha
3430.1.A6	Andoa
3430.1.A83	Ashaninca
3430.1.A85	Asto
	Aymara, *see* F2230.2.A9
	Bora, *see* F2270.2.B6
3430.1.C3	Campa
3430.1.C32	Candoshi
3430.1.C34	Capanahua
3430.1.C35	Cashibo
	Cashinawa, *see* F2520.1.C38
3430.1.C37	Chachapoya
3430.1.C4	Chanca
	Chavín culture, *see* F3429.1.C48
3430.1.C43	Chayahuita
3430.1.C46	Chimu
3430.1.C48	Cholone
3430.1.C5	Chupacho
3430.1.C55	Cocama
3430.1.C6	Colla
	Conibo, *see* F3430.1.S5
	Culina, *see* F2520.1.C84
3430.1.C8	Cupisnique
3430.1.E78	Ese Ejja
3430.1.H78	Huambisa
3430.1.H8	Huanca

	South America
	Peru
	Antiquities. Indians
3430.1.A-.1.Z	Tribes (Ancient and modern), A-Z — Continued
3430.1.H83	Huari
	Incas, *see* F3429+
3430.1.I68	Iquito
3430.1.I8	Iscaycinca
3430.1.I85	Itucale
	Jivaro, *see* F3722.1.J5
	Kechua, *see* F2230.2.K4
3430.1.M3	Machiganga
3430.1.M38	Mashco
3430.1.M4	Mayna
3430.1.M45	Mayoruna
3430.1.M6	Mochica
3430.1.N3	Nasca
3430.1.O25	Ocaina
3430.1.O5	Omagua
3430.1.O74	Orejón
3430.1.P3	Pano
3430.1.P33	Panoan Indians
3430.1.P4	Peban
	Pioje, *see* F3722.1.P5
3430.1.P5	Piro
3430.1.P6	Pocra
3430.1.P8	Puquina
3430.1.Q47	Quero
3430.1.S35	Senci
3430.1.S4	Setibo
3430.1.S47	Shapra
3430.1.S48	Sharanahua
3430.1.S5	Shipibo-Conibo. Sipibo
	Tacana, *see* F3320.2.T3
3430.1.W35	Wamani
	Witoto, *see* F2270.2.W5
3430.1.Y3	Yagua
3430.1.Y34	Yanaconas
3430.1.Y8	Yunca
	Zaparo, *see* F3722.1.Z3
	History
3430.3	Chronological tables. Outlines, syllabi, etc. Questions and answers, etc.
	Historiography
3430.4	General works
	Biography of historians
3430.5	Collective
3430.6.A-.6.Z	Individual, A-Z
	GALE NOTE *See note at the head of Table F5 at the end of the text for further instructions on how to subdivide this number*
3430.7	Study and teaching
3431	General works
	Including political history
	General special
3432	Military and naval history
	Diplomatic history. Foreign and general relations
3433	General works
3434.A-.Z	Relations with individual countries, A-Z
	By period
	Pre-Columbian period, *see* F3429+

	South America
	Peru
	History
	By period — Continued
3442	1522-1548
	Including Spanish conquest, civil wars, etc.
	Including biography: Francisco Pizarro, Gonzalo Pizarro, etc.
	For Indians of Peru and the Inca Empire before 1531, see F3429
3444	1548-1820
	Including Viceroyalty of Peru, 1542-1824; Insurrection of Tupac Amaru, 1780-1781; sporadic revolts, 1805-1814
	Including biography: Vega, Garcilaso de la; Francisco de Toledo; Micaela Villegas; etc.
3446	1820-1829
	Including Independence from Spain proclaimed, 1821; battles at Zepita (1823), Colpahuaico (1824), Ayacucho (1824)
	Including biography: Juan Antonio Álvarez de Arenales, José de Lamar y Cortazar, William Miller, José Silverio Olaya, etc.
	For battle of Portete de Tarqui, see F2275
	For loss of Upper Peru, 1825, see F3324
	1829-
3446.5	General works
3447	1829-1919
	Including civil wars; Battle of Yanacocha, 1835; Confederación Perú-Boliviana, 1835-1839; Spanish question, 1864; War with Spain, 1865-1866; Bombardment of Callao, 1866; Revolution of 1872; period of reconstruction, 1884-1919
	Including biography: Ramón Castilla, Agustín Gamarra, Augusto Bernardino Leguia, Nicolás de Piérola, Leoncio Prado, Mariano Ignacio Prado, Felipe Santiago Salaverry, etc.
	For War of the Pacific, 1879-1884, see F3097
	Cf. D501+, World War I, 1914-1918
	Cf. F3095, War with Spain, 1865-1866
	Cf. F3451.P94, Putumayo atrocities
3448	1919-1968
	Including rise of liberalism; the Apristas; anti-axis policies
	Including biography: Oscar Raimundo Benavides, Víctor Raúl Haya de la Torre, Manuel Artura Odría, Manuel Prado y Ugarteche, etc.
	Cf. D731+, World War II, 1939-1945
	Cf. F2281.B7P1+, Leticia Dispute, 1932-1934
	1968-
3448.2	General works
	Biography
3448.3	Collective
3448.4.A-.4.Z	Individual, A-Z
	GALE NOTE *See note at the head of Table F5 at the end of the text for further instructions on how to subdivide this number; The cutter number(s) listed below have been given only as examples by the Library of Congress*
3448.4.V4	Velasco Alvarado, Juan
3451.A-.Z	Regions, departments, etc., A-Z
3451.A4	Amazonas
	Amazonas, Bajos, *see* F3451.B3
3451.A43	Anan Yauyo (Province)
3451.A45	Ancachs (Ancash)
	Including Callejon de Huaylas
3451.A48	Andahuaylas (Province)
3451.A5	Andes Mountains, Peru
	Including Cordillera Blanca
	Cf. F2212, General
3451.A54	Andrés Avelino Cáceres
3451.A6	Apurímac

	South America
	Peru
3451.A-.Z	Regions, departments, etc., A-Z — Continued
3451.A7	Arequipa
	Including Coropuna, El Misti (Volcano)
	Arica (Department), *see* F3231
3451.A87	Ayabaca (Province)
3451.A9	Ayacucho
3451.B3	Bajo Amazonas
	Province was named Maynas in 1943
	Boundaries
3451.B7	General
3451.B71	Bolivia
	Brazil, *see* F2554.P4
3451.B73	Chile
	Cf. F3097.3, Tacna and Arica question
	Colombia, *see* F2281.B7
3451.B75	Ecuador
	Leticia question, *see* F2281.B7P1+
	Cáceres Region, *see* F3451.A54
3451.C2	Cajamarca
3451.C23	Calca (Province)
3451.C25	Callao
3451.C28	Canchis
3451.C3	Carabaya (Province)
	Cerro Salcantay, *see* F3451.C9
3451.C46	Chancay (Province)
3451.C5	Chincha Valley
3451.C55	Chota (Province)
3451.C6	Chucuito (Province)
3451.C7	Contumazá (Province)
	Cordillera Blanca, *see* F3451.A5
3451.C76	Corongo (Province)
3451.C85	Cutervo (Province)
3451.C9	Cuzco (Cusco)
	Including Nevado Sarcantay (Cerro Salcantay), Pampaconas River, Urubamba River
	Ene River and Valley, *see* F3451.J9
3451.G73	Grau Region
3451.H7	Huamalies (Province)
3451.H75	Huancané (Province)
3451.H76	Huancavelica
3451.H78	Huancayo
3451.H79	Huanta
3451.H8	Huánuco
	Including Pozuzo colony
3451.H83	Huaral (Province)
	Huaura River and Valley, *see* F3451.L7
	Huaylas, Callejon de, *see* F3451.A45
3451.I3	Ica
3451.J33	Jaén (Province)
3451.J9	Junín
	Including Ene River and Valley
	La Libertad, *see* F3451.L3
3451.L2	Lambayeque
3451.L23	Lampa
3451.L3	Libertad
3451.L7	Lima
	Including Huaura River and Valley, Marcahuasi Plateau
	Cf. F3601, Lima (City)

	South America
	Peru
3451.A-.Z	Regions, departments, etc., A-Z — Continued
3451.L8	Loreto
	Including Amazon River and Valley, Peru, Marañón River, Pichis River, and Ucayali River
3451.M2	Madre de Dios
	Including Madre de Dios River
	Marcahuasi Plateau, *see* F3451.L7
	Maynas (Province), *see* F3451.B3
	Misti (Volcano), *see* F3451.A7
3451.M6	La Montaña (region)
3451.M8	Moquegua
	Nevado Sarcantay, *see* F3451.C9
3451.N67	Nor Oriental del Marañón
3451.O16	Ocsabamba (Oxapampa) colony
3451.P14	Pachitea (Province)
3451.P19	Pacific coast
3451.P245	Parinacochas (Province)
3451.P247	Pasco
3451.P25	Paucartambo (Province)
3451.P48	Pisco (Province)
3451.P5	Piura
	Pozuzo (Posuso) colony, *see* F3451.H8
3451.P9	Puno
	Including Peruvian section of Lake Titicaca
	Cf. F3341.T6, General, and Bolivia
3451.P94	Putumayo River and Valley
	Including rubber atrocities
	Cf. F2281.P9, Colombia
	Cf. F2546, Brazil, where river is called "Içá"
3451.R6	Rodríguez de Mendoza (Province)
	Salcantay, Cerro, *see* F3451.C9
3451.S2	San Marcos (Province)
3451.S24	San Martín
3451.S244	Sandia (Province)
3451.S25	Santa Cruz (District)
	Sarcantay, *see* F3451.C9
	Tacna (Department), *see* F3231
	Tarapacá, *see* F3241
	Lake Titicaca region, *see* F3451.P9
3451.T7	Trujillo (Province)
3451.T8	Tumbes
	Ucayali River and Valley, *see* F3451.L8
	White Cordillera, *see* F3451.A5
3451.Y38	Yauyos (Province)
3451.Y47	Yerupaja (El Carnicero, The Butcher)
	Cities, towns, etc.
	Including individual biography
3601	Lima
	Subarrange by Table F1 at the end of the text
	Including earthquakes of 1687, 1746, etc.; occupation by Chilean forces, 1881-1883
3611.A-.Z	Other, A-Z
	GALE NOTE *The cutter number(s) listed below have been given only as examples by the Library of Congress*
3611.A7	Arequipa
3611.C2	Callao
3611.C9	Cusco
3611.H8	Huancavelica
3611.H82	Huancayo

	South America
	Peru
	Cities, towns, etc.
3611.A-.Z	Other, A-Z — Continued
3611.I6	Iquitos
3611.S84	Sullana
3611.T8	Trujillo
	Elements in the population
	Including foreign elements (General), minorities, race conflicts and problems
	For interpretation, see F1392.A+
3619.A1	General works
3619.A2-.Z	Individual elements, A-Z
3619.A5	Americans
3619.B55	Blacks
3619.B7	British
3619.C34	Canary Islanders
3619.C5	Chinese
3619.G3	Germans
	Indians, *see F3429+*
3619.I8	Italians
3619.J3	Japanese
3619.J4	Jews
3619.M47	Mestizos
	Negroes, *see F3619.B55*
3619.P64	Poles
3619.R87	Russians
3619.Y84	Yugoslavs
	Ecuador
3701	Periodicals. Societies. Collections
	Collected works
3702	Several authors
3703	Individual authors
	Including collected papers, addresses, essays
3703.5	Museums. Exhibitions, exhibits
3704	Gazetteers. Dictionaries. Geographic names
3704.5	Directories
	Biography
3705	Collective
	Individual, *see F3726, F3733-3738.4*
3708	General works
3708.5	Juvenile works
	Pamphlets, addresses, essays
3709	General
3709.3	Anecdotes, legends, pageants, etc.
	Cf. Subclasses PN, PQ, etc., Literature
3709.5	Guidebooks. Handbooks
3709.7	Historic monuments (General)
3710	Social life and customs. Civilization. Intellectual life
	Including national characteristics
	For race conflicts and problems, see F3799
3710.9	Geography
	Description and travel. Views
3711	Early to 1808
3714	1809-1950
3715	1951-1980
3716	1981-
	Antiquities. Indians
3721	General works

South America
    Ecuador
        Antiquities. Indians — Continued

3721.1.A-.1.Z	Local (Ancient and modern), A-Z
	GALE NOTE *The cutter number(s) listed below have been given only as examples by the Library of Congress*
3721.1.C2	Carchi (Province)
3721.1.G9	Guayas (Province)
3721.1.I3	Imbabura (Province)
3721.1.L36	La Plata Island
3721.1.M2	Manabi
3721.1.T65	Tomebamba
3721.3.A-.3.Z	Topics (Ancient and modern), A-Z
3721.3.A35	Agriculture
3721.3.A67	Architecture
3721.3.A7	Art
3721.3.C64	Commerce
3721.3.D35	Dances
	Drugs, *see* F3721.3.N35
3721.3.E25	Economic conditions
3721.3.E35	Education
3721.3.E84	Ethnic identity
3721.3.E85	Ethnobotany
3721.3.F65	Folklore. Legends
3721.3.F7	Food
3721.3.G45	Genealogy
3721.3.G68	Government relations
3721.3.I4	Implements
3721.3.M37	Material culture
3721.3.M38	Mathematics
3721.3.M4	Medicine
3721.3.M45	Metalwork
3721.3.M6	Missions
	Mythology, *see* F3721.3.R44
3721.3.N35	Narcotics
3721.3.P74	Politics and government
3721.3.P76	Population
3721.3.P8	Pottery
3721.3.R44	Religion. Mythology
3721.3.S24	Salt
3721.3.S65	Social conditions
3721.3.S7	Social life and customs
3721.3.T18	Taxation. Tribute
3721.3.T2	Teeth mutilation and decoration
3721.3.T47	Textile industry and fabrics
	Tribute, *see* F3721.3.T18
3721.3.U73	Urban residence
3721.3.W35	Wars
3721.3.W65	Women
3722	Modern Indians (General)
3722.1.A-.1.Z	Tribes (Ancient and modern), A-Z
	Achuale, *see* F3430.1.A25
	Andoa, *see* F3430.1.A6
	Arawak, *see* F2230.2.A7
3722.1.C2	Cañari
3722.1.C23	Canelo
3722.1.C25	Cara
3722.1.C3	Cayapa
3722.1.C67	Cofán
3722.1.C7	Colorado

	South America
	Ecuador
	Antiquities. Indians
3722.1.A-.1.Z	Tribes (Ancient and modern), A-Z — Continued
3722.1.C83	Cuaiquer
3722.1.E8	Esmeralda
3722.1.G82	Guayacundo
3722.1.H8	Huancavilca
3722.1.H83	Huao
	Incas, *see* F3429
3722.1.J5	Jivaro. Shuar
	Kechua, *see* F2230.2.K4
3722.1.M3	Manta
3722.1.O8	Otavalo
3722.1.P35	Panzaleo
	Pasto, *see* F2270.2.P44
3722.1.P5	Pioje
3722.1.P8	Puruhá
3722.1.Q48	Quijo
3722.1.Q5	Quitu
3722.1.S43	Secoya
	Shuar, *see* F3722.1.J5
	Tucuna, *see* F2520.1.T925
3722.1.Z3	Zaparo
	History
3723	Chronological tables. Outlines, syllabi, etc. Questions and answers, etc.
	Historiography
3724	General works
	Biography
3725	Collective
3726.A-.Z	Individual, A-Z
	GALE NOTE *See note at the head of Table F5 at the end of the text for further instructions on how to subdivide this number*
3727	Study and teaching
3731	General works
	Including political history
	General special
3731.5	Military and naval history
	Diplomatic history. Foreign and general relations
3732	General works
3732.5.A-.5.Z	Relations with individual countries, A-Z
3732.9	Other (not A-Z)
	By period
	Pre-Columbian period, *see* F3721+
3733	1526-1809. Colonial period
	Including discovery and conquest; civil war among the conquistadores; under viceroyalty of Peru, 1539-1717; under viceroyalty of Nueva Granada, 1717-1723; under viceroyalty of Peru, 1723-1740; under viceroyalty of Nueva Granada, 1740 to independence
	Including biography: Sebastián de Belalcázar, Francisco Javier Eugenio, Santa Cruz y Espejo, etc.
3734	1809-1830. Wars of independence
	Including revolts against Spain, 1809-1810; Battle of Pichincha, 1822; member of Confederacy known as Republic of Colombia, 1822-1830
	Including biography: Abdón Calderón, etc.
	1830-
	Republic of Ecuador created in 1830 by secession from confederacy
3735	General works
3736	1830-1895. Age of Moreno, 1860-1895
	Including civil wars; Concordat of 1862; Theocratic state, 1860-1895; etc.

	South America
	Ecuador
	History
	By period
	1830-
3736	1830-1895. Age of Moreno, 1860-1895 — Continued
	Including biography: Juan José Flores, Gabriel García Moreno, Federico González Suárez, Vicente Rocafuerte, Luis Vargas Torres, etc.
	For War with Spain, 1865-1866, see F3447
3737	1895-1944
	Including rule of liberals; restriction of church influence; loss of territory to Brazil in 1904, to Peru in 1942; etc.
	Including biography: Eloy Alfaro, Carlos Alberto Arroyo del Río, Isidro Ayora, Federico Páez, Leónidas Plaza Gutiérrez, etc.
	For Leticia dispute, 1932-1934, see F2281.B7P1+
	Cf. D501+, World War I, 1914-1918
	Cf. D731+, World War II, 1939-1945
3738	1944-1984
	Including revolts and counter revolutions; earthquake of 1949; etc.
	Including biography: Galo Plaza Lasso, José María Velasco Ibarra, etc.
	1984-
3738.2	General works
	Biography
3738.3	Collective
3738.4.A-.4.Z	Individual, A-Z
	GALE NOTE *See note at the head of Table F5 at the end of the text for further instructions on how to subdivide this number*
3741.A-.Z	Regions, provinces, etc., A-Z
3741.A6	Andes Mountains, Ecuador
	Cf. F2212, General
	Archipiélago de Colón, *see F3741.G2*
3741.A9	Azuay
3741.B5	Bolívar
3741.B7	Boundaries (General)
	For Colombia, see F2281.B7
	For Leticia question, see F2281.B7P1+
	For Peru, see F3451.B75
3741.C25	Cañar
3741.C3	Carchi
	Including Rumichaca Grotto
3741.C5	Chimborazo
	Colón, Archipiélago de, *see F3741.G2*
3741.C6	Cotopaxi (León)
3741.E4	El Oro
	Enchanted Islands, *see F3741.G2*
3741.E6	Esmeraldas
	Including Isla de la Tola (Tolita)
3741.G2	Galápagos (Encantadas, Enchanted) Islands. Archipiélago de Colón
3741.G9	Guayas
	Cf. F3741.G2, Galápagos Islands
3741.I6	Imbabura
	León, *see F3741.C6*
3741.L5	Llanganati (Mountains)
3741.L6	Loja
3741.L7	Los Ríos
3741.M2	Manabí
3741.N3	Napo-Pastaza
	Including Oriente (Región oriental)
	For Peruvian boundary dispute, see F3451.B75

	South America
	Ecuador
3741.A-.Z	Regions, provinces, etc., A-Z
3741.N3	Napo-Pastaza — Continued
	Cf. F3741.S3, Santiago-Zamora
	Oriente (Región oriental), *see* F3741.N3
	El Oro, *see* F3741.E4
3741.P32	Pacific Coast
3741.P4	Pichincha
	Región oriental, *see* F3741.N3
	Los Ríos, *see* F3741.L7
3741.S3	Santiago-Zamora
	For Oriente (Región oriental), see F3741.N3
	Sierra, *see* F3741.A6
3741.S93	Sucumbíos
3741.T7	Tungurahua
	Cities, towns, etc.
3781	Quito
	Subarrange by Table F1 at the end of the text
3791.A-.Z	Other, A-Z
	GALE NOTE *The cutter number(s) listed below have been given only as examples by the Library of Congress*
3791.A6	Ambato
3791.C9	Cuenca
3791.G9	Guayaquil
3791.I3	Ibarra
3791.J3	Jipijapa (Canton)
3791.L3	Latecunga
3791.L6	Loja
3791.R6	Riobamba
3791.T8	Tulcán
3791.V7	Vinces
	Elements in the population
	For interpretation, see F1392.A+
3799.A1	General works
3799.A2-.Z	Individual elements, A-Z
3799.B55	Blacks
	Indians, *see* F3721+
3799.J4	Jews
	Negroes, *see* F3799.B55
3799.S3	Salesians

TABLE E1 FOR INDIVIDUAL BIOGRAPHY

	GALE NOTE *".x" represents the cutter number for the individual*
.xA2	Collected works. By date
.xA25	Selected works. Selections. By date
	Including quotations
.xA3	Autobiography, diaries, etc. By date
.xA4	Letters. By date
.xA5	Speeches, essays, and lectures. By date
.xA6-.xZ	Biography and criticism

TABLE E2 FOR INDIVIDUAL BIOGRAPHY (1 NO.)

.A3	Autobiography, diaries, etc. By date
.A4	Letters. By date
.A6-.Z	Biography and criticism

TABLE E2A FOR INDIVIDUAL BIOGRAPHY (CUTTER NUMBER)

GALE NOTE *".x" represents the cutter number for the individual*

.xA3	Autobiography, diaries, etc. By date
.xA4	Letters. By date
.xA6-.xZ	Biography and criticism

TABLE E3 FOR COLLECTED WORKS OF AMERICAN STATESMEN

GALE NOTE *".x" represents the cutter number for the individual*

.x	Collected works. By date
.x2	Selected works. Selections. By date
	Including quotations
	Autobiography, diaries, etc., *see* Table E2 or biography number of individual presidents
	Letters, *see* Table E2 or biography number of individual Presidents
.x4	Essays. By date
.x5	Speeches. By date
.x9A-.x9Z	Special libraries. By author, A-Z

TABLE F1 FOR ONE NUMBER CITIES IN THE AMERICAS

.A2	Periodicals. Societies. Collections
.A3	Museums. Exhibitions, exhibits
.A4	Guidebooks. Gazetteers. Directories
.A5-.Z	General works. Description
.1	Monumental and picturesque
.13	Pamphlets, addresses, essays
.15	Antiquities
.2	Social life and customs. Intellectual life
	History
	Biography
.23.A2	General. Collective
.23.A3-.23.Z	Individual
.25	Historiography. Study and teaching
.3	General works
	Sections. Districts, etc.
.4.A2	General. Collective
.4.A3-.4.Z	Individual
	Cemeteries
.42.A2	General. Collective
.42.A3-.42.Z	Individual
	Monuments. Statues
.5.A2	General. Collective
.5.A3-.5.Z	Individual
	Parks. Squares. Circles
.6.A2	General. Collective
.6.A3-.6.Z	Individual
	Streets
.7.A2	General. Collective
.7.A3-.7.Z	Individual
	Buildings
.8.A2	General. Collective
.8.A3-.8.Z	Individual
	Elements in the population
.9.A2	General. Collective
.9.A3-.9.Z	Individual, A-Z

For lists of cutter numbers, see E184, United States; F1035, Canada; F1392, Mexico; F1477, Guatemala; etc.

TABLE F2 FOR CUTTER NUMBER CITIES IN THE AMERICAS

GALE NOTE *".x" represents cutter number for city*

.x	Periodicals. Societies. Collections
.x2	Museums. Exhibitions, exhibits
.x3	Guidebooks. Gazetteers. Directories
.x4	General works. Description
.x43	Monumental and picturesque
.x45	Pamphlets, addresses, essays
.x47	Antiquities
.x5	Social life and customs. Intellectual life
	History
	Biography
.x53A2-.x53A29	General. Collective
.x53A3-.x53Z	Individual
.x55	Historiography. Study and teaching
.x57	General works
	Sections. Districts, etc.
.x6A2	General. Collective
.x6A3-.x6Z	Individual
	Cemeteries
.x62A2	General. Collective
.x62A3-.x62Z	Individual
	Monuments. Statues
.x65A2	General. Collective
.x65A3-.x65Z	Individual
	Parks. Squares. Circles
.x7A2	General. Collective
.x7A3-.x7Z	Individual
	Streets
.x75A2	General. Collective
.x75A3-.x75Z	Individual
	Buildings
.x8A2	General. Collective
.x8A3-.x8Z	Individual
	Elements in the population
.x9A2-.x9A29	General. Collective
.x9A3-.x9Z	Individual, A-Z

For lists of cutter numbers, see E184, United States; F1035, Canada; F1392, Mexico; F1477, Guatemala; etc.

TABLE F3 FOR COUNTRIES, ISLANDS, REGIONS

.A2	Periodicals. Societies
.A3	Sources and documents. Collections
.A5-.Z	General works
.2	Description and travel. Guidebooks. Gazetteers
.3	Antiquities. Indians
.4	Social life and customs. Civilization
.42	Elements in the population
	History
.5	General works
.6	Biography and memoirs (Collective)
	Political and diplomatic history
.62	General works
.63.A-.63.Z	Relations with individual countries, A-Z
	By period
	Early
.65	General works
	Biography and memoirs
.66	Collective
.67	Individual, A-Z
	Colonial
.7	General works
	Biography and memoirs
.72	Collective
.73.A-.73.Z	Individual, A-Z
	Independent
.8	General works
	Biography and memoirs
.82	Collective
.83.A-.83.Z	Individual, A-Z
.9.A-.9.Z	Local, A-Z

TABLE F4 FOR INDIVIDUAL BIOGRAPHY (ONE NO.)

	Use this table to subarrange cutter numbers for individual persons under each class number of the F schedule providing for biography and memoirs. However, in cases where individual biography is classed in numbers designating individual periods, two cutters are assigned, one for the name of the biographee, and one for the author
.A2	Collected works. By date
	Including collected or selected works by the individual on general historical or political topics pertaining to the period in which he lived
	For his collected or selected works on a special topic, see the topic
.A25	Selected works. By date
	Including collected or selected works by the individual on general historical or political topics pertaining to the period in which he lived
	For his collected or selected works on a special topic, see the topic
.A3	Autobiography, diaries, etc. By date
.A4	Letters. By date
	Speeches, essays, and lectures
	Including collected or selected works by the individual on general historical or political topics pertaining to the period in which he lived
	For his collected or selected works on a special topic, see the topic
	Including interviews
.A49-.A499	Serials. By title
.A5	Monographs. By date
.A6-.Z	Biography and criticism

TABLE F5 FOR INDIVIDUAL BIOGRAPHY (CUTTER NO.)

> *Use this table to subarrange cutter numbers for individual persons under each class number of the F schedule providing for biography and memoirs, e.g. F1788.22.C3, Castro, Fidel. However, in cases where individual biography is classed in numbers designating individual periods, two cutters are assigned, one for the name of the biographee, and one for the author*
> GALE NOTE *".x" represents the cutter number for the individual*

.xA2	Collected works. By date
	Including collected or selected works by the individual on general historical or political topics pertaining to the period in which he lived
	For his collected or selected works on a special topic, see the topic
.xA25	Selected works. By date
	Including collected or selected works by the individual on general historical or political topics pertaining to the period in which he lived
	For his collected or selected works on a special topic, see the topic
.xA3	Autobiography, diaries, etc. By date
.xA4	Letters. By date
	Speeches, essays, and lectures
	Including collected or selected works by the individual on general historical or political topics pertaining to the period in which he lived
	For his collected or selected works on a special topic, see the topic
	Including interviews
.xA49-.xA499	Serials. By title
.xA5	Monographs. By date
.xA6-.xZ	Biography and criticism

INDEX TO CLASSES E-F

Aguada (Puerto Rico): F1981.A26
Aguapehy River (Brazil): F2631
Aguaruna Indians: F3430.1.A35
Aguascalientes, Mexico (State): F1241
Aguilar, Jerónimo de: E125.A3
Aguilera, Francisco Vicente: F1785
Aguirre, Lope de: E125.A35
Aguirre Cerda, Pedro: F3099+
Ahtena Indians: E99.A28
Aisén, Chile (Province): F3134
Akatek Indians: F1465.2.A34
Aklavik (Mackenzie District): F1100.5.A4
Akoerio Indians: F2420.1.A35
Akron (Ohio): F499.A3
Akuri Indians: F2420.1.A35
Akuria Indians: F2420.1.A35
Akurijo Indians: F2420.1.A35
Akurio Indians: F2420.1.A35
Akwa'ala Indians: F1221.A4
Akwē-Shavante Indians: F2520.1.A4
Alabama: F321+
    Afro-Americans: E185.93.A3
    Confederate history: E551.1+
    Counties, etc.: F332.A+
    Indians: E78.A28
    Reconstruction, 1865-1877: F326
    Slavery: E445.A3
    Wars
        Civil War: E495.1+
            Military operations: E470.6,
            E470.7, E471+
        War of 1898: E726.A3
Alabama (Confederate cruiser): E599.A3
Alabama Indians: E99.A4
Alacaluf Indians: F2986
Alagoas, Brazil (State): F2541
Alajuela (Costa Rica): F1556.A6
Alamán, Lucas: F1232
Alamo, Siege of the, 1836: F390
Alaska: F901+
    Afro-Americans: E185.93.A4
    Counties, etc.: F912.A+
    Early exploration and settlement: F907
    Indians: E78.A3
    Purchase by U.S.: F907
Alaska, Gulf of: F912.A43
Alaska Commercial Company, 1868-1940:
    F912.P9
Alaska Highway (General): F1060.9
Albán (Mexico): F1219.1.O11
Albanians in the United States: E184.A3
Albany: F129.A3
Albemarle (Ram): E599.A4
Albemarle region (North Carolina):
    F262.A33
Albemarle settlement (North Carolina): F257
Albeni Falls Dam and Region (Idaho):
    F752.A55
Alberni region (British Columbia): F1089.A4
Albert Co. (New Brunswick): F1044.A4
Alberta: F1075+
    Indians: E78.A34
Albuquerque (New Mexico): F804.A3

Alcan Highway (General): F1060.9
Alcatraz Island (California): F868.S156
Alcohol use, Indian: E98.L7
    Mexico: F1219.3.A42
    Peru: F3429.3.A45
Alessandri, Arturo: F3099+
Aleutian Islands (Alaska): F951
Aleuts: E99.A34
Alexander VI (Pope)
    Demarcation line of: E123
Alexander, Andrew Jonathan: E467.1.A3
Alexander, Robert: E278.A3
Alexander, William (Lord Sterling):
    E207.A3
Alexandria (Virginia): F234.A3
Alexis, Pierre Nord: F1926
Alfaro, Eloy: F3737
Alger Hiss case: E743.5
Algeria, U.S. War with, 1815: E365
Algodones Dunes (California): F868.I2
Algoma District (Ontario): F1059.A3
Algonkin Indians: E99.A349
Algonquian Indians: E99.A35
Algonquin Provincial Park (Ontario):
    F1059.A4
Alibamu Indians: E99.A4
Alien and sedition laws, 1798: E327
Alien enemies, Treatment of United States
    War of 1812: E358
Allagash River and Valley (Maine): F27.A4
Allatoona, Battle of, 1864: E476.87
Allegany State Park (New York): F127.A43
Alleghany Mountains: F217.A3
Allegheny Mountains: F217.A3
Allegheny River and Valley (New York):
    F127.A45
Allegheny River and Valley (Pennsylvania):
    F157.A5
Allen, Charles: E340.A4
Allen, Ethan: E207.A4
Allen, Henry Watkins: E467.1.A4
Allen, Ira: F52
Allen, Jolley: E278.A4
Allen, William: F496
Allen Parish (Louisiana): F377.A4
Allende, Salvador: F3101.A4
Allende y Unzaga, Ignacio José: F1232
Allens Creek and Valley (New York):
    F127.M6
Allerton, Isaac: F68
Almaguin Highlands (Ontario): F1059.A44
Alsatians in the United States: E184.A4
Alsea Indians: E99.A45
Alta Pimería: F799
Alta Vela (Island): F1939.A4
Alta Verapaz (Guatemala): F1469.V3
    Indian antiquities: F1435.1.A38
Altar de Sacrificios, Guatemala (Mayas):
    F1435.1.A4
Altgeld, John Peter: F546
Altiplano (South America): F2212
Alto Paraná, Paraguay (Dept.): F2691.A4
Alto Velo, Isla: F1939.A4
Alton (Illinois): F549.A4
    Military Prison (Civil War): E616.A4

Altona Flat Rock (New York): F127.C77
Altun Ha site (Mayas): F1435.1.A57
Alvarado, Pedro de: F1437
Alvarado (Veracruz, Mexico), 1846, Battle
    of: E406.A48
Álvarez, Juan: F1232.5
Álvarez de Arenales, Juan Antonio: F3446
Alvear, Marcelo Torcuato de: F2848
Amador Guerrero, Manuel: F1566.5
Amahuaca Indians: F3430.1.A5
Amapá, Brazil (Territory): F2543
Amapala, Insurrection of, 1910: F1507.5
Amargosa River and Valley (Nevada):
    F847.A42
Amarillo (Texas): F394.A4
Amazon River and Valley: F2281.A4, F2546
    Indian antiquities: F2519.1.A6
Amazon River and Valley (Peru): F3451.L8
Amazonas
    Brazil (State): F2546
    Peru (Dept.): F3451.A4
    Venezuela (Territory): F2331.A3
Amazonas, Bajo, Peru (Province): F3451.B3
Ambato, Ecuador: F3791.A6
Ambergris Cay (Belize): F1449.A53
Ambrister, Robert
    Execution: E83.817
Ambulance service
    United States
        Civil War: E621+
Amelia Island
    Seized by MacGregor, 1817: F314
Amelia Island (Florida): F317.N3
America
    Antiquities: E51+, E75+
    Atlantic coast: F106, F1035.8, F2214
    Description
        Earliest to 1810: E141+
    Discovery and exploration: E101+
    Folklore
        Indians: E98.F6
    Indians: E51+
    Pacific coast
        North and South: F851
        South: F2213
    Pan-American relations: F1415+
America (The name): E125.V6
America Day: E120
American aborigines: E75+
American Civil War: E461+
American colonial tracts monthly: E187.A5
American Colonization Society: E448
American conferences, International:
    F1404+
American Indians: E75+
American Indians, Education of: E97+
American institutions, European origin of:
    E189
American Knights: E458.8
American loyalists: E277+
American political tracts
    Colonial history: E187.A53
American Republics, International Bureau
    of: F1403+

American Revolution: E201+
American River and Valley (California): F868.A44
American Scenic and Historic Preservation Society: E151
Americanists, Societies of: E51
Americanization
    United States: E169.1+
Americanized citizens
    Argentina: F3021.A64
    Brazil: F2659.A5
Americans in Argentina: F3021.A5
Americans in Brazil: F2659.A5
Americans in Canada: F1035.A5
Americans in Central America: F1440.A54
Americans in Chile: F3285.A5
Americans in Cuba: F1789.A45
Americans in foreign countries: E184.2
Americans in Mexico: F1392.A5
Americans in Nicaragua: F1537.A5
Americans in Peru: F3619.A5
Americans in Venezuela: F2349.A5
Ames, Fisher: E302.6.A5
Amézaga, Juan José: F2728
Amherst College and the Civil War: E541.A5
Amish in the United States: E184.M45
Amishgo Indians: F1221.A58
Amistad
    Slave ship: E447
Amnesty after Civil War
    United States: E668
Amucho Indians: F1221.A58
Amueixa Indians: F3430.1.A54
Amuesha Indians: F3430.1.A54
Amuexa Indians: F3430.1.A54
Amusement, Places of: F73.627, F128.627, F158.627, F548.627
Amusgo Indians: F1221.A58
Amuzgo Indians: F1221.A58
Anacapa Island (California): F868.V5
Anacostia River and Valley (District of Columbia): F202.A5
Anales de Tecamachalco: F1219.56.A52
Analosten Island (District of Columbia): F203.4.T5
Anan Yauyo, Peru (Province): F3451.A43
Anasazi culture: E99.P9
Ancachs (Ancash), Peru (Dept.): F3451.A45
    Indian antiquities: F3429.1.A45
Anchieta, José de: F2528
Anchorage, Alaska: F914.A5
Ancón, Peru
    Indian antiquities: F3429.1.A5
Ancón, Treaty of, 1883: F3097.3
Andahuaylas, Peru (Province): F3451.A48
Andalgala (Argentina)
    Indian antiquities: F2821.1.A3
Andaqui Indians: F2270.2.A6
Anderson, Richard Heron: E467.1.A54
Anderson Valley (California): F868.M5
Andersonville, Ga. Military prison
    Civil War: E612.A5
Andes, Los, Argentina (Territory): F2853

Andes Mountains: F2212, F2281.A5, F2331.A5, F2851, F3111, F3341.A5, F3451.A5, F3741.A6
Andoa Indians: F3430.1.A6
Andrada e Silva, José Bonifacio de: F2536
André, John: E280.A5
Andrés Avelino Cáceres (Peru): F3451.A54
Andrew, John Albion: E513.1+
Andrews' Railroad Raid, 1862: E473.55
Andros, Edmund: F7.5
Androscoggin, Lake: F27.A5
Androscoggin Co: F27.A5
Androscoggin River and Valley: F27.A53
Anecdotes, Historical: E296; F19.6, F1008.4
Angaco, Battle of, 1841: F2846.3
Angeles, Mount (Washington): F897.C52
Angeles National Forest: F868.A5
Angell, Israel: E263.R4
Angell, James Burrill: E664.A55
Anglicans and the Revolution
    United States: E269.C5
Anglo-German Blockade, 1902 (Venezuela): F2325
Anguilla (West Indies): F2033
Aniakchak National Monument and Preserve (Alaska): F912.A54
Ann, Cape (Massachusetts): F72.E7
Ann Arbor (Michigan): F574.A6
Annadel State Park (California): F868.S7
Annapolis (Maryland): F189.A6
Annapolis Co. (Nova Scotia): F1039.A2
Annapolis Royal (Nova Scotia): F1039.5.A16
Anniversaries
    United States
        Civil War: E641+
        Revolution: E285+
            1976 Bicentennial: E285.3+
        War of 1812: E363
        War of 1898: E733
        War with Mexico: E413
Anserma Indians: F2270.2.A63
Ansermas (Indians): F2270.2.A63
Ante-bellum South: F213, F230, F258
Antes, Henry: F152
Anthony, Henry Bowen: E664.A6
Anthropology
    Indians
        North America: E51+, E75+
Anthropology, Physical (Indians): E98.P53
Anthropometry, Afro-American: GN57.A35
Anthropometry, Indian: E98.A55; F1219.3.A5, F1219.76.A62, F1434.2.A55, F1435.3.A56, F2230.1.A4, F2270.1.A58, F2319.3.A5, F2519.3.A5, F3429.3.A5
    Pre-Comumbian America: E59.A5
Anticosti Island: F1054.A6
Antietam, Battle of, 1862: E474.65
Antietam Campaign, 1862: E474.61
Antietam Creek (Maryland): F187.W3
Antietam National Cemetery: E474.65
Antigonish Co. (Nova Scotia): F1039.A25
Antigua (Guatemala): F1476.A5
Antigua and Barbuda (West Indies): F2035

Antilles, Greater: F1741+
Antilles, Lesser: F2001+
Antioquia, Colombia (Dept.): F2281.A6
Antiquities
    Aboriginal American: E51+
    Non-Indian
        America: E21.5
        United States: E159.5
Antislavery leaders
    United States: E446, E449+
Antislavery movements
    United States: E440.92+
        Kansas troubles: F685
Antofagasta (Chile)
    City: F3281.A45
    Province: F3116
Antuco (Volcano), Chile: F3136
Anza-Borrego Desert State Park (California): F868.S15
Anzoátegui, José Antonio: F2324
Anzoátegui, Venezuela (State): F2331.A55
Apache Indians: E99.A6
    War, 1883-1886: E83.88
Apache Mohave (Yavapai) Indians: E99.Y5
Apalachee Indians: E99.A62
Apalachicola Indians: E99.A63
Apalachicola River and Valley: F317.A6
Apalai Indians: F2520.1.A6
Apalakiri Indians: F2520.1.A63
Apapocuva Indians: F2520.1.A632
Apapokuva Indians: F2520.1.A632
Apatzingan, Mexico (District)
    Indian antiquities: F1219.1.M55
Apiacá Indians: F2520.1.A64
Apinagé Indians: F2520.1.A65
Apolista Indians: F3320.2.A6
Apostle Islands (Wisconsin): F587.A8
Appalachian Mountains: F106
Appalachian Mountains, Southern: F217.A65
Appalachian Region
    Indians: E78.A66
Appalachian Trail: F106
Applegate, Jesse: F880
Applegate River and Valley (Oregon): F882.A65
Appomattox Campaign, 1865: E477.67
Apristas, The (Peru): F3448
Apure, Venezuela (State): F2331.A65
Apurímac, Peru (Dept.): F3451.A6
Apytere Indians: F2679.2.M34
Aquidneck (Island): F87.R4
Arabs in Argentina: F3021.A59
Arabs in Brazil: F2659.A7
Arabs in Canada: F1035.A7
Arabs in Chile: F3285.A7
Arabs in Honduras: F1517.A73
Arabs in Paraguay: F2699.A72
Arabs in South America: F2239.A7
Arabs in the Dominican Republic: F1941.A73
Arabs in the United States: E184.A65
Aragua, Venezuela (State): F2331.A7
Araguaya River (Brazil): F2566, F2576, F2586

Arahuna Indians: F2230.2.A68
Araona Indians: F2230.2.A68
Arapaho Indians: E99.A7
Arara Indians: F2520.1.A7
Ararawa Indians: F2520.1.A7
Araua Indians: F2520.1.A75
Arauca Department
   Colombia: F2281.A7
Araucania (Chile): F3126
Araucanian Indians: F3126
Araucanian wars (Chile): F3091
Arauco, Chile (Province): F3126
Araujo, Manuel Enrique: F1487.5
Arauna Indians: F3320.2.A7
Aravaipa Canyon (Arizona): F817.A73
Arawak Indians: F2230.2.A7
Araweté Indians: F2520.1.A77
Arawna Indians: F2230.2.A68
Arbenz Guzmán, Jacobo: F1466.5
Arbuthnot, Alexander: E83.817
Arce, Manuel José: F1438
Archaeological Institute of America: E51
Archaeological research methods in the
   United States: E57
Archaeology, Prehistoric American: E61
Arches National Park (Utah): F832.A7
Archipiélago de Colón: F3741.G2
Architecture, Indian: E98.A63, F1219.3.A6,
   F1219.76.A74, F1435.3.A6,
   F1505.3.A72, F2230.1.A5,
   F2821.3.A78, F3320.1.A68,
   F3429.3.A65, F3721.3.A67
   Pre-Columbian American: E59.A67
Archives, Indian: E97.9
Arctic Bay, Franklin District (Trading post):
   F1105.5.A7
Arctic regions of Canada: F1090.5
Aré Indians: F2520.1.H48
Arecibo (Puerto Rico): F1981.A6
Arecuna Indians: F2380.1.A7
Arekaina Indians: F2319.2.A73
Arekena Indians: F2319.2.A73
Arenales, Juan Antonio Álvarez de: F3446
Arequena Indians: F2319.2.A73
Arequipa (Peru)
   City: F3611.A7
   Department: F3451.A7
      Indian antiquities: F3429.1.A7
Arévalo, Juan José: F1466.5
Argenteuil County (Québec): F1054.A67
Argentina: F2801+
   La Plata region before 1806: F2841
   Military history
      Argentine-Brazilian wars: F2725,
         F2846.3
      Civil wars: F2846, F2847
      Paraguayan War, 1865-1870: F2687
      Seven Reductions, War of the, 1754-
         1756: F2684
      War of Independence, 1810-1817:
         F2845
   Misiones question with Brazil: F2626,
      F2916
   Perón regime, 1943-1955: F2849
   Rosas period, 1829-1852: F2846.3

Argonauts (California): F865
Argyle Island (Georgia): F277.S3, F292.S3
Arhuaco Indians: F2270.2.A67
Ariari River (Colombia): F2281.M49
Arias de Saavedra, Hernando: F2841
Arias Madrid, Arnulfo: F1566.5
Arica (Former Peruvian territory): F3231
Arica, Chile (City): F3281.A6
Arica-Tacna question: F3097.3
Arikara Indians: E99.A8
Arikara War, 1823: E83.818
Arista, Mariano: F1232.5
Arizona: F806+
   Afro-Americans: E185.93.A7
   Confederate history: E552.1+
   Counties, etc.: F817.A+
   Indians: E78.A7
   Wars
      Apache War, 1883-1886: E83.88
      Civil War, 1861-1865
         Military operations: E470.9
Arizona Strip (Arizona): F817.A75
Arkansas: F406+
   Afro-Americans: E185.93.A8
   Confederate history: E553.1+
   Counties, etc.: F417.A+
   Indians: E78.A8
   Reconstruction, 1865-1877: F411
   Wars
      Civil War
         Military operations: E470.4+,
           E470.8, E470.9, E471.57
Arkansas (Confederate ironclad): E474.11
Arkansas, Grand Canyon of the: F782.F8
Arkansas Delta (Arkansas): F417.A67
Arkansas National Forest: F417.O8
Arkansas Post, Expedition against, Jan. 1863:
   E474.48
Arkansas River and Valley: F417.A7
   Colorado: F782.A7
   Kansas: F687.A7
   Oklahoma: F702.A7
Arlington (Virginia): F234.A7
Arlington House: F234.A7
Arlington Memorial Bridge (Washington,
   D.C.): F203.7.A6
Arlington National Cemetery: F234.A7
Armand Bayou Park and Nature Center
   (Texas): F392.H38
Armenians in Argentina: F3021.A64
Armenians in Brazil: F2659.A75
Armenians in Canada: F1035.A74
Armenians in the United States: E184.A7
Armies
   Canada
      American Revolution: E263.C2
      Intercolonial wars: E196, E197, E198
      War of 1812: E359.85
   Confederate States of America
      Civil War: E470.2+, E545+, E608
         Afro-American troops: E585.A35
         Registers: E548
   Great Britain
      American Revolution: E267+
      War of 1812: E359.8

Armies — Continued
   Mexico
      War with U.S.: E409.8
   Spain
      War of 1898: E725.9
   United States
      Civil War: E491+, E608
      Revolution: E255
      War of 1812: E359+
      War of 1898: E725+
      War with Mexico: E409+
Arms and armor, Indian: E98.A65;
   F2230.1.A6
   Pre-Columbian America: E59.A68
Armstrong, John: E302.6.A7
Army life
   U.S. Civil War: E607
Army of Northern Virginia (C.S.A.):
   E470.2+
Army of Tennessee (C.S.A.): E470.5
Army of the Cumberland: E470.5
Army of the James: E470.2+
Army of the Pacific: E470.9
Army of the Potomac: E470.2+
Army of the Tennessee: E470.5
Army of Virginia: E470.2+
Army of West Virginia: E470.4+
Arnold, Benedict: E278.A7
   Treason, 1780: E236
Arnold, Margaret (Shippen): E278.A72
Aroostook River and Valley: F27.A7
   New Brunswick: F1044.A7
Aroostook War, 1839: E398
Arosaguntacook Indians: E99.A82
Arosemena, Pablo: F1566.5
Arrows, Indian: F2519.3.B6
Arrowsmith, George: E467.1.A78
Arroyo de San Antonio Estate (California):
   F868.S7
Arroyo del Río, Carlos Alberto: F3737
Art, Indian: E98.A7; F1219.3.A7,
   F1219.76.A78, F1434.2.A7,
   F1435.3.A7, F1465.3.A7, F1525.3.A7,
   F1545.3.A7, F1565.3.A7, F2230.1.A7,
   F2270.1.A7, F2319.3.A7, F2380.2.A7,
   F2420.2.A7, F2519.3.A7,
   F2679.3.A77, F2821.3.A8,
   F3069.3.A7, F3320.1.A7, F3429.3.A7,
   F3721.3.A7
   Pre-Columbian America: E59.A7
Art and the war
   War with Mexico: E415.2.A78
Arthabaska Co. (Quebec): F1054.A7
Arthur, Chester A.
   Administration, 1881-1885: E691
Articles of Confederation
   United States: E303
Artigas, José Gervasio: F2725
Artigas, Uruguay (Dept.): F2731.A7
Arts, Indian: E98.A73
   Pre-Columbian America: E59.A73
Aruac Indians: F2270.2.A67

Aruba (West Indies): F2038
Ascension Island: F3030.3
Ascension Parish (Louisiana): F377.A7
Ash Swamp, New Jersey, Battle of, 1777: E241.S53
Ashaninca Indians: F3430.1.A83
Ashburton Treaty, 1842: E398
Ashby, Turner: E461.1.A8
Asheville (North Carolina): F264.A8
Ashley River and Valley (South Carolina): F277.A84
Ashluslay Indians: F2230.2.A78
Ashurst Colony (California): F868.S13
Asian influences, Indian: E98.A84
Asians in America: E29.O6
Asians in Brazil: F2659.A84
Asians in Canada: F1035.O6
Asians in Latin America: F1419.A84
Asians in United States: E184.O6
Asians, South, in Canada: F1035.S66
Aspen (Colorado): F784.A7
Assassination attempts
    Franklin Delano Roosevelt: E807.3
    Gerald R. Ford: E866.3
    Ronald Reagan: E877.3
Assateague Indians: E99.A83
Assateague Island National Seashore (Maryland): F187.W7
Assiniboia: F1067
Assiniboin Indians: E99.A84
Association of the Territorial Company of Philadelphia: F442.1
Assumption Parish (Louisiana): F377.A75
Assunguy Colony (Brazil): F2596
Assyrians in Canada: F1035.A87
Assyrians in the United States: E184.A8
Asto Indians: F3430.1.A85
Astoria (Oregon): F884.A8
Astrology, Indian: F1219.76.A83, F1435.3.A8, F3429.3.C14
Astronomy
    Indians: E98.A88, F1219.3.A85, F1219.76.A84, F2230.1.A85, F2519.3.A84
    Peru: F3429.3.A76
    Pre-Columbian America: E59.A8
Asturians in Cuba: F1789.A7
Asturians in Latin America: F1419.A87
Asunción (Paraguay): F2695.A8
Asurini Indians: F2520.1.A84
Atacama (Former Bolivian territory): F2853, F3116
Atacama, Chile (Province): F3131
    Indian antiquities: F3069.1.A8
Atacama Desert, Chile: F3131
Atacameño Indians: F3070.1.A7
Atchafalaya River and Swamp (Louisiana): F377.A78
Athabasca region (Alberta): F1079.A8
Athabasca Sand Dunes Provincial Wilderness Park (Saskatchewan): F1074.A75
Athapascan Indians: E99.A86
Atitlán, Lake (Guatemala): F1469.S64
    Indian antiquities: F1465.1.A8

Atlanta (Georgia): F294.A8
    Capture of, 1864: E476.7
Atlanta (Ram): E599.A8
Atlanta Campaign, 1864: E476.7
Alantic, South (Region): F3030
Atlantic City (New Jersey): F144.A8
Atlantic coast of Brazil: F2548
Atlantic coast of Canada: F1035.8
    Nova Scotia: F1039: A74
Atlantic coast of Colombia: F2281.A79
Atlantic coast of Nicaragua: F1529.M9
Atlantic coast of North America: F106
Atlantic coast of South America: F2214
Atlantic coast of United States: F106
    Georgia: F292.A74
    Maine: F27.A75
    New England: F12.A74
    New Jersey: F142.A79
    South Carolina: F277.A86
Atlantic coast of Uruguay: F2731.A84
Atlantic Provinces (Canada): F1035.8
Atlantic States: F106
    Indians: E78.A88
Atlántico, Colombia (Dept.): F2281.A8
Atrocities, Putumayo rubber: F3451.P94
Atsina Indians: E99.A87
Atsugewi Indians: E99.A875
Attacapa Indians: E99.A88
Attakapas District (Louisiana): F377.A8
Atticmospicayes Indians: E99.T4
Au Sable Chasm (New York): F127.E8
Au Sable River and Valley (New York): F127.E8
Auca Indians: F3722.1.H83
Audiencia of Caracas: F2322
Audiencia of Charcas: F3322
Audiencia of Guadalajara: F1296
Audiencia of Guatemala: F1437
Audiencia of New Granada: F2272
Audiencia of Santo Domingo: F1621
Audio-visual materials catalogs (Latin America): F1409.9.Z9
Auditorium Building (Chicago): F548.8.A9
Augusta (Georgia): F294.A9
Augusta (Maine): F29.A9
Augutge Indians: F2520.1.G37
Austin, Stephen Fuller: F389
Austin (Nevada): F849.A9
Austin (Texas): F394.A9
Austin's Colony (Texas): F389
Australians in Paraguay: F2699.A87
Austrians in Brazil: F2659.A9
Austrians in Canada: F1035.A94
Austrians in the United States: E184.A9
Auxiliaries, French
    American Revolution: E265
Auyuittuq National Park (Northwest Territories, Canada): F1105.A89
Ava-Canoeiro Indians: F2520.1.A93
Ava-mbiha Indians: F2679.2.M34
Avachiripá Indians: F2230.2.A82
Avákatúeté Indians: F2230.2.A82
Avalon (Baltimore colony): F1123
Avellaneda, Nicolás: F2847

Avellaneda (Argentina)
    City: F3011.A9
    Partido: F2861
Avery Island (Louisiana): F377.F57
Aves Islands (Venezuela): F2331.A9
Avila, Pedro Arias de: F1437
Ávila Camacho, Manuel: F1234
Avila Mountain (Venezuela): F2331.A93
Avoyelles Parish (Louisiana): F377.A9
Awahun Indians: F3430.1.A35
Awikenox Indians: E99.O68
Awikyenoq Indians: E99.O68
Axes, Indian: F3429.3.A9
Ayabaca Province (Peru): F3451.A87
Ayacucho, Battle of, 1824: F3446
Ayacucho, Peru (Dept.): F3451.A9
Ayala, Eusebio: F2688
Aycock, Charles Brantley: F259
Aymara Indians: F2230.2.A9
Ayora, Isidro: F3737
Aysén, Chile (Province): F3134
Azero, Bolivia (Province): F3341.A9
Azilia: F289
Azoreans in the United States: E184.A95
Aztec Club of 1847: E401.1
Aztec codices: F1219.54.A98
Aztec Ruins National Monument
    New Mexico: E99.P9
Aztecs: F1219.73+
    Wars: F1219.3.W37
Azuay, Ecuador (Province): F3741.A9

B

B.E.F.: F199
Bache, Benjamin Franklin: E302.6.B14
Back Creek and Valley
    Virginia: F232.B24
    West Virginia: F247.B14
Back River and Valley
    Keewatin: F1110.B33
    Mackenzie: F1100.B33
Bacon, Robert: E664.B123
Bacon's Rebellion, 1676: F229
Badlands (North Dakota): F642.L5
Badlands (South Dakota): F657.B24
Báez, Buenaventura: F1938.4
Baffin Island and Land: F1105.B3
Bahamas: F1650+
Bahia (Brazil)
    City: F2651.S13
        Capture by Dutch, 1625: F2532
    State: F2551
        Indian antiquities: F2519.1.B3
Bahia Blancha, Argentina: F3011.B3
Baía (Brazil): F2651.S13
Baie Saint-Paul region (Quebec): F1054.B35
Bailey, Anne: F241
Bailey, Joseph Weldon: E664.B2
Bailey, Theodorus: E467.1.B14
Bainbridge, William: E353.1.B2
Bainbridge Island (Washington): F897.K5
Baja California (Mexico): F1246+
Baja California (State)
    Mexico: F1246.2

Baja California Sur (Mexico): F1246.3
Baja Vera Paz, Guatemala (Dept.): F1469.V4
Bajío Region (Mexico): F1246.6
Bajo Amazonas, Peru (Province): F3451.B3
Bakairi Indians: F2520.1.B3
Baker, Edward Dickenson: E467.1.B16
Baker, Mount (Washington): F897.W57
Baker Lake (Trading post): F1110.5.B3
Baker River (Chile): F3134
Balberta
    Mayas: F1435.1.B35
Balboa, Vasco Núñez de: E125.B2
Balboa Island (California): F868.O6
Balcones Canyonlands National Wildlife
        Refuge (Texas): F392.F17
Bald Head Island (North Carolina): F262.B9
Bald Mountains
    North Carolina: F262.B3
    Tennessee: F443.B3
Baldwin, Abraham: E302.6.B17
Baldwin, Simeon: E302.6.B19
Balize: F1441+
Ball's Bluff, Battle of, 1861: E472.63
Balmaceda, José Manuel: F3098
Balsas River (Mexico): F1247
Baltimore, Cecilius Calvert, 2d Baron of:
        F184
Baltimore, George Calvert, 1st Baron of:
        F184
    Colony of Avalon: F1123
Baltimore (Maryland): F189.B1
    Battle of, 1814: E356.B2
    Conflict between U.S. troops and mob,
        1861: E472.13
    Riot, 1812: F189.B1
Baltimore colony of Avalon: F1123
Bancroft, George: E340.B2
Banda Oriental del Uruguay: F2723
Bandeiras: F2528
    São Paulo: F2631
Bandelier National Monument: F802.B25
Banff National Park (Alberta): F1079.B5
Bangladeshis in the United States: E184.B13
Bangor (Maine): F29.B2
Baniba Indians: F2520.1.B35
Baniva Indians: F2520.1.B35
Bank of the United States
    Removal of deposits: E384.7
Bankhead, John Hollis: F326
Banks, Nathaniel Prentice: E467.1.B23
Banks, The (Islands): F262.O96
Bannock Indians: E99.B33
Baptista, Mariano: F3325
Baptists and the American Revolution:
        E269.B2
Bar Harbor (Maine): F29.B3
Baracoa (Cuba): F1849.B2
Baranof Island (Alaska): F912.B14
Baranov, Aleksandr Andreevich: F907
Barasana Indians: F2270.2.B27
Barbacoa Indians: F2270.2.B3
Barbados (West Indies): F2041

Barbary States
    Relations with U.S.: E335
        War with Algeria, 1815: E365
        War with Tripoli, 1801-1805: E335
Barbosa, Ruy: F2537
Barbuda (West Indies): F2035
Baré Indians: F2520.1.B4
Barinas, Venezuela (State): F2331.B3
Barlow, Francis Channing: E467.1.B25
Barnegat Bay (New Jersey): F142.O2
Barnes, James: E467.1.B26
Barney, Joshua: F353.1.B26
Barona Valley (California): F868.S15
Barquisimeto (Venezuela): F2341.B3
Barrácas al Sud (Argentina): F3011.A9
Barranquilla (Colombia): F2291.B3
Barrios, Justo Rufino: F1466.45
Barron, James: E335
Barros Arana, Diego: F3076.B3
Barrow, Point (Alaska): F912.B2
Barrundia, José Francisco: F1438
Barry, John: E207.B2
Bartholdi's Statue of Liberty (New York):
        F128.64.L6
Bartica (British Guiana): F2389.B3
Bartlett, Josiah: E302.6.B2
Bartlett, William Francis: E467.1.B29
Bartlett Island (Maine): F27.M9
Barú Island (Colombia): F2281.B6
Baruch, Bernard Mannes: E748.B32
Bas-Saint-Laurent: F1054.B36
Basket-Maker Indians: E99.B37
Basket making, Indian: F1435.3.B37
Basketry, Indian: E98.B3
    Pre-Columbian America: E59.B3
Baskets
    Indians
        Venezuela: F2319.3.B37
Basques
    Discovery of America
        Pre-Columbian: E109.B3
Basques in America: E29.B35
Basques in Argentina: F3021.B2
Basques in Canada: F1035.B3
Basques in Chile: F3285.B3
Basques in Colombia: F2299.B37
Basques in Latin America: F1419.B37
Basques in Mexico: F1392.B3
Basques in South America: F2239.B3
Basques in United States: E184.B15
Basques in Uruguay: F2799.B2
Basques in Venezuela: F2349.B3
Bass Islands (Ohio): F497.O8
Basse-Terre Island (Guadeloupe): F2066
Bat Indians: F2520.1.C38
Bates, Frederick: F466
Bathurst District (Ontario): F1059.B36
Baticola Indians: F2679.2.M34
Batlle y Ordóñez, José: F2728
Baton Rouge (Louisiana): F379.B33
    Operations against, 1862: E474.11
Baton Rouge District of West Florida:
        F377.F6
    Before 1812: F301
Battery, New York: F128.65.B3

Battle Abbey (Richmond): F234.R5
Battle Harbour, Labrador (Fishing port):
        F1139.B3
Battle Valley (Alberta and Saskatchewan):
        F1079.B55
Battlement National Forest (Colorado):
        F782.B33
Battles
    United States: E181, E182
    Civil War: E470+
    Indian wars: E81+
    Revolution: E231+
    War of 1812: E355+
    War of 1898: E717+
    War with Mexico: E405+
Baxter Springs, Kansas, Battle of, 1863:
        E474.9
Baxter State Park (Maine): F27.P5
Bay City (Michigan): F574.B3
Bay Islands, Honduras (Dept.): F1509.B3
Bay of Fundy (Nova Scotia): F1039.F9
Bay of Quinte (Ontario): F1059.Q6
Bayamo (Cuba): F1849.B3
Bayard, George Dashiell: E467.1.B3
Bayard, James Asheton: E302.6.B3
Bayard, John: E263.P4
Bayard, Nicholas: F122+
Bayard, Thomas Francis: E664.B3
Bayou Chene (Louisiana): F377.A78
Bayou Teche (Louisiana): F377.T4
Beacon Hill (Boston): F73.68.B4
Beacon Hill Monument (Boston): F73.64.B4
Beadwork, Indian: E98.B46; F1219.3.B4
    Pre-Columbian America: E59.B43
Beale, Edward Fitzgerald: F593
Bean, Roy: F391+
Bean Creek and Valley
    Michigan: F572.B36
    Ohio: F497.B3
Bear Butte (South Dakota): F657.M4
Bear Flag War, 1846: F864
Bear River and Valley (Utah): F832.B3
Bear Valley (California): F868.S14
Beard, Charles Austin: E175.5.B38
Bearlake Indians: E99.B376
Beartooth Mountains
    Montana: F737.B35
    Wyoming: F767.B23
Beauce Co., Quebec: F1054.B38
Beaufort Sea region (Alaska): F912.B24
Beaumont (Texas): F394.B3
Beauregard, Pierre Gustave Toutant:
        E467.1.B38
Beauregard Parish (Louisiana): F377.B4
Beaver, James Addams: E467.1.B39
Beaver Creek and Valley (Colorado):
        F782.E15
Beaver Dam Creek, Battle of, 1862: E473.68
Beaver Dams, Ontario, Battle of, 1813:
        E356.B3
Beaver Indians
    Athapascan tribe: E99.T77
Beaver Island (Michigan): F572.B38
Beaver Kill (New York): F127.B4

Beaver Kill Valley (New York): F127.B4
Beaver Lake (Indiana): F532.N5
Beaver River and Valley (Pennsylvania): F157.B23
Becan site (Mexico): F1435.1.B4
Beckworth Trail (California): F868.S5
Bedard, Pierre Stanislas: F1053
Bedford, N.Y. (Westchester Co.), Battle of, 1779: E241.B33
Bedford Co. (Tennessee): F443.B35
Bedinger, George Michael: F455
Bedloe's Island (New York). Statue of Liberty: F128.64.L6
Beecher Island, Battle of, 1868: E83.868
Behaim, Martin: E110
Belalcázar, Sebastián de: F3733
Belém (Brazil): F2651.B4
Belgians in Brazil: F2659.B4
Belgians in British Honduras: F1457.B4
Belgians in Canada: F1035.B4
Belgians in United States: E184.B2
    Civil War: E540.B4
Belgrano, Manuel: F2845
Belice: F1441+
Belize (British Honduras)
    City: F1456.B4
    District: F1449.B4
Bell, John: E415.9.B4
Bella Coola/Chilcotin Road (British Columbia): F1089: B43
Bella Coola River and Valley (British Columbia): F1089.B44
Bellabella Indians: E99.H45
Bellacoola Indians: E99.B39
Bellamar Cave (Cuba): F1819.B4
Belle Isle Prison, Richmond: E612.B3
Bellechasse Co. (Québec): F1054.B45
Bellevue (Nebraska): F674.B4
Bellevue Valley (Missouri): F472.B38
Belly River, Battle of, 1870: E83.8697
Belmont, August
    Collected works: E415.6.B45
Belmont, Perry: E664.B5
Belmont (Missouri), Engagement at, 1861: E472.28
Belo Horizonte (Brazil): F2651.B42
Beltrami Co. (Minnesota): F612.B43
Ben Lomond (Utah): F832.W3
Benavides, Oscar Raimundo: F3448
Benedict, Lewis: E467.1.B397
Bengalis in the United States: E184.B26
Beni, Bolivia (Dept.): F3341.B4
Benjamin, Judah Philip: E467.1.B4
Bennett, Richard Belford: F1033
Bennington (Vermont): F59.B4
Bennington, Battle of, 1777: E241.B4
Benton, Thomas Hart: E340.B4
Bent's Old Fort National Historic Site (Colorado): F782.A7
Beothuk Indians: E99.B4
Berbice (British Guiana): F2389.N4
Berbice (Dutch Colony): F2383, F2423
Berbice Co. (British Guiana): F2387.B4
Bering Sea: F951
Berkeley (California): F869.B5

Berkshire Hills: F72.B5
Bermuda Hundred (Virginia), Operations at, 1864: E476.57
Bermudas: F1630+
    American Revolution: E263.W5
Berry, Hiram Gregory: E467.1.B5
Berthier Co. (Quebec): F1054.B54
Betancourt, Rómulo: F2326
Betancourt Cisneros, Gaspar: F1783
Betancourt y Dávalos, Pedro de Estanislao: F1786
Bethel, Battle of, 1861: E472.14
Betoyan Indians: F2270.2.T77
Beverages, Indian: F1219.76.B48
Biblioteca nazionale centrale di Firenze. Manuscript. Magl. XIII, 3: F1219.56.B53
Bibliothèque nationale (France). Manuscript. Mexicain 40 (Codices): F1219.56.B58
Bibliothèque Nationale de France. Manuscript 210 (Codices): F1219.56.B56
Bickerdyke, Mary Ann: E621
Biddle, Charles: F153
Biddle, James: E353.1.B5
Biddle, Nicholas: E207.B48
Biddle, Owen: E207.B5
Bidwell, John: E864
Bienville, Jean Baptiste Le Moyne de: F372
Bienville Parish (Louisiana): F377.B5
Big Bald Mountain
    North Carolina: F262.B3
    Tennessee: F443.B3
Big Bear Lake (California): F868.S14
Big Bear Valley
    California: F868.S14
Big Bend National Park (Texas): F392.B53
Big Bend region (Florida): F317.B54
Big Bend region (Texas): F392.B54
Big Bethel, Engagement at, 1861: E472.14
Big Blue, Battle of, 1864: E477.16
Big Blue River (Kansas): F687.B6
Big Bone Lick (Kentucky): F457.B65
Big Coal River and Valley (West Virginia): F247.B54
Big Fork River and Valley (Minnesota): F612.K7
Big Hole Battle: E83.877
Big Hole River and Valley (Montana): F737.B48
Big Horn Canyon National Recreation Area (Montana and Wyoming): F737.B49
Big Horn Post No. 2 (Montana): F737.Y4
Big Horn River and Valley (Wyoming): F767.B4
Big Oak Flat Road (California): F868.B5
Big Pine Creek and Valley (North Carolina): F262.M25
Big Sandy River and region (Arizona): F817.B5
Big Sandy River and Valley (Kentucky): F457.B5
Big Sioux River and Valley
    Iowa: F627.B5

Big Sioux River and Valley — Continued
    South Dakota: F657.B5
Big Tancock Island (Nova Scotia): F1039.T35
Big Thicket (Texas): F392.H37
Big Thompson Canyon (Colorado): F782.B45
Big Thompson River and Valley (Colorado): F782.B45
Big Tree, Treaty of, 1797: F127.H7
Big Tree National Forest (Caliveras, California): F868.C14
Big Wood River and Valley (Idaho): F752.B55
Bigelow, John: E664.B55
Bigelow, Timothy: E207.B58
Bigot, François: F1030
Billings (Montana): F739.B5
Billy the Kid: F786
Billys Island (Georgia): F292.O5
Biloxi (Mississippi): F349.B5
Biloxi Indians: E99.B5
Bingham, Harry: F39
Binney, Horace, 1790-1875: E340.B57
Bío-Bío, Chile (Province): F3136
Biography (Collective)
    Argentina: F2805
    Bahamas: F1650.9
    Bermudas: F1630.9
    Bolivia: F3305
    Brazil: F2505
    British America: F1005
    British Guiana: F2365
    British Honduras: F1442.7
    Canada: F1005
    Central America: F1426
    Chile: F3055
    Colombia: F2255
    Costa Rica: F1542.7
    Cuba: F1755
    Dominican Republic: F1933
    Dutch Guiana: F2405
    Ecuador: F3705
    French Guiana: F2445
    Guatemala: F1462.7
    Haiti: F1914
    Honduras: F1502.7
    Jamaica: F1865
    Latin America: F1407
    Mexico: F1205
    Nicaragua: F1522.7
    Panama: F1562.7
    Paraguay: F2665
    Peru: F3405
    Puerto Rico: F1955
    Salvador: F1482.7
    South America: F2205
    Spanish America: F1407
    United States
        West, The: F590.5
    Uruguay: F2705
    Venezuela: F2305
    West Indies: F1607

Biology
 Indians: E98.B54
Birch Coulee, Battle of, 1862: E83.86
Birch Creek Valley (Idaho): F752.B63
Bird-Truax Trail (Idaho): F752.B64
Birmingham (Alabama): F334.B6
Birney, David Bell: E467.1.B6
Birney, James Gillespie: E340.B6
Biscayne Bay (Florida): F317.D2
Bismarck (North Dakota): F644.B6
Bissot, Jean Baptiste, sieur de Vincennes:
 F1030
Bisti (New Mexico): F802.B58
Bitter Root River and Valley (Montana):
 F737.B6
Bizard Island (Quebec): F1054.B58
Black, Jeremiah Sutherland: E415.9.B6
Black Canyon of the Gunnison National
 Monument (Colorado): F782.B5
Black Caribs: F1505.2.C3
Black Conspiracy, 1844: F1783
Black Eagle Conspiracy, 1830: F1783
Black Hawk
 Sauk chief: E83.83
Black Hawk War, 1832: E83.83
 Lincoln's participation: E457.35
Black Hawk War (Utah), 1865-1872:
 E83.867
Black Hills (South Dakota): F657.B6
Black Lake (New York): F127.S2
Black Mountains (North Carolina): F262.B4
Black Range (New Mexico): F802.B63
Black River (New York): F127.B48
Black River and Valley (Wisconsin):
 F587.B55
Black Rock Desert (Nevada): F847.B53
Black studies: E184.7
Blackfoot River and Valley (Montana):
 F737.B62
Blackfoot (Sihasapa) Dakota Indians:
 E99.S53
Blackfoot (Siksika) Algonquian Indians:
 E99.S54
Blacks
 Relations with: F3429.3.R27
Blacks in America: E29.N3
Blacks in Canada: F1035.N3
Blacks in Central America: F1440.B55
 British Honduras: F1457.B55
 Costa Rica: F1557.B55
 Honduras: F1517.B55
 Nicaragua: F1537.B55
 Panama: F1577.B55
 Salvador: F1497.B55
Blacks in Latin America: F1419.N4
Blacks in Mexico: F1392.B55
Blacks in South America: F2239.B55
 Argentina: F3021.B55
 Bolivia: F3359.B55
 Brazil: F2659.N4
 Chile: F3285.B53
 Colombia: F2299.B55
 Ecuador: F3799.B55
 French Guiana: F2471.B55
 Peru: F3619.B55

Blacks in South America: F2239.B55 —
 Continued
 Surinam: F2431.N3
 Uruguay: F2799.N3
 Venezuela: F2349.B55
Blacks in the Caribbean: F2191.B55
Blacks in West Indies: F1629.B55
 Bahamas: F1660.B55
 Bermudas: F1640.B55
 Cuba: F1789.N3
 Dominican Republic: F1941.B55
 Haiti: F1930.B55
 Jamaica: F1896.N4
 Puerto Rico: F1983.N4
Blacks Run and Valley (Virginia): F232.R7
Blackstone, William: F73.4
Blackstone Harbour Provincial Park
 (Ontario): F1059.B53
Blackstone River and Valley
 General and Rhode Island: F87.B55
 Massachusetts: F72.B57
Blackwater River and Valley (Maryland):
 F187.D6
Bladensburg, Battle of, 1814: E356.B5
Blaine, Harriet (Bailey): E664.B62
Blaine, James Gillespie: E660.B6, E664.B6
 Foreign policy, 1881: E686
Blair House (Washington, D.C.): F204.B5
Blancos (Uruguay): F2726
Bland, Richard Parks: E664.B64
Bland, Theodorick: E263.V8
Blankets, Indian: E98.T35
Blennerhassett Island (West Virginia):
 F247.B56
Blisland Parish (Virginia): F232.B55
Bliss, Aaron Thomas: F566
Blissland Parish (Virginia): F232.B55
Block Island (Rhode Island): F87.B6
Blockades, Naval
 United States
 Civil War: E480, E600
 War of 1812: E360
Blondin, Pierre Edouard: F1034
Bloom, Sol: E748.B63
Bloomingdale (New York): F128.68.B6
Bloomington (Illinois): F549.B65
Blount, William: E302.6.B6
Blue Hill Bay (Maine): F27.B49
Blue Licks, Battle of the, 1782: E241.B65
Blue Mountain Lake (Arkansas): F417.L75
Blue Mountain Lake (New York): F127.H2
Blue Mountains (Pennsylvania): F157.B65
Blue Ridge Mountains: F217.B6
Blue Valley (Kansas): F687.B6
Bluegrass region (Kentucky): F457.B6
Bluff Island (Maine): F27.Y6
Blumenau (German colony in Brazil): F2626
Boats
 Indians: E98.B6; F2230.1.B6,
 F2519.3.B5
 Peru: F3429.3.B63
 Pre-Columbian American: E59.C2
Bob Marshall Wilderness (Montana):
 F737.B66

Bocas del Toro, Panama (Province):
 F1569.B6
Bocootawwonauke Indians: E99.B6
Boerum, Simon: E263.N6
Bogardus, Annetje Jane: F128.4
Bogotá (Colombia): F2291.B6
Bogotá River (Colombia): F2281.C9
Bogue Banks (North Carolina): F262.C23
Bogue Island (North Carolina): F262.C23
Bohemia Manor (Maryland): F187.C3
Bohemians in the United States: E184.B67
Bois-Francs (Quebec): F1054.A7
Boise (Idaho): F754.B65
Boise River and Valley (Idaho): F752.B673
Bolas: F2821.3.B6
Bolívar, Colombia (Dept.): F2281.B6
Bolívar, Ecuador (Province): F3741.B5
Bolívar, Simón: F2235.3
Bolívar, Venezuela (State): F2331.B6
Bolivar Peninsula (Texas): F392.B57
Bolivia: F3301+
 Acre Territory controversy: F2540
 Charcas (Audiencia): F3322
 Confederación Perú-Boliviana, 1835-
 1839: F3447
 Military history
 Chaco War, 1932-1935: F2688.5
 Civil wars: F3324-3325
 Peru-Bolivian Confederation War with
 Chile, 1836-1839: F3447
 War of Independence, 1809-1825:
 F3323
 War of the Pacific, 1879-1884: F3097
 Tacna-Arica question: F3097.3
Bolivians in Argentina: F3021.B65
Bolivians in the United States: E184.B674
Bomoseen, Lake (Vermont): F57.R9
Bon Echo Provincial Park (Ontario):
 F1059.B64
Bonaire (West Indies): F2048
Bonampak (Mexico)
 Mayas: F1435.1.B6
Bonaparte, Charles Joseph: E664.B69
Bonaventure Co. (Quebec): F1054.B6
Bonaventure Island (Quebec): F1054.B63
Bone carving, Indian: F1219.3.B6
Bone Cave (Missouri): F472.M45
Boni in Surinam: F2431.B64
Bonilla, Manuel: F1507.5
Bonilla, Policarpo: F1507.5
Bonita Creek and Valley (Arizona): F817.G7
Bonneville, Lake (Utah): F832.B6
Bonney, William H.: F786
Bonus Expeditionary Force, 1932 and 1933
 Veterans' march, Washington, D.C.: F199
Boomer, George Boardman: E467.1.B7
Boon Island (Maine): F27.Y6
Boon Lake (Massachusetts): F72.M7
Boone, Daniel: F454
Booth, John Wilkes: E457.5
Boquet River, Engagement at, 1814:
 E356.B6
Bora Indians: F2270.2.B6

Borah, William Edgar: E748.B7

Border life: E161.5+

Border ruffians
  Kansas: F685

Border Slave States, Convention of, 1861:
  E440.5

Border warfare
  In Civil War
    United States: E470.45
  Indian
    North America: E81+

Borinqueño Indians: F1969

Boriquén: F1951+

Borno, Louis: F1927

Bororo Indians: F2520.1.B75

Borrego Desert State Park (California):
  F868.S15

Borrego Valley (California): F868.S15

Boruca Indians: F1545.2.B6

Bossier Parish (Louisiana): F377.B6

Boston (Massachusetts): F73
  Anthony Burns case, 1854: E450
  Garrison mob, 1835: E450
  Massacre, 1770: E215.4
  Siege, 1775-1776: E231

Boston Common (Boston): F73.65

Boston Port Bill, 1774: E215.8

Boston Tea Party: E215.7

Boston Ten Townships: F127.T6

Botany, Economic
  Indian: E98.B7; F2230.1.B7

Botelho de Magalhães, Benjamin Constant:
  F2536

Botocudo Indians: F2520.1.B76

Boucher, Pierre: F1030

Boudinot, Elias: E302.6.B7

Bound Brook, Battle of, 1777: E241.B76

Boundaries
  Canada: F1027.5, F1039.B7
  United States: E179.5
    Alaska: F912.B7
    Louisiana: F374
    Mexico: F786
    Northeast: E398
    Northern: F550.5+, F597
    Northwest: F854, F880
    Southeast (Before 1819): F317.B7
    Southwest: F392.B7, F786

Boundary Waters Canoe Area (Minnesota):
  F612.B73

Bounties, Military
  United States
    Civil War: E491+, E545+
    Revolution: E255
    War of 1812: E359.4
    War with Mexico: E409.4

Bouquet, Henry: E83.76

Bourassa, Henri: F1034

Boves, José Tomás: F2324

Bowdoin, James: F69

Bowdoin College and the Civil War:
  E541.B7

Bowen, John Steven: E467.1.B73

Bowen Island (British Columbia):
  F1089.B74

Bowery (New York): F128.67.B6

Bows and arrows, Indian: F2519.3.B6

Boyacá, Battle of, 1819: F2274

Boyacá, Colombia (Dept.): F2281.B8

Boyd's Creek and Valley (Tennessee):
  F443.B74

Boyer, Jean Pierre: F1924

Boyl, Bernardo: E125.B7

Boyle, John: F545

Braddock's defeat, 1755: E199

Braddock's Rock (Washington, D.C.):
  F203.4.B7

Bradford, William: F68

Bradley, Stephen Row: E302.6.B8

Bradley, William Albert: F198

Bradstreet, John: E199

Bragg, Braxton: E467.1.B75

Branch, John: E340.B67

Brandeis, Louis Dembitz: E664.B819

Brandon (Manitoba): F1064.5.B73

Brandywine, Battle of, 1777: E241.B8

Brandywine Creek and Valley
  Delaware: F172.B78
  Pennsylvania: F157.B77

Brant Co. (Ontario): F1059.B82

Brasilia, Brazil
  City: F2647
  Federal District: F2647

Brass Ankles in the United States:
  E184.B676

Brattleboro (Vermont): F59.B8

Bravo, Nicolás: F1232

Bravo, Pascual: F2276

Brazil: F2501+
  Cisplatine province, 1821-1824: F2725
  Contests over Colonia: F2723
  Dutch conquest, 1624-1654: F2532
  French Guiana, Occupation of (1809-
    1817): F2462
  Military history
    Argentine-Brazilian wars
      1825-1828: F2725
      1849-1852: F2846.3
    Paraguayan War, 1865-1870: F2687
    Revolution of 1930: F2538
    Revolution of the Farrapos, 1835-
      1845: F2621
    São Paulo Revolution, 1932: F2631
    War of Independence, 1889: F2536
    War of the Seven Reductions, 1754-
      1756: F2684
  Portuguese court in Brazil, 1808-1821:
    F2534
  Rio de Janeiro (French colony): F2529

Brazilians in Bolivia: F3359.B73

Brazilians in foreign countries: F2510.5

Brazilians in Paraguay: F2699.B67

Brazilians in the United States: E184.B68

Brazilians in Uruguay: F2799.B7

Brazos River and Valley (Texas): F392.B842

Breckenridge Creek and Valley (West
  Virginia): F247.B6

Breckinridge, John: E302.6.B84

Breckinridge, John Cabell: E415.9.B79

Breed's Hill, Battle of, 1775: E241.B9

Brethren, Hutterite, in the United States:
  E184.H97

Brewster, William: F68

Bribri Indians: F1545.2.B7

Bridge River and Valley (British Columbia):
  F1089.B8

Bridger, James: F592

Bridger Pass Overland Trail
  Colorado: F782.O94
  Wyoming: F767.O94

Bridges (U.S.): F73.67, F158.67.A+,
  F203.7.A+, F548.67

Bridgewater, Ont., Battle of, 1814: E356.L9

Brier Island (Nova Scotia): F1039.F9

Brighton (Massachusetts): F74.B73

Brightwood (Washington, D.C.): F202.B8

Brinton, John Hill: E621

Brión, Pedro Luis: F2324

Bristoe (Virginia), campaign, Oct. 1863:
  E475.75

Bristol Bay (Alaska): F912.B74

Bristol Parish (Virginia): F232.B8

British America: F1001+
  Bahamas: F1650+
  Bermudas: F1630+
  British Guiana: F2361+
  British Honduras: F1441+
  British West Indies: F2131
  Canada: F1001+
  Falkland Islands: F3031

British Cartagena expedition, 1741: F2272.5

British colonies in America: E162
  British Honduras: F1447

British Columbia: F1086+
  Hudson's Bay Company and Northwest
    Company of Canada: F1060+
  Indians: E78.B9
  Oregon country: F880

British Guiana: F2361+
  Dutch colonies, 1667-1803: F2383, F2423

British Honduras: F1441+

British in America: E29.B75

British in Argentina: F3021.B86

British in Brazil: F2659.B7

British in Canada: F1035.B7

British in Chile: F3285.B7

British in Mexico: F1392.E5

British in Paraguay: F2699.B7

British in Peru: F3619.B7

British in South America: F2239.B8

British in United States: E184.B7

British Library. Manuscript Egerton 2895
  (Codices): F1219.56.B74

British North America: F1001+

British West Florida: F301

British-West Indian Federation (Proposed):
  F1886

British West Indies: F2131
  Individual islands: F1630+, F1861+,
    F2006+

Broad River and Valley
  North Carolina: F262.B89
  South Carolina: F277.B73

Broadway (New York): F128.67.B7
Brock, Sir Isaac: E353.1.B8
Brockenbrough, William Henry: E340.B8
Broderick, David Colbreth: E415.9.B84
Brome Co. (Quebec): F1054.B8
Bronx (Borough): F128.68.B8
Bronx Parkway (New York): F128.65.B8
Brookland (Washington, D.C.): F202.B9
Brooklyn (New York) (Borough, New York City): F129.B7
Brooks, P.S
    Assault on Senator Sumner: E434.8
Brooks Range (Alaska): F912.B75
Broom, Jacob: F168
Brotherton Indians: E99.B7
Brown, Albert Gallatin: F341
Brown, George: F1032
Brown, Guillermo: F2845
Brown, Jacob: E353.1.B9
Brown, James: E340.B88
Brown, John, 1744-1780: E207.B8
Brown, John, 1800-1859: E451
    Kansas: F685
    Raid at Harper's Ferry (West Virginia), 1859: E451
Brown, Joseph Newton: E467.1.B77
Brown University and the Civil War: E541.B8
Browning, Orville Hickman: E415.9.B88
Brownlow, William Gannaway: E415.9.B9
Brown's Ferry, Skirmish at, 1863: E475.92
Brown's Hole: F767.G7
Brown's Park (Wyoming): F767.G7
Brownstown, Mich., Battle of, 1812: E356.B8
Bruce Co. (Ontario): F1059.B95
Brulé, Étienne: F1030.13
Brulé Indians: E99.B8
Brule River and Valley
    Michigan: F572.B86
    Wisconsin: F587.B85
Brum, Baltasar: F2728
Bruneau River and Valley (Idaho): F752.O97
Brunswick (Maine): F29.B9
Brunswick Proprietors: F29.B9
Bruzual (Venezuela): F2331.B75
Bryan, William Jennings: E660.B87, E664.B87
Bryan-Chamorro Treaty, 1916: F1526.3
Bryce Canyon National Park: F832.B9
Bucaramanga (Colombia): F2291.B77
Buccaneers
    Caribbean Sea: F2161
    Cuba: F1779
Buchanan, James: E437
    Administration, 1857-1861: E436
    Family: E437.1
Buckeye Lake (Ohio): F497.B86
Buckingham, William Alfred: E499.1+
Buckshot War, 1838: F153
Buen Ayre (West Indies): F2048
Buena Vista, Mexico, Battle of, 1847: E406.B9

Buenos Aires
    Province: F2861
        Indian antiquities: F2821.1.B8
Buenos Aires (Argentina)
    City: F3001
    Federal District: F3001
Buenos Aires (Viceroyalty): F2841
Buffalo (New York): F129.B8
Buffalo, Indian: E98.B8
Buffalo Bill (W.F. Cody): F594
Buffalo Creek and Valley (Pennsylvania): F157.U5
Buffalo Hill region (Alberta): F1079.B8
Buffalo River and Valley (Arkansas): F417.B85
Buga, Colombia: F2291.B8
Bulgarians in Argentina: F3021.B93
Bulgarians in Canada: F1035.B84
Bulgarians in South America: F2239.B9
Bulgarians in United States: E184.B8
Bulkley River and Valley (British Columbia): F1089.B9
Bull Run, 1st Battle of, 1861: E472.18
Bull Run, 2d Battle of, 1862: E473.77
Bull Run Campaign, July 1861: E472.18
Bull Shoals Lake and region
    Arkansas: F417.B86
    Missouri: F472.B94
Bullock, Rufus Brown: F291
Bullock Creek and Valley (South Carolina): F277.Y6
Bull's Ferry, N.J., Engagement at, 1780: E241.B87
Buneau-Varilla-Hay Treaty, 1903: F1566.5
Bunker Hill, Battle of, 1775: E241.B9
Bureau of the American Republics: F1403
Burges, Tristam: E340.B9
Burgoyne, John
    Campaign of 1777: E233
Burial customs, Indian: E98.M8, F3429.3.M7
Burlington (Iowa): F629.B9
Burlington (Vermont): F59.B9
Burnet, David Gouverneur: F389
Burnet, Jacob: F495
Burnet, William: F122+
Burnett, Thomas Pendleton: F584
Burns, Anthony: E450
Burnside, Ambrose Everett: E467.1.B8
    Expedition to North Carolina, 1862: E473.3
Burr, Aaron: E302.6.B9
    Conspiracy: E334
Burr, Esther (Edwards): E302.6.B93
Burrington, George: F257
Bush, George.: E881
Bush, George W.: E902+
Bushnell, Asa Smith: F496
Business, Negroes in: E185.8
Business enterprises, Indian: E98.B87
Busquipani Indians: F3430.1.C34
Bustamente y Sirvén, Antonio Sánchez de: F1787
Butch Cassidy (G.L. Parker): F595
Butcher, The (Cerro Yerupaja): F3451.Y47

Butler, Benjamin Franklin (1795-1858): E340.B98
Butler, Benjamin Franklin (1818-1893): E467.1.B87
    Government of Louisiana: E510.1+
Butler, Smedley Darlington: E182
Butler, Walter: E278.B9
Butler, William Orlando: E403.1.B9
Butler's Indian Campaign, 1778: E234
Butler's rangers
    Loyalist: E277.6.B9
Butte (Montana): F739.B8
Butte Valley (California): F868.S6
Butte, Battle of the, 1877: E83.8765
Butterfield, Daniel: E467.1.B9
Butternuts: E458.8
Buzzards Bay region: F72.B9
Byelorussians in Canada: F1035.W5
Byelorussians in the United States: E184.W6

C

C.S.A.: E482+
Caá Guazú, Battle of, 1841: F2891
Caaygua Indians: F2679.2.M34
Cabahiba Indians: F2520.1.P4
Cabecar Indians: F1545.2.C33
Cabinet National Forest: F737.C14
Cabiyari Indians: F2270.2.C22
Caboclos in Brazil: F2659.C32
Cabot, George: E302.6.C11
Cabot, John: E129.C1
Cabot, Sebastian: E129.C1
Cabot Trail (Nova Scotia): F1039.C2
Cabral, Pedro Alvares: E125.C11
Cabrillo, Juan Rodríguez: E125.C12
Cacapon River and Valley (West Virginia): F247.C24
Cacaxtla
    Mexico: F1434.1.C32
Cáceres Region (Peru): F3451.A54
Cache National Forest: F832.C35
Cache River and Valley (Illinois): F547.C13
Cache Valley (Utah): F832.C3
Cactus Canyon (Arizona): F788
Caddo Indians: E99.C12
Caddo Lake
    Louisiana: F377.C15
    Texas: F392.C17
Caddo Parish (Louisiana): F377.C15
Caddoan Indians: E99.C13
Cadioéo Indians: F2520.1.C3
Cadron Creek and Valley (Arkansas): F417.C27
Caguas (Puerto Rico): F1981.C24
Cahaba, Ala. Military Prison: E612.C2
Cahal Pech
    Mexico: F1435.1.C33
Cahita Indians: F1221.C3
Cahokia Indians: E99.C15
Cahuilla Indians: E99.C155
Caicos Island: F1659.T9
Caingua Indians: F2230.2.C3
Cajamarca, Peru (Dept.): F3451.C2
Cajuns in the United States: E184.A2

Canyonlands National Park (Utah):
F832.C37

Cap Français (Haiti): F1929.C3

Cap-Haïtien (Haiti): F1929.C3

Capanahua Indians: F3430.1.C34

Capanawa Indians: F3430.1.C34

Capay Valley (California): F868.Y5

Cape Ann (Massachusetts): F72.E7

Cape Breton Co. (Nova Scotia): F1039.C15

Cape Breton Island: F1039.C2
Siege and capture, 1745: E198

Cape Canaveral (Florida): F317.B8

Cape Cod (Massachusetts): F72.C3

Cape Cod Bay (Massachusetts): F72.C3

Cape Fear (North Carolina): F262.B9

Cape Fear River (North Carolina): F262.C2

Cape Hatteras National Seashore (North
Carolina): F262.O96

Cape Horn
Chile: F3186
Voyages to California via: F865

Cape Krusenstern National Monument
(Alaska): F912.C34

Cape Nome region (Alaska): F912.N7

Cape Sable Island: F1039.C3

Cape Verdeans in the United States:
E184.C24

Capim River (Brazil): F2586

Capinota, Bolivia (Province): F3341.C27

Capitals (Cities)
National: F191+
State, provincial, etc.: F73, F129.A3,
F334.T9

Capitals, State (U.S.): E159, F73.8.S8

Capitol building (Washington, D.C.):
F204.C2

Capitol Hill (Washington, D.C.): F202.C2

Capitol Reef National Park (Utah):
F832.W27

Caplan River and Valley (Quebec):
F1054.C22

Capon River and Valley (West Virginia):
F247.C24

Capote Indians: E99.C2

Captivities, Indian
Pre-Columbian America: E59.C22

Captivities, Indians: E85+

Capulin Volcano National Monument (New
Mexico): F802.U5

Caquetá (Colombia): F2281.C26

Caquetio Indians: F2319.2.C28

Cara Indians: F3722.1.C25

Carabaya, Peru (Province): F3451.C3

Carabobo, Battle of, 1821: F2324

Carabobo, Venezuela (State): F2331.C3

Caracas (Audiencia): F2322

Caracas (Venezuela): F2341.C2

Caracas Valley (Venezuela): F2331.C5

Caracol, Belize (Mayas): F1435.1.C37

Caraja Indians: F2520.1.C35

Carapana Indians: F2270.2.C26

Carchi, Ecuador (Province): F3741.C3
Indian antiquities: F3721.1.C2

Cárdenas, Lázaro: F1234

Cárdenas (Cuba): F1819.C3

Carib Indians: F2460.1.C37
Black Caribs: F1505.2.C3

Cariban Indians: F2001

Caribbean, English-speaking: F2130

Caribbean Sea: F2155+

Caribbeans in the United States: E184.C27

Caribbees: F2001+

Cariboo District (British Columbia):
F1089.C3

Caricatures and cartoons
United States
Lincoln, Abraham: E457.63
Wars
Civil War: E647
Wars
Revolution: E298

Carihona Indians: F2270.2.C27

Carijó Indians: F2520.1.F8

Carijona Indians: F2270.2.C27

Caripuna Indians: F2520.1.C37

Carleton, Guy: F1032

Carleton Co. (New Brunswick): F1044.C3

Carleton Co. (Ontario): F1059.C3

Carleton Island (New York): F127.T5

Carleton's Raid, 1778: E241.C2

Carlsbad Caverns (New Mexico): F802.C28

Carlsbad Caverns National Park: F802.C28

Carmel (California): F869.C27

Carnegie Institution of Washington. Division
of Historical Research: E175.4.C3

Carnicero (Cerro Yerupaja): F3451.Y47

Carnijó Indians: F2520.1.F8

Caro, Miquel Antonio: F2277

Carolana grant, 1629: F272

Carolina, Province of (1663-1712): F272
Northern Carolina settlements: F257
Queen Anne's War, 1702-1713: E197

Carolina grants
1629: F272
1663: F257

Carolinas
Separation: F272
Wars
Civil War Campaign, 1865: E477.7
Revolution Campaign, 1781: E237

Caroline (Steamer)
Burning, 1837: F1032

Caron, René Edouard: F1053

Carpenter, Matthew Hale: E664.C29

Carpenters' Hall (Philadelphia): F158.8.C2

Carpetbag rule: E668

Carquinez Strait (California): F868.S156

Carranza, Venustiano: F1234

Carrera, José Miguel: F3094

Carrera, Rafael; F1466.45

Carrier (Takulli) Indians: E99.T17

Carroll, Anna E.
Claim: E472.9

Carroll, Charles: F302.6.C3

Carroll, Daniel: E302.6.C33

Carson, Christopher: F592

Carson City (Nevada): F849.C3

Carson River and Valley (Nevada):
F847.C37

Cartagena (Colombia)
City: F2291.C3
Sieges
1585, 1697: F2272
1741: F2272.5
Province: F2281.C27

Cartago (Costa Rica): F1556.C3

Carter, Jimmy: E872+

Carteret, Sir George: F137

Cartier, Jacques: E133.C3

Cartier, Sir George Étienne: F1033

Cartography, Indian: E98.C17;
F1219.76.C37
Pre-Columbian America: E59.C25

Cartwright, Labrador (Fishing port):
F1139.C3

Cartwright, Peter: F545

Cartwright, Richard: F1058

Carutana Indians: F2520.1.B35

Carvajal, Luis de: F1231

Carver, Jonathan: F597

Cary, Archibald: F230

Casa Blanca Land Grant (Texas): F392.C287

Casa Grande National Monument
Arizona: F817.C35

Casa Yrujo, Carlos Martínez de Yrujo y
Tacón, marqués de: E313+

Casas, Bartolomé de las: E125.C4

Casas Grandes (Mexico)
Indian antiquities: F1219.1.C3

Casas Revolution: F389

Cascade Range: F851.7

Cascade Range in Oregon: F882.C3

Cascade Range in Washington (State):
F897.C3

Casco Bay: F27.C3

Cashibo Indians: F3430.1.C35

Cashinahua Indians: F2520.1.C38

Cashinawa Indians: F2520.1.C38

Casper (Wyoming): F769.C3

Casper Mountain (Wyoming): F767.N2

Cass, Lewis: E340.C3

Cassiar District (British Columbia):
F1089.C35

Castañeda Castro, Salvador: F1488

Castilla, Ramón: F3447

Castillo Armas, Carlos: F1466.5

Castle Island (Massachusetts): F73.68.C3

Castleguard, Mount (Alberta): F1079.B5

Castleton Island State Park (New York):
F127.C28

Castro, Cipriano: F2325

Castro, Fidel: F1788.22.C3

Cat Cay and Island (Bahamas): F1659.C37

Catahoula Parish (Louisiana): F377.C3

Catalans
Discovery of America
Pre-Columbian: E109.C37

Catalans in America: E29.C37

Catalans in Argentina: F3021.C3

Catalans in Cuba: F1789.C3

Catalans in Mexico: F1392.C3

Catalans in the Dominican Republic:
F1941.C37

Catalans in the United States: E184.C29

Chan Kom, Mexico
  Mayas: F1435.1.C47
Chañabal Indians: F1221.T58
Chanca Indians: F3430.1.C4
Chancay, Peru (Province): F3451.C46
Chancay culture (Peru)
  Indian antiquities: F3429.1.C47
Chancay Valley (Peru)
  Indian antiquities: F3429.1.C47
Chancellorsville campaign, 1863: E475.35
Chandalar Kutchin Indians: E99.N22
Chandler, John: E278.C4
Chandler, Zachariah: E664.C4
Chandler River and Valley (Alaska):
  F912.C43
Chané Indians: F3320.2.C37
Chango Indians: F3070.1.C5
Channel Islands (California): F868.S232
Chantilly, Battle of, 1862: E473.77
Chapa Indians: F3430.1.S47
Chapacura Indians: F3320.2.C38
Chapala, Lake (Mexico): F1254
Chaplains, Military
  United States
    Civil War: E635
Chappaquiddick Island (Massachusetts):
  F72.M5
Chapra Indians: F3430.1.S47
Chapultepec, Battle of, 1847: E406.C47
Charcas (Audiencia): F3322
Charcas, Bolivia (City): F3351.S94
Charitable contributions
  Indians
    North America: E98.C47
Charles River (Massachusetts): F72.C46
Charleston (South Carolina): F279.C4
  Settlement at: F272
  Siege, 1780: E241.C4
  Siege, 1863: E475.62
Charleston (West Virginia): F249.C4
Charleston, Lake and region (Ontario):
  F1059.C53
Charleston Harbor (South Carolina)
  Civil War
    Engagements and operations, 1863-
      1864: E473.96, E475.6+,
      E476.41
    Fort Sumter, 1861: E471.1
    Siege, 1863-1865: E470.65
Charleston Insurrection, 1822: F279.C4
Charleston Mountain (Nevada): F847.C5
Charlestown (Massachusetts): F74.C4
Charlevoix Region (Quebec): F1054.C445
Charlotte, Consort of Maximilian: F1233
Charlotte (North Carolina): F264.C4
Charlotte and Mecklenburg County (North
  Carolina): F264.C4
Charlottetown (Prince Edward Island):
  F1049.5.C5
Charrua Indians: F2719.2.C5
Chase, Camp (Columbus, Ohio)
  Civil War prison: E616.C4
Chase, Salmon Portland: E415.9.C4
Chase, Samuel: E302.6.C4
Chasta Indians: E99.C48

Chastacosta Indians: E99.C483
Chatata Creek and Valley (Tennessee):
  F443.B8
Chateauguay, N.Y., Battle of, 1813: E356.C4
Chateauguay Co. (Quebec): F1054.C45
Chatino Indians: F1221.C47
Chattahoochee River and Valley: F292.C4
  Alabama: F332.C4
  Florida: F317.J2
Chattahoochee River Valley: F217.C45
  Indians: E78.C45
Chattanooga (Tennessee): F444.C4
  Attack on, 1862: E473.59
Chattanooga Railroad Expedition, 1862:
  E473.55
Chattanooga region
  Military operations, 1861-1865: E470.5
Chattanooga-Ringgold campaign, 1863:
  E475.97
Chattooga River and Valley: F217.C45
Chautauqua Creek and Valley (New York):
  F127.C7
Chautauqua Lake (New York): F127.C7
Chavante-Akwẽ Indians: F2520.1.A4
Chavante Indians: F2520.1.A4
Chavín (Peru)
  Indian antiquities: F3429.1.C48
Chavín culture (Peru)
  Indian antiquities: F3429.1.C48
Chayahuita Indians: F3430.1.C43
Cheat Mountain (West Virginia): F247.R2
Cheat River, Cave of Dry Fork of (West
  Virginia): F247.R2
Chehalis Indians: E99.C49
Chelan Indians: E99.C4925
Chelsea, Mass., Battle of, 1775: E241.C48
Chemehuevi Indians: E99.C493
Chemung River and Valley: F127.C73
  Pennsylvania: F157.C37
Chenango Canal (New York): F127.C765
Chenango River and Valley (New York):
  F127.C765
Cheneaux Islands (Michigan): F572.L57
Chennault, Claire Lee: E745
Chequamegon Bay (Wisconsin): F587.A8
Cheraw Indians: E99.C495
Cherente Indians: F2520.1.S47
Cherokee (Steamer): E595.C5
Cherokee Indians: E99.C5
Cherokee National Female Seminary,
  Tahlequah, Okla.: E97.6.C35
Cherokee Outlet (Oklahoma): F702.C42
Cherokee Strip, Oklahoma: F702.C42
Cherokee War, 1759-1761: E83.759
Cherry Valley, N.Y., massacre, 1778:
  E241.C5
Chesapeake and Ohio Canal area: F187.C47
Chesapeake Bay and region: F187.C5
  Virginia: F232.C43
Chesapeake Bay expedition, 1813: E355.4
Chesapeake-Leopard Affair, 1807: E357.3
Chester Parish (Maryland): F187.K3
Chesterfield Inlet, Keewatin District
  (Trading post): F1110.5.C5

Chestnut Hill, Battle of, 1777: E241.C52
Chesuncook Lake (Maine): F27.P5
Chetco Indians: E99.C526
Chetlain, Augustus Louis: E467.1.C52
Chew, Benjamin: F153
Cheyenne (Wyoming): F769.C5
Cheyenne Indians: E99.C53
Cheyenne Mountain (Colorado): F782.E3
Cheyenne outbreak: E83.875
Cheyenne War, 1864: E83.863
Chezzetcook Inlet: F1039.H3
Chiapa de Corso Site (Mexico): F1435.1.C49
Chiapanec Indians: F1221.C5
Chiapas, Mexico (State): F1256
Chibcha Indians: F2270.2.C4
  Conquest by Colombia, 1536-1538:
    F2272
Chicago: F548+
  Massacre, 1812: E356.C53
Chicago River (Illinois): F547.C45
Chicanná Site (Mayas): F1435.1.C494
Chichén Itzá (Mexico)
  Mayas: F1435.1.C5
Chichimec Indians: F1219.8.C55
Chichimeca-Jonaz Indians: F1221.C53
Chickamauga and Chattanooga National
  Military Park: E475.81
Chickamauga campaign, 1863: E475.81
Chickamauga Lake and region (Tennessee):
  F443.C47
Chickasaw Indians: E99.C55
Chickasaw National Recreation Area
  (Oklahoma): F702.M84
Chickasaw War, 1739-1740: E83.739
Chicoutimi Co. (Quebec): F1054.C49
Chignecto Isthmus: F1039.C5
Chihuahua, Mexico (State): F1261
Chihuahua campaign, 1846-1848: E405.4
Chihuahuan Desert (Mexico): F1262
Chihuahuan Desert (New Mexico):
  F802.C52
Chilako River and Valley (British
  Columbia): F1089.C3
Chilcotin Indians: E99.T78
Chilcotin River and Valley (British
  Columbia): F1089.C42
Child soldiers
  Civil War
    Confederate Army: E585.C54
Children
  Jews: E184.36.S65
Children
  Afro-American: E185.86
  Indian: E98.C5; F1219.76.C56,
    F1435.3.C47; F2230.1.C5
  Mexico: F1219.3.C45
  Pre-Columbian America: E59.C46
Children and grandchildren of Presidents:
  E176.45
Children in the United States
  Civil War: E540.C47
Children of the American Revolution:
  E202.9
Children of the Confederacy: E483.55

Chile: F3051+
  Boundaries: F3131.A1+
    Argentina: F2851, F2853
    Peru: F3451.B73
    Tacna and Arica question: F3097.3
  Military history
    Civil wars: F3095
    Revolution of 1891: F3098
    War of Independence, 1810-1824:
      F3094
    War of the Pacific, 1879-1884: F3097
    War with Peru-Bolivian
      Confederation, 1836-1839:
      F3447
    War with Spain, 1865-1866: F3095
    Occupation of Lima, 1881-1883: F3601
Chileans in Canada: F1035.C48
Chileans in United States: E184.C4
Chilkat Indians: E99.C552
Chillán (Chile): F3281.C46
Chillicothe (Ohio): F499.C4
  Virginia military lands
    Old Northwest: F483
Chilliwack Indians: E99.C5523
Chilliwack River and Valley (British
    Columbia): F1089.C45
Chilliwhack Indians: E99.C5523
Chiloé, Chile (Province): F3146
Chilote Indians: F3126
Chilton, William Parish: F326
Chilula Indians: E99.C553
Chimane Indians: F3320.2.C387
Chimariko Indians: E99.C56
Chimborazo, Ecuador (Province): F3741.C5
Chimila Indians: F2270.2.C5
Chimmesyan Indians: E99.C565
Chimu Indians: F3430.1.C46
Chinantec Indians: F1221.C56
Chinatown
  New York: F128.68.C47
  Washington, D.C.: F202.C46
Chinautla (Guatemala)
  Indian antiquities: F1465.1.C5
Chincha Valley (Peru): F3451.C5
Chincoteague Island (Virginia): F232.A2
Chinese
  Discovery of America
    Pre-Columbian: E109.C5
Chinese in America: E29.C5
Chinese in British Guiana: F2391.C5
Chinese in Canada: F1035.C5
Chinese in Central America
  Panama: F1577.C48
Chinese in Cuba: F1789.C53
Chinese in Jamaica: F1896.C5
Chinese in Mexico: F1392.C45
Chinese in Peru: F3619.C5
Chinese in South America: F2239.C48
Chinese in United States: E184.C5
Chinese influences
  Mayas: F1435.3.C49
Chinkultic Site (Mexico): F1435.1.C54
Chinook Indians: E99.C57
Chinookan Indians: E99.C58
Chipaya Indians: F3320.2.C388

Chipewyan Indians: E99.C59
Chippewa, Ont., Battle of, 1814: E356.C55
Chippewa Indians: E99.C6
Chippewa River and Valley (Wisconsin):
    F587.C5
Chippewa War, 1898: E83.895
Chiquito Indians: F3320.2.C39
Chiquitos, Bolivia (Province): F3341.C5
Chiricahua Indians: E99.C68
Chiricahua National Monument (Arizona):
    F817.C5
Chiriguano Indians: F3320.2.C4
Chiripá Indians: F2679.2.C5
Chiriquí, Laguna de (Panama): F1569.B6
Chiriquí, Panama (Province): F1569.C5
Chisholm Trail: F596
Chitimacha Indians: E99.C7
Chittenden, Thomas: F52
Choate, Joseph Hodges: E664.C45
Choate, Rufus: E340.C4
Chocho Indians: F1221.C567
Chocó, Colombia (Dept.): F2281.C5
Choco Indians: F2270.2.C6
Chocolate Mountains (California): F868.I2
Choctaw Indians: E99.C8
Choke Canyon Reservoir (Texas): F392.F92
Chol Indians: F1221.C57
Cholchagua, Chile (Province): F3151
Cholone Indians: F3430.1.C48
Choltí Indians: F1221.C57
Choluteca, Honduras (Dept.): F1509.C4
Chono Indians: F3070.1.C6
Chontal Indians: F1221.C58
Chontales (Nicaragua): F1529.C53
Choqquequirau (Peru)
  Indian antiquities: F3429.1.C5
Chorotega Indians: F1545.2.C48
Choroti Indians: F3320.2.C5
Chorti Indians: F1465.2.C5
Chota, Peru (Province): F3451.C55
Chouart, Médard, sieur des Groseilliers:
    F1060.7
Christ Church (Philadelphia): F158.62.C5
Christ Church Parish (Maryland): F187.C15
Christian Commission, United States: E635
Christian (Moravian) Indians: E99.M9
Christiana Riot, 1851: E450
Christians and the Civil War
  United States: E540.C5
Christie, James: E278.C5
Christina Lake and region (British
    Columbia): F1089.C47
Christina River (Creek) (Delaware): F172.N5
Chronological tables
  Argentina
    History: F2827
  Bahamas
    History: F1655.3
  Belize
    History: F1445.5
  Bermudas
    History: F1635
  Boliva
    History: F3320.3

Chronological tables — Continued
  Brazil
    History: F2520.3
  Central America
    History: F1435.4
  Chile
    History: F3073
  Colombia
    History: F2270.3
  Costa Rica
    History: F1545.5
  Cuba
    History: F1772
  Ecuador
    History: F3723.3
  French Guiana
    History: F2460.3
  Guyana
    History: F2380.3
  Haiti
    History: F1918
  Honduras
    History: F1505.5
  Jamaica
    History: F1878
  Mexico
    History: F1223
  Panama
    History: F1565.5
  Paraguay
    History: F2679.35
  Peru
    History: F3430.3
  Puerto Rico
    History: F1970
  Salvador
    History: F1485.5
  South America
    History: F2230.3
  Surinam
    History: F2420.3
  Uruguay
    History: F2720
  West Indies
    History: F1620
Chronology
  Indian: F1219.3.C2, F1435.3.C14,
    F3429.3.C14
Chronology, Historical
  America: E18.5
  Dominican Republic: F1937
  Latin America: F1409.6
  North America: E174.5
Chronology, Indian: E98.C55
  Pre-Columbian America: E59.C5
Chubut, Argentina (Territory): F2881
  Indian antiquities: F2821.1.C5
Chucuito, Peru (Province): F3451.C6
Chuj Indians: F1221.C585
Chumash Indians: E99.C815
Chumashan Indians: E99.C815
Chupacho Indians: F3430.1.C5
Chuquisaca, Bolivia (City): F3351.S94
Chuquisaca, Bolivia (Dept.): F3341.C6

Church of England and the American
　　Revolution: E269.C5
Churches (U.S.): F73.62, F128.62
Churches, Negro: E185.7
Churches and the Civil War 1861-1865:
　　E540.C5
Churches and the War of 1898: E725.5.C5
Churchill River and Valley
　　Manitoba: F1064.C58
　　Saskatchewan: F1074.C58
Churchill River Watershed (Sask. and Man.):
　　E78.C5
Church's expedition to the eastward, 1704:
　　E197
Churoya Indians: F2270.2.C63
Churubusco, Battle of, 1847: E406.C5
Churumata Indians
　　Bolivia: F3320.2.C62
Cibola: F799
Ciboney Indians: F1769
Cicero (Illinois): F549.C56
Ciego de Avila Province (Cuba): F1851+
Cienfuegos (Cuba): F1829.C5
Cienfuegos Province (Cuba): F1852+
Cilley, Jonathan: E340.C5
Cilley, Joseph: E263.N4
Cimientos Site (Mexico): F1435.1.C56
Cimmaron River and Valley (Oklahoma):
　　F702.C53
Cincinnati (Ohio): F499.C5
　　Symmes Tract: F483
Cincinnati, Daughters of the: E202.2
Cincinnati, Society of the: E202.1
Cinta Larga Indians: F2520.1.C64
Cisne, Islas del: F1509.B3
Cisnes River (Chile): F3181
Cisplatine Province, 1821-1824: F2725
City Hall Park (New York): F128.65.C5
City Island (New York): F128.68.C5
City of Rocks National Reserve (Idaho):
　　F752.C35
City planning, Indian: F1219.76.C59,
　　F1435.3.C57
　　Pre-Columbian America: E59.C55
Ciudad de los Césares: F3072
Civil rights
　　Indians: F1434.2.C58, F2270.1.C58,
　　　　F3320.1.C57, F3429.3.C56
　　Mayas: F1435.3.C58
　　United States
　　　　Afro-Americans: E185.61
Civil War, 1861-1865: E461+
　　Aerial operations: E492.7, E546.7
　　Anniversaries: E641+
　　Armies
　　　　Confederate: E545+
　　　　Union: E491+
　　Biography: E467+
　　Chronology: E468.3
　　Commerce: E480
　　Diplomatic history: E469+, E488
　　Finance: E480
　　Historiography: E468.5
　　History: E468+
　　Lee's surrender, 1865: E477.67

Civil War, 1861-1865: E461+ — Continued
　　Medical and hospital services: E621+
　　Monuments and memorials: E641+
　　Naval operations: E591+
　　Opening events: E471+
　　Personal narratives: E464
　　Political history: E458+, E459, E487
　　Press, censorship, etc.: E609
　　Prisons: E611+
　　Relief: E629+
　　Religious aspects: E540.A+, E635
　　Secret service: E608
　　Societies
　　　　Patriotic, etc.: E462+
　　　　　　Confederate: E483
　　Travel: E167
　　Veterans' societies: E462+
　　　　Confederate: E483
　　Women's work: E628
　　　　Nurses: E621+
Claiborne, William: F184, F229
Claiborne, William Charles Cole: F374
Claiborne Parish (Louisiana): F377.C5
Claims against the United States
　　Civil War: E480
　　Indian: E98.C6+
　　Revolution: E249, E255
　　War of 1812: E359.4
　　War with Mexico: E409.4
Clallam Indians: E99.C82
Clamorgan land grant (Arkansas and
　　Missouri): F417.C5
Clapps Mill, N.C., 1781
　　Battle of: E241.C56
Clarence Cannon Reservoir (Missouri):
　　F472.C47
Clarendon settlement (North Carolina): F257
Clarion River (Pennsylvania): F157.C52
Clark, Abraham: E302.6.C55
Clark, Champ: E664.C49
Clark, George Rogers: E207.C5
　　Expedition against Detroit, 1781: E237
　　Expedition to the Illinois, 1778: E234
Clark, William
　　Lewis and Clark Expedition: F592.3+
Clark Fork and Valley
　　Idaho: F752.C57
　　Montana: F737.C55
Clark Lake (Alaska): F912.C47
Clark Mountain (Virginia): F232.O6
Clarke, Elijah: F290
Clarke, John: F82
Clatsop Fort National Memorial (Oregon):
　　F882.C53
Clay, Cassius Marcellus: E415.9.C55
Clay, Henry: E340.C6
　　Charge of bargain with John Quincy
　　　　Adams: E375
　　Collected works: E337.8.C55
　　Omnibus Bill: E423
Clayoquot Indians: E99.C83
Clayoquot Sound (British Columbia):
　　F1089.V3

Clayton, Augustin Smith: E340.C62
Clayton, John Middleton: E415.9.C6
Clayton-Bulwer Treaty, 1860: F1438
Clear Creek and Valley (Big Horn County-
　　Sheridan County)
　　Wyoming: F767.C55
Clear Creek and Valley (Colorado):
　　F782.C59
Clear Fork River and Valley
　　Kentucky: F457.C58
　　Tennessee: F443.C56
Clearwater River and Valley (Idaho):
　　F752.C62
Cleburne's Division
　　Confederate Army: E547.C6
Clergy and the Civil War, 1861-1865:
　　E540.C5
Clergy and the Revolution, 1775-1783:
　　E210+
Clermont State Historic Site (New York):
　　F127.L73
Clermont State Park (New York): F127.L73
Cleveland, Grover: E697
　　Administrations, 1885-1889, 1893-1897:
　　　　E696+, E706+
　　Family: E697.5
Cleveland (Ohio): F499.C6
Cliff dwellings in America: E61
　　Pueblo Indians: E99.P9
　　Mesa Verde National Park (Colorado):
　　　　F782.M52
Clifty Falls State Park (Indiana): F532.J5
Clinch River and Valley
　　Tennessee: F443.C57
　　Virginia: F232.C65
Clingman, Thomas Lanier: E415.9.C63
Clinton, Bill: E885+
Clinton, De Witt: E340.C65
Clinton, George: E302.6.C6
Clinton, James: E207.C62
Clinton administration: E885+
Clinton Lake (Kansas): F687.W4
Clover Creek (Washington): F897.P6
Clovis culture: E99.C832
Coachella Valley (California): F868.R6
Coahuila, Mexico (State): F1266
Coahuila and Texas (State): F389
Coahuilla Indians: E99.C155
Coahuiltecan Indians: E99.C834
Coaiker Indians: F3722.1.C83
Coaiquer Indians: F3722.1.C83
Coalcomán, Mexico (District): F1306
Coast Range (British Columbia): F1089.C7
Coast Salish Indians: E99.S21
Coastal Bend (Texas): F392.C517
Cobá Indians: F1435.1.C63
Cobaría Indians: F2270.2.T8
Cobb, Howell: F290
Cobb Island (Maryland): F187.C6
Cobbeos Indians: F2270.2.C8
Cobbosseecontee, Lake (Maine): F27.K2
Coburn, Abner: E511.1+
Cocalico Creek and Valley (Pennsylvania):
　　F157.C67
Cocama Indians: F3430.1.C55

Columbus, Christopher: E111+ —
  Continued
    Monument, Washington, D.C.: F203.4.C7
    Quincentennial, 1992-1993: E119.2
Columbus (Georgia): F294.C7
  Capture, 1865: E477.96
Columbus (Kentucky), Demonstration upon,
    1861: E472.28
Columbus (Ohio): F499.C7
Columbus Day: E120
Colville Indians: E99.C844
Colville River and Valley (Washington):
    F897.S9
Comalcalco Site (Mexico): F1435.1.C67
Comanche Indians: E99.C85
Comanche War, 1840: E83.837
Comayagua (Honduras): F1516.C72
Comechingone Indians: F2823.C5
Comic histories
  United States
    Revolution, 1775-1783: E298
Commerce
  Indians: E98.C7; F1219.3.C6,
      F1435.3.C6, F2230.1.C75,
      F3069.3.C66, F3429.3.C59
    Central America: F1434.2.C65
    Pre-Columbian America: E59.C59
Commerce, Restrictions on
  United States
    Colonial period: E215.1
    1800-1810: E336+
Commerce Building, Department of
    (Washington, D.C.): F204.D43
Committee of Seventy (Louisiana): F375
Committees of correpondence and safety:
    E216
Commonwealth Caribbean: F2130+
Communication
  Indians
    Brazil: F2519.3.C65
    Peru: F3429.3.C594
    North America: E98.C73
Communist Revolution of 1935 (Brazil):
    F2538
Communist spies in Canada: F1034
Communist spies in United States: E743.5
Community colleges, Indian: E97.55
Comodoro Rivadavia (Argentina): F2884
Comonfort, Ignacio: F1232.5
Comox Indians: E99.C86
Comox Valley (British Columbia): F1089.V3
Compagnie du Scioto: F483
Company of New France: F1030
Company of the West Indies: F1030
Compromise of 1850: E423
Compton Co. (Quebec): F1054.C7
Comstock Lode (Nevada): F849.V8
Comuneros, Insurrection of the, 1781: F2272
Conant, Roger: F67
Concepción (Chile)
  City: F3281.C5
  Province: F3156

Concepión, Paraguay
  City: F2695.C7
  Department: F2691.C6
Concepción de la Vega (Dominican
    Republic): F1939.L3
Concho River and Valley (Texas):
    F392.C773
Concord (Massachusetts): F74.C8
Concord (New Hampshire): F44.C7
Concord, Battle of, 1775: E241.C7
Concord River (Massachusetts): F72.M7
Concordat of 1862: F3736
Concordia Parish, La.: F377.C7
Conejo Valley (California): F868.C74
Conemaugh River and Valley: F157.C73
Conestoga Creek (Pennsylvania): F157.L2
Conestoga Indians: E99.C87
Conewago Creek and Valley (Pennsylvania):
    F157.C75
Coney Island (New York): F129.C75
Confederación de Centro América (1823-
    1838/1842): F1438
  Costa Rica: F1547
  Guatemala: F1466.4
  Honduras: F1507
  Nicaragua: F1526.25
  Salvador: F1487
Confederación Granadina: F2276
Confederación Perú-Boliviana: F3447
Confederate Memorial Day: E645
Confederate Memorial Literary Society:
    E483.75
Confederate operations in Canada: E470.95
Confederate States of America: E482+;
    JK9663+
  Construction of war vessels in England:
      E469+
  Description and travel: F214
  Flags: E646
  Military history: E551+
  Naval history: E591+
  Political history: E487
  Propaganda in foreign countries: E488.5
  Slavery: E453
  Social conditions: F214
  Travel: F214
Confederate sympathizers in the North:
    E458.8
Confederate Veteran Association of
    Kentucky: E483.2
Confederate Veterans' Association of Fulton
    County, Georgia: E483.99.C78
Confederated Southern Memorial
    Association: E483.72
Confederates in Canada: E470.95
Confederation, 1783-1789
  United States: E303
Confederation, Articles of, 1778
  United States: E303
Confederation of Granada: F2276
Confiscations
  United States
    Civil War: E480
    Revolution: E277

Congaree Swamp and Region (South
    Carolina): F277.C85
Congress Hall (Philadelphia): F158.8.C7
Congress of Panama, 1826: F1404
Congressional Cemetery (Washington,
    D.C.): F203.1.C7
Conibo Indians: F3430.1.S5
Conkling, Roscoe: E664.C75
Conneaut Lake (Pennsylvania): F157.C77
Connecticut: F91+
  Afro-Americans: E185.93.C7
  Counties, etc.: F102.A+
  Dutch posts: F97
  Indians: E78.C7
  Old Northwest cession: F483
  Slavery: E445.C7
  Wars
    Civil War: E499.1+
    French and Indian War: E199
    Indian wars: E83.63, E83.67
    Revolution: E230+, E263.C5
    War of 1812: E359.5.C7
    War of 1898: E726.C7
    War with Mexico, 1845-1848:
        E409.5.C6
  Western Reserve: F497.W5
  Wyoming Valley claims: F157.W9
Connecticut Gore: F157.W9
Connecticut Reserve (Ohio): F497.W5
Connecticut River and Valley
  Connecticut: F102.C7
  Massachusetts: F72.C7
  New England: F12.C7
  New Hampshire: F42.C65
  Vermont: F57.C7
Conner, David: E403.1.C7
Connolly, John: E278.C7
Conococheague Creek and Valley: F157.F8
  Maryland: F187.W3
Conoy Indians: E99.C873
Consanguinity, Indian (Peru): F3429.3.C6
Conselheiro Insurrection (Brazil): F2537
Consolidated province of New England: F7.5
Conspiracies
  U.S. Civil War: E458.8
Constitution
  United States: E303
Constitution Avenue (Washington, D.C.):
    F203.7.C7
Constitution Island (New York): F127.C83
Continental army
  United States: E259+
Continental Congress, 1774-1788: E303
Continental Hall, Memorial (Washington,
    D.C.): F204.M5
Contrabands: E453
Contracts, Government
  United States
    Civil War: E480
Contreras, Battle of, 1847: E406.C6
Contumazá, Peru (Province): F3451.C7
Convention of Border Slave States
    Frankfort, Kentucky: E440.5
Conway Cabal: E255

Crockett, David: F436
Croghan, George: E353.1.C8
Croker, Richard: F128.47
Crook, George: E83.866
Crooked Billet, Battle of the, 1778:
　　E241.C94
Crooked Creek, Battle of, 1859: E83.8577
Crosby, Enoch: E280.C95
Crow Indians: E99.C92
Crown Coffee House (Boston): F73.8.C9
Crown Point (New York)
　　French and Indian War: E199
Crowsnest Pass
　　Alberta: F1079.C76
　　British Columbia: F1089.C77
Crowsnest River and Valley
　　Alberta: F1079.C76
　　British Columbia: F1089.C77
Crozat's Grant, 1712-1717: F372
Cruises down the river
　　Mississippi River and Valley: F354
Crystal Lake (Michigan): F572.B4
Crystal Park (Colorado): F782.E3
Cuaiker Indians: F3722.1.C83
Cuaiquer Indians: F3722.1.C83
Cuauhtemoc, Emperor of Mexico:
　　F1219.75.C83
Cuba: F1751+
　　American occupation, 1906-1909: F1787
　　Annexation question: F1786
　　Discovery and exploration: E101+
　　English occupation, 1762-1763: F1781
　　Filibusters: F1784
　　Military history
　　　　Insurrections
　　　　　　1849-1851 (López expeditions):
　　　　　　　　F1784
　　　　　　1868-1878 (Ten Years' War):
　　　　　　　　F1785
　　　　　　Little War, 1879-1880: F1785
　　　　　Revolutions
　　　　　　1895-1898: F1786
　　　　　　1906: F1787
　　　　　　1933: F1788
　　　　　War of 1898: E717.1
　　Ostend Manifesto, 1854: E431
　　Spanish West Indies: F1783
Cubagua Island (Venezuela): F2331.C7
Cuban missile crisis: E841+
Cuban question
　　1895-1898: F1786
Cubans in Mexico: F1392.C8
Cubans in Puerto Rico: F1983.C83
Cubans in United States: E184.C97
Cubans in Venezuela: F2349.C83
Cubeo Indians: F2270.2.C8
Cuelap (Peru)
　　Indian antiquities: F3429.1.C8
Cuello Site (Belize): F1435.1.C84
Cuenca (Ecuador): F3791.C9
Cuesta Encantada (California): F868.S18
Cuestas, Juan Lindolfo: F2726
Cueva Indians: F1565.2.C77
Cuiba Indians: F2319.2.C78
Cuicatec Indians: F1221.C84

Cuiva Indians: F2319.2.C78
Cul de Sac (Haiti) (Plain): F1929.C8
Culebra Island (Puerto Rico): F1981.C9
Culina Indians: F2520.1.C84
Cultural assimilation, Indian: E98.C89;
　　F1525.3.C84, F2519.3.C85
Cultural relations (General)
　　Spain with Latin America: F1414
　　United States
　　　　20th century: E744.5, E840.2
Culture, Indian: F2230.1.C9
Cumaná (Venezuela): F2341.C8
Cumana Indians: F2319.2.C8
Cumberland, Army of the: E470.5
Cumberland, Fort, N.B., Battle of, 1776:
　　E241.C96
Cumberland (Frigate): E595.C9
Cumberland Caverns (Tennessee): F443.W2
Cumberland Gap (Tennessee), Evacuation of
　　Sept.-Oct. 1862: E474.38
Cumberland Gap campaign, Mar.- June
　　1862: E473.52
Cumberland Gap National Historical Park:
　　F457.C77
Cumberland Island (Georgia): F292.C94
Cumberland Island National Seashore
　　(Georgia): F292.C94
Cumberland Mountains: F457.C8
Cumberland Parish (Virginia): F232.C94
Cumberland River and Valley
　　Kentucky: F457.C9
Cumberland Road (Pennsylvania): F157.C85
Cumberland Valley
　　Kentucky and Tennessee: F442.2,
　　　　F457.C9
　　　　Civil War
　　　　　　Military operations: E470.5
　　Pennsylvania: F157.C9, F157.F8
Cuna Indians: F1565.C8
Cundinamarca (Colombia): F2269.1.C95
Cundinamarca, Colombia (Dept.): F2281.C9
Cunningham Chapel Parish (Virginia):
　　F232.C59
Cupeño Indians: E99.C94
Cupisnique Indians: F3430.1.C8
Curaçao (West Indies): F2049
Curicó, Chile (Province): F3166
Curitiba, Brazil: F2651.C83
Curler, Arent van: F122.1
Curley, James Michael: F70
Current River and Valley (General, and Mo.):
　　F472.C9
Curripaco Indians: F2270.2.C87
Curtis, Benjamin Robbins: E415.9.C96
Curtis, Samuel Ryan: E467.1.C97
Curuguaty (Paraguay): F2695.C9
Curupaity, Battle of, 1866: F2687
Curwen, Samuel: E278.C9
Cuscatlán, El Salvador (Dept.): F1489.C8
　　Indian antiquities: F1485.1.C8
Cushing, Caleb: E415.9.C98
Cushing, William Barker: E467.1.C98
Custer, Fort (Montana): F737.Y4

Custer, George Armstrong: E467.1.C99
Custer State Park (South Dakota): F657.C92
Custis-Lee Mansion
　　Arlington, Virginia: F234.A7
Custom House (Chicago): F548.8.C9
Cutervo, Peru (Province): F3451.C85
Cutler, Manasseh: F483
Cuttyhunk Island (Massachusetts): F72.E5
Cuyahoga River and Valley (Ohio):
　　F497.C95
Cuyo (Province): F2911
Cuzco (Peru)
　　City: F3611.C9
　　　　Indian antiquities: F3429.1.C9
　　Department: F3451.C9
Cypress Creek and Valley (Arkansas):
　　F417.C7
Cypress Creek and Valley (Kentucky):
　　F457.U5
Cypress Hills (Alta. and Saska.): F1079.C9
Cypress Hills Provincial Park
　　(Saskatchewan): F1074.C92
Czechs in America: E29.C94
Czechs in Canada: F1035.C9
Czechs in Chile: F3285.C94
Czechs in Latin America: F1419.C94
Czechs in Mexico: F1392.C93
Czechs in the United States: E184.B67
　　Civil War: E540.C94
Czolgosz, L.F.: E711.9

D

D.A.R.: E202.5
Dahlgren, John Adolphus Bernard:
　　E467.1.D13
Dahlgren, Ulric
　　Raid, 1864: E476.27
Dakota Indian wars
　　1855-1856: E83.854
　　1862-1865: E83.86
　　1876: E83.876
　　1890-1891: E83.89
Dakota Indians: E99.D1
Dakota region before 1861: F655
　　Indian War, 1855-1856: E83.854
Dakota Territory (1861-1889): F655
　　Indians: E78.D2
Dalhousie, George Ramsay, 9th Earl of:
　　F1053
Dallas, Alexander James: E302.6.D14
Dallas, George Mifflin: E340.D14
Dallas (Texas): F394.D21
Dalles of the Wisconsin: F587.W8
Dames of 1846: E401.7
Dames of the Loyal Legion: E462.25
Dana, Francis: E302.6.D16
Dana, Richard Henry: E415.9.D15
　　Collected works: E415.6.D16
Danbury (Connecticut)
　　Burning by the British, 1777: E241.D2
Dance
　　Indians
　　　　Bolivia: F3320.1.D35
　　　　South America: F2230.1.D35

Dewey, Thomas Edmund: E748.D48
Dexter, Samuel: E302.6.D45
Dhegiha Indians: E99.D4
Día de Colón: E120
Diaguita Indians
   Argentina: F2823.D5
   Chile: F3070.1.D5
Diamantina Plateau (Brazil): F2551
Diamond Cave (Kentucky): F457.B2
Dias, Henrique: F2532
Dias, Marcillio: F2536
Díaz, Adolfo: F1526.3
Díaz, Porfirio: F1233.5
Díaz del Castillo, Bernal: F1230
Dickinson, Anna Elizabeth: E415.9.D48
Dickinson, Daniel Stevens: E415.9.D5
Dickinson, John: E302.6.D5
Dickinson, Walter Mason: E714.6.D55
Diefenbaker, John George: F1034.3.D5
Diegueño Indians: E99.D5
Digby Co. (Nova Scotia): E1039.D5
Dingley, Nelson, Jr.: E664.D58
Dinosaur National Monument: F832.D5
Dinwiddie Courthouse, Battle of, 1865:
   E477.67
Diriamba (Nicaragua): F1536.D5
Disappointment Creek and Valley
   (Colorado): F782.D57
Disasters
   United States: E179
Discoveries and exploration
   America: E101+
      Columbian: E111+
      Post-Columbian: E121+
      Pre-Columbian: E103+
Discovery Day: E120
Discrimination, Racial
   United States
      Afro-Americans: E185.61
Diseases, Indian: E98.D6; F1219.3.D5,
   F2821.3.D5, F3429.3.D6,
   F3721.1.D58, F3721.3.D58
   Pre-Columbian America: E59.D58
Disloyal organizations
   U.S. Civil War: E458.8
Dismal Swamp
   North Carolina: F262.D7
   Virginia: F232.D7
District of Columbia: F191+
   Afro-Americans: E185.93.D6
   Indians: E78.D6
   Retrocession of Alexandria Co., 1846:
      F195
   Slavery: E445.D6
   Wars
      Civil War: E501.1+
         Military operations: E470.2+,
            E476.66
        War of 1812: E355.6
           Burning of Washington: E356.W3
        War with Mexico: E409.5.D6
District of West Augusta (Virginia):
   F157.W5
Dix, John Adams: E415.9.D6
Dix, John Alden: F124

Dixie: F206+
Djore-Xikrin Indians: F2520.1.X5
Dochet Island: F27.W3
Dodge, Augustus Caesar: F621
Dodge, Grenville Mellen: E467.1.D6
Dodge, Henry: E340.D7
Doe, Charles: F39
Dog Rib Indians: E99.T4
Dolls, Indian: E98.D65, F1219.76.D64
   Pre-Columbian America: E59.D66
Domestic animals
   Indians
      North America: E98.D67
      Peru: F3429.3.D69
      Pre-Columbian America: E59.D69
      South America: F2230.1.D65
Domestic relations, Indian: F3429.3.D72
Dominica (West Indies): F2051
Dominican Republic: F1931+
   Annexation to U.S. proposed: E673
   Pre-Columbian period: F1909
   Spanish colony, 1492-1795: F1911
Dominicans (Dominican Republic) in Puerto
   Rico: F1983.D65
Dominicans (Dominican Republic) in United
   States: E184.D6
Dominion of Canada: F1001+
Dominion of New England, 1686-1689: F7.5
Don River and Valley (Ontario): F1059.Y6
Donck, Adriaen van der: F122.1
Donelson, Emily Tennessee (Donelson):
   E382.1.D6
Donelson, Fort
   Siege and capture, 1862: E472.97
Dongan, Thomas, Earl of Limerick: F122+
Doniphan, Alexander William: E403.1.D6
   Expedition in Mexican War: E405.2
Donner, Lake (California): F868.N5
Donner party expedition: F868.N5
Dorado, El: E121+
Dorask Indians: F1565.2.D6
Dorchester, Guy Carleton, Baron: F1032
Dorchester (Massachusetts): F74.D5
Dorchester Co. (Maryland): F187.D6
Dorchester Co. (Quebec): F1054.D4
Dorchester Company: F67
Dorr, Thomas Wilson: F83.4
Dorrego, Manuel: F2846
Dos Pilas (Mexico): F1435.1.D67
Douglas, Camp, Chicago, Illinois
   Military prison
      Civil War: E616.D7
Douglas, Sir James: F1088
Douglas, Stephen Arnold: E415.9.D73
   Debates with Lincoln, 1858: E457.4
Douglas, Thomas, 5th Earl of Selkirk: F1063
Douglass, Frederick: E449
Doukhobors in Canada: F1035.D76
Dover (Delaware): F174.D74
Dover (New Hampshire): F44.D7
Drachita Indians: F2823.D5
Draft riot (New York), 1863: F128.44
Drake, Sir Francis: E129.D7
Drama, Indian: E98.D8, F1219.3.D8

Drayton, John: E263.S7
Dred Scott case: E450
Drew, Daniel: F124
Drinking horns: F2230.1.D75
Drinking vessels, Indian: F2230.1.D75
Droop Mountain, Battle of, 1863: E475.76
Drug use, Indian: F1219.3.D83,
   F2230.1.D78, F3429.3.D79
Drugs, Indian: E98.N5, F2230.1.N37,
   F2270.1.N35, F3721.3.N35
Drummond, Lake (Virginia): F232.D7
Drummond Island (Michigan): F572.D88
Druzes in the United States: E184.D78
Dry Fork River and region (West Virginia):
   F247.D79
Dry Tortugas
   Civil War operations, 1861: E471.53
Du Pont, Samuel Francis: E467.1.D9
Duane, James: E302.6.D8
Duane, William: E302.6.D82
Duane, William John: F153
Duarte, Juan Pablo: F1938.4
Dubuque (Iowa): F629.D8
Duché letters: E216
Duck Creek (Ohio): F497.H2
Duck Mountain Provincial Park (Manitoba):
   F1064.D8
Dudley, Thomas: F67
Dudley Indians: E99.D8
Dudley's defeat, 1813: E356.D8
Dufferin Co. (Ontario): F1059.D88
Dukhobors in Canada: F1035.D76
Dulany, Daniel: E278.D94
Dulce, Golfo (Costa Rica): F1549.D8
Dulles, John Foster: E748.D868
Duluth (Minnesota): F614.D8
Duncan, Joseph: F545
Dunes of
   Illinois: F547.M56
   Indiana: F532.M67
Dunes region (Indiana): F532.M67
Dunes State Park (Indiana): F532.I5
Dunmore, Lake (Vermont): F57.A2
Dunmore's War, 1774: E83.77
Dunn, William McKee: E415.9.D9
Dunne, Edward Fitzsimons: F546
Duportail, Louis Lebegue de Presle: E207.D9
Durand de Villegagnon, Nicolas: F2529
Durango, Mexico (State): F1276
Durant, Thomas Jefferson: F374
Durazno, Uruguay (Dept.): F2731.D8
Durfee, Amos: F1032
Durham Co. (Ontario): F1059.D93
Durward's Glen (Wisconsin): F587.S2
Dutch
   Discovery and exploration of America
      Post-Columbian: E135.D9
      Pre-Columbian: E109.D9
Dutch America
   Dutch Guiana: F2401+
Dutch American Union, 1828-1845
   Dutch Guiana: F2424
Dutch attack on Puerto Rico, 1625: F1973
Dutch Blockade of Venezuela, 1908: F2325

Dutch colonies in America
  Brazil (1624-1654): F2532
  Connecticut: F97
  Dutch Guiana: F2423
  Dutch West Indies: F2141
  Guiana (Early colonies): F2383, F2423
  New Netherlands (1610-1664): F122+
  New Sweden (1629-1664): F167
Dutch conquest of Brazil, 1624-1654: F2532
Dutch conquest of Delaware, 1655: F167
Dutch conquest of New Sweden: F167
Dutch conquest of New York: F122+
Dutch Guiana: F2401+
  Early history of separate colonies: F2383
  Raleigh's explorations, 1595-1617:
    E129.R2
Dutch in Argentina: F3021.D87
Dutch in Brazil: F2659.D7
Dutch in Canada: F1035.D8
Dutch in South America: F2239.D8
Dutch in the American Revolution:
  E269.D88
Dutch in United States: E184.D9
Dutch in Venezuela: F2349.D8
Dutch-Indian War, 1643-1645: E83.65
Dutch West India Company
  Dutch Guiana: F2423
Dutch West Indies: F2141
Dutra, Eurico Gasper: F2538
Duwamish Indians: E99.D9
Dwellings
  Indian: E98.D9, F1219.3.D9,
    F2519.3.D84, F3320.1.D83
    Pre-Columbian America: E59.D9
Dzibilchaltún (Mexico): F1435.1.D85
Dzibilnocac Site (Mexico): F1435.1.D87

E

Eagle Creek and Valley, Alberta: F1079.E24
Eagle Lake (California): F868.L33
Eagles Mere (Pennsylvania): F157.S67
Earle, Thomas: F153
Early, Jubal Anderson: E467.1.E13
Earthquakes
  Costa Rica: F1556.C3
  Guatemala: F1466.4, F1466.45
  Jamaica: F1884, F1886
  Salvador: F1488
  Venezuela: F2324
East, Dept. of the, June-Aug., 1863: E475.5
East Baton Rouge Parish (Louisiana):
  F377.E17
East Bay (California): F868.E22
East Boston (Massachusetts): F73.68.E2
East Carroll Parish (Louisiana): F377.E2
East Europeans in Canada: F1035.E28
East Europeans in the United States:
  E184.E17
East Feliciana Parish (Louisiana): F377.E3
East Florida: F314
  Revolution: E263.F6
East Gallatin River (Montana): F737.G2
East Hampton (New York): F129.E13

East Indians
  Discovery of America
    Pre-Columbian: E109.E2
East Indians in America: E29.E37
East Indians in British Guiana: F2391.E2
East Indians in Canada: F1035.E3
East Indians in Jamaica: F1896.E2
East Indians in Surinam: F2431.E2
East Indians in the Caribbean: F2191.E27
East Indians in the United States: E184.E2
East Jersey, 1676-1702: F137
East Maine Conference Seminary,
  Bucksport, and the Civil War:
  E541.E13
East North Central States: F476+
East Orange (New Jersey): F144.O6
East St. Louis (Illinois): F549.E2
East Syrians in the United States: E184.C36
East Tennessee: F442.1
  Mountain whites of the South: F210
East Tennessee campaign, 1863: E475.85
Easter Island (Chile): F3169
Eastern Indian wars (New England), 1722-
  1726: E83.72
Eastern North American Indians: E78.E2
Eastern shore of Maryland: F187.E2
Eastern shore of Virginia: F232.E2
Eastern Townships (Quebec): F1054.E13
Eaton, William: E302.6.E16
Ebey's Landing National Historical Preserve
  (Washington): F897.I7
Ecab, Mexico (Mayas): F1435.1.E32
Ece'je Indians: F3430.1.E78
Echeverría, Esteban: F2846
Echeverría, Luis: F1235.5.E25
Ecleto Creek and Valley (Texas): F392.W7
Economic conditions
  Afro-Americans: E185.8
  Indians: E98.E2, F1219.3.E2,
    F2319.3.E26, F3069.3.E2,
    F3429.3.E2, F3721.3.E25
    Pre-Columbian America: E59.E3
  Jews: E184.36.E25
Ecuador: F3701+
  Leticia dispute, 1932-1934: F2281.B7P1+
  Member of Republic of Colombia, 1822-
    1830: F2274, F3734
  Military history
    Civil wars: F3736
      Conquistadors: F3733
    Wars of independence, 1809-1830:
      F3734
Ecuadorians in the United States: E184.E28
Eden Valley (Wyoming): F767.S9
Edisto Island (South Carolina): F277.B3
Edmonton (Alberta): F1079.5.E3
Education
  Indians: E96+, F2519.3.E2, F2679.3.E38,
    F3320.1.E4, F3429.3.E3
  Chile: F3069.3.E38
  French Guina: F2460.2.E38
  Pre-Columbia America: E59.E4
Edwards, Ninian: F545
Edward's Ferry, Action near, 1861: E472.63

Edwards Plateau (Texas): F392.E33
Edzná Site (Mexico): F1435.1.E37
Egg Harbor, N.J., Skirmish of, 1778:
  E241.L7
Egyptian influences, Indian: F3429.3.E35
Egyptians
  Discovery of America
    Pre-Columbian: E109.E3
Egyptians in the United States: E184.E38
Eiriksson, Leiv: E105
Eisenhower, Dwight David: E742.5.E37,
  E836
  Administrations, 1953-1961: E835+
  Family: E837
Eisenhower, Mamie (Doud): E837
Ekab, Mexico: F1435.1.E32
El Arbolillo (Mexico)
  Indian antiquities: F1219.1.T43
El Beni, Bolivia (Dept.): F3341.B4
El Camino Real (California): F868.E28
El Caney, Battle of, 1898: E717.1
El Dorado: E121+
El Dorado Lake (Kansas): F687.B9
El Gran Chaco: F2876
El Loa (Chile): F3170
El Malpais National Conservation Area (New
  Mexico): F802.C54
El Malpais National Monument (New
  Mexico): F802.C54
El Misti (Volcano): F3451.A7
El Morro National Monument (New
  Mexico): F802.E5
El Oro, Ecuador (Province): F3741.E4
El Paso (Texas): F394.E4
El Salvador: F1481+
Elbert, Samuel: E207.E3
Electoral Commission, 1877: E680
Electronic information resource catalogs
  United States history: E175.88
Eleven Point Wild and Scenic River
  (Missouri): F472.E4
Elgin Co. (Ontario): F1059.E4
Elizabeth (New Jersey): F144.E4
  Battle of, 1780: E241.E39
Elizabeth City (North Carolina)
  Capture, 1862: E473.3
Elizabeth City Parish (Virginia): F232.E6
Elizabeth Islands (Massachusetts): F72.E5
Elizabethtown, North Carolina, Battle of,
  1781: E241.E4
Elk Island National Park (Alberta): F1079.E5
Elk River and Valley (B.C.): F1089.E38
Elk River and Valley (West Virginia):
  F247.E4
Ellery, William: E302.6.E3
Ellesmere Island (Nunavut): F1144.E44
Elliott, Jesse Duncan: E353.1.E4
Elliott, Stephen: E467.1.E4
Elliott Island (Maryland): F187.D6
Ellsworth, Ephraim Elmer: E467.1.E47
Ellsworth, Oliver: E302.6.E4
Ellsworth Canyon (Nevada): F847.N9

Elmira (New York)
  Military prison
    Civil War: E616.E4
Elmwood (Pennsylvania): F158.68.E4
Eloida Lake region (Ontario): F1059.E46
Elsinore, Lake and region (California):
  F868.R6
Emancipation of slaves
  United States: E453
Emancipation Proclamation: E453
Embargo, 1794: E313+
Embera Indians: F2270.2.E43
Embroidery, Indian: E98.E5, F1435.3.E52
Emerald Bay and region (California):
  F868.O6
Emerillon Indians: F2460.1.E5
Emigrant Trail (California): F868.S5
Empire Mine State Historic Park
    (California): F868.N5
Employment
  Indians: F1219.76.E47, F2319.3.E46,
      F3069.3.E46, F3429.3.E45
    Pre-Columbian America: E59.E3
Enauenê-Nauê Indians: F2520.1.S24
Encantadas (Islands), Ecuador: F3741.G2
Encarnación (Paraguay): F2695.E5
Enchanted Hill (California): F868.S18
Enchanted Islands (Ecuador): F3741.G2
Enchanted Rock State Natural Area (Texas):
  F392.E64
Endecott, John: F67
Endless Caverns (Virginia): F232.S47
Endless Mountains (Pennsylvania):
  F157.E45
Ene River and Valley (Peru): F3451.J9
English colonies in America: E162, E188
  Bahamas: F1650+
  Bermudas: F1630+
  British Guiana: F2383
  British West Indies: F2131
  Cuba: F1781
  Falkland Islands: F3031
  Florida, East and West (1763-1783): F314
  Florida, West and East: F301
  Jamaica (1655-): F1861+
  Labrador: F1140
  New Haven Colony: F98
  New Plymouth Colony: F68
  Newfoundland: F1121+
  Roanoke Colonies (Virginia), 1584-1590:
    F229
  Thirteen North American colonies (before
    1776): E162, E163, E186+
English conquest of
  Delaware, 1664: F167
  New France, 1629: F1030
  New Netherlands, 1664: F122.1, F167
English explorers of America: E127+
English invasion of Nicaragua, 1780-1781:
  F1526.25
English settlements
  Dutch Guiana: F2423
  French Guiana: F2462
  Illinois: F547.E3

English-speaking Canadians: F1035.E53
English-speaking Caribbean: F2130
English West Indian expeditions, 1654-1655,
    1695: F1621
English West Indian expeditions, 1739-1742:
    F2272.5
Enid (Oklahoma): F704.E6
Entiat Indians: E99.E42
Entre Rios, Argentina (Province): F2896
  Indian antiquities: F2821.1.E5
Epena Saija Indians: F2270.2.E53
Epidemics
  Guatemala: F1466.45
Ericson (Ericsson), Leif: E105
Ericsson Monument (Washington, D.C.):
  F203.4.E6
Erie (Pennsylvania): F159.E7
Erie, Fort
  Siege, 1814: E356.E5
Erie, Lake, Battle of, 1813: E356.E6
Erie, Lake, region: F555
  New York: F127.E65
  Ohio: F497.E6
  Ontario: F1059.E6
  Pennsylvania: F157.E6
Erie Canal
  Local history: F127.E5
Erie Indians: E99.E5
Escalante Canyon (Colorado): F782.E82
Escobedo, Mariana: F1233
Escondido Valley (California): F868.S15
Ese Ejja Indians: F3430.1.E78
Eskimauan Indians: E99.E7
Esmeralda Indians: F3722.1.E8
Esmeraldas, Ecuador (Province): F3741.E6
Esopus Indian wars, 1659-1664: E83.663
Esopus Indians: E99.E8
Española Valley (New Mexico): F802.E8
Espionage in the United States: E743.5
Espírito Santo (Brazil): F2561
Espiritu Pampa, Peru
  Indian antiquities: F3429.1.E7
Essequibo (Dutch colony): F2383, F2423
Essequibo Co. (British Guiana): F2387.E8
Essex (U.S. ironclad): E474.11
Essex Co. (Ontario): F1059.E7
Estates, Trust
  Indians: E98.F3
Estatoe River (North Carolina): F262.A9
Estes Park region (Colorado): F782.L2
Esther Mountain
  New York: F127.A2
Estigarribia, José Félix: F2689
Estimé, Dumarsais: F1927
Estonians in Brazil: F2659.E8
Estonians in Canada: F1035.E85
Estonians in the United States: E184.E7
Estrada Cabrera, Manuel: F1466.45
Estrada Palma, Tomás: F1787
Ethics, Indian: E98.E83
Ethiopians in the United States: E184.E74
Ethnic elements in the population (America):
  F1392.A+, F1419.A+

Ethnic identity
  Indians
    Brazil: F2519.3.E83
    Ecuador: F3721.3.E84
    Guatemala: F1465.3.E84
    Mayas: F1435.3.E72
    Nicaragua: F1525.3.E74
    North America: E98.E85
    Peru: F3429.3.E84
    Pre-Columbian America: E59.E75
  Jews: E184.36.E84
Ethnic relations
  Jews: E184.36.E86
Ethnobiology
  Indians: E98.B54
    Mayas: F1435.3.E73
    Nicaragua: F1525.3.E76
Ethnobotany
  Afro-American: E185.89.E8
  Indian: E98.B7, F1435.3.E74,
      F2230.1.B7, F3429.3.E86
Ethnozoology, Indian: F1219.3.E83,
    F1435.3.E76, F2230.1.E87
Eugene (Oregon): F884.E9
European intervention in Mexico, 1861-
    1867: F1233
Europeans in America: E29.E87
Europeans in Brazil: F2659.E95
Europeans in Latin America: F1419.E87
Europeans in the United States: E184.E95
Evacuation Day
  New York City: E239
Evangeline Parish (Louisiana): F377.E8
Evans, John: F780
Evans, Robley Dunglison: E182
Evanston (Illinois): F549.E8
Evansville (Indiana): F534.E9
Evarts, William Maxwell: E664.E88
Everard, Sir Richard: F257
Everett, Edward: E340.E8
  Collected works: E337.8.E9
Everett, Mount (Massachusetts): F72.B5
Everglades (Florida): F317.E9
Everglades National Park: F317.E9
Ewell, Richard Stoddert: E467.1.E86
Ewing, Charles: E467.1.E9
Ewing, Thomas: E340.E9
Ex-slaves, Afro-American: E185.2,
    E185.93.A+
Excavations
  Archaeology: E51+
Expansion
  United States: E179.5
Expunging resolutions, 1834-1835: E384.7
Extraterrestrial influences, Indian:
  F1435.3.E87
Eyak Indians: E99.E9
Eyre, Edward John: F1886

Folk, Joseph Wingate: F466
Folk literature
  Venezuela
    Indians: F2319.3.F58
Folk literature, Indian: E98.F58,
    F2230.1.F56
Folklore
  Eskimos: E99.E7
  Indian: F2679.3.F64, F2821.3.F6,
    F3429.3.F6
  Indians: E98.F6, F1435.3.F6, F1465.3.F6,
    F2230.1.F6, F2519.3.F6
    Chile: F3069.3.F64
    Panama: F1516.3.F64
    Pre-Columbian America: E59.F6
    Venezuela: F2319.3.F6
Folly Island (South Carolina): F277.C4
Folsom culture: E99.F65
Fonseca, Manuel Deodoro da: F2537
Food
  Indian: E98.F7, F1435.3.F7,
    F2519.3.F63, F2821.3.F7,
    F3429.3.F65
    Bolivia: F3320.1.F64
    Pre-Columbian America: E59.F63
Foote, Andrew Hull: E467.1.F68
Foote, Henry Stuart: E415.9.F7
Footwear, Indian: E98.F73
Foraker, Joseph Benson: E664.F69
Forbes Road (Pennsylvania): F157.F65
Force, Peter
  Tracts and other papers: E187.F69
Ford, Gerald R.: E865+
Ford, Thomas: E545
Ford Theatre (Washington, D.C.): F204.F6
Fordham Manor (New York): F127.W5
Foreign intervention in Cuba: F1786
Foreign intervention in Mexico, 1861-1867:
  F1233
Foreign intervention in Nicaragua, 1848- :
  F1526.27
Foreign intervention in Uruguay: F2726
Foreign public opinion
  United States
    Civil War: E469.8
    Revolution: E249.3
Foreign relations
  United States: E183.7+
    By period
      Revolution, 1775-1783: E249
      1783-1789: E303
      War of 1812: E358
      War with Mexico, 1845-1848:
        E408
      Civil War, 1861-1865: E469+
      1865-1900: E661.7
      20th century: E744+, E840+
Foreigners in the United States
  American Revolution: E269.F67
  Civil War: E540.F6
Forest Lawn Memorial Park (Glendale,
  California): F869.G5
Forest of Nisene Marks State Park
  (California): F868.S3

Forest reserves
  United States
    Parks: E160
Forests, National
  United States: E160
Forestville State Park (Minnesota): F612.F4
Formosa, Argentina (Territory): F2901
Fornio Indians: F2520.1.F8
Forrest, Nathan Bedford: E467.1.F72
  Expedition into West Tennessee, 1861-
    1863: E474.46
  Expedition into West Tennessee and
    Kentucky: E476.17
Forrest's Cavalry Corps
  Confederate Army: E547.F6
Fort Ancient culture: E99.F67
Fort Anne Park (Nova Scotia): F1039.A2
Fort Beauséjour National Park (New
  Brunswick): F1044.F6
Fort Chambly National Historic Park
  (Quebec): F1054.C44
Fort Churchill Historic State Monument
  (Nevada): F847.F6
Fort Clatsop National Memorial (Oregon):
  F882.C53
Fort Custer (Montana): F737.Y4
Fort Dearborn Massacre, 1812: E356.C53
Fort Frederica National Monument: F292.F7
Fort Jefferson National Monument: F317.M7
Fort Loudoun Lake (Tennessee): F443.L9
Fort Louisbourg National Historic Park
  (Nova Scotia): F1039.5.L8
Fort McHenry National Monument and
  Historic Shrine: E356.B2
Fort Pillow State Park (Tennessee):
  F443.L35
Fort Raleigh National Historic Site (North
  Carolina): F262.R4
Fort Ridgely Battle, 1862: E83.86
Fort Rock Valley (Oregon): F882.L15
Fort Ross, Franklin District (Trading post):
  F1105.5.F6
Fort Shaw Indian School (Great Falls,
  Mont.): E97.6.F66
Fort Sisseton State Park (South Dakota):
  F657.R6
Fort Smith, Mackenzie District: F1100.5.F6
Fort Snelling (Minnesota): F614.F7
Fort Wayne (Indiana): F534.F7
Fort Worth (Texas): F394.F7
Fortaleza (Brazil): F2651.F6
Fortress of Louisbourg National Historic
  Park (Nova Scotia): F1039.5.L8
Forty Mile Coulee and Valley (Alberta):
  F1079.F67
Forty Mile Coulee Reservoir (Alberta):
  F1079.F67
Forty-Second Street, New York: F128.67.F7
Foster, Sir George Eulas: F1033
Founders and Patriots of America: E186.6
Four Corners Region: F788.5
Fourth of July: E286.A1+
Fowler, John: E302.6.F6
Fox Indians: E99.F7

Fox Islands (Michigan): F572.L45
Fox River and Valley
  Illinois: F547.F77
  Wisconsin
    Columbia Co.-Brown Co.: F587.F72
    Waukesha Co.: F587.F7
France
  Attacks on Venezuela, 1679: F2322
  Attempted invasion of Jamaica, 1694,
    1782, 1806: F1884
  Blockade of
    Argentine coast, 1838: F2846.3
    Río de la Plata, 1845-1848: F2846.3
  Conquest of British Guiana, 1782: F2383
  Discovery and exploration of America:
    E131+
  Military history in America
    American Revolution: E265
  Naval operations in West Indies, 1775-
    1783: E271
  Relations with U.S., 1789-1797: E313+
  Sale of Louisiana: E333
  Troubles with Mexico, 1838-1839: F1232
  Troubles with U.S., 1796-1800: E323
Frances Lake (Yukon): F1095.F7
Francia, Juan Carlos: F2686
Franciscan missions
  California: F862, F864
Franco, Rafael: F2688
Franconia Notch: F41.6.F8
Frankford (Pennsylvania). Arsenal:
  F158.8.A7
Frankfort (Kentucky): F459.F8
Frankland: F436
Franklin, Benjamin: E302.6.F7+
  Collected works: E302.F8
Franklin, William: F137
Franklin, William Buel: E467.1.F83
Franklin (State): F436
Franklin (Tennessee), Battle of, 1864:
  E477.52
Franklin District (Canada): F1101+
  Eskimos: E99.E7
  Indians: E78.F73
Franklin Mountains, Mackenzie District:
  F1100.F7
Franklin Parish (Louisiana): F377.F7
Franklin Park (Boston): F73.65
Franquistas (Paraguay): F2689
Fraser River and Valley (British Columbia):
  F1089.F7
Frayser's Farm, Battle of, 1862: E473.68
Frederick Parish (Virginia): F232.C59
Fredericksburg (Virginia): F234.F8
Fredericksburg, Battle of, 1862: E474.85
Fredericksburg and Spotsylvania County
  National Military Park: E474.85
Fredericksville Parish (Virginia): F232.F76
Fredericton (New Brunswick): F1044.5.F8
Fredonian Insurrection, 1826-1827: F389
Free Afro-Americans: E185, E185.97.A+
  The North: E185.9
  The South before 1863: E185.18
Free states (U.S.), Slaves in: E450

Gardner, Augustus Peabody: E664.G2

Garfield, James Abram: E660.G2, E687
  Administration, 1881: E686
  Memorial, Philadelphia: F158.64.G3
  Statue, Washington, D.C.: F203.4.G2

Garfield Co. (Colorado): F782.G3

Garfield Colony (Alabama): F332.B6

Garibaldi, Giuseppe: F2536

Garibaldi Provincial Park (British
    Columbia): F1089.G3

Garner, James Nance: E748.G23

Garrison, William Lloyd: E449

Garrison mob, Boston, 1835: E450

Garry, Fort (Lower) (Manitoba): F1064.G22

Gaspar Rodríguez, José: F2686

Gaspé District (Quebec): F1054.G2

Gaspé Peninsula (Quebec): F1054.G2

Gaspee affair, June 1772: E215.6

Gaspésie, La (Quebec): F1054.G2

Gaston, William: E340.G2

Gates, Horatio: E207.G3

Gates of the Arctic National Park and
    Preserve (Alaska): F912.G36

Gateway National Recreation Area
  New Jersey: F142.G37
  New York: F127.G15

Gatineau River and Valley
  Quebec: F1054.G26

Gauchos: F2217
  Argentina: F2926
  Brazil: F2621
  Paraguay: F2682.9
  Uruguay: F2722.9

Gaviões Indians: F2520.1.G37

Gayarré, Charles Étienne Arthur: F374

Gaynor, William Jay: F128.5

Gazos Creek and Valley (California):
    F868.G39

Gê Indians: F2520.1.G4

Geary, John White: E467.1.G29

Geffrard, Fabre Nicolas: F1926

Geisel, Ernesto: F2538.27.G44

Gem Valley (Idaho): F752.C3

Genealogía de Zolín (Codices):
    F1219.56.G46

Genealogy
  Ecuador: F3721.3.G45
  Peru: F3429.3.G4
  United States
    Afro-Americans: E185.96+
    American colonists: E187.5, E302.5
    Indians: E98.G44
    West, The: F590.5

General Grant Grove area (California):
    F868.K48

General Grant National Park (California):
    F868.K48

General Slocum (Steamboat)
  Disaster, 1904: F128.5

Genet, E.C.: E313+

Genoa Columbus celebration, 1892: E119

Gentile Valley (Idaho): F752.C3

Geode State Park (Iowa): F627.H5

Geography, Historical
  America: E21.7

Geography, Historical — Continued
  Latin America: F1408.8
  United States: E179.5

George, Fort (Ontario)
  Battle, 1812: E356.G4

George, James Zachariah: E664.G34

George, Lake (New York): F127.G3
  Battle, 1775: E199

George III, "Olive branch" petition to (1775):
    E215.95

George Dawson, Mount (British Columbia):
    F1089.C7

George Rogers Clark Memorial Park (Ohio):
    F497.C5

George Washington Memorial Parkway
    (Virginia): F232.G38

George Washington Parkway: F232.G38

George Washington-Robert Morris-Haym
    Salomon Monument (Chicago,
    Illinois): F548.64.G4

Georgetown (British Guiana): F2389.G3

Georgetown (District of Columbia): F202.G3
  Saint John's Church: F203.2.S14

Georgia: F281+
  Afro-Americans: E185.93.G4
  Cession of western lands: F290
  Confederate history: E559.1+
  Counties, etc.: F292.A+
  Indians: E78.G3
  Reconstruction, 1865-1877: F291
  Saint Augustine expeditions, 1740, 1743:
    F314
  Slavery: E445.G3
  South Carolina cession, 1787: F292.B7
  Wars
    Civil War: E503.1+, E559.1+
      Military operations: E470.6,
        E470.65
    Indian wars: E83.813, E83.817,
      E83.836
    Queen Anne's War, 1702-1713: E197
    Revolution: E263.G3
      Military operations: E230+
    War of 1812: E355, E359.5.G4

Georgia, North: F291.7

Georgia, South: F291.8

Georgia, Strait of, Region (British
    Columbia): F1089.G44

Georgia (Colony): F289

Georgian Bay region (Ontario): F1059.G3

Georgians (Transcaucasians) in the United
    States: E184.G27

German-Anglo Blockade of Venezuela,
    1902: F2325

German colonies in America
  Brazil
    Espírito Santo: F2561
    Peru (Pozuzo colony): F3451.H8
    Rio Grande do Sul: F2621
    Santa Catharina: F2626
  Venezuela
    Welser colony: E135.G3, F2322

German explorers of America: E135.G3

German mercenaries in the American
    Revolution: E268

Germans in America: E29.G3

Germans in Argentina: F3021.G3

Germans in Bolivia: F3359.G3

Germans in Brazil: F2659.G3

Germans in Canada: F1035.G3

Germans in Central America: F1440.G3

Germans in Chile: F3285.G3

Germans in Colombia: F2299.G3

Germans in Costa Rica: F1557.G3

Germans in Guatemala: F1477.G3

Germans in Latin America: F1419.G3

Germans in Mexico: F1392.G4

Germans in Nicaragua: F1537.G47

Germans in Paraguay: F2699.G3

Germans in Peru: F3619.G3

German in South America: F2239.G3

Germans in the United States: E184.G3
  American Revolution: E268, E269.G3
  Civil War: E540.G3
  War of 1898: E725.5.G3

Germans in Uruguay: F2799.G3

Germans in Venezuela: F2349.G3
  Welsers: F2322

Germantown (Pennsylvania): F159.G3

Germantown, Battle of, 1777: E241.G3

Gerry, Elbridge: E302.6.G37

Gettysburg, Battle of, 1863: E475.53

Gettysburg address: E475.55

Gettysburg National Cemetery: E475.55

Gettysburg National Military Park: E475.56

Ghanaians in the United States: E184.G44

Ghent, Treaty of, 1814: E358

Gibara (Cuba): E1849.G5

Gibbon Falls (Wyoming): F767.Y44

Gibson, John Bannister: F153

Giddings, Joshua Reed: E415.9.G4

Gila River and Valley
  Arizona: F817.G52
  New Mexico: F802.G54

Gilbert, Sir Humphrey: E129.G4

Gilbert, Thomas: E278.G4

Giles, William Branch: E302.6.G47

Gillem's raid, 1865: E477.9

Gilmore, J.R.
  Conference with Davis, 1854: E469+

Gilmore Ranch (Idaho): F752.I2

Gilpin, Edward Woodward: F169

Gilpin, Henry Dilworth: E340.G48

Gilpin, William: F593

Ginkgo Petrified Forest State Park
    (Washington): F897.K53

Girty, Simon: F517

Gitksan Indians: E99.K55

Glace Bay (Nova Scotia): F1039.5.G5

Glacier Bay (Alaska): F912.G5

Glacier Bay National Monument (Alaska):
    F912.G5

Glacier National Park: F737.G5

Glacier National Park (British Columbia):
    F1089.G55

Glass, Carter: E748.G53

Glen Canyon National Recreation Area
    (Ariz. and Utah): F832.G5

Glendale, Battle of, 1862: E473.68
Glendale (California): F869.G5
Glengarry Co. (Ontario): F1059.G5
Glenwood Canyon (Colorado): F782.G3
Glenwood Cemetery (Washington, D.C.):
    F203.1.G5
Globe (Arizona): F819.G5
Glover, John: E207.G56
Goajira, Colombia (Territory): F2281.G8
Goajira peninsula (Colombia): F2281.G8
Goajiro Indians: F2270.2.G6
Goat Island (California): F869.S3
Goat Island (New York): F127.N8
Gobernador Canyon (New Mexico):
    F802.G62
Godfrey, Edward: F23
Goebel, William: F456
Goiás State (Brazil): F2566
    Indian antiquities: F2519.1.G68
Goiaz State (Brazil): F2566
Gold Creek and Valley (Alaska): F912.G64
Gold discoveries
    Alaska: F909
    California: F865
Golden Gate National Recreation Area
    (California): F868.S156
Golden Isles (Georgia): F292.G58
Goldsborough (North Carolina), Expedition
    to, Dec. 1862: E474.52
Goldwork
    Aztecs: F1219.76.G64
    Indians: F1219.3.G57, F1434.2.G6,
        F1545.3.G65, G3429.3.G5
        Pre-Columbian America: E59.G55
        South America: F2230.1.G64
Golfo Dulce (Costa Rica): F1549.D8
Goliad State Park (Texas): F392.G6
Gómez, Esteban: E125.G6
Gómez, Juan Carlos: F2726
Gómez, Juan Gualberto: F1787
Gómez, Juan Vicente: F2325
Gómez, Laureano: F2278
Gómez y Báez, Máximo: F1783
Gonave Island (Haiti): F1929.G6
Gonzáles, Joaqu in Víctor: F2848
Gonzalez Island (Chile): F3131
Gonzáles Suárez, Federico: F3736
Gooding, Oliver Paul: E467.1.G6
Goodnight, Charles: F391+
Goodpasture, Jefferson Dillard: F436
Gookin, Daniel: F67
Goose Creek Island (North Carolina):
    F262.P2
Gorda, Sierra: F1339
Gordon, John Brown: E467.1.G66
Gore, Christopher: F69
Gorgas, Josiah: E467.1.G68
Gorham, Nathaniel: E302.6.G66
Gorman, Arthur Pue: E664.G67
Gorman, Willis Arnold: F606
Gorsuch, Edward
    Christiana riot, 1851: E450
Gorton, Samuel: F82
Gosiute Indians: E99.G67
Gosnold, Bartholomew: F7

Goulart, Joao Belchior Marques:
    F2538.22.G6
Goulart administration (Brazil): F2538.2+
Gourds, Indian: F1219.3.G59
Gourgues, Dominique de: F314
Government, Indian: F2519.3.P58
    Central America: F1545.3.P57
    Ecuador: F3721.3.P74
    Pre-Columbian America: E59.P73
Government agencies dealing with Indians:
    E91+
Government and politics
    Bolivia
        Indians: F3320.1.P56
Government relations
    Indians
        Argentina: F2821.3.G65
        Bolivia: F3320.1.G6
        Brazil: F2519.3.G6
        Chile: F3069.3.G6
        Ecuador: F3721.3.G68
        Panama: F1565.3.G68
        Paraguay: F2679.3.G67
        Peru: F3429.3.G6
        Pre-Columbian America: E59.G6
Government services for Indians: E91+
Governor Shirley's War: E198
Governor's Island (New York): F128.68.G7
Governor's Land Archaeological District
    (Virginia): F232.C43
Goyataca Indians: F2520.1.G6
Goyaz, Brazil (State): F2566
    Indian antiquities: F2519.1.G68
Graceland Cemetery (Chicago):
    F548.612.G72
Gracias (Honduras): F1516.G7
Grady, Henry Woodfin: E664.G73
Graham, Joseph: E263.N8
Graham, William Alexander: E415.9.G7
Graham Co.
    Arizona: F817.G7
Graham Land (Palmer Peninsula): F3031+
Gran Chaco, El: F2876
Gran Montana (Venezuela): F2331.A93
Granada, Confederation of: F2276
Granada, Nicaragua (City): F1536.G72
    Rivalry with León: F1526.25
Granary Burial Ground (Boston): F73.61
Grand Army of the Republic: E462.1
Grand Camp Confederate Veterans,
    Department of Virginia: E483.28
Grand Canyon National Park: F788
Grand Canyon of the Arkansas (Colorado):
    F782.F8
Grand Canyon of the Colorado River: F788
Grand Central Passenger Station (Chicago):
    F548.8.G7
Grand Coulee Dam region (Washington):
    F897.C7
Grand Falls (Labrador): F1138.G7
Grand Falls (Newfoundland): F1124.5.G7
Grand Forks (North Dakota): F644.G8
Grand Gulf State Military Park (Mississippi):
    F347.C5

Grand Island
    Michigan: F572.G45
    Nebraska: F674.G7
    New York: F129.G68
Grand Isle (Louisiana): F377.J4
Grand Lake (Lake)
    Colorado: F782.G7
Grand Manan Island: F1044.G7
Grand Mesa (Colorado): F782.G73
Grand Rapids (Michigan): F574.G7
Grand River and Valley
    Colorado: F782.C7
    Michigan: F572.G46
    Ontario: F1059.G78
    Utah: F832.C7
Grand Staircase-Escalante National
    Monument (Utah): F832.G66
Grand Teton National Park (Wyoming):
    F767.T3
Grand Traverse Bay region (Michigan):
    F572.G5
Grandchildren of Presidents: E176.45
Grande Island Bay (Brazil): F2611
Grandfather Mountain (North Carolina):
    F262.B6
Grant, General National Park (California):
    F868.K48
Grant, Sir John Peter: F1886
Grant, Ulysses Simpson: E672
    Administrations, 1869-1877: E671
    Collected works: E660.G756
    Controversy with Sumner: E671
    Memorial (Washington, D.C.): F203.4.G7
    Monument and tomb (New York):
        F128.64.G7
Grant-Kohrs Ranch National Historic Site
    (Montana): F737.P88
Grant Parish (Louisiana): F377.G7
Grass Valley (Nevada): F847.G7
Grasslands National Park (Saskatchewan):
    F1074.G72
Grau Region
    Peru: F3451.G73
Grau San Martín, Ramón: F1788
Gravelly Run (Virginia), Battle of, 1865:
    E477.67
Graves-Cilley duel: E340.C5
Grays Harbor (Washington): F897.G84
Great Basin: F789
Great Basin Indians: E78.G67
Great Basin National Park (Nevada):
    F847.G73
Great Bear Lake, Mackenzie District:
    F1100.G7
Great Bridge (Virginia), Battle of, 1775:
    E241.G6
Great Britain
    Colonies in America: E162
    Discovery and exploration of America:
        E127+
    Military history
        Conquests of Jamaica, 1596, 1643,
            1655: F1884
        Invasion Haiti, 1793-1798: F1923

Great Britain — Continued
  Military history in America
    American Revolution: E230+
    Attacks on
      Venezuala, 1595-1598: F2322
    Blockade of
      Argentine coast, 1838: F2846.3
      Venezuela, 1902: F2325
    Capture of Martinique, 1809: F2081
    Conquests of British Guiana: F2383
    Invasion of
      La Plata, 1806-1807: F2845
      Nicaragua, 1780-1781: F1526.25
    Siege of Havana, 1762: F1781
    West Indian expeditions and
      campaigns
        1645-1655: F1621
        1739-1742: F2272.5
        1793-1815: F1621
  Mosquito coast, Nicaragua (Protectorate):
    F1529.M9
  Naval history
    American Revolution: E271
    War of 1812: E360
  Nootka Sound Controversy, 1789-1790:
    F1089.N8
  Occupation of
    Cuba, 1762-1763: F1781
    Oregon jointly with U.S., 1818-1846:
      F880
  Relations with U.S.: E183.8.A+
Great Falls (Montana): F739.G7
Great Falls of the Potomac: F187.M7
Great Gott Island
  Maine: F27.H3
Great Kanawha River and Valley (West
  Virginia): F247.K3
Great Lakes
  Indians: E78.G7
Great Miami River and Valley (Ohio):
  F497.M64
Great Onyx Cave (Kentucky): F457.B2
Great Pedee River (South Carolina): F277.P3
Great Plains: F590.3+
Great Plains Indians: E78.G73
Great Salt Lake, Desert, and region (Utah):
  F832.G7
Great Sand Dunes National Monument
  (Colorado): F782.G78
Great Savannah (Venezuela): F2331.B6
Great Smoky Mountains (Tennessee):
  F443.G7
Great Smoky Mountains National Park:
  F443.G7
Greater Antilles: F1741+
Greater New York: F128.5
Greeks
  Discovery of America
    Pre-Columbian: E109.G7
Greeks in Canada: F1035.G7
Greeks in South America: F2239.G74
Greeks in the United States: E184.G7
Greeks in Uruguay: F2799.G74

Greeley, Horace: E415.9.G8
Greeley (Colorado): F784.G7
Green, Andrew Haswell: F128.47
Green Bay (Wisconsin): F589.G7
Green Bay region: F587.G6
  Michigan: F572.G87
Green Island (Quebec): F1054.I5
Green Mountain boys: F52
Green Mountains (Vermont): F57.G8
Green River and Valley
  Kentucky: F457.G85
  Wyoming: F767.G7
Green Valley (Texas): F392.D4
Greenbrier River Trail (West Virginia):
  F247.G73
Greene, George Sears: E467.1.G79
Greene, Nathanael: E207.G9
Greenhalge, Frederic Thomas: F70
Greenville (South Carolina): F279.G79
Greenwater Lake Provincial Park
  (Saskatchewan): F1074.G74
Greenwich Village (New York): F128.68.G8
Grenada (West Indies): F2056
Grenadians in the United States: E184.G75
Grenadines (West Indies): F2061
Grenell Island (New York): F127.T5
Grenfell, Sir William Thomason: F1137
Grey Co. (Ontario): F1059.G84
Greylock Mountain (Massachusetts): F72.B5
Greytown (Nicaragua): F1536.S2
Grierson's Cavalry Raid, 1863: E475.23
Grijalva, Juan de: E125.G8
Grijalva River (Mexico): F1279
Grimes, James Wilson: E415.9.G85
Grindstone Island
  New York: F127.T5
Grinnell, Josiah Bushnell: E415.9.G86
Grinnell Land: F1105.G7
Groseilliers, Médard Chouart, sieur de:
  F1060.7
Grosse Île (Quebec): F1054.S3
Groton (Massachusetts): F74.G9
Groton Heights, Battle of, 1781: E241.G8
Grout, William Wallace: E467.1.G88
Groveton, Battle of, 1862: E473.77
Grow, Galusha Aaron: E415.9.G89
Grues, Île aux (Quebec): F1054.C8
Grundy, Felix: E340.G8
Grupo oficiales unidos (Argentina) Coup,
  1943: F2849
Guacanahua Indians: F3430.1.E78
Guachichile Indians: F1219
  Modern: F1221.G79
Guadalajara (Audiencia): F1296
Guadalajara (Mexico): F1391.G9
Guadalupe Club of 1848, Washington, D.C.:
  E401.2
Guadalupe Hidalgo, Treaty of, 1848: E408
Guadalupe Mountains
  New Mexico: F802.G93
  Texas: F392.G86
Guadalupe Mountains National Park:
  F392.G86

Guadeloupe (West Indies): F2066
Guaharibo Indians: F2520.1.G68
Guahibo Indians: F2319.2.G8
Guaica Indians: F2520.1.W3
Guáimaro (Cuba): F1839.G8
Guaíra Falls (Brazil): F2596
Guajajara Indians: F2520.1.T4
Guajira, Colombia (Territory): F2281.G8
Guale Indians: E99.G82
Guana Indians: F2520.1.G718
Guanabacoa (Cuba): F1799.G8
Guanabara: F2567
Guanacaste, Costa Rica (Province):
  F1549.G9
Guanajuato (Mexico)
  City: F1391.G98
  State: F1281
Guanano Indians: F2520.1.G72
Guane Indians: F2270.2.G8
Guantanamo, Cuba (Province): F1850+
Guaporé, Brazil (Territory): F2624
Guaraira Repans, Venezuela: F2331.A93
Guarani Indians: F2230.2.G72
Guarani War, 1754-1756: F2684
Guararapes, Battles at, 1648, 1649: F2532
Guarasu Indians: F3320.2.P37
Guarayo Indians: F3320.2.G8
Guarayo Indians (Tacanan): F3430.E78
Guarayú-tá Indians: F3320.2.P37
Guardia, Tomás: F1547.5
Guarequena Indians: F2319.2.A73
Guárico, Venezuela (State): F2331.G8
Guarijío Indians: F1221.G82
Guarino Indians: F2270.2.G83
Guarpe Indians: F2823.G8
Guartelá (Brazil)
  Region: F2596
Guasco River (Chile): F3131
Guatemala: F1461+
  Claims in British Honduras:
    F1449.B7G1+
  Confederación de Centro América:
    F1466.4
  Wars with
    Honduras: F1466.45, F1507.5
    Salvador: F1466.45, F1487.5
Guatemala (Audiencia): F1437
Guatemala (Dept.): F1469.G9
Guatemala Antigua: F1476.A5
Guatemala City (Guatemala): F1476.G9
Guatemalans in the United States: E184.G82
Guató Indians: F2520.1.G75
Guatuso Indians: F1545.2.G77
Guayacán Bay (Chile): F3161
Guayacundo Indians: F3722.1.G82
Guayacuruan Indians: F2230.2.G78
Guayaki Indians: F2679.2.G9
Guayama (Puerto Rico): F1981.G7
Guayana Indians: F2230.2.G75
Guayana Region (Venezuela): F2331.G83
Guayaqui Indians: F2679.2.G9
Guayaquil (Ecuador): F3791.G9
Guayaquil meeting, 1822: F2235.36

Guayas, Ecuador (Province): F3741.G9
  Indian antiquities: F3721.1.G9
Guaycuruan Indians: F2230.2.G78
Guaymi Indians: F1565.2.G8
Guayra Falls (Brazil): F2596
Güemes, Martín Miguel: F2845
Güenoa Indians: F2719.2.G84
Guenoc Valley (California): F868.L2
Guerrero, Mexico (State): F1286
Guerrillas in Civil War, 1861-1865: E470.45
Guetar Indians: F1545.2.G8
Guiana: F2351+
  Discovery and exploration: E111+,
    E121+, E129.R2
  Dutch settlements: F2383, F2423
  English settlements: F2383, F2423, F2461
  French settlements: F2462
  Raleigh's expeditions: E129.R2
  Willoughby and Hyde grant, 1663: F2423
Guiana, British: F2361+
Guiana, Dutch: F2401+
Guiana, French: F2441+
Guidebooks
  United States
    West, The: F590.3
Guilford Court House, Battle of, 1781:
  E241.G9
Guiteau, C.J.: E687.9
Gujaratis in the United States: E184.G84
Gulf, Department of the
  General Butler's administration, 1862:
    E510.1+
Gulf coast (U.S.): F296, F372
  Alabama: F332.G9
  Florida: F317.G8
  Louisiana: F377.G9
  Mississippi: F347.G9
  Texas: F392.G9
Gulf Islands (British Columbia): F1089.G8
Gulf Islands National Seashore
  Florida: F317.G8
  Mississippi: F347.G9
Gulf of Morrosquillo (Colombia): F2281.S82
Gulf of Panama: F1569.P35
Gulf States: F296
Gunby, John: E263.M3
Gunnison National Monument (Colorado):
  F782.B5
Gurupy (Gurupi) River (Brazil): F2571,
  F2586
Guthrie (Oklahoma): F704.G9
Guyana: F2361+
Guyanese in the United States: E184.G86
Guysborough Co. (Nova Scotia): F1039.G8
Guzmán Blanco, Antonio: F2325
Gwinnett, Button: E302.6.G95
Gwynn Island (Virginia): F232.M3
Gwynn's Island (Virginia): F232.M3
Gyitkshan Indians: E99.K55

H

Habeas corpus, Suspension of writ of
  U.S. Civil War: E458.8
Hackensack Indians: E99.H15
Hackensack Meadowland (New Jersey):
  F142.H35
Hackensack River and Valley (New Jersey):
  F142.B4
Hacker's Creek and Valley (West Virginia):
  F247.H17
Hackett, William Henry Young: F38
Hagerman Fossil Beds National Monument
  (Idaho): F752.T8
Haida Indians: E99.H2
Haisla Indians: E99.H23
Haiti (Island): F1900+
  French or Haitian colony: F1923, F1938.3
  Pre-Columbian history: F1909
  Spanish colony, 1492-1795: F1911
    Withdrawal of Spain, 1795: F1923
  Spanish colony, 1808-1822: F1938.3
  Union of whole island, 1822-1844:
    F1924, F1938.3
Haiti (Republic): F1912+
  Military history
    War of Independence, 1791-1804:
      F1923
Haitians in Canada: F1035.H34
Haitians in the American Revolution:
  E269.H3
Haitians in the Dominican Republic:
  F1941.H3
Haitians in the United States: E184.H27
Haldimand, Sir Frederick: F1032
Hale, John Parker: E415.9.H15
Hale, Nathan: E280.H2
Hale's Bar Dam Region
  Tennessee: F443.M32
Half Dome (California): F868.Y6
Haliburton, Sir Brenton: F1038
Haliburton, Thomas Chandler: F1038
Haliburton Co. (Ontario): F1059.H27
Halifax (Nova Scotia): F1039.5.H17
Halifax Co. (Nova Scotia): F1039.H3
Hall, Benjamin Franklin: F780
Hall, Lyman: E263.G3
Hall of Fame, New York University: E176.6
Halleck, Henry Wager: E467.1.H18
Hamblin, Jacob: F826
Hamer, Thomas Lyon: E403.1.H2
Hamilton (Bermuda Islands): F1639.H3
Hamilton (Ontario): F1059.5.H2
Hamilton, Alexander
  Collected works: E302.6.H2
Hamilton, Andrew: F152
Hamilton, Elizabeth (Schuyler): E302.6.H22
Hamilton Parish (Virginia): F232.H2
Hamlin, Hannibal: E415.9.H2
Hammond, Charles: E340.H2
Hammond, James Henry: F273
Hampton, Wade, 1754-1835: E353.1.H2
  Lake Champlain Campaign, 1813: E355.4
Hampton, Wade, 1818-1902: E467.1.H19

Hampton Institute, Hampton, Virginia:
  E97.6.H3
Hampton National Historic Site (Maryland):
  F187.B2
Hampton Plantation (South Carolina):
  F277.C4
Hampton Plantation State Park (South
  Carolina): F277.C4
Hampton Roads (Virginia): F232.H23
  Naval engagement in, 1862: E473.2
Hampton Roads Conference, 1865: E469+
Hampton's Cavalry Division Confederate
  Army: E547.H2
Han Indians: E99.H26
Hancock, Dorothy (Quincy): E302.6.H24
Hancock, John: E302.6.H23+
Hancock, Winfield Scott: E467.1.H2
Handicapped, Indian: E98.H35
Handicraft, Indian: E98.I5
Hanging Rock iron region, Ohio: F497.H35
Hanna, Marcus Alonzo: E664.H24
Hanover Parish
  Jamaica: F1891.H2
Hanson, John: E302.6.H27
Hants Co. (Nova Scotia): F1039.H4
Hanway trial
  Christiana riot: E450
Harakmbet Indians: F3430.1.M38
Harbors (U.S.): F73.63, F128.63, F158.63
Hardin, Benjamin: E340.H26
Harding, Florence Kling: E786.2
Harding, Warren Gamaliel: E786
  Administration, 1921-1923: E785
Hare Indians: E99.K28
Hare's Hill (Virginia), Battle of, 1865:
  E477.61
Harkers Island (North Island): F262.C23
Harlan, James: E664.H27
Harlem (New York): F128.68.H3
Harlem Heights, Battle of, 1776: E241.H2
Harlem River: F128.68.H4
Harmar's Expedition, 1790: E83.79
Harmon, Daniel Williams: F1060.7
Harney, William Selby: E181
Harney's Expedition: E83.854
Harper, Robert Goodloe: E302.6.H29
Harpers Ferry (West Virginia): F249.H2
  John Brown Raid, 1859: E451
  Military operations, 1864: E476.66
  Siege, 1862: E474.61
Harris, Benjamin Gwinn: E415.9.H28
  Court-martial, 1865: E458.8
Harris, Isham Green: E664.H31
Harrisburg (Pennsylvania): F159.H3
Harrisburg Convention, 1788: F153
Harrisburg Insurrection, 1838: F153
Harrison, Benjamin: E660.H29, E702
  Administration, 1889-1893: E701
Harrison, Fort
  Battle of, 1812: E356.H3
  Capture of, Sept. 1864: E477.21
Harrison, William Henry: E392
  Administration, 1841: E391
  Expedition, 1812: E355.2
  Northwestern campaign, 1813: E355.4

Harrod, James: F454

Harry S. Truman Dam and Reservoir (Missouri): F472.B4

Harstine Island (Washington): F897.M4

Hartford (Connecticut): F104.H3

Hartford (Sloop): E595.H2

Hartford Convention, 1814: E357.7

Hartranft, John Frederick: E467.1.H4

Hartstene Island (Washington): F897.M4

Hartstine Island (Washington): F897.M4

Harvard University and the Civil War: E541.H2

Harvard University and the War of 1898: E725.6.H3

Hasinai Indians: E99.H28

Haskin, John Bussing: E415.9.H35

Hastings (Nebraska): F674.H3

Hatcher Pass (Alaska): F912.H37

Hatteras Indians: E99.C91

Hatton, Robert: E467.1.H44

Haureaux, Ulises: F1938.4

Havana (City): F1799.H3
Siege, 1762-1763: F1781

Havana (Province): F1791+

Havasu Canyon (Arizona): F788

Havasupai Indians: E99.H3

Haverhill (Massachusetts)
Massacre, 1697: E196
Massacre, 1708: E197

Hawaii (State)
Afro-Americans: E185.93.H3

Hawaiians in Canada: F1035.H36

Hawaiians in the United States: E184.H3

Hawkins, Sir Richard: E129.H4

Hawley, Joseph: E263.M4

Hay, John: E664.H41

Hay-Buneau-Varilla Treaty, 1903: F1566.5

Hay-Herrán Treaty of 1903: F1566.5

Hay-Pauncefote Treaty, 1901: F1438

Haya de la Torre, Victor Raúl: F3448

Hayes, Rutherford Birchard: E682
Administration, 1877-1881: E681
Family: E682.1

Hayne, Robert Young: E340.H4

Hazard, Ebenezer
Historical collections: E187.H42

Hazel Creek and Valley (North Carolina): F262.S95

Health, Indian
North America: E98.D6

Health statistics
Civil War, 1861-1865: E621+

Hearne, Samuel: F1060.7

Hearst Castle (California): F868.S18

Hearst-San Simeon State Historical Monument (California): F868.S18

Heathcote, Caleb: F122+

Hecla Provincial Park (Manitoba): F1064.H42

Heiltsuk Indians: E99.H45

Hein, Pieter Pieterszoon
Capture of the Spanish silver-fleet: F1779

Helena, Arkansas, Battle of, 1863: E474.9

Helena (Montana): F739.H4

Hells Canyon National Recreation Area
Idaho: F752.H44
Oregon: F882.H44

Hemlock Lake (New York): F127.L7

Henderson, Richard: F454

Hendricks, Thomas Andrews: E664.H49

Hennepin, Louis: F1030.4
In Mississippi Valley: F352

Henrico Parish (Virginia): F232.H5

Henry, Alexander (1739-1824): F1060.7

Henry, Fort
Capture of, 1862: E472.96

Henry, John: E302.6.H4

Henry, John (British): E360.6.H5

Henry, Patrick: E302.6.H5

Henshaw, David: F69

Heredia, Costa Rica (Province): F1549.H5

Hereditary Order of Descendants of Colonial Governors: E186.99.H55

Hereditary patriotic societies
United States: E172.7+

Hereditary societies
United States
War of 1812: E351.3+

Herrán, Pedro Alcántara: F2276

Herrán-Hay Treaty of 1903: F1566.5

Herrera, Luis Alberto de: F2728

Herrera y Obes, Julio: F2726

Herring Lake (Michigan): F572.B4

Hessians in the American Revolution: E268

Heta Indians: F2520.1.H48

Hewitt, Abram Stevens: F128.47

Heyn, Piet: F1779

Hiawatha Island (New York): F127.S96

Hickey Plot, 1776: E277

Hickok, James Butler: F594

Hicks, Thomas Holliday: E415.9.H6

Hidalgo y Costilla, Míguel: F1232

Hidalgo, Mexico (State): F1291

Hidatsa Indians: E99.H6

Hiester, Joseph: F153

Higginson, Stephen: F69

Highland Lake (Connecticut): F102.L6

Highlands (New York): F127.H8

Hill, Benjamin Harvey: E664.H53

Hill, Isaac: F38

Hill Country (Texas): F392.T47

Hillegas, Michael: E302.6.H6

Hillhouse, James: E302.6.H63

Hilliard, Henry Washington: E415.9.H65

Hilton Head Island (South Carolina): F277.B3

Hinckley, John
Biography: E877.3

Hincks, Sir Francis: F1032

Hindman, William: E302.6.H65

Hindman, Fort, Arkansas
Operations against, Jan. 1863: E474.48

Hindu influences, Indian
Pre-Columbian America: E59.H54

Hindus in Canada: F1035.H54

Hispanic Americans in the United States: E184.S75

Hispaniola: F1900+

Hispano-American War, 1898: E714+

Hiss case, Alger: E743.5

Historians, American: E175.45+

Historic monuments
United States: E159, F20

Historiography
Central America: F1445.5+

Historiography, Indian: F3429.3.H5

History, Local, of the United States: F1+

Hitchiti Indians: E99.H65

Hmong (Asian people) in French Guiana: F2471.H56

Hmong (Asian people) in the United States: E184.H55

Hmu (Asian people) in the United States: E184.H55

Hmung (Asian people) in the United States: E184.H55

Hoar, George Frisbee: E664.H65

Hoar, Samuel: F70

Hobart, Garret Augustus: E664.H73

Hocking River and Valley, Ohio: F497.H7

Hodgenville (Kentucky). Lincoln Memorial Building: E457.32

Hoffman, Harold Giles: F139

Hoh River and Valley (Washington): F897.H63

Hohenau (Paraguay): F2695.H7

Hohokam culture: E99.H68

Holden, William Woods: F259

Holguín (Cuba): F1849.H6

Holguín Province
Cuba: F1854+

Holland Purchase (New York): F127.H7

Hollywood (California): F869.H74

Holmans Creek (Virginia): F232.S47

Holmes Creek and Valley
Alabama: F332.H56
Florida: F317.H73

Holston River and Valley (Tennessee): F443.H7

Holy Cross, Mount of the (Colorado): F782.H6

Holyoke, Mount (Massachusetts): F72.H3

Home Island (Connecticut): F102.F2

Homosexuality
Indians
North America: E98.S48

Honduras: F1501+
Confederación de Centro América: F1507
Wars with
Guatemala: F1466.45, F1507.5
Salvador: F1487.5, F1507.5

Hone, Philip: F128.44

Honey Hill (South Carolina), Engagement at, 1864: E477.44

Hood, John Bell: E467.1.H58

Hood, Mount (Oregon): F882.H85

Hood Canal region (Washington): F897.P9

Hood River and Valley (Oregon): F882.H9

Hooker, Joseph: E467.1.H6

Hooper, William: E302.6.H7

Hoosic River and Valley: F127.H73
Massachusetts: F72.B5
Vermont: F57.B4

Hoosier National Forest
    Indiana: F532.H75
Hoover, Herbert Clark: E742.5.H66, E802+
    Administration, 1929-1933: E801
    Family: E802.1
Hoover, Lou (Henry): E802.1
Hopatcong, Lake (New Jersey): F142.H7
Hope region, British Columbia: F1089.H6
Hopedale, Labrador (Fishing port):
    F1139.H6
Hopewell culture: E99.H69
Hopi Indians: E99.H7
Hopkins, Benjamin Franklin: F586
Hopkins, Ezek: E207.H7
Hopkins, Samuel
    Expedition, 1812: E355.2
Hopkins, Stephen: E302.6.H78
Hornby Island (British Columbia):
    F1089.H63
Horses
    Riding gear, Indian: E98.R5
    Use by Indians of North America:
        E98.H55
Horseshoe Lake (Illinois): F547.A3
Hosmer, Titus: E302.6.H8
Hospital services, Military
    United States
        Civil War: E621+
        Revolution: E283
        War of 1812: E362.5
        War of 1898: E731
        War with Mexico: E412.5
Hostos y Bonilla, Eugenio María de: F1973
Hot Springs (Arkansas): F419.H8
Hotels, taverns, etc. (U.S.): F73.625,
    F128.625, F158.625, F203.35
Houghton Lake (Michigan): F572.R6
Houma Indians: E99.H72
Housatonic River and Valley: F102.H7
    Massachusetts: F72.H7
House of Representatives
    United States
        Election of speaker, 1856: E434.5
Housing, Indian: E98.H58
Houston, Samuel: F390
Houston, William Churchill: F138
Houston (Texas): F394.H8
Hovey, Alvin Peterson: E467.1.H7
Howard, John Eager: E263.M3
Howard, Oliver Otis: E467.1.H8
Howe, John: E280.H8
Howe, Joseph: F1038
Howe, Robert: E207.H85
Howe, Samuel: F69
Howe, William Howe, 5th Viscount,
    Occupation of Philadelphia, 1777:
        E233
Hualapai Indians: E99.H75
Huamachuco, Peru (Province)
    Indian antiquities: F3429.1.H8
Huamalies, Peru (Province): F3451.H7
Huambisa Indians: F3430.1.H78
Huanca Indians: F3430.1.H8
Huancané, Peru (Province): F3451.H75

Huancavelica, Peru
    City: F3611.H8
    Department: F3451.H76
Huancavilca Indians: F3722.1.H8
Huancayo (Peru)
    City: F3611.H82
    Province: F3451.H78
Huanta, Peru (Province): F3451.H79
Huánuco (Peru): F3451.H8
Huao Indians: F3722.1.H83
Huaorani Indians: F3722.1.H83
Huaral
    Peru
        Province: F3451.H83
Huarayo Indians (Tacanan): F3430.1.E78
Huari (Peru)
    Indian antiquities: F3429.1.H828,
        F3430.1.H83
Huari Indians: F3430.1.H83
Huasco, Chile (Province)
    Indian antiquities: F3069.1.H8
Huasco River (Chile): F3131
Huastec Indians
    Modern: F1221.H8
    Pre-Columbian: F1219.8.H83
Huasteca, Mexico (Region): F1294
Huatuso Indians: F1545.2.G77
Huaura River and Valley (Peru): F3451.L7
Huave Indians: F1221.H85
Hubbardton, Battle of, 1777: E241.H8
Hudson, Henry: E129.H8
Hudson Bay: F1060+
Hudson-Fulton Celebration, 1909: F127.H8
Hudson River and Valley: F127.H8
    New Jersey: F142.H83
Hudson River Palisades: F127.H8
Hudson Strait: F1105.7
Hudson Valley: F127.H8
    Dutch colony, 1610-1664: F122+
    Indians: E78.H83
    Revolution, 1775-1783
        Military operations: E230.5.N4
        Washington's retreat, 1776: E232
Hudson's Bay Company: F1060+
Hueco Mountains
    New Mexico: F802.H84
    Texas: F392.H82
Huehuetenango, Guatemala (Dept.):
    F1469.H8
Huerta, Victoriano: F1234
Huetar Indians: F1545.2.G8
Huexotzinco codex: F1219.56.H83
Hughes, Charles Evans: E664.H86
Hughes, Sir Sam: F1033
Huguenots in America: E29.H9
Huguenots in Canada: F1035.H76
Huguenots in the United States: E184.H9
    Florida, 1562-1565: F314
Huichica Creek and Valley
    California: F868.N2
Huichol Indians: F1221.H9
Huila, Colombia (Dept.): F2281.H8
Huilliche Indians: F3126
Hull, Cordell: E748.H93
Hull, Isaac: E353.1.H8

Hull, William: E353.1.H9
Hull (Quebec): F1054.5.H8
Hullicos Indians: F3126
Humber River and Valley (Ontario):
    F1059.H9
Humboldt Bay (California): F868.H8
Humboldt River and Valley (Nevada):
    F847.H85
Humor, Indian: E98.H77
Humor of American history: E178.4
Humphreys, Andrew Atkinson: E467.1.H885
Humphreys, David: E302.6.H89
Humung (Asian people) in the United States:
    E184.H55
Hungarians in Canada: F1035.H8
Hungarians in South America: F2239.H85
Hungarians in the United States: E184.H95
    Civil War: E540.H6
Hungerford, Daniel Elihu: E403.1.H87
Hungry Mother Creek and Valley (Virginia):
    F232.S6
Hunkpapa Indians: E99.H795
Hunt, Henry Jackson: E467.1.H89
Hunter, David: E467.1.H9
Hunter, Robert Mercer Taliaferro: E415.9.H9
Hunting, Indian: E98.H8; F2230.1.H84,
    F2519.3.H85, F2821.3.H8
    Mayas: F1435.3.H85
Hunting Island (South Carolina): F277.B3
Huntingdon, Benjamin: E302.6.H9
Huntington, Jabez Williams: E340.H9
Huntington, Mount (Alaska): F912.H8
Huntington (West Virginia): F249.H95
Huntington Co. (Quebec): F1054.H9
Hupa Indians: E99.H8
Huron, Lake, region: F554
    Michigan: F572.H92
    Ontario: F1059.H95
Huron Co. (Ontario): F1059.H92
Huron Indians: E99.H9
Huron-Manistee National Forests
    Michigan: F572.H93
Huron Mountains (Michigan): F572.M33
Hurricanes
    Jamaica: F1895.P6
    United States: E179; F9, F316
Husbands, Herman: E302.6.H93
Hutchinson, Anne (Marbury): F67
Hutchinson, Thomas: F67
Hutchinson (Kansas): F689.H9
Hutterians in the United States: E184.H97
Hutterite Brethren in the United States:
    E184.H97
Hutterites in the United States: E184.H97
Hyde and Willoughby's grant, 1663
    (Guiana): F2423
Hyde Park (New York): F129.H99

I

Ibáñez del Campo, Carlos: F3099+
Ibarra (Ecuador): F3791.I3
Iberia Parish (Louisiana): F377.I15
Iberville, Pierre Le Moyne d': F372
Iberville Parish (Louisiana): F377.I2
Ibiapaba (Brazil): F2567.3
Ica, Peru (Dept.): F3451.I3
Içá River (Brazil): F2546
Icelanders in Canada: F1035.I2
Icelanders in United States: E184.I3
Ichilo, Bolivia (Province): F3341.I25
Ickes, Harold Le Claire: E748.I28
Idaho: F741+
    Afro-Americans: E185.93.I15
    Counties, etc.: F752.A+
    Indians: E78.I18
    Wars
        Indian wars: E83.83, E83.877
Idaho Co.: F752.I2
Idaho Falls (Idaho): F754.I2
Ide, William Brown: F864
Idiarte Borda, Juan: F2726
Iglesias, Rafael: F1547.5
Iguape, Ribeira de (Brazil): F2631
Iguazú, Parque Nacional del (Argentina):
    F2916
Iguazú Falls
    Argentina: F2909
    Brazil: F2596
Iguazú River and Falls (Brazil): F2596
Ijca Indians: F2270.2.A67
Île aux Coudres (Quebec): F1054.I3
Île aux Grues (Quebec): F1054.C8
Île aux Noix (Quebec): F1054.I35
Île Bizard (Québec): F1054.B58
Île Jésus (Québec): F1054.J47
Île Percée (Quebec): F1054.G2
Île Royale (Nova Scotia): F1039.C2
Île Verte (Quebec): F1054.I5
Îles de Mingan (Québec): F1054.M59
Îles du Salut (French Guiana): F2467.I4
Îles Madeleine (Quebec): F1054.M18
Illinois: F536+
    Afro-Americans: E185.93.I2
    Clark's campaign, 1778-1779: E234
    Counties, etc.: F547.A+
    Indians: E78.I3
    Quebec Act, 1774: F1032
    Slavery: E445.I2
    Treaty of Paris, 1783: E249
    Wars
        Civil War: E470.4+, E470.8, E505.1+
        Indian wars: E83.83
        War of 1812: E355+, E359.5.A+
        War of 1898: E717, E726.I2
        War with Mexico: E405+, E409.5.I4
Illinois and Michigan Canal National
    Heritage Corridor (Illinois): F547.I13
Illinois country: F544
Illinois Indians: E99.I2
Illinois military tract: F547.M6
Illinois River and Valley: F547.I2
Imbabura, Ecuador (Province): F3741.I6
    Indian antiquities: F3721.1.I3

Immigrant lists
    The thirteen colonies
        English: E187.5
Immigrants in the United States
    Civil War: E540.F6
Impeachment, Proposed, of Richard Nixon:
    E861
Impeachment of President Johnson: E666
Imperial Valley (California): F868.I2
Imperialism
    United States: E713
Implements, Indian: E98.I4, F1219.3.I4,
    F1435.3.I46, F1619.3.I6, F2230.1.I4,
    F2519.3.I4, F2821.3.I5, F3320.1.I45,
    F3721.3.I4
    Pre-Columbian America: E59.I4
Impresarios (Texas): F389
Impressment
    War of 1812: E357.2
Incas: F3429+
    Insurrection of Tupac-Amaru, 1780-1781:
        F3444
Independence, Declaration of: E221
Independence, Mount
    Revolution, 1775-1783: E230.5.V3
Independence Day: E286.A1+
Independence Hall (Philadelphia): F158.8.I3
Independence National Historical Park
    (Philadelphia): F158.65.I3
Independence Rock (Wyoming): F767.I38
Independence Square (Philadelphia):
    F158.67.I33
Indian campaigns of the
    Revolution, 1775-1783: E230+
    War of 1812: E355
Indian community colleges
    North America: E97.55
Indian country, west of Arkansas and
    Missouri: F697
Indian Creek and Valley (West Virginia):
    F247.R6
Indian masonry: E98.S75
Indian massacres: E81+, E83
    Virginia: F229
Indian reservation police
    North America: E98.C87
Indian reservations: E91+
Indian rights associations: E91+
Indian River (Florida): F317.B8
Indian sandpaintings: E98.S3
Indian schools
    Canada: E96.6.A+
    United States: E97.5+
Indian Stream (New Hampshire): F42.C7
Indian Territory
    History
        To 1890: F697
        1890-1907: F698
    Indians: E78.I5
    Wars
        Civil War, 1861-1865: E470.9,
            E471.57, E505.95, E561
Indian tribal government: E98.T77

Indian tribes
    Central America: F1445.2.A+,
        F1465.2.A+, F1485.2.A+,
        F1505.2.A+, F1525.2.A+,
        F1545.2.A+, F1565.2.A+
    Mayas: F1435.1.A+
    Mexico: F1219.1.A+, F1221.A+
    North America: E99.A+
    South America: F1434.3.A+,
        F2230.2.A+, F2270.2.A+,
        F2319.2.A+, F2380.1.A+,
        F2420.1.A+, F2460.1.A+,
        F2520.1.A+, F2679.2.A+,
        F2719.2.A+, F2823.A+,
        F3070.1.A+, F3320.2.A+,
        F3430.1.A+, F3722.1.A+
    West Indies: F1619.2.A+
Indian warfare: E98.W2, F1545.3.W2,
    F3429.3.W2
    Scalping: E98.W2
Indian wars
    Aztecs: F1219.76.W37
    Bolivia: F3320.1.W37
    Central America: F1219.3.W37,
        F1434.2.W37, F1435.3.W2,
        F1465.3.W37
    North America: E81+
        Chronological list: E83
    Peru: F3429.3.W27
    South America: F2230.1.W37,
        F2519.3.W37
Indian Wells Valley (California): F868.K3
Indiana: F521+
    Afro-Americans: E185.93.I4
    Counties, etc.: F532.A+
    Indians: E78.I53
    Slavery: E445.I3
    Wars
        Civil War: E506.1+
            Military operations: E470.4+
        Indian wars: E83.81
        Morgan's raid, 1863: E475.18
        Revolution: E263.I5
        War of 1812: E359.5.I53
        War of 1898: E726.I3
        War with Mexico: E405.1+, E409.5.I7
Indiana Dunes State Park: F532.I5
Indianapolis (Indiana): F534.I3
Indians
    Biography
        North America: E89+
    Economic conditions (South America):
        F1219.76.E36, F1435.3.E27,
        F1465.3.E2, F2230.1.E25,
        F2270.1.E3, F3429.3.E2,
        F3721.3.E25
    Education
        Canada: E96.2+
        United States: E97+
    Government relations
        Latin America (To 1601): F1411
        North America: E91+
    Mixed bloods: E99.M693, F3069.3.M55,
        F3320.1.M5, F3429.3.M63
    Origin: E61

Iroquoian Indians: E99.I69
Iroquois (New York). Thomas Indian School:
    E97.6.T4
Iroquois Indians: E99.I7
Irrigation, Indian: E98.I75; F2230.1.I77,
    F3429.3.I77
Irvine Park (California): F868.O6
Irvine Regional Park (California): F868.O6
Irving Park (Illinois): F548.68.I7
Isabela (Dominican Republic): F1939.I8
Iscaycinca Indians: F3430.1.I8
Island No. 10
    Military operations, 1862: E473.15
Island Park region (Idaho): F752.I7
Islas de las Perlas (Panama): F1569.P3
Islas del Cisne (Honduras): F1509.B3
Islas Malvinas: F3031
Isle of Orleans (Quebec): F1054.O7
Isle of Pines (Cuba): F1799.I8
Isle Royale (Michigan): F572.I8
Isle Verte (Quebec): F1054.I5
Isles de Pierres Indians: E99.S55
Isles of Shoals: F42.I8
Islesboro Island (Maine): F27.W16
Isleta Indians: E99.I8
Israelis in the United States: E184.I7
Isthmus of Central America
    Voyages to California via: F865
Isthmus of Panama: F1561+
Isthmus of Tehuantepec: F1359
Itajahy (Itajaí) River and Valley (Brazil):
    F2626
Italian Jews in the United States: E184.3+
Italians
    Discovery and exploration of America
        Post-Columbian: E135.I8
        Pre-Columbian: E109.I8
Italians in America: E29.I8
Italians in Argentina: F3021.I8
Italians in Brazil: F2659.I8
Italians in Canada: F1035.I8
Italians in Chile: F3285.I8
Italians in Latin America: F1419.I8
Italians in Mexico: F1392.I82
Italians in Paraguay: F2699.I8
Italians in Peru: F3619.I8
Italians in South America: F2239.I8
Italians in United States: E184.I8
    Civil War: E540.I8
Italians in Uruguay: F2799.I8
Italians in Venezuela: F2349.I8
Italy
    Anglo-German-Italian Blockade of
        Venezuela, 1902: F2325
Itamaracá Island (Brazil): F2601
Itasca Lake (Minnesota): F612.I8
Itasca State Park (Minnesota): F612.I8
Itene Indians: F3320.2.I8
Itucale Indians: F3430.1.I85
Itúrbide, Augustín de: F1232
Iturrigaray y Aróstegui, José de: F1231
Ituzaingó, Battle of, 1827: F2725
Itza Indians: F1465.2.I87
Iuka (Mississippi), Engagement at, Sept
    1862: E474.42

Ivaparé Indians: F2520.1.H48
Ixil Indians: F1465.2.I95
Ixmiquilpan, Mexico (District): F1291
Izabal, Guatemala (Dept.): F1469.I9

J

Jacalteca Indians: F1465.2.J3
Jackson (Mississippi): F349.J13
    Campaign, 1863: E475.29
Jackson, Andrew: E337.8.J3, E382
    Administrations, 1829-1837: E381+
    Execution of the Tennessee militiamen:
        E83.813
    Family: E382.1.A1+
    Governor of Florida: F315
    Vote of censure, 1834: F384.7
Jackson, Fort
    Bombardment and capture, 1862: E472.88
Jackson, John Peter: F139
Jackson, Rachel (Donelson): E382.1.J2
Jackson, Thomas Jonathan: E467.1.J15
Jackson Hole (Wyoming): F767.T28
Jackson Hole National Monument
        (Wyoming): F767.J3
Jackson Lake (Wyoming): F767.T3
Jackson Parish (Louisiana): F377.J2
Jackson Purchase region (Kentucky):
    F457.J23
Jackson River and Valley
    Virginia: F232.J13
    West Virginia: F247.J22
Jackson Whites: E184.R3
Jacksonville (Florida): F319.J1
Jacob's Cavern (Missouri): F472.M13
Jacques Cartier Park (Québec): F1054.P36
Jacuhype River (Brazil): F2551
Jacuípe River (Brazil): F2551
Jaén (Peru)
    Province: F3451.J33
Jalama Beach Park (California): F868.S23
Jalapa (Mexico)
    Canton: F1371
    City: F1391.J2
Jalisco, Mexico (State): F1296
Jamaica: F1861+
    Separation of British Honduras from,
        1884: F1447
Jamaicans in the United States: E184.J27
James, Army of the: E470.2+
James, Jesse: F594
James Bay region (Ontario and Quebec):
    F1059.J3
James Island (South Carolina)
    Engagement at, 1862: E473.92
James River (Virginia)
    Campaign from the Rapidan, 1864:
        E476.52
    Operations on south side, 1864: E476.57
James River and Valley (Alberta): F1079.J27
James River and Valley (Virginia): F232.J2
Jamestown (Virginia): F234.J3
Jamestown settlement: F229
Japanese in America: E29.J3

Japanese in Argentina: F3021.J36
Japanese in Bolivia: F3359.J3
Japanese in Brazil: F2659.J3
Japanese in Canada: F1035.J3
Japanese in Colombia: F2299.J3
Japanese in Cuba: F1789.J3
Japanese in Latin America: F1419.J3
Japanese in Mexico: F1392.J3
Japanese in Paraguay: F2699.J35
Japanese in Peru: F3619.J3
Japanese in South America: F2239.J3
Japanese in the Dominican Republic:
    F1941.J3
Japanese in the United States: E184.J3
Japanese in Uruguay: F2799.J36
Japurá River (Brazil): F2546
Jaquess, J.F.
    Conference with Davis, 1864: E469+
Jarvis, Leonard: E340.J3
Jasper National Park (Alberta): F1079.J3
Javanese in Dutch Guiana: F2431.J3
Javarí River (Brazil): F2546
Jay, John: E302.6.J4
    Treaty with Great Britain: E314
Jay, William: E449
Jeddore Harbour (Nova Scotia): F1039.J43
Jedediah Island (British Columbia):
    F1089.J43
Jefferson, Fort (Dry Tortugas)
    Civil War operations, 1861: E471.53
    Fort Jefferson National Monument:
        F317.M7
Jefferson, Thomas
    Administrations, 1801-1809: E331+
    Family: E332
    Memorial, Washington, D.C.: F203.4.J4
Jefferson City (Missouri): F474.J4
Jefferson Davis Parish (Louisiana): F377.J43
Jefferson Parish (Louisiana): F377.J4
Jekyl Island (Georgia): F292.G58
Jemez Indians: E99.J4
Jemez Mountains (New Mexico): F802.S3
Jenckes, Thomas Allen: E415.9.J5
Jenkins, Charles Jones: F291
Jenny Lake (Wyoming): F767.T3
Jequitinhonha River (Brazil): F2581
Jersey City: F144.J5
Jersey Shore: F142.J4
Jesuit province of Paraguay: F2684
Jesuit reductions: F2684
Jesuit relations (North America): F1030.7+
Jesuits
    Expulsion from
        Brazil: F2528
        Mexico: F1231
    Missions
        Mount Desert Island station, 1609:
            F1038
        New France: F1030.7+
        Paraguay reductions (1609-1769):
            F2684
            War of the Seven Reductions, 1754-
                1756: F2684
        Pimería Alta: F799

Jesup, Thomas Sydney: E83.836
Jesus Island (Quebec): F1054.J47
Jewelry, Indian: F1435.3.J48
    Costa Rica: F1545.3.J48
    Mexico: F1219.3.J48
    North America: E98.J48
Jewish colony in British Guiana, 1658-1666:
    F2381
Jews, Relations with
    United States Presidents: E176.472.J47
Jews in America: E29.J5
Jews in Argentina: F3021.J5
Jews in Bolivia: F3359.J47
Jews in Brazil: F2659.J5
Jews in Canada: F1035.J5
Jews in Central America: F1440.J48
Jews in Chile: F3285.J4
Jews in Colombia: F2299.J5
Jews in Costa Rica: F1557.J4
Jews in Cuba: F1789.J4
Jews in Dutch Guiana: F2431.J4
Jews in Ecuador: F3799.J4
Jews in Jamaica: F1896.J48
Jews in Latin America: F1419.J4
Jews in Mexico: F1392.J4
Jews in Panama: F1577.J4
Jews in Paraguay: F2699.J4
Jews in Peru: F3619.J4
Jews in South America: F2239.J5
Jews in the Dominican Republic: F1941.J4
Jews in the United States: E184.3+
    Civil War: E540.J5
    Revolution: E269.J5
    War of 1812: E359.9.J5
    War of 1898: E725.5.J4
Jews in Uruguay: F2799.J4
Jews in Venezuela: F2349.J48
Jicarilla Indians: E99.J5
Jim Thorpe
    Pennsylvania: F159.M4
Jiménez, Ricardo: F1547.5
Jiménez de Quesada, Gonzalo: F2272
Jinotega, Nicaragua (Dept.): F1529.J4
Jipijapa, Ecuador (Canton): F3791.J3
Jiquilpan, Mexico (District): F1306
Jivaran Indians: F2230.2.J58
Jivaro Indians: F3722.1.J5
João VI, King of Portugal
    Court in Brazil, 1808-1821: F2534
Joaquin Miller Trail (Oregon): F882.J73
Jocko Indian Reservation
    Montana: E99.S2
John Brown's Raid, 1859: E451
John Day River and Valley (Oregon):
    F882.J76
John Fenwick's colony: F142.S2
John Marshall Day: E302.6.M4
John Muir Trail (California): F868.S5
Johnson, Andrew: E667
    Administration, 1865-1869: E666+
    Collected works: E415.6.J65
    Impeachment: E666
    Military governor of Tennessee: E531.1+
Johnson, Herschel Vespasian: F290

Johnson, John Albert: F606
Johnson, Lyndon Baines: E847
    Administration, 1963-1969: E846+
    Family: E848
Johnson, Richard Mentor: E340.J69
Johnson, Sir William: E195+
Johnson, Thomas: E302.6.J65
Johnson, Tom Loftin: F496
Johnson, William Samuel: E302.6.J7
Johnson's Indian School, White Sulphur
    (Kentucky): E97.6.J69
Johnson's Island (Lake Erie)
    Military prison: E616.J7
Johnston, Albert Sidney: E467.1.J73
Johnston, Joseph Eggleston: E467.1.J74
Johnstown (Pennsylvania): F159.J7
Joliet, Louis: F1030.3
    In Mississippi Valley: F352
Joliet (Illinois): F549.J7
Jonathan Lemmon slave case, 1860: E450
Jonaz-Chichimeca Indians: F1221.C53
Jones, Anson: F389
Jones, George Wallace: E415.9.J6
Jones, J. Glancy: E415.9.J7
Jones, Jacob: E353.1.J7
Jones, John Paul: E207.J7
Jones, William: E57
Jones Mountain (Virginia): F232.S48
Jonesboro (Jonesborough), Battle of, 1864:
    E476.7
Jordão, Campos do (Brazil): F2631
Jornada del Muerto Road (New Mexico):
    F802.J67
Jornada del Muerto Wilderness (New
    Mexico): F802.J67
Joseph, Lake (Ontario): F1059.M9
Joseph Plains (Idaho): F752.I2
Joshua Tree National Monument
    (California): F868.J6
Juan de Fuca Strait region (Washington):
    F897.J9
Juan Fernández Islands (Chile): F3171
Juan José Mora District (Venezuela):
    F2331.J82
Juaneño Indians: E99.J8
Juárez, Benito Pablo: F1233
Jubilee College State Park (Illinois): F547.P4
Judiciary, Indian: F3429.3.J8
Judith River and Valley (Montana): F737.J83
Jujuy, Argentina (Province): F2906
    Indian antiquities: F2821.1.J9
Jukumani Indians: F3320.2.J84
Julian, George Washington: E415.9.J95
    Collected works: E415.6.J94
July Fourth: E286.A1+
Jumano Indians: E99.J9
Jumel, Eliza (Bowen): E302.6.B91
Jumel Mansion (New York): F128.8.M8
Juneau (Alaska): F914.J9
Juniata River and Valley (Pennsylvania):
    F157.J7
Junín, Peru (Dept.): F3451.J9
Junípero, Father: F864

Juquiá River (Brazil): F2631
Jurua River (Brazil): F2546
Juruna Indians: F2520.1.J8
Justo, Juan Bautista: F2848
Jutaí River (Brazil): F2546
Jutiapa, Guatemala (Dept.): F1469.J8
Juvenile delinquency among Indians:
    E98.C87

K

Kaaterskill Park (New York): F127.C3
Kachemak Bay State Park (Alaska):
    F912.K26
Kachemak Bay State Wilderness Park
    (Alaska): F912.K26
Kadiak Island (Alaska): F912.K62
Kagaba Indians: F2270.2.K3
Kagwahiv Indians: F2520.1.P4
Kaieteur Falls (British Guiana): F2387.E8
Kainah Indians: E99.K15
Kaingang Indians: F2520.1.K3
Kaingangue Indians: F2520.1.K3
Kalamazoo (Michigan): F574.K1
Kalamazoo River and Valley (Michigan):
    F572.K22
Kalapuyan Indians: E99.K16
Kalb, Jean, Baron de: E207.K14
Kalispel Indians: E99.K17
Kalmyks in the United States: E184.K3
Kamaiurá Indians: F2520.1.K35
Kamia Indians: E99.K18
Kamloops District (British Columbia):
    F1089.K4
Kamouraska Co. (Quebec): F1054.K2
Kananaskis Country (Alberta): F1079.K34
Kanarese in the United States: E184.K35
Kanawha River and Valley (West Virginia):
    F247.K3
Kandoshi Indians: F3430.1.C32
Kanjobal Indians: F1465.2.K36
Kankakee River and Valley: F532.K2
    Illinois: F547.K27
    Indians: E78.K15
Kankakee-St. Joseph portage (Indiana):
    F532.S2
Kansa Indians: E99.K2
Kansas: F676+
    Afro-Americans: E185.93.K16
    Counties, etc.: F687.A+
    Indians: E78.K16
    Quivira: F799
    Slavery: E445.K16
        Pro- and anti-slavery party struggles:
        F685
    Wars
        Civil War: E508.1+
            Military operations: E470.9
        War of 1898: E726.K2
Kansas City (Kansas): F689.K2
Kansas City (Missouri): F474.K2
Kansas (Kansa) Indians: E99.K2
Kansas-Nebraska Bill, May, 1854: E433
Kansas River and Valley: F687.K3
Karankawa Indians: E99.K23
Karijona Indians: F2270.2.C27

Kariri Indians: F2520.1.K4
Karok Indians: E99.K25
Karutana Indians: F2520.1.B35
Kashaya Indians: E99.K258
Kashinaua Indians: F2520.1.C38
Kashubes in Canada: F1035.K36
Kaska Indians: E99.K26
Kaskaskia Indians: E99.K264
Katcinas: E98.R3
Kathadin, Mount (Maine): F27.P5
Katmai National Monument (Alaska):
    F912.K3
Kato Indians: E99.K267
Kavanagh, Edward: E302.6.K3
Kawaiisu Indians: E99.K269
Kawartha Lakes (Ontario): F1059.K2
Kawchodinne Indians: E99.K28
Kawchottine Indians: E99.K28
Kawia Indians
    Shoshoneans: E99.C155
Kayabi Indians: F2520.1.K45
Kazan River and Valley (General and
    Mackenzie): F1100.K39
Kazan River and Valley (Keewatin):
    F1100.K39
Kearny, Fort: E83.866
Kearny, Philip: E467.1.K24
Kearny, Stephen Watts: E403.1.K2
    New Mexico campaign: E405.2
Kearsarge (Corvette): E595.K2
Kearsarge, Mount (New Hampshire):
    F42.C3, F42.M5
Kechua Indians: F2230.2.K4
Keeche Indians: E99.K3
Keewatin District (Canada): F1106+
    Eskimos: E99.E7
    Indians: E78.K25
    Ontario boundary: F1059.B7
Keith, Sir William: F152
Kejimkujik Lake and region (Nova Scotia):
    F1039.K43
Kejimkujik National Park (Nova Scotia):
    F1039.K44
Kekchi Indians: F1465.2.K5
Kelley, Alfred: F495
Kelleys Island (Ohio): F497.E5
Kelly, John: F128.47
Kelly's Ford (Virginia), Battle of, 1863:
    E475.3
Kenai Fjords National Park (Alaska):
    F912.K4
Kenai Peninsula (Alaska): F912.K4
Kendall, Amos: E340.K33
Kennebago Lake (Maine): F27.R2
Kennebec Patent (Maine): F27.K3
Kennebec Purchase (Maine): F27.K3
Kennebec River and Valley: F27.K32
Kennebunk (Maine): F29.K3
Kennedy, John Fitzgerald: E842+
    Administration, 1961-1963: E841+
    Family: E843
Kennedy, John Pendleton: E415.9.K35
Kennedy, Robert F.: E840.8.K4
Kennesaw Mountain, Battle of, 1864: E476.7

Kennesaw Mountain National Battlefield
    Park: E476.7
Kenosha (Wisconsin): F589.K3
Kensington rune stone: E105
Kent, James: F123
Kent Co. (Ontario): F1059.K3
Kent Island, Maryland: F187.C5
    Kent Island and Claiborne: F184
Kenton, Simon: F517
Kentucky: F446+
    Afro-Americans: E185.93.K3
    Confederate history: E564.1+
    Counties, etc.: F457.A+
    Indians: E78.K3
    Slavery: E445.K5
    Virginia claims withdrawn: F454
    Wars
        Civil War: E509.1+, E564.1+
            Military operations: E472.4
        Indian wars: E83.79
        Revolution: E263.K4
        War of 1812: E359.5.K5
        War of 1898: E726.K37
        War with Mexico: E409.5.K4
Kentucky (District): F454
Kentucky and Virginia Resolutions: E328
Kentucky County and District (Virginia):
    F454
Kentucky Lake: F457.K29
Kentucky River and Valley: F457.K3
Keresan Indians: E99.K39
Kernstown, Battle of, 1862: E473.72
Kerr, Michael Crawford: E664.K4
Ketchikan (Alaska): F914.K4
Kettle Creek, Georgia, Battle of, 1779:
    E241.K48
Kettle River and Valley
    British Columbia: F1089.K57
    Washington: F897.K3
Keuka Lake: F127.K4
Keweenaw Peninsula (Michigan): F572.K43
Key West (Florida): F319.K4
Khmers in Canada: F1035.C27
Khmers the United States: E184.K45
Khotana Indians: E99.K79
Kiawah Island (South Carolina): F277.B3
Kichai Indians: E99.K396
Kicho Indians: F3722.1.Q48
Kickapoo Indians: E99.K4
Kickapoo River and Valley (Wisconsin):
    F587.K4
Kidnapping of slaves: E450
Kieft's War: E83.65
Kilby, Thomas Erby: F326
Kiliwa Indians: F1221.K5
Killarney Provincial Park (Ontario):
    F1059.K5
Killbear Provincial Park (Ontario):
    F1059.K52
Killdeer Mountain, Battle of, 1864: E83.86
Killdeer Mountain Park (North Dakota):
    F642.D9
Killdeer Mountains (North Dakota): F642.D9

Kilpatrick's expedition against Richmond,
    1864: E476.27
King, Ernest Joseph: E182
King, Horatio: E415.9.K52
King, John Alsop: F123
King, Rufus: E302.6.K5
King, William: F24
King, William Lyon Mackenzie: F1033
King, William Rufus: E340.K54
King George's Parish (Maryland): F187.P9
King George's War, 1744-1748: E198
King Philip's War, 1675-1676: E83.67
King Ranch (Texas): F392.K47
King William Island (Franklin District):
    F1105.K5
King William's War, 1689-1697: E196
Kings and rulers
    Indians: F1219.3.K55, F1435.3.K55
        Brazil: F2519.3.K53
        Peru: F3429.3.K53
Kings Bay (Georgia): F292.C17
Kings Canyon National Park: F868.K48
King's Chapel Burial Ground (Boston):
    F73.61
Kings Co.
    New Brunswick: F1044.K5
    Nova Scotia: F1039.K5
    Prince Edward Island: F1049.K5
Kings Mountain, Battle of, 1780: E241.K5
Kings Mountain National Military Park
    (South Carolina): F277.K5
Kingston (Jamaica): F1895.K5
Kingston (New York)
    Burning by the British, 1777: E241.K6
Kingston Parish (Virginia): F232.K54
Kingston Peninsula (New Brunswick):
    F1044.K53
Kino, Eusebio Francisco: F799
Kinship
    Indians
        North America: E98.K48
        Mayas: F1435.3.K57
Kinship, Indian: F1219.76.K55, F2230.1.K5,
    F2270.1.K55, F2519.3.K55,
    F3429.3.K55
Kiowa Apache Indians: E99.K52
Kiowa Indians: E99.K5
Kirkpatrick, Andrew: F138
Kirkwood, Samuel Jordan: E507.1+
Kissimmee River and Valley (Florida):
    F317.K57
Kissinger, Henry: E840.8.K58
Kitksan Indians: E99.K55
Kittochtinny Valley (Pennsylvania):
    F157.C9
Kiyuksa Indians: E99.K59
Klamath Falls (Oregon): F884.K62
Klamath Indians: E99.K7
Klamath River and Valley (California):
    F868.K55
Klikitat Indians: E99.K76
Klondike gold fields: F1095.K5
Klondike Gold Rush National Historical Park
    (Alaska): F912.K56

Klondike region (Yukon Territory):
F1095.K5
Knife River and Valley (North Dakota):
F642.K54
Knights of the Golden Circle: E458.8
Knights of the Order of the Sons of Liberty:
E458.8
Knik Arm (Alaska): F912.K58
Knives, Indian: E98.K54
Knott, Aloysius Leo: F186
Knowles, Sir Charles, in Cuba: F1779
Knox, Henry: E207.K74
Knoxville (Tennessee): F444.K7
Knoxville campaign, 1863: E475.94
Koaiker Indians: F3722.1.C83
Koasati Indians: E99.K77
Kobena Indians: F2270.2.C8
Kobuk River and Valley (Alaska): F912.K6
Kodiak Island (Alaska): F912.K62
Kofán Indians: F3722.1.C67
Kohunlich Site (Mexico)
Mayas: F1435.1.K64
Kokomish Indians: E99.S64
Kongo (African people) in South America:
F2239.K65
Kootenay District, River, and Valley
British Columbia: F1089.K7
Korean Air Lines Incident, 1983: E183.8.A+
Koreans in Canada: F1035.K65
Koreans in Mexico: F1392.K65
Koreans in South America: F2239.K67
Koreans in the United States: E184.K6
Korekaru Indians: F2520.1.B35
Körner, Gustave Philip: E415.9.K7
Kósciusko, Tadeusz Andrzej: E207.K8
Kotzebue Sound and region (Alaska):
F912.K66
Kourou expedition in French Guiana, 1763-
1765: F2462
Koyukon Indians: E99.K79
Koyukuk River and Valley (Alaska):
F912.K67
Koyukukkhotana Indians: E99.K79
Kraho Indians: F2520.1.C67
Kreen-Akarore Indians: F2520.1.K7
Krusenstern, Cape, National Monument
(Alaska): F912.C34
Ku-Klux Klan: E668
Alabama: F326
Louisiana: F375
Kubitschek, Juscelino: F2538.22.K8
Kubitschek administration (Brazil):
F2538.2+
Kuitsh Indians: E99.K82
Kuskokwim River and Valley (Alaska):
F912.K85
Kusso Indians: E99.K83
Kutchin Indians: E99.K84
Kutenai Indians: E99.K85
Kwaiker Indians: F3722.1.C83
Kwakiutl Indians: E99.K9

L

La Antigua (Guatemala): F1476.A5
La Crosse (Wisconsin): F589.L1
La Fontaine, Sir Louis Hippolyte: F1032
La Guajira Dept. (Colombia): F2281.G8
La Guardia, Fiorello Henry: E748.L23
La Jonquière, P.J. de Taffanel, marquis de:
F1030
La Junta de los Rios (Texas): F392.L33
La Lagunita Site (Guatemala): F1435.1.L24
La Libertad, Peru (Dept.): F3451.L3
La Pampa, Argentina (Province): F2924
La Paz (Bolivia)
City: F3351.L2
Department: F3341.L3
La Plata (Argentina): F3011.L4
La Plata (Viceroyalty): F2841
La Plata, Bolivia (City): F3351.S94
La Plata Island (Ecuador)
Indian antiquities: F3721.1.L36
La Plata region: F2801+
La Plata River (South America): F2909
La Rioja (Argentina)
City: F3011.L45
Province: F2956
Indian antiquities: F2821.1.R58
La Sal National Forest: F832.M3
La Salle, Robert Cavelier, sieur de: F1030.5
In Mississippi Valley: F352
La Salle National Forest: F832.M3
La Salle Parish (Louisiana): F377.L3
La Salle's Colony, 1685-1687: F352
La Tour, C.A. de Saint-Étienne, sieur de:
F1038
La Unión, El Salvador (Dept.): F1489.L3
La Vega (Dominican Republic) (City):
F1939.L3
La Venta, Mexico (Tabasco)
Indian antiquities: F1219.1.T13
La Verendrye, Pierre Gautier de Varennes,
sieur de: F1060.7
Labrador: F1135+
Eskimos: E99.E7
Indians: E78.L3, E99.A+
Ungava: F1054.N5
Labrador Peninsula: F1140
Labrador: F1135+
Lac La Hache region (British Columbia):
F1089.L3
Lacandon Indians: F1221.L2
Lackawanna River and Valley
(Pennsylvania): F157.L17
Ladies of the Grand Army of the Republic:
E462.17
Lafayette, Fort (New York)
Military prison: E616.L2
Lafayette, Marquis de: E207.L2
Lafayette, Order of: E202.99.O63
Lafayette National Park: F27.M9
Lafayette Parish (Louisiana): F377.L2
Lafayette Park (Washington, D.C.):
F203.5.L2
Lafitte, Jean: F374
LaFollette, Robert Marion: E664.L16
Lafourche Bayou (Louisiana): F377.L24

Lafourche Parish (Louisiana): F377.L25
Lagoa Santa (Brazil)
Indian antiquities: F2519.1.L3
Laguna de Chiriquí (Panama): F1569.B6
Laguna de On Site (Belize): F1435.1.L23
Laguna Indians: E99.L2
Laguna region (Mexico): F1266
Lagunita Site (Guatemala): F1435.1.L24
Laja River and Valley (Chile): F3174
Lake Boon (Massachusetts): F72.M7
Lake Clark National Park and Preserve
(Alaska): F912.C47
Lake Meredith National Recreation Area
(Texas): F392.H95
Lake Quinsigamond (Massachusetts):
F72.W9
Lake region (U.S.): F550.5+
Lake Roosevelt National Recreation Area
(Washington): F897.L35
Lakes Indians: E99.S546
Lamar, Lucius Quintus Cincinnatus:
E664.L2
Lamar, Mirabeau Bonaparte: F390
Lamar culture: E99.L25
Lamar y Cortazar, José de: F3446
Lamb, John: E207.L22
Lambayeque, Peru (Dept.): F3451.L2
Lambton Co. (Ontario): F1059.L23
Lamèque Island (New Brunswick):
F1044.L35
Lamoille River and Valley (Vermont):
F57.L22
Lampa (Peru): F3451.L23
Lanark Co. (Ontario): F1059.L3
Lanaudière (Quebec): F1054.L17
Land tenure
Indians: E98.L3, F1219.3.L34,
F1219.76.L35, F1545.3.L34,
F2230.1.L35, F2270.1.L3,
F2519.3.L36, F2679.3.L35,
F2821.3.L35, F3320.1.L35,
F3429.3.L3
Central America: F1434.2.L35
Mayas: F1435.3.L35
Pre-Columbian America: E59.L3
Venezuela: F2319.3.L35
Land transfers, Indian: E91+
Landon, Alfred Mossman: F686
Lane, Harriet: E437.1
Lane, Harry: F881
Lane, James Henry: F685
Lane, Joseph: E415.9.L2
Langdon, John: E302.6.L26
Lanier, James Franklin Doughty: F526
Lanier, Lake
Georgia: F292.S53
Lanín, Parque Nacional (Argentina): F2921
Lansing (Michigan): F574.L2
Laos in the United States: E184.L27
Lara, Venezuela (State): F2331.L3
Laramie (Wyoming): F769.L2
Larecaja Province
Bolivia: F3341.L35
Laredo Brú, Federico: F1788
Larrazolo, Octaviano Ambrosio: F801

Las Casas Revolution: F389
Las Vegas (Nevada): F849.L35
Las Villas, Cuba (Province): F1821+
Lassen, Peter: F864
Lassen Peak (California): F868.L34
Lassen Volcanic National Park: F868.L34
Lassik Indians: E99.L3
L'Assomption Co. (Quebec): F1054.L2
Latecunga (Ecuador): F3791.L3
Latin America: F1401+
    Aborigines: E65
    Description
        1607-1810: E141+
        Since 1810: F1409
    Discovery and exploration to 1600:
        E101+
    Foreign and general relations: F1415+
    History: F1409.6+
    Indian
        Folklore: F1465.3.F6
    Indians: E65, F1218.5, F1434+, F2229+,
        F2269+
    Relations with United States: F1418
Latin American wars of independence
        (General): F1412
Latin Americans in Canada: F1035.L27
Latorre, Lorenzo: F2726
Latrobe, Benjamin Henry
    U.S. Capitol: F204.C2
Latvians in Brazil: F2659.L38
Latvians in Canada: F1035.L3
Latvians in United States: E184.L4
Laudonnière, R.G. de: F314
Laurens, Henry: E302.6.L3
Laurentian Mountains: F1054.S3
Laurier, Sir Wilfred: F1033
Lava Beds National Monument (California):
    F868.L38
Laval de Montmorency, F.X. de: F1030
Lavalle, Juan Galo de: F2846
Lavalleja, Uruguay (Dept.): F2731.L3
Lawrence, Abbott: E340.L4
Lawrence, Amos: F69
Lawrence, Amos Adams: E415.9.L38
Lawrence, Fort (Nova Scotia): F1039.C5
Lawrence, James: E353.1.L4
Lawrence, William Beach: E415.9.L4
Lawrence (Kansas): F689.L4
    Massacre, 1863: E474.97
Le Conte, Mount (Tennessee): F443.S45
Le Droit Park (Washington, D.C.): F202.L4
Le Moyne de Bienville, Jean Baptiste: F372
Le Moyne d'Iberville, Pierre: F372
Leadville (Colorado): F784.L4
Leadville National Forest: F782.L4
League Island (Pennsylvania): F158.68.L4
League of Córdoba: F2847
Leather District (Boston): F73.68.L43
Leatherwood Creek and Valley
    Ohio: F497.L4
Leatherwork, Indian: E98.L4
    Pre-Columbian America: E59.L4
Leavenworth, Elias Warner: F123
Leavenworth (Kansas): F689.L5
Lebanese in Brazil: F2659.L42

Lebanese in Canada: F1035.L43
Lebanese in Colombia: F2299.L42
Lebanese in Costa Rica: F1557.L42
Lebanese in Mexico: F1392.L4
Lebanese in the United States: E184.L34
Lebanese in Uruguay: F2799.L4
Lebanese in Venezuela: F2349.L43
Lebanon (Connecticut). Moor's Indian
    Charity School: E97.6.M5
Lechiguanas Islands (Argentina): F2861
Lechuguilla Desert (Arizona): F817.Y9
Lecompton Constitution
    Kansas: F685
LeConte, Mount (Tennessee): F443.S45
Ledesma, A.A. de: F2322
Lee, Charles: E207.L47
Lee, Henry: E207.L5
Lee, Jason: F880
Lee, John Doyle: F826
Lee, Richard Henry: E302.6.L4
Lee, Robert Edward: E467.1.L4
    Gettysburg Campaign: E475.53
    Mansion
        Arlington, Virginia: F234.A7
    Memorial
        Arlington, Virginia: F234.A7
    Surrender, 1865: E477.67
Lee, Thomas: F273
    Ohio Company (1747-1779): F517
Leeds Co. (Ontario): F1059.L4
Lee's legion
    Continental Army: E260
Leesburg (Virginia)
    Military operations near, 1861: E472.63
Leetes Island (Connecticut): F102.N5
Leeward Islands: F2006
Legal status, laws, etc. (Indian): F1219.3.L4
Legaré, Hugh Swinton: E340.L5
Legends, Indian
    Chile: F3069.3.F64
    Pre-Columbian America: E59.F6
Legion of Loyal Women, Washington, D.C.:
    E462.18
Leguía, Augusto Bernardino: F3447
Lehigh (Monitor): E595.L5
Lehigh River and Valley (Pennsylvania):
    F157.L6
Lehman, Herbert Henry: F124
Leif the Lucky: E105
Leisler, Jacob: F122+
Leisler's Rebellion, 1689: F122+
Leiv Eiriksson: E105
Lemmon, Jonathan: E450
Lemon, John A.: F154
Lenca Indians: F1505.2.L4
L'Enfant, Pierre C.
    Plan for Washington, D.C.: F195
Lengua Indians: F2679.2.L4
Lennox, Fort (Quebec): F1054.I35
Lennox and Addington Co. (Ontario):
    F1059.L5
Lennox Co. (Ontario): F1059.L5
Lenox, Walter: F198
León, Ecuador (Province): F3741.C6

León, Nicaragua (City): F1536.L4
    Rivalry with Granada: F1526.25
León, Nuevo: F1316
Leonard, Daniel: E278.L5
Les Cheneaux Islands (Michigan): F572.L57
Les Saintes (West Indies): F2070
Lescot, Élie: F1927
Lesser Antilles: F2001+
Lesser Slave Lake (Alberta): F1079.L47
Lethbridge (Alberta): F1079.5.L5
Leticia question: F2281.B7P1+
Lévis, François Gaston: E199
Levis Co. (Quebec): F1054.L3
Lewis, Ellis: F153
Lewis, Francis: E302.6.L6
Lewis and Clark Cavern State Park
    (Montana): F737.L65
Lewis and Clark Expedition: F592.3+
Lewis Mountain
    Virginia: F232.S48
Lewisburg (West Virginia), Expeditions
    against, 1863: E475.76
Lewiston (Idaho): F754.L6
Lexington (Kentucky): F459.L6
Lexington (Massachusetts), Battle of, 1775:
    E241.L6
Lexington (Missouri), Siege of, 1861:
    E472.25
Libby Prison (Richmond): E612.L6
Liberal Republicans
    United States history: E671
Liberia
    American Colonization Society: E448
Liberians in the United States: E184.L53
Libertad, Peru (Dept.): F3451.L3
Liberty, Statue of (New York): F128.64.L6
Liberty and Union Convention
    Nashville, Tennessee: E531.1+
Liberty Bell: F158.8.I3
Liberty Gap (Tennessee): F443.B35
Libraries and Indians: E97.8
Lieber, Francis: E415.9.L7
Liechtensteiners in the United States:
    E184.L55
Lienzo de Parapan (Codices): F1219.56.L48
Lienzo de Tepetícpac (Codices):
    F1219.56.L52
Lienzo de Tiltepec (Codices):
    F1219.56.L525
Lienzo de Tlaxcala (Codices): F1219.56.L53
Lienzo of Petlacala (Codices): F1219.56.L54
Lienzo Totomixtlahuaca (Codices):
    F1219.56.L55
Lienzos de Acaxochitlan: F1219.56.L57
Liggon's Tobacco Warehouse Prison,
    Richmond: E612.L7
Lilienthal, David Eli: E748.L7
L'ile de Pâques (Chile): F3169
Lillooet District (British Columbia):
    F1089.L7
Lillooet Indians: E99.L4

Lima, Peru
  City: F3601
  Department: F3451.L7
    Indian antiquities: F3429.1.L7
Lime Creek and Valley (Colorado):
  F782.S18
Limerick, Thomas Dongan, Earl of: F122+
Limón (Costa Rica): F1556.L5
Limón Province (Costa Rica): F1549.L55
Linares, Chile (Province): F3176
Lincoln, Abraham: E456+
  Administrations, 1861-1865: E456
  Douglas debates: E457.4
  Elections 1864: E440, E458.4
  Emancipation Proclamation: E453
  Family: E457.25, E457.32
  Gettysburg address: E475.55
  Home in Springfield: F549.S7
  Memorial (Washington, D.C.):
    F203.4.L73
  Museum, Washington, D.C.: E457.65
  Tomb
    Springfield, Illinois: E457.52
  Writings: E457.91+
Lincoln, Mary (Todd): E457.25
Lincoln, Nancy (Hanks): E457.32
Lincoln, Sarah (Bush) Johnston: E457.32
Lincoln, Thomas: E457.32
Lincoln, Thomas (Tad): E457.25
Lincoln (Nebraska): F674.L7
Lincoln Boyhood National Memorial
  (Indiana): F532.S6
Lincoln Day: E457.7
Lincoln-Douglas debates: E457.4
Lincoln Parish (Louisiana): F377.L6
Lincoln Park (Chicago): F548.65.L7
Lincoln's Birthday: E457.7
Lincoln's Cooper Institute address: E438
Lindley's Mill, Battle of, 1781: E241.L65
Lindo, Juan: F1507.5
Liniers y Bremond, Santiago Antonio María
  de: F2845
Linn, Lewis Fields: E340.L7
Lipan Indians: E99.L5
Liquor use, Indian: E98.L7
Lisbôa, Joaquim Nabuco, marques de
  Tamandare: F2536
L'Islet Co. (Quebec): F1054.L57
Litchfield (Connecticut): F104.L7
Litchfield Hills (Connecticut): F102.L6
Lithuanians in Brazil: F2659.L5
Lithuanians in Canada: F1035.L5
Lithuanians in South America: F2239.L7
Lithuanians in the United States: E184.L7
Litters, Indian (Peru): F3429.3.L5
Little Big Horn Battle, 1876: E83.876
Little Colorado River and Valley (Arizona):
  F817.L5
  Indians: E78.L58
Little Cranberry Island (Maine): F27.H3
Little Egg Harbor, New Jersey, Skirmish of,
  1778: E241.L7
Little Gott Island
  Maine: F27.H3

Little Laurel Creek and Valley (North
  Carolina): F262.L64
Little Long Island (Connecticut): F102.F2
Little Miami River and Valley (Ohio):
  F497.L7
Little Missouri Badlands (North Dakota):
  F642.L5
Little Nine Partners Patent (New York):
  F127.D8
Little Pedee River (South Carolina): F277.P3
Little Pipestone Creek and Valley
  (Saskatchewan): F1074.L5
Little River and Valley
  Arkansas: F417.L64
  Oklahoma: F702.L55
  Tennessee: F443.L63
Little Rock (Arkansas): F419.L7
  Advance of Union forces upon, 1863:
    E474.96
Little Tennessee River and Valley (Georgia
  and Tennessee): F443.L64
Little Traverse Bay region: F572.L7
Little War, 1879-1880 (Cuba): F1785
Littlefield, George Washington: F391+
Lituya Bay (Alaska): F912.L57
Livermore, Edward St. Loe: E302.6.L66
Livermore Valley (California): F868.A3
Livingston, Anne Home (Shippen):
  E302.6.L67
Livingston, Edward: E302.6.L68
Livingston, Louise (Davezac) Moreau:
  E302.6.L684
Livingston, Philip: E302.6.L7
Livingston, Robert R.: E302.6.L72
Livingston, William: E302.6.L75
Livingston Manor (New York): F127.L73
Livingston Parish (Louisiana): F377.L6
Llaima, Chile (Dept.): F3141
  Indian antiquities: F3069.1.L5
Llanganati Mountains (Ecuador): F3741.L5
Llano Estacado (Texas): F392.L62
Llanos Orientales (Colombia): F2281.L52
Llanquihue, Chile (Province): F3181
Llanquihue Lake (Chile): F3181
Loa (Chile): F3170
Loa River and Valley
  Indian antiquities: F3069.1.L6
Lobos, Point (Monterey Co., California):
  F868.M7
Local history of the United States: F1+
Lochea River and Valley (Idaho): F752.I2
Locke, John
  Fundamental constitutions (South
    Carolina): F272
Lodge, Henry Cabot: E660.L75, E664.L7
Lodore, Canyon of (Colorado): F782.M65
Loess Hills
  General and Iowa: F627.L76
  Missouri: F472.L88
Logan (Utah): F834.L8
Logan, George: E302.6.L8
Logan, James: F152
Logan, John Alexander: E664.L83
Logan, Thomas Muldrup: E467.1.L5

Loja (Ecuador)
  City: F3791.L6
  Province: F3741.L6
Loltun Cave (Mexico): F1435.1.L64
Loma Tina: F1939.T5
Lombardo, Guillén: F1231
London (Ontario): F1059.5.L6
London, Virginia Company of: F229
Lonesome Lake and region (British
  Columbia): F1089.L75
Long, Huey Pierce: E748.L86
Long Beach (California): F869.L7
Long Beach (New Jersey): F142.O2
Long Beach Island (New Jersey): F142.L65
Long Branch Lake and region (Missouri):
  F472.M2
Long Bridge (Washington, D.C.): F203.7.L8
Long Cove (Texas): F392.L66
Long Island, Battle of, 1776: E241.L8
Long Island (Connecticut): F102.F2
Long Island (Maine): F27.H3
Long Island (New York): F127.L8
Long Island (Prince of Wales-Outer
  Ketchikan Census Area)
  Alaska: F912.L65
Long Island City (New York): F129.L78
Long Lake (Michigan): F572.I6
Long Lake (New York): F127.H2
Long Point (Ontario): F1059.L8
Long Tom River and Valley
  Oregon: F882.L78
Longs Peak (Colorado): F782.L83
Longstreet, James: E467.1.L55
Lonquimay (Volcano): F3196
Lookout, Point (Maryland)
  Military prison: E616.L8
Lookout, Point (Arenac Co.)
  Michigan: F572.A7
Lookout Mountain (Tennessee): F443.L8
  Battle of, 1863: E475.97
López, Alfonso: F2277
López, Francia Carlos Antonio: F2686
López, Francisco Solano: F2686
López, José Hilario: F2276
López, Narciso: F1784
López Contreras, Eleazar: F2326
López expeditions to Cuba, 1849-1851:
  F1784
Lopez Island (Washington): F897.S2
López Mateos, Adolfo: F1235.5.L6
López Portillo, José: F1235.5.L65
Lorenzan Indians: F3430.1.A54
Loreto, Peru (Dept.): F3451.L8
Lorretto Indians: F3722.1.C23
Los Alamos (New Mexico): F804.L6
Los Andes, Argentina (Territory): F2853
Los Angeles (California): F869.L8
Los Angeles River (California): F868.L8
Los Padres National Forest (California):
  F868.L83
Los Ríos (Ecuador)
  Province: F3741.L7
Losantiville (Ohio): F499.C5
Lost Cove (Tennessee): F443.C32
Lost River and Valley (Indiana): F532.O63

Loudoun, Fort (Tennessee): F443.M7
Louisburg (Nova Scotia): F1039.5.L8
　Siege and capture, 1745, 1758: E198,
　　E199
Louisburg National Historic Park (Nova
　　Scotia): F1039.5.L8
Louise, Lake (Alberta): F1079.L8
Louisiana: E366+
　Afro-Americans: E185.93.L6
　Confederate history: E565.1+
　French control: F372-373
　Indians: E78.L8
　Parishes (Counties), etc.: F377.A+
　Purchase by U.S., 1803: E333
　Reconstruction, 1865-1877: F375
　Slavery: E445.L8
　Spanish control: F372-373
　Wars
　　Civil War: E510.1+, E565.1+
　　　Military operations: E470.7
　　Indian wars: E83.739
　　Revolution: E263.L68
　　War of 1812: E359.5.L8
　　War of 1898: E726.L8
Louisiana, French: F372-373
Louisiana, Spanish: F373
Louisiana (Colony): F372-373
Louisiana (Province), 1803-1804: F374
Louisiana Purchase, 1803: E333
　Boundary question with Spanish territory:
　　F374
Louisville (Kentucky): F459.L8
Loup River and Valley (Nebraska): F672.L8
Lovejoy, Owen: E415.9.L89
Lovering Lake and region (Saskatchewan):
　　F1074.L65
Low, Seth: F128.5
Lowden, Frank Orren: F546
Lowe, Enoch Louis: F185
Lowe, Mount (California): F868.L8
Lowell, Charles Russell: E467.1.L6
Lower Canada: F1051+
Lower counties on the Delaware: F167
Lower Mississippi River and Valley: F396
Lower Peninsula, Michigan (Northern part):
　　F572.N7
Lowes area (Virginia): F232.L8
Lowes Island (Virginia): F232.L8
Loyada Lake region (Ontario): F1059.E46
Loyal League of Union Citizens: E463
Loyal Legion of the United States, Military
　　Order of the: E462.2
Loyal National League of the State of New
　　York: E463
Loyal Publication Society: E463
　Collected pamphlets: E458
Loyalists, American: E277+
Lua River and Valley (Honduras): F1509.U4
Lubaantun, Belize (Mayas): F1435.1.L83
Lucas, Robert: F621
Lucayan Indians: F1655
Lucayos: F1650+
Ludington, Henry: E263.N6
Luiseño Indians: E99.L9
Luján (Argentina): F3011.L8

Lule Indians: F2823.L8
Lumbee Indians: E99.C91
Lummi Indians: E99.L95
Lundy's Lane, Battle of, 1814: E356.L9
Lunenburg Co. (Nova Scotia): F1039.L9
Luperón, Gregorio: F1938.4
Luray Caverns (Virginia): F232.P2
Lusatian Sorbs in the United States:
　　E184.S68
Lutuamian Indians: E99.L98
Luxemburgers in the United States:
　　E184.L88
Luz y Caballero, J.C. de la: F1783
Luzerne, Lake (New York): F127.W2
Lygonia (Colony): F23
Lynch, Sir Thomas: F1884
Lynchburg campaign, 1864: E476.65
Lyndon B. Johnson Historical Park (Texas):
　　F392.L87
Lynn (Massachusetts): F74.L98
Lynnhaven Parish (Virginia): F232.P87
Lyon, Nathaniel: E467.1.L9
Lytle Creek Canyon
　California: F868.S14

M

Maca Indians: F2679.2.M25
Macanché Island (Guatemala): F1435.1.M22
MacArthur, Douglas: E745
Macauley, Edward Yorke: E182
MacDonald, Sir John Alexander: F1033
Macdonough, Thomas: E353.1.M2
Macedonians in Canada: F1035.M33
Macedonians in the United States: E184.M3
Maceo, Antonio: F1786
MacGregor, Gregor
　Invasion of Florida, 1817: F314
Machaculi Indians: F2520.1.M27
Machado, Jose Gomes Pinheiro Machado:
　　F2537
Machado y Morales, Gerardo: F1787
Machiganga Indians: F3430.1.M3
Machu Picchu (Peru)
　Indian antiquities: F3429.1.M3
Maciel, Antonio Vicente Mendes: F2537
Mackay, John Williams: F841
Mackenna, Juan: F3094
Mackenzie, Sir Alexander: F1060.7
Mackenzie, William Lyon: F1032
Mackenzie District (Canada): F1096+
　Eskimos: E99.E7
　Indians: E78.M16
Mackenzie River and Valley: F1100.M3
Mackinac, Fort: F572.M14
Mackinac, Straits of: F572.M14
Mackinac Island: F572.M16
　Capture, 1812: E356.M15
Mackinac Island, Mich. (City): F572.M16
Mackinac region: F572.M14
Mackinaw (Michigan): F574.M17
Mackinaw Island: F572.M16
Maclay, William: E302.6.M14
Maclay, William Brown: E415.9.M16
Macomb, Alexander: E353.1.M3
Macon, Nathaniel: E302.6.M17

Macon (Georgia): F294.M2
　Military Prison
　　Civil War: E612.M1
　　Wilson's raid, 1865: E477.96
Macu Indians: F2520.1.M2
Macuna Indians: F2270.2.M33
Macusi Indians: F2380.1.M3
Madawaska Co. (New Brunswick):
　　F1044.M3
Madehsi Indians: E99.M115
Madeira River (Brazil): F2624
Madeleine, Îles (Quebec): F1054.M18
Madeline Island (Wisconsin): F587.A8
Madero, Francisco Indalecio: F1234
Madison, Dolly: E342.1
Madison, Dorothy (Payne) Todd: E342.1
Madison, James: E302.M19, E302.M72+,
　　E342
　Administrations, 1801-1817: E341+
　Family: E342.1
Madison (Georgia). Military Prison:
　　E612.M2
Madison (Wisconsin): F589.M1
Madison Parish (Lousiana): F377.M2
Madison River and Valley
　Montana: F737.M24
　Wyoming: F767.M34
Madre de Dios, Peru (Dept.): F3451.M2
Madre de Dios River (Peru): F3451.M2
Madrid
　Columbus celebration, 1892: E119
Madrid, José Fernandez: F2274
Madrid, Treaty of
　1670: F1884
　1750: F2684
Maffitt, John Newland: E467.1.M35
Magallanes y Antártica Chilena: F3186
Magalloway Valley (Maine): F27.M18
Magdalen Islands (Quebec): F1054.M18
Magdalena, Colombia (Dept.): F2281.M2
Magdalena River and Valley (Colombia):
　　F2281.M23
Magellan, Strait of: F3191
Magic, Indian: E98.M2, F1219.3.M34,
　　F1219.76.M35, F2230.1.M24,
　　F3429.3.M3
Magloire, Paul Eugéne: F1928
Magothy River and Valley (Maryland):
　　F187.C5
Mahan, Alfred Thayer: E182
Mahican Indians: E99.M12
Mahone, William: F231
Mahoning River and Valley: F497.M2
　Pennsylvania: F157.M3
Maidu Indians: E99.M18
Maine: F16+
　Afro-Americans: E185.93.M15
　Ancient boundary of Acadia: F1039.B7
　Annexed to Massachusetts: F23-24
　Counties, etc.: F27.A+
　Indians: E78.M2
　Land patents: F27.K3, F27.M95, F29.B9
　Wars
　　Aroostook War, 1839: E398
　　Civil War: E511.1+

Maine: F16+
  Wars — Continued
    Indian wars, 1722-1726: E83.72
    Revolution: E263.M4
      Military operations: E230+
Maine (Battleship)
  Destruction, 1898: E721.6
Maine (Colony): F23
Maiongking Indians: F2319.2.Y4
Maipo, Battle of, 1818: F3094
Maipure Indians: F2319.2.M3
Makah Indians: E99.M19
Makka Indians: E99.M19
Malakoff Diggins State Historic Park
  (California): F868.N5
Malargüe, Argentina (Province): F2911
Maldonado (Uruguay)
  City: F2791.M3
  Department: F2731.M2
Malecite Indians: E99.M195
Malians
  Pre-Columbian discovery of America:
    E109.M34
Maligne Lake and region (Alberta): F1079.J3
Mall, The (Washington, D.C.): F203.5.M2
Malleco, Chile (Province): F3196
Malloa (Chile)
  Indian antiquities: F3069.1.M25
Malpelo Island (Colombia): F2281.M3
Maltese in Canada: F1035.M35
Maltese in the United States: E184.M34
Malungeons in the United States: E184.M44
Malvern Hill, Battle of, 1862: E473.68
Malvinas, Islas: F3031+
  War of 1982: F3031+
Mam Indians: F1465.2.M3
Mamaindê Indians: F2520.1.M24
Mammoth Cave (Kentucky): F457.M2
Mammoth Cave National Park (Kentucky):
  F457.M2
Mana River and Valley (French Guiana):
  F2467.M25
Manabí, Ecuador
  Province: F3741.M2
    Indian antiquities: F3721.1.M2
Manacica Indians: F3320.2.M26
Managua (Nicaragua): F1536.M26
Manahoac Indians: E99.M198
Manassas
  1st Battle of, 1861: E472.18
  2d Battle of, 1862: E473.77
Manassas Battlefield Confederate Park:
  E472.182
Manassas National Battlefield Park:
  E472.183
Manatee River (Florida): F317.M2
Manche Indians: F1465.2.M65
Manchester (New Hampshire): F44.M2
Mancos River and Valley (Colorado):
  F782.M7
Mandan Indians: E99.M2
Mangue Indians: F1545.2.M3
Mangum, Willie Person: E340.M3

Manhasset Neck (New York): F127.N2
Manhattan Indians: E99.M22
Maniba Indians: F2520.1.B35
Manila Bay, Battle of, 1898: E717.7
Manisees Island (Rhode Island): F87.B6
Manitoba: F1061+
  Indians: E78.M25
  Riel Rebellion, 1885: F1060.9
Manitou (Colorado): F784.M3
Manitoulin Island: F1059.M27
Maniva Indians: F2520.1.B35
Manley, Charles: F258
Mann Creek and Valley (Idaho): F752.W3
Manning Provincial Park (British Columbia):
  F1089.M3
Mansfield, Mount (Vermont): F57.M3
Mansions, Historic
  United States: E159
Manso Indians: E99.M23
Manta Indians: F3722.1.M3
Mantawa River and Valley: F1054.M2
Manti Canyon (Utah): F832.S42
Manti La Sal National Forest (Utah and
  Colorado): F832.M3
Manti National Forest: F832.M3
Mantua (Cuba): F1809.M4
Manzanar National Historic Site (California):
  F868.I6
Manzano Mountains (New Mexico):
  F802.M34
Mapa de Cuauhtinchan núm.3:
  F1219.56.M33
Mapa de Santiago Guevea (Codices):
  F1219.56.M36
Mapa de Tepechpan (Codices):
  F1219.56.T46
Mapuche Indians: F3126
Maquiritare Indians: F2319.2.Y4
Mar del Plata (Argentina): F3011.M29
Mar Mountains (Brazil): F2567.9
Maracaibó (Venezuela): F2341.M2
Maracaibo Lake Region (Venezuela):
  F2331.M27
Maracay (Venezuela): F2341.M25
  Indian antiquities: F2319.1.M3
Marajó, Brazil (Island): F2568
Maraka Indians: F2319.2.Y8
Maranga (Peru)
  Indian antiquities: F3429.1.M35
Maranhão, Brazil (State): F2571
  Indian antiquities: F2519.1.M37
Marañón River (Peru): F3451.L8
Marathas in the United States: E184.M37
Marcahuasi Plateau (Peru): F3451.L7
Marcelina Kué Site (Paraguay):
  F2679.15.M35
Marco da Nizza, Father: E125.M3
Marco Gonzalez Site (Belize): F1435.1.M26
Marcy, William Learned: E415.9.M18
Margarita (Island), Venezuela: F2331.M3
Marias Pass (Montana): F737.R8
Maricopa Indians: E99.M25
Maricopa Wells, Battle of, 1857: E83.8565
Marie Galante (West Indies): F2076

Marietta (Georgia)
  Chattanooga Railroad Expedition, 1862:
    E473.55
Marietta (Ohio): F499.M3
  Ohio Company (1786-1795): F483
Marietta College and the Civil War:
  E541.M3
Marin Peninsula (California): F868.M3
Marion, Francis: E207.M3
Mariposa estate (California): F868.M4
Maritime Provinces (Canada): F1035.8
  Indians: E78.M28
Market Street (Philadelphia): F158.67.M34
Maroba Indians: F2520.1.M26
Maroni River and Valley
  Dutch Guiana: F2427.M3
  French Guiana: F2467.M3
Maroon War, 1795-1796: F1884
Marova Indians: F2520.1.M26
Marquette, Jacques: F1030.2
  In Mississippi Valley: F352
Marriage customs and rites
  Indians
    Bolivia: F3320.1.M37
    Mexico: F1219.3.M38
    North America: E98.M27
    Peru: F3429.3.M34
    South America: F2230.1.M28
Marroquín, José Manuel: F2276.5
Marrowstone Island (Washington): F897.J4
Marsh, John: F865
Marshall, George Catlett: E745
Marshall, Humphrey: E302.6.M35
Marshall, James Wilson: F865
Marshall, John: E302.6.M4
Martha's Vineyard (Massachusetts): F72.M5
Martí, José: F1783
Martiau, Nicolas: F229
Martin, Morgan Lewis: F586
Martín Garcia (Island): F2909
Martinez, Macimiliano Hernandez: F1487.5
Martínez de Irala, Domingo: F2841
Martínez Trueba, Andrés: F2728
Martinique (West Indies): F2081
Martis culture: E99.M27
Maruba Indians: F2520.1.M26
Marubo Indians: F2520.1.M26
Maryland: F176+
  Afro-Americans: E185.93.M2
  Cession to the District of Columbia: F197,
    F202.G3
  Confederate history: E566.1+
  Counties, etc.: F187.A+
  Indians: E78.M3
  Reconstruction, 1865-1877: F186
  Slavery: E445.M3
  Wars
    Civil War: E512.1+, E566.1+
      Military operations: E470.2+
    French and Indian War: E199
    Revolution: E230+, E263.M3
    War of 1812: E359.5.M2
      Baltimore Riot, 1812: F189.B1
    War with Mexico: E409.5.M2
Maryland, Western: F186.9

Maryland campaigns
   1862: E474.61
   1863: E475.51
   1864: E476.66
Maryland Heights (Maryland): F187.W3
Maryland Loyalists Regiment: E277.6.M2
Masacali Indians: F2520.1.M27
Masco Indians: F3430.1.M38
Mascouten Indians: E99.M3
Mashacali Indians: F2520.1.M27
Mashco Indians: F3430.1.M38
Mashpee Indians: E99.M4
Masko Indians: F3430.1.M38
Masks, Indian: E98.M3; F1219.3.M4,
   F1435.3.M3, F1465.3.M36,
   F2230.1.M3, F3320.1.M38
   Pre-Columbian America: E59.M3
Masó, Bartolomé: F1786
Mason, Armistead Thomson: E302.6.M432
Mason, Charles: E415.9.M19
Mason, George: E302.6.M45
Mason, James Murray: E415.9.M2
Mason, Jeremiah: E340.M34
Mason, John: F37
Mason, Stevens Thomson: F566
Mason and Dixon's line: F157.B7
Mason's Grant (New Hampshire): F37
Massabesic, Lake (New Hampshire): F42.R7
Massachuset Indians: E99.M42
Massachusetts: F61+
   Afro-American citizens of Massachusetts
      in South Carolina, 1845: F273
   Afro-Americans: E185.93.M3
   Counties, etc.: F72.A+
   Indians: E78.M4
   Lands in western New York: F127.H7,
      F127.T6
   Maine separated from, 1820: F24
   Shays' Rebellion: F69
   Slavery: E445.M4
   Wars
      Civil War: E513.1+
      Indian wars: E83.67, E83.72
      Intercolonial wars, 1689-1763: E196,
         E197, E199
      Revolution: E263.M4
         Military operations: E230+
         Preliminaries: E210+
      War of 1812: E359.5.M3
      War of 1898: E726.M4
   Western lands ceded, 1787: E309, F483
Massachusetts (Province): F67
Massachusetts Bay Company: F67
Massachusetts Ten Townships: F127.T6
Massacre of 1856 (Panama): F1566.45
Massawomeck Indians: E99.M424
Massey, John Edward: F231
Massie, Nathaniel: F483
Massue Seigniory (Quebec): F1054.M35
Mataco Indians: F2823.M3
Matagorda Bay (Texas): F392.M4
Matamoros, Battle of, 1846: E406.M3
Matane Co. (Quebec): F1054.M4

Matanuska River and Valley (Alaska):
   F912.M3
Matanzas (Cuba)
   City: F1819.M4
   Province: F1811+
Matanzas Bay (Cuba)
   Capture of the Spanish silver-fleet, 1628:
      F1779
Matapédia River and Valley: F1054.M42
Material culture
   Indians: F1435.3.M32, F3721.3.M37
      Aztecs: F1219.76.M37
      Mexico: F1219.3.M42
      Paraguay: F2230.1.M34
      Pre-Columbian America: E59.M33
Mathematics
   Indians
      Aztecs: F1219.76.M38
      Brazil: F2519.3.M37
      Ecuador: F3721.3.M38
      Mayas: F1435.3.M35
      Peru: F3429.3.M36
      Pre-Columbian America: E59.M34
Mather, Cotton: F67
Mather, Increase: F67
Matinicus Island (Maine): F27.M3
Matlatzinca Indians
   Modern: F1221.M27
   Pre-Columbian: F1219.8.M38
Mato Grosso (Brazil): F2576
   Jesuit missions of Paraguay: F2684
Mato Grosso do Sul (Brazil): F2578
Matrícula de tributos (Codices):
   F1219.56.M37
Matthew, Lyon: E302.6.L9
Matto Grasso (Brazil)
   Indian antiquities: F2519.1.M4
Mattole Indians: E99.M43
Maua, Irineo Evangelista de Souza, visconde
   de: F2536
Mauch Chunk
   Pennsylvania: F159.M4
Maue Indians: F2520.1.M3
Maule, Chile (Province): F3201
Maumee River and Valley
   Indiana: F532.M62
   Ohio: F497.M4
Mauricius, Jan Jacob: F2423
Maury, Dabney Herndon: E415.9.M3
Maury, Lake (Virginia): F232.W27
Maxakali Indians: F2520.1.M27
Maximilian, Emperor of Mexico: F1233
Maxwell Land Grant: F802.M38
Maya astrology: F1435.3.A8
Mayagüez (Puerto Rico): F1981.M4
Mayas: F1435+
   British Honduras: F1445+
   Guatemala: F1465
   North America: E99.M433
   Yucatán: F1376
Mayflower (Ship): F68
Mayflower Descendants, Society of: F68
Mayna Indians: F3430.1.M4
Maynas, Peru (Province): F3451.B3
Mayntzhusen, Colonia: F2691.A4

Mayo Indians: F1221.M3
Mayoruna Indians: F3430.1.M45
Mazahua Indians: F1221.M33
Mazama, Mount (Oregon): F882.C8
Mazatec Indians: F1221.M35
Mazzei, Filippo: E263.V8
Mbaya Indians: F2679.2.M3
Mbwiha Indians: F2679.2.M34
Mbya Indians: F2679.2.M34
McAlpine, John: E278.M13
McArthur, Duncan: E353.1.M15
McCarren, Patrick Henry: F124
McCarthyism: E743.5
McClellan, George Brinton: E467.1.M2
McCrea, Jane: E233
McCulloch, Ben: E467.1.M24
McDonald, Charles James: F290
McDonald, Lake (Montana): F737.G5
McDonald, William Jesse: F391+
McDuffie, George: E340.M17
McEnery, Samuel Douglas: F375
McGee, Thomas D'Arcy: F1032
McGregor, Mount (New York): F127.S26
McHenry, Fort
   Bombardment of, 1814: E356.B2
McHenry, James: E302.6.M12
McKean, Thomas: E302.6.M13
McKinley, Ida (Saxton): E711.95
McKinley, Mount, National Park (Alaska):
   F912.M23
McKinley, Mount (Alaska): F912.M2
McKinley, William: E660.M14, E711.6+
   Administrations, 1897-1901: E711+,
      E751+
   Statue (Philadelphia): F158.64.M2
McLean, John: E340.M2
McLeod, Alexander
   Murder of Amos Durfee: F1032
McLeod, John: F1060.8
McLoughlin, John: F880
McMahon, John Van Lear: F185
McNabs Island (Nova Scotia): F1039.H3
McRae, Thomas Chipman: F411
Mdewakanton Indians: E99.M435
Meacham, Alfred Benjamin: F881
Mead, Lake, National Recreation Area
   (Arizona, Colorado, and Nevada):
      F788
Meade, George Gordon: E467.1.M38
   Monument (Washington, D.C.):
      F203.4.M5
Meade, Richard Worsam: E182
Meadow Lake Provincial Park
   (Saskatchewan): F1074.M4
Meagher, Thomas Francis: E467.1.M4
Mechanicsville, Va., Battle of, 1862:
   E473.68
Mecklenburg Resolves, 1775: E215.9
Meco Indians: F1221.C53
Meco Site (Mexico): F1435.1.M32
Medal of Honor Legion of the United States:
   E181
Medals, Indian: E98.M35
Medellín (Colombia): F2291.M4
Medical Lake (Washington): F897.S7

Medical services, Military
   United States
      Civil War: E621+
      Revolution: E283
      War of 1812: E362.5
      War of 1898: E731
      War with Mexico: E412.5
Medicine, Indian: E98.M4; F1219.3.M5,
   F1219.76.M43, F1435.3.M4,
   F1465.3.M4, F1525.3.M43,
   F2230.1.M4, F2270.1.M43,
   F2380.2.M44, F2519.3.M43,
   F3320.1.M4, F3429.3.M4,
   F3721.3.M4
   Argentina: F2821.3.M4
   Pre-Columbian America: E59.M4
Medicine Bow Mountains
   Colorado: F782.M43
   Wyoming: F767.M42
Medicine Bow National Forest (Wyoming):
   F767.M43
Medicine Hat (Alberta): F1079.5.M4
Medicine-man, Indian: E98.M4
Medina Angarita, Isaías: F2326
Meek, Joseph L.: F880
Meenahga, Mount (New York): F127.U4
Meeting of Consultation of Ministers of
   Foreign Affairs of American States:
   F1405.5
Megantic Co. (Quebec): F1054.M45
Mehinacu Indians: F2520.1.M44
Meigs, Fort, Battle of, 1813: E356.M5
Mekranoti Indians: F2520.1.M45
Melgarejo, Mariano: F3324
Mellon, Andrew William: E748.M52
Melungeons in the United States: E184.M44
Melville Peninsula: F1110.M5
Memminger, Christopher Gustavus:
   E415.9.M4
Memorial Bridge (Washington, D.C.):
   F203.7.A6
Memorial Continental Hall (Washington,
   D.C.): F204.M5
Memorial Day: E642
Memphis (Tennessee): F444.M5
Memphremagog, Lake, region
   Quebec: F1054.M5
   Vermont: F57.M5
Mendocino Headlands State Park
   (California): F868.M5
Mendota, Lake (Wisconsin): F587.D3
Mendoza, Antonio de, conde de Tendilla:
   F1231
Mendoza (Argentina)
   City: F3011.M45
   Province: F2911
Menefee, Richard Hickman: E340.M4
Menéndez de Avilés, Pedro: F314
Mennonites in Belize: F1457.M45
Mennonites in Canada: F1035.M45
Mennonites in Latin America: F1419.M45
Mennonites in Paraguay: F2699.M44
Mennonites in the United States: E184.M45
Menocal, Mario García: F1787

Menominee Indians: E99.M44
Menominee Range
   Michigan: F572.M516
   Wisconsin: F587.M49
Menominee River and Valley: F572.M52
   Wisconsin: F587.M5
Meo (Asian people) in the United States:
   E184.H55
Mercedes (Uruguay): F2791.M55
Mercenaries, German, in the American
   Revolution: E268
Mercer, Charles Fenton: E340.M5
Mercer, Fort, N.J., Battle of, 1777: E241.M5
Mercer, Hugh: E207.M5
Mercier, Honoré: F1053
Meredith, Lake, National Recreation Area
   (Texas): F392.H95
Meredith, William Morris: E415.9.M5
Mérida (Mexico): F1391.M5
Mérida (Venezuela)
   City: F2341.M5
   State: F2331.M5
Mérida, Cordillera de: F2331.M52
Meridian (Mississippi): F349.M5
   Expedition, 1864: E476.14
Merrimac (Frigate): E599.M5
Merrimac and Monitor, Battle between,
   1862: E473.2
Merrimac River and Valley
   Massachusetts: F72.M6
   New Hampshire: F42.M4
Mesa Verde National Park (Colorado):
   F782.M52
Mesaba range (Minnesota): F612.M36
Mescalero Indians: E99.M45
Mesilla (New Mexico), Skirmish at, 1861:
   E472.32
Mesilla Valley (New Mexico): F802.M4
Messiah War: E83.89
Mestizos in Peru: F3619.M47
Mestizos in the United States: E184.M47
Meta Department (Colombia): F2281.M49
Metalwork
   Indians
      Bolivia: F3320.1.M43
      Central America: F1434.2.M4
      Chile: F3069.3.M4
      Ecuador: F3721.3.M45
      Mexico: F1219.3.M52
      North America: E98.M45
      Peru: F3429.3.M42
      Pre-Columbian America: E59.M47
      South America: F2230.1.M43
Metapán, El Salvador (District): F1489.M46
Metchosin District (British Columbia):
   F1089.V3
Methodists and the Civil War
   United States: E540.M5
Methow Indians: E99.M46
Methow River and Valley (Washington):
   F897.O4
Métis: E99.M47
Métis Rebellion, 1869-1870: F1063
Métis Rebellion, 1885: F1060.9
Metztitlán, Mexico (District): F1291

Mexican War, 1846-1848: E401+
Mexicans and the Civil War
   United States: E540.M54
Mexicans in foreign countries: F1210.5
   United States: E184.M5
Mexico: F1201+
   Annexation and separation of
      Central America (1822-1823): F1438
      Guatemala (1822-1823): F1466.4
   Boundaries: F1249
   Cession of 1848: E408, F786
   Claims in British Honduras:
      F1449.B7M1+
   European intervention, 1861-1867: F1233
   Frontier troubles: F1232-1234
      United States: F786
      Texas: F391
   Mayas: F1435.1.A+
   Military history
      Spanish conquest of, 1519-1550:
         F1230
      Texan Mier Expedition, 1842: F390
      Texan War of Independence, 1835-
         1836: F390
      War with the United States, 1845-
         1848: E405+
      Wars of Independence, 1810-1821:
         F1232
   Naval history
      War with the United States, 1845-
         1848: E410
   Revolution of 1910- : F1234
   Rule over Honduras, 1822-1823: F1507
   Troubles with France, 1838-1839: F1232
Mexico (Archdiocese): F1301
Mexico (City): F1386
   Capture of, 1847: E406.M6
   Indian antiquities: F1219.1.M5
Mexico (Empire)
   Itúrbide, 1821-1823: F1232
   Maximilian, 1864-1867: F1233
Mexico (Federal District): F1386
Mexico (State): F1301
Mexico (Viceroyalty): F1231
Mexico, Gulf of: F296
Mexico, Gulf of (Caribbean area): F2155+
Mexico, Valley of: F1302
Mezquital Valley (Mexico): F1291
Miami (Florida): F319.M6
Miami Indians: E99.M48
Miami Purchase: F483
Miami River and Valley (Ohio): F497.M64
Miao (Asian people) in the United States:
   E184.H55
Miccosukee Indians: E99.M615
Michaelius, Jonas: F122.1
Michelena, Santos: F2325
Michigan: F561+
   Afro-Americans: E185.93.M5
   Counties, etc.: F572.A+
   Indians: E78.M6
   Wars
      Civil War: E514.1+
      Indian wars: E83.76, E83.81

Michigan: F561+
  Wars — Continued
    Revolution
      Clark's Expedition against Detroit, 1781: E237
      Toledo War, 1836: F497.B7
      War of 1812: E355+
      War of 1898: E726.M6
Michigan, Lake, region: F553
  Illinois: F547.M56
  Indiana: F532.M67
  Michigan: F572.M57
  Wisconsin: F587.M57
Michigan Association of Veterans of the War with Mexico: E401.34
Michilimackinac: F572.M16
Michilimackinac Island (Michigan): F572.M16
Michoacán, Mexico (State): F1306
Micmac Indians: E99.M6
Middle America: F1421+, F1601+
Middle Atlantic States (Middle States): F106
  Colonial history: E188
  Indians: E78.M65
  Revolution: E230.5.M6
Middle Columbia Salish Indians: E99.S55
Middle Tennessee: F442.2
Middle West: F350.5+
  Indians: E78.M67
Middleburg, Battle of, 1863: E475.5
Middlesex Co. (Ontario): F1059.M6
Middlesex Fells Reservation (Massachusetts): F72.M7
Middletown (Virginia), Battle of, 1864: E477.33
Midwest (Midwestern States): F350.5+
Mier Expedition, 1842: F390
Mifflin, Thomas: E207.M6
Migrations, Indian: F2230.1.M47
  Mexico: F1219.3.M54
Mikasuki Indians: E99.M615
Mikinakwadshiwininiwak Indians: E99.M62
Miles, Nelson Appleton: E83.866
Military biography
  United States: E181, E745
    Wars
      Civil War: E457, E467+
      Revolution: E206+
      War of 1812: E353+
      War of 1898: E714.5+
      War with Mexico: E403+
Military history in America
  Attacks on
    Puerto Rico, 1585, 1598, 1791: F1973
Military lands
  Illinois: F547.M6
  New York: F127.M4
Military museums
  United States
    Civil War: E646
    Revolution: E289
    War of 1898: E734

Military Order of Foreign Wars of the United States: E181
Military Order of Pulaski: E202.99.M64
Military Order of the Loyal Legion of the United States: E462.2
  Papers read before: E464
Military Order of the Medal of Honor: E462.3
Military Order of the Purple Heart: E181
Military service, Compulsory
  United States
    Civil War
      Confederate Army: E545, E551.4
      Union Army: E491
Military societies
  United States: E181
Military Society of the War of 1812: E351.5
Military tracts
  Illinois: F547.M6
  New York: F127.M4
  Virginia
    Old Northwest: F483
Militia
  United States
    War of 1812: E359.3
Milk River and Valley: F1079.M54
  Alberta: F1079.M54
  Montana: F737.M48
Mill Creek (Ohio): F497.H2
Mill Creek and Valley (Pennsylvania): F157.L2
Mill Creek Indians: E99.M625
Mill Creek War, 1857-1865: E83.858
Mill River (Massachusetts): F72.H3
Miller, William: F3446
Millers River and Valley (Massachusetts): F72.M73
Milliken's Bend, Battle of, 1863: E475.4
Mills, David: F1033
Millstone River and Valley (New Jersey): F142.M64
Milner, Moses Embree: F594
Miluk Indians: E99.C8742
Milwaukee (Wisconsin): F589.M6
Mimbreño Indians: E99.M63
Mimbres culture: E99.M76
Mimbres River and Valley (New Mexico): F802.G7
Minaco Indians: F2520.1.M44
Minas Geraes, Brazil (State): F2581
Mine Run (Virginia), campaign, 1863: E475.78
Mineral King Valley (California): F868.T8
Mingan Islands (Quebéc): F1054.M59
Mingo Indians: E99.M64
Miniconjou Indians: E99.M642
Mining, Indian: F1219.3.M58
Minisink, N.Y., Battle of, 1779: E241.M6
Minisink Indians: E99.M65
Minisink Patent (1704): F142.B7
Minisink region (New York): F127.M5
Minneapolis (Minnesota): F614.M5
Minneapolis and St. Paul (Minnesota): F614.M6

Minnedosa River and Valley (Manitoba): F1064.M5
Minnesota: F601+
  Afro-Americans: E185.93.M55
  Counties, etc.: F612.A+
  Indians: E78.M7
  Wars
    Civil War: E515.1+
    Indian wars: E83.86, E83.863
    War of 1898: E726.M7
Minnesota River and Valley: F612.M4
Minnetonka, Lake (Minnesota): F612.H5
Minnewaska, Lake (New York): F127.U4
Minook Creek and Valley (Alaska): F912.M55
Minorcans in the United States: E184.M53
Minorities (America): F1035.A+, F1419.A+, F1440.A+, F1629.A+, F2239, F3021.A+
Minuit, Peter: F122.1
Minute Man National Historical Park (Massachusetts): F72.M7
Minute Men of 1861: E493.9
Minutemen
  United States Revolution: E263.A+
Miquelon: F1170
Miramichi River and Valley (New Brunswick): F1044.M5
Miranda, Francisco de: F2323
Miranda, Venezuela (State): F2331.M6
Miranda's Expedition to Venezuela, 1806: F2323
Miró, Esteban: F373
Miscegenation
  Negroes
    United States: E185.62
Mishikhwutmetunne Indians: E99.C8742
Misiones, Argentina (Province): F2916
  Jesuit missions of Paraguay: F2684
  Part awarded to Brazil: F2626
Miskigula Indians: E99.P26
Miskito Indians: F1529.M9
Mission buildings, Spanish: F862
Missionary Ridge, Battle of, 1863: E475.97
Missions, Indian
  Central America: F1434.2.M6, F1435.3.M53, F1465.3.M57, F1525.3.M57
  North America: E98.M6
    Mexico: F1219.3.M59
    United States: F864
  Pre-Columbian America: E59.M65
  South America: F2230.1.M5, F2270.1.M5, F2319.3.M5, F2519.3.M5, F2679.3.M5, F2821.3.M5, F3069.3.M5, F3320.1.M47, F3429.3.M6, F3721.3.M6
Missisauga Indians: E99.M68
Missisquoi Co. (Quebec): F1054.M6
Missisquoi River and Valley
  Quebec: F1054.B8
  Vermont: F57.M7
Mississippi: F336+
  Afro-Americans: E185.93.M6

Montezuma I, Emperor of Mexico:
F1219.75.M75
Montezuma II, Emperor of Mexico: F1219,
F1230
Montezuma Castle National Monument
(Arizona): F817.M57
Montgomery, Richard: E207.M7
Montgomery, Sir Robert: F289
Margravate of Azilia: F289
Montgomery (Alabama): F334.M7
Monticello (Virginia): E332.74
Montmagny Co. (Quebec): F1054.M79
Montmorency Co. (Quebec): F1054.M8
Montpelier (Vermont): F59.M7
Montreal (Quebec): F1054.5.M8
Montreal District (Quebec): F1054.M83
Monts, Pierre de Guast, sieur de: F1030
Montserrat (West Indies): F2082
Montt, Manuel F.A.J.: F3095
Monument Cemetery (Philadelphia):
F158.61.M8
Monument Valley (Arizona): F817.M6
Monuments
United States
Persons: E312.45+, E332.73
Wars and battles: E641+, E733
Monuments, Indian (Mexico): F1219.3.M6
Monuments, National (U.S.): F292.F7
Moody, James: E278.M8
Moore's Creek Bridge, N.C., Battle of, 1776:
E241.M8
Moor's Indian Charity School (Lebanon,
Connecticut): E97.6.M5
Moose Mountain Provincial Park
(Saskatchewan): F1074.M66
Moosehead Lake region (Maine): F27.M8
Mopan Indians: F1465.2.M65
Moquegua, Peru (Dept.): F3451.M8
Moquelumnan Indians: E99.M89
Mora, Juan Rafael: F1547.5
Morant Bay Rebellion, 1865-1866: F1886
Moravian Indians: E99.M9
Moravians in the United States: E184.M7
Revolution, 1775-1783: E269.M6
Morazán, Francisco: F1438
Morehead, John Motley: F258
Morehouse Parish (Louisiana): F377.M7
Morelia (Mexico): F1391.M8
Morelos, Mexico (State): F1311
Morelos y Pavón, José María Teclo: F1232
Moreno, Mariano: F2845
Moreno Creek and Valley (New Mexico):
F802.C7
Moreno Valley (California): F868.R6
Morgan, Daniel: E207.M8
Morgan, George: E302.6.M6
Morgan, John Hunt: E467.1.M86
First Kentucky raid, July 1862: E474.32
Kentucky raid, May-June 1864: E476.82
Raid in Kentucky, Indiana, and Ohio,
1863: E475.18
Second Kentucky raid, 1862-1863:
E474.75
Morgan's Cavalry Division
Confederate Army: E547.M8

Morillo y Morillo, Pablo: F2324
Moriníngo Martínez, Higinio: F2689
Mormons
Settlements
Utah: F826
Rebellion, 1857-1859: F826
Mormons in Canada: F1035.M67
Mormons in Mexico: F1392.M6
Mormons in the United States: E184.M8
Moro Indians: F2679.2.M6
Morrill, Justin Smith: E664.M8
Morris, Charles: E353.1.M8
Morris, Gouverneur: E302.6.M7
Morris, Margaret (Hill): E263.N5
Morris, Mary (White): E302.6.M81
Morris, Richard Valentine: E335
Morris, Robert: E302.6.M8
Morris, Thomas: E340.M8
Morris Creek and Valley (West Virginia):
F247.B6
Morris Island (South Carolina), Military
operations on, 1863: E475.63
Morris Mansion (New York): F128.8.M8
Morris River and Valley (Manitoba):
F1064.M67
Morrisania Manor (New York): F128.68.B8
Morrison Cave (Montana): F737.L65
Morristown National Historical Park (New
Jersey): F142.M85
Morro, El, National Monument (New
Mexico): F802.E5
Morro Bay (California): F868.S18
Morro Island (Panama): F1569.P3
Morrow, Dwight Whitney: E748.M75
Morrow, Jeremiah: E340.M83
Mortality and health statistics
United States
Civil War: E621+
Morton, Camp, Indianapolis
Military prison: E616.M8
Morton, Julius Sterling: E664.M82
Morton, Levi Parsons: E664.M85
Morton, Oliver Perry: F506.1+
Mortuary customs, Indian: E98.M8;
F1435.3.M6, F2230.1.M6,
F2821.3.M6, F3429.3.M7
Pre-Columbian America: E59.M8
Mosby, John Singleton: E467.1.M87
Moseten Indians: F3320.2.M6
Mosier Hills (Oregon): F882.W3
Moslems in Latin America: F1419.M87
Moslems in the United States: E184.M88
Mosquera, Tomás Cipriano de: F2276
Mosquitia, Honduras (District): F1509.M9
Mosquitia, Nicaragua (Region): F1529.M9
Mosquito Coast (Nicaragua): F1529.M9
Transfer to Nicaragua by Great Britain,
1893: F1526.27
Mosquito Indians: F1529.M9
Mosquito Reservation (Nicaragua):
F1529.M9
Motagua River (Guatemala): F1469.M68
Mother Neff State Park (Texas): F392.C8
Mothers of U.S. Presidents: E176.3

Motherwell Farmstead National Historic
Park (Saskatchewan): F1074.W28
Motilon Indians: F2319.2.M6
Motilone Indians: F2319.2.M6
Motilones (Indians): F2319.2.M6
Motion pictures about the war
Civil War, 1861-1865: E656
Motochintlec Indians: F1221.M74
Motozintlec Indians: F1221.M74
Motoztintlec Indians: F1221.M74
Mott, Lucretia (Coffin): E449
Moultrie, Fort, Battle of, 1776: E241.M9
Moultrie, William: E207.M85
Mound builders: E73, E78.A+
Mounds: E73, E78.A+
Mounds, Cave of the (Wisconsin): F587.D3
Mount Adams (Washington): F897.K6
Mount Castleguard (Alberta): F1079.B5
Mount Desert Island
Jesuit station, 1609: F1038
Maine: F27.M9
Mount Diablo State Park (California):
F868.C76
Mount Hope Cemetery (Boston): F73.61
Mount Le Conte (Tennessee): F443.S45
Mount LeConte (Tennessee): F443.S45
Mount McKinley (Alaska): F912.M2
Mount McKinley National Park (Alaska):
F912.M23
Mount Moosilaukee (New Hampshire):
F42.G7
Mount Orford Park (Québec): F1054.P37
Mount Pleasant (District of Columbia):
F202.M9
Mount Rainier National Park (Washington):
F897.R2
Mount Rushmore National Memorial:
F657.R8
Mount Tamalpais State Park (California):
F868.M3
Mount Vernon: E312.5
Mount Vernon Memorial Highway
(Virginia): F232.G38
Mountain Lake (Virginia): F232.G4
Mountain Meadows Massacre, 1857: F826
Mountain people
Ramapo Mountains: E184.R3
Mountain whites: E184.M83
Mountain whites of the South (General):
F210
Mountaineer (Montagnais) Indians:
E99.M87
Mouse River and Valley
Manitoba: F1064.S6
Saskatchewan: F1074.S67
Mowat, Sir Oliver: F1058
Moxie Pond (Maine): F27.S7
Moxos, Bolivia (Province): F3341.M9
Moylan, Stephen: E207.M9
Mozambicans in Brazil: F2659.M69
Mt. Castleguard (Alberta): F1079.B5
Mt. Le Conte (Tennessee): F443.S45
Mt. LeConte (Tennessee): F443.S45
Muckleshoot Indians: E99.M917
Mucury Colony (Brazil): F2581

Muename Indians: F2270.2.M75
Muenane Indians: F2270.2.M75
Muhlenberg, John Peter Gabriel: E207.M95
Muinana Indians: F2270.2.M75
Muinane-Bora Indians: F2270.2.M75
Muinane Indians: F2270.2.M75
Muinani Indians: F2270.2.M75
Muir Glacier (Alaska): F912.M9
Muir Trail (California): F868.S5
Muir Woods National Monument
    (California): F868.M3
Mul-Chic (Mexico): F1435.1.M84
Mulattoes
    United States: E185.62
Mulberry Island (Virginia): F232.J2
Mullica River (New Jersey): F142.M9
Mulligan, Hercules: E302.6.M88
Mulluk Indians: E99.C8742
Multnomah Indians: E99.M92
Mummies, Indian
    Peru: F3429.3.M8
Mundurucu Indians: F2520.1.M8
Münkü Indians: F2520.1.I7
Munsee Indians: E99.M93
Mura Indians: F2520.1.M9
Murfreesboro (Tennessee), Action at and
    surrender of, July 1862: E474.34
Murfreesboro campaign, 1862-1863:
    E474.77
Murphy, Henry Cruse: F123
Murphys Lake (Louisiana): F377.N4
Murray, James: E278.M98
Murray, Lake, and Region (South Carolina):
    F277.M87
Murray, William Henry: F700
Murrell, John A.: F396
Murrieta, Joaquin: F865
Muscatine (Iowa): F629.M9
Muscle Shoals (Topography): F332.T2
Muscongus lands (Maine): F27.M95
Muscongus (Waldo) Patent (Maine):
    F27.M95
Muskeget Island (Massachusetts): F72.N2
Muskegon (Michigan): F574.M9
Muskhogean Indians: E99.M95
Muskingum River and Valley (Ohio):
    F497.M92
Muskogee (Oklahoma): F704.M9
Muskoka District (Ontario): F1059.M9
Muskoka Lake region (Ontario): F1059.M9
Muslims in Canada: F1035.M87
Muslims in Latin America: F1419.M87
Muslims in the United States: E184.M88
Mustang Island State Park (Texas): F392.N8
Mutilones (Indians): F2319.2.M6
Mutiny Act, 1765: E215.4
Mutiny of the Pennsylvania line, 1781: E255
Muzo Indians: F2270.2.M8
Myakka River State Park (Florida):
    F317.M92
Mystery Mountain (British Columbia):
    F1089.C7
Mythology, Indian
    Pre-Columbian America: E59.R38

N

Nabesnatana Indians: E99.T187
Nabuco, Joaquim: F2536
Naches River and Valley (Washington):
    F897.Y18
Nacimiento River and Valley (California):
    F868.N16
Nacogdoches District (Texas): F392.N24
Nahane Indians: E99.N125
Nahoas: F1221.N3
Nahua Indians
    Modern: F1221.N3
    Pre-Columbian: F1219.73+
Nahuatl Indians: F1221.N3
Nahuatlecas: F1221.N3
Nahuel Huapí, Lake (Argentina): F2951
Nahuel Huapí, Parque Nacional de
    (Argentina): F2951
Naj Tunich
    Mayas: F1435.1.N35
Nakimu Caves (British Columbia): F1089.S4
Nambicuara Indians: F2520.1.N3
Names, Indian: E98.N2, F1219.76.N35,
    F1485.3.N35, F1525.3.N35,
    F2319.3.N5, F2519.3.N35,
    F2821.3.N3
Names, Negro: E185.89.N3
Nancy Hanks Lincoln Memorial (Indiana):
    F532.S6
Nanticoke Indians: E99.N14
Nanticoke River and Valley: F172.N35
    Delaware: F172.N35
    Maryland: F187.N35
Nantucket Island (Massachusetts): F72.N2
Napo Indians: F3722.1.Q48
Napo-Pastaza, Ecuador
    Province: F3741.N3
Naranjo Site (Guatemala): F1435.1.N37
Narcotics, Indian: E98.N5, F2230.1.N37,
    F2270.1.N35, F3320.1.N37,
    F3721.3.N35
    Pre-Columbian America: E59.N5
Nariño, Antonio: F2274
Nariño, Colombia (Dept.): F2281.N3
Narraganset Indians: E99.N16
Narragansett Bay region: F87.N2
Narragansett country: F82
Narváez, Pánfilo de: E125.N3
Nasca Indians: F3430.1.N3
Nash, Francis: E207.N2
Nashawena Island (Massachusetts): F72.E5
Nashua (New Hampshire): F44.N2
Nashville (Tennessee): F444.N2
    Battle of, 1864: E477.52
    Southern Convention, 1850: E423
Naskapi Indians: E99.N18
Nassau (Bahamas): F1659.N3
Nat Turner's Insurrection, 1831: F232.S7
Natchesan Indians: E99.N19
Natchez (Mississippi): F349.N2
Natchez District of West Florida: F341
Natchez Indians: E99.N2
Natchez Massacre, 1729: E83.73

Natchez Trace: F217.N37
Natchitoches Parish (Louisiana): F377.N4
National Alliance, Daughters of Veterans:
    E462.99.D2
National Association of Army Nurses of the
    Civil War: E621
National Association of Naval Veterans:
    E462.5
National Association of Veterans of the
    Mexican War: E401.3
National capital, Location of (U.S.): F195
National Cathedral (Washington, D.C.):
    F204.C3
National cemeteries
    United States: F234.A7
        Rolls of interment
            Civil War
                Confederate Army: E548
                Union Army: E494
National characteristics
    America: E169.1
National Convention of the Soldiers of the
    War of 1812: E351.2
National parks
    United States: E160
National Road (Pennsylvania): F157.C85
National Society of the Colonial Dames of
    America: E186.4
National Society of the Colonial Daughters
    of America: E186.99.N33
National Society of the United States
    Daughters of 1812: E351.6
National Soldiers Historical Association:
    E462.98
National Theatre (Washington, D.C.):
    F204.N23
National Veteran Club of the United States:
    E462.99.N27
Natsitkutchin Indians: E99.N22
Natural Bridge (Virginia): F232.R68
Naugatuck Indians: E99.N23
Naugatuck River and Valley (Connecticut):
    F102.N2
Nauset Indians: E99.N25
Naushon Island (Massachusetts): F72.E5
Navaho War, 1858-1868: E83.859
Navajo Indians: E99.N3
Naval and Military Order of the Spanish-
    American War: F714.3.N2+
Naval biography
    United States: E182, E746
    Wars
        Civil War: E467+
        Revolution: E206+
        War of 1812: E353+
        War of 1898: E714.5+
        War with Mexico: E403+
Naval blockades
    Civil War: E480
Naval Order of the United States: E182
Naval revolt (Brazil): F2537
Naval societies
    United States: E182
Naval veterans' organizations
    United States: E182

Naval war with France (U.S.), 1798-1800: E323

Navarrese in Latin America: F1419.N38

Navassa: F1991

Navesink River and Valley (New Jersey): F142.M7

Navies
  Spain
    War of 1898: E727.8
  United States
    Revolution: E271
    War of 1812: E360
    War of 1898: E727

Navigation laws, British Enforcement (1775-1783): E215.1

Navy Island (Ontario): F1059.W36

Nayarit, Mexico (State): F1313

Nazareth Hall, Nazareth, Pa., and the Civil War: E541.N2

Nazca (Peru)
  Indian antiquities: F3429.1.N3

Nazca culture (Peru)
  Indian antiquities: F3429.1.N3

Nebraska: F661+
  Afro-Americans: E185.93.N5
  Civil War: E518.1+
  Counties, etc.: F672.A+
  Indians: E78.N3
  Slavery: E445.N2

Nebraska-Kansas Bill, May 1854: E433

Necessity, Fort: E199

Neches River and Valley (Texas): F392.N35

Negro emancipation
  Haiti: F1923
  Jamaica: F1886

Negro insurrections
  Jamaica, 1831: F1886

Negro River (Brazil): F2546

Negroes in British Guiana: F2391.N4

Nehalem Indians: E99.N45

Neiva, Colombia (Province): F2281.N5

Nelson, Knute: E664.N4

Nenana River and Valley (Alaska): F912.N45

Nendiume Site (Mexico): F1435.1.C49

Nepisiguit River and Valley (New Brunswick): F1044.N7

Nespelim Indians: E99.N46

Netherlands
  Attack on Puerto Rico, 1625: F1973
  Blockade of Venezuela, 1908: F2325

Netherlands Guiana: F2401+

Netherlands West Indies: F2141

Netsikutchin Indians: E99.N22

Neuquén, Argentina (Territory): F2921
  Indian antiquities: F2821.1.N4

Neuquén River (Argentina): F2921

Neuse River and Valley (North Carolina): F262.N48

Neutral Nation Indians: E99.N48

Neutral trade, American, 1800-1810: E336+

Neutrality proclamation, 1793: E313+

Nevada: F836+
  Afro-Americans: E185.93.N52

Nevada: F836+ — Continued
  Civil War: E519.1+
  Counties, etc.: F847.A+
  Indians: E78.N4

Nevado Sarcantay (Peru): F3451.C9

Nevis (West Indies): F2084

New Albion Grant: F137

New Amsterdam (British Guiana): F2389.N4

New Amsterdam (New York before 1775): F128.4

New Bern (North Carolina)
  Battle of, March 1862: E473.34
  Expedition against, 1864: E476.23
  Expedition from, Dec. 1862: E474.52

New Brunswick (Canada): F1041+
  American Revolution: E263.N9
    Loyalists: E277
  Boundary troubles with U.S.: E398
  Indians: E78.N46

New Deal period
  United States history: E806

New England: F1+
  Colony and province: F7-7.5
  Council for: F7
  Dominion of, 1686-1689: F7.5
  Hurricane, 1938: F9
  Indians: E78.N5
  Nova Scotia settlement, 1760-1761: F1038
  United colonies, 1643-1684: F7
  Wars
    Indian wars: E83.63, E83.67, E83.72
    Intercolonial wars, 1689-1763: E196-199
    Revolution of 1689: F7.5
    War of 1812, Federalist opposition to: E357.6+

New England Association of Soldiers of the War of 1812: E351.27

New England Emigrant Aid Company: F685

New France
  Acadia: F1036+
  Conflicts with British colonies, 1689-1763: E196, E197, E199
  English conquests: F1030, F1030.9
  Explorations: E131+
    Mississippi River and Valley: F351
  Hudson's Bay Company: F1060+
  Indian wars: E81+
  Intercolonial wars: E199
    Quebec Campaign, 1759: E199

New France, Company of, 1629-1663: F1030

New Granada
  Audiencia: F2272
  Republic, 1842-1858: F2276
  State, 1831-1842: F2275
  United Provinces, 1811-1816: F2274
  Viceroyalty: F2272

New Hampshire: F31+
  Afro-Americans: E185.93.N53
  Counties, etc.: F42.A+
  Indians: E78.N54

New Hampshire: F31+ — Continued
  Wars
    Civil War: E520.1+
    French and Indian War: E199
    Indian wars: E83.72
    Revolution: E263.N4
      Military operations: E230+
    War of 1812: E359.5.N3
    War of 1898: E726.N3

New Hampshire Grants: F52

New Harmony (Indiana): F534.N5

New Haven (Connecticut): F104.N6
  Invasion, 1779: E241.N5

New Haven Colony: F98

New Hope Church, Battle of, 1864: E476.7

New Jersey: F131+
  Afro-Americans: E185.93.N54
  Counties, etc.: F142.A+
  East Jersey, 1676-1702: F137
  Fenwick's colony: F142.S2
  Indians: E78.N6
  Slavery: E445.N54
  Wars
    Civil War: E521.1+
    Colonial wars: E199
    Revolution: E263.N5
      Military operations: E230+
      Washington's retreat, 1776: E232
    War of 1812: E359.5.N4
    War of 1898: E726.N4

New Jersey Coastal Heritage Trail (New Jersey): F142.N48

New Jersey Palisades: F142.B4

New Jersey Volunteers
  Loyalist regiment: E277.6.N5

New London (Connecticut): F104.N7

New Madrid (Missouri)
  Military operations, 1862: E473.15

New Market (Virginia): F234.N48
  Engagement at, 1864: E476.64

New Market Endless Caverns (Virginia): F232.S47

New Melones Lake and region (California): F868.N52

New Mexico: F791+
  Afro-Americans: E185.93.N55
  Confederate history: E571.1+
  Counties, etc.: F802.A+
  Indians: E78.N65
  Mexican state, 1822-1848: F800
  New Southwest: F786, F799+
  Occupation by U.S.
    War with Mexico: E405.2
  Slavery: E445.N55
  Spanish province before 1822: F799
  Texan Santa Fe Expedition, 1841: F390
  Texas purchase of 1850: F801
  Wars
    Civil War: E522.1+, E571.1+
      Military operations: E470.9
    Indian wars: E83.88
    War with Mexico: E405.2

New Netherlands: F122+
  Conquest of New Sweden: F167

New Netherlands: F122+ — Continued
  Hudson Valley: F127.H8
  Indian wars: E83.655
  Posts on Connecticut River: F97
New Northwest: F597
New Orleans
  Battle of, 1815: E356.N5
  General Butler's administration, 1862:
    E510.1+
  Occupation of, 1862: E472.88
  War of 1812: E355.6
New Orleans (Louisiana): F379.N5
New Plymouth Colony: F68
New Providence (Bahamas): F1659.N3
New Quebec District (Quebec): F1054.N5
New River and Valley
  North Carolina: F262.N6
  Virginia: F232.N5
  West Virginia: F247.N5
New River and Valley (Onslow Co., North
  Carolina): F262.O5
New Southwest: F785.3+
New Spain (Viceroyalty): F1231
New Sweden: F167
New Ulm Battle, 1862: E83.86
New World, Allusions to the: E139
New York (City): F128+
  British occupation, 1776: E232
  Draft riots, 1863: F128.44
  Evacuation, 1783: E239
New York City College and the Civil War:
  E541.N5
New York (County): F128+
New York (State): F116+
  Afro-Americans: E185.93.N56
  Counties, etc.: F127.A+
  Dutch conquest, 1673: F122+
  Hudson's explorations: E129.H8
  Indians: E78.N7
  New Hampshire Grants: F52
  Slavery: E445.N56
  Wars
    Civil War: E523.1+
    Indian wars: E83.655, E83.663
    Intercolonial wars: E199
    Revolution: E263.N6
      Military operations: E230+
    War of 1812: E359.5.N6
    War of 1898: E726.N5
    War with Mexico: E409.5.N6
    Western lands ceded, 1787: E309, F483
New York Avenue Presbyterian Church
  (Washington, D.C.): F203.2.N4
New York Indian Uprising, 1655: E83.655
New York military tracts: F127.M4
New York State Convention of the Soldiers
  of the War of 1812: E351.28
New York State Seaway Trail (New York):
  F127.N38
New York University. Hall of Fame: E176.6
Newark (New Jersey): F144.N6
Newbern (North Carolina): E474.52
Newberry District (South Carolina): F277.N5

Newberry National Volcanic Monument
  (Oregon): F882.D4
Newburgh addresses: E255
Newburgh Bay (New York): F127.O8
Newfound Lake (New Hampshire): F42.G7
Newfoundland: F1121+
  Annexation of Labrador: F1137
  Indians: E78.N72
  Provincial status, 1949: F1123
Newport (Rhode Island): F89.N5
  Union of plantations: F82
Newsmen
  U.S. Civil War: E609
Newtown, New York, Battle of, 1779:
  E241.N59
Nez Percé Indians: E99.N5
Nez Percé War, 1877: E83.877
Nezahualcóyotl, King of Texcoco:
  F1219.75.N49
Niagara (Ontario): F1059.5.N5
Niagara, Fort
  French and Indian War, 1755-1763: E199
Niagara campaign, 1759: E199
Niagara Falls, Battle of, 1814: E356.L9
Niagara Falls (New York): F127.N8
Niagara Falls (Ontario): F1059.5.N55
Niagara Falls Park, Queen Victoria:
  F1059.Q3
Niagara frontier: F127.N6
Niagara-on-the-Lake (Ontario): F1059.5.N5
Niagara peninsula (Ontario): F1059.N5
Niagara region
  War of 1812: E355.6
Niagara River region
  New York: F127.N6
  Ontario: F1059.N5
Niantic Indians: E99.N6
Nicaragua: F1521+
  Confederación de Centro América:
    F1438, F1526.25
  Conflicts with El Salvador: F1527
  English Invasion, 1780-1781: F1526.25
  Filibuster War, 1855-1860: F1526.27
  Revolutions of 1909-1910, 1912, 1926-
    1929: F1526.3
  United States intervention, 1909-1933:
    F1526.3
Nicaragua, Lake, region: F1529.N5
Nicaragua Canal: F1526.27
Nicaraguans in Costa Rica: F1557.N5
Nicaraguans in the United States: E184.N53
Nicarao Indians: F1525.2.N5
Nicolet, Jean: F1030.15
Nicoya Peninsula (Costa Rica): F1549.N5
Nictheroy (Brazil): F2651.N5
Nieuw Nickerie (Dutch Guiana): F2429.N5
Nievería (Peru)
  Indian antiquities: F3429.1.N5
Nigerians in the United States: E184.N55
Nile Creek and Valley (Washington):
  F897.Y18
Nim Li Punit Site (Belize): F1435.1.N55
Nimrod Lake and Region (Arkansas):
  F417.N56
Nine Partners Patent (New York): F127.D8

Nineteen Seventy Six (1976) Bicentennial
  United States: E285.3+
Ninety-Six District (South Carolina):
  F277.N6
Niobrara River and Valley
  Nebraska: F672.N56
  Wyoming: F767.N52
Nipissing District (Ontario): F1059.N55
Nipissing Indians: E99.N65
Nipmuc Indians: E99.N7
Niquiranos: F1525.2.N5
Nisenan Indians: E99.N73
Nishinam Indians: E99.N73
Niska Indians: E99.N734
Nisqualli, Fort (Washington): F897.P9
Nisqually Indians: E99.N74
Niterói (Brazil): F2651.N5
Nixon, Richard Milhous: E855+
No Man's Land (Oklahoma): F702.N6
No Mans Land Island (Massachusetts):
  F72.N6
Noah, Mordecai Manuel: E335
Noatak National Preserve (Alaska): F912.N6
Nobles Trail (California): F868.S5
Nohmul Site (Belize): F1435.1.N64
Noix, Île aux (Quebec): F1054.I35
Nome (Alaska): F914.N6
Nome, Cape: F912.N7
Nome-Taylor Highway (Alaska): F912.N73
Nomlaki Indians: E99.N815
Nonamesset Island (Massachusetts): F72.E5
Nonimportation agreements of 1768-1769:
  E215.3
Nooksack Indians: E99.N84
Nootka Indians: E99.N85
Nootka Sound, British Columbia: F1089.N8
Nootka Sound Controversy, 1789-1790:
  F1089.N8
Nor Oriental del Marañón (Peru): F3451.N67
Nor Yungas, Bolivia (Province): F3341.N67
Norbeck, Peter: F656
Nord Alexis, Pierre: F1926
Nordeste brasileiro: F2583
Nordeste do Brasil (Region): F2583
Norfolk (Virginia): F234.N8
  Expedition against, 1813: E355.4
  Occupation of, 1862: E473.64
Norfolk Co. (Ontario): F1059.N6
Norman, Lake (North Carolina): F262.N67
Norman (Oklahoma): F704.N6
Norman Wells (Mackenzie District):
  F1100.5.N6
Norridgewock Indians: E99.N9
Norris, George William: E748.N65
Norris Lake (Tennessee): F443.N67
Norsemen
  Pre-Columbian discovery of America:
    E105
Norte de Santander, Colombia (Dept.):
  F2281.N6
North America: E31+
  Aborigines: E75+
  Atlantic coast: F106
    Canada: F1035.8

North America: E31+ — Continued
  Discovery: E101+
  Ethnology: E51+
  Indians: E98.F6
  Pacific coast: F851.72+
North Carolina: F251+
  Afro-Americans: E185.93.N6
  Confederate history: E573.1+
  Counties, etc.: F262.A+
  Indians: E78.N74
  Raleigh's colonies, 1584-1590: F229
  Reconstruction, 1865-1877: F259
  Slavery: E445.N8
  Wars
    Civil War: E524.1+, E573.1+
      Military operations: E470.6,
        E470.65, E477.7
      Indian wars: E83.71, E83.759
      Regulator Insurrection, 1766-1771:
        F257
      Revolution: E236-237, E241.A+,
        E263.N8
      War of 1812: E359.5.N7
      War of 1898: E726.N8
      War with Spaniards of Florida, 1740:
        F314
      Western lands ceded to the U.S.: E309;
        F483
North Carolina, Western: F261
North Carolina University and the Civil War:
  E586.N8
North Cascades National Park: F897.C3
North Central States: F476+, F597
North Chile: F3205
North Dakota: F631+
  Afro-Americans: E185.93.N7
  Counties, etc.: F642.A+
  Dakota Indian War, 1890-1891: E83.89
  Indians: E78.N75
North End (Boston): F73.68.N65
North Fork, Coeur d'Alene River (Idaho):
  F752.C65
North Fork Skokomish River (Washington):
  F897.S54
North Georgia: F291.7
North Mexico: F1314
North Park (Colorado): F782.J3
North Penn Village (Philadelphia):
  F158.68.N8
North Platte River and Valley: F672.N8
  Wyoming: F767.N8
North Point, Battle of 1814: E356.B2
North River (Massachusetts): F72.P7
North Shore (Chicago): F548.68.N7
North Shore (Massachusetts): F72.E7
North Shore (Quebec): F1054.S3
North Shore of the Saint Lawrence Gulf:
  F1054.S3
North Shrewsbury River (New Jersey):
  F142.M7
North Toe River and Valley (North
  Carolina): F262.A9
Northeast Argentina: F2921.5
Northeast Brazil: F2583

Northeast coast region (North Carolina):
  F262.A33
Northeast Washington (District of
  Columbia): F202.N5
Northeastern boundary
  United States: F27.B7, F42.B7
  Disputes, 1783-1845: E398
Northeastern States (Indians): E78.E2
Northern boundary (U.S.): F550.5+, F597
Northern California: F867.5
Northern Liberties (Philadelphia):
  F158.68.N9
Northern Michigan: F572.N7
  Upper Peninsula: F572.N8
Northern Neck (Virginia): F232.N86
Northern Peninsula (Michigan): F572.N8
Northern regions of Canada (General):
  F1090.5
Northern Virginia, Army of (C.S.A.):
  E470.2+
Northmen
  Pre-Columbian discovery of America:
    E105
Northumberland Co. (Ontario): F1059.N65
Northwest, Canadian: F1060+
Northwest, Department of the
  United States Army
    Military operations, 1862: E473.8
Northwest, New: F597
Northwest, Old: F476+
Northwest, The (U.S.): F597
Northwest Angle (Minnesota): F612.L4
Northwest Argentina: F2922
Northwest boundary (U.S.): F854, F880
Northwest coast Indians: E78.N78
Northwest Company of Canada: F1060+
Northwest Miramichi River and Valley (New
  Brunswick): F1044.N83
Northwest Ordinance, 1787: E309
Northwest Rebellion, 1885: F1060.9
Northwest Territories (Canada): F1060+
Northwest Territories, Indians of: E78.N79
Northwest Territory (U.S.): F476+
Northwest Washington (District of
  Columbia): F202.N7
Northwestern Conspiracy, 1864: E458.8
Northwestern Indian wars (Ohio Valley),
  1790-1795: E83.79
Norton Sound and region (Alaska):
  F912.N75
Norwalk Islands (Connecticut): F102.F2
Norwegians in Canada: F1035.N6
Norwegians in South America: F2239.N6
Norwegians in the United States: E184.S2
Norwich (Connecticut): F104.N93
Norwich (Vermont): F59.N9
Nottoway Indians: E99.N93
Nouel y Bobadilla, Adolfo Alejandro:
  F1938.4
Nova Scotia: F1036+
  American Revolution: E263.N9
    Loyalists: E277, F1038
  Indians: E78.C2, E78.N9
  Wars: E83.72

Nova Scotia: F1036+ — Continued
  Settlement by New Englanders, 1760-
    1761: F1038
Ntlakyapamuk Indians: E99.N96
Ñuble, Chile (Province): F3206
Nueces River, Battle of, 1862: E473.4
Nueces River and Valley (Texas): F392.N82
Nueva Esparta, Venezuela (State): F2331.N8
Nueva Galicia: F1296
Nueva Viscaya: F1261
Nuevitas (Cuba): F1839.N9
Nuevo Reino de León: F1316
Nuevo Santander: F1356
Nukak Indians: F2270.2.N8
Nullification
  United States
    Jackson's administration: E384.3
Numa Indians: E99.N97
Numeral systems, Indian: F1219.3.N9
  Pre-Columbian America: E59.N8
Numeration
  Mayas: F1435.3.M35
Numic Indians: E99.N97
Nunavik
  Quebec: F1054.N93
Nunavut: F1141+
Núñez, Rafael: F2276
Núñez Cabeza de Vaca, Alvar: E125.N9
Nurses
  United States Civil War: E621+
    Confederate: E625
Nutley area (New Jersey): F142.E8
Nym Lake and region (Ontario): F1059.T5

O

O-wee-kay-no Indians: E99.O68
Oaica Indians: F2520.1.W3
OAK: E458.8
Oak Hill Cemetery (Washington, D.C.):
  F203.1.O12
Oak Island (Nova Scotia): F1039.O35
Oak Park (Illinois): F549.O13
Oak Ridge (Tennessee): F444.O3
Oakland (California): F869.O2
OAS: F1402
Oaxaca (Mexico)
  City: F1391.O12
  State: F1321
    Indian antiquities: F1219.1.O11
Oberlin College and the Civil War: E541.O2
Oberlin-Wellington rescue, 1858: E450
Obligado, Battle of, 1845: F2846.3
Obregón, Álvaro: F1234
O'Brien, Jeremiah: E207.O13
Ocaina Indians: F3430.1.O25
Occaneechi Indians: E99.O22
Occidente, Mexico (State): F1322
Occultism, Indian: E98.R3
Ocean Pond, Florida, Battle of, 1864:
  E476.43
Ochoco National Forest: F882.O16

Ocloya Indians: F2823.O34
Ocmulgee River (Georgia): F292.O27
Ocoee District (Tennessee): F442.1
Oconee River and Valley (Georgia): F292.O33
Ocorona Indians: F3320.2.O3
Ocracoke Island (North Carolina): F262.H9
Ocsabamba colony (Peru): F3451.O16
Octagon House (Washington, D.C.): F204.O2
Octoraro Creek and Valley (Maryland): F187.O27
Octoraro Creek and Valley (Pennsylvania): F157.O26
O'Daniel, Wilbert Lee: F391+
Odiorne Point State Park (New Hampshire): F42.R7
Odría, Manual Artura: F3448
Ogden (Utah): F834.O3
Ogeechee River and Valley (Georgia): F292.O38
Oglala Indians: E99.O3
Oglethorpe, James Edward: F289
O'Gorman, James Aloysius: F124
O'Higgins, Bernardo: F3094
O'Higgins, Chile (Province): F3211
O'Higgins Land (Palmer Peninsula): F3031+
Ohio: F486+
    Afro-Americans: E185.93.O2
    Counties, etc.: F497.A+
    Indians: E78.O3
    Old Northwest: F476+
    Wars
        Civil War: E470.4+, E525.1+
            Morgan's raid, 1863: E475.18
        Indian wars: E83.81
        Revolution: E263.O3
        Toledo War, 1836: F497.B7
        War of 1812: E359.5.O2
        War of 1898: E726.O3
        War with Mexico: E409.5.O3
Ohio Company (1747-1779): F517
Ohio Company (1786-1795): F483
Ohio Company of Virginia: F517
Ohio Land Company: F483
Ohio River and Valley: F516+
    Illinois: F547.O4
    Indiana: F532.O4
    Kentucky: F457.O3
    Ohio: F497.O3
    Pennsylvania: F157.B2
    West Virginia: F247.O4
Ohio State Association of Mexican War Veterans: E401.36
Ohio Valley: F516+
    Indians: E78.O4
    Wars
        Civil War: E470.4+
        French and Indian War: E199
        Indian wars: E83.79
        Revolution: E230.5.O3
Ohlone Indians: E99.O32
Ojai Valley (California): F868.V5
Ojarikoelle Indians: F2420.1.O8

Ojibwa Indians: E99.C6
Okanagan River and Valley (British Columbia): F1089.O5
Okeechobee, Lake (Florida): F317.O4
Okefenokee Swamp (Georgia): F292.O5
Okinagan Indians: E99.O35
Oklahoma: F691+
    Afro-Americans: E185.93.O4
    Counties, etc.: F702.A+
    Indian country: F697
    Indian Territory: F697-698
    Indians: E78.I5, E78.O45
    Oklahoma Territory: F699
Oklahoma City (Oklahoma): F704.O41
Oklahoma Panhandle (Oklahoma): F702.N6
Oklawaha River and Valley (Florida): F317.O46
Okoboji Lake (Iowa): F627.D5
Olancho, Honduras (Dept.): F1509.O4
Olaya, José Silverio: F3446
Olaya Herrera, Enrique: F2277
Old Capitol Prison, Washington, D.C.
    Civil War: E616.O4
Old Colony Historical Society (Massachusetts): F74.T2
Old Emigrant Trail (California): F868.S5
Old Man of the Mountain (New Hampshire): F41.6.P9
Old Northwest: F476+
Old Order Amish in the United States: E184.M45
Old Southwest: F396
Old State House (Boston): F73.8.O4
Old Westmoreland Co. (Pennsylvania): F157.W5
Oldroyd Collection of Lincoln Relics: E457.65
Oley Valley (Pennsylvania): F157.B3
Olinda (Brazil)
    Capture by Dutch, 1630: F2532
Olive branch petition to George III, 1775: E215.95
Oliveira Lima, Manuel de: F2537
Oliver, Peter: F67
Oliver Dam (Alabama): F332.T9
Olmec Indians: F1219.8.O56
Olmsted, Arthur George: F154
Olson, Floyd Bjornsterne: F606
Olustee, Florida, Battle of, 1864: E476.43
Olympia (Washington): F899.O5
Olympic Mountains: F897.O5
Olympic National Park: F897.O5
Omagua Indians: F3430.1.O5
Omaha (Nebraska): F674.O5
Omaha Indians: E99.O4
Omasuyos, Bolivia (Province): F3341.O5
Omineca River and Valley (British Columbia): F1089.O55
Omnibus Bill, Clay's: E423
Ompompanoosuc Parish (Vermont): F57.O56
Ona Indians: F2986
Oneida Indians: E99.O45
Oneida Lake (New York): F127.O52
O'Neill Ranch (California): F868.S34

Oneota Indians
    Great Plains: E99.O5
Onondaga Indians: E99.O58
Onondaga Lake (New York): F127.O6
Ontario: F1056+
    American loyalists: F1058
    Canadian Rebellion, 1837-1838: F1032
    History to 1791: F1030-1032
    Indians: E78.C2, E78.O5
    War of 1812: E355+
Ontario (California): F869.O5
Ontario, Lake, region: F556
    New York: F127.O72
    Ontario: F1059.O6
Ontario Co. (Ontario): F1059.O5
Ontario Colony (California): F869.O5
Ontonagon River and Valley (Michigan): F572.O62
Oohenonpa Indians: E99.O63
Oowekeeno Indians: E99.O68
Opata Indians: F1221.O6
Opaye Indians: F2520.1.O63
Opeongo Lake (Ontario): F1059.A4
Opequan Creek, Battle of, 1864: E477.33
Orange (New Jersey): F144.O6
Orange County Park (California): F868.O6
Orangeburgh District (South Carolina): F277.O6
Oratory, Indian: E98.O7
Orcas Island (Washington): F897.S2
Ord, Edward Otho Cresap: E467.1.O7
Ordás, Diego de: E125.O58
Order of American Freemen: E462.94
Order of American Knights: E458.8
Order of Colonial Lords of Manors in America: E186.99.O6
Order of La Fayette: E202.99.O63
Order of Stars and Stripes: E462.99.O65
Order of the Descendants of the Signers of the Secret Pact or prior Declaration of Independence: E202.99.O65
Order of the Founders and Patriots of America: E186.6
Order of the Lone Star: E458.8
Order of the Purple Heart, Military: E181
Order of the Sons of Liberty: E458.8
Order of Washington: E202.7
Orderly books
    American Revolution: E231+
Ordinance of 1787: E309
Oregon: F871+
    Afro-Americans: E185.93.O7
    Counties, etc.: F882.A+
    Indians: E78.O6
    International boundary: F854
    Wars
        Civil War: E526.1+
        Indian wars: E83.84, E83.87, E83.877
Oregon country: F880
Oregon question: F880
Oregon Trail: F597
    Oregon: F880
Orejón Indians: F3430.1.O74
Orellano, Francisco de: E125.O6

Organ Pipe Cactus National Monument
    (Arizona): F817.O7
Organization of American States: F1402
Organization of Central American States:
    F1439
Oribe, Manuel: F2726
Oriente
    Bolivia: F3341.O6
Oriente, Cuba (Province): F1841+
Oriente, Ecuador (Region): F3741.N3
Origin, Indian: F1435.3.O73
Original narratives of early American
    history: E187.O7
Orinoco River and Valley (Venezuela):
    F2331.O7
Oriskany, Battle of, 1777: E241.O6
Oriskany Campaign, 1777: E233
Orizaba (Mexico)
    Canton: F1371
Orleans, Isle of (Quebec): F1054.O7
Orleans, Territory of, 1804-1812: F374
Orleans Parish (Louisiana): F377.O7
Ornaments, Indian: E98.C8
Oro, El, Ecuador (Province): F3741.E4
Orphanages
    Indians: E98.O76
Orr's Island, Maine: F27.C9
Orsainville, Jean Talon, comte d': F1030
Ortiz de Rosas, J.M.J.D.: F2846.3
Oruro, Bolivia
    City: F3351.O7
    Department: F3341.O7
Osa Gulf (Costa Rica): F1549.D8
Osa Peninsula (Costa Rica): F1549.O83
Osage Indians: E99.O8
Osage River and Valley (Missouri):
    F472.O74
Osawatomie, Battle of, 1856: F685
Osborn, Chase Salmon: F566
Oshkosh (Wisconsin): F589.O8
Osorio, Oscar: F1488
Ospina, Pedro Nel: F2277
Ospina Peréz, Mariano: F2278
Ossipee Mountain (New Hampshire): F42.C3
Ossipee Mountain Park (New Hampshire):
    F42.C3
Ostend Manifesto, October 1854: E431
Österreichische Nationalbibliothek.
    Manuscript. Mexicanus 1 (Codices):
    F1219.56.O84
Otavalo Indians: F3722.1.O8
Otero, Antonio Miguel: F801
Otis, Harrison Gray: E340.O8
Otis, James: E302.6.O8
Oto Indians: E99.O87
Otomaco Indians: F2319.2.O8
Otomi Indians
    Modern: F1221.O86
    Pre-Columbian: F1219.8.O87
Ottawa (Ontario): F1059.5.O9
Ottawa Indians: E99.O9
Ottawa region (Quebec): F1054.O94
Ottawa River and Valley
    Ontario: F1059.O91

Ottawa River and Valley — Continued
    Quebec: F1054.O9
Otuquis Indians: F3320.2.O8
Ouachita Mountains
    Arkansas: F417.O77
    Oklahoma: F702.O9
Ouachita National Forest: F417.O8
Ouachita Parish (Louisiana): F377.O78
Ouachita River and Valley
    Arkansas: F417.O83
    Louisiana: F377.O8
Ouayeoue Indians: F2380.1.W25
Ouro Preto, Brazil: F2651.O9
Outaouais region (Quebec): F1054.O94
Outer Banks (North Carolina): F262.O96
Overland journeys to the Pacific (1848-
    1860): F593
Overland Trail: F597
    Colorado: F782.O94
    Wyoming: F767.O94
Overwharton Parish (Virginia): F232.O9
Oweekano Indians: E99.O68
Oweekayo Indians: E99.O68
Owens River and Valley (California):
    F868.O9
Owikeno Indians: E99.O68
Owyhee Mountains region (Idaho, Nevada,
    and Oregon): F752.O97
Owyhee River and Valley
    Idaho: F752.O98
    Nevada: F847.O98
    Oregon: F882.O98
Owyhees in the United States: E184.H3
Oxapampa colony (Peru): F3451.O16
Oxford Co. (Ontario): F1059.O98
Oxford Hills (Maine): F27.O9
Oxford Township (Pennsylvania):
    F158.68.O8
Oxkintok (Mexico): F1435.1.O94
Oyambi Indians: F2460.1.O9
Oyapok River (French Guiana)
    English settlements: F2462
Oyaricoulet Indians: F2420.1.O8
Oyster Bay (New York): F129.O98
Ozark Mountains
    Arkansas: F417.O9
    Indians: E78.O9
    Missouri: F472.O9
Ozonia Lake (New York): F127.S2

P

Pacaguara Indians: F3320.2.P3
Pachacamac, Peru
    Indian antiquities: F3429.1.P2
Pachitea, Peru (Province): F3451.P14
Pachuca, Mexico (District): F1291
Pacific, Army of the: E470.9
Pacific Coast
    California: F868.P33
    Ecuador: F3741.P32
    Oregon: F882.P34
Pacific coast of America: F851
    British Columbia: F1089.P2

Pacific coast of America: F851 —
    Continued
    North America: F850.5+
        Exploring expeditions
            After 1769: F864, F880, F907,
                F1088
            Before 1769: F851.5
        Indians: E78.P2
        Overland journeys (1848-1860): F593
        Voyages by Cape Horn or the isthmus
            (1848-1856): F865
    South America: F2213
        Colombia: F2281.P23
        Peru: F3451.P19
Pacific Crest Trail
    Indians: E78.P24
Pacific Islanders in the United States:
    E184.P25
Pacific Northwest: F851.72+
Pacific Ocean
    U.S. insular possessions: F970
Pacific Rim National Park (British
    Columbia): F1089.V3
Pacific States: F850.5+
Padre Island (Texas): F392.P14
Padrones de Tlaxcala del siglo XVI
    (Codices): F1219.56.P33
Paducah (Kentucky)
    Demonstration from, 1861: E472.28
Páez, Federico: F3737
Páez, José Antonio: F2322.8
Paez Indians: F2270.2.P3
Page, Walter Hines: E664.P15
Pageants
    United States history: E179, F4.6
        Colonial: E189
        Wars
            War with Mexico: E415
Pahsimeroi River and Valley (Idaho):
    P752.P23
Paia Indians: E99.P32
Paiaia Indian: E99.P32
Paialla Indians: E99.P32
Paiaya Indians: E99.P32
Paine, Robert Frost: E302.6.P14
Painguá Indians: F2230.2.C3
Paint Rock River
    Alabama: F332.P34
    Tennessee: F443.P34
Painted Desert (Arizona): F817.P2
Painting, Indian: E98.P23, F1219.3.P25,
    F1219.76.P35, F1435.3.P34,
    F3429.3.P34, F3721.1.P35,
    F3721.3.P35
Paiute Indians: E99.P2
Pajarito Plateau (New Mexico): F802.P25
Pajaro River and Valley (California):
    F868.S3
Pakaa Nova Indians: F2520.1.P32
Pakistanis in America
    Canada: F1035.P34
    the United States: E184.P28
Palafox y Mendoza, Juan de: F1231
Palaihnihan Indians: E99.P215
Palatines in Canada: F1035.P36

Palatines in the United States: E184.P3
Palenque Indians: F1435.1.P2, F2319.2.P3
Palermo
    Columbus celebration, 1892: E119
Palestinian Arabs in Central America:
    F1440.P34
Palestinians in the United States: E184.P33
Palicur Indians: F2460.1.P3
Palisades of New Jersey: F142.B4
Palisades of the Hudson (Interstate park):
    F127.H8
Palmares, Brazil: F2651.P15
Palmer, John McAuley: E664.P2
Palmer House, Chicago: F548.8.P17
Palmer Peninsula: F3031+
Palo Alto, Battle of, 1846: E406.P3
Palo Duro Canyon (Texas): F392.P16
Palo Duro State Park (Texas): F392.P16
Palomar Mountain (California): F868.S15
Paloos Indians: E99.P22
Palouse River and Valley
    Idaho: F752.P25
    Washington: F897.P24
Pame Indians: F1221.P3
Pamlico Indians: E99.P225
Pampa, Argentina (Province): F2924
Pampaconas River (Peru): F3451.C9
Pampas, Argentina (Region): F2926
Pampean Indians: F2823.P3
Pamplona, Colombia (Province): F2281.P3
Pamunkey Indians: E99.P23
Pamunkey River and Valley (Virginia):
    F232.P25
Pan-American conferences: F1404+
Pan-American Highway: F1409, F1547.5
Pan American Union: F1403+
Panama: F1561+
    Scots' Colony of Darien: F2281.D2
    Secession from Colombia: F2276.5
    Under U.S. protection, 1903-1936:
        F1566.5
    War of Independence, 1903: F1566.45
Panama (City): F1576.P2
    American Congress, 1826: F1404
Panama (Province): F1569.P3
Panama, Gulf of: F1569.P35
Panama, Isthmus of: F1561+
Panama Bay: F1569.P35
Panama Canal: F1569.C2
Panama Canal Zone: F1569.C2
Panama Congress, 1826: F1404
Panama Expeditions: F1566.45
Panamanians in the United States: E184.P35
Panamint Indians: E99.P24
Panare Indians: F2319.2.P34
Pancaldo, León: E125.P2
Pancararu Indians: F2520.1.P35
Pando, Bolivia (Department): F3341.P3
Panhandle, Texas: F392.P168
Panhandle culture
    Indians: E99.P244
Paniquita Indians: F2270.2.P4
Panjabis in the United States: E184.P36
Pano Indians: F3430.1.P3
Panoan Indians: F3430.1.P33

Pánuco, Mexico (Province): F1323
Panzaleo Indians: F3722.1.P35
Paoli Massacre, 1777: E241.P2
Papago Indians: E99.P25
Paper and paper making, Indian: F1219.3.P3,
    F1219.76.P37
Papigochic River and Valley (Mexico):
    F1261
Papineau, Louis Joseph: F1032
Papineau Rebellion, 1837-1838: F1032
Pâques, L'ile de (Chile): F3169
Pará (Brazil)
    City: F2651.B4
    State: F2586
        Indian antiquities: F2519.1.P2
        Marajó Island: F2568
Paracas, Peru
    Indian antiquities: F3429.1.P25
Paradise Valley (Nevada): F847.H8
Paraguaná Peninsula (Venezuela): F2331.F2
Paraguay: F2661+
    Chaco region: F2691.C4, F2876,
        F3341.C4
    Jesuit province: F2684
    Military history
        Chaco War, 1932-1935: F2688.5
        Paraguayan War, 1865-1870: F2687
        War of Independence, 1810-1811:
            F2683
        War of the Seven Reductions, 1754-
            1756: F2684
    Reductions (1609-1769): F2684
    United States Expedition, 1858-1859:
        F2686
Paraguay (Province): F2683-2684
Paraguay River and Valley: F2691.P3
Paraguayan War, 1865-1870: F2687
Parahyba, Brazil (State): F2591
Parahyba do Sul River (Brazil): F2611
Paraíba, Brazil (State): F2591
Paraibuna River (Brazil): F2581
Paramaribo, Dutch Guiana: F2429.P3
Paramona Indians: F2380.1.P3
Paramonga (Peru)
    Indian antiquities: F3429.1.P28
Paraná, Brazil (State): F2596
    Indian antiquities: F2519.1.P3
Paraná River
    Argentina: F2909
    Brazil: F2596, F2631
Paraná Valley, Argentina
    Indian antiquities: F2821.1.P22
Paraphernalia, Political: E183.3
Paraujano Indians: F2319.2.P37
Parc de la Jacques-Cartier (Québec):
    F1054.P36
Parc de Plaisance (Quebec): F1054.P365
Parc des Hautes-de-la-Rivière-Malbaie
    (Quebec): F1054.P367
Parc du Mont-Orford (Québec): F1054.P37
Parinacochas, Peru (Province): F3451.P245
Parintintin Indians: F2520.1.P4
Paris, Treaty of
    1778: E249
    1783: E249

Paris, Treaty of — Continued
    1803: E333
    1814: F2424, F2463
Park Avenue (New York): F128.67.P3
Park Street (Boston): F73.67.P3
Parkateyê Indians: F2520.1.G37
Parker, George Le Roy: F595
Parker, Joel: E521.1+
Parker House (Boston): F73.8.P3
Parks
    Canada
        National: F1011, F1044.F6
        Provincial: F1059.A4
    United States: E160
        City: F73.65, F128.65.A+,
            F158.65.A+, F203.5.A+,
            F548.65
        National: F232.S48
        National military: E475.81
        State: F547.L3
Parley's Canyon (Utah): F832.S2
Parmachenee Lake (Maine): F27.O9
Parnahyba River (Brazil): F2606
Parque Nacional del Iguazú (Argentina):
    F2916
Parque Nacional lLanínr (Argentina): F2921
Parris Island (South Carolina): F277.B3
Parsons, Lewis Baldwin: E467.1.P26
Parsons, Samuel Holden: E207.P2
Parsons, Theophilus: F69
Parsons' Cause, 1763: F229
Parú River (Brazil): F2586
Pasadena (California): F869.P3
Pascagoula Indians: E99.P26
Pasco, Peru (Dept.): F3451.P247
Pascua, Isla de (Chile): F3169
Pasquaney Lake (New Hampshire): F42.G7
Pasque Island (Massachusetts): F72.E5
Passaic River and Valley: F142.P3
Passamaquoddy Bay and region: F27.P3
    New Brunswick: F1044.P3
Passamaquoddy Indians: E99.P27
Pasto (Colombia): F2291.P28
Pasto Indians: F2270.2.P44
Pastorius, Francis Daniel: F152
Pastour, Philippe de, sieur de Costebelle:
    F1123
Patachó Indians: F2520.1.P43
Patagonia
    Argentina: F2936
        Indian antiquities: F2821.1.P29
    Chilean: F3146
Patapsco Neck and River (Maryland):
    F187.B2
Patarabueye Indians: F1221.P35
Patashó Indians: F2520.1.P43
Pataxó Indians: F2520.1.P43
Pataxte (Guatemala)
    Mayas: F1435.1.P25
Paterson, John: E207.P3
Paterson, William: E302.6.P3
Paterson (New Jersey): F144.P4
Patía River and Valley, Colombia:
    F2281.P37

Patos, Isla de, Venezuela: F2331.P3
Patriotic hereditary societies
 United States: E172.7+
Patriotic societies
 United States
  Civil War: E462+, E483
  Colonial period: E186.3+
  War of 1812: E351.3+
  War of 1898: E714.3.A+
  War with Mexico: E401.1+
Patriots' Day, April 19: E231
Patton, George Smith: E745
Patuxent River and Valley (Maryland):
 F187.P38
Patwin Indians: E99.P29
Paucartambo, Peru (Province): F3451.P25
Paugusset Indians: E99.P292
Pauishana Indians: F2520.1.P45
Pauisiana Indians: F2520.1.P45
Pauixana Indians: F2520.1.P45
Paul Revere's ride: E216
Paula, Francisco Julião Arruda de:
 F2538.27.P38
Paula Santander, Francisco de: F2273
Paulding, Hiram: E182
Paulding, John: E280.A5
Paulina Lake (Oregon): F882.D4
Paulint, Antoine: E263.C2
Paulmier de Gonneville, Binot: E133.P3
Paulus Hook, Battle of, 1779: E241.P24
Pauserna Indians: F3320.2.P37
Pavón, Battle of, 1861: F2846
Paw Paw Lake (Michigan): F572.B5
Paw Paw River and Valley (Michigan):
 F572.P38
Pawleys Island (South Carolina): F277.G35
Pawnee Indians: E99.P3
Pawtucket (Wamesit) Indians: E99.W19
Pawtuxet River and Valley (Rhode Island):
 F87.P3
Paxil (Mexico)
 Mayas: F1435.1.P38
Paxton boys: F152
Paya Indians: F1505.2.P3
Payagua Indians: F2679.2.P3
Payai Indians: E99.P32
Payalla Indians: E99.P32
Payay Indians: E99.P32
Payaya Indians: E99.P32
Payaye Indians: E99.P32
Payette River and Valley (Idaho): F752.P33
Payne, Davis Lewis: F697
Payne Hollow (Kentucky): F457.T65
Paynes Prairie (Florida): F317.A4
Paysandú (Uruguay)
 City: F2791.P54
 Department: F2731.P3
Paz, José María: F2846
Paz Estenssoro, Victor: F3326
Pea Ridge, Battle of, 1862: E473.17
Pea River and Valley (Alabama): F332.P37
Peace Conference at Washington: E440.5
Peace River and Valley (British Columbia):
 F1089.P3

Peace River District (Alberta): F1079.P3
Peachtree Creek, Ga., Battle of, 1864: E476.7
Peak Island (Maine): F27.C9
Peak-to-Peak Highway (Colorado):
 F782.P37
Pearce, James Alfred: E340.P3
Pearl Islands (Panama): F1569.P3
Pearl River
 Louisiana: F377.P3
 Mississippi: F347.P3
Pearson, Lester B.: F1034.3.P4
Peaux-de-Lièvres Indians: E99.K28
Peay, Austin: F436
Peban Indians: F3430.1.P4
Pecos Indians: E99.P34
Pecos River and Valley
 New Mexico: F802.P3
 Texas: F392.P3
Pedee region (South Carolina): F277.P3
Pedee River
 North Carolina: F262.Y2
 South Carolina: F277.P3
Pedro I, Emperor of Brazil: F2536
Pedro II, Emperor of Brazil: F2536
Pedro IV, Emperor of Brazil: F2536
Pee Dee Indians: E99.P35
Pee Dee River and Valley
 North Carolina: F262.Y2
 South Carolina: F277.P3
Peel Co. (Ontario): F1059.P25
Peguenche Indians: F3126
Pehuenche Indians: F3126
Peirpoint, Francis Harrison: E534.1+
Peixe River (Brazil): F2631
Peixoto, Floriano: F2537
Pejepscot Company: F29.B9
Pejepscot Patent and Purchase (Brunswick),
 Maine: F29.B9
Pelham Manor (New York): F128.68.B8
Pellegrini, Bartolomé Mitre Carlos: F2847
Pell's Point, Battle of, 1776: E241.P3
Peltier Creek and Valley (North Carolina):
 F262.P35
Pemaquid (Maine): F22
Pemberton, John Clifford: E467.1.P365
Pemberton Valley (British Columbia):
 F1089.P4
Pembina River and Valley (Alberta):
 F1079.P36
Pemon Indians: F2319.2.P45
Peñalosa, Diego Dionisio de: F799
Peñaranda Castillo, Enrique: F3326
Pendleton, Edmund: F230
Pendleton, George Hunt: E415.9.P4
Pendleton, William Nelson: E467.1.P37
Pendleton (Oregon): F884.P39
Pendleton District (South Carolina):
 F277.P35
Penikese Island (Massachusetts): F72.E5
Peninsula Lake (Muskoka, Ontario):
 F1059.M9
Peninsular campaign, 1862: E473.6
Penn, William: F152.2
 Grant to, 1681: F152, F167

Penn family (Proprietors of Pennsylvania):
 F152.2
Pennacook Indians: E99.P4
Penn's Cave (Pennsylvania): F157.C3
Pennsylvania: F146+
 Afro-Americans: E185.93.P41
 Connecticut claims in northeast: F157.W9
 Counties, etc.: F157.A+
 Fries' Rebellion, 1798-1799: E326
 Indians: E78.P4
 Lower counties on the Delaware: F167
 New Sweden: F167
 Slavery: E445.P3
 Virginia claims in southwest: F157.W5
 Wars
  Buckshot War, 1838: F153
  Civil War: E527.1+
   Military operations: E470.2+
  French and Indian War: E199
  Indian wars: E83.76
  King George's War: E199
  Revolution: E263.P4
  War of 1812: E359.5.P3
  War of 1898: E726.P4
  War with Mexico: E409.5.P3
  Whisky Rebellion, 1794: E315
Pennsylvania, Insurrection of, 1795: E315
Pennsylvania Association of the Defenders of
 the Country in the War of 1812:
 E351.23
Pennsylvania Avenue (Washington, D.C.):
 F203.7.P4
Pennsylvania Dutch Country (Pennsylvania):
 F157.P44
Pennsylvania Dutch region (Pennsylvania):
 F157.P44
Pennsylvania German region (Pennsylvania):
 F157.P44
Pennsylvania Hall (Philadelphia): F158.8.P4
Pennsylvania Invasion, 1863: E475.51
Pennsylvania line mutiny: E255
Pennsylvania Station (New York): F128.8.P4
Pennsylvania University and the Civil War:
 E541.P4
Pennypacker, Samuel Whitaker: F154
Pennypacker Memorial (Philadelphia):
 F158.64.P4
Penobscot Bay region (Maine): F27.P37
Penobscot Expedition, 1779: E235
Penobscot Indians: E99.P5
Penobscot River and Valley (Maine): F27.P4
Penrose, Boies: F664.P41
Pensacola (Florida): F319.P4
Pensacola District of West Florida
 First Seminole War, 1817-1818: E83.817
 History
  Before 1819: F301
  Since 1819: F317.W5
 Treaty of 1819: F314
Pensions, Indian: E98.P3

Pickwick Landing Reservoir: F217.T3
Pico do Monte Roraima (Brazil): F2609
Pictou Co. (Nova Scotia): F1039.P6
Pictou Island (Nova Scotia): F1039.P6
Picture writing, Indian
    Pre-Columbian America: E59.W9
Pictured Rocks National Lakeshore
    (Michigan): F572.P5
Picunche Indians: F3126
Picuris Indians: E99.P575
Piedmont Region: F217.P53
Piegan Indians: E99.P58
Piémont des Appalaches (Quebec):
    F1054.P54
Pierce, Franklin: E432
    Administration, 1853-1857: E431+
    Family: E432.2
Piérola, Nicolás de: F3447
Pierpont, Francis Harrison: E534.1+
Pierre (South Dakota): F659.P6
Pietri, Juan: F2325
Pigeon River and Valley (Michigan):
    F572.P53
Pigeon River Country State Forest
    (Michigan): F572.P53
Pigeon Roost Massacre, 1812: E356.P6
Pigwacket Fight, 1725: E83.72
Pijao Indians: F2270.2.P64
Pike, Montgomery
    Exploration in the West: F592
Pike, Zebulon Montgomery: F592
Pike National Forest (Colorado): F782.P63
Pikes Peak (Colorado): F782.P63
Pilaga Indians: F2823.P5
Pilar Site (Belize): F1435.1.P53
Pilchuck, Mount (Washington): F897.S66
Pilcomayo River
    Paraguay-Argentina boundary question:
        F2857.P2
Pilgrim Society (Plymouth): F68
Pilgrims: F7, F68
Pilgrims, The
    Patriotic society: E186.99.P6
Pillow, Fort, Massacre at, 1864: E476.17
Pillow, Gideon Johnson: E403.1.P6
    Court-martial: E405.6
Pilot Knob, Battle of, 1864: E477.16
Pima Indians: E99.P6
Piman Indians: E99.P62
Pinao Indians: F2270.2.P64
Pinar del Rio (Cuba)
    City: F1809.P5
    Province: F1801+
Pinchot, Gifford: E664.P62
Pinckney, Charles: E302.6.P54
Pinckney, Charles Cotesworth: E302.6.P55
Pinckney, Eliza (Lucas): F272
Pinckney, Thomas: E302.6.P57
Pine Barrens (New Jersey): F142.P5
Pine Creek (Potter County-Lycoming
    County)
    Pennsylvania: F157.P63
Pine Creek Gorge Natural Area
    Pennsylvania: F157.P64

Pine Ford Dam and Reservoir (Missouri):
    F472.P64
Pine Ford Lake (Missouri): F472.P64
Pine Island (Florida): F317.L3
Pine Lawn Valley (New Mexico): F802.P5
Pinelands National Reserve (New Jersey):
    F142.P5
Piñero, Jesús T.: F1975
Piney Woods (Mississippi): F347.P63
Pinkney, William: E302.6.P6
Pinon Canyon (Colorado): F782.L3
Pinzón, Martín Alonso: E125.P5
Pinzón, Próspero: F2276.5
Pinzón, Vincente Yáñez: E125.P52
Piocobgês Indians: F2520.1.G37
Pioje Indians: F3722.1.P5
Pioneer life: E161.5+
Pioneer Valley (Massachusetts): F72.C7
Pipe Spring National Monument (Arizona):
    F817.M5
Pipes, Tobacco
    Indian: E98.T6
        Pre-Columbian America: E59.T6
Pipil Indians: F1485.2.P5
Piqua, Ohio, Battle of, 1780: E241.P55
Piracicaba River
    Brazil: F2631
Pirahá Indians: F2520.1.M9
Pirates
    Caribbean Sea: F2161
    Tripolitan War, 1801-1815: E335
    U.S. War with Algeria, 1815: E365
Piray River and Valley (Bolivia): F3341.S2
Piro Indians: F3430.1.P5
Piro Pueblo Indians: E99.P63
Pisagua, Chile (Dept.): F3214
Piscataqua River and Valley
    Maine: F27.P48
    New Hampshire: F42.P4
Piscataway Indians: E99.C873
Piscataway Park (Maryland): F187.P56
Pisco, Peru (Province): F3451.P48
Pisinahua Indians: F3430.1.S48
Pitcairn, John: E207.P68
Pitney, Henry Cooper: F139
Pitt Lake and region (British Columbia):
    F1089.P5
Pittsburgh (Pennsylvania): F159.P6
Pittsburgh Landing, Battle of, 1862: E473.54
Piura, Peru (Dept.): F3451.P5
Pizarro, Francisco: F3442
Pizarro, Gonzalo: F3442
Places of amusement: F73.627, F128.627,
    F158.627, F548.627
Placilla, Battle of, 1891: F3098
Plains Indians: E78.G73
Plaisted, Harris Merrill: F25
Planchon de las Figuras (Mexico)
    Mayas: F1435.1.P55
Plano en papel maguey (Codices):
    F1219.56.P56
Plantation life
    United States: F213, F214
        Slave life on plantations: E443

Plantations, Union of, 1636-1643: F82
Plaquemines Parish (Louisiana): F377.P45
Plate River: F2909
Plateau Indians: E78.G67
Plateau Shoshonean Indians: E99.N97
Plats-Côtes-de Chien Indians: E99.T4
Platt, Orville Hitchcock: E664.P7
Platt, Thomas Collier: E664.P72
Platt Amendment (Cuba): F1787
    Abrogation, 1934: F1788
Platt National Park (Oklahoma): F702.P7
Platte Bridge Fight, July 1865: E83.86
Platte Purchase: F466
Platte River and Valley (Nebraska): F672.P6
Plattsburg, N.Y., Battle of, 1814: E356.P7
Plaza Gutiérrez, Leónidas: F3737
Plaza Lasso, Galo: F3738
Pleasant Hill, Battle of, 1864: E476.33
Pleasant Valley (Arizona): F817.G5
Plough (Patent): F23
Plowden's New Albion Grant (New Jersey):
    F137
Plum Island (Massachusetts): F72.P6
Plumb, Preston B.: E664.P73
Plumer, William: E302.6.P73
Plymouth (Massachusetts): F74.P8
Plymouth Colony: F68
Plymouth Company (1606): F7
Plymouth Company (1749-1816): F27.K3
Pocahontas: E99.P85
Pocasset Indians: E99.P64
Pocatello (Idaho): F754.P7
Pocomoke River (Maryland): F187.E2
Pocono Mountains: F157.M6
Pocra Indians: F3430.1.P6
Pocumtuck Valley (Massachusetts): F72.F8
Poetical works
    United States history: E178.9
Poindexter, George: E340.P75
Poinsett, Joel Roberts: E340.P77
Point Barrow (Alaska): F912.B2
Point Lobos (California): F868.M7
Point Lookout (Arenac Co.)
    Michigan: F572.A7
Point Lookout (Maryland)
    Military prison: E616.L8
Point Pleasant Battle, 1774: E83.77
Point Reyes (California): F868.P9
Point Roberts (Washington): F897.P65
Pointe Coupee Parish (Louisiana): F377.P55
Pokagon State Park (Indiana): F532.S8
Pokomam Indians: F1465.2.P6
Polar Bear Provincial Park (Ontario):
    F1059.P65
Poles in America: E29.P6
    Canada: F1035.P6
    Latin America: F1419.P65
    Mexico: F1392.P6
    South America: F2239.P6
        Argentina: F3021.P6
        Brazil: F2659.P7
            Espírito: F2561
        Peru: F3619.P64
    the West Indies
        Haiti: F1930.P64

Presbyterians (U.S.) and the Civil War:
E540.P9
Presbyterians (U.S.) and the Revolution:
E269.P9
Prescott, William: E207.P75
Presidential campaigns (U.S.)
1796: E320
1800: E330
1804: E333.7
1808: E337
1812: E349
1816: E370
1824: E375
1828: E380
1832: E383
1836: E385
1840: E390
1844: E400
1848: E420
1852: E430
1856: E435
1860: E440
1864: E458.4
1868: E670
1872: E675
1876: E680
1880: E685
1884: E695
1888: E700
1892: E705
1896: E710
1900: E738
1904: E758
1908: E760
1912: E765
1916: E769
1920: E783
1924: E795
1928: E796
1932: E805
1936: E810
1940: E811
1944: E812
1948: E815
1952: E816
1956: E837.5
1960: E837.7
1964: E850
1968: E851
1972: E859
1976: E868
1980: E875
1984: E879
1988: E880
1992: E884
1996: E888
2000: E889
Presidents
United States
Biography: E176.1
Mothers: E176.3
Pets: E176.48
Wives: E176.2
Inaugural ceremonies
New York City, 1789: F128.44

Presidents
United States
Inaugural ceremonies — Continued
Philadelphia, 1793, 1797: F158.44
Washington, D.C., 1801-1957:
F197+
Press censorship
U.S. Civil War: E609
Preston, Francis: E302.6.P93
Pribilof Islands (Alaska): F912.P9
Price's Missouri Expedition, 1864: E477.16
Prickly Pear Creek and Valley (Montana):
F737.P93
Priest Lake and Region
Idaho: F752.B677
Primería, Alta: F799
Prince Albert National Park (Saskatchewan):
F1074.P7
Prince Co. (Prince Edward Island): F1049.P7
Prince Edward (Ontario): F1059.P75
Prince Edward Island: F1046+
Prince Frederick Parish (South Carolina):
F277.P95
Prince George (British Columbia):
F1089.5.P7
Prince George's Parish
Frederick Co. (Maryland).: F187.F8
Montgomery Co. (Maryland): F187.M7
Prince of Wales Island (Alaska): F912.P95
Prince of Wales-Outer Ketchikan Census
Area
Alaska: F912.L65
Prince William Forest Park (Virginia):
F232.P86
Prince William Sound region (Alaska):
F912.P97
Prince William's Parish (South Carolina):
F277.P97
Princess Louisa Inlet and region (British
Columbia): F1089.P77
Princeton, Battle of, 1777: E241.P9
Princeton (Frigate)
Explosion: E396
Princeton University and the Civil War:
E541.P9
Princeton University and the Revolution:
E270.P9
Princeton University and the War of 1898:
E725.6.P7
Prison ships
United States Revolution: E281
Prisoners of state
United States
Civil War: E458.8
Prisoners of war
United States
Civil War: E611+
Revolution: E281
War of 1812: E362
War of 1898: E730
War with Mexico: E412

Prisons, Military
United States
Civil War: E611+
Revolution: E281
War of 1812: E362
War of 1898: E730
War with Mexico: E412
Privateers
United States
Civil War: E596+
Revolution: E271
War of 1812: E360
Profile (New Hampshire): F41.6.P9
Propaganda
United States: E743.5
Civil War: E468.9
Propaganda, Confederate, in foreign
countries: E488.5
Property, Indian: E98.P9
Proprietors of Kennebec Purchase: F27.K3
Prosperity Lake and region (Missouri):
F472.J3
Prosperity Reservoir (Missouri): F472.J3
Protection Island (Washington): F897.J4
Providence
United States sloop: E273.P75
Providence (Rhode Island): F89.P9
Providence Island
Colombia: F2281.S15
Providence plantations: F82
Provincetown (Massachusetts): F74.P96
Provo (Utah): F834.P3
Psychology, Indian: F1219.3.P84,
F3320.1.P8
Peru: F3429.3.P85
Pre-Columbian America: E59.P87
Psychosocial factors, Afro-American:
E185.625
Public buildings, Historic
United States: E159, F5
Public domain
United States: E179.5
Public opinion
War with Mexico: E415.2.P82
Public opinion, Foreign
United States
Civil War: E469.8
Revolution: E249.3
Public opinion about Indians: E98.P99
Pre-Columbian America: E59.P89
Public opinion about pre-Columbian and
modern Indians: F1219.3.P87
Public welfare, Indian
Pre-Columbian America: E59.P92
Puebla (Mexico)
City: F1391.P6
State: F1326
Pueblo (Colorado): F784.P9
Pueblo Indians: E99.P9
Puelche Indians: F2823.P8
Puelo River (Chile): F3181
Puerco River and Valley (General and New
Mexico): F802.P83
Puerto Barrios (Guatemala): F1476.P8

Puerto Plata, Dominican Republic (City):
F1939.P9
Puerto Principe, Cuba
City: F1839.C3
Province: F1831+
Puerto Rican campaign, 1898: E717.3
Puerto Ricans in the United States: E184.P85
Puerto Rico: F1951+
Annexation by U.S.: F1975
Commonwealth: F1976+
Military history
Revolts against Spain in 1812, 1867:
F1973
Spanish-American War, 1898
Puerto Rican campaign: E717.3
Spanish rule: F1973
Territory of the U.S.: F1975
Pueyrredón, Juan Martín de: F2845
Puget Sound region (Washington): F897.P9
Indians: E78.P8
Puget Sound Salish Indians: E99.S21
Puinave Indians: F2270.2.P8
Pukóbye Indians: F2520.1.G37
Pulaski, Fort
Bombardment and capture, 1862: E472.79
Pulaski, Military Order of: E202.99.M64
Pulpos Island (Mexico): F1335
Puno, Peru (Dept.): F3451.P9
Indian antiquities: F3429.1.P8
Punta Ballema (Uruguay): F2731.M2
Puquina Indians: F3430.1.P8
Purcell Range (British Columbia): F1089.P8
Puri Indians: F2520.1.P8
Puritans
Massachusetts: F67
New England: F7
Purple Heart, Military Order of the: E181
Puruhá Indians: F3722.1.P8
Purus River (Brazil): F2546
Indian antiquities: F2519.1.P8
Put-in-Bay (Ohio): F497.O8
Perry Memorial: E356.E6
Putnam, Israel: E207.P9
Putnam, Rufus: F483
French and Indian War, 1755-1763: E199
Putumayo Department (Colombia):
F2281.P9
Putumayo River and Valley
Colombia: F2281.P9
Peru: F3451.P94
Putumayo River Valley (Peru)
Indian antiquities: F3429.1.P86
Putumayo rubber atrocities: F3451.P94
Puuc Region (Mexico)
Mayas: F1435.1.P88
Puxití Indians: F2520.1.A4
Puyallup Indians: E99.P98
Pyramids, Indian: F1219.3.P9

Q

Quabbin Reservoir (Massachusetts): F72.S94
Quadra Island (British Columbia): F1089.V3
Quadros administration (Brazil): F2538.2+
Quaichs: F2230.1.D75
Quantrill's raid into Kansas, August 1863:
E474.97
Quapaw Indians: E99.Q2
Qu'Appelle River and Valley
Manitoba: F1064.Q34
Saskatchewan: F1074.Q34
Quay, Matthew Stanley: E664.Q2
Quebec
Wars
American Revolution: E231
Quebec (City): F1054.5.Q3
Capture, 1759: E199
Siege, 1775-1776: E231, E241.Q3
Quebec (Province): F1051+
American loyalists: E278.A+; F1058
History to 1791: F1030
Indians: E78.C2, E78.Q3
Treaty of Paris, 1783: E249
Wars
American Revolution: E263.C2
French and Indian War: E199
Intercolonial wars: E197
Rebellion, 1837-1838: F1032
War of 1812: E355+, E359.85
Quebec Act, 1774: F1032
Quebec campaign, 1759: E199
Quebec Co. (Quebec): F1054.Q4
Quebec District: F1054.Q5
Quebec District, New: F1054.N5
Quebec expeditions
1711: E197
1775: E231
Quechua Indians: F2230.2.K4
Queen Anne's Parish (Maryland): F187.P9
Queen Anne's War, 1702-1713: E197
Queen Charlotte Islands (British Columbia):
F1089.Q3
Queen Elizabeth Islands: F1105.Q44
Queen Victoria Niagara Falls Park (Ontario):
F1059.Q3
Queens (Borough) (New York): F128.68.Q4
Queens Co.
Nova Scotia: F1039.Q3
Prince Edward Island: F1049.Q6
Queen's Rangers
Loyalist: E277.6.Q6
Queenston Heights, Battle of, 1812: E356.Q3
Querandi Indians: F2823.Q4
Querétaro (Mexico)
City: F1391.Q4
State: F1331
Quero Indians: F3430.1.Q47
Queros
Indians
South America: F2230.1.D75
Quesada, Gonzalo de: F1787
Quetico Provincial Park (Ontario): F1059.Q4

Quezaltenango (Guatemala)
City: F1476.Q8
Department: F1469.Q5
Quichés: F1465.2.Q5
Quichua Indians: F2230.2.K4
Quijeros Mountains (Arizona): F817.P5
Quijo Indians: F3722.1.Q48
Quijotoa Mountains (Arizona): F817.P5
Quileute Indians: E99.Q5
Quillacinga Indians: F2270.2.Q54
Quilpué (Chile)
Indian antiquities: F3069.1.Q6
Quimbaya Indians: F2270.2.Q8
Quinaielt Indians: E99.Q6
Quincy, Josiah (1744-1775): E263.M4
Quincy, Josiah (1772-1864): E302.6.Q7
Quincy (Illinois): F549.Q6
Quindío, Colombia (Province): F2281.Q55
Quinnipiac Indians: E99.Q7
Quiñónez Molina, Alfonso: F1487.5
Quintana Roo (Mexico)
Mayas: F1435.1.Q78
Territory: F1333
Quinte, Bay of, Ontario: F1059.Q6
Quipu: F3429.3.Q6
Quiroga, Juan Facundo: F2846
Quitman, John Anthony: E403.1.Q8
Quito (Ecuador): F3781
Quitu Indians: F3722.1.Q5
Quivera: F799
Quixo Indians: F3722.1.Q48

R

Race identity, Afro-American: E185.625
Race problems: E184.A1, F1027, F1419.A+
Race relations
United States
Afro-Americans: E185.61
Racial discrimination
United States
Afro-Americans: E185.61
Racial elements in the population (America):
F1035.A+
Racine (Wisconsin): F589.R2
Radisson, Pierre Esprit: F1060.7
Railroads (U.S.): F73.67, F158.67.A+,
F203.7.A+
Rainbow Bridge (Utah): F832.R3
Rainbow Bridge National Monument (Utah):
F832.R3
Rainbow Canyon (Nevada): F847.R33
Rainier, Mount (Washington): F897.R2
Rainsford Island (Massachusetts): F73.68.R2
Rainy River region (Minnesota): F612.R18
Raisin River, Battle of, 1813: E356.R2
Râle, Sébastien: E83.72
Raleigh, Sir Walter
Explorations, 1595-1617: E129.R2
Virginia colonies, 1584-1590: F229
Raleigh (North Carolina): F264.R1
Rama Indians: F1525.2.R3
Ramapo Mountain people: E184.R3
Ramapo River and Valley (New Jersey):
F142.R16
Ramsay, George, Earl of Dalhousie: F1035

Ramseur, Stephen Douglas: E467.1.R2
Rancagua, Battle of, 1814: F3094
Ranch life
  Canadian Northwest: F1060.94
  U.S.: F596
    North Dakota: F636
    Texas: F391+
    Wyoming: F761
Rancho El Tejon (California): F868.K3
Rancho Santa Margarita (California):
  F868.S34
Rancho Santa Margarita y las Flores
  (California): F868.S34
Rancocas Valley (New Jersey): F142.B9
Randolph, Edmund: E302.6.R18
Randolph, John: E302.6.R2
Rangeley Lakes (Maine): F27.R2
Ranqueles Indians: F2823.R2
Ransom, Truman Bishop: E403.1.R2
Raousset-Boulbon, Gaston Raoux, comte de:
  F1232.5
Rapa Nui (Chile): F3169
Rapid City (South Dakota): F659.R2
Rapid City Indian School: E97.6.R35
Rapidan River and Valley (Virginia):
  F232.R18
Rapides Parish (Louisiana): F377.R25
Rappahannock Indians: E99.R18
Raquette Lake (New York): F127.H2
Raritan River and Valley (New Jersey):
  F142.R2
Rasles (Rasle), Sébastien: E83.72
Raven Rocks (Ohio): F497.B4
Rawlins, John Aaron: E467.1.R25
Ray Roberts Lake (Texas): F392.R22
Read, George: E302.6.R27
Read, John: F67
Reading (Pennsylvania): F159.R2
Reagan, Ronald: E876+
Recife (Brazil): F2651.R4
Reconstruction (U.S.), 1865-1877: E668
  The South: F216
Recreation
  Indians: E98.G2
    Pre-Columbian America: E59.G3
Red Bank, Battle of, 1777: E241.R3
Red Cloud War, 1866-1867: E83.866
Red Cross
  War of 1898: E731
Red Deer River and Valley (Alberta):
  F1079.R4
Red Hills (Florida): F317.R43
Red Mountain Mining District (Colorado):
  F782.R36
Red River (Louisiana), campaign, 1864:
  E476.33
Red River (New Mexico): F802.T2
Red River and Valley
  Arkansas: F417.R3
  Kentucky: F457.R4
  Louisiana: F377.R3
  New Mexico: F802.R36
  Oklahoma: F702.R3
  Texas: F392.R3
Red River expedition, 1864: E476.33

Red River Gorge (Kentucky): F457.R4
Red River of the North and Valley
  Manitoba: F1064.R3
  Minnesota: F612.R27
  North Dakota: F642.R3
Red River Parish (Louisiana): F377.R32
Red River Rebellion, 1869-1870: F1063
Red River Settlement: F1063
Red River War, 1874-1875: E83.875
Red Rock Canyon National Conservation
  Area (Nevada): F847.C5
Reductions, Jesuit (1609-1769): F2684
Redwood National Park (Humboldt and Del
  Norte Counties) (California): F868.R4
Redwood Park (California): F868.S3
Reed, James: E207.R32
Reed, Joseph: E302.6.R3
Reed, Thomas Brackett: E664.R3
Reed Gold Mine State Historic Site (North
  Carolina): F262.R25
Reelfoot Lake and Region (Tennessee):
  F443.R34
Reemelin, Charles: F496
Refugees, Political, to the United States:
  E429
Refugees, Southern: E458.7
Regimental histories
  United States
    Civil War
      Confederate Army: E545+
      Union Army: E491+
    Revolution
      Loyalists: E277.6.A+
    War of 1812: E359
    War of 1898: E725+
    War with Mexico: E409
Regiments, Afro-American
  Civil War: E492.9
Regina (Saskatchewan): F1074.5.R3
Region de los Lagos (Chile): F3218
Región oriental (Ecuador): F3741.N3
Registers, lists, etc., Military
  Confederate States Army: E548
    Prisoners: E611
    Veterans: E548
  Great Britain. Army
    American Revolution: E267+
  Spain. Army
    War of 1898: E725.9
  United States. Army
    Civil War: E494
    Revolution: E255
      Auxiliaries: E265
      By state: E263.A+
    War of 1898: E725.8
    War with Mexico: E409.7
Regulars
  United States Army
    War of 1812: E359.2
    War with Mexico: E409.2
Regulator Insurrection, 1766-1771: F257
Regulators
  Vigilante groups: E179
Reid, Whitelaw: E664.R35

Relations with Blacks (Indians):
  F3429.3.R27
Relations of seceded states to the Union,
  1865-1877: E668
Relations with women
  United States presidents: E176.4
Relief, Financial, Indian: E98.F3
Relief agencies and associations
  United States
    Civil War: E629+
Religion
  Abraham Lincoln: E457.2
  George Washington
    Letters: E312.75.R3+
Religion, Indian
  Pre-Columbian America: E59.R38
Religion and mythology of Indians:
  F2679.3.R44, F3069.3.R44
  Katcinas: E98.R3
  Shamanism: E98.R3
Religion in the armed forces
  United States
    Civil War: E635
Religion of Indians
  Totems: E98.T65
Religious elements in the population
  United States
    Civil War
      Confederate Army: E585.A+
      Union Army: E540.A+
      Revolution: E269.A+
Religious toleration in colonial Maryland:
  F184
Remedios (Cuba): F1829.R4
Remón, José Antonio: F1567
Removal, Indian: E98.R4; F1465.3.R44
Removal of deposits
  Bank of United States: E384.7
Renfrew Co. (Ontario): F1059.R4
Reno (Nevada): F849.R4
Rensselaerswyck (New York): F127.R32
Reporters, News
  U.S. Civil War: E609
Republic, 1889- : F2537
Republic of Florida, 1812-1816: F314
Republic of Texas, 1836-1846: F390
Republican River Valley (Nebraska and
  Kansas)
  Indians: E78.R37
Republicans, Liberal
  United States history: E671
Resaca, Battle of, 1864: E476.7
Resaca de la Palma, Battle of, 1846: E406.R4
Reservations, Indian: E91+
  North America: E78.A+, E99.A+,
    F2270.1.G6
  South America: F2270.1.G6
Reservations, National
  United States: E160
Resignation of Richard Nixon: E861
Revere, Paul: F69
  Paul Revere's ride: E216
Revilla Gigedo Islands (Mexico): F1333.5
Revillagigedo Island (Alaska): F912.R48

Robinson Creek and Valley (Oklahoma): F702.L5

Robson River and Valley (British Columbia): F1089.R62

Roca, Julio Argentino: F2847

Rocafuerte, Vicente: F3736

Rocha, Uruguay (Dept.): F2731.R6

Rochambeau, J.B.D. de Vineur, comte de: E265

Roche de la Croix (Missouri): F472.P4

Rochester (Minnesota): F614.R6

Rochester (New York): F129.R7

Rock Creek Park (Washington, D.C.): F203.5.R6

Rock Island (Illinois): F549.R6
  Military Prison
    Civil War: E616.R6

Rock Island (Wisconsin): F587.D7

Rock paintings
  Indians: E98.P34, F1219.3.P46, F1435.3.P44, F2270.1.P4, F2319.3.P4, F2821.3.P6, F3429.3.P47
    Pre-Columbian America: E59.P42.

Rock River and Valley: F547.R7
  Wisconsin: F587.R63

Rockaway Beach (New York): F129.R8

Rockaway Peninsula (New York): F129.R8

Rockefeller Center (New York): F128.8.R7

Rockford (Illinois): F549.R7

Rocking Chair Ranche (Texas): F392.R64

Rocky Mountain National Park (Colorado): F782.L2, F782.R59

Rocky Mountains and region: F721
  Canada: F1090
  Colorado: F782.R6
  Indians: E78.R63
  Montana: F737.R8
  New Mexico: F802.R68

Rocky River and Valley (Ohio): F497.R7

Roddey's Raid, 1863: E475.87

Rodgers, John: E353.1.R7

Rodman, William: F153

Rodney, Caesar: E302.6.R6

Rodney, Caesar Augustus: E302.6.R61

Rodney, George Brydges, Baron
  St. Eustatius, 1781: F2097
  West Indies (Seven Years' War, 1756-1763): F1621

Rodney, Thomas: E263.D3

Rodríguez, José Gaspar: F2686

Rodríguez, Simón: F2235.5.R6

Rodríguez de Mendoza, Peru (Province): F3451.R6

Roe, Francis Asbury: E182

Rogers, Robert: E199

Rogue River and Valley: F882.R6

Rogue River War, 1850: E83.84

Rojas, Arístides: F2328

Rojas Pinilla, Gustavo: F2278

Rollins, Edward Henry: E415.9.R75

Rollins, James Sidney: E415.9.R76

Romanians in Canada: F1035.R65

Romanians in the United States: E184.R8

Romero Bosque, Pío: F1487.5

Rondônia, Brazil (Territory): F2624

Rondônia State (Brazil): F2624

Roosevelt, Eleanor: E807.1

Roosevelt, Franklin Delano: E807
  Administrations, 1933-1945: E806
  Collected works: E742.5.R6
  Family: E807.1
  Hyde Park Home (National Historic Site): F129.H99

Roosevelt, Theodore: E757
  Administrations: E756+
  Collected works: E660.R7
  Family: E757.3
  Rough Riders
    War of 1898: E725.45
  Sagamore Hill (Oyster Bay, New York): F129.O98

Roosevelt Island (District of Columbia): F203.4.T5

Roosevelt-Sequoia National Park (Proposed): F868.S4

Root, Elihu: E664.R7

Roque Island (Maine): F27.W3

Roraima (Brazil): F2609

Roraima, Mount (Brazil): F2609

Roroima Mountain (Brazil): F2609

Rosario (Argentina): F3011.R7

Rosario Islands (Colombia): F2281.B6

Rosario Valley (Mexico): F1435.1.R67

Rosas, J.M.J.D. Ortiz de: F2846.3
  War against: F2846.3

Rosbrugh, John: E263.P4

Rosebud Creek and Valley (Montana): F737.R96

Rosebud River and Valley (Alberta): F1079.R66

Rosecrans, William Starke: E467.1.R7

Roseland (Illinois): F548.68.R8

Rosemont Plantation (South Carolina): F277.L3

Roslindale (Boston): F73.68.R67

Ross, Betsy (Griscom): E302.6.R77

Ross, George, 1730-1779: E302.6.R79

Ross, George, 1841-1894: F154

Ross, James: E302.6.R8

Rossiĭsko-Amerikanskai︠a︡ kompanii︠a︡: F907

Rouges Creek and Valley (Alabama): F332.J4

Rough Riders: E725.45

Round Valley, California: F868.M5

Routt National Forest (Colorado): F782.R8

Rowan, Andrews Summers: E714.6.R8

Rowan, Stephen Clegg: E182

Roxbury (Massachusetts): F74.R9

Royal Gorge (Colorado): F782.F8

Royale, Île (Nova Scotia): F1039.C2

Royale, Isle (Michigan): F572.I8

Royall, Anne (Newport): E340.R88

Rubber atrocities (Putumayo): F3451.P94

Ruffin, Edmund: F230

Ruffin, Thomas: F258

Ruggles, Timothy: F67

Rugs, Indian: E98.T35

Ruins
  Aboriginal America: E51+

Ruiz Cortines, Adolfo: F1235.5.R8

Rulers
  Aztecs: F1219.76.K53

Rulers, Indian
  Peru: F3429.3.K53

Rumichaca grotto (Ecuador): F3741.C3

Rupert River and Valley (Quebec): F1054.R87

Rupert's Land: F1060+

Rush, Benjamin: E302.6.R85

Rush, Richard: E340.R9

Rush Creek Valley (Minnesota): F612.W7

Rushmore, Mount, National Memorial: F657.R8

Rusk, Jeremiah McLain: E664.R93

Rusk, Thomas Jefferson: F389

Russell Lake region (Saskatchewan): F1074.R8

Russia
  Sale of Alaska to United States: E669, F907

Russian-American Company: F907

Russian exploration and settlement in Alaska: F907

Russian Germans in America: E29.R83

Russian Germans in Argentina: F3021.R87

Russian Germans in Canada: F1035.R79

Russian Jews in the United States: E184.3+

Russian River and Valley (California): F868.R9

Russians in Canada: F1035.R8

Russians in Paraguay: F2699.R8

Russians in Peru: F3619.R87

Russians in the United States: E29.R84, E184.R9

Russo-Japanese War, 1904-1905
  U.S. policy: E756

Rustic Canyon (California): F868.L8

Ruthenians in Canada: F1035.U5

Rutledge, Ann: E457.35

Rutledge, John, 1739-1800: E302.6.R89

Rutledge, John, 1766-1819: E302.6.R9

Ruyter's attack on Barbados, 1655: F2041

Rwandans in the United States: E184.R93

Ryswick, Treaty of, 1697: F1923

S

Sá, Mem de: F2528

Saavedra, Cornelio de: F2845

Saba (West Indies): F2088

Sabine Parish (Louisiana): F377.S115

Sabine Pass, Battle of, 1863: E475.4

Sabine Pass Battlefield State Historical Park (Texas): F392.J33

Sabine River and Valley (Louisiana): F377.S116

Sabine River and Valley (Texas): F392.S12

Sable Island (Nova Scotia): F1039.S13

Sacasa, Juan Bautista: F1526.3

Sacasa, Roberto: F1526.27

Sacatepéquez, Guatemala (Dept.): F1469.S13

Sackets Harbor, N.Y., Battle of, 1813: E356.S34

Saclan Indians: E99.S14

Saco, José Antonio: F1774.S3
Saco Bay (Maine): F27.Y6
Saco River and Valley: F27.S15
Saconet Indians: E99.S16
Saconnet Indians: E99.S16
Sacramento (California): F869.S12
Sacramento River and Valley (California):
    F868.S13
Sacrificios, Isla de (Mexico)
    Indian antiquities: F1219.1.V47
Sáenz Peña, Roque: F2847
Sagamore Hill (Oyster Bay, N.Y.): F129.O98
Saginaw, Fort (Michigan): F572.S15
Saginaw (Michigan): F574.S15
Saginaw Bay region: F572.S15
Saginaw River and Valley (Michigan):
    F572.S2
Sagua la Grande (Cuba): F1829.S12
Saguaro National Monument (Arizona):
    F817.S18
Saguaro National Park (Arizona): F817.S18
Saguenay Co. (Quebec): F1054.S13
Saguenay River and Valley (Quebec):
    F1054.S14
Sailly, Peter: E302.6.S13
Saint Albans Confederate Raid, 1864:
    E470.95
Saint Ambrose Island (Chile): F3131
Saint Andrews Bay (Florida): F317.W3
Saint Andrews Island (Colombia):
    F2281.S15
Saint Anne's Parish (Maryland): F187.A6
Saint Ann's Bay and region (Nova Scotia):
    F1039.S18
Saint Augustine (Florida): F319.S2
Saint Augustine colony: F314
Saint Augustine expeditions, 1740, 1743:
    F314
Saint Barthélemy (West Indies): F2089
Saint Bartholomew (West Indies): F2089
Saint Bernard Parish (Louisiana): F377.S12
Saint Boniface (Manitoba): F1064.5.S13
Saint Charles Parish (Louisiana): F377.S124
Saint Christopher (West Indies): F2091
Saint Clair, Arthur: F483
    Campaign, November 1791: E83.79
Saint Clair, Lake, region
    Michigan: F572.S34
    Ontario: F1059.S3
Saint Cloud (Minnesota): F614.S25
Saint Croix (West Indies) (Island): F2096
Saint Croix Island (Maine): F27.W3
Saint Croix River and Valley (General and
    Wisconsin): F587.S14
Saint Croix River and Valley (Maine):
    F27.S2
Saint Croix River and Valley (Minnesota):
    F612.S2
Saint Croix River and Valley (New
    Brunswick): F1044.S17
Saint Domingue, 1677-1803: F1923
Saint Elias, Mount (Alaska): F912.S15
Saint Elias-Wrangell National Park and
    Preserve (Alaska): F912.W74

Saint Eustatius (West Indies): F2097
Saint Felix Island (Chile): F3131
Saint Francis River and Valley (Arkansas):
    F417.S2
Saint Francis River and Valley (Missouri):
    F472.S25
Saint Francis River and Valley (Québec):
    F1054.S254
Saint George Island (Bermudas): F1639.S3
Saint George (George's) River (Maine):
    F27.S25
Saint-Georges (French Guiana): F2469.S3
Saint-George's Cay (Belize): F1449.S24
Saint-Georges-de l'Oyapock (French
    Guiana): F2469.S3
Saint George's Parish
    Maryland: F187.H2
    Virginia: F232.S15
Saint Helena, Mount (California): F868.S132
Saint Helena Island (South Carolina):
    F277.B3
Saint Helena Mountain (California):
    F868.S132
Saint Helena Parish (Louisiana): F377.S13
Saint Helens, Mount (Washington):
    F897.S17
Saint Helen's Island (Quebec): F1054.S26
Saint Helens Mountain (Washington):
    F897.S17
Saint Hyacinthe Co. (Quebec): F1054.S264
Saint Ignatius Mission (Montana): F737.L3
Saint James Parish
    Jamaica: F1891.S14
    Louisiana: F377.S134
Saint James' Parish (Maryland): F187.A6
Saint Joe River and Valley (Idaho): F752.S74
Saint John (New Brunswick): F1044.5.S14
Saint John (West Indies): F2098
Saint John Lake (Quebec): F1054.S267
Saint John River and Valley
    Maine: F27.S3
    New Brunswick: F1044.S2
Saint John the Baptist Parish (Louisiana):
    F377.S135
Saint John's (Newfoundland): F1124.5.S14
Saint Johns' Church (Georgetown, D.C.):
    F203.2.S14
Saint Johns River and Valley (Florida):
    F317.S2
Saint Joseph (Missouri): F474.S18
Saint Joseph Island (Ontario): F1059.S33
Saint Joseph-Kankakee portage (Indiana):
    F532.S2
Saint Joseph River and Valley
    Indiana: F532.S3
    Michigan: F572.S43
Saint Kitts (West Indies): F2091
Saint Kitts-Nevis (West Indies): F2084
Saint Landry Parish (Louisiana): F377.S14
Saint-Laurent (French Guiana): F2469.S5
Saint-Laurent-du-Maroni (French Guiana):
    F2469.S5
Saint Lawrence, Gulf of: F1050

Saint Lawrence Island (Alaska): F912.S2
Saint Lawrence River and Valley: F1050
    New York: F127.S23
    Ontario: F1059.S4
    Quebec: F1054.S3
Saint Lawrence River campaign, 1813
    War of 1812: E355.4
Saint Leger's invasion, 1777: E233
Saint Louis (Missouri): F474.S2
Saint Lucia (West Indies): F2100
Saint Margaret's Bay and region (Nova
    Scotia): F1039.S19
Saint Maries River and Valley (Idaho):
    F752.S28
Saint Mark's Parish
    South Carolina: F277.S2
    Virginia: F232.S2
Saint Martin (West Indies): F2103
Saint Martin Parish (Louisiana): F377.S16
Saint Mary Anne's Parish (Maryland):
    F187.C3
Saint Mary Parish
    Jamaica: F1891.S2
    Louisiana: F377.S2
Saint Marys Bay and region (Nova Scotia):
    F1039.S20
Saint Marys River and Valley
    Florida: F317.S3
    Georgia: F292.S2
Saint Maurice River and Valley (Quebec):
    F1054.S33
Saint-Ours (Seigniory) (Quebec): F1054.S34
Saint Paul (Minnesota): F614.S4
Saint Peter and Saint Paul, Cathedral of
    (Washington, D.C.): F204.C3
Saint Peter's Parish (Virginia): F232.N3
Saint Petersburg (Florida): F319.S24
Saint Philip, Fort
    Bombardment and capture, 1862: E472.88
Saint Pierre and Miquelon: F1170
Saint Regis Indians: E99.M8
Saint Simon's Island (Georgia): F292.G58
Saint Tammany Parish (Louisiana): F377.S3
Saint Thomas (West Indies): F2105
Saint Thomas and Saint Denis Parish (South
    Carolina): F277.S24
Saint Vincent (West Indies): F2106+
Saint Vincent and the Grenadines (West
    Indies): F2106
Saint Vrain Creek and Valley (Colorado):
    F782.S15
Sainte-Foy, Battle of, 1760: E199
Saintes, Les (French West Indies): F2070
Saklan Indians: E99.S14
Sakonnet Indians: E99.S16
Sakonnet River and Region (Rhode Island):
    F87.S25
Salado culture: E99.S547
Salado River and Valley (Argentina): F2957
Salaverry, Felípe Santiago: F3447
Salcantay, Cerro (Peru): F3451.C9
Salcedo, Dominican Republic (Province):
    F1939.S15

Salem (Massachusetts): F74.S1
    Columbus celebration, 1892: E119
Salem (Oregon): F884.S2
Salesians in Ecuador: F3799.S3
Salinan Indians: E99.S17
Salinas National Monument (New Mexico):
    F802.S13
Salinas River and Valley (California):
    F868.S133
Salisbury (North Carolina). Military Prison:
    E612.S15
Salish Coastal Indians: E99.S2
Salish Indians: E99.S2
Salishan Indians: E99.S21
Saliva Indians: F2319.2.S3
Salmon River and Valley (Idaho): F752.S35
Salmon River and Valley (Oregon):
    F882.S18
Salomon, Haym: E302.6.S17
Salomon, Louis Étienne Félicité: F1926
Salondé Indians: F2520.1.S24
Salt, Indians: E98.S26, F1435.3.S24,
    F3721.3.S24
Salt Creek and Valley (Oklahoma): F702.O7
Salt Lake City (Utah): F834.S2
Salt Lake Co. (Utah): F832.S2
Salt Lick Creek and Valley (Kentucky):
    F457.S24
Salt River and Valley (Arizona): F817.S2
Salt Spring Island (British Columbia):
    F1089.S2
Salt Valley
    Idaho: F752.S37
    Wyoming: F767.S37
Salta (Argentina)
    City: F3011.S2
    Province: F2958
        Indian antiquities: F2821.1.S15
Salto (Uruguay)
    City: F2791.S2
    Department: F2731.S2
Salto Grande Department (Uruguay)
    Indian antiquities: F2719.1.S24
Saltonstall, Leverett: E340.S18
Saltspring Island (British Columbia):
    F1089.S2
Saluma Indians: F2520.1.S24
Salut, Îles du (French Guiana): F2467.I4
Salvador: F1481+
    Confederación de Centro América:
        F1438, F1487
    Military history
        Wars with
            Guatemala: F1466.45, F1487.5
            Honduras: F1487.5, F1507.5
            Nicaragua (Invasion): F1527
Salvador (Brazil): F2651.S13
Salvador, Charter of, 1951: F1439
Salvadorans in the United States: E184.S15
Salzburgers in Georgia: F295.S1
Samaná (Dominican Republic): F1939.S18
Samaypata (Bolivia)
    Indian antiquities: F3319.1.S2
Sambrano Revolution: F389

Sami Americans in the United States:
    E184.S16
Samish Indians: E99.S2115
Samoan Americans: E184.S17
Sampson State Park (New York): F127.S235
Samucan Indians: F3320.2.S3
Samucu Indians: F3320.2.S3
San Agustin (Colombia): F2269.1.S24
San Agustín culture: F2270.2.S35
San Ambrosio Island (Chile): F3131
San Andres Mountains (New Mexico):
    F802.S15
San Andrés y Providencia, Colombia
    (Territory): F2281.S15
San Antonio (Texas): F394.S211
San Antonio, Arroyo de (Estate) (California):
    F868.S7
San Antonio de los Baños (Cuba): F1799.S2
San Antonio River and Valley (Texas):
    F392.S19
San Augustine, Surrender of Union forces at,
    1861: E472.32
San Bernardino National Forest (California):
    F868.S144
San Bernardino Valley (California):
    F868.S14
San Blas coast (Panama): F1569.S3
San Cristóbal (Venezuela): F2341.S13
San Diego (California): F869.S22
San Felipe de Puerto Plata (Dominican
    Republic): F1939.P9
San Felipe Indians: E99.S212
San Félix Island (Chile): F3131
San Fernando Valley (California): F868.L8
San Francisco (California): F869.S3
San Francisco Bay region: F868.S156
San Gabriel River and Valley (Texas):
    F392.S234
San Gabriel Valley (California): F868.L8
San Gervasio Site (Mexico)
    Indians: F1435.1.S26
San Ildefonso, Treaty of, 1777: F2723
San Ildefonso Indians: E99.S213
San Jacinto River and Valley (California):
    F868.R6
San Joaquin River and Valley (California):
    F868.S173
San Jorge River (Colombia): F2281.B6
San José (Costa Rica)
    City: F1556.S2
    Province: F1549.S15
San José, Uruguay (Dept.): F2731.S3
San Juan (Argentina)
    City: F3011.S218
    Province: F2961
San Juan (Puerto Rico): F1981.S2
San Juan de la Frontera (Argentina):
    F3011.S218
San Juan de Ulúa Island (Mexico): F1335
San Juan del Norte (Nicaragua): F1536.S2
San Juan Hill, Battle of, 1898: E717.1
San Juan Island (Mexico): F1335
San Juan Islands (Washington): F897.S2
San Juan Mountains (Colorado): F782.S18

San Juan National Monument (Puerto Rico):
    F1981.S2
San Juan region (Colorado): F782.S19
San Juan River (Nicaragua): F1529.S35
San Juan River and Valley (Costa Rica):
    F1549.S17
San Juan Teotihuacán (Mexico)
    Indian antiquities: F1219.1.T27
San Juan Valley (California): F868.S136
San Luis, Argentina (Province): F2966
San Luis Park (Colorado) (Valley): F782.S2
San Luis Potosí (Mexico)
    City: F1391.S19
    State: F1336
        Indian antiquities: F1219.1.S22
San Marcos (Province)
    Peru: F3451.S2
San Marcos, Guatemala (Dept.): F1469.S17
San Martín, Colombia (Territory):
    F2281.M49
San Martín, José de: F2235.4
San Martín, Juan de: F2841
San Martín, Peru (Dept.): F3451.S24
San Martín, Ramón Grau: F1788
San Mateo, Treaty of, 1812: F2323
San Mateo Mountains (New Mexico):
    F802.V3
San Miguel de Tucumán (Argentina):
    F3011.T89
San Miguel Island (California): F868.S23
San Pablo Villa de Mitla, Mexico (Oaxaca)
    Indian antiquities: F1219.1.M6
San Pasqual, Battle of, 1846: E406.S2
San Pasqual Valley (California): F868.S15
San Pedro River and Valley
    Arizona: F817.S25
    Mexico: F1346
San Pedro Sula (Honduras): F1516.S3
San Rafael River and Valley (Utah):
    F832.S415
San Rafael Swell (Utah): F832.S415
San Ramon Valley (California): F868.S2
San Salvador (Salvador)
    City: F1496.S2
    Department: F1489.S2
San Simeon Estate (California): F868.S18
San Vicente Valley (California): F868.S15
Sanavirona Indians: F2520.1.S3
Sánchez, Francisco del Rosario: F1938.4
Sánchez, Gabriel
    Columbus letter to: E116
Sanclemente, Manuel Antonio: F2276.5
Sancti-Spíritus (Cuba)
    City: F1829.S2
    Province: F1853+
Sand Creek Massacre, 1864: E83.863
Sand Hills (Nebraska): F672.S17
Sand Island boundary controversy: F882.B7
Sanders, Fort, Attack upon, 1863: E475.94
Sandhills
    Georgia: F292.S25
    North Carolina: F262.S34
    South Carolina: F277.S27
Sandhills (Nebraska): F672.S17
Sandia, Peru (Province): F3451.S244

Sandia Indians: E99.S214
Sandia Mountains (New Mexico): F802.S28
Sandino, Augusto César: F1526.3
Sandoz, Jules Ami: F666
Sandpaintings, Indian: E98.S3
Sands, Benjamin Franklin: E182
Sandusky Bay (Ohio): F497.S23
Sandusky River and Valley (Ohio): F497.S23
Sandy Beaver Canal (Ohio): F497.C6
Sangamon River and Valley (Illinois): F547.S33
Sangre de Cristo grant (Colorado): F782.C8
Sangre de Cristo Mountains
   Colorado: F782.S26
   New Mexico: F802.S32
Sanibel Island (Florida): F317.S37
Sanitary commissions
  United States
    Civil War: E631+
Sanitary fairs
  United States
    Civil War: E632
Sanitary services, Military
  United States
    Civil War: E621+
    War of 1898: E731
Sanpoil Indians: E99.S215
Sans Arc Indians: E99.S217
Santa Ana (Salvador): F1496.S35
Santa Ana Mountains (California): F868.S21
Santa Ana River and Valley (California): F868.S22
Santa Anna, Antonio López de: F1232
Santa Bárbara de Samaná (Dominican Republic): F1939.S18
Santa Barbara Islands (California): F868.S232
Santa Barbara Valley (California): F868.S23
Santa Catalina Island (California): F868.L8
Santa Catalina Mountains (Arizona): F817.S28
Santa Catarina (Catharina), Brazil (State): F2626
Santa Catarina Island (Brazil): F2626
Santa Clara (Cuba)
  City: F1829.S3
  Province: F1821+
Santa Clara, California, Battle of, 1847: E406.S25
Santa Clara Valley (California): F868.S25
Santa Clarita Valley (California): F868.L8
Santa-Cruz, Andrés: F3324
Santa Cruz, Argentina (Territory): F2971
Santa Cruz, Peru (District): F3451.S25
Santa Cruz (Bolivia)
  City: F3351.S3
  Department: F3341.S2
Santa Cruz del Sur (Cuba): F1839.S23
Santa Cruz Island (California): F868.S23
Santa Cruz Mountains (California): F868.S33
Santa Cruz River and Valley (Arizona): F817.S33
Santa Cruz y Espejo, F.J.E.: F3733

Santa Fé (Argentina)
  City: F3011.S26
  Province: F2976
Santa Fe (New Mexico): F804.S2
Santa Fe Expedition, 1841: F390
Santa Fe Trail: F786
Santa Margarita Ranch (California): F868.S34
Santa Margarita River and Valley (California): F868.S34
Santa Margarita y las Flores Ranch (California): F868.S34
Santa Maria River and Valley (California): F868.S23
Santa Marta, Sierra Nevada de (Colombia): F2281.M2
Santa Marta Lagoon region (Colombia)
  Indian antiquities: F2269.1.S25
Santa Monica Bay region (California): F868.L8
Santa Monica Canyon (California): F868.L8
Santa Monica Mountains National Recreation Area (California): F868.S355
Santa Rosa Island (California): F868.S355
Santa Rosa Lake and Region (New Mexico): F802.G9
Santa Rosino Indians: F3722.1.Q48
Santa Ynez River and Valley (California): F868.S23
Santana, Pedro: F1938.4
Santander, Colombia (Dept.): F2281.S3
Santander, Francisco de Paula: F2273
Santander, Norte de, Colombia (Dept.): F2281.N6
Santangel, Luis de
  Columbus letter to: E115+
Santee Indians: E99.S22
Santee Normal Training School, Santee (Nebraska): E97.6.S2
Santee River and system (South Carolina): F277.S28
Santiago, Battle of, 1898: E717.1, E727
Santiago, Chile (Province): F3221
Santiago campaign, 1898: E717.1
Santiago de Chile (City): F3271
  Columbus celebration, 1892: E119
Santiago de Cuba
  City: F1849.S3
  Province: F1841+
Santiago de Cuba, Society of the Army of: E714.3.S67+
Santiago del Estero, Argentina (Province): F2981
  Indian antiquities: F2821.1.S23
Santiago-Zamora, Ecuador (Province): F3741.S3
Santiam National Forest (Oregon): F882.S2
Santo Domingo (Audiencia): F1621
Santo Domingo (French colony), 1677-1803: F1923
Santo Domingo (National District and City): F1939.S4

Santo Domingo (Spanish Colony): F1911
  1492-1795
    Withdrawal of Spain, 1795: F1923
    1808-1822: F1938.3
Santo Domingo Indians: E99.S223
Santo Tomas, Guatemala (District): F1469.S2
Santos, Eduardo: F2277
Santos, Máximo: F2726
Santos (Brazil): F2651.S15
São Francisco River and Valley (Brazil): F2629
São Paulo (Brazil)
  City: F2651.S2
  State: F2631
    Indian antiquities: F2519.1.S2
São Paulo Revolution, 1932 (Brazil): F2631
São Salvador (Brazil): F2651.S13
Saone Indians: E99.S225
Sapelo Island (Georgia): F292.M15
Saponi Indians: E99.S226
Sapuya Indians: F2520.1.K4
Saramacca (Surinam people): F2431.S27
Saramaccaner (Surinam people): F2431.S27
Saramaka (Surinam people): F2431.S27
Saranac Lakes (New York): F127.F8
Sarandi, Battle of, 1825: F2725
Saratoga, Battle of, 1777: E241.S2
Saratoga Campaign, 1777: E241.S2
Saratoga Springs (New York): F129.S3
Saravia, Aparicio: F2726
Sarcantay (Peru): F3451.C9
Sargent, Winthrop: F341
Sarmiento, Domingo Faustino: F2846
Sarmiento de Gamboa, Pedro: E125.S23
Sarsi Indians: E99.S227
Saruma Indians: F2520.1.S24
Saskatchewan: F1070+
  Assiniboia: F1067
  Indians: E78.S2, E99.A+
Saskatchewan Rebellion, 1885: F1060.9
Saskatchewan River and Valley: F1074.S3
Saskatoon (Saskatchewan): F1074.5.S3
Saugus River (Massachusetts): F72.E7
Sauk Indians: E99.S23
Sault Ste. Marie (Michigan): F574.S3
Sauvies Island (Oregon): F882.S3
Savage Station, Battle of, 1862: E473.68
Savannah (Georgia): F294.S2
  Campaign, 1864: E477.41
  Siege, 1779: E241.S26
Savannah (Privateer): E599.S2
Savannah River and Valley
  Georgia: F292.S3
  South Carolina: F277.S3
Sawtooth Mountains and Valley (Idaho): F752.B65
Sawyer, Frederick Adolphus: F274
Sawyer, Lemuel: E302.6.S3
Sayil Site (Mexico)
  Mayas: F1435.1.S29
Scalping by Indians: E98.W2
Scandinavians in Canada: F1035.N6, F1035.S3
Scandinavians in South America: F2239.N6

Scandinavians in the United States:
E184.S18, E184.S2
Scaticook Indians
Connecticut: E99.S25
New York: E99.S252
Schaerer, Eduardo: F2688
Schenck, Robert Cumming: E467.1.S32
Schenectady (New York)
Destruction, 1690: E196
Schlatter, Michael: F152
Schley, Winfield Scott: E714.6.S3
Courtmartial: E727
Schmidel, Ulrich: E125.S3
Schofield, John McAllister: E467.1.S35
Schoharie Creek and Valley (New York):
F127.S3
Schokleng Indians: F2520.1.S5
Schurz, Carl: E660.S3, E664.S39
Schuyler, Philip John: E207.S3
Schuylkill, Falls of (Pennsylvania):
F158.68.F2
Schuylkill River and Valley (Pennsylvania):
F157.S33
Science
Indians
North America: E98.S43
Pre-Columbian America: E59.S35
Scioto companies, American and French:
F483
Scioto Land Company: F483
Scioto River and Valley (Ohio): F497.S32
Scocomish Indians: E99.S64
Scotch in Canada: F1035.S4
Scotch in the United States: E184.S3
Scotch in Venezuela: F2349.S36
Scotch-Irish in the United States: E184.S4
Scots' Colony at Darien: F2281.D2
Scots-Irish in the American Revolution:
E269.S36
Scott, Charles
Expedition, May 1791: E83.79
Scott, Dred: E450
Scott, Hugh Lenox: E181
Scott, Winfield: E403.1.S4
Campaign in Mexico, 1847: E405.6
Scott's Expedition, 1791: E83.79
Scotty's Castle (California): F868.D2
Scouts, Military
United States
Civil War: E608
Revolution: E279+
Scranton (Pennsylvania): F159.S4
Sculpture
Indians: F1219.3.S38, F1219.76.S35,
F1435.3.S34, F1525.3.S38,
F1545.3.S35, F1619.3.S38,
F2230.1.S37, F3429.3.S39
Bolivia: F3320.1.S38
Central America: F1434.2.S38
Pre-Columbian America: E59.S37
Sea Islands (South Carolina): F277.B3
Negroes: E185.93.S7
Seabrook Island (South Carolina): F277.C4
Seaconnet Indians: E99.S16

Seamen
United States
Impressment
War of 1812: E357.2
Search, Right of
War of 1812: E357.2
Searles Valley (California): F868.S37
Seattle (Washington): F899.S4
Seaway Trail (New York): F127.N38
Sebastian, Benjamin: F455
Sebec Lake (Maine): F27.P5
Secession
United States
Civil War period: E440.5, E458.1
Southern States: F213, F230, F258
Secessionville (South Carolina)
Engagement at, 1862: E473.92
Sechelt Indians: E99.S258
Seconet Indians: E99.S16
Secoya Indians: F3722.1.S43
Secret service, Military
United States
Civil War: E608
Revolution: E279+
War of 1812: E360.5+
War with Mexico: E415.2.S43
Sectionalism
United States
Civil War period: E440.5, E458.1,
E468+
Southern States: F213, F230, F258
Sedge Islands (New Jersey): F142.O2
Sedgwick, John: E467.1.S4
Sedition laws, 1798: E327
Seiad Creek and Valley (California):
F868.S6
Seibal, Guatemala (Mayas): F1435.1.S44
Seigneuries
New France: F1030
Quebec: F1054.M35
Sekani Indians: E99.S26
Sekoya Indians: F3722.1.S43
Self-destruction, Indian: E98.S9
Selkirk, Thomas Douglas, 5th Earl of: F1063
Selkirk Range (British Columbia): F1089.S4
Selma (Alabama)
Wilson's raid, 1865: E477.96
Seminole Indians: E99.S28
Seminole War, 1st, 1817-1818: E83.817
Seminole War, 2d, 1835-1842: E83.835
Seminole War, 3d, 1855-1858: E83.855
Semitic influences on Indians: F2230.1.S44
Semmes, Raphael: E467.1.S47
Senci Indians: F3430.1.S35
Seneca Indians: E99.S3
Seneca Lake (New York): F127.S43
Sequatchie River and Valley (Tennessee):
F443.S36
Sequoia National Forest: F868.S4
Sequoia National Park: F868.S4
Serbs in Canada: F1035.S47
Serbs in the United States: E184.S5
Serente Indians: F2520.1.S47
Sergief Island (Alaska): F912.S27
Sergipe, Brazil (State): F2636

Seri Indians: F1221.S43
Sermons, Wartime
United States
Civil War: E649+
Revolution: E297
War of 1812: E364.5
War with Mexico: E415
Serra, Junípero (Miguel José): F864
Serrano Indians: E99.S31
Serrato, José: F2728
Service Men of the Spanish War (1899-
1904): E714.3.S48+
Services for Indians
North America: E98.S46
Setá Indians: F2520.1.H48
Sete Quedas (Guayra Falls): F2596
Setibo Indians: F3430.1.S4
Seven cities of Cibola: F799
Seven Days' Battles, 1862: E473.68
Seven Pines, Battle of, 1862: E473.65
Seven Ranges
Old Northwest: F483
Seven Reductions, War of the, 1754-1756:
F2684
Seven Years' War, 1756-1763
West Indies: F1621
Severn River and Valley (Maryland):
F187.A6
Severn River and Valley (Ontario):
F1059.S49
Severn-Trent Waterway (Ontario): F1059.T7
Sevier, John: E302.6.S45
Sewall, Samuel: F67
Seward, Mount (New York): F127.F8
Seward, William Henry: E415.9.S4
Collected works: E415.6.S51
Seward Peninsula (Alaska): F912.S3
Sewee Indians: E99.S32
Sexual behavior
Indians: E98.S48, F3429.3.S45
Mexico: F1219.3.S45
Pre-Columbian America: E59.S45
Seymour, Horatio: E415.9.S5
Shahaptian Indians: E99.S325
Shakamak State Park (Indiana): F532.S47
Shakers in the United States: E184.S53
Shamanism: E98.R3
Shapera Indians: F3430.1.S47
Shapra Indians: E3430.1.S47
Sharanahua Indians: F3430.1.S48
Shark River (New Jersey): F142.M7
Sharpshooters
United States
Civil War: E492.7
Shasta, Mount (California): F868.S6
Shasta Indians: E99.S33
Shasta Mountains (California): F868.S495
Shastan Indians: E99.S332
Shaver Lake (California): F868.F8
Shawangunk Mountains (New York):
F127.U4
Shawnee Indians: E99.S35
Shay's Rebellion, 1786-1787: F69

Sheepscot River and Valley (Maine):
F27.W16
Sheffield Island (Connecticut): F102.F2
Shefford Co. (Quebec): F1054.S48
Shelburne Co. (Nova Scotia): F1039.S5
Shelby, Isaac: F455
Shelby's raid in Arkansas and Missouri,
1863: E474.98
Shell beads
Indians
South America: F2230.1.S54
Shell engraving, Indian
Pre-Columbian America: E59.S54
South America: F2230.1.S54
Shell jewelry
Indians
South America: F2230.1.S54
Shelter Cove (California): F868.H8
Shelter Island (New York): F127.S54
Shelton Laurel Creek and Valley (North
Carolina): F262.M25
Shenandoah (Cruiser): E599.S5
Shenandoah National Park: F232.S48
Shenandoah River and Valley
Virginia: F232.S5
West Virginia: F247.S5
Shenandoah Valley
Civil War
Military operations: E470.3, E472.16,
E473.74, E476.66, E477.33
Shenango River and Valley (Pennsylvania):
F157.S47
Shepherd, Alexander Robey: F198
Sherbrooke (Quebec): F1054.5.S55
Sherente Indians: F2520.1.S47
Sheridan, Philip Henry: E467.1.S54
Sherman, Ellen (Ewing): E467.1.S552
Sherman, John: E664.S57
Sherman, Roger: E302.6.S5
Sherman, William Tecumseh: E467.1.S55
March to the sea (May 1864-April 1865):
E476.69
Sheta Indians: F2520.1.H48
Shields, James: E403.1.S5
Shiloh, Battle of, 1862: E473.54
Shiloh National Military Park: E473.54
Shinnecock Indians: E99.S38
Ship Island (Mississippi): F347.H3
Shipibo-Conibo Indians: F3430.1.S5
Shirianán Indians: F2520.1.Y3
Shirley, William: E195+
Shoals, Isles of: F42.I8
Shokleng Indians: F2520.1.S5
Short Hills, New Jersey, Battle of, 1777:
E241.S53
Short Hills Provincial Park (Ontario):
F1059.S58
Shoshone National Forest: F767.S57
Shoshone River and Valley (Wyoming):
F767.S58
Shoshonean Indians: E99.S39
Shoshoni Indians: E99.S4
Shoshoni War, 1863-1865: E83.863
Shreveport (Louisiana): F379.S4

Shreveport, La. Centenary College of
Louisiana and the Civil War: E586.S5
Shuar Indians: F3722.1.J5
Shubenacadie River and Valley (Nova
Scotia): F1039.S55
Shuswap Indians: E99.S45
Shuswap Lake (British Columbia):
F1089.S46
Shuyak Island State Park (Alaska): F912.S38
Sia Indians: E99.S5
Sibley, Henry Hastings: F606
Sibundoy Valley (Colombia): F2281.P9
Sickles, Daniel Edgar: E415.9.S53
Sicuane Indians: F2319.2.S52
Side Lake (Minnesota): F612.S25
Sidney Lanier, Lake
Georgia: F292.S53
Sierra de la Espuma: F817.S9
Sierra de Perijá (Colombia): F2281.P4
Sierra Gorda: F1339
Sierra Madre (Mexico): F1340
Sierra Nevada de Mérida: F2331.M52
Sierra Nevada de Santa Marta (Colombia):
F2281.M2
Sierra Nevada Mountains (California):
F868.S5
Sierra Norte de Puebla: F1326
Sierra Popoluca Indians: F1221.P62
Sierras, The (California): F868.S5
Sieur de Monte National Monument (Maine):
F27.M9
Sifton, Sir Clifford: F1033
Sigel, Franz: E467.1.S58
Sign language, Indian: E98.S5
Signal Corps
United States Civil War: E608
Signers of the Declaration of Independence:
E221
Sihasapa Indians: E99.S53
Sikhs in Canada: F1035.S54
Sikhs in the United States: E184.S55
Siksika Indians: E99.S54
Siletz Indians: E99.S544
Silva, José Bonifacio de Andrada e: F2536
Silva Paranhos, José Maria da: F2537
Silva Xavier, Joaquim José da: F2534
Silversmithing, Indian: E98.S55
Silverwork
Indians
Argentina: F2821.3.S54
Peru: F3429.3.S54
Simcoe, John Graves: F1058
Simcoe, Lake (Ontario): F1059.S59
Simcoe Co. (Ontario): F1059.S6
Similkameen River and Valley
British Columbia: F1089.S48
Washington (State): F897.S48
Simpson, Sir George: F1060.8
Simpson, Thomas: F1060.8
Sin Aikst Indians: E99.S546
Sinagua culture: E99.S547
Sinaloa, Mexico (State): F1341
Sincayuse Indians: E99.S55

Sinissippi Valley (Wisconsin): F587.R63
Sinkiuse-Columbia Indians: E99.S55
Sinkyone Indians: E99.S56
Sinnamahoning Creek (Pennsylvania):
F157.S49
Sinos River and Valley (Brazil): F2638
Sinú River (Colombia): F2281.B6
Siouan Indians: E99.S6
Sioux City (Iowa): F629.S6
Sioux Falls (South Dakota): F659.S6
Sioux (Dakota) Indians: E99.D1
Sioux wars: E83.854
1862-1865: E83.86
1876: E83.876
Sipibo Indians: F3430.1.S5
Siriono Indians: F3320.2.S5
Sisal hemp, Mayan: F1435.3.S5
Siskiyou Mountains (Oregon): F882.S56
Sisseton, Fort (South Dakota): F657.R6
Sisseton Indians: E99.S62
Sisseton State Park (South Dakota): F657.R6
Sitka (Alaska): F914.S6
Sitting Bull
Dakota chief: E99.D1
Death: E83.89
Siuslaw Indians: E99.S622
Siuslaw National Forest: F882.S58
Siwanoy Indians: E99.S623
Sixteenth Street (Washington, D.C.):
F203.7.S6
Skagit Indians: E99.S627
Skagit River and Valley (Washington):
F897.S52
Skagway (Alaska): F914.S7
Skakabish Indians: E99.S64
Skakamish Indians: E99.S64
Skakobish Indians: E99.S64
Skaquahmish Indians: E99.S64
Skaquamish Indians: E99.S64
Skasquamish Indians: E99.S64
Skeena River and Valley (British Columbia):
F1089.S5
Skiquamish Indians: E99.S64
Skitswish Indians: E99.S63
Skokamish Indians: E99.S64
Skokobc Indians: E99.S64
Skokomish Indians: E99.S64
Skokomish River and Valley (Washington):
F897.S54
S'Komish Indians: E99.S64
Skoskomish Indians: E99.S64
Slave Indians: E99.S65
Slave insurrections
British Guiana, 1823: F2384
Haiti (Revolution, 1791-1804): F1923
Jamaica
Maroon War, 1795-1796: F1884
Slave insurrections (1831, 1865):
F1886
United States: E447, E450
Charleston (South Carolina), 1822:
F279.C4
New York Afro-American plot, 1741:
F128.4

Slave insurrections
  United States: E447, E450 — Continued
    Richmond Insurrection, 1800:
      F234.R5
    Southampton Insurrection, 1831:
      F232.S7
Slave trade
  Jamaica (Trade abolished, 1807): F1884
  United States: E442
    Attempts to revive: E438, E446
    Internal slave trade: E442
    Mutiny on slave ships: E447
    Slave markets and auctions: E442
Slavery
  America
    Confederate States of America: E453
    United States: E440.92+, E453
      Abolition: E453
      Abolition agitation, 1830-1863:
        E449
      Antislavery movements: E440.92+
        Kansas: F685
      Compromise attempts: E440.5
      Economic aspects: E440.92+
      Extension to the territories: E415.7,
        E416, E423, E438, F685
      Free state slaves: E450
      Fugitive slaves: E450
      History: E441
        To 1830: E446+
        1830-1863: E449+
      Justification: E449
      Lincoln's attitude: E457.2
      Masters and overseers: E443
      Moral aspects: E440.92+
      Personal liberty laws: E450
      Political aspects
        1801/1809-1845: E338, E449
        1845-1849: E416
        1845-1861: E415.7
          1849-1853: E423
          1853-1857: E433
          1857-1861: E438, E440.5
        Civil War, 1861-1865: E453,
          E458+
  Slavery, Indian: E98.S6; F1219.3.S5,
    F1219.76.S53
Slaves
  United States
    Biography: E444, E450
    Colonization: E448
    Emancipation: E453
    Free state slaves: E450
    Fugitive slaves: E450
    Kidnapping: E450
    Legal status in free states: E450
    Life, duties, etc.: E443
    Markets and auctions: E442
    Overseers: E443
    Pensions: E185.2
    Personal liberty laws: E450
    Personal narratives: E444
  Slavs in Canada: F1035.S6

Slavs in Latin America: F1419.S5
Slavs in the United States: E184.S6
Sleeping Bear Dunes National Lakeshore
  (Michigan): F572.S8
Slidell, John: E415.9.S58
Sloat, John Drake: E403.1.S6
Slocum, Henry Warner: E467.1.S63
Slovaks in Argentina: F3021.S6
Slovaks in Canada: F1035.S63
Slovaks in the United States: E184.S64
Slovenes in Argentina: F3021.S62
Slovenes in Brazil: F2659.S45
Slovenes in Canada: F1035.S64
Slovenes in the United States: E184.S65
Smith, Alfred Emanuel: E748.S63
Smith, Benjamin: F258
Smith, Gerrit: E415.9.S64
Smith, Henry: F390
Smith, Jedediah Strong: F592
Smith, Jeremiah: E302.6.S57
Smith, John: F229
Smith, William Farrar: E467.1.S75
Smith, William Stephens: E302.6.S59
Smith Island
  Maryland: F187.C5
  North Carolina: F262.B9
Smith's Island (Connecticut): F102.F2
Smokies, The (Tennessee): F443.G7
Smoking, Indian: E98.T6
Smoky Hill River and Valley
  Colorado: F782.S53
  Kansas: F687.S84
Smoky Mountains (Tennessee): F443.G7
Smoot, Reed: E664.S68
Smyth, Alexander
  Niagara campaign, 1812: E355.2
Smyth, John Ferdinand Dalziel: E278.S6
Snake (Shoshoni) Indians: E99.S4
Snake River and Valley
  Idaho: F752.S7
  Oregon: F882.S6
  Washington: F897.S6
Snoqualmie River and Valley (Washington):
  F897.S67
Snow Falls
  Maine: F27.A5
Snows, The, Islands (Michigan): F572.L57
Snowy Cross Mountain (Colorado): F782.H6
Snyder, Adam Wilson: F545
Sobremonte, Rafael de, marqués de
  Sobremonte: F2841
Social conditions
  Indian: E98.S67, F1219.3.S57,
    F1219.76.S63, F1434.2.S62,
    F1435.3.S68, F1465.3.S6,
    F2230.1.S68, F2270.1.S63,
    F2519.3.S58, F2679.3.S65,
    F3320.1.S62, F3429.3.S59,
    F3721.3.S65
  El Salvador: F1485.3.S6
  Nicaragua: F1525.3.S63
  Pre-Columbian America: F59.S64
  Jews: E184.36.S65

Social life and customs: F1219.76.S64
  Afro-Americans: E185.9+
    Slave life: E443
  America: E20
    United States: E161.5+
  Indians: E98.S7, F1219.3.S6,
    F1434.2.S63, F1435.3.S7,
    F1465.3.S62, F1505.3.S63,
    F2230.1.S7, F2270.1.S64,
    F2519.3.S6, F3429.3.S6,
    F3721.3.S7
    Guyana: F2380.2.S63
    North America: E98.S7
    Venezuela: F2319.3.S62
  Jews: E184.36.S65
  Other countries: F1021+, F1210, F1430,
    F1443.8, F1463.5, F1483.8,
    F1503.8, F1523.8, F1543.8,
    F1563.8, F1609.5, F1633, F1654,
    F1760
Societies
  Indians: E98.S75
    Mexico: F1219.3.S64
Society for Correct Civil War Information:
  E462.99.S6
Society of American Wars of the United
  States: E181
Society of Colonial Wars: E186.3
Society of Mayflower Descendants: F68
Society of the Army and Navy of the
  Confederate States, Maryland:
  E483.25
Society of the Army and Navy of the Gulf:
  E462.99.S62
Society of the Army of Santiago de Cuba:
  E714.3.S67+
Society of the Cincinnati: E202.1
  Washington's letters: E312.75.S6+
Society of the Second War with Great Britain
  in the State of New York: E351.32
Society of the War of 1812: E351.3
Sokoki Indians: E99.S665
Sol, Isla del (Bolivia): F3341.T6
Solano López, Francisco: F2686
Soldiers
  Almanacs
    U.S. Civil War: E468.8
  Indians of North America as: E98.M5
  Lincoln's relations with: E457.2
Soldiers' and Sailors' National Union League
  of Washington, D.C.: E462.92
Sololá (Guatemala): F1469.S64
Solomon River and Valley (Kansas):
  F687.S85
Solomon's Fork, Battle of 1857: E83.8575
Solomons Island (Maryland): F187.C15
Somalis in Canada: F1035.S65
Somalis in the United States: E184.S67
Somers, Richard: E335
Somers Islands: F1630+
Somoza, Anastasio: F1527
Sonoma, Lake (California): F868.S7

Sparrow Lake (Ontario)
    Muskoka District and Simcoe County:
        F1059.S65
Sparta Mine (Arkansas): F417.C3
Spartanburg (South Carolina): F279.S7
Speaker of the House, Election of, 1856:
    E434.5
Speed, James: E415.9.S74
Spencer Butte (Oregon): F882.C3
Spencer's Butte (Oregon): F882.C3
Spies in the United States: E743.5
    Wars
        Civil War: E608
        Revolution: E279+
        War of 1812: E360.5+
Spirit Lake (Iowa): F627.D5
Spirit Lake Massacre, 1857: E83.857
Split Rock Creek and Valley
    Minnesota: F612.S64
    South Dakota: F657.S73
Spokan Indians: E99.S68
Spokane (Washington): F899.S7
Spokane Expedition, 1858: E83.84
Spokane River and Valley (Washington):
    F897.S7
Spoon River and Valley (Illinois): F547.S65
Sports
    Indians
        North America: E98.G2
        Pre-Columbian America: E59.G3
Spotswood, Alexander: F229
Spottsylvania, Battle of, 1864: E476.52
Spring Hill (Tennessee), Battle of, 1864:
    E477.52
Spring Mill State Park (Indiana): F532.L4
Springfield
    Illinois: F549.S7
    Massachusetts: F74.S8
    Missouri: F474.S7
    New Jersey
        Battle of, 1780: E241.S6
    Ohio: F499.S7
Squatter sovereignty: E415.7
Squaw Valley (California): F868.S5
Squawmish Indians: E99.S7
St. Elias-Wrangell National Park and
    Preserve (Alaska): F912.W74
Staff
    United States Presidents: E176.47
Staked Plain (Texas): F392.L62
Stalo Indians: E99.S72
Stamford (Connecticut): F104.S8
Stamp Act, 1765: E215.2
Stamp Act Congress, Oct. 1765: E215.2
Standish, Miles: F68
Stanford, Leland: E664.S78
Stanstead Co. (Quebec): F1054.S7
Stanton, Edwin McMasters: E467.1.S8
Stanwix, Fort, N.Y Siege, 1777: E241.S7
Star Island (Minnesota): F612.B43
Stark, John: E207.S79
Starved Rock State Park (Illinois): F547.L3
State, Prisoners of
    United States
        Civil War: E458.8

State House (Boston): F73.8.S8
State militia
    United States
        Revolution: E263.A+
        War of 1812: E359.5.A+
        War of 1898: E726.A+
        War with Mexico: E409.5.A+
State Street (Boston): F73.67.S7
Staten Island (New York): F127.S7
Statesmen
    United States
        Biography
            Revolutionary period: E302.5+
            19th century: E339+, E415.8+
Statistics, Indian: F1219.3.S7
    Pre-Columbian America: E59.S7
Statue of Liberty (New York): F128.64.L6
Stedman, Fort, Battle of, 1865: E477.61
Steedman, Charles: E182
Steedman, James Barrett: E467.1.S84
Steele, Robert Wilbur: F781
Stein River and Valley (British Columbia):
    F1089.S77
Stephens, Alexander Hamilton: E467.1.S85
Stephens, Linton: F290
Stephenson, Fort, Ohio, Defense of, 1813:
    E356.S7
Steuben, Friedrich Wilhelm, Baron von:
    E207.S8
Steunenberg, Frank: F746
Stevens, Fort, Battle of, 1864: E476.66
Stevens, Isaac Ingalls: F880
Stevens, Thaddeus: E415.9.S84
Stevens Pass (Washington): F897.C3
Stevenson, Adlai Ewing: F546
Stevenson, Andrew: E340.S75
Stewart, Charles: E353.1.S8
Stewart, William Morris: F841
Stikine River and Valley
    Alaska: F912.S85
    British Columbia: F1089.S85
Stillaquamish Indians: E99.S75
Stillwater, Battle of, 1777: E241.S2
Stimson, Frederic Jesup: E748.S88
Stirling, William Alexander, *called* Lord:
    E207.A3
Stirling, William Alexander, Earl of: F1038
Stockbridge Indians: E99.S8
Stockton, Richard: E302.6.S85
Stockton, Robert Field: E403.1.S8
    California campaign
        Mexican War: E405.2
Stone, Charles Pomeroy: E467.1.S87
Stone Mountain Memorial (Georgia):
    F292.S85
Stoneman, George
    Raid, 1863: E475.38
    Raid, 1865: E477.9
Stone's River campaign, 1862-1863:
    E474.77
Stones River National Military Park:
    E474.77
Stonington (Connecticut)
    Bombardment, 1814: E356.S8
Stony Lake (Ontario): F1059.P4

Stony Point, Battle of, 1779: E241.S8
Stormont, Dundas and Glengarry (Ontario):
    F1059.S89
Straight River and Valley (Steele and Rice
    Counties)
    Minnesota: F612.S86
Strait of Magellan: F3191
Stratford Hall (Virginia): F234.S865
Strathcona (Alberta): F1079.S7
Strathcona and Mount Royal, Donald
    Alexander Smith, 1st baron: F1033
Stratton Island (Maine): F27.Y6
Straus, Oscar Solomon: E664.S896
Strawberry Mansion (Philadelphia):
    F158.8.S8
Streets (U.S.): F73.67, F128.67.A+,
    F158.67.A+, F203.7.A+, F548.67
Streight, A.D.
    Raid toward Rome, Ga., 1863: E475.1
String figures, Indian: F2380.2.S7
String Lake (Wyoming): F767.T3
Strong, Caleb: F69
Stuart, Alexander Hugh Holmes: E415.9.S88
Stuart, Granville: F731
Stuart, James Ewell Brown: E467.1.S9
    Expedition into Maryland and
        Pennsylvania, Oct. 1862: E474.67
    Raid, June 1862: E473.66
Stuart Lake and region (British Columbia):
    F1089.S88
Stuartburn (Manitoba): F1064.S79
Study and teaching
    Canadian history: F1025
    Indians
        Argentina: F2819
        Maine history: F18.5
        United State history: E175.8
Stuyvesant, Peter: F122.1
Stuyvesant Village (New York): F128.68.S9
Subtiaba Indians: F1525.2.S7
Suburbs (U.S.): F73.68.A+, F128.68.A+,
    F158.68.A+, F548.68
Subversive activities in the U.S: E743.5
Sucre, Antonio José de: F2235.5.S9
Sucre, Bolivia (City): F3351.S94
Sucre, Venezuela (State): F2331.S8
    Indian antiquities: F2319.1.S8
    Sucre Department (Colombia):
        F2281.S82
Sucumbíos (Ecuador): F3741.S93
Sud Chichas (Bolivia): F3341.S9
Sudanese in the United States: E184.S77
Sudbury River and Valley (Massachusetts):
    F72.S86
Suffrage, Indian: E91+
Sugar Creek and Valley, Macoupin County
    and Sangamon County (Illinois):
    F547.S94
Sugarlands (Tennessee): F443.S45
Sugarloaf Provincial Park (New Brunswick):
    F1044.S9
Sugliak: F1110.S6
Suicidal behavior, Indian: F2519.3.S94
Suicide, Indian: E98.S9

Sulgrave Manor House: E312.195
Sullana, Peru: F3611.S84
Sullivan, John: E207.S9
    Indian campaign, 1779: E235
Sullivans Island (South Carolina): F277.S77
Sullivan's Island, Battle of, 1776: E241.M9
Sulphur Springs Valley (Arizona): F817.C5
Sumapaz Region (Colombia): F2281.S86
Sumidero (Mexico)
    Mayas: F1435.1.S92
Summerside (Prince Edward Island):
    F1049.5.S8
Summit Springs, Battle of, 1869: E83.8695
Sumner, Charles: E415.9.S9
    Brooks' assault on: E434.8
    Collected works: E415.6.S93
    Controversy with President Grant: E671
Sumo Indians: F1525.2.S8
Sumter, Fort
    Bombardment, 1861: E471.1
    Bombardment, 1863: E475.65
Sumter, Thomas: E207.S95
Sumter (Cruiser): E599.S8
Sun, Island of the (Bolivia): F3341.T6
Sun River and Valley (Montana): F737.S84
Sunapee Lake (New Hampshire): F42.S9
Sunset Crater Volcano National Monument
    (Arizona): F817.C6
Sunshine Coast (British Columbia):
    F1089.S94
Superior, Lake, region: F552
    Indian antiquities: E78.S87
    Michigan: F572.S9
    Minnesota: F612.S9
    Ontario: F1059.S9
    Wisconsin: F587.S9
Superior (Wisconsin): F589.S95
Superior National Forest: F612.S95
Superior Roadless Primitive Area
    (Minnesota): F612.B73
Superstition Mountains (Arizona): F817.S9
Supreme Court Building (Washington, D.C.):
    F204.S9
Suquamish Indians: E99.S85
Sur de Occidente, Venezuela (State):
    F2331.B3
Surette's Island (Nova Scotia): F1039.Y3
Surface Creek and Valley (Colorado):
    F782.D4
Surinam (Dutch colony): F2423
Suriname: F2401+
Surini Indians: F2520.1.A84
Surprise Valley (California): F868.M6
Surratt, J.H.: E457.5
Surratt, Mary E. (Jenkins): E457.5
Surui Indians: F2520.1.S86
Susitna River and Valley (Alaska): F912.S95
Susquehanna claims: F157.W9
Susquehanna Company: F157.W9
Susquehanna Indians: E99.S95
Susquehanna River and Valley
    Maryland: F187.S8
    New York: F127.S96
    Pennsylvania: F157.S8

Susquehanna Valley
    Indian antiquities: E78.S9
Sutter, John Augustus: F865
Suwannee River and Valley (Florida):
    F317.S8
Suya Indians: F2520.1.S89
Sverdrup Islands: F1105.S8
Swabians in Canada: F1035.S88
Swabians in the United States: E184.S78
Swan Islands (Honduras): F1509.B3
Swan River and Valley
    Manitoba: F1064.S9
    Saskatchewan: F1074.S9
Swans Island (Maine): F27.H3
Sweatbaths, Indian: E98.S94
Sweden, New: F167
Swedes in America: E29.S83
Swedes in Argentina: F3021.S86
Swedes in Brazil (Espírito Santo): F2561
Swedes in Canada: F1035.S9
Swedes in South America: F2239.S8
Swedes in the United States: E184.S23
    Civil War: E540.S8
    Revolution: E269.S8
Swedish settlements on the Delaware River:
    F167
Sweet Grass Hills (Montana): F737.T6
Sweetwater Valley (Tennessee): F443.S97
Swift River Valley (Massachusetts): F72.S94
Swiss in Argentina: F3021.S88
Swiss in Canada: F1035.S94
Swiss in Chile: F3285.S9
Swiss in South America: F2239.S9
Swiss in the United States: E184.S9
Sydenham, C.E.P. Thomson, Baron: F1032
Sydney (Nova Scotia): F1039.5.S9
Symmes, John Cleves: E302.6.S98
    Symmes Purchase: F483
Syrians in the United States: E184.S98

T

Tabasco, Mexico (State): F1351
    Indian antiquities: F1219.1.T13
Tabeguache Indians: E99.T114
Taboga, Isla (Panama): F1569.P3
Tacana Indians: F3320.2.T3
Táchira, Venezuela (State): F2331.T2
Tacna, Chile (Dept., 1883-1929): F3231
Tacna, Peru (Dept., 1929-): F3231
Tacna (Former Peruvian territory): F3231
Tacna-Arica question: F3097.3
Tacoma (Washington): F899.T2
Tacoma, Mount (Washington): F897.R2
Taconic Mountains (New York): F127.R3
Tacuarembó, Uruguay (Dept.): F2731.T3
Taensa Indians: E99.T115
Taft, Alphonso: E415.9.T12
Taft, Helen (Herron): E762.1
Taft, Robert Alphonso: E748.T2
Taft, William Howard: E660.T11, E762+
    Administration, 1909-1913: E761+
    Family: E762.1
Tahlequah, Okla. Cherokee National Female
    Seminary: E97.6.C35

Tahltan Indians: E99.T12
Tahoe, Lake (California): F868.T2
Tahoe National Forest (California): F868.T2
Tail Creek Region (Alberta): F1079.T3
Taino Indians: F1619.2.T3
Tairona Indians: F2270.2.T3
Tait, Charles: E302.6.T18
Taiwanese in the United States: E184.T35
Taiwano Indians: F2270.2.T32
Takelma Indians: E99.T15
Taku River and Valley
    Alaska: F912.T32
    British Columbia: F1089.T14
Takulli Indians: E99.T17
Talamanca, Costa Rica (District): F1549.T13
Talamantes Salvador y Baeza, Melchor de:
    F1231
Talbot, Silas: E207.T13
Talbot Settlement (Ontario): F1059.T34
Talca (Chile)
    City: F3281.T17
    Province: F3236
Talcahuano (Chile): F3281.T2
Tallahassee (Florida): F319.T14
Tallmadge, Benjamin: E302.6.T2
Talmadge, Eugene: F291
Talon, Jean, comte d'Orsainville: F1030
Taltal, Chile (Dept.): F3238
Tamanca Indians: F2319.2.T25
Tamandare, J.M. Lisbôa, marques de: F2536
Tamaroa Indians: E99.T18
Tamaulipas, Mexico (State): F1356
Tamiscamingue, Lake (Quebec): F1054.T6
Tampa (Florida): F319.T2
Tampico (Mexico): F1391.T2
Tanai Indians: E99.T185
Tanana Indians: E99.T187
Tancook Island (Nova Scotia): F1039.T35
Tangier Island (Virginia): F232.T15
Tangipahoa Parish (Louisiana): F377.T3
Tanglewood Park (North Carolina): F262.F7
Tanimuca-Retuama Indians: F2270.2.T34
Tannehill Historical State Park (Alabama):
    F332.T17
Tanner, John Riley: F546
Tanning, Indian: E98.L4
    Pre-Columbian America: E59.L4
Taos (New Mexico): F804.T2
Taos Indians: E99.T2
Tapajo Indians: F2520.1.T2
Tapajos River (Brazil): F2586
Tapia y Rivera, Alejandro: F1970.6.T3
Tapirapé Indians: F2520.1.T25
Tapuya Indians: F2520.1.T3
Taquari-Antas River and Valley (Brazil):
    F2621
Tarahumara Indians: F1221.T25
Tarapacá, Chile (Province): F3241
Tarasco Indians
    Modern: F1221.T3
    Pre-Columbian: F1219.8.T37
Taria Indians: F2520.1.T32
Tariana Indians: F2520.1.T32
Tarija, Bolivia (Dept.): F3341.T2
Tarqui, Battle of, 1829: F2275

Tarryall Mountains (Colorado): F782.T37

Taruma Indians: F2380.1.T3

Tatham, William: F436

Tatlayoco Lake (British Columbia): F1089.T17

Tatlayoka Lake (British Columbia): F1089.T17

Tatlayoko Lake (British Columbia): F1089.T17

Tatshenshini River and Valley (British Columbia): F1089.T18

Tattooing, Indian: E98.T2, F3429.3.T2

Taunton (Massachusetts): F74.T2

Taurepan Indians: F2380.1.A7

Tawakoni Indians: E99.T315

Taxation, Indian: E98.T24, F1219.3.T3, F1219.76.T39, F1465.3.T3, F3320.1.T38, F3429.3.T28, F3721.3.T18

   Colombia: F2270.1.T38

Taxation and representation (American colonies): E215.5

Taxco (Mexico): F1391.T23

Taylor, Alfred Alexander: F436

Taylor, John: E302.6.T23

Taylor, Robert Love: F436

Taylor, Zachary: E422

   Administration, 1849-1850: E421+

   Campaign in Mexico, 1846-1847: E405.1

Te Pito te Henua (Chile): F3169

Tea Farm Park (South Carolina): F277.C4

Tea tax

   American colonies: E215.7

Teapot Dome oil scandal: E785

Teche, Bayou (Louisiana): F377.T4

Teco Indians: F1219.8.T43

Tecuexe Indians: F1221.T33

Teeth, Indian: F3429.3.T29

Teeth mutilation and decoration, Indian: F3721.3.T2

Tegakouita, Catharine: E90.T2

Tegucigalpa (Honduras)

   City: F1516.T4

   Province: F1509.T2

Tehuantepec, Isthmus of: F1359

Tehuexe Indians: F1221.T33

Tejon Ranch (California): F868.K3

Telegraph service, Military

   United States

      Civil War: E608

Telkwa River and Valley (British Columbia): F1089.T2

Teller, Henry Moore: E664.T2

Tellico Creek and Valley (North Carolina): F262.M2

Temecula Creek and Valley (California): F868.R6

Temecula Massacre, 1847: E83.838

Temiscaming, Lake (Quebec): F1054.T6

Témiscamingue Co. (Quebec): F1054.T6

Temiscouata Co. (Quebec): F1054.T29

Temiskaming Co. (Quebec): F1054.T6

Temple Heights (Washington, D.C.): F202.T4

Temple Mound culture: E99.M6815

Temuco (Chile): F3281.T4

Ten Years' War, 1868-1878: F1785

Tenampua (Honduras)

   Indian antiquities: F1505.1.T2

Tenankutchin Indians: E99.T187

Tenayuca San Bartolo, Mexico (Pyramid): F1219.1.T24

Tendilla, Antonio de Mendoza, conde de: F1231

Tenetehara Indians: F2520.1.T4

Tenino Indians: E99.T32

Tenleytown (Washington, D.C.): F202.T43

Tenmile Creek and Valley (West Virginia): F247.T4

Tennessee: F431+

   Afro-Americans: E185.93.T3

   Confederate history: E579.1+

   Counties, etc.: F443.A+

   Franklin (State): F436

   Indians: E78.T3

   Reconstruction: F436

   Slavery: E445.T3

   Wars

      Civil War: E531.1+, E579.1+

         Military operations: E470.4+, E470.5, E470.8

      Indian wars: E83.813

      Revolution: E263.T4

      War of 1898: E726.T4

      War with Mexico: E409.5.T4

Tennessee, Army of (C.S.A.): E470.5

Tennessee, Army of the: E470.5

Tennessee, East: F442.1

Tennessee, Middle: F442.2

Tennessee, West: F442.3

Tennessee militiamen, Jackson's execution of: E83.813

Tennessee River and Valley: F217.T3

   Alabama: F332.T2

   Kentucky: F457.T3

   Tennessee: F443.T3

Tennessee River Region

   Indians: E78.T33

Tennessee River Reopening, 1863: E475.92

Tennessee Valley

   Military operations

      Civil War: E470.5

   Texas: F392.B34

Tensas Parish (Louisiana): F377.T45

Teotihuacán (Mexico): F1301

   Indian antiquities: F1219.1.T27

Tepanec Indians: F1219.8.T47

Tepecano Indians: F1221.T37

Tepehua Indians: F1221.T39

Tepehuan Indians: F1221.T4

Tepic, Mexico (Territory): F1361

Tepoztlán (Mexico): F1391.T3

Teque Indians: F2319.2.T4

Tequesta Indians: E99.T325

Teremembe Indians: F2520.1.T43

Terena Indians: F2520.1.T45

Tereno Indians: F2520.1.T45

Terra, Gabriel: F2728

Terraba Indians: F1545.2.T4

Térraba River and Valley (Costa Rica): F1549.R5

Terre Haute (Indiana): F534.T3

Terrebonne Co. (Quebec): F1054.T4

Terrebonne Parish (Louisiana): F377.T5

Territorial Company of Philadelphia, Association of the: F442.1

Territorial expansion (Canada): F1027.5

Territorial expansion (U.S.): E179.5

   Acquisition by cession, purchase, etc.

      Alaska purchase, 1867: E669, F907

      Canal Zone: F1569.C2

      Danish West Indies purchase: E768, F2136

      Florida cessions (1798-1819): F301, F314

      Gadsden Purchase, 1853: F786

      New Southwest: F786

      Northwest Ordinance, 1787: E309

      Old Northwest: E309, F483

      Oregon: F314

      Western lands, 1787: E309, F483

   Political question: E713

   Proposed annexations

      Canada: F1033

Territorio Nacional de Colonias (Bolivia): F3341.T3

Territory of Orleans, 1804-1812: F374

Territory south of the Ohio: F431+

Terry, David Smith: F864

Teslin River and Valley (British Columbia): F1089.T25

Teslin River and Valley (Yukon): F1095.T47

Têtes de Boule Indians: E99.T33

Teton Indians: E99.T34

Teton Mountains (Wyoming): F767.T29

Teton River and Valley (Idaho): F752.T5

Tewa Basin (New Mexico): F802.T47

Tewa Indians: E99.T35

Texada Island (British Columbia): F1089.T3

Texan Mier Expedition, 1842: F390

Texas: F381+

   Afro-Americans: E185.93.T4

   Burr Conspiracy, 1805-1807: E334

   Confederate history: E580.1+

   Counties, etc.: F392.A+

   Fredonian Insurrection: F389

   Indians: E78.T4

   International boundary: F786

   La Salle's Colony, 1685-1687: F352

   New Mexico (1836-1848): F800

   Northwest lands sold to U.S.: F801

   Reconstruction, 1867-1877: F391

   Santa Fe Expedition, 1841: F390

   Slavery: E445.T47

   Wars

      Civil War: E532.1+, E580.1+

         Military operations: E470.7, E470.9

      Revolution: E263.T45

      War of 1812: E359.5.T47

      War of Independence, 1835-1836: F390

      War with Mexico: E409.5.T45

Tongass National Forest (Alaska): F912.T64
Tongue River, Battle of, 1877: E83.8765
Tongue River and Valley
   Montana: F737.T55
   Wyoming: F767.T65
Tonikan Indians: E99.T73
Tonina (Guatemala)
   Mayas: F1435.1.T65
Tonkawa Indians: E99.T75
Tonocote Indians: F2823.T8
Tonto River and Valley (Arizona): F817.T66
Toombs, Robert Augustus: E415.9.T6
Topeka (Kansas): F689.T6
Topoxté (Mexico)
   Mayas: F1435.1.T67
Tordesillas, Treaty of, 1494: E123
Tories, American: E277+
Toromona Indians: F3320.2.T6
Toronto (Ontario): F1059.5.T68
   Capture, 1813: E356.T68
Toronto Islands (Ontario): F1059.O6
Torre, Lisandro de la: F2848
Torriente y Peraza, Cosme de la: F1787
Tory estates, Sale of: E277
Tory regiments: E277.6.A+
Toscanelli, Paolo del Pozzo: E110
Tosta, Vicente: F1507.5
Totem poles, Indian: E98.T65
Totems, Indian: E98.T65
Totonac Indians
   Modern: F1221.T6
   Pre-Columbian: F1219.8.T68
Totonicapán, Guatemala (Dept.): F1469.T7
Toussaint Louverture, François Dominique:
   F1923
Tower Rock (Missouri): F472.P4
Townsend, Robert: E280.T7
Townshend Acts, 1767: E215.3
Trade laws, British
   Enforcement in American colonies:
      E215.1
Trails, Indian
   North America: E98.T7
   Peru: F3429.3.R6
   Pre-Columbian America: E59.R6
Traitors
   United States
      Civil War: E458.8
      Revolution: E277
Trans-Mississippi Department
   Confederate Army: E470.9
Trans-Mississippi Region: F590.3+
Transatlantic influences, Indian: E98.T73;
   F1219.3.T73
Transcontinental journeys (U.S.), 1848-
   1860: F593
Transpacific influences, Indian
   Pre-Columbian America: E59.T73
Transylvania: F454
Trapping, Indian: E98.T75
Traverse region (Michigan): F572.G5
Treaties
   Indians of North America
      Individual: E78.A+, E99.A+
Treatment of Indians: F1411, F2230.1.T7

Treaty of Washington, 1819: F314
Treinta y Tres, Uruguay (Dept.): F2731.T6
   Indian antiquities: F2719.1.T74
Trelawney Plantation (Maine): F23
Tremont Street (Boston): F73.67.T7
Trent Affair, Nov. 8, 1861: E469+
Trent Canal (Ontario): F1059.T7
Trent River and Valley (Ontario): F1059.T7
Trent-Severn Waterway (Ontario): F1059.T7
Trent Valley, Ontario: F1059.T7
Trenton, Battle of, 1776: E241.T7
Trenton (New Jersey): F144.T7
Trephining, Indian: F3429.3.T7
Tres Marias Islands (Mexico): F1368
Tres Zapotes (Mexico)
   Indian antiquities: F1219.1.T7
Tribal colleges
   North America: E97.55
Tribal government, Indian: E98.T77
   Pre-Columbian America: E59.T75
Tribute, Indian: F3429.3.T28, F3721.3.T18
Trike Indians: F1221.T7
Trimble, Allen: F495
Trinidad (Cuba): F1829.T8
Trinidad (West Indies): F2119+
Trinidad and Tobago (West Indies): F2119+
Trinity Alps (California): F868.T58
Trinity River and Valley (Texas): F392.T83
Trio Indians: F2420.1.T7
Triometesem Indians: F2420.1.A35
Triple Alliance, War of the, 1865-1870:
   F2687
Tripoli, War with, 1801-1805: E335
Tripoline War: E335
Tripolitan War: E335
Trique Indians: F1221.T7
Trois Rivières Co. (Quebec): F1054.T5
Trojan
   Pre-Columbian discovery of America:
      E109.T74
Trophies, Military
   United States
      Civil War: E646
      War of 1898: E734
Trujillo, Venezuela (State): F2331.T7
Trujillo (Peru)
   City: F3611.T8
   Province: F3451.T7
      Indian antiquities: F3429.1.T8
Trujillo Molina, Rafael Leónidas: F1938.5
Trumai Indians: F2520.1.T7
Truman, Harry S.: E814
   Administrations, 1945-1953: E813+
   Collected works: E742.5.T6
   Family: E814.1
Trumbell, Jonathan: E263.C5
Trumbell, Lyman: E415.9.T86
Truro Parish (Virginia): F232.T8
Trust estates, Indian: E98.F3
Trustee for establishing the colony of
   Georgia: F289
Truth, Sojourner: E185.97.T8
Truxtun, Thomas: E182
Tryon, William: F257

Tsattine Indians: E99.T77
Tsetsaut Indians: E99.T772
Tsilkotin Indians: E99.T78
Tsimshian Indians: E99.T8
Tsuva Indians: F2520.1.S89
Tubatulabal Indians: E99.T83
Tucano Indians: F2520.1.T9
Tucanoan Indians: F2270.2.T77
Tuck, Amos: E415.9.T88
Tucker, John Randolph: E467.1.T8
Tucker, Samuel: E207.T8
Tucker-Prentiss Duel: E340.P9
Tuckernuck Island (Massachusetts): F72.N2
Tucson (Arizona): F819.T9
Tucumán (Ancient gobernación): F2991
Tucumán (Argentina)
   City: F3011.T89
   Province: F2991
      Indian antiquities: F2821.1.T89
Tucuna Indians: F2520.1.T925
Tug Hill region (New York): F127.T83
Tukanoan Indians: F2270.2.T77
Tukkuthkutchin Indians: E99.T845
Tukuarika Indians: E99.T85
Tula de Allende (Mexico): F1219.1.T8
Tula Site (Mexico): F1219.1.T8
Tulalip Indians: E99.T87
Tulare Lake and region (California):
   F868.S173
Tulcán (Ecuador): F3791.T8
Tule Lake (California): F868.S6
Tullahoma campaign, 1863: E475.16
Tulsa (Oklahoma): F704.T92
Tulum (Mexico)
   Mayas: F1435.1.T8
Tumacacori National Monument: F817.T8
Tumbes, Peru (Dept.): F3451.T8
Tumuc-Humac Mountains (French Guiana):
   F2467.T9
Tunebo Indians: F2270.2.T8
Tungurahua, Ecuador (Province): F3741.T7
Tunica Indians: E99.T875
Tunisians in Canada: F1035.T85
Tunja (Colombia)
   City: F2291.T8
   Province: F2281.T8
Tunxis Indians: E99.T88
Tuolumne River and Valley (California):
   F868.T92
Tupac Amaru, Insurrection of, 1780-1781:
   F3444
Tupambaé, Battle of, 1904: F2728
Tupari Indians: F2520.1.T933
Tupelo (Mississippi), Expedition to, 1864:
   E476.84
Tupi Indians: F2230.2.T84
Tupinamba Indians: F2520.1.T94
Tupper, Sir Charles: F1033
Tupungato, Argentina (Dept.): F2911
Turkey Run State Park (Indiana): F532.P2
Turks and Caicos Islands (Bahamas):
   F1659.T9
Turks in the United States: E184.T88
Turnagain Arm (Alaska): F912.C6

Waco (Texas): F394.W12
Waco Indians: E99.W125
Waddington, Mount (British Columbia):
    F1089.C7
Wade, Benjamin Franklin: E415.9.W16
Wadmalaw Island (South Carolina): F277.C4
Wadsworth, Fort (South Dakota): F657.R6
Wadsworth, James Samuel: E467.1.W13
Wadsworth Trail (Minnesota): F612.W15
Wager (Ship), Wreck of the: F3146
Wagner, Battery, 1863: E475.63
Wahpekute Indians: E99.W13
Wahpeton Indians: E99.W135
Waica Indians: F2520.1.W3
Waika Indians: F2520.1.W3
Wailaki Indians: E99.W15
Waimiri Indians: F2520.1.W34
Wainright, Jonathan Mayhew: E745
Waite, Davis Hanson: F781
Waiwai Indians: F2380.1.W25
Waiwe Indians: F2380.1.W25
Wakarusa River and Valley (Kansas):
    F687.W4
Wakashan Indians: E99.W16
Walden Pond (Mass.): F72.M7
Waldo Patent (Maine): F27.M95
Waldron Island (Washington): F897.S2
Walker, Frank C.: E748.W225
Walker, James John: F128.5
Walker, Robert James: E415.9.W2
Walker, William: F1526.27
    Filibuster expeditions: F1232.5, F1507.5
Wall Street (New York): F128.67.W2
Walla Walla Indians: E99.W18
Walla Walla River and Valley (Washington):
    F897.W2
Wallace, Henry Agard: E748.W23
Wallace, Lewis: E467.1.W2
Wallace, William Alexander Anderson: F390
Wallace, William Henry Lamme: E467.1.W3
Walloomsac, New York, Battle of, 1777:
    E241.B4
Walloon Lake (Michigan): F572.W24
Walloons in the United States: E184.W35
Wallowa Lake (Oregon): F882.W2
Wallowa National Forest: F882.W25
Walpapi Indians: E99.W185
Wama Indians: F2420.1.A35
Wamani Indians: F3430.1.W35
Wamesit Indians: E99.W19
Wampanoag Indians: E99.W2
Wampum: E98.M7, F1219.3.M597
    Pre-Columbian America: E59.M7
Wanamaker, John: E664.W24
Wanapum Indians: E99.W3
Wao Indians: F3722.1.H83
Waodädi Indians: F3722.1.H83
Wapisiana Indians: F2380.1.W3
Wappinger Indians: E99.W34
Wappo Indians: E99.W35
War, prisoners of
    Civil War: E611+

War, prisoners of — Continued
    Revolution: E281
    War of 1812: E362
    War of 1898: E730
    War with Mexico: E412
War against Rosas, 1849-1852: F2846.3
War between the States: E461+
War correspondents
    U.S. Civil War: E609
    War of 1812: E351+
    War of 1898: E714+
War of Independence (Texas), 1835-1836:
    F390
War of the American Revolution: E201+
War of the Pacific, 1879-1884: F3097
War of the Regulators (North Carolina):
    F257
War of the Seven Reductions, 1754-1756:
    F2684
War of the Triple Alliance, 1865-1870:
    F2687
War relief work
    United States
        Civil War: E629+
        War of 1898: E731
War songs
    United States
        Songs and ballads
            Civil War: E647
            War of 1898: E735
            War with Mexico: E415
Warao Indians: F2319.2.W3
Ward, Artemas: E207.W2
Ward, Samuel: E207.W26
Ware River and Valley (Massachusetts):
    F72.S94
Warekena Indians: F2319.2.A73
Warfare, Indian
    Pre-Columbian America: E59.W3
Warm Springs Apache Indians: E99.W36
Warner, Seth: E207.W27
Warrau Indians: F2319.2.W3
Warren, Gouverneur Kemble: E467.1.W4
    Court-martial: E477.675
Warren, Joseph: E263.M4
Warren Wagon Train Massacre, 1871:
    E83.866
Wars, Indian
    Chile: F3069.3.W37
Warwick (Rhode Island)
    Union of plantations: F82
Wasco Indians: E99.W37
Washburn, Cadwallader Colden: F586
Washburn, Israel: E511.1+
Washington, Booker Taliaferro: E185.97.W4
Washington, Bushrod: E302.6.W15
Washington, D.C. Old Capitol Prison
    Civil War: E616.O4
Washington, D.C. Old Guard: E462.93
Washington, Fort, Capture of, 1776:
    E241.W3
Washington, George: E312+
    Administrations, 1789-1797: E311

Washington, George: E312+ — Continued
    Expeditions to the Ohio: E312.23
    Family: E312.19
    Mansion (Philadelphia, Pennsylvania):
        F158.8.W3
    Masonic Memorial (Alexandria,
        Virginia): F234.A3
    Military career: E312.25
        French and Indian War: E312.23
        Northwestern Indian wars: E83.79
        Revolution: E201+
    Monument (Washington, D.C.):
        F203.4.W3
    Monuments (Philadelphia): F158.64.W3
    Presidential speeches and messages:
        E312.9
    Writings: E312.7+
Washington, Lake (Washington): F897.K4
Washington, Martha (Dandridge) Custis:
    E312.19
Washington, Mount (New Hampshire):
    F41.6.W3
Washington, Order of: E202.7
Washington, Treaty of
    1819: F314
    1842: E398
Washington (District of Columbia): F191+
    Bonus Expeditionary Force, 1932, 1933:
        F199
    Burning by British, 1814: E356.W3
    L'Enfant's plan: F195
    Monuments, memorials, statues, etc.:
        F203.4.A+
    Peace Conference, 1861: E440.5
    Princeton (Frigate) explosion, 1844: E396
Washington (North Carolina)
    Siege, 1863: E474.55
Washington (State): F886+
    Afro-Americans: E185.93.W3
    Columbia River Highway: F882.C63
    Counties, etc.: F897.A+
    Indians: E78.W3
    Sand Island controversy: F882.B7
    Sauvies Island: F882.S3
    Vancouver Island: F1089.V3
    Wars
        Civil War: E535.1+
        Indian wars: E83.84
Washington Heights (New York):
    F128.68.W2
Washington Island (Wisconsin): F587.D7
Washington Memorial Parkway (Virginia):
    F232.G38
Washington-Morris-Salomon Monument
    (Chicago, Illinois): F548.64.G4
Washington Parish (Louisiana): F377.W3
Washington Society of Maryland: E202.8
Washington Street (Boston): F73.67.W3
Washington's birthday: E312.6
Washita Campaign, 1868-1869: E83.869
Washita River and Valley
    General and Texas: F392.W33
    Oklahoma: F702.W36

Wheeler Lake and region (Alabama): F332.W48
Wheeler's Cavalry Corps
  Confederate Army: E547.W5
Wheeling (West Virginia): F249.W5
Whidbey Island (Washington): F897.I7
Whipple, William: E302.6.W5
Whiskeytown-Shasta-Trinity National
  Recreation Area (California): F868.S49
Whisky Insurrection, 1794: E315
White, Hugh Lawson: E340.W53
White, Thomas Clark: F666
White Cordillera (Peru): F3451.A5
White House (Washington, D.C.): F204.W5
White Mountains: F41
White Plains, Battle of, 1776: E241.W5
White River and Valley (Arkansas and
  Missouri): F417.W5
  Arkansas: F417.W5
  Missouri: F472.W5
White River and Valley (Colorado and Utah): F782.R4
  Colorado: F782.R4
  Utah: F832.U4
White Russians in Canada: F1035.W5
White Russians in the United States: E184.W6
White Sands Missile range (New Mexico): F802.W44
White Sands National Monument
  New Mexico: F802.W45
White Sulphur (Kentucky). Johnson's Indian
  School: E97.6.J69
White Sulphur Springs (West Virginia): F249.W6
White Walnut Creek and Valley (Illinois): F547.P45
Whitehorse (Yukon): F1095.5.W5
White's Island (Connecticut): F102.F2
Whiteshell Provincial Park (Manitoba): F1064.W47
Whitestone Hill, Battle of, 1863: E83.86
Whitewater River and Valley (Indiana): F532.W59
Whiting, William Henry Chase: E467.1.W61
Whitman, Marcus: F880
Whitman Mission National Historic Site
  (Washington): F897.W65
Whitman National Monument: F897.W65
Whitney, Mount (California): F868.W6
Wichita (Kansas): F689.W6
Wichita Indians: E99.W6
Wichita Mountains and region
  Oklahoma: F702.W55
Wickes, Lambert: E207.W63
Wier's Cave (Virginia): F232.A9
Wife abuse, Indian: E98.W49
Wikanee Indians: E99.O68
Wikeinoh Indians: E99.O68
Wikeno Indians: E99.O68
Wild Bill Hickok (J.B. Hickok): F594
Wilder, John Thomas: E467.1.W69
Wilderness, Battle of, 1864: E476.52

Wilke, Wendell Lewis: E748.W7
Wilkes-Barre (Pennsylvania): F159.W6
Wilkins, Isaac: E278.W6
Wilkinson, Eliza (Yonge): E263.S7
Wilkinson, James: E353.1.W6
  Burr's conspiracy: E334
  Campaigns, 1813: E355.4
  Expedition, Aug. 1791: E83.79
Willamette River and Valley (Oregon): F882.W6
Willett, Marinus: E207.W65
William B. Bankhead National Forest
  Alabama: F332.W54
William Bacon Oliver Dam (Alabama): F332.T9
William Henry, Fort
  French and Indian War: E199
Williams, Alpheus Starkey: E467.1.W72
Williams, David: E280.A5
Williams, John Sharp: E664.W675
Williams, Otho Holland: E207.W7
Williams, Roger: F82
Williams, William: E302.6.W55
Williams, William Sherley: F592
Williams College and the Civil War: E541.W7
Williamsburg, Battle of, 1862: E473.63
Williamsburg (Virginia): F234.W7
Williamson, Hugh: E302.6.W6
Willing, Thomas: E302.6.W62
Willoughby and Hyde's Grant, 1663
  (Guiana): F2423
Willoughby Lake (Vermont): F57.O7
Willow Creek and Valley (Illinois): F547.K27
Willow Creek State Recreation Area
  (Alaska): F912.W56
Wills, Indian: E98.P9
Wilmington (Delaware): F174.W7
Wilmot, David: E340.W65
Wilmot Proviso: E416+
Wilson, Edith (Bolling): E767.3
Wilson, Henry: E415.9.W6
Wilson, James: E302.6.W64
Wilson, James Harrison: E467.1.W74
Wilson, Woodrow
  Administrations, 1913-1921: E766+
  Collected works: E660.W71
  Family: F767.3
Wilson Lake (Kansas): F687.W73
Wilson Reservoir (Kansas): F687.W73
Wilson's Creek, Battle of, 1861: E472.23
Wilson's raid to Selma, Ala., and Macon,
  Ga., 1865: E477.96
Wiminuche Indians: E99.W65
Winá Indians: F2270.2.D4
Winchester, Battle of
  Mar. 1862: E473.72
  Sept. 1864: E477.33
Winchester, Expedition from, 1865: E477.65
Wind Cave (South Dakota): F657.W7
Wind Cave National Park (South Dakota): F657.W7

Wind River and Valley (Wyoming): F767.W5
Wind River Range (Wyoming): F767.W5
Windermere Lake (British Columbia): F1089.W55
Windmill Island (Pennsylvania): F158.68.W7
Windom, William: E664.W76
Windsor (Ontario): F1059.5.W5
Windward Islands: F2011
Windward Passage (West Indies): F1741
Wingate, Paine: E302.6.W67
Winn Parish (Louisiana): F377.W6
Winnebago Indians: E99.W7
Winnipauk Island (Connecticut): F102.F2
Winnipeg (Manitoba): F1064.5.W7
Winnipeg, Lake, region (Manitoba): F1064.W5
Winnipesaukee, Lake: F42.W7
Winona (Minnesota): F614.W7
Winooski River (Vermont): F57.W73
Winslow, John Ancrum: E467.1.W77
Winslow's expedition for the expulsion of
  the Acadians, 1755: F1038
Winston-Salem (North Carolina): F264.W8
Winter Island (California): F868.C76
Winthrop, John (1588-1649): F67
Winthrop, John (1606-1676): F97
Winthrop, Robert Charles: E340.W73
Wintu Indians: E99.W78
Wintun Indians: E99.W79
Wiregrass Country: F217.W57
Wirt, William: F340.W79
Wisconsin: F576+
  Afro-Americans: E185.93.W58
  Counties, etc.: F587.A+
  French rule and exploration: F584
  Indians: E78.W8
  Slavery: E445.W8
  Wars
    Civil War: E537.1+
    War of 1898: E726.W6
Wisconsin River and Valley: F587.W8
Wisconsin Territory: F585
Wise, Henry Alexander: E415.9.W8
Wisner, Henry: E302.6.W68
Wissahickon Creek: F158.68.W8
Wistar, Isaac Jones: E467.1.W81
Witherspoon, John: E302.6.W7
Witoto Indians: F2270.2.W5
Wives of U.S. presidents: E176.2, E312.19, E342.1
Wiwa Indians: F2270.2.W54
Wiyat Indians: E99.W8
Wolcott, Edward Oliver: E664.W8
Wolcott, Oliver: E302.6.W85
Wolcott, Roger: F70
Wolf Mountain, Battle of, 1877: E83.8765
Wolf National Scenic Riverway (Wisconsin): F587.W86
Wolf River (Wisconsin): F587.W86
Wolfe, James
  Capture of Quebec: E199
Wolf's Point, Chicago: F548.68.W8

Yoncalla Indians: E99.Y77

Yopi Indians: F1221.Y64

York, Ontario, Battle of, 1813: E356.T68

York (Maine): F29.Y6

York Co. (New Brunswick): F1044.Y65

York Co. (Ontario): F1059.Y6

York District (South Carolina): F277.Y62

York Regional Municipality (Ontario): F1059.Y6

York Road (Pennslyvania): F157.Y7

Yorktown (Virginia): F234.Y6
    Siege, 1862: E473.61
    Surrender of Cornwallis, 1781: E241.Y6

Yoro, Honduras (Dept.): F1509.Y6

Yoruba in Cuba: F1789.Y6

Yoruba in the United States: E184.Y66

Yosemite National Park (California): F868.Y6

Yosemite Valley (California): F868.Y6

Youghiogheny River and Valley
    Maryland: F187.Y68
    Pennsylvania: F157.Y72
    West Virginia: F247.Y68

Young, Owen D.: E748.Y74

Young Men's Christian Associations and the Civil War: E635

Younger, Cole: F594

Youngstown (Ohio): F499.Y8

Yount, George Calvert: F864

Youth
    Jews: E184.36.S65

Youth, Indian: E98.Y68

Youth, Negro: E185.86

Yucatán, Mexico (State): F1376
    Indian antiquities: F1219.1.Y8
    Mayas: F1435.1.Y89

Yucatán Peninsula (Mexico): F1376

Yuchi Indians: E99.Y9

Yuco Indians: F2319.2.Y8

Yucpa Indians: F2319.2.Y8

Yucuna Indians: F2270.2.Y87

Yugoslavs in Argentina: F3021.Y7

Yugoslavs in Chile: F3285.Y8

Yugoslavs in Peru: F3619.Y84

Yugoslavs in South America: F2239.Y83

Yugoslavs in the United States: E184.Y7

Yukian Indians: E99.Y92

Yuko Indians: F2270.2.Y9

Yukon River and Valley
    Alaska: F912.Y9
    Canada: F1095.Y9

Yukon Territory: F1091+
    Alaska boundary: F912.B7
    Eskimos: E99.E7
    Indians: E78.Y8
    Klondike region: F1095.K5

Yukpa Indians: F2319.2.Y8

Yulee, David Levy: E415.9.Y9

Yuma Indians: E99.Y94

Yuman Indians: E99.Y95

Yunca Indians: F3430.1.Y8

Yupa Indians: F2319.2.Y8

Yuqui Indians: F3320.2.Y78

Yurok Indians: E99.Y97

Yurucari Indians: F3320.2.Y8

Yuruna Indians: F2520.1.J8

Yvaparé Indians: F2520.1.H48

Z

Zaca Lake (California): F868.S23

Zacapa, Guatemala (Dept.): F1469.Z3

Zacatecas (Mexico)
    City: F1391.Z2
    State: F1381

Zaculeu (Guatemala)
    Mayas: F1435.1.Z3

Zamora, Venezuela (State): F2331.B3

Zamorano, Augustín Juan Vicente: F864

Zamucoan Indians: F3320.2.Z3

Zangara, Giuseppe
    Biography: E807.3

Zanjon, Treaty of, 1878: F1785

Zaparo Indians: F3722.1.Z3

Zapata, Emiliano: F1234

Zapatera Island
    Indian antiquities: F1525.1.Z3

Zapotec Indians
    Modern: F1221.Z3
    Pre-Columbian: F1219.8.Z37

Zayas y Alfonso, Alfredo: F1787

Zelaya, José Santos: F1526.27

Zelaya, Nicaragua (Dept.): F1529.Z4

Zeledon-Wyke Treaty, 1860: F1438

Zeno, Antonio: E109.I8

Zeno, Niccolò: E109.I8

Zepita, Battle of, 1823: F3446

Zion National Park: F832.Z8

Zoological Park (New York): F128.65.Z6

Zoque Indians: F1221.Z6

Zoró Indians: F2520.1.Z65

Zulia, Venezuela (State): F2331.Z9